# The Literature of the American West

*Edited by*

## J. GOLDEN TAYLOR

*Colorado State University*

HOUGHTON MIFFLIN COMPANY · BOSTON

*New York · Atlanta · Geneva, Illinois · Dallas · Palo Alto*

Library of Congress Catalog Card Number:
71-132448
ISBN: 0-395-05458-3

*For Ethel*

# Preface

## SOME BASIC ASSUMPTIONS

THE DIVERSITY, richness, and challenge of life in the American West during the past century and a half, and the excellence and variety of the portrayal of that life in literature are very little known in these United States—even in the West itself. My primary purpose in editing *The Literature of the American West* has been to establish these facts by selecting and making available in one inexpensive volume some of the best selections of western literature in the various genres. If my first criterion of selection has been quality, my second has been representativeness.

I have planned this anthology, first of all, as a basic textbook for the course, Western American Literature, which is now taught in most of the colleges and universities this side of the Missouri River. There is some evidence that it can also serve well as a supplementary text for the American Literature Survey—since the thirty-seven single- and multiple-volume anthologies on my shelves purporting to survey American literature with few exceptions attest to a certain literary innocence about the West. Finally, the body of literature presented here should thoroughly dispel not only for students of American literature, but also for general readers and students of American civilization the baneful television "Western" image.

In this book, then, I work from the assumption that the western experience has been significant and that much of the literature based upon it is eminently worth studying. I believe with Frederick Jackson Turner, Bernard De Voto, and others that the westward movement was a unique, culminating experience for the American character and imagination. I also agree with James Bryce, that eminent English visitor to the West, who observed (even before Turner) that ". . . the West is the most American part of America; that is to say, the part where those features which distinguish America from Europe come out in the strongest relief." Such views have long suggested to me the need for the systematic study of the literature of the American West.

## THE WESTERN EXPERIENCE AND WESTERN LITERATURE

In my study of western American literature I have assumed that one might reasonably expect that the literature of a region would have some resemblance to the lives of its people. As all life is the province of the artist, western writers can be expected to use imaginatively all kinds of people and themes in the life of the West, its ever-changing present as well as its colorful past. The best books properly subordinate local color peculiarities of the West and transcend their settings by showing man in the West involved in mankind's universal struggles. No one needs to be told that America has developed such regions as New England and the South and that the distinguishing cultural features of these regions are notably represented in the works of literature that have these respective regional habitations.

The West, however, has not been so fortunate in achieving the recognition that its literature actually represents a full and accurate image of its culture. The idea that there is a significant body of western American literature that is a distinguished part of American literature and worthy of the attention of discriminating readers has not been fully recognized. And since I have had such a satisfactory experience for a number of years teaching, writing, editing, and doing research in this area, I have felt it worth while to edit this anthology in order to make an adequate representation of western life and literature although I have major scholarly interests in Thoreau and Hawthorne. My own justification for the study of western literature began with my conviction (as I have expressed it elsewhere) that literary scholars in all regions of America (no matter what their specialties) ought to develop a mature appreciation of the literature of their own region and an understanding of the historic cultural forces that underlie it.

There is something to be said for the study of the literature of a region. Not only is the general tone of life in a region best reflected in its literature, often with a shock of recognition; but the quality of life itself may be ultimately enhanced by what a great book reveals about mankind, by showing man involved in the peculiar stresses of a regional culture. The West can learn a great deal from what New England and the South have done: not only has each produced a great literature; but also, through scholarly critical endeavor they have educated the readers of their regions and elsewhere to an awareness of what *is* their best literature and a recognition of where its merits lie. The values of the society and its conflicts are portrayed meaningfully; and when the artist is successful, his work says something about mankind—not just men and women in a local-color tale. Life in the plains, mountains, and deserts of the West has already proved adequate to inspire a good number of western writers to create significant human drama in their work. Many of the selections in this book meet this standard.

Though I believe we Westerners should give much more scholarly attention to the literature of the West, I certainly am not advocating a prickly parochialism which would prefer the sentimental effusions of a local versifier or annalist to the sublimity of Milton or Homer. Nor am I in any way decrying the study of the best that has been written or created in the world. I like Chaucer and Shakespeare as well as anyone. I am asserting, rather, that Westerners may actually reflect in their lives and their literature some of the best values America—or the world—has ever learned to stand for. I have long suspected, also, that if one ignores or neglects to study the culture of the people among whom he lives, his generalizations about life in societies on the other side of the world are likely to be doctrinaire.

Everyone recognizes, of course, that one does not study American culture in isolation from the rest of the world. But I submit that it is as important to recognize that America has developed in the West a distinctive regional culture worthy of separate study as it is to acknowledge the values of studying the many separate European, African, and Asian cultures, to which American thought and institutions are often closely related.

Americans today live in a "thousand-eyed present" such as Emerson could not have imagined, and the discoveries from research are so diverse and the publications so vast that they exceed the capacity of any individual or the resources of any institution. There has certainly not been an American Leonardo since Jefferson rather successfully took all knowledge for his province; and no university can collect and maintain the ideally complete record of universal knowledge. Perhaps in our world of unprecedented intellectual cross-currents we Westerners would do well to return to ourselves more often, not only to our own direct observation of man in our home regions but more importantly to nature as it can be experienced uniquely in the West—and to the literature which effectively reflects that life.

The austere Plains, the Great American Desert, the Rocky Mountains, the lush river and coastal valleys—and water—have been from the first such important forces in shaping and conditioning life in the West that they function in much of its literature in a sense as major characters. The first explorers and mountain men, who ventured across the wide Missouri into the great plains saw in the West a dimension in nature unknown and unimagined. The abundance of its natural wealth, the stark grandeur and variety of the landscapes, the fearful vastness of its arid reaches have given challenge to the legitimate aspirations of the human spirit as well as to the endurance of the human body. Many of those who spread like a flood into fertile western valleys were the dispossessed of the world or the ostracized at home—such as the Mormons—and they created on their precariously held homesteads the self-reliance and self-respect that still gives luster to the name of pioneer. Unknown thousands of settlers, unprepared or unequal to the task of subduing a wilderness, wore themselves out and ended in defeat. The frontier, likewise, has given scope to the anti-social exploiters of all kinds—the petty sluice robber, the bandit, the rustler, the confidence man, and the robber-baron. The West has not been immune to anything. Man's confrontations with nature and his involvement with the stresses of human nature have since Lewis and Clark's epic narrative of a century and a half ago received interesting and vivid treatment in the literature of the West.

## ORGANIZATION OF THE TEXT

*The Literature of the American West* is organized into nine sections according to genre, each with a brief introduction and recommendations for further reading. The individual instructor will no doubt wish to assign and discuss selections according to his own thematic preferences. The settings chronologically go far back to the pre-white man world of Little Bear in Schaefer's *The Canyon* and the legendary beginnings of the Kiowas in Momaday's *The Way to Rainy Mountain*. Almost every decade in the nineteenth and twentieth centuries is represented by one or more selections, either in setting or in time of composition; and thus a wide variety of tone, style, and techniques is represented. In a chronological-thematic approach Schaefer's novella about Little Bear, a pre-white-man Cheyenne who tries to live according to his vision, would come first. Whether *The Way to Rainy Mountain* would come next is an interesting problem, for it deals with Kiowa legend as far back as the setting of *The Canyon* but blends events reflected in Mr. Momaday's mind down to 1969 when it was published.

## BACKGROUND READING

Anyone who teaches Western American Literature will likely want to be familiar with the major aspects of the westward movement. There is a wealth of original diaries and reminiscences in print, one of the most revealing and articulate accounts being that of Elisha Douglass Perkins, *Gold Rush Diary*. Biographies abound also; notable among them are such classics as Dale Morgan's *Jedediah Smith*, Juanita Brooks' *John Doyle Lee*, and Mari Sandoz' *Crazy Horse*. There are comprehensive and specialized histories and essays on the West by Frederick Jackson Turner—and a good deal of re-examination of Turner, such as *Turner and the Sociology of the Frontier* (1968)—Walter Prescott Webb, Ray Allen Billington, and Bernard De Voto. *Across the Wide Missouri* is for me one of the very best. John A. Hawgood's prize-winning work, *America's Western Frontiers* (1967) is concise and clear. *The Book of the American West*, compiled by nine authorities, is a very good account of the major aspects of the westward movement.

The various state historical journals—such as those of Arizona, Montana, Oregon, and Utah—are especially valuable sources as are *The American West* and the newly established *Western Historical Quarterly*, both sponsored by The Western History Association. The files of *Western Folklore* and the *Journal of American Folklore* are basic sources of western lore. Many literary quarterlies have occasionally published critical studies of western literature. *The South Dakota Review* since its founding in 1963 has published one issue a year on western literature. And journals like *The Prairie Schooner* and *The New Mexico Quarterly* have long traditions of high-quality western literary scholarship. *Western American Literature*, now in its fifth volume, is the only journal devoted exclusively to western literary history, criticism, bibliography, and reviews of current western books. It carries annually in the fourth issue (February) reports on Annual Bibliography of Studies in Western American Literature (books and articles); Research in Western American Literature, and a Membership Directory of The Western Literature Association.

*Western Words: A Dictionary of the American West* by Ramon F. Adams, New Edition Revised and Enlarged (1968), is very helpful; but Adams' *Six-Guns and Saddle Leather* (1969) is indispensable. This latter is a most knowledgeably annotated bibliography of 2491 books and pamphlets on western outlaws and gunmen. Actually, it assesses books on all phases of life in the West. Another valuable bibliography is J. Frank Dobie's *Guide to Life and Literature of the Southwest* (1952). In literary history, Franklin Walker's *San Francisco's Literary Frontier* (1939, 1969) and Spiller et al., *Literary History of the United States* are authoritative. A few of the books I have listed in *Further Reading* are collections and references; but most of them are paperbacks recommended as possible supplementary texts for courses based on this anthology.

## ACKNOWLEDGMENTS

I recognize that through the years I have incurred a literary indebtedness to many teachers, colleagues, and friends, which can no longer be identified or adequately acknowledged. I have benefitted, more specifically, during the past decade from correspondence and discussion with more than two hundred western writers and scholars whose ideas have contributed significantly to my understanding of western literature; and the authors of the many manuscripts submitted to *Western American Literature* which I have assessed have broadened the scope of my knowledge of western writing.

I would like to express my special thanks to a few people who through imaginative or scholarly interpretations of the West, correspondence, discussion, and friendship and encouragement have contributed particularly to the nature of this book: John A. Barsness, John S. Bullen, Walter Van Tilburg Clark, Vardis Fisher, James K. Folsom, W. H. Hutchinson, Thomas J. Lyon, Frederick Manfred, Michael McCloskey, John R. Milton, John G. Neihardt, Jack Schaefer, C. L. Sonnichsen, Don D. Walker, Frank Waters, Max Westbrook, and Delbert E. Wylder.

*Fort Collins, Colorado*                    J. GOLDEN TAYLOR

# Contents

# ONE

# The Novel

THIS SECTION CONSISTS OF discussions *about* the western novel since it is obviously impossible to reprint full-length novels in an anthology such as this. A very large proportion of current western literary criticism is devoted to the study of novels, but most of what is written about novels applies to the shorter forms of fiction as well.

Don Walker's essay is a pleasant spoof in the Pooh Perplex tradition on literary critics who assess the western novel. A good start can be made in the study of western literature if we recognize that there might just creep into our critical pronouncements certain elements of bias and irrelevancies such as those that Walker identifies. The insidious sin of pride is the bane of contemporary literary critics—as it was once of Puritan ministers.

Max Westbrook's essay on realism places him in the forefront of those contemporary critics who are attempting to identify what is distinctively western in the novel. John R. Milton has done more than anyone else in interviewing and getting into print and on television tape what major western writers think about the West and western writing. The *Symposium* is as revealing of the personalities of the novelists as it is of their art.

Since *The Grapes of Wrath, The Ox-Bow Incident*, and *Little Big Man* have received extensive critical acclaim and are three of the most popular novels with students in western literature classes, I have included one outstanding essay on each of these novels.

# Critical and Creative Approaches

## DON D. WALKER

### *The Rise and Fall of Barney Tullus*

Late in the spring of 1962 a small novel issued from the presses of an Eastern publishing house. Coming as it did rather late in the critical season, it attracted little attention from the reviewers. The *Times* simply noted that it had appeared; the *Wednesday Review* gave it a three-line summary; and the *American Saddle and Bridle Gazette* allowed it one substantial paragraph, noting particularly that the saddle mentioned on page 104 seemed to be a genuine Peotone Rider, with leathers hand-shaped over the seat and side bars of the tree hand-formed with a drawing knife.

*The Rise and Fall of Barney Tullus*, however, was destined for a more serious and extended critical consideration. Early in the winter of that same year scholars in Western American literature apparently discovered it. There followed a series of full-length critical essays, explicating *Barney* from various points of view. By the end of 1964 he was in quality paperback, and when the academic year opened in September, 1965, he was required or recommended optional reading in a dozen classes at a dozen different colleges and universities. Just a few years later one can say that *The Rise and Fall of Barney Tullus* has become a minor classic in American letters. And one can predict with considerable confidence the ultimate appearance of a work entitled *The Art of Barney Tullus* or perhaps *Barney Tullus: Text, Sources, and Criticism*.

A critical history of *Barney Tullus* of course remains to be written, although earnest graduate students may already be at work upon such a project. However, while waiting for the completion of such a study—a more definitive analysis and a more complete summary of critical dis-

This paper was delivered at the annual meeting of the Western Literature Association in Albuquerque, New Mexico, in October 1967.

*Reprinted from* WESTERN AMERICAN LITERATURE,
*Vol. III, No. 2 (Summer 1968), by permission of the editor.*

coveries—we can usefully survey briefly some of the major interpretations that have demonstrated the novel's importance.

Since some readers may not know the book, let me quote in full a key episode, the one from which the novel seems to have derived its title and upon which the critics have chosen to focus.

Barney slowly sat up and sleepily reached for his boots. The warm afternoon air had partly dried his socks, but after he had pulled on the left boot the right boot stuck, and he thought again, as he had thought so many times, why does one goddamn foot have to be bigger than the other? Or why can't a man go into a store and say, give me that little boot and give me that big boot and put 'em both in the same goddamn box?

The exertion stirred the old beer again. He could feel it rumble beneath his broad belt buckle. He wished now he had saved the fourth bottle for another time.

Booted at last, he rose unsteadily. He tipped backward; he tipped forward; he caught himself in gentle sway. He spread his legs; the boot heels dug deeper into the soft earth; he stood solid at last.

It can's be the beer, he thought. It must be the sun.

He pulled the rag of a handkerchief from his left rear pocket, wiping his sweaty face. "Goddamn," he said. "Even a man's dainties stink of horse sweat and dust."

Lifting the coil of rope from the dry juniper limb, he squinted toward the watering trough a hundred yards away. They were still there all right, the mare stirring the dust with her big feet and brushing black flies with her tail. Even with the flies, they'd just as soon wait awhile, he thought.

The saddle lay dumped where he had dropped it a couple of hours ago, the blanket still damp with the morning's sweat. I've come to the crossroads of life, he thought: I can pack this stinking saddle all of the way down to that horse, or I can lead that stinking horse all of the way back to this saddle.

He chose the second way. That way didn't look any easier, but he could put off the hardest part a little longer. Maybe he could carry himself and the rope those hundred yards, but if he had to put that saddle on his own back he'd be dead. He'd be down in the brush before he'd stumbled a hundred feet, let alone a hundrd yards. And it wasn't the brush he hated so much as that goddamn itchy june grass.

So he took a quick aim and launched himself. The sagebrush wavered hotly around him; the steel blue sky seemed too bright to look at; he stumbled weakly across the tilting world. But he spread his arms like balancing wings; he spread his uneasy legs across the hot earth; he moved steadily again. My legs are already too short, he thought; I need to be up there to see where the hell I am headed; but even if my ass does drag the brush, I'm still going.

He reached the mare, and she stood for him, her tail still steadily sweeping her rump. He reached the rope around her neck and turned a half hitch over her nostrils. I'm pooped again, he thought. I couldn't lift that saddle even if it hung right now on my strong right arm. If I had that fourth bottle, which I should have saved, I'd drink it now to give me strength. The tail continued to swing.

Barney was at the crossroads again. He could either stumble back through the brush with the mare on the end of his rope, or he could make a gigantic effort to lift himself across her bare back. It'll be sweaty either way, he thought. But one way she'll do the sweating; she'll do the sweating, even if it does end up on me.

She was a tall mare; Barney was a short man; it would truly take a gigantic leap. Even with a stirrup, he thought, it's a long way up. Every time he had stretched his left leg and felt the denim tighten across his crotch, he had thought, maybe they ought to put those goddamn rivets in other places too.

Now he placed his boots solidly for the leap. With his left hand he fastened a sweaty grip on her withers. For his right hand there was only the fat back and slick hair, but if he could get an elbow on the other side he could hang in balance; he could kick himself upward; at last he could spread his legs and sit as a man was made to sit: astride, man and horse become the centaur.

The warm earth gave him strength. He leaped upward. He pawed the air and the ungrippable hair, hung like a kicking sack for an instant upon the apex, then tumbled headdown to the earth again. His head struck the pile of dung; his legs flew loosely into the sagebrush; he lay face upward, the delicate dung dust settling about him, his boots a yard apart in the twisted gray green branches. He could look up and see the old teats of the mare, black, slightly wrinkled and unused. She hadn't moved. She hadn't even stopped stirring the flies.

"Goddamn," he said to himself gently. Then he thought, maybe I'll just stay here until the sun goes down.

One of the first to note the real complexity of *Barney Tullus* was Professor Ernest Dewlap of Two Forks Junior College. In an article entitled "Style and Structure in *Barney Tullus*," he developed the thesis that whatever its seeming indifference to literary design, it is in reality a highly complicated, closely wrought text, with a great many literary devices functioning effectively to deepen and heighten meaning.

"Structurally," writes Professor Dewlap, "the story is a triangle, an isoscles triangle, with one side the rise, one side the fall, and the base the horizontal earthly experience of the hero. The title of course makes this clear. However, even without the title, the triangularity of the design would be strongly revealed.

"Consider the first description of Barney as he stands 'booted at last.' 'He spread his legs; the boot heels dug deeply into the soft earth; he stood solid at last.' Barney thus becomes a human triangle, and in his triangularity he becomes strong upon the earth. The same image is picked up a bit later, and again Barney is able to order his experience. 'He spread his uneasy legs across the hot earth; he moved steadily again.'

"Note, too, that the mare herself is a triangle in her relationship to Barney. Her withers are both the apex of her own solid structure and the high point of Barney's rise. And as he lies prostrate looking up at her, he in a sense completes the form which gives her strength.

"Furthermore, in the development of such structural design, the style functions with special effectiveness. Note the three-clause shape of a great many sentences, and note that in many of these sentences the third clause binds the form. Steadiness, control come in the very design of the sentences. An already quoted passage illustrates this stylistic feature: 'He spread his legs; the boot heels dug deeper into the soft earth; he stood solid at last.' Note, too, that even the alliteration moves in threes: 'broad belt buckle,' 'still steadily sweeping,' and 'delicate dung dust.'

"The triangularity of design is thus clear. However, lest the reader take this for mere mechanical contrivance, the imposition of rigid forms upon the naturally amorphous human experience, note the way the form really reinforces the ambiguity of the human predicament. The apex signifies aspiration, perhaps hubris, but it is also the point of fragile balance and fall. And in the fall, which may be the failure of aspiration, is a return to that which may be mundane but that which is the plane of strength. All of this is imaged also in the figure of Barney himself: his head, which is the human apex, becomes giddy at times but becomes steady in its dependence on the legspread grounding to the dusty earth."

Still another dimension of the novel was revealed by Professor Alister Outlook, writing in *The Balsam Review*. In an essay entitled "Mythic Patterns in *Barney Tullus*," Professor Outlook argued convincingly that the real power of the novel comes from its evocation of great mythic themes. "The first evidence," he noted, "comes in the word *gigantic*, in 'he could make a gigantic effort to lift himself across her bare back,' and repeated shortly after in 'it would truly take a gigantic leap.' Now Barney is clearly not a giant in any strictly physical sense, yet an aura of the superhuman begins to surround him. Thus when he falls in weakness and lies close again upon the earth, we say to ourselves at once: this is not Barney Tullus; this is Antaeus. And we can be certain, though the novel does not tell us explicitly, that Barney will regain his strength and rise again.

"Less immediately obvious is another mythic allusion. As he makes his way to the horses, Barney moves through a field of sagebrush. After his fall he lies with his boots 'a yard apart in the twisted gray green branches.' Now it is never clear whether this is black sagebrush (*Artemisia nova*) or big sagebrush (*Artemisia tridentata*), but in either case it is *Artemisia*. And, as every one knows, Artemisia derives through association with wormwood and mugwort from Artemis. Although Barney is probably not a virgin in any strictly physical sense, he is nevertheless a hunter. And thus the relevance of the myth becomes overwhelmingly clear."

If Professor Outlook suggested that Barney will rise again in all of his old strength, Professor L. B. H. Fescue seemed to have his doubts, though he did not state them in a direct and dogmatic manner. In an article entitled "Barney Tullus as American: An Old Theme Restated," he saw the hero finally as a changed man. "If Barney goes up one side of the mare an innocent," he wrote, "he comes down the other side a fallen man. This realization takes us at once from the dung dust of the West deep into the central development of American self-awareness—or lack of self-awareness. If Jonathan remains a hick, Manly has never been one; yet in his pompous goodness—indeed his manliness—he has no insight into his own nature. If he comes out well in other conflicts, he will do so by good luck, the good luck of the cultural circumstances which save his kind of nature—or should we say allow for it. His heroism is ambiguous, or at least let us say that his creator has an ambivalent attitude toward him. In one sense, he—that is, the hero—is a barbarian, and we suspect that if he were to take his Americanness to Europe a century later, although he would have little patience with the pretensions of his fellow American tourists, as he has little patience with the Anglomaniacal Dimple, he would nevertheless prefer a shiny, well preserved Da Vinci to a faded and cracked one. And certainly were he to encounter Newman, who, as Leslie Fiedler so aptly points out, might well have come upon that other innocent barbarian, the conversation would fail, not merely because a century lies between them but also because for one—that is, for Newman—at least one wall, the outer wall to self-discovery, has been penetrated. Yet even Newman, as he stares too eagerly up at the masterpiece he wants to know, is substituting—or at least trying to—an American frontier energy for the reflective awareness that is the knowledge and burden of centuries-old traditions. And even as he turns finally to see if the little paper is in fact consumed, he has played the game to the end in his own way. As Mrs. Tristram must point out to him, it is his remarkable good nature that has saved *them*, as it has saved *him*, kept them a facade of innocence as it has kept him the real purity of his moral intent." Thus concludes Professor Fescue.

So far the school of authenticism had not been heard from. However, at last the word got around that here was a novel about a cowboy. "We'll see," said Dr. Angus McFrisby, Professor of English at the Upper Pahvant College for Girls and one of the leading authenticators in Western letters.

"There is some evidence here," began Dr. McFrisby, "that the author of *The Rise and Fall of Barney Tullus* knows something about the real West. At least he has read widely. Although his sources may be difficult to identify with satisfactory scholarly precision, one can be confident that if necessary he can provide a solid bibliography and a comforting foundation of specific notes.

"Having said this, we are sorry that we must object to a few matters which make uncertain the complete authenticity of this account of Western life. Reference is made in the story to the mare's brushing black flies with her tail. We assume that these flies are the black-bodied gnats of the dipterous family *Simuliidae*. If this assumption is correct, then within the limited historical context of Barney's experience these flies may be slightly anachronistic. Let us consider the time of Barney's rise and fall. The author mentions the extreme heat; indeed the hotness is the dominant climatic note. He mentions the itchy June grass, which we take to be cheatgrass (*Bromus tectorum*). Now June grass is itchy only when it is ripe, and it ripens only in late June or early July, with the possibility, when the spring is long, wet, and cool, of reaching maturity only in mid July. The heat and the itchy June grass (one does feel more comfortable calling it *cheatgrass*) do thus seem to belong together. But what about the black flies? As everybody knows, the larvae of the black gnat are aquatic. They thus develop only in the wetness of the late spring, coming to their most vicious maturity by mid-June. Dates will differ here, according to latitudes, elevations, and particular circumstances of weather patterns, but it is my personal observation that the black flies have passed out of the picture by June 29 or by July 2 at the latest. In short, if one scratches his legs in June, he probably scratches the bite of the black fly. If he scratches in July, he probably scratches the cheatgrass caught in his socks. Although he may possibly scratch both in the same period of time, such simultaneity would, I believe, be highly unusual.

"Furthermore, we are sorry that we must add that some signs of a phony literary West still flaw the book. It is good—indeed it is delightful—to have dust and sweat and stink in the story, but we are more than mildly troubled about the word dung. Dung it must be, to be sure, but haven't literary conventions won out here? Hasn't the author given in to the temptations of the pleasantly alliterative 'd' and the poetically euphonious *ung* when he ought to give way manfully to linguistic realities? To sum up, for the writer about the West a spade must be a spade, or, to paraphrase slightly, a horse turd must be a horse turd."

This completes my survey of formal criticism, but one more critic ought I think to be included in this brief study. I know an old fellow who sometimes reminds me of Barney, in the little things he sometimes does, in the little things he says, even in the way he looks. I have to be careful about fusing reality and fiction here because this old guy is in other ways unlike Barney. He sometimes shoes my horses, and although he seems to insist on calling my gelding a mare, I still have confidence in his horse sense. In a certain way he is a cowboy. I reasoned that he would do as an informed lay critic.

When his wife met me at the front door, she said, "Jim's in the basement watching television." I knew that if I announced boldly that I wanted her to tell him that I wanted him to read something, he'd spook and probably climb out a window. "Tell him to come up a minute," I said. "Just tell him I want to ask him something." She opened the door to the basement stairs and yelled down. "Some one wants to see you." "What about?" I heard him say. "Come on up and see," she said. I could hear him growling, so I walked across the room to the door and yelled down in my own way. "Come on up a minute, Jim. I need your opinion on something." "Okay," he answered, "as soon as I slip on these goddamn boots."

When he saw the book, he did spook. But I had him trapped. He couldn't do anything but sit down at the table and read the pages I shoved in front of him.

"That's pretty rough language for a book," he said.

"Never mind that," I said. "Just get to the part about falling off the horse."

He read slowly, smiling slightly.

"Well, what do you think?" I finally said.

"What do you mean, what do I think?" he said.

"I mean, is it true."

"How the hell should I know?" he said. "I don't know the guy."

"I mean, does it seem true? Could it happen?"

"Sure it could happen," he said. "Happened to me once."

There was a bit of silence; then he added, "But I wouldn't write a book about it."

I think I understand why my friend Jim would not write a book about falling off a horse. The books he knows simply do not give attention to such seemingly unimportant human experiences. However, there is no good reason why a writer should not write about falling off a horse. Perhaps it would be difficult to make such an experience or even one of the major experiences, but if that experience, trivial, unexciting, unromantic or whatever it may seem to Jim, can function with other experiences to define and illuminate something important about a man, then clearly it can have a rightful place in the story. The rightness will depend upon the understanding and skill of the writer. Some writers cannot make falling off a thousand foot cliff important; Henry James could make taking off a glove important.

A part of that skill may well be a close attention to the sounds of words, the rhythms of sentences, the patterns of imagery, the larger structures of chapters and sections and of the short story or novel itself. At his best, and when he has the active cooperation of an intelligent and sensitive reader, these things, these devices, should function in the fictional persuasion without the help of the critic. After all, a novel should be read as a novel, and this goes for *The Sound and the Fury* as much as for *David Copperfield* or *The Man of Property*. If as readers we come armed with or prepared by maps, genealogical charts, handbooks to this and that, we are no longer reading a novel. We are playing an academic literary game. But perhaps I make reading too simple. Obviously some young readers need help in developing that kind of awareness, those habits in which the skills of the writer can really have their say. But obviously, too, critics can help too much. Innocent readers can still, I believe, read Cooper with pleasure. College junior and senior English majors, trained to quiver at the least exquisite twist and turn of a phrase, have their difficulties.

Furthermore, a part of the understanding and skill involves an awareness of the mythic dimensions of human experience, although *awareness* may be misleading here since what is meant is not just the central controlling consciousness but the unconscious as well. So in the long view I don't object to relating Barney to Antaeus, providing the pattern of mythic allusions does really illuminate the *human* dimension of Barney. The trouble with Professor Outlook is that he is not really interested in Barney. And poor old Barney will do better carrying that stinking saddle than toting all that classical pedantry.

With one exception, I really have no quarrel with the critical assumptions of the eminent men I have quoted. I confess that McFrisby stirs me up. For the real enemy of Western American literature, in my opinion, is the high priest of authenticism. He thinks he is a literary critic, but he is not really a critic, for he has none of the qualities of mind that make a critic. He is really a bastard type, fathered by a third-rate historian and mothered by a retarded literary lady who never got over the shock of learning that Shakespeare *lied* when he added those years to young Prince Hal. What can he know of the acts of the creative imagination, when he has none of his own? He is convinced that Western American literature began—and perhaps ended—with Andy Adams and *The Log of a Cowboy*. He says to the young writer, get those cows in there, and rub a little shit on their hides, when he ought to be saying, keep reading Andy Adams because he can teach you honesty, but don't forget to read Hawthorne also and even Henry James. He discovered a cardboard literary West and learned to call it phony. Indeed *phony* is his favorite word, but he really doesn't understand what makes it phony. He assumes it is phony because it lacks historical fact or because it rearranges historical fact, because it has too many guns, too many women, not enough cows and too many horses. He thinks Taisie Lockhart is phony because she is a woman, when a woman didn't belong on the trail. But the critical truth is that Taisie is phony because she isn't a woman. She is a cardboard doll. And no supply of footnotes could have given her life. Only a novelist's imagination could have done that.

# MAX WESTBROOK

## *Conservative, Liberal, and Western: Three Modes of American Realism*

> *My task which I am trying to achieve is, by the power of the written word to make you hear, to make you feel—it is, before all, to make you see.*—JOSEPH CONRAD, PREFACE TO *The Nigger of the Narcissus.*

JOSEPH CONRAD'S FAMOUS PREFACE is widely admired, but its meaning has not been understood by those who attempt an ideological definition of

*Reprinted from the Summer, 1966 issue of* SOUTH DAKOTA REVIEW *with the permission of the editor, John R. Milton.*

American literary realism. If fiction does not teach us what to believe but, rather, what to see, then the proper subject for study is a reality we are made to feel and see, not ideas and themes prepared for discussion. For the philosopher, the real is the property of metaphysics. For the novelist—if Conrad is right—the real is the property of epistemology. Literature is more concerned with *how* we know than with *what* we know.

Conrad, however, is not separating the *how* from the *what*. He is not saying that art should be technique merely or sensation merely. As an artist, he wants to make the reader "see." He wants that, "and no more." But making the reader see, he adds, "is everything." Like the new critics and the formalists of a later generation, Conrad is contending that the artist should try to make the reader feel and see the truth of human experience, that the concretions and forms of art constitute a distinct way of making an insight into reality. Our efforts to define American literary realism, then, might well begin with a study of how relevant authors believe it is possible to see and to learn, with a look at the modes of apprehension which lie behind what are usually called themes.

While not making any claims whatsoever about being exclusive or exhaustive, I want to distinguish three modes of apprehension which I believe to represent three major types of realism in American literature. The three names I have selected are Conservative, Liberal, and Western, though I hold no brief for my choice of terms. My purpose, more specifically, is to show that the Conservative and the Liberal are opposite one another in their interpretations of the place of subjective insight and formal tradition in the hero's effort to see realistically. Conservative and Liberal, nonetheless, have a common frame of reference in their mutual emphasis on consciousness and will. The Western realist, by contrast, is grounded in sources that are alien to the main streams of American experience as that experience is commonly understood in the Northern and Eastern and Southern states.

Before distinguishing types of realism, however, it is necessary to discuss two problems associated with the word itself.

First, the effort to understand differing modes of realism is made especially difficult because man's sensibility tends to be partisan: we are inclined to believe that our own language is qualitative but that the language of our opponent is quantitative. A Catholic may make qualitative distinctions about the Confession, while reducing the Baptist belief in individual freedom to a quantitative rule and thus an advocacy of license rather than freedom. A Baptist may reverse the process, making qualitative distinctions between his own belief in freedom and his own rejection of license, while reducing the Catholic Confession to an advocacy of automatic and mechanical forgiveness. It is much the same in other religions, in politics, and in beliefs generally: we tend to use our own beliefs as principles while reducing the beliefs of others to rules.

A common ground, of course, is an aid to our broadmindedness. A Liberal critic, for example, if he is reasonably fairminded, may pardon James Gould Cozzens (in *Guard of Honor*) for giving his Liberal Lieutenant the disgusting habit of picking his nose. Liberal novelists, after all, tend to be equally prejudicial in selecting a rather low species for their examples of Conservatives (Hemingway in *To Have and Have Not* for example). The point is that Cozzens and Hemingway, despite being in opposite camps, share a belief in the importance of consciousness and the will. It is possible for the members of one camp to say merely that the members of the other camp are taking a wrong-headed approach to reality. With the Western realist, however, it is a different matter. John Steinbeck's use of the term "Timshel" in *East of Eden,* for example, will not be taken as a sign of a known bias. Both Liberal and Conservative, having little or no common ground with the Western realist, will read "Timshel" as a sign that Steinbeck is indulging in fantasy, in illusions that are not wrong-headed but, rather, irrelevant. An examination of the Western mode of apprehension, however, will suggest a way of knowing—and thus a relevance—not possible in the world views of the Conservative or the Liberal.

Second, it is necessary to remember that "historical realism"—as a term referring to a period in American literature—must be distinguished from "realism" as a generic term. The "realism" of "historical realism" need not be taken as an invidious term. Certainly, all good writers are realistic in the sense that they are not merely idle; in the sense that what they say— with ghosts, symbols, or whatever—is germane to the actual lives of actual men. And it is the generic sense I have in mind when I speak of types of realism. Historical realism, by contrast, may be defined as works published primarily between 1865 and 1920 and containing an implicit or explicit attack on books which are patently stereotyped, sentimental, slick, escapist, and—typically—popular expressions of cultural attitudes which were also popular.

During the period 1865 to 1920, major authors often wrote in direct attack on popular romancers. And it was relevant for a William Dean Howells to write the story of Silas Lapham with at least the partial motive of showing that popular novelists like Horatio Alger made an inaccurate association between virtue and success. It is not now relevant, however, for a Bernard Malmud to write a novel showing that "Mission Impossible" is unrealistic. The audience he writes for does not need the information.

Because of special pressures, many Western realists, by contrast, are still concerned with the relativistic wars of historical realism. Hollywood and television "westerns," the still popular cowboy paperback, and the general feeling that Western writing is regional rather than American are three of the major forces of this pressure; and the pressure is antagonistic to the finer potential of Western writers. Defining a Western type of realism, it is hoped, will help to designate those Western writers who have overcome the special problems of their region.

The Conservative mode of apprehension is illustrated by James Russell Lowell's defense of institutions and laws as the necessary corrective of man's subjective bias. The individual, Lowell argues, cannot see objectively:

Truth, after all, wears a different face to everybody, and it would be too tedious to wait till all were agreed. She is said to lie at the bottom of a well, for the very reason, perhaps, that whoever looks down in search of her sees his own image at the bottom, and is persuaded not only that he has seen the goddess, but that she is far better-looking than he had imagined.[1]

Since the objects of experience are a mirror, reflecting what the individual observer wants to see, revealing merely his own bias, his subjective self, the individual cannot use personal experience as a mode of apprehension to discover an objective reality outside himself. Institutions and laws, therefore (in a general sense, traditions), are the necessary corrective of subjective bias.

The second mode of realism, the Liberal, is characterized by the opposite position: it is only by looking to personal experience that man can hope to get outside his subjective bias and discover the objectively real. Emerson is the obvious example, as shown by representative quotations from his major essays:

To believe your own thought, to believe that what is true for you in your private heart is true for all men,—that is genius. Speak your latent conviction, and it shall be the universal sense.

Nothing is at last sacred but the integrity of your own mind.

No law can be sacred to me but that of my nature.

If it were only for a vocabulary, the scholar would be covetous of action. Life is our dictionary.[2]

Personal experience, then, is for the Liberal the dictionary which honest and courageous observers use to discover an objective reality outside themselves.

The opposition between Conservative and Liberal appears also in their attitudes toward use of the traditional as a mode of apprehension. For the Conservative, the real is best apprehended through the language and discipline of traditionalist experience. In Hawthorne, for example, characters who use a non-traditionalist approach to the real (Rappaccini's science, Zenobia's transcendentalism, Dimmesdale's merely subjective expiation) fail to get outside themselves to the objectively real. Certainly, a literal or a tyrannical employment of traditionalist language also fails; but, as we see in "The Celestial Railroad" and especially in the spiritual triumph of Hester Prynne, it is only by means of a genuine and individualistic use of the traditional mode that man can overcome subjective illusion and apprehend a reality that enjoys ontological status. In the writings of Liberal thinkers, the traditionalist mode is assigned the opposite function. The language of tradition, according to Emerson, is a deceitful mode of perception, luring man with the promise of temporal reward, feeding his subjective ambition,

[1] See paragraph 13 of his essay entitled "Democracy."

[2] The first three quotations are from "Self-Reliance"; the fourth is from "The American Scholar."

and blinding him to those universal values the institution serves in name only.

The political version of this profound difference is directly comparable to the literary. The political Conservative considers himself realistic on the grounds that he has the common sense and moral courage to recognize man's innate culpability. What the political Conservative feels should be done about man's culpability changes with the times. Perhaps the earliest strategy was that of the Puritan theocracy. Quite different was the later and more strictly political form founded in the five pillars of aristocracy —beauty, wealth, birth, genius, and virtue—and taking the practical form of federalism. John Jay's remark that "Nothing is more certain than the indispensable necessity of government"[3] may be contrasted with "Civil Disobedience," a Liberal document in which Thoreau argues the superiority of the individual to the government and hopes for a day when men will be good enough to need no government at all. John Jay, believing that man is culpable by nature, asserts that the traditionalist language of government will always be needed to serve as a check against the innate evil of the individual.

Around the turn of the century, aberrant forms of Conservative thought appeared, with the five virtues of aristocracy now in ill-repute before the spread of democracy, while the pragmatic virtues of Horatio Alger heroes and "Captains of Industry" became increasingly popular as a Conservative language which was appropriate for the move from farm to city. More recently, during the Kennedy-Johnson era, the tradition was obscured for the casual observer because the central government—which supported capital around the turn of the century, even going so far as to use troops to break strikes—frequently became the instrument of Liberal thinkers; and thus we had the confusing turn-about illustrated by John Birchers who quoted with approval Thoreau's opposition to governmental intervention in private affairs. Without indicating the absurdity of this citation of Thoreau, suffice it to say that the continuing opposition of the Liberal and the Conservative modes of political thought is clearly seen in the struggle against federal authority—in the name of individual rights as the primary right—by such groups as the S.D.S.

In writers like Nathaniel Hawthorne, Henry James, T. S. Eliot, and James Gould Cozzens, the most continuing interest of the literary version of the Conservative mode seems to be a fascination with the theme of "conscious detachment."[4] Since reality, according to the Conservative, can be viewed objectively only through a traditionalist mode (a sense of the past, church ritual, an established and respected code of social and moral values), the paradigm of human hopes and failures is a study of the man who views life through his own impotent vision and thus develops a monster or bastard illusion of reality. Hawthorne's scientists, whose emphasis

[3] The Federalist, No. II, paragraph two.
[4] The term is from Henry James's *The Ambassadors*, chapter one.

on their own reason cuts them off from the legitimate generative power of God, become detached; and what they create is "spiritualized," that is, birthed apart from God's ontology, and thus has about it a glow of horror. In "The Birthmark," for example, Georgiana reads Aylmer's notebook and sees that even his most brilliant experiments are failures: they have life, but they are not real. Aylmer's refusal to accept the fact that he and Georgiana are made of clay is a refusal to accept that human limitation which makes it necessary for man to work through a traditionalist mode.

Henry James's studies of failure in Conservative apprehension are illustrated by Winterbourne, whose detachment from either European or American traditions results in his inability to "see" Daisy Miller; by Lambert Strether's "double consciousness," which causes him to create out of personal sensibility an illusion he must later, painfully, relinquish; by Isabel Archer's naive rejection of traditional duty in favor of her rights as an individual with personal insight and a free spirit, and by her learning, finally, that the utmost in self development lies in the performance of a duty which can be apprehended only by use of a traditionalist language.

T. S. Eliot writes from a comparable viewpoint when he describes Gerontion's "wilderness of mirrors," the terror of life in a wasteland in which man's sensibility—disassociated from the meaning and generative power of traditionalism—simply reflects back upon itself, mirroring an impoverished soul into an infinity of horrors.

Such Conservativist rejections of the subjective, it must be remembered, do not constitute a formula. It is the little mind, of whatever pursuasion, that reduces a mode to a formula. The finer spokesmen of the Conservative mode can think with traditionalist language and attack a Gilbert Osmond, whose allegiance to form is a perverted one; or a Mrs. Newsome, whose traditionalism is narrow-minded, insensitive, self-righteous. Comparable is James Gould Cozzens' concern with discriminations of realism as understood by the Conservative imagination. Both *Guard of Honor* and *By Love Possessed* feature heroes who learn, even in their mature years, of folk compromises which are the most noble level of traditionalist responsibility.

The second major characteristic of Conservative realism is the belief that there is a chemistry in the relation between the mode of apprehension and the physical world. The method of seeing can change souls, sometimes physical objects. Traditionalist modes of apprehension have an ontological status that is primary to the physical nature of an object apprehended by the personal insight of an individual. It is therefore realistic—especially in the fictive worlds of Hawthorne and James—for a mode of apprehension to have the power to change physical composition. Thus, in *The Scarlet Letter*, Dimmesdale's cowardly failure to confess through the pre-established mode of public confession marks an "A" on his breast. Hawthorne's equivocation before the question of the literal existence of the mark is a reluctant concession to the narrow factualist and to the individual who believes in personal insight: the "A," which may or may not be apprehended through personal insight, is real. The changing portrait and the withered chickens in *The House of the Seven Gables, The Marble Faun* passim, the hints of violations of physical laws at the end of "The Artist of the Beautiful" and in many other stories, and the general tendency to provide a physical reflection of internal values (the light and dark women for example) are cases in point. A symbol, in short, can have generative power, on the plot level, in relation to the physical world.

Though admitting that the ghost story is a possibility for any writer, I would hold that Henry James's affinity for stories like "The Private Life" is evidence of his interest in the physical potency of modes of apprehension. Relevant also are the deaths of Miles (in *The Turn of the Screw*) and Daisy Miller, who are killed by qualities of moral meaning more than by fright or the Roman fever. And, in *The Spoils of Poynton*, the manor house and its artifacts (judged true works of art by an act of personal sensitivity, and thereby falsely judged) are burned by a fire which has a symbolic rather than a physical cause.

The Liberal, by contrast, subscribes to the physical integrity of natural objects as to an article of faith. Witness Twain's famous attack on Fenimore Cooper, or Hemingway's efforts in *Green Hills of Africa* to write with such fidelity about actual experience that the quality of an imaginative work might be achieved. The Liberal's devotion to accurate observation, I want to emphasize, is different in kind from that common sense interest in accuracy which can be found in almost any successful writing. Since the Liberal holds that concrete personal experience is the language for getting to an objective reality outside one's self, he has assigned an ontological status to the integrity of natural objects. The belief is different from that of the Conservative, who admires accurate observation in a negative way (as a shibboleth in protection from illusions) but who is too pessimistic about natural depravity and personal bias to assign philosophical status to individual insight. The belief is different also from that of Melville. Though he accepted the Liberal's belief in personal experience as a language one might use to apprehend the real, Melville felt that each object contained its opposite, that the means of giving objective status to personal experience was thereby undercut; and thus Melville could lean toward transcendentalism but always find it unrealistic, untenable.

As the Conservative mode of apprehension leads to an interest in "conscious detachment" and in the chemical powers of viewpoint, so does the Liberal mode lead to an interest in stories of initiation. If man's personal mode of seeing is his best approach to objective reality, then studies of that effort would naturally be considered fundamental comments on the nature of reality. Again, the finer spokesmen of a type of realism do not reduce it to formula. Personal observation is no more a mechanical guarantee for the Liberal than external form is an automatic sign of achievement for the Conservative. In *The Sun Also Rises*, for example, Robert Cohn attempts to reduce the Hemingway code to a formula ("love" is reduced to "get a mistress" or "worship the pretty lady"; integrity becomes an instance of phony heroics) and fails to learn what is in front of him to learn. Others, like Frederic Henry in *A Farewell to Arms*, find it difficult to hold on to what they have learned or, like Henry Morgan in *To Have and Have Not*, come ill-equipped and in a bad time so that what they learn (in this case, the necessary brotherhood) they learn too late. Perhaps the most convincing examples, though, are *Huckleberry Finn* and *The Red Badge of Courage*, both stories of youths who learn of universal values through their own observations and who find that traditionalist modes reveal the world in distorted form.

Though the contrasts between the two modes of apprehension are profound, both the Liberal and the Conservative believe in the ethical importance of a good will, the necessity of man's being conscious of the meaning of his decisions, and in the association of will and rationality. Their dispute, to a significant degree, is the old and honorable debate about the rights of the individual and the rights of the group. A good Republican and a good Democrat, without betraying party loyalty, can agree that both are for the welfare of the common man, the difference being that one thinks this end is best served by some special attention to capital while the other thinks it better to pay some special attention to labor. In literature, there are similar points of contact. A Conservative novelist like Henry James does not advocate education in place of the practical experience which is so highly valued by the Liberal, nor does he want allegiance to traditions to be given by that mechanical obedience which is so fervently attacked by the Liberals.[5] And Liberals like Twain, Crane, and Hemingway, in turn, may show a fine appreciation of education—though nervous on the point—and they may even reveal a latent preference for a tough or roguish version of the gentleman. Such overlappings do not undercut the fundamental opposition, but they do suggest that the debate is grounded in a common belief: the importance of good will and of conscious understanding as necessary values in a realistic world view.

The third major American realism, the Western, holds that a heightened state of consciousness is a bifurcation of the human being and results in a disenfranchisement of the human soul. Authors like John Steinbeck, Walter Van Tilburg Clark, Wright Morris, Willa Cather (at least in *The Professor's House* and *A Lost Lady*), Glenway Wescott (in early works like *The Apple of the Eye* and *The Grandmothers*), Vardis Fisher, Frederick Manfred, Wallace Stegner, and Frank Waters have a sacred as opposed to a profane mode of apprehension. Events are real or unreal according to whether or not they recreate the relevant original act, the primordial act which is the source of meaning. Mircea Eliade's *The Sacred and the Profane* and *Cosmos and History* and Arnold Van Gennep's *Rites of Passage* are standard—and excellent—sources for study of this primordial sense of life.

---

[5] See the concluding chapter of *The Ambassadors*.

To the Western realist, the Conservative is right to appeal to pre-established forms (the primordial is after all the ultimate on this score), but pathetically wrong in that modern forms are barren, profane. The modern church, modern society, and contemporary values generally reflect no sense of the sacred unity of all life, no contact with the unconscious, with the *anima*. They are man's mental inventions, and they are without blood. Modern traditions have lost contact with the source, with sex, God, land . . . with the generative primordial. And the fact that the modern Conservative does have traditional forms is all the more dangerous, for he has thereby just enough show of ritual to mislead him into thinking his forms are real, just enough to passify his primordial needs (provided the stresses are not major, provided he can use creature comforts as temporary mitigation), just enough to lure him toward that inevitable day when the soul he has betrayed and the dark inner self he has denied will demand something more than a form barren of creative energy. Then comes the day of horror, which modern man calls, euphemistically, a "nervous breakdown."

Western realism also contrasts sharply with the Liberal viewpoint. C. G. Jung, whose psychology the Westerner prefers to Freud's, put it this way: "It is, to my mind, a fatal mistake to consider the human psyche as a merely personal affair and to explain it exclusively from a personal point of view."[6] Jung's criticism is aimed at those who—whether Conservative or Liberal—hold that a belief can be real to an individual only when the belief is clear to his rational consciousness. Later in the same essay, Jung intends to warn all men as he comments on one of his patients: "He has forced everything under the inexorable law of his reason, but somewhere nature escaped and came back with a vengeance in the form of perfectly unassailable nonsense."[7] Mark Twain, like his own Hank Morgan in *A Connecticut Yankee,* placed his faith in reason as an ability which distinguishes man from beast, only to find that reason ran thin and seemed, finally, to have no satisfactory connection with human nature or with human history, to have—the Westerner would say—very little to do with what *is*. Reason (or the probing consciousness as it appears in the Liberal mode) is held by the Westerner to be unrealistic. And the hard-nosed level of the Liberal viewpoint—his insistence on grounding observation in factual accuracy—is also judged unrealistic, in Jung's terms, as an "undervaluation of the human soul."[8]

Thus the traditions of the Conservative, the disciplined experience of the Liberal, and the reason (under whatever name) of both viewpoints are, for the Western imagination, three signs of the modern impoverishment of the soul. Western realism is founded in the belief that man cannot approach a universal through modern traditions or through personal experience, for both require an effort of will, an act which betrays the uncon-

[6] *Psychology and Religion* (New Haven, 1963), Yale University Press, p. 16.
[7] *Ibid.*, p. 18.
[8] *Ibid.*

scious and precludes a harmony of the whole being with the whole of reality, precludes that unity which is essential to Western ontology.

The characteristic voice of this ontology is the *anima*, the soul:

> The anima is not the soul in the dogmatic sense, not an *anima rationalis*, which is a philosophical conception, but a natural archetype that satisfactorily sums up all the statements of the unconscious, of the primitive mind, of the history of language and religion . . . it is life behind consciousness that cannot be completely integrated with it, but from which, on the contrary, consciousness arises. For, in the last analysis, psychic life is for the greater part an unconscious life that surrounds consciousness on all sides.[9]

Here is an overt explanation of the fundamental distinction suggested earlier: in profane realisms the conscious mind is primary; in Western realism the unconscious mind is primary. The Westerner is required, however, when there is no instruction from the *anima*, to be strictly obedient to objective reality and, it follows, to use his reason. But when the *anima* speaks, he is required to listen absolutely, even if this means he must treat objective reality as the merest appearance of the moment. Profane realists ask the Westerner for his guidelines: by what standard does he heed the discipline of objective reality at one time, the voice of the *anima* at another? But since profane realists require guidelines in terms of conscious reasoning (characteristic of the Conservative) or the reasoning intuition (characteristic of the Liberal), they can only conclude that the Westerner's answer is arbitrary, leading to a world view that will be unrealized and to novels that will be unstructured. They cannot see that the Western realist —who owes no allegiance to what he considers an intellectual and bifurcating concept of the real, who associates the reason with mere practicality and not with ontology—moves between fact and dream according to the sometimes voice of his dark and inner self.

This willingness to accept the authority of the *anima* suggests to the profane realist that the Westerner is an escapist type of romantic. The Westerner argues, however, that it is the other way around, since he can accept facts that do not fit his theory, while the profane man restricts the world to suit his theory. Both the Conservative and the Liberal believe that a universal cannot be proved by empirical means. It is possible, by empirical methods, to show merely that an hypothesis has not been disproved in whatever number of instances one has studied. The profane man believes that man can *discover* the real (in the discipline of historicity for the Conservative, in the discipline of personal experience for the Liberal), but both believe this act of discovery must be or become a conscious act in order to be genuine for the individual.

For the Western realist, by contrast, it is possible to believe in universals without a rationale, possible to base universals on empirical evidence. The real lies in dark caverns of the unconscious and cannot be penetrated

[9] "Archetypes of the Collective Unconscious," in *The Basic Writings of C. G. Jung* (New York, 1959), Random House, p. 311.

by the rational (or conscious) mind. We think with the conscious mind, but thereby apprehend only the effects of the unconscious, rather than its true nature, and thus we have only empirical evidence of the nature of the real, that is, of the archetypal symbols of the real as they voluntarily appear in the unconscious.

I make the distinction, obviously, in its purest form. In practice, philosophical clarity is blurred with rough edges by all parties. The Western artist, for his part, has long since chafed under the majority emphasis on rational modes, and he is inclined to tease the Easterner or to deliberately misunderstand him as a perverse testament of loyalty to the unconscious mind. But even in the skilled exaggerations of D. H. Lawrence the basic position is clear. Lawrence, a British cousin of the American West, names morality as the essential function of art, denies the didactic (rational) type of morality, and explains that he means a "passionate, implicit morality . . . a morality which changes the blood, rather than the mind," for the mind merely "follows later, in the wake."[10] Consciousness, that is, has an empirical function. It cannot create. It can merely record the effects of that real morality which is deeper than rational thought. Lawrence is illustrative also in his denigration of the will: "A thing that you sincerely believe in cannot be wrong, because belief does not come at will. It comes only from the Holy Ghost within."[11] And when this "Holy Ghost within" (a type of the *homunculus* or little man within, a term used by Lawrence, Walter Clark, and others) is betrayed by the consious mind, he turns beast, "howling like a wolf or a coyote under the ideal windows."[12]

And yet the Western rejection of will is not a rejection of *any* function of the will; it is rather an insistence that will keep its proper place and not be used to betray the primary unconscious. The point is that will cannot control the unconscious. For the Western realist, an intuition *occurs*. As Jung put it, "you do not *make* an intuition. On the contrary, it always comes to you; you *have* a hunch, it has produced itself and you only catch it if you are clever or quick enough."[13] A climactic scene in H. L. Davis's *Honey in the Horn* is a characteristic literary expression of the primacy of the unconscious:

> Not to take her [Luce, the heroine] would mean setting up enmity between them, and it would be an enmity of her body, which couldn't understand such matters as moral responsibility and ethical scruples. He [Clay, the hero] dared not risk that, no matter what it got him into.[14]

For the profane man, whether Conservative or Liberal, this decision will be viewed through a conscious mode of apprehension and found to be— in the most pejorative sense of the term—romantic. For the Westerner,

[10] *Studies in Classic American Literature* (New York, 1964), The Viking Press, p. 171.
[11] *Ibid.*, p. 102.
[12] *Ibid.*, p. 9.
[13] *Psychology and Religion*, p. 49.
[14] *Honey in the Horn* (New York, 1935), Avon Book Division, p. 259.

who will view the scene through the unconscious mode of apprehension, Clay's decision is realistic; and any other decision would be non-substantive or irrelevant use of rational faculties totally unable to assess an "enmity of body." The conscious mind can reflect on the unconscious, but never merge with it, control it, or reduce it to rational meanings.

There are many causes of the war between critics associated with Western American literature and critics associated with the East, but one of the most substantive causes is the Western critic's belief in the kind of unity found in writers like Davis. Since the Eastern critic tends to judge both the real and the actual worlds with a conscious mode of apprehension, he places a high value on a consistent approach to both and on the necessary dualism of mind and body. He will conclude, therefore, that a novel like Walter Clark's *The City of Trembling Leaves* is unsuccessfully resolved. Timothy Hazard, the hero, confronts problems of the practical world: his career in music, his family, his friends. He seems, most importantly, to be a quest hero in search of unity within multiplicity. The method of his quest centers around his art, and includes his youthful adventures as an athlete and frustrated lover; but the balance he so desperately seeks seems to come mainly in ritualistic mountain hikes during which he observes and respects a variety of "sprites." At the end, he has married his childhood sweetheart and is last seen watering his front yard, watching his children play. For the Eastern critic, typically, there is neither a traditionalist nor an experiential connection between a communion with mountain sprites and a domestic scene of the hero watering his front yard. The unconscious mode, however, from its primitive to its contemporary versions, does not permit the *anima* to be tamed or brought under conscious management. The ending of *The City of Trembling Leaves* represents, for the Westerner, one instance of the only resolution which is possible: that which comes when the dark and inner self has been given its due, when the mystic unity of sprite and home results in a sense of the sacrality of *all* life. For Clark, in short, it is *realistic* to hold the sacred in a profane hand. It is *unrealistic* to deny either fact or spirit and to subsume one under the standards of the other. Unity is the goal, but it is a goal that will never be achieved by the conscious mind.

John Steinbeck's *East of Eden*, for similar reasons, has also been misreviewed by Eastern critics. The reader who grounds his morality in consciousness is disturbed to find that Aron Trask's will toward the good collapses under realistic pressures, with the clear implication that his goodness is improperly motivated; while Cal Trask's evil—which seems to have a biological, a deterministic foundation—turns toward moral heroism. Since good and evil are clearly stated by the intruding author to be the certain realities of human existence, since rational terms are used yet irrational conclusions reached, since free will is praised yet a major character (Cathy) is called an unhuman monster by birth rather than by will, the novel is incoherent. Steinbeck, many reviewers felt, should have returned to the kind of thing he did in *The Grapes of Wrath*, where his dramatization of interconnectedness made sense in terms of economic problems felt to be substantive by Americans of all regions. Economic problems, however, are not fundamental to Steinbeck's vision. The difference between *The Grapes of Wrath* and *East of Eden,* in terms of their critical reception, is that sacrality in *The Grapes of Wrath* was misread as transcendentalism or social protest or Protestant brotherhood and thus felt to be authentic, whereas *East of Eden* lacked an obvious tie to national problems and thus Eastern reviewers could not discover a way to misread it into legitimacy.

But the presence of a biological (and moral) sport like Cathy does not disrupt the ontology of Steinbeck's fictive world, for, like Jung, like Walter Clark, like Manfred, Waters, and others, he is not bothered by what he does not know in rational terms. What he consciously knows of ultimate reality is merely "effect" anyway, and it is arrogant to turn the one-cell flashlight of man's intellect into the blinding light of the sun and pronounce theories in explanation. Thus, for the Western realist, determinism and belief in the human spirit can live side by side. Neither, after all, can be fully assessed. Both, empirical observation tells us, exist. The fate of Aron and Cal Trask is offensive to profane sensibilities because it seems an emotional and perverse testimony to a romantic bias against the man of good will. The collapse of Aron, however, is realistic to the Westerner, not because of bias against the intellect, but because Aron's "goodness" is based on the conscious intellect and is, therefore, unrealistic in its foundations. Cal's evil, on the contrary, includes an honest awareness of his dark and inner self, of the wolf within all men; and he is thus more realistically prepared for morality than is his brother, whose intellect leads him to deny a part of his being which, under stress, breaks loose, sending his shattered consciousness into terror.

These three realisms, I repeat, are neither exclusive nor exhaustive. Qualifications and differentiations are needed. Exceptions and combinations are plentiful. I merely claim, here, that they are fundamental types of realism, and I believe their distinctiveness can be summarized by the three different ways of apprehending human inclinations.

For the Conservative realist, inclinations are animalistic, and the rational mind, through the mode of traditionalist experience, should restrain them. The Conservative believes it is realistic to recognize that inclinations are the true source of evil, are basic to human nature, and that it is wise, therefore, for reason to use the guidelines and language of tradition. The Liberal realist, by contrast, associates inclinations with earthly corruption, and he distinguishes between an inclination which is the residue of that corruption and an *intuition* which is man's spark of the divine (or capacity for reason or sensitivity to the real). Thus he believes it is at least possible for man to overcome a temporal corruption and develop the finer and more fundamental side of his being; working in this direction, the Liberal feels, is certainly more realistic than a cynical surernder to an evil which lies in the nature of human foibles and creations rather than in the souls of men. The Western realist, revealing that he is an alien to both camps, believes that inclinations (both good and evil, though not aptly called by either name) are our contact with the primordial. To grant the integrity of the inner self—however disturbing its voice—is realistic; to deny it, to chain it with rational reasons, to be ashamed of it, is a betrayal of multiplicity to the false comfort of intellectual single-mindedness, and the bargain is fatal.

# JOHN R. MILTON
## Moderator and Editor

## *The Western Novel—A Symposium*

FOR A LONG TIME we have felt that some novelists living on or near the Great Plains have been unduly neglected by critics and by professors of literature. The reasons for this neglect are several. Western writers, except those living on the Pacific Coast, are geographically isolated, and so it is difficult to think of them as a group or school. Persons interested in literary history speak easily of the New England school, the Southern group, or the Midwest writers; but the serious Western novelists live so far apart and work in such solitude that they have never been considered as a group. Furthermore, it is not entirely understood that they have any wish to be taken as a group. In the West, the last remnants of frontier individualism (which we still fondly but perhaps mistakenly call "American") linger in the strength, independence, orneriness, and quiet courage of capable novelists. These men are just beginning to fraternize to a certain extent, and they want to know and respect each other as men and writers. In their work, however, each stubbornly goes his own way, and this is as it should be. In spite of charges laid against their work (formlessness, wordiness, crudeness, etc.) they are highly concerned with the novel as both storytelling and as art. They wish to preserve those people, places, and values which have often been distorted by mythmaking and tourism.

The exploitation by commercialism of the sensational and adventurous aspects of the West has clouded our eyes to those novels of or from the West which have literary stature. The term "western" has been applied to all novels produced in the West, even though this popular term is better applied to only the pulp novel or the romance or the descendents of the dime novel. The frontier spirit lives on in our wishful thinking, in our

*Reprinted from the Autumn, 1964 issue of* SOUTH DAKOTA REVIEW
*with the permission of the editor, John R. Milton.*

television series, and in the thousands of almost worthless hack jobs which pass as paperback novels in the railroad, bus, and plane terminals. This phenomenon is interesting, certainly, but it does not represent all the writing which might be called western. And, in judgment, if Luke Short is not better than Kathleen Norris, or Raymond Chandler, then perhaps Frederick Manfred and Walter Clark are no worse than Faulkner and Crane. The difficulty comes in getting the professors and critics (and often they are the same persons) to put aside the long-established misconceptions of Western American fiction and take a fresh look at this literature.

The fresh look calls for a certain amount of courage and for independent evaluation, because western fiction is relatively new and there is no back-log of criticism to which the student may turn. For the past ten years it has been a matter of a few isolated teachers and writers in the West putting in a good word—sometimes quietly, sometimes noisily—for those novels which seemed to deserve attention. Gradually and persistently they have won ground. Vardis Fisher, Frank Waters, Frederick Manfred, H. L. Davis, and others, have found their way into M.A. and Ph.D. theses. It is not unlikely that the Western American novel will achieve respectability within the next decade.

The novelists who participate in the following symposium have at least one thing in common (Michael Straight excepted)—they live, or have lived, in the arid and semi-arid region of the United States which Walter Prescott Webb has defined as the West. This region differs from the Eastern United States in its natural rhythms, its geography, its climate, and therefore its society. These differences are reflected in the art of the two regions, even though there are also many similarities, as one would expect in art. The purpose of this symposium is to provide information and to expose the insights of the writer whose concerns and problems center upon the West. The questions vary in their intent. Some are too complex to be answered within the limitations of the symposium. At least one, as Vardis Fisher points out, is perhaps childish. Others may seem obvious. Each question, however, was designed to evoke (or provoke) a variety of responses, so that in this first public discussion by a group of Western writers there might emerge both the similarities and differences among these men.

The novelists: Frederick Manfred lives in Luverne, Minnesota, with the Midwest at this back and the West in front of him. Frank Waters is a native Southwesterner who maintains a winter home in Taos and a summer home in Arroyo Seco, both in the northern mountains of New Mexico. Walter Clark recently left San Francisco and returned to Reno, Nevada. Vardis Fisher is in Hagerman, Idaho. Harvey Fergusson spent the major portion of his life in New Mexico, although he now lives in California. Forrester Blake has also lived in New Mexico but is currently in Idaho. Paul Horgan originated in New York, spent most of his writing life in New Mexico, and has recently moved to Connecticut. Michael Straight was invited to join this group because he is an Easterner who has gone to the West for the subjects of his two fine novels and is able to speak as a perceptive and intelligent "outsider." All told, these men have produced more than one hundred books.

In the symposium an abbreviated question appears in the text with each answer, for the sake of convenience. The full questions which were posed to the eight novelists are as follows:

1. Are you conscious of being a *western* writer (regional), and what does this mean to you in terms of what you are trying to do in fiction?

2. What do you consider the chief characteristics of the American West? As a region, or place, and the subject for fiction, how does it differ from the East, the South, or the Midwest? What is its chief force, ie, the force which might be said to lie behind or to motivate the fiction written in the West?

3. Because of locale, western fiction seems to pay more attention to nature, usually in a somewhat romantic way (and often through symbolism). Are you conscious of this emphasis in your own work?

4. It has been said that characterization is weak in the western novel, and that the cause of this may be the emphasis given to locale or setting. Do you feel this to be true? Does the eastern novel, or the southern novel, succeed better in characterization?

5. How can we account for the fact that there are few western novels with a contemporary setting as opposed to an historical setting?

6. Of those novels within the 20th century which deal with the area bounded roughly by the Mississippi River, the Pacific coastal mountains, and the Mexican and Canadian borders, would you name the ones which you consider outstanding and make a comment about them? (Include, if you wish, novels written by "outsiders" who have come into the region for their subject matter.)

7. Which of your own novels do you consider the best one, or the most satisfactory to you? Why?

8. Does the American West have, or suggest to you, a major theme? Or, in your own work, is there something which stands behind the individual concerns in the novels and provides a thematic (or other) continuity?

9. Does the western novelist have any special problems, because of his subject matter and/or his regional background? How can these be overcome?

10. How do you account for the fact that the major western novelists have not received the kind of recognition accorded to eastern or southern novelists?


## FREDERICK MANFRED

1. *Are you conscious of being a* western *writer, and how does this affect your writing?*

I am no more conscious of being a western writer than Homer was of being a Greek or Hardy a Wessex Englishman or Tolstoi a Russian or Faulkner a Mississippi Southern. I just happened to be born here; I like it here; and by great good luck it also happens to be one helluva wonderful place to live in. It is open; and the stallion in me feels free to roam and create.

*2.   What are the characteristics of the American West, especially the chief motivating force on fiction?*

I don't care much for either the East or the South when I visit there. The east is too congested (the Greeks came to great flower in an Athens with a population under 200,000); it is too dependent on Europe and its whimsies; it is terribly provincial, even ignorant; and the creative forces seem dead. The South is another matter. There is force in the South. But it is a force that has been eaten into by an acid of bitterness. Someday, though, when black blood and white blood have finally become one, it may provide the greatest creative explosion of them all. The Midlands west of the Mississippi I like. We have room here. We have time to brood on things in an easy, casual, even luxurious fashion. Our soil is incredibly rich from thousands upon thousands of years of buffaloes manuring it, which gives us seething blood. And there is still enough left of wild nature to subdue (or to learn to get along with) for us to be called upon to be inventive. But it all still comes down to individuals, men who are ruggedly individualistic, and this "Western country" still doesn't mind too much having them around. Throw a Western lad stark naked out into freezing weather in the middle of the winter with no resources except a knife and he is more likely to survive than is a lad from the East or the South. And to survive as a writer in any society at all takes the most guts of all.

*3.   Is there an emphasis on nature in your work, perhaps romantic or symbolic?*

No. I just take orders from the Old Lizard. If he is romantic, that's a surprise. Perhaps it's because he's still young and vigorous. Behind the Lizard I hear the Old Ones talking to me. Behind the Old Ones I hear the Land itself. Generally speaking, the people and their artists voice the spirit of a place. So far we haven't disturbed the spirits of the Old Ones too much, and some of us still hear them talking.

*4.   Is the western novel weak in characterization?*

No. I think the characterization is powerful. But it also happens that nature and its phenomena are overpowering, so that sometimes it seems the characters are overshadowed. A giant standing in the shadow of a mountain is still a bigger man than a pigmy standing next to an anthill. (Faulkner had the same problem in *his South.*)

*5.   Why do few western novels have a contemporary setting?*

Time. Also, let's ask a man from another civilization the same question. "Mr. Sophocles, how do you account for the fact that so few of your dramas deal with contemporary settings as opposed to historical settings?"

*6.   Which western novels do you consider outstanding?*

*Dark Bridwell* by Vardis Fisher. Reminds one of a stark play by Aeschylus.

*Tale of Valor* by Vardis Fisher. Reminds one of Xenophon's *Anabasis*.

*The Mothers* by Vardis Fisher. Reminds one of *The Suppliants* by Aeschylus.

*Orphans in Gethsemane* by Vardis Fisher. This one just simply stands alone.

*People of the Valley* by Frank Waters. Presents Maria del Valle, one of the great characters of American literature.

*The Man Who Killed the Deer* by Frank Waters. Contemporary or "historical" (and I don't like the distinction, since I doubt if any good writer worth his salt ever thinks of such a distinction), this is just about the best Indian novel ever written.

*The City of Trembling Leaves* by Walter Van Tilburg Clark. Who can surpass this penetrating and yet at the same time dreamlike novel? It is nobler than a symphony by Mahler.

*The Track of the Cat* by Walter Van Tilburg Clark. Read over the title several times and you will realize that greatness has been afoot in the land.

*The Big Rock Candy Mountain* by Wallace Stegner. Mr. Stegner has made the trip to the Shining Mountains.

*East of Eden* by John Steinbeck. A much better novel than many people have been willing to admit. And it should have been titled *West of Eden,* or *Eden West.*

7.   *Which of your own novels do you like best?*

The one I'm about to write is the best one. I love all of my children, idiot and genius alike. Or, let's put it this way: so far, I dove the deepest in *Morning Red,* rose the highest in *Conquering Horse,* rambled the furtherest afield in *Wanderlust,* and so on.

8.   *Does the American West (or your own work) have a major theme?*

Presenting the latest member, the youngest child, in the family called Western Civilization. The youngest son has arrived on the scene and now it is his turn to speak.

9.   *Does the western novelist have any special problems?*

He works more in solitude than have most writers. And this is perfect since a writer should be, and is, slightly more of an individual, a person apart, an aristocrat (if there be any), than any other member of society. The isolation works to his advantage. Critics, performers, virtuosos, entertainers need to live near or in crowds most of the time. So it isn't a matter of overcoming anything; it is a matter of taking advantage of a natural, a given, asset.

10.   *Why haven't the major western novelists received recognition?*

We don't have a big publishing center of our own; most of the nation's communication media are in the hands of aliens; and, finally, we haven't paid too much attention to the problem in the first place. If you really have talent you don't start out wondering about recognition so much as you do about what is the task. You're too busy pitching the game to notice the crowd. Because, you see, what really counts is not you but the Book. Now that we have *Hamlet* and *Oedipus Rex,* who really cares very much about the private joys and pains of Shakespeare and Sophocles? In doing The Work you are lost in a larger thing. I've had a little recognition, not much, yet I can say that up to this minute I cannot conceive of anyone having had a happier life. Give me forty years more and you can have eternity.

# FRANK WATERS

*1. Are you conscious of being a* western *writer, and how does this affect your writing?*

All writers, whether they like it or not, are regional writers—of the American West or South, or of any special region anywhere in the world. The tag merely identifies the locale of most of their work. Lesser writers are limited by their geographical settings. The good ones, like Herman Melville, Joseph Conrad, and William Faulkner, create art that transcends its subject matter. The writer is not different from the painter. To neither of them are the subject and its background primarily important. If the creator is successful, they serve only as the idiom in which he speaks the universal language of the heart, of all mankind.

*2. What are the characteristics of the American West, especially the chief motivating force on fiction?*

The characteristic of the American West which differentiates it from all other sections of the country is the conception of it as a great untrammeled wilderness offering unbounded freedom to the individual to express himself fully. In the great era of westward expansion this conception coincided with fact. Here during the days of the Big Grab a man could carve out for himself an empire of cattle range or virgin forest, stake out a mountain of gold and silver, without restrictions. He could shoot down a personal enemy, or dispossess an entire tribe of Indians without much fear of the law—and sometimes with its tacit approval.

The fact has vanished today, but the conception remains. As individualism vanishes under conformity to mass mediocrity, the conception of the free wild West grows stronger and spreads even wider. It is no paradox that Western Americana is spreading at a phenomenal rate not only in America but throughout Europe. *Westerners* clubs and corrals are mushrooming in England and Scotland, and Western-style saloons in Germany. For all the world the American West symbolizes a boundless realm of individual freedom; a psychological realm where men are men, and women like it.

This is the theme that motivates traditional Western fiction.

*3. Is there an emphasis on nature in your work, perhaps romantic or symbolic?*

Western fiction emphasizes nature because it is still a paramount fact of life. No one can ignore the lowest deserts and highest mountain peaks, the deepest canyons, widest plateaus, and wildest rivers in America, all jumbled together here in one fabulous area. Some early writers like Harold Bell Wright romanticized nature to the point of nauseous sentimentality. Barbara Worth in her ten-gallon hat etched against the picture-postcard sunset! No doubt about it. Noble nature, uncontaminated by the gross touch of humanity, brought out the best in man.

It also brought out the worst. The overwhelming immensity of the land with its limitless plains and huge brooding mountains not only dwarfed man to an infinitesimal speck. Its haunting timelessness overemphasized his own brief and dangerous span. Everywhere he was confronted by the force of alien natural laws inherent in the landscape itself—the ineffable spirit-of-place of a new continent to which he was not yet attuned. How wonderfully this is acknowledged in a little-known book by the popular author of those romanticized tales of the Mohicans which deserve so little attention, by J. Fenimore Cooper. *The Prairie*, for perhaps the first time, grapples with the invisible ghosts that stalk the land.

Nor can we glibly dismiss Zane Grey because his prototypal Western stories failed to achieve the stature of literature. The millions of copies of his fifty-nine novels sold throughout the world achieved an effect that cannot be denied. It is more pertinent to inquire what made them so popular in their time.

For one thing, Zane Grey had the remarkable knack of picking out as locales the very regions richest in scenery; and he took the time, as writers of current Westerns do not, to describe them to a public not yet familiar with them. And always they had some effect upon his characters, puppets though they were. It is amazing to find how many of his characters came into the West carrying the memory of some wrong done them or a sense of some fanciful guilt. Here in the empty wastelands they were freed of all their inhibitions, free to act out the dictates of their compulsions without restraint—and all his novels are stories of violent action. Nature with her sublime beauty and diabolic cruelty served as a psychiatrist's couch, as it were, to heal their wounds or else it offered an escape from the realities of society. "Roll the stone, Lassiter!" Lock us within this hidden valley, forever safely immured from all mankind! It is all there in his most popular romance, *The Riders of the Purple Sage*.

*4.    Is the western novel weak in characterization?*

Characterization is weak in the Western novel not only because emphasis is given to the setting, but because characterization is the test of all novels wherever their settings are laid. Great literature does not rely upon action, the intricacies of plot structure, the manipulation of events. It depends upon the unfoldment of character.

Few Western novels meet this test. It has been far easier to depend upon the built-in drama of Indian depredations, cattle and sheep wars, battles over water rights and mining claims, of pushing through railroads, and damming wild rivers. Stock characters easily manipulated are sufficient: the Trapper, Trader, and Mountain Man, the Settler, the dashing Dragoon, the renegade Mormon, the Cattle King, the Prospector, the Outlaw, and above all, the savage Redskin.

Even non-fiction is inclined to re-model historical characters on these fictional prototypes. It makes no difference that Wyatt Earp has been proved an itinerant saloon-keeper, cardsharp, bigamist, bunco artist, confidence man, and gunman masquerading as a law officer under a tin badge. Yet a hundred novels, as well as a dozen movies and a TV series, glorify him as the greatest Frontier Marshal in the history of the West. And they will probably continue doing so. We are not a people to be told that George Washington did *not* cut down that cherry tree. Little wonder that our most successful fiction, those block-busting Book-of-the-Month selections, adhere to the general pattern followed by *Warlock, Blood Brother,* and others of the kind.

What chance, a struggling new writer may inquire, does an ordinary character have against such an imposing cast of stock principals so long endeared to their admiring public?

*5.   Why do so few western novels have a contemporary setting?*

The reason why there are few Western novels with a contemporary setting as opposed to an historical setting seems obvious.

The West today no longer coincides in fact with the traditional conception of it as a boundless realm offering individual freedom. It's all fenced in. Arizona—home of the murderin' Apache, hell-roarin' Tombstone, the Bad Man with his six-shooters, and the rugged individualist—is today the most conservative and reactionary of all the Western states, if not of the United States. Roughly two-thirds of its land is government owned or government controlled. Without government subsidies and payrolls the State economy would collapse. The same holds true, more or less, for every Western state.

A novel of the current West must be written within this framework. This is not to say great novels cannot or will not be written. For great novels are written about people, not places. But the characters must reflect this unromantic political, economic, and missile-base background which is far different from the empty landscape of Zane Grey.

*6.   Which Western novels do you consider outstanding?*

To assess the novels of the West written within the 20th Century is a job requiring months of work from a most hardy critic. I wouldn't attempt it. A few pop readily into mind. *The Big Sky* by A. B. Guthrie is laid in the period of the mountain men. So is *Lord Grizzly* by Frederick Manfred who has staked out as distinctly his own that literary domain he calls Sioux-land. *The Conquest of Don Pedro* by Harvey Fergusson, always dependable, features a Jewish peddler in an early Spanish village on the lower Rio Grande. A larger picture of the Mexican border around El Paso is Tom Lea's *The Wonderful Country*, a beautiful book. Walter Van Tilburg Clark's *The Oxbow Incident* and *Track of the Cat* are both laid in

Nevada. *Coarse Gold* by Edwin Corle is the story of a Mojave Desert ghost mining town coming to life in the technological present. *The Rounders* by Max Evans is the humorous tale of two cowpokes on a drunken spree, authentic and promising much. Due to our unbroken racial prejudice against Indians, there are so few good novels about them that only two come readily to mind: *Crazy Weather* by Charles McNichols, and *Apache* by Will Levington Comfort, both classics. To these should be added a book of short stories by Dorthy M. Johnson, *Indian Country*. Undoubtedly I have skipped a dozen more to be treasured, but these illustrate a great diversity of time periods, locations, subject matter, and individual writing styles. They all have one thing in common; they are written from the inside out, not with one eye on Hollywood, and they achieve a depth of creative maturity. To the phony claim that good Western books can be written only by regional Western writers, I must mention here the non-fiction *Midnight on the Desert* by J. B. Priestly, a visiting Englishman, to illustrate the sensitively felt and acutely observed West that can be recorded by anyone with the right apparatus.

7.   *Which of your own novels do you like best?*

*The Man Who Killed the Deer* may be my own best novel. It is a story that attempts to distill the essence of Pueblo Indian life in its own introverted and mystical terms, rather than to record it from an outside viewpoint in the usual terms of extroverted action. Advertised as something on the order of a Hiawatha love story, the book was first published within a month of Pearl Harbor and was an instantaneous flop. But for some strange reason after it had gone out of print, copies came to be collectors' items. It was then that Alan Swallow, director of the University of Denver Press, gave it a new birth by issuing a small reprint edition. He then, upon establishing his own small publishing house in Denver, continued to re-issue it. To him this maverick book—and myself—owes its long and stubborn life.

Now, more than twenty years since it was first published, it has been re-issued in the United States five times, published in Great Britain, and translated into French and German; and it has been placed on required reading lists of schools in Colorado, Arizona, and New Mexico.

To me it is a pleasing example of how an initially disregarded book can in time win its own small niche in an unfamiliar world.

8.   *Does the American West (or your own work) have a major theme?*

The major theme of any novel laid in the American West or anywhere else is life itself; and life is too full and diverse, contradictory and changeful, to be pinned down with a tidy theme. Still, a primary concern of all peoples everywhere is their relationship to their land. This has been the basic source of conflict between the White and Red races on this continent. To the newly arrived European immigrants in America, the land was but an inanimate treasure house to be exploited for their material benefit. To the Indians, the land was a living entity, their Mother Earth; not only their immemorial homeland, but their "church" with its sacred peaks and shrines.

Hence the White's usurpation of lands constituted for the Indians a re-ligious war. This theme of their conflicting relationships to their earth has provided something of a thematic continuity in all my books, novels and non-fiction. The world is now concerned with the same problem in South America, Africa, and Asia where similar indigenous peoples are insisting on the freedom to develop their own life-patterns, like plants and animals, from their own native soil rather than from the dictates of waning Colo-nialism of waxing Totalitarianism. I look to see this theme developed in coming novels by writers of these areas.

*9. and 10.   Does the western novelist have any special problems? Why haven't the major western novelists received recognition?*

Practically all major publishing houses are located in New York. They depend for the sale of their books on the populous East which still regards the West as a backward province, suitable enough for a summer vacation, but far awash from the current of contemporary thought and not quite up to metropolitan standards. No small publishing house in the West has broken their virtual monopoly simply because it hasn't the prestige to sell enough books to its own comparatively scanty population.

The Western, and especially the Southwestern writer, is thus confronted with a special problem if he writes about his own neighbors and immediate background. A subway strap-hanger in Brooklyn is not interested in a dirty Greaser or a savage Redskin if the one is not sitting in the sun and rolling cigarettes and the other war-whooping under a bonnet of eagle-feathers before he is shot down by the noble Cowboy. Having never been farther west than the Mississippi, he can't be expected to know—at least from the most popular Western novels—that times have changed out this way.

Or have they? Our Nobel Prize Winner, John Steinbeck, recently traveled over all the United States to report in his *Travels with Charley* that all the people he encountered, of whatever racial extraction, had amalgamated into one common American culture. The only section he drove through without mention was the vast area of the Southwest threaded by U. S. Highway 66. I wonder why. It is a pity that with his observant eye and love for underdog minorities, he did not turn off a few miles through the largest Indian Reservation in the country to the oldest Indian pueblo in America. Or even stop to talk a moment in one of the little Spanish villages. Perhaps it's just as well he didn't. I think his sweeping conclusion would have been badly dented.

For here are Spanish people whose ancestors settled the Southwest long before the Pilgrims landed on Plymouth Rock; who built the cathedral here in my home town before the Declaration of Independence; and who make New Mexico still a bi-lingual state. As for the Indians, thousands of them are still living in many-storied, adobe pueblos built long before Columbus officially discovered America. These people, Spanish and Indian, are not small minorities here. They are important segments of the population with their own language, mores, customs, and traditions—not yet amalgamated

into the American culture common to the east and south. It is all so exotic
and erotic. So foreign really! It is. All of America east of the Mississippi
owes its birthright and allegiance to Europe. But the motherland of the
Southwest is Mexico with its ancient heritage.

Western writers, then, are writing about a people and a country virtually
foreign to most readers. They can adhere to the romantic pattern of the
past with all its cliches. Or they can gloss over the difference to make their
wares more palatable. At least many of them can and do. They shouldn't
be censured for doing so, for I'm convinced that no man can successfully
"write down" to the public; there would be more of us doing it. A man
writes as he can, with his own temperament, the talent allotted him, and
the tools at his hand. But if he aspires to greater truth, he must realize that
his problem is not the publisher nor the reading public. It is the perception
he brings to his own task. That no man can define. But if he feels deeply
enough and sees clearly enough those people who serve as his medium, he
may find himself bestowed with the strength and courage to speak in terms
of the common humanness that links us all, whoever and wherever we are,
in one indivisible whole. That is accomplished seldom and is its own
reward.

# WALTER VAN TILBURG CLARK

*1.   Are you conscious of being a* western *writer, and how does this affect
your writing?*

Yes, I am conscious of being a western writer, in the sense that, since
the American west is the world I know best and care most about, it is also
the world from which most of my stories have emerged. I can't see, however, that this means anything in terms of my purposes, or those of anyone
trying to write well about the West (certainly it shouldn't, anyhow) that
it wouldn't to a writer from any other region. No story is without a world.
Every world has its individual characteristics which furnish certain problems for the writer. But the effort of any writer must always be to make
the actualities of his world say something of more than local and passing
validity.

*2.   What are the characteristics of the American West, especially the
chief motivating force on fiction?*

The only important difference between the West and any other American region—if we are talking country—seems to me to be still what it has
always been, that it is a vast land with a relatively small population, so
that other aspects of nature than man must count for more than they
usually do elsewhere. Nature, we might say, must become actor, not backdrop. Which, in good part, answers question 3.

*3.   Is there an emphasis on nature in your work, perhaps romantic or
symbolic?*

Certainly I am conscious of paying attention, even primary attention, to nature in my writing, and also of doing so symbolically at times. I am not aware of doing so "romantically" however, if romantically means sentimentally. The view that it is romantic to pay serious attention to country and to other forms of life than man, essentially an urban and self-consciously "literary" view, strikes me as being not only the product of the worst kind of egocentric sentimentality itself, but also a very dangerous, possibly, at last a suicidal view. As for the use of natural symbols—hasn't it always been done? Is there any reason why a mountain, or a desert, or a wild animal can't be made to convey more than literal meanings at least as well as a cocktail glass, a taxi, a woman's shoe? I'll take William Faulkner's bear, for instance, over the bill-board eye in *The Great Gatsby*, or the taxi-cab that opens and closes *The Sun Also Rises*. Any day.

*4. Is the western novel weak in characterization?*

Characterization, in this literary sense, is chiefly the result of man's involvement with man. Older and more settled regions naturally give rise to a greater degree of such involvement.

*5. Why do so few western novels have a contemporary setting?*

The history of any region is the seed-bed of its human meanings and values. The west is still in the process of establishing the conscious continuity with its past which has long been taken for granted in the East and the South.

*6. Which Western novels do you consider outstanding?*

I don't read regionally, and this question, it seems to me, cannot be usefully answered save at impossible length, even by someone who has done western reading widely and systematically enough to have a right to an opinion. I can only mention a few writers who seem to me to have contributed importantly to the development of western fiction: A. B. Guthrie, Vardis Fisher, Frank Waters, Frederick Manfred, William Eastlake, H. L. Davis, Wallace Stegner and, for he is, to my mind, often a western writer in the real sense, despite the fact that he doesn't fall within the geographical limitations set here, John Steinbeck.

*7. Which of your own novels do you like best?*

I've published only three novels to date. They came far apart, and they are very different in kind and in manner. I don't have any distinct preference. It may be that if I manage to complete any important part of what I still want to write, *The Track of the Cat* will turn out to be more fully and directly related to my intention as a whole than either of the other two.

*8. Does the American West (or your own work) have a major theme?*

So, yes, I have, both philosophically and fictionally, a continuity in mind, or rather in feeling—where it counts more—which may emerge if I ever get enough done. But such things, it seems to me, should appear in something like a full way before they are talked about at all, and even then no writer should talk about his own. I can only say that what may possibly emerge as major or controlling theme in my work is not, I hope, altogether western in its implications.

*9. Does the western novelist have any special problems?*

My answers to the first five questions have already answered this one, even a bit redundantly, I'm afraid. I might add, however, that the long-popular formula westerns, and still more, now, the movies and TV shows which stem from them, have not yet ceased to make all western writing a little suspect with certain kinds of "serious" readers and critics. I have no solution for any of these problems. Enough time and enough good writing out of the West will take care of all of them, and I can't see how anything else will.

*10.   Why haven't the major western novelists received recognition?*

One is tempted to say that it is because such recognition comes almost entirely, so far, by way of eastern and southern critics who do not really believe that there is a West. That is true, I believe, as far as it goes, but it's only a small part of the truth. Major novelists don't appear often in any region, or even in any literature, and when they appear it is always, in good part, because they have been born into more or less mature social and cultural complexes. The West is young, and its good writing is even younger. In my sense of the term, at least, I don't believe it has produced a major novelist yet. But in the same sense I would add that the South has produced only William Faulkner and the East only Herman Melville, Henry James (if the East can claim him) and possibly Nathaniel Hawthorne.


# VARDIS FISHER

*1.   Are you conscious of being a* western *writer, and how does this affect your writing?*

I have never thought of myself as a regional writer.

*2.   What are the characteristics of the American West, especially the chief motivating force on fiction?*

I know the East only a little and the South hardly at all. I think the Midwest has far more in common with the Rocky Mountains West than California has with it, and especially such areas as Los Angeles. I have thought of myself as a mountain man, as my father was and his father was. I suppose some characteristics of mountain men (about whom I am writing a novel) are self-reliance, abhorrence of cities and of a crowded humanity anywhere, passionate devotion to the beauty of great mountains and mountain valleys, unpolluted streams, vast spaces, and all the marvelous colors and scents of clean mountain country. Lawrence Gilman, the distinguished critic of music, has written:

". . . Pierre Janet holds that those who, at different times in the history of the world's civilization, have manifested a strong attraction to the natural world, have always been persons of a definite and particular type: emotional, subject to exaltation of mood, impatient of hampering traditions, essentially anticonventional. Mr. Havelock Ellis, in his study of the psychology of the love of wild Nature, characterizes all such persons as, in a greater or less degree, 'temperamentally exceptional.' In the strongest and simplest manifestations of the type, these lovers of wild Nature have been persons who were instinctively repelled by their ordinary environment. . . . Chateaubriand, who had small use for mountains except as 'the sources of rivers, a barrier against the horrors of war,' is balanced by Petrarch, who climbing Mont Ventoux . . . observed that his soul 'rose to lofty contemplations on the summit'. . . . The strongest appeal of natural beauty has always, then, been chiefly to individuals of emotional habit, and especially to those of untrammeled imagination and non-conformist tendencies; in other words, to poetically minded radicals in all times and regions. It is probable that the curious and enlightened inquirer, bearing in mind these facts, would not be surprised to find, in studying the various expressions of this attraction as they are recorded in the arts, that the uniquely sensitive and eloquent art of music has long been the handmaid of the Nature-lover; and he would be prepared to find the Nature-lover himself appearing often in the guise of that inherently emotional and often heterodox being, the music-maker."

Wrote Historian DeVoto: "but the loveliest myth of all America was the far West . . . a lost impossible province . . . where men were not dwarfs and where adventure truly was. For a brief season, consider, the myth so generously begotten became fact. For a few years Odysseus Jed Smith and Siegfried Carson and the wing-shod Fitzpatrick actually drew breath in this province of fable. Then suddenly it was all myth again. Wagons were moving down the trails, and nowhere remained any trace of the demigods who had passed this way." Of the mountain men he wrote: "But he was a man. He possessed, too, a valor hardly to be comprehended. He went forth into the uncharted peaks and made his way." Perhaps no class of men on the face of the earth, said Washington Irving, had been "more enamored of their occupations."

Of "western" writers I would guess that Clark and Waters are mountain men at heart.

*3.  Is there an emphasis on nature in your work, perhaps romantic or symbolic?*

This is covered in 2.

*4.  Is the western novel weak in characterization?*

Who has said it? The so-called literary critics, who find progress in the suffocating togetherness of the welfare states, in the barbarous horrors of over-population, in the ugly noisy foul-smelling litter called cities, haven't the background, the knowledge, or the temperament to pass judgment on the kind of artists Gilman and Ellis had in mind.

*5.  Why do so few western novels have a contemporary setting?*

For the reason here, as with the bonanza towns, that the riches are back there. Contemporary life in the Rocky Mountains areas is only an unhappy truce between a way of life that is all but gone, and the haste and frenzy and status-seeking (see *Forbes Magazine*, April 15, page 35) that are obliterating the last traces of it.

*6.   Which Western novels do you consider outstanding?*

I have had too many thousands of books to read to have time for the work of my fellow-writers.

*7.   Which of your own novels do you like best?*

This question asked endlessly of writers, has always seemed to me to be childish.

*8.   Does the American West (or your own work) have a major theme?*

I don't know that such a matter can be put into words. I would suspect that a major theme or meaning is the open society, at its best in such qualities as self-reliance, self-sufficiency, self-healing and self-discovering, in contrast to the closed society, now being established all over the world, in which God is replaced by Government, high political figures are becoming father-images, and the frankly avowed aim is the control and management of whole peoples by their father-images. For the mountain man such a system is utterly detestable and can only lead to the robotization of mankind.

*9.   Does the western novelist have any special problems?*

I have never been conscious of any.

*10.   Why haven't the major western novelists received recognition?*

I think I have touched on some of the reasons. The whole spirit of the Rocky Mountain area was not only non-urban but anti-urban. Nearly all the literary judges back East have urbanized minds. This kind of mind has revealed itself to me in a question put by some people, "Why Idaho, of all places?" The leading news magazine gave to a venomous review of one of my books the title, "Strictly from Idaho." These emotional illiterates probably have never seen Idaho, and in any case have much the same attitude toward such grandeurs as the Rocky Mountains as I have towards the Manhattans, where they live in their ant-swarms. When I was director of the Federal Writers Project in Idaho and Regional Editor of the Rocky Mountains area there came one day an excited letter, or telegram (they loved long telegrams), saying that they had just learned of an official primitive area (in North Carolina, I think it was) and wanted us all to know about it. I replied that Idaho had a primitive area into which they could toss the dinky one back there and never find it in a year's search. I doubt that a member of the national staff had ever been west of Shenandoah and the Great Smokies. What could such people be expected to write about the magnificence out here?

In California a hundred years ago, a group of the Forty-Niners organized the State of Rough and Ready, adopted a constitution, and seceded from the Union. One explanation that historians have given is that these miners were fed up to the ears with the manners and ways and pretensions of the people among them from New England. The attitude of those people was similar to that of Sir Henry Vere Huntley, an English prig who openly sneered at Americans out there. He wrote ,"Dined at Hickman's Ranche. Tripe and pork! What a combination of nauseous horrors! Went to bed; one long room held about twenty of us, here and there two in a bed. I was single—the California Americans say the Britishers don't make 'kinder sociable' bedfellows. . . . It is absurd to say that a people possessed of a natural good principle and feeling could, by having transferred themselves to another country, instantly become so lost to all humanity and decency."

Poor Henry! He would make a nice top bureaucrat in a welfare state.

In 1849, a group of New England prigs, with an itch for gold momentarily overriding their culture, left in the chartered ship *Edward Everett* to take Bibles to the rude men on the western coast; and with them went the ringing injunction of the president of Harvard College, that they should do their best to set the light of the cultured East above the rumpots and whores in the placer diggins.

The English condescension to the colonies and, later, the states, has found its way into countless books. In their turn the people of the Atlantic seaboard have cultivated a sneering condescension toward those who live in Idaho, of all places—or Montana or Arizona or Utah—and in a less virulent form (for they have heard of Aspen) toward those in Colorado—or Nevada, for a lot of them have emptied their purses in Las Vegas or Reno. California they have had to treat with a little more respect, for the reason that in the range of its physical marvels and beauties no other state can be compared to it.

"Western" writers have no choice but to be patient, knowing that there will be more knowledgeable and less prejudiced judges somewhere in the years to come.

## HARVEY FERGUSSON

*1.  Are you conscious of being a* western *writer, and how does this affect your writing?*

The truth is that I have a strong aversion to wearing the regional label. The range of my work and my interest is much wider than the region with which I am always identified. It is true that four of the best known of my ten novels are laid in nineteenth century New Mexico, but none of these is a typical "Western," they do not appeal to the lovers of cowboy romance, yet they never escape the stigma which has long been the curse of everything called "Western," in American literature. Every time I find myself designated in print as a Western writer, or worse yet as a writer of Westerns, I feel like quoting the immortal words of the Virginian: "When you call me that, smile."

*6.  Which Western novels do you consider outstanding?*

I am not qualified to comment on Western fiction because I have not read it, although I know some of it is good.

*7.  Which of your own novels do you like best?*

*Grant of Kingdom* and *The Conquest of Don Pedro* are to me my best work on the nineteenth century West, partly because all the characters seem to be very much alive, but also because the first book is my best attempt to record the heroic aspect of pioneer life, while the second is anti-heroic, being a portrait of a nonviolent man in a violent and romantic world.

*10.    Why haven't the major western novelists received recognition?*

The failure of readers and reviewers to deal adequately with novels about the West is due primarily to the immortal popularity of the cowboy romance. It has steadily deteriorated over the years into a stereotyped fable with stereotyped characters. It may well be the feeblest product of American imagination with the possible exception of the comic strip. Yet it is still a staple product of the paper-backs, the movies and television, our children are raised on it and it was President Eisenhower's favorite literary pablum. Any attempt to write seriously about the movement of the American population from the Mississippi to the Golden Gate is inevitably identified with and drowned in this flood of trash. The mere word Western alienates a horde of readers. Also most American reviewers and critics live in New York, care nothing about the West and know nothing about it except that any novel dealing with "the great open spaces" must be treated with a certain condescension.

# FORRESTER BLAKE

*2.    What are the characteristics of the American West, especially the chief motivating force on fiction?*

The American West is space: light: time: motion. The West is tension: the picaresque, seeking freedom to wander, contends against set unities of time, place, and action. For contemporary writers of the West, the problem becomes that of encasing lines within a sphere, without destroying the reader's awareness of the lines or comprehension of the sphere.

*4.    Is the western novel weak in characterization?*

The American West, as a natural influence upon character, is its own best agent. One frequently hears the visitor from Manhattan complain: "The West is so huge: it makes one feel so small."

*6.    Which Western novels do you consider outstanding?*

a. Owen Wister's *The Virginian*. (The classic of the cattle era, and prototype of the modern romantic novel of the West. It is more than this, of course: it is noteworthy for its optimism and whimsy, and for its opposed currents of realism and mysticism.)

b. Willa Cather's *Death Comes for the Archbishop*. (Spanish New Mexico in mid-Nineteenth Century, with emphasis upon the centers of hierarchical power. Noted for its simplicity and beauty of line.)

c. Oliver La Farge's *Laughing Boy*. (A tone poem of the desert; a Navajo sand painting.)

d. John Steinbeck's *The Grapes of Wrath*. (Highway 66, now "Bloody 66," during times of the Great Depression. A bitter novel of social protest, overdrawing its characterizations of the Oklahoma emigrants to California. This novel reveals but one facet, or hemisphere, of the concept: it describes neither the Spanish nor the Anglo-Saxon people who remained upon the land throughout the years of dust and depression and who emerged as the central victors in that struggle.)

e. Vardis Fisher's *In Tragic Life*. (In no novel of the West is there a harsher or more poignant presentation of homestead life as it was known in the Northern Rockies seventy years ago, along the Upper Snake River.)

f. H. L. Davis' *Honey in the Horn*. (This novel of Western Oregon, in pioneer times, is structurally diffuse. Even so, for its style and response to scene it is invaluable.)

g. John Steinbeck's *Tortilla Flat*. (Satire in Monterey sunlight and fog. Wry humor; long history; uneasy law and order of the conqueror; man's restlessness; ultimate violence, and tragedy.)

h. Conrad Richter's *The Lady*. (This short novel of frontier Las Vegas, New Mexico, on the Rio Gallinas, is one of the most powerful studies of evil yet presented in a Western American setting.)

i. A. B. Guthrie, Jr.'s *The Big Sky*. (A long, loosely linked narrative in the tradition of the American West. One of the few presentations of frontier life along the upper rivers, it trails beyond the rivers to northern cordilleras and attains, in many passages, the quality of epic.)

j. Walter Van Tilburg Clark's *The Oxbow Incident*. (This novel of the Nevada frontier draws broadly upon ethnic and historical resources of the West. Its use of language to impart the atmosphere of Puritan New England; its contrasts between a small Nevada cowtown and the Oxbow high in timbered mountains; its involuntary treatment of protagonists: these elements, especially, mark *The Oxbow Incident* as a distinguished Western American novel.)

*8. Does the American West (or your own work) have a major theme?*

If the American West possesses a single major theme, that theme must be America herself. That is one reason why the West is so difficult to place between the covers of a single book.

*10. Why haven't the major western novelists received recognition?*

For the first time in its history, the Northeast, centered upon Boston and Newport, Hartford and Westchester, New York and Philadelphia, finds itself engaged in a rear-guard action against the developing South, Middle West, and Trans-Mississippi West.

A century after military defeat, the South is achieving economic triumph over New England. The Middle West, long past its era of subservience to the Northeast, is establishing its own economic empire and expanding its cultural influences, through its universities, to every section. Most swiftly and aggressively of all, the Trans-Mississippi West is moving to claim its full and equal place within the nation.

Manhattan publishing concerns, entrenched in the Northeast, confront the challenges common to their region. Accustomed to monopolistic con-

trol of the nation's publishing affairs, too often intolerant of ideas and fearful of experimentation, these concerns are holding with increasing unreality
to restricted literary periods and attitudes, including the Nineteenth Century romantic tradition of the American West.

Western American writers, today, know they cannot hold exclusively
to past literary attitudes, forms and techniques. They know that they
cannot disregard either history or the new currents which race like storms
through the West. Growth forces change. These writers will write as they
must, upon the Western American subjects of their choice.

# PAUL HORGAN

*1.   Are you conscious of being a* western *writer, and how does this affect
your writing?*

Since I have written about many parts of the United States, I do not
wear comfortably the title "regionalist."

I am a native of New York state and my childhood from twelve years
on was spent in New Mexico and the last three years of my adolescence
were passed in Rochester, New York. In the three periods of greatest im-
pressionability I was thus exposed to life in both East and West, and my
life ever since has reflected this variety.

I have loved the landscape in all parts of the country, I have had deep
affinity for the history of the Southwest, I have derived most of my education informally from the cultural expressions best exemplified in the
intellectual and artistic life of the East and of Europe, and I have been
concerned with people without regard exclusively to the "typical" character imposed on either eastern or western environment by other writers
or observers.

My first published novel was set in New York state, though it was
written in New Mexico. My second was set in both East and West. My
next few were set almost wholly in the West, within both modern and
historical periods. In certain early works I held to a romantic intensity
about *west*, and tried to capture what seemed essentially true to *west*. But
the various play of my interest always encountered in each new book a
new sort of problem to solve in design or form, and though at first glance
the succession of my books might seem to proclaim a discontinuity of
vision and style, I think that the whole body of my work may be seen to
outline the coherent terms of my geographical, intellectual, and artistic
sensibility.

In a word, I am not a "regionalist" in the accepted sense because my
"region" lies wherever I find subject and emotion that compel my writing,
which means that I am not committed to be a celebrant of any one locale
for its own sake.

In my work both as novelist and historian it has been the creation of
an appropriate and shapely vessel to contain a literary or factual image of

truth which has most engaged me. Regionalism, as such, seems to me to have not much determining relevance to this interest.

2. *What are the characteristics of the American West, especially the chief motivating force on fiction?*

Typical observers and interpreters of *west* seem to be held by a lyric, often mournful, often proud, sense of the spacious and the simple, the chivalrous and the physical, the visionary and the heroic, which do not appear so plainly in the cultures of other regions of the nation.

If the outer landscape is vast and dramatically lighted, so the mindscape of man in *west* seems to reflect large simplifications of act and philosophy and self-image. If there is a single pervasive theme in writing about *west*, perhaps, with all its variations, it could be identified as the theme of man, alone, against the grand immensity of nature—the nature of the land, reflected in his own soul. You often see a doleful holiness ascribed to western life by literary celebrants not because it is life but because it is western life. Too often this represents a naive frontiersmanship that will not hold up in any aesthetic sense; but it is often excused by its innocence, and talent trapped within it will eventually break out as it must. What is sad and funny is that, initially, under cult judgments, the regional value is confused with the literary or artistic value. A true artist—like Harvey Fergusson—will write about his region without ever being limited by "regionalism," with its crippling self-consciousness.

In *east* it is society in its complexity which offers opposition to the individual. In *west* it is the raw wilderness, with a sparse society reflecting rawness, which offers opposition. In *west* a man triumphs over or succumbs to primal nature—or used to: present urbanization and technological sophistication now proceed at so wildly rapid a rate that the old theme is disappearing, and presently the unique equation of man and *west* will vanish.

3. *Is there an emphasis on nature in your work, perhaps romantic or symbolic?*

See 2. Yes—I was conscious of the great significance of nature in my early books with *west* settings. But for me this has less a symbolic value than a value related to landscape as seen by a painter—for though I have not made any career as a painter I have something of the painter's knack of seeing. I believe there is much evidence of this in all my books, of both history and fiction.

4. *Is the western novel weak in characterization?*

If characterization is weak in much writing about *west* it may be because of the symbolic or allegorical role required of man alone as he faces the vastness of *west*, as suggested in 2. Characterization often rises to great aesthetic value when it is most complex and least allegorical.

Complex people rarely appear in the literature of *west* because the drama—to simplify perhaps outrageously—is more often about water rights or hippophily or the hazards inherent in vast distances than about complex human interaction or subjective conflict.

The literature of *east* seems to concern itself more with private than with public nature, so to speak, and so has more opportunity to create character of extended variety and complexity.

The literature of *south* seems bound by its own regional stereotype, made up of degrees of decadence, savagery, and cynical whimsy, not essentially different from the popular hillbilly images of cartoons, radio and TV, despite elaborate rhetorical furnishings or preciosities.

*5.  Why do so few western novels have a contemporary setting?*

Perhaps even now too few serious writers have been born and have grown up in the West to let us have a luxuriant authentic literature of contemporary *west*.

Furthermore, the "big" themes as related to *west* are all to be found in the past—the westward movement, the conquest of the frontier, the taming of wilderness, the making of towns, etc., in which uncomplicated monolithic man is dominant. Big themes related to non-monolithic man could be laid as well in any locality, so rendering *west* and *region* irrelevant to the question.

Apart from landscape and—so far, generally—the indestructibility of its vast splendors, the contemporary *west* is only *tourist west;* and nothing much can be said about it in literary regional terms except in accents of satire, dealing with dude ranch life, or wistful escapism from over-industrialized *east*, or the pathos of the desire to hold on to an honest but already defeated atavistic longing for wilderness, etc.

We are left with false *west*, which is rapidly killing vestiges of real *west* in commercial exploitation through motels, roadside "museums," summer caterings, clever merchandising ideas, and the rest. When a·region becomes self-conscious it begins to destroy what gave it particular character.

*6.  Which Western novels do you consider outstanding?*

Here I must list:

a. Willa Cather's *A Lost Lady, The Professor's House* (for Book Two, "Tom Outland's Story"), *The Song of the Lark* (for its lovely early chapters laid in a southern Colorado railroad town), and of course *Death Comes for the Archbishop*. In all of these there is a glowing presence of the land and the light over it, against which, without undue limitation by regional reverence, the universal human concerns of her characters call into play Miss Cather's quiet art. Yet she does, of course, catch most evocatively the particular homeliness of her western places, and we enjoy these for what they are.

b. Harvey Fergusson's novels, all of them, with perhaps my own emphasis on *In Those Days* as that book of his I value most for its beautiful design and its unsentimental nostalgia. It is a book laid in the past—and the past was just over his own shoulder, for he grew up in the Albuquerque whose story he told. No other novelist seems to me to match his claim to primacy as the best novelist to have written for the most part about the *west*. His subject matter condemns him to classification as a *regionalist;* his artistry releases him from it.

c. *The House of Breath* (novel) and various stories by William Goyen, a true artist who has found themes in Texas and has transcended their background, however valuable it may be to his design.

d. Walter Van Tilburg Clark's novels which give the effect of raising regional anecdote to the spaciousness of myth.

7. *Which of your own novels do you like best?*

This question is not really very meaningful to me, since all my books grew out of compelling artistic impulses which I cannot judge comparatively. If I give an answer at all, I must do it in two parts, with two choices:

a. *No Quarter Given,* for the variety of its settings, (*east* and *west*), and characters, ("regional" and "non-regional"), which illustrates my biographical claim to trans-continental artistic citizenship.

b. *Far From Cibola,* which perhaps satisfies best among my works that concern which is for me the most interesting of the artist's problems—the solution of form.

8. *Does the American West (or your own work) have a major theme?*

Regarding the major theme of *west,* see 2, 4. Regarding my own work: in the face of evidence for the tragic view of life, my underflowing persuasion has always been to transcend the tragic by simple recognition of its existence.

All my works in one way or another present this view; and it is a view which allows permutations without loss of the original concept. It carries with it a repudiation of cynicism in favor of love for the organic life, in which growth and aspiration seem more truly illustrative of the significant human condition than qualities like willful destructiveness or a taste for futility.

This means two things—first, that I regard the act of art as an act of love: the artist's response to any and all aspects of life, whether seen subjectively or otherwise; second, that however quietly I may state or imply it, my humble relation to creativity is an expression of my religious belief.

9. *Does the western novelist have any special problems?*

Yes: he faces the difficult problems established for him by the vulgarization of almost every aspect of *west* by the popular media of film, TV, radio and formula fiction. What was once material of genuine artistic energy and interest has become a mass of cliches; and it takes thinking twice to try handling any of the basic subject matter in any serious way nowadays.

I confess to having tried to do it in a recent novel, *A Distant Trumpet,* in which I quite deliberately opened up a panoramic story about the United States Army in the 19th Century, which necessarily involved the frontier Indian problems, and other themes peripheral to the western setting and life. I wanted to deal with these things as if nobody had ever heard of them before. It was my belief that if I wrote a rich enough book, and a true one, it would survive the current slang of *west* and come to be seen in time as a worthwhile novel whose "westernness" was not necessarily the determining thing about it.

As a matter of fact, about one-third of the book is laid in the eastern and middle-western parts of the country. It is, actually, like others of my novels, transcontinental in its touch upon subject matter and place.

*10.   Why haven't the major western novelists received recognition?*

Perhaps because:

a. They have tended to be detached from literary cliques or movements which govern reputations elsewhere;

b. The famous major theme or subject matter of *west* has always been expressed more in physical or social action than through applications or systematic psychology (often carried to clinical extremes) and with social decadence such as have engaged writers of high reputation elsewhere.


# MICHAEL STRAIGHT

*1.   Are you conscious of being a western writer, and how does this affect your writing?*

As a writer, I'm conscious only of my own isolation.

*2.   What are the characteristics of the American West, especially the chief motivating force on fiction?*

The West drew me into fiction; the circumstances are easier to identify than the reasons.

In 1956, I came to the end of a twenty year stretch in politics. I'd written myself out; I needed to break away.

I spent that summer in the Big Horns, near the ruins of Fort Phil Kearny. I drove past the ruins; I rode around them; after a time, they reached out and took hold of me. I read all that was known about the brief, disastrous history of the Fort. I worked from the story, and let the story guide me. It led in turn to a second story, closely related in its time and its setting, but different in the direction in which it pointed. The two stories enabled me to recapitulate my own experiences in an indirect, and therefore, a disciplined way. When they were finished, the West had done what it could for me.

*3.   Is there an emphasis on nature in your work, perhaps romantic or symbolic?*

The grandeur of the setting is one attraction which the West exerts on romantic writers. Its timeliness is also an advantage for those who lack imagination, and who write what they know. (It is hard now, to picture George Washington riding through the woods of Manhattan, or to describe the soldiers of the Union and the Confederacy fighting and dying among the split-level bungalows of Gettysburg.)

Symbolism seems to me to be, too often a substitute for narrative content, or intellectual precision. A few symbols moved by themselves into my narratives. I tried to limit their appearances, and to keep them submerged.

*4.   Is the western novel weak in characterization?*

Characterization is certainly weak in my novels. The causes, apart from my own incapacity, are threefold.

First, my interest centered, not in personalities as such, but in two incidents (The Fetterman Massacre and The Sand Creek Massacre). My novels were directed to the question: why did these events occur? The individuals I dealt with were developed only in relation to these overriding events.

Second, I worked from the Aristotelian rule that character is seen in action. This rule accorded with my own beliefs, and it seemed particularly appropriate to the time and setting of the Western frontier. It precluded any thorough-going exploration of the inward aspects of personality through which a complete characterization may be achieved.

Third, in my novels, I was dealing with events which occurred a century ago, and with men and women who took part in these events. I could of course have changed the names of people and places and so, claimed the right to give my imagination free rein. But, this seemed to me to be a form of deception. I accepted the gift of plot from the past; I felt bound in return to yield some freedom of action in developing character. I had of course, to move into the realm of motivation—there was no justification, short of this step, for treating the story as fiction rather than as history. But, I could not feel free from all restraint in writing about men and women who lived once and who could not rise to reply in their own defense. Nor could I dwell, with any conviction, upon the purely private lives of my characters. I could watch them on the parade ground where others watched them; I could stand behind them as they wrote out their dispatches. I could not spend much of my time hidden under their beds.

*5.   Why do so few western novels have a contemporary setting?*

Again, I can speak only for myself.

By breaking away from the present, I felt able to discard the unimportant, transitory details that serve to obstruct our vision. I hoped also, that by breaking away, I would be able to strip from myself, the vestiges of the reporter and the editor, and so gain the wholly different frame of mind of the novelist. My first novel dealt with the limitations of humanism, and the second with the containment of fanaticism; both were themes that flowed in part from my own experiences. But, had I set the two novels in the present, they would have been simple political tracts.

*6.   Which Western novels do you consider outstanding?*

I'm ashamed to say that I've read very few contemporary novels.

*7.   Which of your own novels do you like best?*

I doubt if novelists should try to assess their own works. They must believe in themselves; they should be their own, most exacting critics. If they speak frankly, they will be misunderstood.

*8.   Does the American West (or your own work) have a major theme?*

The West is, for me, the frontier at the time of the Indian Wars. The continuing theme is conflict and its resolution.

A novel is in some measure, an allegory of the author's life. The author tries, through his novels, to come to terms with his experiences. I grew up in Europe, in the Thirties. The dominants were for me, the collapse of order, the rise of fanaticism, the resort to violence, ending in war. I could not come to terms with these experiencees in any direct way. I felt able to deal with them indirectly, in the stories of Fort Phil Kearny and Sand Creek. Both novels were written to stand as history and as story-telling. But, being fiction, they relate in style and in spirit to 1964 rather than to 1864. Their themes are important to me because they are contemporary; their characters, although none are drawn from life, are all familiar; the man who bears responsibility in a hopeless situation; the man who sets out to do good, and finds that he has been an accomplice of evil; the man who in the name of one faith or another, arrogates to himself the power to decree life or death for his fellow men; the man who foresees catastrophe and who attempts to forestall it by a reconciliation of enemies; who fails, but who, in failing, keeps the way open for the restoration of the balance between good and evil that will come.

*9.    Does the western novelist have any special problems?*

The opening of the West is the one unique experience in our history. It holds people in all lands enthralled.

"Western" in contrast, is a dirty word in literary circles. And some of the dirt clings.

No matter; the Victorian weeklies were not up to the literary standards of the Partisan Review. The fiction they published seems as dated as their patterns for ladies dresses. But, it was in these magazines that the works of Dickens and Hardy appeared.

*10.    Why haven't the major western novelists received recognition?*

Willa Cather, for one, has been placed in the small company of novelists whose work will last. If no other Western novelists have joined her, isn't that because we haven't yet produced a Faulkner or a Fitzgerald? In any case, recognition seems to me to be evanescent as an objective, rough as a measure of achievement, and, as a reward, secondary to the writers own sense of succeeding in what he has set out to do.

# Critical Analyses of Three Novels

## FREDERIC I. CARPENTER

### The Philosophical Joads

A POPULAR HERESY has it that a novelist should not discuss ideas—especially not abstract ideas. Even the best contemporary reviewers
concern themselves with the entertainment value of a book (will it please
their readers?), and with the impression of immediate reality which it
creates. *The Grapes of Wrath*, for instance, was praised for its swift action
and for the moving sincerity of its characters. But its mystical ideas and
the moralizing interpretations intruded by the author between the narrative
chapters were condemned. Presumably the book became a best seller in
spite of these; its art was great enough to overcome its philosophy.

But in the course of time a book is also judged by other standards.
Aristotle once argued that poetry should be more "philosophical" than
history; and all books are eventually weighed for their content of wisdom.
Novels that have become classics do more than tell a story and describe
characters; they offer insight into men's motives and point to the springs
of action. Together with the moving picture, they offer the criticism of
life.

Although this theory of art may seem classical, all important modern
novels—especially American novels—have clearly suggested an abstract
idea of life. *The Scarlet Letter* symbolized "sin," *Moby Dick* offered an
allegory of evil. *Huck Finn* described the revolt of the "natural individual"
against "civilization," and *Babbitt* (like Emerson's "Self-reliance") de-
nounced the narrow conventions of "society." Now *The Grapes of Wrath*
goes beyond these to preach a positive philosophy of life and to damn that
blind conservatism which fears ideas.

*"The Philosophical Joads" originally appeared in the January,
1941 issue of* COLLEGE ENGLISH. *It was collected in Frederic I.
Carpenter's Volume,* AMERICAN LITERATURE AND THE DREAM
*(New York: Philosophical Library, 1955) pp. 167–176.
Reprinted with the permission of the National Council of
Teachers of English and Frederic I. Carpenter.*

I shall take for granted the narrative power of the book and the vivid reality of its characters: modern critics, both professional and popular, have borne witness to these. The novel is a best seller. But it also has ideas. These appear abstractly and obviously in the interpretative interchapters. But more important is Steinbeck's creation of Jim Casy, "the preacher," to interpret and to embody the philosophy of the novel. And consummate is the skill with which Jim Casy's philosophy has been integrated with the action of the story, until it motivates and gives significance to the lives of Tom Joad, and Ma, and Rose of Sharon. It is not too much to say that Jim Casy's ideas determine and direct the Joads's actions.

Beside and beyond their function in the story, the ideas of John Steinbeck and Jim Casy possess a significance of their own. They continue, develop, integrate, and realize the thought of the great writers of American history. Here the mystical transcendentalism of Emerson reappears, and the earthy democracy of Whitman, and the pragmatic instrumentalism of William James and John Dewey. And these old philosophies grow and change the book until they become new. They coalesce into an organic whole. And, finally, they find embodiment in character and action, so that they seem no longer ideas, but facts. The enduring greatness of *The Grapes of Wrath* consists in its imaginative realization of these old ideas in new and concrete forms. Jim Casy translates American philosophy into words of one syllable, and the Joads translate it into action.

### I

"Ever know a guy that said big words like that?" asks the truck driver in the first narrative chapter of *The Grapes of Wrath*. "Preacher," replies Tom Joad. "Well, it makes you mad to hear a guy use big words. Course with a preacher it's all right because nobody would fool around with a preacher anyway." But soon afterward Tom meets Jim Casy and finds him changed. "I was a preacher," said the man seriously, "but not no more." Because Casy had ceased to be an orthodox minister and no longer uses big words, Tom Joad plays around with him. And the story results.

But although he is no longer a minister, Jim Casy continues to preach. His words have become simple and his ideas unorthodox. "Just Jim Casy now. Ain't got the call no more. Got a lot of sinful idears—but they seem kinda sinsible." A century before, this same experience and essentially these same ideas had occurred to another preacher: Ralph Waldo Emerson had given up the ministry because of his unorthodoxy. But Emerson had kept on using big words. Now Casy translates them: "Why do we got to hang it on God or Jesus? Maybe it's all men an' all women we love; maybe that's the Holy Sperit—the human sperit—the whole shebang. Maybe all men got one big soul ever'body's a part of." And so the Emersonian oversoul comes to earth in Oklahoma.

Unorthodox Jim Casy went into the Oklahoma wilderness to save his soul. And in the wilderness he experienced the religious feeling of identity with nature which has always been the heart of transcendental mysticism: "There was the hills, an' there was me, an' we wasn't separate no more. We was one thing. An' that one thing was holy." Like Emerson, Casy came to the conviction that holiness, or goodness, results from this feeling of unity: "I got to thinkin' how we was holy when we was one thing, an' mankin' was holy when it was one thing."

Thus far Jim Casy's transcendentalism has remained vague and apparently insignificant. But the corollary of this mystical philosophy is that any man's self-seeking destroys the unity or "holiness" of nature: "An' it (this one thing) on'y got unholy when one mis'able little fella got the bit in his teeth, an' run off his own way. . . . Fella like that bust the holiness." Or, as Emerson phrased it, while discussing Nature: "The world lacks unity because man is disunited with himself. . . . Love is its demand." So Jim Casy preaches the religion of love.

He finds that this transcendental religion alters the old standards: "Here's me that used to give all my fight against the devil 'cause I figured the devil was the enemy. But they's somepin worse'n the devil got hold a the country." Now, like Emerson, he almost welcomes "the dear old devil." Now he fears not the lusts of the flesh but rather the lusts of the spirit. For the abstract lust of possession isolates a man from his fellows and destroys the unity of nature and the love of man. As Steinbeck writes: "The quality of owning freezes you forever into 'I,' and cuts you off forever from the 'we.'" Or, as the Concord farmers in Emerson's poem "Hamatreya" had exclaimed: " ''Tis mine, my children's and my name's," only to have "their avarice cooled like lust in the chill of the grave." To a preacher of the oversoul, possessive egotism may become the unpardonable sin.

If a society has adopted "the quality of owning" (as typified by absentee ownership) as its social norm, then Protestant nonconformity may become the highest virtue, and even resistance to authority may become justified. At the beginning of his novel Steinbeck had suggested this, describing how "the faces of the watching men lost their bemused perplexity and became hard and angry and resistant. Then the women knew that they were safe . . . their men were whole." For this is the paradox of Protestantism: when men resist unjust and selfish authority, they themselves become "whole" in spirit.

But this American ideal of nonconformity seems negative: how can men be sure that their Protestant rebellion does not come from the devil? To this there has always been but one answer—faith: faith in the instincts of the common man, faith in the ultimate social progress, and faith in the direction in which democracy is moving. So Ma Joad counsels the discouraged Tom: "Why, Tom, we're the people that live. They ain't gonna wipe us out. Why, we're the people—we go on." And so Steinbeck himself affirms a final faith in progress: "When theories change and crash, when schools, philosophies . . . grow and disintegrate, man reaches, stumbles forward. . . . Having stepped forward, he may slip back, but only half a step, never the full step back." Whether this be democratic faith, or mere transcendental optimism, it has always been the motive force of our American life and finds reaffirmation in this novel.

II

Upon the foundation of this old American idealism Steinbeck has built. But the Emersonian oversoul had seemed very vague and very ineffective— only the individual had been real, and he had been concerned more with his private soul than with other people. *The Grapes of Wrath* develops the old idea in new ways. It traces the transformation of the Protestant individual into the member of a social group—the old "I" becomes "we." And it traces the transformation of the passive individual into the active participant—the idealist becomes pragmatist. The first development continues the poetic thought of Walt Whitman; the second continues the philosophy of William James and John Dewey.

"One's-self I sing, a simple separate person," Whitman had proclaimed. "Yet utter the word Democratic, the word En-Masse." Other American writers had emphasized the individual above the group. Even Whitman celebrated his "comrades and lovers" in an essentially personal relationship. But Steinbeck now emphasizes the group above the individual and from an impersonal point of view. Where formerly American and Protestant thought has been separatist, Steinbeck now faces the problem of social integration. In his novel the "mutually repellent particles" of individualism begin to cohere.

"This is the beginning," he writes, "from 'I' to 'we.'" This is the beginning, that is, of reconstruction. When the old society has been split and the Protestant individuals wander aimlessly about, some new nucleus must be found, or chaos and nihilism will follow. "In the night one family camps in a ditch and another family pulls in and the tents come out. The two men squat on their hams and the women and children listen. Here is the node." Here is the new nucleus. "And from this first 'we,' there grows a still more dangerous thing: 'I have a little food' plus 'I have none.' If from this problem the sum is 'We have a little food' the thing is on its way, the movement has direction." A new social group is forming, based on the word "en masse." But here is no socialism imposed from above; here is a natural gouping of simple separate persons.

By virtue of his wholehearted participation in this new group the individual may become greater than himself. Some men, of course, will remain mere individuals, but in every group there must be leaders, or "representative men." A poet gives expression to the group idea, or a preacher organizes it. After Jim Casy's death, Tom is chosen to lead. Ma explains: "They's some folks that's just theirself, an' nothin' more. There's Al [for instance] he's jus' a young fella after a girl. You wasn't never like that, Tom." Because he has been an individualist, but through the influence of Casy and of his group idea has become more than himself, Tom becomes "a leader of the people." But his strength derives from his increased sense of participation in the group.

From Jim Casy, and eventually from the thought of Americans like Whitman, Tom Joad has inherited this idea. At the end of the book he sums it up, recalling how Casy "went out in the wilderness to find his own soul, and he found he didn't have no soul that was his'n. Says he foun' he jus' got a little piece of a great big soul. Says a wilderness ain't no good 'cause his little piece of a soul wasn't no good 'less it was with the rest, an' was whole." Unlike Emerson, who had said goodbye to the proud world, these latter-day Americans must live in the midst of it. "I know now," concludes Tom, "a fella ain't no good alone."

To repeat: this group idea is American, not Russian; and stems from Walt Whitman, not Karl Marx. But it does include some elements that have usually seemed sinful to orthodox Anglo-Saxons. "Of physiology from top to toe I sing." Whitman had declared, and added a good many details that his friend Emerson thought unnecessary. Now the Joads frankly discuss anatomical details and joke about them. Like most common people they do not abscond or conceal. Sometimes they seem to go beyond the bounds of literary decency: the unbuttoned antics of Grandpa Joad touch a new low in folk comedy. The movies (which reproduced most of the realism of the book) could not quite stomach this. But for the most part they preserved the spirit of the book, because it was whole and healthy.

In Whitman's time almost everyone deprecated this physiological realism, and in our own many readers and critics still deprecate it. Nevertheless, it is absolutely necessary—both artistically and logically. In the first place, characters like the Joads do act and talk that way—to describe them as genteel would be to distort the picture. And, in the second place, Whitman himself had suggested the necessity of it: just as the literature of democracy must describe all sorts of people, "en masse," so it must describe all of the life of the people. To exclude the common or "low" elements of individual life would be as false as to exclude the common or low elements of society. Either would destroy the wholeness of life and nature. Therefore, along with the dust-driven Joads, we must have Grandpa's dirty drawers.

But beyond this physiological realism lies the problem of sex. And this problem is not one of realism at all. Throughout this turbulent novel an almost traditional reticence concerning the details of sex is observed. The problem here is rather one of fundamental morality, for sex had always been a symbol of sin. *The Scarlet Letter* reasserted the authority of an orthodox morality. Now Jim Casy questions that orthodoxy. On this first meeting with Tom he describes how, after sessions of preaching, he had often lain with a girl and then felt sinful afterward. This time the movies repeated his confession, because it is central to the motivation of the story. Disbelief in the sinfulness of sex converts Jim Casy from a preacher of the old morality to a practitioner of the new.

But in questioning the old morality Jim Casy does not deny morality. He doubts the strict justice of Hawthorne's code: "Maybe it ain't a sin. Maybe it's just the way folks is. Maybe we been whippin' the hell out of ourselves for nothin'." But he recognizes that love must always remain responsible and purposeful. Al Joad remains just "a boy after a girl." In place of the old, Casy preaches the new morality of Whitman, which used sex to symbolize the love of man for his fellows. Jim Casy and Tom Joad have become more responsible and more purposeful than Pa Joad and Uncle John ever were: they love people so much that they are ready to die for them. Formerly the only unit of human love was the family, and the family remains the fundamental unit. The tragedy of *The Grapes of Wrath* consists in the breakup of the family. But the new moral of this novel is that the love of all people—if it be unselfish—may even supersede the love of family. So Casy dies for his people, and Tom is ready to, and Rose of Sharon symbolically transmutes her maternal love to a love of all people. Here is a new realization of "the word democratic, the word en masse."

### III

"An' I got to thinkin', Ma—most of the preachin' is about the poor we shall have always with us, an' if you got nothin', why, jus' fol' your hands an' to hell with it, you gonna git ice cream on gol' plates when you're dead. An' then this here Preacher says two get a better reward for their work."

Catholic Christianity had always preached humility and passive obedience. Protestantism preached spiritual nonconformity, but kept its disobedience passive. Transcendentalism sought to save the individual but not the group. ("Are they *my* poor?" asked Emerson.) Whitman sympathized more deeply with the common people and loved them abstractly, but trusted that God and democracy would save them. The pragmatic philosophers first sought to implement American idealism by making thought itself instrumental. And now Steinbeck quotes scripture to urge popular action for the realization of the old ideals.

In the course of the book Steinbeck develops and translates the thought of the earlier pragmatists. "Thinking," wrote John Dewey, "is a kind of activity which we perform at specific need." And Steinbeck repeats: "Need is the stimulus to concept, concept to action." The cause of the Okie's migration is their need, and their migration itself becomes a kind of thinking—an unconscious groping for the solution to a half-formulated problem. Their need becomes the stimulus to concept.

In this novel a kind of pragmatic thinking takes place before our eyes: the idea develops from the predicament of the characters, and the resulting action becomes integral with the thought. The evils of absentee ownership produce the mass migration, and the mass migration results in the idea of group action: "A half-million people moving over the country. . . . And tractors turning the multiple furrows in the vacant land."

But what good is generalized thought? And how is future action to be planned? Americans in general, and pragmatists in particular, have always disagreed in answering these questions. William James argued that thought was good only in so far as it satisfied a particular need and that plans, like actions, were "plural"—and should be conceived and executed individually. But Charles Sanders Peirce, and the transcendentalists before him, had argued that the most generalized thought was best, provided it eventually resulted in effective action. The problems of mankind should be considered as a unified whole, monistically.

Now Tom Joad is a pluralist—a pragmatist after William James. Tom said, "I'm still layin' my dogs down one at a time." Casy replied: "Yeah, but when a fence comes up at ya, ya gonna climb that fence?" "I climb fences when I got fences to climb," said Tom. But Jim Casy believes in looking far ahead and seeing the thing as a whole: "But they's different kinda fences. They's folks like me that climbs fences that ain't even strang up yet." Which is to say that Casy is a kind of transcendental pragmatist. His thought seeks to generalize the problems of the Okies and to integrate them with the larger problem of industrial America. His solution is the principle of group action guided by conceptual thought and functioning within the framework of democratic society and law.

And at the end of the story Tom Joad becomes converted to Jim Casy's pragmatism. It is not important that the particular strike should be won, or that the particular need should be satisfied; but it is important that men should think in terms of action, and that they should think and act in terms of the whole rather than the particular individual. "For every little beaten strike is proof that the step is being taken." The value of an idea lies not in its immediate but in its eventual success. That idea is good which works —in the long run.

But the point of the whole novel is that action is an absolute essential of human life. If need and failure produce only fear, disintegration follows. But if they produce anger, then reconstruction may follow. The grapes of wrath must be trampled to make manifest the glory of the Lord. At the beginning of the story Steinbeck described the incipient wrath of the defeated farmers. At the end he repeats the scene. "And where a number of men gathered together, the fear went from their faces, and anger took its place. And the women sighed with relief . . . the break would never come as long as fear could turn to wrath." Then wrath could turn to action.

## IV

To sum up: the fundamental idea of *The Grapes of Wrath* is that of American transcendentalism: "Maybe all men got one big soul ever'body's a part of." From this idea it follows that every individual will trust those instincts which he shares with all men, even when these conflict with the teachings of orthodox religion and of existing society. But his self-reliance will not merely seek individual freedom, as did Emerson. It will rather seek social freedom or mass democracy, as did Whitman. If this mass democracy leads to the abandonment of genteel taboos and to the modification of some traditional ideas of morality, that is inevitable. But whatever happens, the American will act to realize his ideals. He will seek to make himself whole—i.e., to join himself to other men by means of purposeful actions for some goal beyond himself.

But at this point the crucial question arises—and it is "crucial" in every sense of the word. What if this self-reliance lead to death? What if the individual is killed before the social group is saved? Does the failure of the individual action invalidate the whole idea? "How'm I gonna know about you?" Ma asks. "They might kill ya an' I wouldn't know."

The answer has already been suggested by the terms in which the story has been told. If the individual has identified himself with the oversoul, so that his life has become one with the life of all men, his individual death and failure will not matter. From the old transcendental philosophy of identity to Tom Joad and the moving pictures may seem a long way, but even the movies faithfully reproduced Tom's final declaration of transcendental faith: "They might kill ya," Ma had objected.

"Tom laughed uneasily, 'Well, maybe like Casy says, a fella ain't got a soul of his own, but on'y a piece of a big one—an' then—'

" 'Then what, Tom?'

" 'Then it don' matter. Then I'll be aroun' in the dark. I'll be ever'where —wherever you look. Wherever they's a fight so hungry people can eat, I'll be there. Wherever they's a cop beating up a guy, I'll be there. If Casy knowed, why, I'll be in the way guys yell when they're mad, an'—I'll be in the way kids laugh when they're hungry an' they know supper's ready. An' when our folks eat the stuff they raise an' live in the houses they build —why, I'll be there. See?' "

For the first time in history, *The Grapes of Wrath* brings together and makes real three great skeins of American thought. It begins with the transcendental oversoul, Emerson's faith in the common man, and his Protestant self-reliance. To this it joins Whitman's religion of the love of all men and his mass democracy. And it combines these mystical and poetic ideas with the realistic philosophy of pragmatism and its emphasis on effective action. From this it develops a new kind of Christianity—not otherworldly and passive, but earthly and active. And Oklahoma Jim Casy and the Joads think and do all these philosophical things.

# MAX WESTBROOK

## *The Archetypal Ethic of* The Ox-Bow Incident

ONE OF THE MOST SENSIBLE of all critical principles warns the reader that he must not choose indiscriminately what questions he will ask of a work of art. To ask a significant question is to impose the conditions of possible meanings. Philosophers and literary theorists—Susanne Langer, for example, in *Philosophy in a New Key*—have written learned and convincing studies of the principle and its applications. The legal mind is alert to this principle in the court room, realizing that what is admitted as evidence depends as much on questions asked as on answers given. The practical critics of Walter Van Tilburg Clark's *The Ox-Bow Incident*, however, have allowed circumstances to mislead them into asking the wrong questions; and the evidence thereby granted relevance has confused our reading of the novel.

In 1940, when it was first published, *The Ox-Bow Incident* was immediately recognized as an exception, as a cowboy story of literary merit; and it is still conceded to be, on critical grounds, the best or at least one of the best cowboy novels ever written. Some such judgment has prompted reviewers and critics to ask why this cowboy story is superior to other cowboy stories. But the question suggests that the excellence of *The Ox-Bow Incident* consists in Clark's having handled skillfully what is normally not handled skillfully in works of sub-literary merit. The approach might have worked had critics compared the novel with the fiction of Western writers like Willa Cather, John Steinbeck, Frederick Manfred, Vardis Fisher. The comparison, however, is between *The Ox-Bow Incident* and the formula cowboy story, which is about as profitable as trying to find the meaning and excellence of *Moby Dick* by limiting yourself to a discussion of ways in which it does not fall into clichés and ineptitudes of the formula sea story. Clark's critics have tried to analyze the novel by negation—the narrative is not loose, the cavalry (in this case the sheriff) does not gallop unrealistically to the rescue—and the result is an impoverished criticism amounting to little more than praise for a tight and suspenseful narrative.[1] Placing a work of art in its proper genre is essential to criticism,

[1] See, for example, Ben Ray Redman, "Magnificent Incident," *Saturday Review of Literature* (October 26, 1940), XXIII, p. 6. Redman is representative in that his review is very favorable, with only minor reservations, and yet contains no significant analysis.

*"The Archetypal Ethic of the Ox-Bow Incident"* originally appeared in WESTERN AMERICAN LITERATURE, *Vol. 1, No. 2 (Summer, 1966). It was published in Max Westbrook's volume* WALTER VAN TILBURG CLARK (*New York: Twayne Publishers, Inc., 1969) pp. 54–67. Reprinted by permission of Twayne Publishers, Inc, and Max Westbrook.*

but the discovery of that proper genre must itself be an act of criticism.

Certainly Clark chose the setting with reason. *The Ox-Bow Incident* is Western in a significant way, and its craftsmanship is excellent. The novel, however, cannot be called a cowboy story except in some perversely abstract sense, except in that sense in which *The Scarlet Letter* is a true-confessions story or *Hamlet* a detective-mystery. Nor can the injustice of lynch-law be called the subject of the novel, for surely the subject of a work of art must be something which is investigated. Hemingway's *A Farewell to Arms*, for example, includes an investigation of the subject of loyalty. Frederic Henry is a conscientious volunteer who deserts, and neither his devotion to duty nor his desertion is overtly condemned. The problem is subjected to aesthetic study. But in *The Ox-Bow Incident* there is no evidence that lynching, under any circumstances, is just or even expedient. Most men consider lynching wrong, both legally and morally, and the novel does not question that judgment. It questions something else.

If the reader is not distracted by comparisons with the formula cowboy story—or by the belief that the book is an allegorical warning against Nazi tyranny, an approach which, in 1940, appealed to reviewers and even to Clark himself—he will find, I think, that the story itself suggests a quite different and much more rewarding set of questions.

Why does the novel begin and end with Art Croft and Gil Carter despite the fact that neither plays a major role in those events which are central to the novel? What is the relevance of the long gambling scene which opens the novel? What is the relevance of the discussion of Art and Gil's emotional problems built up on winter range? What sense are we to make of Davies, who seems the most admirably moral character in the novel and is yet allowed to disintegrate into pathetic helplessness? Why is Gerald Tetley—the novel's second most articulate spokesman for morality —made to be so weak that he is disgusting to Art Croft the narrator? Why does Clark spend so much time—in an economical novel—getting the lynchers started, and why is the lynching not stopped? If Davies' academic explanation is wrong, what is the answer? If Davies is right, what is the relevance of his finely-drawn distinctions to the hard-headed realism which

---

For the most part, he praises the tension in the novel, the suspense, Clark's abilities in craftsmanship. Typical of the general criticism on Clark is Chester E. Eisinger's essay in his *Fiction of the Forties* (Chicago, 1963), The University of Chicago Press. Eisinger writes that Clark has no interest in "society" or in "ideology" (p. 310) and then describes *The Ox-Bow Incident* as a philosophical novel, as a "deliberate commingling of social and moral issues" (p. 331). Eisinger's basic strategy is also typical: Clark is a transcendentalist, his novels do not constitute an accurate development of transcendentalism. Instead of concluding that it is therefore mistaken to call Clark a transcendentalist, Eisinger stubbornly concludes that Clark is therefore incoherent. Vernon Young does the same thing in his "Gods Without Heroes: The Tentative Myth of Van Tilburg Clark." *Arizona Quarterly* (Summer, 1951, VII, pp. 110–119. Two critics I do not agree with, but whose positions I respect and whose articles I recommend, are John Portz, "Idea and Symbol in Walter Van Tilburg Clark," *Accent* (Spring, 1957), XVII, pp. 112–128; and Herbert Wilner, "Walter Van Tilburg Clark," *The Western Review* (Winter, 1956), XX, pp. 103–122. Easily the best article on Clark, in my judgment, is John R. Milton's "The Western Attitude: Walter Van Tilburg Clark," *Critique* (Winter, 1959), II, pp. 57–73.

characterizes the tone of the novel?

The passages which give rise to these and to comparable questions share a common emphasis. Clark repeatedly focuses our attention on pent-up emotions and internal meanings, on the difficulty of giving external shape to the internal, and on the danger of fragmented projections of the inner self. In the opening paragraph, the land, not yet unpent from winter, is working its way out into Spring. It is the same with Art Croft and Gil Carter, for "winter range stores up a lot of things in a man, and spring roundup hadn't worked them all out."[2] Once in the saloon, working off their "edge" with drinks and kidding, Art and Gil discover that the ranchers around Bridger's Wells are also pent-up, also on "edge," for someone has been stealing cattle. Gil joins a poker game and begins to win heavily, but "with his gripe on he [does not take] his winning right," (21) and Art begins to worry about Farnley, who "wasn't letting off steam in any way." (22) The scene becomes structurally relevant when Farnley does "let off steam" by becoming the symbolic leader of the lynch mob. The pattern continues with Major Tetley, the actual leader, and with Davies and Gerald Tetley, who are the voices of conscience, and with numerous minor characters: inner feelings must be projected into practical action, but there must be an integrity if that projection is to be healthy, and there is the constant danger—in small matters as well as in the lynching— that what is inside man will be given a distorted projection, and the result will be a horror, at best a helplessness. This value-system, I think, underlies language and event throughout the novel, but it is given its most straight-forward expression in a comparatively minor passage. Art Croft, almost parenthetically, offers a brief description of Kinkaid, the cowboy whose supposed death the lynchers want to avenge:

> He was only an ordinary rider, with no flair to give him a reputation, but still there was something about him which made men cotton to him; nothing he did or said, but a gentle, permanent reality that was in him like his bones or his heart, that made him seem like an everlasting part of things. (36)

Kinkaid's character does not consist in deeds or words, that is, in either the pragmatic or the rational, but in some quality of "bones" and "heart" which expresses a sense of "permanent reality" and expresses it with balance and unity, as "an everlasting part of things." These values, I hope to show, are comparable to those which C. G. Jung describes as arche-typal. They are the property of the unconscious mind, and the rational mind—like that of Davies—finds itself incapable in their domain. The rational mind can comment and analyze, even with some validity, but it cannot project its ideas into action. Man can only feel himself into accord with archetypal reality, and then aesthetically and ethically successful

[2] Walter Van Tilburg Clark, *The Ox-Bow Incident* (New York, 1942), The Press of the Readers Club, p. 4. Since this edition seems the most readily available, I have used it for the convenience of my readers. Subsequent references to this edition are cited parenthetically in the text.

action may occur, but the rational mind cannot will a sense of "permanent reality" into the concrete events of human activity.

The American Dream, however, in direct opposition to Jungian principles, has emphasized individuality, which is both the price and privilege of democracy. As it releases man from cultural and political tyranny, individualism also begins to imprison man within the confines of his own temporal powers of creation. Too often, the emphasis on free will leads to an emphasis on ego and degenerates into greed and into an exaggerated evaluation of the male ego. Clark—again like Jung—holds that the male ego tends to separate man from the permanent, to distort projection. The intellect, also severed from the permanent, is associated with a degrading version of the feminine. Thus the lynch mob in *The Ox-Bow Incident* misappropriates for itself a monopoly on virtuous masculinity, and thus the protestations of Davies and Gerald Tetley are repeatedly associated— both in language and action—with a degrading femininity. But unlike Jung, Clark puts the archetypal to work in problems of American democracy, and thus he assigns to man's unconscious an ethical responsibility which is normally associated with the rational mind. Whether playing poker or joining a lynch mob, man is morally responsible for projecting his responsibility onto the human stage of action; and this projection, though it is properly subject to the judgments of the rational mind, cannot be generated by the rational mind. If man balks before the burden, if archetypal energies are betrayed by the fears or by the ambitions of the selfconscious intellect, terror is let loose.

Twenty-eight men, ostensibly led by Major Tetley, pursue, capture, and lynch three men believed to be guilty of cattle rustling and murder. During the pursuit, Gerald Tetley protests to Art Croft that he thinks their mission despicable. Gerald is a character type, the weak and sensitive son of a stern father and a doting mother. His father bullies him, demanding that he develop the pride of aggressive manhood. His mother, now dead, had always interceded, protecting her son from a stern father and a cruel world. Having to face the Major by himself, Gerald is helpless, and he is doomed. Yet what he says represents one extreme of a polarity essential to the structure of *The Ox-Bow Incident*.

Denouncing the "cheap male virtues" of physical courage, (136) Gerald argues that all men fear the pack, the mass of society which bullies its members, forcing each person to become brutish rather than risk exposing to mass contempt his own inner tenderness and weakness. Each man has dreams, but, says Gerald, "nothing could make us tell them, show our weakness, have the pack at our throats," (137) and yet these dreams are true. No man, Gerald continues, wants to hear the truth; no man wants to hear the confessor: "We're afraid that sitting there hearing him and looking at him we'll let the pack know that our souls have done that too, gone barefoot and gaping with horror, scrambling in the snow of the clearing in the black woods, with the pack in the shadows behind them." (138)

Gerald is uncomfortably right, and his rightness can be seen in emotional details which constitute the real cause that led to the effect of lynching three innocent men. Even Art Croft, after hearing Gerald's confession and after admitting to himself the truth of that confession, goads Gerald with the threat of "cheap male virtues": " 'I'm not wrong about your being here, am I?' " (140) It is wrong for Art to question Gerald's loyalty to honest citizenship, to make him protest that he is not on the side of the rustlers, and Art knows it is wrong, and feels "mean" to ask the question, but he does ask it. Clark's irony here is missed unless we remember that neither Art (who later admits to Davies that he felt all along the lynching was wrong) nor Gil (who keeps remembering, though he is reluctant to confess it, an earlier hanging he had seen and been horrified by) wants to join the lynch mob. Both are participating in murder because they fear an inner reality. Both give in to society's divisive value system which associates virtue with a willingness to join the he-man lynch mob. Repeatedly, Art and Gil show themselves ready to fight with fists or with guns in order to show their allegiance to a cause in which they do not believe.

Jung describes the same fear, placing it in the realm of the unconscious and thus in the domain of the archetypal. People, he explains, are "afraid of becoming conscious of themselves." That fear, furthermore, is different from the reserve prompted by the good manners of one's society. "Beyond all natural shyness, shame and tact," Jung writes, "there is a secret fear of the unknown 'perils of the soul.' Of course one is reluctant to admit such a ridiculous fear." Jung's explanation of the danger of "secret fear" is strikingly relevant to *The Ox-Bow Incident:*

> There is indeed reason enough why man should be afraid of those nonpersonal forces dwelling in the unconscious mind. We are blissfully unconscious of those forces because they never, or almost never, appear in our personal dealings and under ordinary circumstances. But if, on the other hand, people crowd together and form a mob, then the dynamics of the collective man are set free—beasts or demons which lie dormant in every person till he is part of a mob. Man in the crowd is unconsciously lowered to an inferior moral and intellectual level, to that level which is always there, below the threshold of consciousness, ready to break forth as soon as it is stimulated through the formation of a crowd.[3]

Man's unconscious, then, for Clark as for Jung, is both his hope for contact with archetypal reality and, when pent-up, when joined with mob-energy instead of with the energy of nature, the source of horror. As mentioned earlier, however, Clark believes man must learn to think through unconscious archetypes for the purpose of making ethical distinctions. We see this most obviously in Art Croft's reflections on Gerald's outburst:

---

[3] C. G. Jung, *Psychology and Religion* (New Haven, 1963), pp. 14, 15, 16. Of particular relevance, also, is "Positive Aspects of the Mother-Complex," part four of Jung's *Psychological Aspects of the Mother Archetype.* The second paragraph of part four would do quite well as a brief statement of Clark's world view.

I realized that queerly, weak and bad-tempered as it was, there had been something in the kid's raving which had made the canyon seem to swell out and become immaterial until you could think the whole world, the universe, into the half-darkness around you: millions of souls swarming like fierce, tiny, pale stars, shining hard, winking about cores of minute, mean feelings, thoughts and deeds. To me his idea appeared just the opposite of Davies'. To the kid what everybody thought was low and wicked, and their hanging together was a mere disguise of their evil. To Davies, what everybody thought became, just because everybody thought it, just and fine, and to act up to what they thought was to elevate oneself. And yet both of them gave you that feeling of thinking outside yourself, in a big place; the kid gave me that feeling even more, if anything, though he was disgusting. You could feel what he meant; you could only think what Davies meant. (139)

Here are the central argument and the typical image of Clark's allegiance to the West. Though his sin, in a general way, is the same as Major Tetley's, Art Croft is an appropriate narrator for a novel of that allegiance in that he is moving toward the acceptance of ethical responsibilities in a world of archetypal realities. He wants to think outside himself, to a reality more objective than the personal projections of the romanticized individualist. The objectively real, furthermore, must be felt, a requirement which suggests mysticism, or knowledge of the real apprehended by a means beyond human analysis. Gerald, however, in stressing the imaginative at the expense of the practical, disgusts Art, who does not like to see a man pour "out his insides without shame"; and Art admits also a deep admiration for Davies, whose intellectual and very unmystical approach also gives "that feeling of thinking outside yourself." Art Croft has thus accepted a Western version of the American paradox. The universal principles of justice, as formulated and intellectualized by Davies, are real. They represent a part of our history, and the American of integrity cannot take D. H. Lawrence's advice (given throughout his *Studies in Classic American Literature*) and ignore an ethical duty because it is not honored with the ontological status that is the exclusive property of the unconscious. Clark's hero is obligated to grant the rights of the internal self, the ethical duties owed to others, and unlike his Eastern counterpart, to accept also the primary reality of the archetypes of the unconscious. He intellectualizes nervously (all of Clark's heroes are painfully rational, none are mindless), he is concerned with the practical world (law in *The Ox-Bow Incident*, adjustment problems from boyhood to manhood in urban America in *The City of Trembling Leaves*, the settling of the West in *The Track of the Cat*), and he realizes or comes to realize that the unconscious mind must be in tune with primordial reality. The goal for Clark, and here again he is of the West, is unity.

Neither the mystical nor the intellectual, it should be emphasized, leads to unity. Throughout Clark's works, characters who seem mystical or unusually sensitive are either disgusting, like Gerald, or ineffectual, like

Arthur in *The Track of the Cat*. The intellectual, like Davies, is sympathetic but ineffectual, and the intellect—when associated with the coolness
of a Major Tetley—tends toward cruelty and self-destruction. Unity,
which Clark associates with balance, cannot be achieved by a narrow personality.

The Reverend Osgood, for example, is right intellectually, and, according to Art, sincere; but he is a failure as a man and as a minister. The fact
that his advice to the lynchers is legal, ethical, and sensible is irrelevant.
His words do not spring from the generative unconscious, and thus they
come stillborn into the world of action, and make men turn away, ashamed.
Osgood, of course, is not a whole man. He represents man's cowardly
severance of parts from a whole he is neither humble enough nor brave
enough to sense. This severance, quite understandably, is for Clark an
ugly operation. And when the human animal devours a part of its own
body, the act is grotesque. The sense of the whole must be felt with such
courage and conviction that it results in a projection which has an honest
face, which is dramatically effective.

Osgood's failure, therefore, is described in aesthetic terms. Since his
position obligates him to stop the lynching, the Reverend tries, but he
goes about it "busily, as if he didn't want to, but was making himself."
(41) His intellectual concept of an official duty, that is, cannot give birth
to genuine emotion or to genuine action. His efforts are fragmented. He
starts, and then stops, unable to get going, unable to speak with force or
persuasion, incapable even of persuading himself. (The lynch mob has
excessive energy, but it is distorted mob-energy, repugnant to man's ethical
sense, and thus the mob too starts and stalls, has difficulty getting under
way.) He waves his hands, nervously, thrusts them in his pockets again,
and looks, at one point, "as if he were going to cry." (40) Art notices that
his "bald head was pale in the sun," that the "wind fluttered his coat and
the legs of his trousers," that he "looked helpless and timid." (41) He "was
trying to do what he thought was right, but he had no heart in his effort,"
(41) and he makes Art feel "ashamed," "disgusted." (41) His voice "was
too high from being forced," and, Art concludes, "He talked with no more
conviction than he walked." (41)

Osgood, as a man, is embarrassing, which is not to say that brave men
have a full head of hair or that men with high voices are cowards. Clark
has chosen to describe Osgood's pathetic and ineffectual efforts in aesthetic
terms because he is concerned with the necessity of the archetypal source.
Osgood flutters his hands as a nervous reaction to his own incompetence.
He speaks in a voice "too high from being forced" because his source is his
own sterile will instead of the energizing archetypes of the unconscious.
He has given himself over to officialdom's grotesque separation of man
from the totality to which he belongs. He has alienated himself from that
essential unity of thought and things—and self-destruction is a disgusting
sight to behold.

This alienation, I think, explains why Clark began the novel with a brief study in restoration. Though close friends, Art and Gil have succumbed to the tension of winter range, and they have argued and fought. They must now ease out of their divisive feelings, but the restoration can take place only if there is a sense of balance, a sense of the whole. They do not "dare talk much," and they are eager "to feel easy together again." (4) The clipped and ironic conversation, the mask of jokes to cover a bitterness which must not be allowed to grow, and the ritual of restraint represent a sense of the whole of which Osgood is unaware.

Art and Gil's entrance into Bridger's Wells, with its suggestions of rites of passage, is immediately contrasted with Monty Smith, whose degraded insensitivity makes him one of the most despicable villains in Clark's archetypal world. He is a "soft-bellied, dirty fellow," who wears a "half-shaved beard with strawberry patches showing through, sore and itchy." (5) Though opposite Davies and Gerald, though worse even that Osgood, he too is an embarrassment. He is a sponge, the town bum, and he cheapens manliness by pretending to be a genuine cowboy able to buy a round in turn. Gil is too much a man of feelings to be an ideal Clark hero, but he does feel with a roughhouse kind of honesty, and the certainty that Monty Smith will try to sponge a drink makes him "sore." He reins his horse sharply, and Art says, "Take it easy." (6) Gil does not reply, nor does he tell Art what he feels. Art has enough insight (he is apparently a writer) to know what his partner feels, and both know that what is important cannot be shaped into words.

Inside Canby's saloon, Art and Gil begin to drink. Behind the bar is a large and ludicrous oil painting entitled *Woman with Parrot,* but called by Canby himself "The Bitching Hour." The painting shows a large woman, half draped, lounging, holding a parrot. Behind the woman appears a man who seems to be sneaking up on her, or perhaps he is being lured by the woman to his destruction. Gil complains that the man "is awful slow getting there" and thinks the woman "could do better." (8) Canby defends the man, who is always "in reach and never able to make it." He thinks the woman has a "mean nature." (8)

The painting, it seems to me, makes an ironic comment on major action. The tension in the painting is frozen, caught for all time and, as a result, melodramatic, unrealistic. The tensions of the real world, by contrast, must be resolved in action. Almost every character in the novel, at one time or another, feels himself unmanned or at least that his manhood is doubted. Because of the high value placed on the male ego (Sparks is about the only one who escapes its tyranny), tension is built up, pent-up emotions demand satisfaction, gross or otherwise. Tyler and Osgood swell around pathetically trying to assert their authority. A feeble old man and an irate woman tongue-lash the reluctant lynchers. Smith, as a fraud, finds his manhood constantly in jeopardy, specifically when he must bum a drink from Art and then leave, "hitching his belt in the doorway to get his conceit back;" (11) and it is this need which makes him eager to participate in the lynching. Even Gil is unsettled for having lost his girl, an unmanly thing to do, and Major Tetley, of course, is determined to prove his own manly leadership and the courage of his son. In general, the ability of Bridger's Wells ranchers to protect their own cattle is in question. As a result of these small and large distortions, the lynching occurs.

This, I think, is the relevance of the opening scene, one instance in which resolution takes place with a sense of the whole, and the means to a better understanding of the entire novel. During the banter about the painting, Art reflects that Gil and Canby "said something like this every time we came in. It was a ritual." (8) And the word *ritual*, of course, suggests that unconscious realities are being shaped into the world of actuality. It is with ceremonial implications, then, that Art takes his cue from Canby, whose "face stayed as set as an old deacon's," (10) and begins describing the fight he had with Gil. Ironic and friendly insults are then swapped by Art and Gil. Gil justifies having knocked Art across a red-hot stove by saying a man has to have exercise. Art, he complains, is not much of a fighter, "but there wasn't anything else handy." (10) Art counters by kidding his partner's inept singing. They are "talking off their edge," and Canby puts "in a word now and then to keep [them] going." (11) The tension built up during winter range cannot be ignored nor can it be allowed its natural expression. It must be shaped.

The ethical, therefore, stands in a curious relation to the aesthetic. There are qualities and shades of qualities. Clark's vision, I think, reveals reason and feeling as neither good nor bad. What is desired is unity, a sense of the whole, with reason and feeling in their proper place, that is, with feeling (or the unconscious) as man's contact with reality and reason as man's conscious recording device for what the unconscious has taught. Davies, after all, pleads for feeling more than for reason. He is not the cold intellectual without heart. His failure is in his effort to make the rational do the work of the unconscious and in his resultant inability to give his beliefs the shape of dramatic conviction, which is not to imply that Clark has stooped to formulas.

Certainly Major Tetley is a master performer, and his ability to control the lynching party is an actor's ability. He speaks to a man without looking at him, keeping his own face full camera, and thus keeps "inferiors" in their place. He knows when to pause, how to ignore an opponent, when to turn rebellion by a soft reply. He has cunning, which is an archetypal characteristic of pent-up and distorted energies. As the master of male ego, he is the natural leader. Gil Carter, for example, offended by Farnley's accusations at the card table, rouses his manliness and knocks Farnley flat. Offended by Major Tetley, he again asserts his manhood, fully prepared for a gunfight, only to be turned into helplessness by Major Tetley's quiet sophistry. Gil is left in the frustrated position of feeling right but looking wrong, which happens, in different ways, to Osgood, Davies, and Gerald, and which happens also, in the climax of the novel, to the three victims of the lynching.

The lynching is simply a culmination, a gross increase of numerous injustices which occur throughout the novel and which are enacted according to the same ground rules that permit murder. The long poker game is a direct preparation for what takes place at the Ox-Bow. Gil begins to win, but he does not win in the right way. He neither apologizes nor gloats. Rather, he rakes in the pot as if he expected it. And Farnley, the heaviest and most disgruntled loser, also refuses to play the game right when he calls for double draw, even though he is not dealing, even though double draw is not "real poker." The judgments made after their fight are made by the same code, except this time Gil does it right. Canby knocks Gil out with a bottle, and then starts to take his gun. Art shakes him off. He knows his buddy, and his buddy will take it in the right way, and that he does, coming out of it slow, but joking. There is a right way to play poker and a wrong way, a right way to fight and a wrong way. One of the final comments in the novel is Gil's statement that he will not fight the sophisticated dude who took his girl. "I don't know how to start a decent fight with that kind of a guy," (287) he says, and readers will be reminded of Art's hope, just before the lynching, that Martin would "make the decent end he now had his will set on." (240) The Mex, who has held center stage and earned the admiration of everyone by removing a bullet from his own leg, spits in contempt when old Hardwick buckles, saying ironically, "This is fine company for a man to be with." (243) But in the end the Mex goes to pieces and screams, talking "panicky in Spanish," (246) and Art comments: "In the pinch Martin was taking it the best of the three." (246) How to die, how to fight, how to play poker, how to stop a lynching: all are studies in the same world view.

After it has become known that the three hanged men are innocent, Davies flaggelates himself, embarrassing Art with a destructive confession. Davies does make some valid points—his denunciation of the sins of omission for example—but his confession is repugnant, for it comes from a part-man. Art, though enough of a moral coward to confine his opposition to "safe" actions like the fetching of Judge Tyler, though he puts aside his conscience and does not vote to delay the hanging, is a more complete being than Davies. His insight into people characterizes the novel, and he has at least some contact with the unity of all things, but he is also remarkably acute in reading the motives of Davies' rational will. He does miss Davies from time to time, but his understanding of the rational mind is a mark of Clark's American revision of Jungian archetypes.

That revision is a fairly complex one. It is certainly bold. By what guilt or fate, then, have twenty-eight men come to the horror of lynching three innocent men? Clark's answer—or the closest thing to it for an author who feels that questions are more legitimate than answers—is his dramatization of the horrors of divisive lives. It is contained in the portraits of Judge Tyler and the Reverend Osgood and the obscene ethic of their narrow little roles as half-men, in the bumbling but honest frustrations and hi-jenks of Gil Carter, in the sympathetic obsession of Davies' doomed but honorable intellectualism, in the embarrassing but insightful confession of the girl-man Gerald Tetley, and even in the melodramatic tyranny of Major Tetley, the master play-actor of male ego.

The reality which lies behind the archetypal ethic of *The Ox-Bow Incident* is a reality one apprehends best by belonging as an "everlasting part of things." Man does not achieve his real self in idea or office or emotion, but as an individual part of a larger whole. Man's only hope is to act from a sense of the integrity of that larger eternity, and his most shocking failure is to murder innocent men on behalf of his own dedication to a severed piece of man called the male ego. When that failure occurs, his victim will be most probably a man like Martin, an innocent, naive in the affairs of the manly world, the natural prey of the mob-beast that grows from man's neglected unconscious.

The subject of *The Ox-Bow Incident*, I have tried to suggest, is not a plea for legal procedure. The subject is man's mutilation of himself, man's sometimes trivial, sometimes large failures to get beyond the narrow images of his own ego. The tragedy of *The Ox-Bow Incident* is that most of us, including the man of sensitivity and the man of reason, are alienated from the saving grace of archetypal reality. Our lives, then, though not without possibility, are often stories of a cruel and irrevocable mistake.

# DELBERT E. WYLDER

## *Thomas Berger's* Little Big Man *as Literature*

ROBERT EDSON LEE's *From West to East* is an exceptionally provocative and controversial study of western American literature. Of Thomas Berger's *Little Big Man*, for example, Lee says "No one pretends it is literature."[1] However, L. L. Lee in his article[2] on this satirical novel, published the same year, implies that *Little Big Man* not only pretends to be literature, it might very well be literature—and rather good literature at that. There are always critical questions that become important in trying to determine whether any novel is good literature; that is, whether or not it succeeds as a work of art. The selection of specific questions first depends on placing the work of art within the proper frame of reference and then

[1] Robert Edson Lee, *From West to East: Studies in the Literature of the American West* (Urbana: University of Illinois Press, 1966), p. 156.
[2] L. L. Lee, "American, Western, Picaresque: Thomas Berger's *Little Big Man*," *The South Dakota Review* IV (Summer, 1966), pp. 35–42.

*Reprinted from* WESTERN AMERICAN LITERATURE, *Vol. III, No. 4 (Winter, 1969), by permission of the editor.*

choosing the questions appropriate to that particular class of novels. Especially in evaluating *Little Big Man,* this first and basic step is of the utmost importance. The novel seems to be a curious mixture of forms or species of the novel and thus the appropriate critical questions are perhaps difficult to arrive at. The critic is able to understand the perplexity with which scientists must have viewed the duck-billed platypus when time came for that animal to be classified. But once *Little Big Man* is labeled, the critical problem becomes more simple, and then other seemingly disturbing questions can be answered.

As L. L. Lee has already noted, the novel grows more serious as it progresses. The tonal change from comic to tragic, however, is only within the story told by Jack Crabb, the 111-year old whose life, or part of it, forms the action of the novel. Crabb's story begins as a farce, with a comical portrait of an Indian chief as one focus of attention; it ends with that same Indian's death in a scene described in mythic and tragic overtones. A major question in determining whether the novel is effective as literature concerns whether or not Berger has successfully controlled his narrative perspective in achieving this change of tone. It seems to me that he has, and that once we identify the area in which Berger is working, and once we examine closely the narrative perspective, then we will arrive at the conclusion that Berger has successfully brought together the comic and the tragic, the satiric and the mythic into meaningful relationship in a novel that might be called a Barthian Western. Most important, it is successful because of the tonal change, which can be seen most clearly through an analysis of Berger's creation and development of the character of Old Lodge Skins.

In relation to L. L. Lee's comments on the change of tone in *Little Big Man,* it is interesting to note that most of the pejorative criticism of Joseph Heller's World War II novel *Catch 22* concentrated on tonal change. The novel was attacked for beginning with a humorously satirical treatment of U. S. Air Corps personnel and activities during World War II and ending with a serious, though exaggerated, commentary on war. Richard Kostelanetz includes Heller in a group with John Barth—the leader of the group —Thomas Pynchon, and Mordecai Richler, to which might also be added the Westerner William Eastlake. Kostelanetz suggests that the approach of these novelists is essentially derived from the European theatre of the absurd

> in that the author creates a series of absurd (i.e., nonsensical, ridiculous) events—repetition of similar action forms the novel's structure—to depict the ultimate absurdity (i.e., meaninglessness) of history and existence. Thus, these works embody absurdity both in the small events and the entire vision, the subject matter and the form.[3]

It is obvious that Berger's *Little Big Man,* like the platypus, does not fit neatly into this category. It is true that the author does create a series of

[3] Richard Kostelanetz, "The New American Fiction," in Richard Kostelanetz (ed.), *The New American Arts* (New York: Collier Books, 1967), p. 202.

absurd events and that Jack Crabb's distorted narration of historical events casts a reflection on the truthfulness and meaningfulness of recorded history. It is also true that the "editor" Ralph Fielding Snell's framelike introduction and epilogue suggest the absurdity of the entire Crabb narrative. But in spite of all this, what remains for the reader is not a picture of absurdity in the "entire vision," but an emphasis on certain virtues espoused by the tragic hero of Crabb's story, Old Lodge Skins. Thus, Berger's novel is Barthian in its approach, but distinctly Western in its attitude toward humanity and human values.

The Barthian recreation of a history of the absurd is noted particularly in the framework of the novel. The narrative of the life of Jack Crabb is introduced by the editor, Ralph Fielding Snell, the "Fielding" an obvious clue to the essential satiric quality of the novel. Furthermore, Snell is an effete, naive and foolish self-styled "man of letters" and Western history devotee. He is an effeminate and rather smug "Prufrock," who is manhandled by his female nurse, is totally subordinate and dependent upon his father, and who finally is unable to edit the Crabb manuscript until he has recovered from a 10-year protracted "mental collapse" suffered while fighting the fraudulent claims of a supposedly illegitimate half-brother. Snell's inability to determine the real from the fraudulent in judging the claims of Jack Crabb are totally confused at the end of the novel when the bookish editor points out that he has caught Crabb in many factual inaccuracies. "As to Crazy Horse's not wearing feathers, we know that statement to be erroneous—his war bonnet, as mentioned in the Preface, presently reposes in my own collection; the dealer who sold it to me is a man of the highest integrity."[4]

The narrative perspective of the framework, then, is absurd. The question of the Crabb story remains to be examined. The situation is one of the most common literary and historical hoaxes—the claims of a man that he was part of the Western experience. Usually, the perpetrator claims a bit more notoriety, although there is something creative and original about Crabb's claim to be the sole survivor of the Battle of the Little Bighorn. One of the more recent attempts to re-establish an identity was Brushy Bill Roberts' confession, in 1950, that he was Billy the Kid.[5] Since most of the claims of the identity-seekers have been rather ridiculous, the story of Jack Crabb's very claim to existence appears from the beginning of his narrative to be fraudulent and absurd.

Although Robert Edson Lee recognizes that the book is a "satire on Westerns,[6] he suggests that at least Chapters 2–8 are realistic. "They are realistic," he says, "because they are based on the incidents and descriptions of Parkman's *The Oregon Trail*. *Little Big Man* is a product of what

[4] Thomas Berger, *Little Big Man* (Greenwich, Conn.: Fawcett Crest Book, 1965), p. 447.

[5] See C. L. Sonnichsen and William V. Morrison, *Alias Billy the Kid* (Albuquerque: University of New Mexico Press, 1955).

[6] *From West to East*, p. 156.

Berger has read, not of what he has seen and experienced."[7] It may, of course, be quite true that these chapters are based on Parkman's work, but Jack Crabb's sardonic vision is hardly that of Parkman. As a matter of fact, Berger's Jack Crabb at the beginnng of the novel sounds more like a local color humorist in his depictions of the West. He gives us a highly comic figure of Old Lodge Skins.

The first time we see Old Lodge Skins, he is leading a small and ragged band of Indians approaching the ill-fated Crabb wagon train. As Crabb tells it,

> The fellow in the plug hat was their leader. He wore one of those silver medals that the government give out to principal men at treaty signings: I think his showed the image of President Fillmore. He was older than the others and he carried an ancient musket with a barrel four foot long.[8]

Crabb's sister Caroline approaches the old Indian, called "Plug Hat" at this point of the story, and

> Plug Hat marched up to her, sticking out his brown right hand while the left hand held the old musket across his front and also kept his red blanket from falling off.
>
> "Right pleased to make your acquaintance," says Caroline, who is a deal bigger than the old chief, and gives him a grip so hard you can see the pain travel up through his hat and down the other arm. He almost lost his blanket.[9]

This character portrait is hardly a Parkman-like creation. It more closely resembles the portrait of Muck-a-Muck, the satiric Cooper-Indian of Bret Harte's "Condensed Novel."

> Over one shoulder a blanket, negligently but gracefully thrown, disclosed a bare and powerful breast, decorated with a quantity of three-cent postage-stamps which he had despoiled from an Overland Mail stage a few weeks previous. A castoff beaver of Judge Tompkin's, adorned by a simple feather, covered his erect head, from beneath which his straight locks descended. His right hand hung lightly by his side, while his left was engaged in holding on a pair of pantaloons, which the lawless grace and freedom of his lower limbs evidently could not brook.[10]

Further, Old Lodge Skins' actions are exaggerated into the absurd in the drinking scene which leads to the murder of all the white men and the rape of almost all the women on the wagon train. Old Lodge Skins is the first to drink. His reaction is ridiculous.

---

[7] *Ibid.* For an understanding of Berger's artistic use of what he has "read," compare the Indian sections of the novel with E. Adamson Hoebel's *The Cheyennes* (New York: Holt-Rinehart-Winston, 1960).

[8] *Little Big Man*, p. 31.

[9] *Ibid.*

[10] Bret Harte, "*Muck-A-Muck:* A Modern Indian Novel After Cooper," *Condensed Novels.*

Old Lodge Skins took the tin cup my Pa handed him and drained it in one swallow, as if it was water or cold coffee, tilting his head back so far the plug hat fell off. The drink was already down his gullet before he altogether comprehended the nature of it, and you might say simultaneous with that recognition he became instantly drunk, his eyes swimming with liquid like two raw eggs. He fell over backwards on the earth and kicked his feet so hard one moccasin flew off and hit the cover of our wagon. His musket dropped, muzzle down, and packed some dirt in the end of the barrel . . .[11]

And at the end of the scene, when all the white men are dead and most of the Indians are completely drunk, we have another picture of Old Lodge Skins.

Old Lodge Skins was pointing at the unconscious body of Spotted Wolf and laughing his guts out. That irked Caroline, but also pleased her, and she flicked her whip sort of flirty at the chief. He flopped onto his back with his arms crucified and laughed his old mouth, dark as a cave full of bats, into the sun. His foot was still bare and his busted gun lay near him like the skeleton of an open umbrella.[12]

The Indian described here is quite obviously neither the Romantic savage unspoiled by civilization nor the hostile barbarian intent upon the destruction of the white man. He is as foolish as Falstaff, but without Falstaff's wit or his ability to hold his liquor. To make matters even more ridiculous, Old Lodge Skins is plagued by jackrabbits. They bring him bad luck and, as Crabb tells it,

Let the toe of his moccasin protrude from the tepee, and up they'd leap for miles about, numerous as sparks when you throw a horseshoe in a forge.[13]

There is such a contrast between Crabb's introduction to the character of Old Lodge Skins and the final picture of him that, put into close juxtaposition, he is hardly recognizable as the same character. At the end of the novel, the blind old Indian climbs powerfully up to the top of a mountain. Crabb, then quite a young man, must stop several times to rest, but the old man forces him on. They reach the top and Crabb looks around at the big sky and finds himself once more at the center of the universe. Crabb turns to Old Lodge Skins and finds that ". . . he had drawn off from me, dropped his blanket, and standing with his scarred old body naked to the falling sun, he yelled in a mighty voice that sounded like thunder echoing from peak to peak."[14] He yells the battle cry of the Cheyenne. Then he challenges Death to come out and fight. When Death does not appear, Old

[11] *Little Big Man*, p. 33.
[12] *Ibid.*, p. 38.
[13] *Ibid.*, p. 48.
[14] *Ibid.*, p. 444.

Lodge Skins prays to the Everywhere Spirit in a manner that Crabb describes as "never sniveling but bold and free."

> "I have killed many men and loved many women and eaten much meat.
> I have also been hungry, and I thank you for that and for the added sweetness that food has when you receive it after such a time.
> "You make all things and direct them in their ways, O Grandfather, and now you have decided that the Human Beings will soon have to walk a new road. Thank you for letting us win once before that happened. Even if my people must eventually pass from the face of the earth, they will live on in whatever men are fierce and strong. So that when women see a man who is proud and brave and vengeful, even if he has a white face, they will cry: "That is a Human Being!"[15]

Then Old Lodge Skins challenges Death once more and asks for his old power to make things happen. Evidently the power is granted, for then follows a rather amazing natural phenomenon.

> . . . he give his war cry once more, and as it went reverberating across that range, an answering roll of thunder come out of the west, and that sky which had been crystal pure suddenly developed a dark mass of cloud above the sun and it began to roll towards us across the vast distance.
> I stood there in awe and Old Lodge Skins started to sing, and when the cloud arrived overhead, the rain started to patter across his uplifted face, mixing with the tears of joy there.
> It might have been ten minutes or an hour, and when it stopped and the sun's setting rays cut through, he give his final thanks and last request.
> "Take care of my son here," he says, "and see that he does not go crazy."
> He laid down then on the damp rocks and died right away.[16]

This is the death of Old Lodge Skins as Jack Crabb describes it. There are a few more comments concerning how Crabb puts the body on a scaffold and walks down the mountain. And that is the point at which Ralph Fielding Snell chooses to end Crabb's story. The death scene is reminiscent of mythological deaths, where the hero is joined to nature or taken to the gods through some stormy natural phenomenon and where the mythological hero chooses to die. He goes out to meet death rather than allowing death to take him. The scene reminds one especially of the death of Oedipus at Colonnus, where the blind old man looses his sordid garments after being called to his dying place by peals of thunder and bolts of lightning. Like Oedipus, Old Lodge Skins is blind. Old Lodge Skins' blindness allows him a different kind of vision for, as he tells the Everywhere Spirit when he thanks the god for his affliction, his blindness allows him to see "further."

His blindness is not the only parallel with Oedipus. Oedipus had committed patricide and incest, the most terrible of sins in Greek civilization.

---

[15] *Ibid.*

[16] *Ibid.*, pp. 444–445.

Old Lodge Skins has committed the most unpardonable sin in Cheyenne civilization. As is made quite clear within the novel, the most horrendous crime for a Cheyenne is to kill another "Human Being," that is another Cheyenne. As early as Chapter Three, the reader is informed that the Indians were highly concerned about their escapades at the wagon train.

> What bothered them was that while drunk they had nearly killed some of themselves; that's the worst thing a Cheyenne could do: kill another Cheyenne. Being drunk is no excuse. It is always regarded as murder, and the murderer rots inside his guts, giving off a stink to other members of the tribe, soiling the Sacred Arrows, and driving the buffalo away.[17]

The concept is further reinforced a bit later in the novel when Little Big Man and his Cheyenne friends see two white men in the distance, one with long yellow hair. The Indians go in the other direction.

> There was a reason why we didn't hanker none to meet these whites: it had begun to mean bad luck for the Cheyenne. You remember what happened at the wagon train of my white family: some Cheyenne had almost killed one another.[18]

The crime that Old Lodge Skins has committed, as well as his father before him, is exactly that of killing a fellow Human Being. The reason that Old Lodge Skins' band had been exiled from the Burnt Artery band is that the chief's father killed a fellow Cheyenne in a quarrel over a woman.

> Now Old Lodge Skins became their leader, having proved himself wise and brave and generous, and the time come when they was invited back to the Burnt Arteries on the occasion of the sun dance where all the tribe joins together. By God if that Indian didn't get into the same kind of trouble as his Dad—a vein of horniness run right through the family—he swiped the wife of a man from the Hair Rope band and though he left two horses as payment the other fellow didn't like the deal and come after him and in the set-to got an arrow through the windpipe and choked to death.[19]

Old Lodge Skins had then taken his band out on the prairie, where they had wandered alone for years. He has been, like Oedipus, essentially an exile.

The result of all of this is a gradual recognition on the part of the reader that Old Lodge Skins is the Cheyenne equivalent of the mythical tragic hero; he is a Cheyenne Oedipus. It is little wonder that we are not surprised at the concluding scene in which Nature honors the old man and his magic. Nor do we wonder at the characterization at this point, for Berger's treatment of Old Lodge Skins through Jack Crabb's narration allows a gradual acceptance of the blind old chief as the heroic type. Al-

[17] *Ibid.*, p. 66.
[18] *Ibid.*, p. 78.
[19] *Ibid.*, p. 104.

though he is introduced comically, there are a number of scenes in which his power and wisdom are displayed. His magical powers are demonstrated in his conquest of the antelope herd, for one example that comes early in the novel. He is also able to see in his dreams the vision of Little Big Man as Jack Crabb having a soda during his stay with the Pendrakes in Missouri. He has seen a vision of the elephant-shaped soda fountain, and knows that there is air in the water. Even the often skeptical Crabb has no explanation for such a vision. As the novel progresses, Crabb frequently alludes to the wisdom and understanding of Old Lodge Skins and, except for an occasional reminder that the old chief gets pretty upset when he sees a jackrabbit, the treatment of Old Lodge Skins loses all its comic flavor.

Crabb is rather consistent as the humorously picaresque anti-hero. He does nothing heroic, although he sometimes bests a historical Western hero through trickery. However, he is not the naturalistic anti-hero, or unhero, who finds his romantic illusions shattered when he faces reality. As a matter of fact, romantic illusion is something which seems to be enhanced by the Jack Crabb story, as long as the illusions are based upon certain basic realities. Both George Armstrong Custer, the historically debunked hero, and an Indian chief with magical powers that have also been scientifically debunked are the heroes that Crabb recreates at the end of his story. They are both proud men. They are both "big" men in the sense that even their faults are magnificent. They are contrasted quite skillfully with the "little" men throughout the novel.

We are never, of course, sure even of the fictional reality of Jack Crabb. Berger's narrative perspective has increased the absurdity of the tale to the limit. Berger is the creator of all the action, but he has invented a completely unrealistic editor to introduce and comment on the Crabb story. Snell, himself, is unbelievable in realistic literary terms. He is a parody of the 18th century man of letters, a man completely unadjusted to the outside world, who is "tumbled about like an infant" by his nurse, and who has absolutely no qualifications for evaluating the truth of Jack Crabb's story. Furthermore, this fictional creation of Berger's may very well have fictionally created the whole story of Jack Crabb. For one thing, he has just recovered, he tells us, from a mental collapse. Snell's tone, however, in the "Editor's Epilogue" is quite serious, although Berger's is not. Snell tells of his doubts of Crabb's validity because he cannot find Crabb's name on the historical lists and because he believes an Indian trader who has sold him Crazy Horse's war bonnet. And Crabb said that Crazy Horse didn't wear one. Thus, the narrative perspective mirrors absurdity back upon itself and seems to suggest that not only are the details absurd, but that the ultimate vision must also be even more absurd.

What actually results from Snell's role as intermediary between Berger and Crabb is an emphasis on the believability, for the reader, of the Crabb story. What results is not absurdity, but an increase in ambiguity and especially upon the satirical aspects of the novel as told from Crabb's sardonic vision, and in Crabb's humorous and curiously irreverently reverent style—a genuinely fake Western narration. Robert Edson Lee's recognition that the book is a satire on Westerns is a valid recognition, but the novel is often, and finally, more than that. The rather powerful concluding scene with the mythical hero challenging death from the mountain-top might well be seen as a satire on traditional and contemporary Indian novels. In William Eastlake's somewhat Barthian novel, *Portrait of an Artist with 26 Horses* for example, the death of old Tomas Tomas is handled, in detail, somewhat sardonically although the substance of the total scene is suggestive of meaningfulness. A more obvious example of the journey of the hero in an Indian novel is Frederick Manfred's *Conquering Horse*, where the hero of the story must, like Oedipus, replace his father as leader of the tribe. At the end of the novel, there is the same type of natural display and the complete disappearance of the old chief. Conquering Horse has been told in his dreams that he is to kill his "real" father and replace him as chief. He is reluctant to do this, for he loves his father, but the old chief, Redbird, and the medicine man Moon Dreamer, the biological father, taunt the younger generation led by Conquering Horse. The Gods have demanded a sacrifice, and the young warriors finally attack.

> Then, just as Conquering Horse and the young warriors climbed into the tumble of red rocks and were about to fall on Redbird, the Thunders spoke. A long pink tongue of fire licked down out of the churning black cloud above and ticked the copper tip of Redbird's lance. There was a dazzling explosion, completely enveloping Redbird. The explosion was so great it hurled Conquering Horse and the young braves entirely out of the tumble of red rocks and threw them backward upon the ground.
>
> When the people looked again, after the lightning spots had cleared from their eyes, Redbird was gone.[20]

Is the death of Old Lodge Skins a satire on this type of literary treatment of mythology and Indian life? Apparently it is not, although it could be. The satire in the novel is more typically Barthian. It is frequently rather epigrammatic, and there are often commentaries, such as "People came and went in them days, but horses was serious,"[21] or "Being primitive ain't the easiest thing in the world to get used to if you know better."[22] Then there is that exceptional commentary, "If you want to really relax sometime, just fall to rock bottom and you'll be a happy man. Most all troubles come from having standards."[23]

The satire is also comparative. Just as Swift's Gulliver allows us to see the foibles of mankind from different perspectives in sizes between Lilliput and Brobdignag, Crabb's movement from Indian society to white society allows us to view each society from a different perspective. We thus see

[20] Frederick Manfred, *Conquering Horse* (New York: Pocket Books, 1960), pp. 330–331.

[21] *Little Big Man*, p. 176.

[22] *Ibid.*, p. 160.

[23] *Ibid.*, p. 164.

the snobbery, for example, of the whites and Indians. And although there is an emphasis on the subjectivity of the Indian life when Crabb finds the feeling that he is at the center of the earth, the narrative perspective allows both ways of life to be satirized. Thus, the novel is more of a commentary on the foibles of mankind itself rather than a simplified statement about the superiority of Indian ways.

The meaningfulness of Crabb's subjective experience, however, keeps this novel from becoming a totally Barthian novel. Many of the artistic devices are there, to be sure, but the reader's gradual acceptance, through Jack Crabb's acceptance, of the subjective life in the natural environment and of Old Lodge Skins as the Oedipus-like hero provides an over-all affirmation of what Max Westbrook discusses as a "Western sacrality."[24] The Western spirit totally dominates the "ultimate vision" of the novel. It is not, however, imposed on the novel. It grows out of the satiric treatment of mankind, even its heroes, combined with a respect for the living of life. Old Lodge Skins' virtues: the lack of a fear of death, the appreciation of the vicissitudes and the joys of life, fierceness and strength, pride, bravery, and even vengefulness; these are meaningful despite death. They dominate the novel through the device of allowing the skeptical and humorous Jack Crabb, with his Western tall-tale type of narration, to tell the story of his gradual acceptance of the Western spirit.

In the Barthian framework, absurdity added to absurdity may total the ultimate absurdity. In Berger's *Little Big Man*, absurdity added to absurdity added to the Western spirit arrives at meaning. Most important, however, Berger has in some manner put together a variety of techniques and infused them with a spirit so that, though this novel may superficially resemble the platypus, it is a functional and successful piece of literature. It is one of the best of American Western novels.

[24] See Max Westbrook, "The Practical Spirit: Sacrality and the American West," *Western American Literature* III (Fall, 1968), pp. 193–205.

# FURTHER READING

Any adequately representative survey of western literature requires the reading and study of a number of novels, and ordinarily one chooses so as to treat Indian, mountain man, cowboy, pioneer, and other aspects of western life. The following novels are taken from my supplementary reading list and are often found in syllabi sent me by my colleagues throughout the West. Almost all are available in paperback.

Edward Abbey
  *The Brave Cowboy* (New York: Dodd, Mead & Company, Inc. 1956).
  *Fire On the Mountain* (New York: The Dial Press, 1962).

Andy Adams   *The Log of a Cowboy* (Boston: Houghton Mifflin Co., 1903).

Thomas Berger   *Little Big Man* (New York: The Dial Press, 1964).

Hal Borland   *When the Legends Die* (Philadelphia: J. B. Lippincott Company, 1963).

Benjamin Capps
  *Sam Chance* (New York: Duell, Sloan and Pearce, 1965).
  *The Woman of the People* (New York: Duell, Sloan and Pearce, 1966).
  *White Man's Road* (New York: Harper & Row, 1969).

Willa Cather
  *My Ántonia* (Boston: Houghton Mifflin Co., 1918).
  *Death Comes for the Archbishop* (New York: Alfred A. Knopf, Inc., 1927).
  *A Lost Lady* (New York: Alfred A. Knopf, Inc., 1923).
  *The Professor's House* (New York: Alfred A. Knopf, Inc., 1925).

Walter Van Tilburg Clark
  *The Ox-Bow Incident* (New York: Random House, Inc. 1940).
  *The City of Trembling Leaves* (Garden City, New York: The Sundial Press, 1946).
  *The Track of the Cat* (New York: Random House, Inc., 1949).

James Fenimore Cooper   *The Prairie* (Boston: Houghton Mifflin Co., 1898).

H. L. Davis   *Honey in the Horn* (New York: Harper, 1935).

William Eastlake   *The Bronc People* (New York: Harcourt, Brace and Company, 1958).

Max Evans   *The Rounders* (New York: Bantam Books, 1965).

Harvey Fergusson
  *In Those Days*   (New York: Alfred A. Knopf, Inc., 1929).

*Grant of Kingdom* (New York: Morrow, 1950).
*The Conquest of Don Pedro* (New York: Morrow, 1954).

Vardis Fisher
*The Mothers* (New York: The Vanguard Press, 1943).
*Mountain Man* (New York: William Morrow & Co., 1965).

A. B. Guthrie    *The Big Sky* (Boston: Houghton Mifflin Co., 1947).

Oliver LaFarge
*Laughing Boy* (Boston: Houghton Mifflin Co., 1929).
*The Enemy Gods* (Boston: Houghton Mifflin Co., 1937).

Tom Lea    *The Wonderful Country* (Boston: Little, Brown & Co., 1952).

Jack London    *The Sea Wolf* (New York: The Macmillan Company, 1904).

Frederick Manfred
*Lord Grizzly* (New York: McGraw Hill, 1954).
*Conquering Horse* (New York: New American Library, 1959).

Larry McMurtry
*Horseman, Pass By* (New York: Harper & Bros., 1961).
*Leaving Cheyenne* (New York: Harper & Row, 1962).
*The Last Picture Show* (New York: The Dial Press, 1966).

N. Scott Momaday    *House Made of Dawn* (New York: Harper & Row, 1968).

Frank Norris    *The Octopus* (New York: Doubleday, Page & Co., 1901).

Eugene Manlove Rhodes    *Stepsons of Light* (Boston: Houghton Mifflin Co., 1921).

Conrad Richter
*Tracey Cromwell* (New York: Alfred A. Knopf, Inc., 1942).
*The Lady* (New York: Alfred A. Knopf, Inc., 1957).

O. E. Rölvaag    *Giants in the Earth* (New York: Harper & Bros., 1927).

Wallace Stegner    *The Big Rock Candy Mountain* (New York: Duell, Sloan and Pearce, 1938).

John Steinbeck
*The Grapes of Wrath* (New York: The Viking Press, Inc., 1939).
*Cannery Row* (New York: The Viking Press, 1945).
*East of Eden* (New York: The Viking Press, 1952).
*Tortilla Flat* (New York: The Viking Press, 1963).

Frank Waters
*People of the Valley* (Denver: Alan Swallow, Publisher, 1941).
*The Man Who Killed the Deer* (Denver: Alan Swallow, 1966).
*The Woman at Otowi Crossing* (Denver: Alan Swallow, 1966).

Owen Wister    *The Virginian* (New York: The Macmillan Company, 1902).

BOOKS RELATING TO THE MYTH OF THE WEST IN GENERAL AND TO THE NOVEL IN PARTICULAR:

R. W. B. Lewis  *The American Adam* (Chicago: The University of Chicago Press, 1955).

David W. Noble  *The Eternal Adam and the New World Garden* (New York: George Braziller, Inc., 1968).

Henry Nash Smith  *Virgin Land* (Cambridge: Harvard University Press, 1950).

James K. Folsom  *The American Western Novel* (New Haven: College & University Press, 1966).

Nicholas J. Koralides  *The Pioneer in the American Novel: 1900–1950* (Norman, Okla.: University of Oklahoma Press, 1966).

Roy W. Meyer  *The Middle Western Farm Novel in the Twentieth Century* (Lincoln, Neb.: University of Nebraska Press, 1965).


THREE OUTSTANDING ARTICLES ON THE WESTERN:

John G. Cawelti  "Prolegomena to the Western," *Western American Literature* (February, 1970).

Bernard DeVoto  "Phaethon on Gunsmoke Trail" *Harpers* (December, 1954).

W. H. Hutchinson  "Virgins, Villains, and Varmints," *The Rhodes Reader* (Norman, Okla.: University of Oklahoma Press, 1957).

# TWO

---

# The Novella

---

JACK SCHAEFER'S STORY of the young Cheyenne, Little Bear, strikes something near the universal in human nature in its portrayal of the struggle
of an individual to develop the integrity of his own character against the
claims of the traditional values of his society. The story is timeless.

*Pasó por Aquí* may well be the best novella ever written about a cowboy. Rhodes is noted for the authenticity with which he represents the
life of the cowboy, and few writers have endowed cowboys with more
character, humanity, and wit. W. H. Hutchinson has shown in *A Bar Cross
Liar* that much of the action in this story actually happened to Rhodes
and some of his friends.

*The Watchful Gods* presents a contemporary youngster engaged in a
man-sized struggle with his conscience, which results in a sort of ecological vision. A very good article analyzing this story is Max Westbrook's
"Internal Debate as Discipline: Clark's *The Watchful Gods*" (*Western
American Literature*, Vol. 1, No. 2, 153–165).

# JACK SCHAEFER

## *The Canyon*

TRACE ON A MAP the high border country, the land of high plains and high mountains that is the vast northern boundary of the western United States. There is no exact demarcation except on the north where the long, unfortified miracle of the Canadian line runs along the upper edge of North Dakota and Montana. Trace this westward to the flat top of the Idaho panhandle. Drop south and east in an irregular arc roughly paralleling the Idaho-Montana line along the main chain of the Rockies and on down into Wyoming. Sweep eastward across Wyoming from the Absaroka range past the lower tip of the Bighorns and on past the Black Hills into South Dakota. Swing northward in another arc near the eastern edge of South Dakota and push straight up across North Dakota to the Canadian line again. Let other people argue the precise location of the latter lines you have run. The area you have enclosed is the heart bulk of the high border country, the great bull-shaped expanse of Montana with an edging of the Idaho panhandle and the upper portion of Wyoming, spreading on over the Dakotas eastward across the wide Missouri to shade away into the lower plains rolling downgrade to Minnesota.

Those are names on our maps. They were not names then. The area was not yet even marked on early maps as it was marked for so many years later in ignorance as part of the Great American Desert. The Sioux, who were to make much of it their own and their last stronghold against the whitemen, were still grounded on foot east of the Missouri. Only the first small straggling parties of their westward migration had penetrated beyond the river to confront the tribes there before them and discover the four-footed freedom of the horse. But the Crows were there, and the Pawnees, and the Comanches, and the Arapahoes. And the Cheyennes, these last moving out ever farther westward from their settlements along the west bank of the Missouri to follow the roving buffalo ever deeper into the high border pasturelands. And far to the east, still remote as though lost on some far other continent, the twelve colonies that would be thirteen fretted the Atlantic coast with advancing civilization and the thought of their independence was still only a vague half-realized flicker in a few minds.

Find now along the southern rim of this high border country, midway between the Missouri and the crescent of the Bighorns and straddling the Wyoming-Dakota line, the roughly circular shading of the Black Hills. They are cradled on the map between the sweeping south fork of the Cheyenne River and the lovely long reach of the north fork that is known as La Belle Fourche. Streams feeding these rivers lead deep into these hills that are not hills but mountains, not soaring and luminous by night as by day like the Bighorns yet strong and rugged in the solid honesty of their rock risings. If you could follow the right one of these streams into the hills from its junction with Belle Fourche and take the right one of its branches fingering out and up into the broken levels, you would come at last to a wall of stone climbing in jagged tiers for more than a hundred feet. The water flows from a fissure at the base. Around and to the left a gently graded upland pasture leads on, rising slowly until it matches the wall height, and you emerge on a plateau that seems to stretch unbroken for a mile and more. You must move carefully now. Suddenly through the tall grasses and occasional low bushes the ground opens before you, a big gash in the basic rock formation dropping sheer for nearly eighty feet to an almost flat floor then rising again on the other side to the plateau level so that even at a short distance the eye is deceived and it cannot be seen. You are looking at the lost canyon of Little Bear. . . .

Ages ago in the strains of the earth's crust thrusting up to form the western mountains, some fault in the rock strata created that canyon. It is shaped like a long blunted triangle. It is relatively narrow at the upper end where a stream flows from the higher levels over the plateau and drops over the rock lip to fall straight down into a pool worn in the floor. It widens steadily to some five hundred yards at the lower end where the stream drops out of sight into its rock fissure. The sides are sheer, nearly vertical, weather-polished. Only a few narrow ledges harbor scant grass tufts and a lonely bush struggling for roothold. He is a fool who would attempt to scale those sides unaided up or down. But at one place, where successive ledges top each other at fifteen- to twenty-foot intervals, there are niches between in the rock. They are similar in shape. They are regularly spaced. They have the unmistakable imprint of the mind and hand of man.

There were no niches in the rock then. There was only the blunted triangle of the canyon, sharp-rimmed around, stretching its hidden depth across the plateau deep in the Black Hills that are not hills but sturdy mountains. The buffalo had found it, nosing over the edge to snort at the dropping away of space beneath and turning from it. Times beyond counting in the endless herd generations an unwary animal, startled in the dark and rushing from suspected danger behind, had plunged over the rim to the instant death of crushing impact below or the slow death of broken bones. And one moonless night far back along the unmeasured years, when the strange sheet lightning of the hills flared through the black and fireballs hung on the horns, a whole herd stampeded across the open and the foremost flowed over the rim and those following struggled to turn and those behind drove forward and the river of living flesh poured over and piled into a mangled bloody heap for the last falling to strike upon. In the first light of dawn there were seven living buffalo in the canyon by the mass of the dead and four dragged broken bones and died lingering deaths dwindling the number and three remained, two cows and a young bull, and these were enough. There were the good grasses and the stream. There were trees for summer shade when the sun stood high overhead. There were sheer rock walls to shed the winter winds and the worst of the driving blizzards. Thereafter the rutting-season battles of bulls and the ruthless impartial pressure of the winters eliminated the weaker and kept the number almost constant, a small herd never more than fifteen, rarely less than eight. . . . There were no man-made niches in the climbing rock then. There were only the canyon and its buffalo and the good grasses and the trees and the running stream. Out of the hills to the west where the headwaters of the Little Missouri start their northward journey and beyond where the valley of the Powder stretches on to the Bighorns the Comanches and the Pawnees were moving their camps as the free-roaming buffalo moved. Closer in to the north and the east the Cheyennes were following other herds and penetrating into the hills to cut fresh lodgepoles in the lesser timber when the winds of autumn gave warning. Do not ask the exact year or years. It is only when the whitemen come into a land that the drastic changes needing dates arrive. The whitemen were still far to the eastward then, just beginning to spill over the Appalachian barrier. Only a few, almost more Indian than white, had advanced to the western Great Lakes and the upper Mississippi, *voyageurs*, fur traders making small impress, working alone or in small groups up from the valley of the Ohio or down from the Hudson Bay area. Their existence was little more than a legend among the western tribes, variously told by old men to children, easily confused with tales of wandering Mexican traders who had reached as far north as the neighborhood of the Bighorns. The lost canyon of Little Bear, neither lost nor named because not yet even found, was quiet in the drift of the seasons deep in the Black Hills of the high border country, the land of high plains and high mountains that lifts in the heart of a continent. . . .

That is the place and that is the time.

The lodges of the Cheyenne village are set in a large circle, ten groupings around the circumference for the ten tribal divisions, with a wider gap between two groupings on the east for the village entrance. Inside the circle, in the southern arc, are two lodges marked with double crosses, the sacred lodges of the medicine arrows and of the buffalo hat. In one of the lodges of the western arc women have prepared a meal and a small, clean-burning fire and have left the lodge because a ceremonial pipe is to be smoked there. Men are entering the lodge. Each enters and steps to the right and pauses while the owner of the lodge, on his couch at the rear, welcomes him and appoints him a place to sit, sometimes of special honor to the left and again of ordinary honor to the right. Each takes his place, careful not to pass between the owner and the fire, the most courteous careful not to pass between anyone and the fire, when necessary passing behind those already seated while they lean forward to give room.

All eat. Even those eat who have already eaten in their own lodges lest they cast dishonor upon the owner of this lodge who is their friend. He finishes and wipes his hands. He waits until all have finished and have wiped their hands. He brings forth his ceremonial pipe and fills it with native tobacco in which a portion of powdered red willow bark has been mixed. He holds the pipe vertical, stem up, before him. He speaks. "My friends. A village of our enemies is camped six days' journey from here. The face of the winter has been hard. It is now the month of the buffalo-begin-to-fill-out moon. Our enemies will be busy. They will not expect us. It is my wish to lead a war party against them to take horses. I ask if you will go with me."

The owner of this lodge is a man who has led war parties before. He has not had to consult an old man of experience and carry offerings to the medicine arrows and perhaps swing to the pole for a full day as a personal sacrifice as would a young man wishing to lead his first war party. He has been able to call his friends together like this, with little notice, without formal preparations, when the wish came upon him. Because he has led successful war parties he has no doubt that many will go with him. He points with the pipestem to the sky above and to the ground beneath and to the four cardinal points around, east and north and west and south, making his prayer for success and the honor of the first coup to the spirits that dwell in those quarters. He lights the pipe and smokes. He passes the pipe to the man at his left

The man at his left holds the pipe upright, bowl down. He waits a long moment. Perhaps he is arguing his decision in his mind. Perhaps he likes to create a feeling of suspense. He is sitting in the place of most honor and what he does will have influence on the others. He raises the pipe. He smokes. He will go.

The pipe passes from man to man. Always it is passed and held vertically, bowl down. Each does with it according to tribal custom and the variations on that custom of his tribal division. And each smokes. Each will go. It will be a good war party. At last the pipe passes to the man second from the doorway on the right. He is like the others yet he is not like them. His ears have been pierced but they carry no ornament. His hair is not caught together behind with pine gum or woven into braids. It hangs straight. His dress is plain. He has no buffalo robe about him. He is there because he is a man and he lives in this lodge and not to be there would be to dishonor it. He is a young man but he is not in the first wishful pride of youth. Even younger men are there and they have gone on war parties and they have counted coups but he has not. Always he has passed the pipe unsmoked. The owner of the lodge is sad that this is so but he would not say or indicate by any show of emotion what is in his heart. The others know this and they are the same. They wait, patient and impassive. They wonder what the man who is like them yet not like them will do with the pipe that he holds in his hand. He sits still looking at the ground. He has not raised his eyes since the pipe was brought forth. He does not raise them now. His breath is heard leaving his chest in what might be a sigh. He holds the pipe upright according to custom. He passes it unsmoked. . . .

That is the man.

I

His name was Little Bear. That was not a formal name given to him by his father's brother or his grandfather together with the gift of a horse. It was what his Suhtai father and Tsistsista mother called him when he was small, a pet name, a term of endearment. He was a fat baby with short arms and legs, shorter than usual, for the Cheyennes of both the Suhtai and Tsistsista related tribes that merged to form the one tribe were a tall and well-formed people. Little-fat-person his parents called him, small-round-one, and when he was crawling and trying to stand upright on his short legs he became their Little Bear. He had no other name. When he was six years old, of an age to be given a formal name, his father and his father's close relatives were dead and so too were his mother and the members of her immediate family. It was a sickness took them, a sickness that crept into the temporary summer camp of good hunters and their families who had followed the buffalo away from the village and when it was gone only one old man and two women and four children were left to return to the village.

No Cheyenne starved when another Cheyenne had meat. No Cheyenne lacked shelter when another Cheyenne had shelter. Little Bear was taken into the lodge of Strong Left Hand. He had food and he had shelter and his foster parents gave him clothing and treated him in all ways as they did their own children. But always Little Bear was conscious of a difference. When he was twelve years old Strong Left Hand gave him a horse, a painted pony sound of limb, as Strong Left Hand had done for his own older son two years before and as he would do for his own younger son in another year. But still Little Bear was conscious of a difference. It was a difference in his own mind. He was an orphan in a lodge that was not the lodge of his father and his mother. He was expected to carry messages and cut the tobacco and herd Strong Left Hand's horses when they were taken out to graze. It was true that the sons of Strong Left Hand did the same things in equal measure because their father was a fair man in all the doings of those who lived in his lodge and the wife of their father was the same in all that pertained to women's work. But the sons of Strong Left Hand were his sons and they did these things by right as members of his family. Little Bear did them because they were expected of him in exchange for what was given him, for the food that he ate and the shelter of the lodge and the clothing that he wore. And he could remember when it had not been so.

He could remember the laughter of his father and the soft voice of his mother and the warmth of their lodge that was more than the warmth of a fire. He could remember his father, a good hunter and a good warrior, tumbling him head-over-heals in the long grasses and telling him he must develop the strength of a grizzly in his arms to make up for the shortness of his legs. He could remember his mother singing soft songs to him even when he was no longer of an age for singing-to-sleep and making him many small moccasins and small fringed leggings because he was her one child and she knew she would have no other. He could remember her telling him that he was not like other boys because his ears had been pierced by Standing All Night. Always she told this in the same way and the same words.

It was at the Medicine Lodge, the midsummer medicine meeting for which all the villages for a long traveling distance around gathered in a great camp on the plain. It was on the third evening of the four days of dances and ceremonies and the dancing of the day and the ceremony of the pipe-cleaning were done and mothers were taking their small children-in-arms to the central meeting place and fathers were asking the old crier to call out and ask certain persons to pierce the ears of their children. It was then that the mother of Little Bear took his father by the arm and whispered for him to ask for Standing All Night. That was a brave thought.

Standing All Night was not a Cheyenne by birth. He was an Arikara. He had not married a Cheyenne woman. He had married a Mandan woman and lived in her village which was near a Cheyenne village. He was still a young man when he left the village and went to live with the Cheyennes because he liked their people and their ways. They were glad that he came because they liked him and his ways. They accepted him into the tribe and he was one of them. He was an old man now. He was known to everyone in even the farthest village for the courage and the wisdom and the dignity that had been with him all his days. He knew more of the tribal lore than did the old men who had been born in the tribe and lived in it all their lives. He was respected as few men were ever respected. He was not a man to be asked to pierce the ears of a fat round baby with short legs from a far small village near the hills. The father of Little Bear heard the whisper beside him and laughed as at a joke. He looked at the mother of Little Bear and at their little-fat-person in her arms. He laughed no more. He took Little Bear in his arms and turned to find the old crier.

Standing All Night heard the voice of the crier in the lodge where he rested from the ceremony of the day. He came forth into the central fire-light. He was tall though he leaned on his walking stick. He was a very old man and the courage and the wisdom and the dignity of his years were on him. He looked at Little Bear in the arms of the laughing hunter father who was not laughing now. He could turn away and no voice would be raised to stay him. He was Standing All Night. He looked at Little Bear and he saw something there others did not see. His voice was strong despite the years that he carried. "This small one has the moon in his eyes." He stood straight and counted a coup for the small one as a man should when he is ready to pierce the ears. It was a coup no one had heard him count before, not once in the long years he had lived with the tribe. It was not like other coups. "Long ago when I lived in the lodge of my father I wished to be a warrior before my age. I crept out from the lodge of my father to follow a war party. I could not find them. I was lost. Three days I wandered without food. I was weak and frightened. A man of the

Crow people found me and fed me and told me how to go. Three springs after that I was with a war party. We entered a Crow village in the night to take horses. A man woke and ran out of his lodge and took hold of me. We fought. I struck him with my war club and he fell. The blood ran from his nose and he died. The moon gave light. I saw it was the man who fed me."

Standing All Night brought forth his knife, the knife with an iron blade that came from a pale-skinned trader eastward across the big river many many years before. He reached with it and pierced the ears of Little Bear according to custom, making a long cut in each ear in the outer margin. Little Bear made a small noise each time when the knife entered but he did not struggle and he did not cry. . . .

These things lived in the mind of Little Bear. They kept him conscious of a difference. Other things did too. The shortness of his legs made a sore in his mind and at last this healed but a scar remained. He could not run as fast as even the slowest among the other boys. They did not want him as a companion in their running games. When they played buffalo hunt and he was a man riding a horse-stick he could not overtake the boys who were buffalo. When they played and he carried a pole on which was impaled a flat leaf of the prickly pear whose thorns represented the horns of a buffalo it was the same. He played as hard as he could. He tossed and struck with the thorns trying to hook the hunters. When one of their play arrows hit the dirt spot on the leaf which represented the heart of the buffalo, he fell and rolled and threw dust and died as a stricken buffalo dies. But it brought little honor to a hunter to kill such a buffalo. He could be overtaken too quickly. His battle rushes could be avoided too easily. And when they played horse-taking he was not help at all. He dropped out of these games and sat cross-legged on rising ground and watched the other boys play and when they were out of sight he still sat and watched the wide rolling world around him and long thoughts grew in his mind.

When he was older and had the painted pony it was better. The pony was good and ran as other ponies ran and he rode it as a Cheyenne rode, a living part of the living animal, moving as it moved in the release of running swiftness. He became a good hunter as his father had been. On the back of the pony he was as tall as any man. He found a laughter on his lips in the hot chase and a courage to ride in close and use the lance. He did not thrust down for the kidneys as some men did, to cripple the buffalo and have it die slowly at a safe distance. He thrust forward, straight for the heart, and if the buffalo tried to turn and fight he held firmly to the lance and pressed with it until his strength and the strength of the pony and the strength of the buffalo straining against each other drove the point to the death. It was when he dismounted to skin the buffalo and prepare the meat for carrying to camp that he remembered the shortness of his legs and the difference they made. And because of that difference which was more than just a shortness of legs it did not seem right to him that he should ornament his ears with rings and beaded hoops or wear his hair according to fashion or sit in a lodge circle in a buffalo robe of fine designs. It seemed to him that he should be simple and unshowing in all things. . . .

He was a good hunter. He helped keep the lodge supplied with meat and fresh skins for the women to work into clothing and sleeping robes as a man should. Strong Left Hand had more time for the warpath and his own sons with him. When these sons were of age and their father nodded his head, they smoked the pipe when the question was asked in their own lodge and in other lodges and became good warriors. They were untiring in travel and they took many horses, more than they lost, and when they returned successful they never failed to give Little Bear one of the best so that he too would have horses and on proper feast days could give presents according to custom. They respected him for his courage in hunting and for his quiet dignity by the lodge fire. Strong Left Hand was proud of the feeling there was between his own sons and the foster son he had taken into his family. But he could not understand and his sons could not understand why this foster son and brother would not smoke the war pipe. And Little Bear himself did not understand. He was glad for his foster brothers that they showed themselves good warriors and thus gained wealth and honor for themselves in the eyes of the village. Yet always when the pipe was passed to him and he looked in his heart for what to do, there was no urge to gain honor for himself in this way. There was only the remembrance of a difference that he could not explain. . . .

Three miles from the village, hidden in a dip of the rolling plain, the successful returning war party stopped to prepare to surprise their people with their triumphant entry. They killed a buffalo and stripped off a large piece of the skin. They hung this over sticks pushed into the ground with the middle hanging down so that it was like a cooking kettle. They drained blood from the carcass and put it into this kettle. They took bunches of rye grass and twisted these into tight bunches and burned the ends and they let ashes fall into the blood. When the mixture was stirred it became dark. They spread their robes on the ground. One of the older men took a pointed stick and dipped it in the mixture and began to draw designs on the robes. He instructed the younger men as he worked, telling them why he did this and why he did that and the proper motions to use for each. He drew parallel lines across the robes and between these drew wolf tracks and bear tracks and other shapes that were not tracks but had meanings of their own. As the paint dried it became black and it adhered tightly to the robes.

When the painting of the robes was done, they burned small bushes and with the dark ashes painted their faces. The younger men made stripes down their foreheads and cheeks but the older men covered their whole faces. They all dressed as they had been dressed during the raid on the enemies. They mounted their war ponies and led the others on rawhide ropes. When they topped the last rise before the village they shouted their war cries and rushed down toward the circle of lodges.

That was a moment of excitement, a moment no warrior could soon forget. The whole village, men and women and children and dogs all shouting and barking, came running out to greet the heroes. Because they came swiftly, not stopping on the top of the rise to signal with waving robes, everyone knew that no men had been lost. Because there were many horses being led, everyone knew that much wealth had been gained and much honor won. People threw their arms about the warriors and helped them from their horses. Tribal singers moved around singing songs about them. Their relatives proved their pride and joy by giving gifts to those less fortunate in having no family representatives in this party.

Soon the feasts were being prepared. Children scurried from lodge to lodge speaking invitations. Sparks flew from smoke holes into the evening dusk as fires were freshly fed. Streaks of firelight through the lodge openings outlined the village circle in the deepening dark. The sound of drums filled the air with its throbbing, the big drums where a social dance was under way, smaller drums for the songs that accompanied gambling games, an intermittent quick-beating tattoo to mark each climax in a big lodge where members of two soldier bands were counting coups in a brave-deed competition.

The hum of activity ran long into the dark hours. At last the fires burned down. People retired to their home couches. The sound of drums and of rattles ceased and the only music heard was the lonely love song of some young man with his flute hovering near the lodge of his sweetheart. This too died away. The last voices faded and the restless stirring of horses tied by the lodges dwindled and dogs curled into their favorite spots in the dust. The final embers winked and were gone and the village was silent in sleep, an inseparable part of the vast plain rolling on to the hills and the great luminous mountains of the high border country. . . .

Little Bear could not sleep. He lay on his couch of sinew-strung willow rods with its mat of woven bulrushes just inside the open entrance of the lodge. The soft light of the late moon through the opening called to him. He rose quietly and went outside and through the village. He walked out onto the open plain. He sat cross-legged in the long grasses and heard the breezes of the night whispering through them. He stared at the moon. He sat still a long time. Far off a coyote howled and another answered and another and the drawn mournful wailing drifted around the horizon and faded and there was silence. Not the silence of no-sound, for in the whispering of the grasses he could hear the Maiyun talking, the spirits that dwell in the ground. "What is it that troubles this one," they said, "that he cannot be as other men? He fights the mighty buffalo, turning not from its sharp horns, but the enemies of his people he will not fight." A sliver of cloud floated across the moon and still Little Bear stared at it and he heard the Maiyun talking. "His mind is too heavy with thoughts," they said, "thoughts that go crosswise to good custom. He must lighten his mind by sacrifice as the old one directs."

Little Bear pondered this many moments and knew what he must do. He rose and went back to the lodge. He took only what he would need, his pipe and a pouch of tobacco and a small bag of pemmican. He put the grass-filled double pads he used for a saddle on the painted pony and rode eastward toward the rising sun.

All day Little Bear rode and all the next night. He stopped only for water and for brief rest and to graze the pony. Near the noon of the next day he came to the village he sought. He knew the lodge by the designs painted on it. A young woman was in front of it by a fire cooking soup in a small kettle. He went past her and through the doorway and stepped to the right and waited. From the couch at the rear, propped up on piled buffalo robes, the old one looked at him with eyes bright in the wrinkled and toothless face, the old one, the great one, Standing All Night, oldest of living Cheyennes, old beyond reckoning, old beyond memory, able now to take food only in fluid form and to move about only with the aid of two sturdy great-grandsons.

The old one pointed to the ground at his feet. Little Bear went there, careful to circle the inside fire and not to cross in front of it. He sat on the ground and looked up. He took out his pipe and filled it. He reached for a burning stick and lit the pipe. When the smoke came well he held the pipe out, stem up, bowl down. The old one reached and took the pipe. He smoked.

Many times Standing All Night drew the fragrant smoke into his old lungs and breathed it forth in slow rhythm. When the pipe was finished he handed it back to Little Bear. His voice was old, an echo of sound from his withered chest. "My friend. What is it you want of me?" And Little Bear spoke quickly the words he had said over and over to himself on the way. "It is in my mind to ask you to go up on a hill with me."

The moment those words were spoken, Little Bear was ashamed. A young man who wished to make sacrifice must ask an older man of experience to instruct him and go with him and take him to a proper place and come for him at the end of the appointed time and lead him down. And he, a foster son only from a far small village who had never counted a coup and who did not even have a formal name given by a grandfather or an uncle, had spoken the words to this old one, this great one, Standing All Night, who was no longer able to walk alone, who was no longer able to go forth any distance from his lodge even supported on the strong shoulders of his great-grandsons.

The shame was big in the breast of Little Bear. He dropped his head and stared at the ground. But the voice of Standing All Night brought his head up again. "My friend, look at me." He looked at Standing All Night and the old one looked at him and saw something in his face others did not see. "My friend, you are the small one who had the moon in his eyes. What is it that troubles you?" And Little Bear could speak, for this was the man who had pierced his ears and the old voice was kind. He spoke of the difference that was always there in his mind. He spoke of the thoughts that grew heavy in him. ". . . and a man has a mare," he said, "and the mare has a colt. Four seasons the man must wait for the colt to be born and twice and three times four seasons for the colt to be grown enough to begin to be a good horse. Yet the man will ride it to war and the horse can be killed in the flash of an arrow or the thrust of a lance. Or it can be that the man takes a horse from an enemy. Yet that enemy in the time before had to wait four seasons for that horse to be born of its mare and twice and three times four seasons for it to be grown enough for good use. And it is gone from him in a moment." And again Little Bear said: "Sometimes it can seem when they smoke the war pipe and go forth on the warpath that they are like children playing at a game. Yet it is a game that can bring wounds and death-mourning to the one village and to the other. Hunting too can bring wounds and death-mourning. But there is a difference in hunting and it is not the same.

Little Bear spoke. When he had no more words he was silent and quietness breathed in the lodge. Standing All Night sat still for many long moments. "My friend," he said, "one man cannot change a tribe. It is good that is so. There would be endless changing this way and that way and much mischief tormenting all people. It is fitting that a man do as the customs of his tribe tell him. It is fitting too that no man do what his heart tells him is wrong. That is hard. He must be certain that his heart speaks truth to him." Standing All Night lay back on the piled buffalo robes. He closed his eyes and with the closing the light of living seemed to be gone from him and he was very still. His eyes opened. There was new strength in them. "My friend. My strange small one to whom the moon calls. You must do what is in your mind. You must go up into the hills for a starving. I will go with you. These old bones and fragments of flesh that still cling to them will remain here and feed on the soups that my great-granddaughter prepares for me. Yet I will be with you. You must do as I tell you and when a single wolf howls and none answers you must listen and I will be with you. . . ."

The land climbed around him, not swiftly but rolling upward. The stream dropped away on his left, twisting and flowing back down the way he had come. He moved slowly for his legs were short and the painted pony was two days' journey to the eastward with the horses of his foster family by the home village. A man who would make sacrifice must go humbly on foot.

He was far into the hills, farther than he had ever been. Other young men who made sacrifice did so close to the village. He was bound by the words of the old one and he obeyed. He was afraid but he obeyed. It was country like this with its hollows dropping between high hills and the climbing rock heights ahead that Heammawihio, the Wise One Above, might leap over with his far-seeing glance when he looked down on the land and the peoples he had created. It was in country like this with its strange rock shapes rising abruptly out of seeming good pastureland that the bad Maiyun dwelled who delighted in causing sickness and dark troubles of the mind. He was afraid but he moved forward and he did not look back.

He came to a double fork of the stream and did not know which one to take. He remembered words of the old one. He plucked a blade of long grass and held it up straight. Out of the still air a breeze came and bent the grass stem in the direction of the second stream fork. He followed this, keeping to the right-hand bank according to custom.

He came to a flat rock close by the stream on the right side. It was a good place. The hills divided to the eastward so that he could see through them to the far horizon where the sun would rise each morning. He laid his things at one end of the rock, his pipe and pouch of tobacco and fire-sticks, and the small bag of pemmican he must not touch now during four days and the nights between. He gathered armfuls of grasses and laid these on the rock for his couch. He brought forth the knife, the knife with an iron blade that came from a pale-skinned trader across the big river in long ago days, the knife that had pierced his ears when he was a small-one-in-arms and the brave laughter of his father and the soft voice of his mother were fresh in those ears to be pierced, the knife that was with him now as a sign that the old one was near. He laid the knife on the flat rock with the blade pointing eastward towards the division in the hills. He lay down on the grasses on the rock with his face turned in the direction the knife pointed. He lay still and let the hours drift over him. . . .

The sun sank behind the great egg-shaped mass of the mountain to the west. Dusk flowed over the hills. He rose and with his fire-sticks made a small fire. He revolved the one stick between the palms of his hands with its point in the hole in the other flattened stick until sparks glowed in the powdered dry buffalo chip around the edges of the hole. He blew on this and fed it with small twigs until the fire was burning. He filled his pipe and lit it and smoked. Three times each day he could do this, when the sun rose and when the sun stood straight overhead and when the sun sank below the western horizon. But he could not eat. He could not drink of the stream flowing near him.

He lay on the grasses on the rock. The small fire burned down and out. The darkness covered him and he was afraid. The night winds moaned now and again through crevices in the far bluffs and the Maiyun of the hills were talking and he could not understand their voices. He shivered in the night-cool and was afraid. A wolf howled and another answered and yet another and the sound rose and fell through far hollows of the hills. He listened and there was nothing. He lay still and was afraid and a wolf howled with a deeper tone and there was no answer. He listened and coming along the night winds he heard and did not hear yet he heard an old voice like an echo from a shrunken chest: "My friend, it is well. I am here. . . ."

There were no dreams in the night. He slept and waked and slept again and the sleep was good because of the weariness of the long journey on foot into the hills. The day following, which was the second day, he lay on the grasses and the sun soaked its warmth into him and food-hunger gnawed like a ground squirrel in his belly. He forced his mind not to think of this and his thoughts roamed out and away through the hills and came back and were still. He lay quiet and the hours drifted over him.

In the night, which was the second night, dreams came. He was falling through a blackness and there was a roaring in his ears. He cried out and woke. He shivered in the night-cool yet he sweated in the fright of falling. A breeze stirred and moved over his face and took the sweat drops away. It was like a hand, wrinkled and old and reassuring. He slept and dreams came again. He was standing in an unknown place. Everywhere he looked rock rose straight around him. He moved forward and passed through the rock and he was walking in a good land and a fine well-sewn lodge was before him and he knew it was his and by the entrance was a woman and she was beckoning to him. He went toward her and she was gone and the lodge was gone and on the ground was a fallen-in pile of rotting lodge poles and small bushes grew among them. A great sadness took hold of him and he fell on the ground and beat at it with his hands and he woke shivering in the night mist. He was lying on his face off the grasses on the hard surface of the flat rock and his hands hurt from striking on the stone. He rose and blew on his hands to ease the hurting. He lay again on the grasses with his head turned eastward toward the division in the hills. He lay still and at last his mind emptied itself of all thinking. And the Maiyun of the hills emerged like smoke from their homes in the far rock bluffs and clustered round him. They took the form of buffalo and starlight shone on their horns and their eyes glowed. "Is this the man," one said, "who will not be as other men?" And another spoke: "He believes he is humble in his difference but there is strong pride in such humbleness." And another spoke: "Shall we visit upon him a sickness that will wither him away?" And yet another spoke: "Let him live his allotted days. That can be more difficult than a withering away. . . ."

In the morning, which was the third day, the sun fought through lingering mist. His clothing was damp. The tobacco in the pouch would not burn. In the ground near the rock he saw many split-hoofed tracks of buffalo and that was strange because the Maiyun had no weight and made no impress on the earth. He lay on the grasses on the rock and the sun conquered the mist and dried his clothing and the hunger was a torment twisting in his belly. When the sun was straight overhead the tobacco in the pouch still would not burn but the hunger was gone. It died away within him and he felt strangely light and giddy as if he climbed in some great height. He lay on the grasses on the rock. His body remained there but his mind floated free and he thought long thoughts about the dreams because he knew that what a man dreamed when he made the sacrifice of a starving must surely come to pass.

The sun dropped toward the egg-shaped mountain and the air grew still and heavy with unseen warnings. The sun dropped behind the mountain and the stillness pressed down upon the hills. His mind came back into his body and he rose and built a small fire and that was difficult because he had trouble holding his mind there in his body to direct its movements. The tobacco was dry and burned well but when he drew the smoke into his lungs it scratched on his dry throat and brought a dizziness with it. He put the pipe beside him on the ground. He sat huddled over the fire and the stillness broke. Winds rushed from many directions and mingled and cried in the upper air. Lightnings leaped out of the dark and fireballs danced in the distance. He leaned closer over the fire and waited for the rain but no rain fell. There were only the leaping lightnings and the crying winds. A wolf howled, deep-toned, near, and there was no answer. He listened and the winds were a voice shouting. "Follow," the voice said. "Follow." He rose to his feet and stood swaying. The lightnings leaped and he saw it, a wolf, low-bellied to the ground, running into the dark, and a fireball clung to its tail. Unthinking, he stooped to gather his things, the knife and the firesticks and the bag of pemmican. Unthinking, with no question in his emptied mind, he followed as the wolf had led.

The way was hard in the dark. Only when the lightnings leaped could he see the ground stretch before him. There was a weakness in his muscles and often he fell and as often he pushed up and his short legs stumbled on. And always the fireball showed the path, disappearing from sight and appearing again farther ahead. It was leading him up along the stream. It led him on and he came against a wall of rock that climbed in jagged tiers high into the darkness. He did not know which way to turn but the fireball appeared across the stream and to the left and he obeyed. He splashed through the shallow running water and followed. The ground was smoother now under bunched sod, gently graded upward, and he moved more easily. The winds died some and the lightnings ceased. His head was no weight on his shoulders but his feet were heavy. He stumbled on and came out on a wide plateau and stopped. The winds had died away to whisperings and the darkness was thick around. He saw a glimmering in the grasses far ahead and to the right and he went toward it. The glimmering faded and he stumbled forward searching with his eyes into the dark distance to see it and his left foot reaching met only air and he pitched downward. Instinctively his body twisted and his arms caught at the rock edge. His fingers gripped and held. He dangled into a deeper darkness and his mind whirled in dizzying circles and his legs thrashed as he sought to swing them up and crawl back over the edge. But the weakness of the starving was upon him. He dangled into the deeper darkness and his body grew limp. Slowly his fingers slipped, then more rapidly, and he fell downward and his left hip struck an outcropping ledge fifteen feet below and with the shock unconsciousness took him and his body somersaulted outward and fell in silent rush and struck into the topmost branches of a thick-bunched pine. The falling weight broke the first branches and smashed down through those below, forcing a way but slowing, and the thick carpet of old needles on the ground softened the sound of final striking. . . .

2

A man goes forth into the moonlight out on the open plain. He steps in the brief striding from the small known and familiar into a vast wideness. Distance opens and moves outward around him. There are no roads and their destinations. There is only the land, limitless and alive, the land that stretches beyond reach of the mind toward the ever-receding horizon.

He bends his knees and sits cross-legged in the thick grasses. The rim of the world rises around him. The level of his eyes has dropped only a few feet yet he is infinitely closer to the heart of earth. He is part of a great quietness that lives and breathes about him and in the quietness he can hear winds whispering among the grass stems. The ancient magic of man's beginnings is there. . . .

Winds whispering through grasses are the voices of spirits that dwell in the earth to a mind that knows such spirits exist. The unseen presence of the spirit of a friend can bridge long miles and be with a man who has faith in that friend and the power of such friendship. A rushing of winds, a leaping of lightnings, a glimpse of an animal in a flash between darknesses, such are signs to a man who has prepared himself for signs and merged himself into the natural forces that surround him. . . .

Those are the things that led Little Bear to his canyon.

He is there. He is a broken heap of flesh and bone on a thick carpet of old needles under a pine tree on the floor of a small canyon deep in the hills that are not hills but mountains along the southern tier of the high border country. He is a flicker of human life in a small rock-walled wilderness that is his alone.

Rain fell. The chill drops gathering on the pine branches and falling brought consciousness back to the tortured flesh. He stirred and pain was a wave sweeping through him and he was unconscious again. The rain ceased. Dawn spread over the plateau and filtered into the canyon and the sun rose. Slowly awareness crept through him. He lay sprawled on his back. His clothing was rent and ripped. Clotted blood clung to his body in many places. His right leg was doubled under him. It was broken a little above the ankle. Pain swelled and receded and swelled in his chest with each hard-drawn breath.

He stared upward at the pine branches for a long time. The sun was almost straight overhead when he moved. An agony streaked through his whole body but life was movement and he moved. He pushed up a little and looked around. He did not know what had happened. He did not know that he was Little Bear, foster son of Strong Left Hand, who had come into the hills for the sacrifice of a starving. He was a simple elemental creature searching for the essentials of survival. His eyes found the bag of pemmican where it had fallen when he pitched downward over the cliff edge. It was not far from him. He dragged himself to it on his belly. Stretched on the ground he tried to eat. His mouth was dry and he could not swallow.

He sat up. He looked around again. He could see farther from this new height. He saw the stream two hundred feet away. He rolled onto his belly again. He gripped the pursed top of the bag in his teeth and pulled at the ground ahead with his hands and pushed at the ground behind with his left foot. He crawled wormlike, to the stream. Flat on the bank, head down, he gulped at the water. It was the same. He could not swallow. He held water in his mouth and lifted his head and some trickled down his throat and the dry muscles in his mouth soaked in the moisture and he could swallow a little at a time. He lowered his head and drank and the inrush of water became too great and he retched violently and jerked back from the stream edge. He put a hand into the bag of pemmican and tried to eat again. His jaws ached and chewing was very hard. But the roasted dried meat, pounded fine, needed no chewing. He crammed it into his mouth and convulsive constrictions of his throat forced it down. He reached for more and in the reaching a blackness dropped on him and unconsciousness took him again. . . .

There was water in his stomach. There was a little food. The chemistry of life worked in him. . . .

Daylight dwindled in the canyon. Darkness grew and held it. The late moon rose silently out of the hills above and silvered the plateau. It climbed and its pale light slid down the far canyon wall and moved slowly across the canyon floor. The soft radiance touched the limp figure outstretched by the stream and crept over it. The figure stirred and its eyes opened. Unconsciousness had passed into sleeping and the sleeping at last into awakening. The eyes looked up at the traveling moon.

He knew who he was. He was Little Bear, foster son of Strong Left Hand, and he was lying on the ground and a stream talked gently close by his head. The falling had been a real falling. He was hurt in many places. His right leg was broken.

He did not know where he was. But the moon above was the same moon that had called him out on the plain by the village to listen to the Maiyun talking. It had not changed.

His muscles were very stiff. To move was to summon the pain. But he was a man again and he could grind his teeth together and fight the pain. He drank from the stream in slow swallows. He ate of the pemmican left in the pouch but not much because the bag was small and already almost empty. He dragged along the ground to a big stone on the stream bank and pulled himself up against it on his left leg. He looked around. Everywhere, on all sides, he saw at last rock wall rising, some of it near, some of it farther away, some of it silvered in the moonlight, some of it dark in shadow, but all of it rock and rising sheer. That was strange and yet not strange. The soft radiance had moved on across the canyon floor as the moon swung overhead. It was close to the near rock wall now. It called to him and pointed for him. It gleamed dully on iron on the edge of the shadow pool of the broken-branched pine. He dropped flat to the ground and dragged himself there and reached and held the knife and the holding was good. He hunted over the ground and found one of the firesticks, the pointed one of hard greasewood. He could not find the other. He began to gather small branches and pieces of old wood, pushing them ahead of him on the ground into a pile. He crawled, wormlike, on the ground and the pile grew. The pain in his moving muscles had subsided into an aching that could be endured but the pain in his right leg was a mounting torment. He fought it and gathered wood. He fought it and was defeated and rolled over gasping on the ground and shuddered and was still. . . .

The sun arched upward over the rim hills and began to slide its rays down the canyon wall. Little Bear, foster son of Strong Left Hand, kneeled on the ground by his pile of wood. His weight was on his left knee. His right knee touched the ground lightly, doing no more than helping him keep his balance. He revolved his greasewood stick rapidly between the palms of his hands and the point spun in the hole in the flattened piece of softer cottonwood he had shaped with the knife. A tiny wisp of smoke came from the dry brown powder of pounded pine needles close about the hole. He revolved the pointed stick faster and the tiny wisp of smoke grew bigger. He dropped the pointed stick and leaned low to blow gently on the powder. It glowed red. Gently he placed small twigs over it and blew again. He guarded the tiny flickering with his hands and blew upon it. He nursed it into a small fire and fed it larger twigs. It burned bravely and he began to feed it from his pile of wood.

The column of smoke rose straight upward. It floated on up and above the canyon. It wavered above the plateau level when day-winds wandered across and straightened again when the air was still. It was a slender plumed signal rising into the sky.

He lay on the ground and waited. When he lay still the pain in his right leg numbed and did not strike at him with each beat of his heart. The fire burned down and he fed it again. He was sparing with his wood.

All morning and into the afternoon he lay on the ground and waited and no one came. He drank from the stream and ate two mouthfuls of pemmican. He found shoots of the wild licorice near the stream and cut these and ate them. The slender column of smoke rose into the sky. He lay on the ground and waited. All afternoon and into the evening he waited. The smoke faded and dimmed into the darkness and disappeared. He lay still and waited and no one came. . . .

There was no one to come.

No one of his own village knew that he had gone into the high hills for his starving. His lips had been sealed in silence lest bad omens follow him. No one knew that he had not done as other young men did when they made sacrifice. They went out on a rise of the rolling plain at most half a day from the village and always within sight of the smoke from its campfires. No one knew that Little Bear had gone farther because his need was greater, had gone into the high hills and deep into those hills where the Maiyun would be stronger and the dreams more powerful. And no old man of experience had gone with him to choose a proper place for him and come back for him at the end of the appointed time. There had gone with him only the spirit of an old one, a great one, Standing All Night, whose ancient bones and the fragments of flesh still clinging to them were far to the eastward tended in the last coughing illness by a sorrowing great-granddaughter.

There was no one to come. No hunting party of any tribe was following buffalo even through the lower edging hills. They were all out in the open plain following the big main herds that were moving in the late spring wandering. Not until fall would parties enter the hills again, to cut lodge-posts and gather stones to be shaped into arrowheads. And they would not penetrate very far.

In the soft radiance of the old moon waning toward extinction and rebirth, Little Bear worked on his swelling right leg. He took hold of the twisted flesh and the pain was so intense that he knew he must have everything ready before he did more. He found and trimmed five short pieces of branch from what remained of his pile of wood, each about the thickness of his middle fingers. He cut away what was left of his leggings on his right leg and took part of the worn leather and sliced it into thin strips. He put a small piece of the leather into his mouth and clamped his teeth into it. He took hold of his right leg with his hands, one hand below the break and the other hand above the break in the bone. It was a clean break but the ends of the bone were pushed past each other. He wrenched apart with his hands and ground his teeth into the leather piece in his mouth and wrenched apart with his hands. He heard the bone ends grind on each other and his mind screamed wordless sounds at the pain and the bone ends were together and the leg was straight from ankle to knee. Quickly, hurrying before the darkness should take him, he bound the five sticks along the leg with the strips of leather and pulled the knots tight. The pain was sweeping in waves through his mind and each was higher than the last and one rose overwhelming him and he fell back on the ground and was still. . . .

All morning Little Bear, foster son of Strong Left Hand, fed his new fire and hoped. But he did not wait. He held a stout stick in his hands and stood on his left leg and hopped about. When he found what he wanted, he dropped to the ground and brought forth the knife. He cut many shoots of the wild licorice. He dug roots of the *pomme blanche*, that resembles the white potato. These were young yet and small and very hard but there was sustenance in them. He found a few bushes of the wild gooseberry with small green berries on them. He had these things in a little heap by the stream and the scrapings remained in the pemmican bag and he could do no more.

He could do no more because the swelling in his right leg was growing and pressed outward against the sticks and leather bindings and the pain was beyond pain and an agony that crowded his mind. The inner flesh, torn by the bone ends, festered beneath the skin and swelled it outward with evil fluids. He forgot to feed the fire and it burned down and out. He fell on the ground. He rolled and clutched at the grass bunches. He lay on his back and stared up at the sky and drifted in and out of awareness and the hours passed over him. . . .

Dark shadows claimed the canyon. Winds of evening wandered over the plateau and sighed softly in the upper air. Little Bear lay still and the pain in his leg throbbed in the rhythm of his heart beating and a fever burned in his blood. Off in the hills a wolf howled, deep-toned, mournful and lingering, and there was no answer. He listened and there was no sound. Again the wolf howled, deep-toned, and the howling moaned along the edges of the winds and dwindled into the outer distances. He listened and there was nothing. There was only the soft sighing of the winds in the empty sky.

Darkness filled the canyon. Little Bear lay still and the pain drove his mind to beat in blunting bitterness on the bones of his skull. It struck him as a club strikes and forced him back and back toward a deeper darkness.

Winds of night wandered over the plateau. They did not drop below the rock walls but they sent exploring streamers through cracks along the rim and these chuckled with a hollow sounding one to another. And the Maiyun of the canyon rocks floated like mist out of their hiding places and searched for him. They came searching and they took the form of rabbits and they found him. They leaped and they laughed at him. They mocked him with a strange haunting laughter that was more terrible than any other sound. Their long ears stood straight up and their laughter jangled in the night air. "Look at this one," they said. "He fights a festering within him and is afraid." Their ears stretched upward like columns of smoke rising and they laughed at him. "The festering is not in his leg alone," they said. "There is a fear that festers in his spirit."

The pain throbbed and the Maiyun laughed and far back in his being where the life-center clung an anger grew and rushed forward and filled him. A great shout sprang in his mind and fought outward to his lips. "The laughter of my brave father is in my mouth! I spit it at you!" And the Maiyun leaped and faded into mist and he was sitting up on the ground and the knife was in his hand, the knife that had known the hand of Standing All Night, the knife that had pierced his ears and was not alien to his flesh. He raised his arm and leaned and drove the blade into the swollen flesh of his right leg. An agony raced like a shriek upward through him and he wrenched with the knife to widen the cut and pulled it forth and the evil fluids, thick and foul-smelling, gushed from the open wound. He dragged himself along the ground to the stream edge. He lay flat close along it. He thrust his right leg into the water and the chill running current closed over it. . . .

From small springs in the high hills the water came, a legacy of winter snows on the heights. Their tiny trickles mingled and flowed downward and others joined in the long descent. The water was clear and cold. It was constantly freshened in the clean air by the play and tumbling of rapids and swift swooping circuits among rocks. It flowed downward and emerged onto the plateau. Slowing there, it moved lazily and built and rebuilt and ever changed small rippled sandbars between its sodded banks and slipped smoothly over the lip of the canyon to fall into the pool below. Out of the pool it ran in gently curving swirls across the canyon floor to drop into its fissure at the wide lower end. Fresh and clear and cold, the water washed around and over the right leg of Little Bear and moved on and the corruption of the flesh went with it. . . .

Three days Little Bear remained there close by the stream. He was very weak. He drank of the clear running water. He ate of the small heap of food. He slept much. He washed his right leg often in the cold freshness of the stream and saw the healing begin. He studied the whole expanse of the canyon around him. He saw the rock walls rising everywhere.

It was early on the first of these days that he saw the buffalo, shaggy humped shapes among the low bushes and tree clumps at the wide lower end of the canyon where the grasses grew best. He counted them. There was an old bull and a young bull, five cows and four calves, eleven in all. His heart leaped high with hope when he saw them. As soon as he was stronger, he would follow their trails and they would show him the way out of the canyon. But by the evening of the third of these days a worry fretted in him. They were always there, always the same number, always the same buffalo. They moved about at the lower end of the canyon. They wandered up along the stream close to where he was and when he shouted and waved his arms they snorted and moved away. But they were always there.

On the morning of the fourth day he unbound his right leg and reset the short sticks and rebound them. He took other thin strips of the leather and knotted them into a thin rope. He made a small loop at one end of this to go around his right ankle and a big loop at the other end to go around his chest over his left shoulder and under his right armpit. When he stood up with the aid of a stout pole as tall as himself, the rope held his right foot from the ground. He held firmly to the stout pole with both hands and reached forward with it and leaned his weight on it and hopped on his left foot. He made strange tracks on the edge of the stream, a moccasin print then a small round hole in the soft ground and then a moccasin print and then again a small round hole. But he did not drag along low to the ground. He was upright as a man should be.

Straight to the near rock wall he went and began to move along its base in a circuit of the canyon. All day that took him. He moved slowly and rested often. He chewed on the roots he had taken with him. The buffalo stared at him and watched him and grazed again and kept a distance from him. They were not frightened and they were not angry. They were wary of a new strange thing.

He came on the fissure where the stream disappeared. It was small and the stream almost filled it. A man stepping in the water could force his body only a few feet in and the rock would press upon him.

He came to the pool and the waterfall at the upper end of the canyon. The water fell straight from the high lip of rock. It made a mist in the air and rainbows floated in this. It was very beautiful. But the rock behind and beside it was as smooth and sheer as the other walls.

He finished the full circuit. Nowhere was there a trail leading up to the high plateau. Nowhere was there a place where a man, even a man with two strong legs, could climb upward to the tall rock edge. There was no way out.

Little Bear sat on the flattened top of a boulder by the pool and waterfall that lifted him enough above the ground so that he could see across the entire canyon floor. His right leg itched and the itching was good. It meant that the leg was healing fast. He wore only his breechclout and the manhood string about the waist on which the breechclout hung. The summer sun was warm on his body. He had food. The gooseberries had passed and the shoots of the wild licorice were no longer good because they had leafed out. But the *pommes blanches* were bigger and softer and better than before. There were plenty of tapering thistles whose stalks, when the thorny skin was peeled, were soft and sweet. He had these and he had fish from the stream, taken as boys took them, by thrusting sticks into the bottom mud in a semicircle downstream from side to side so close that the fish could not pass between them and driving the fish down into the semicircle and scooping some out with quick hand-flips before they all could escape back upstream and away. He even had a tea made from leaves of the elk mint which he boiled in water over a fire in a kettle fashioned from the bag that had held the pemmican. He had all these and once a rabbit that he snared and still a proper strength would not return to his muscles.

It would not return because he did not have the real food of a man. He did not have strong meat. He did not have the stored-up strength of a strong animal to be transformed within him into his own strength. And there, captive in the same canyon with him, meat walked and grazed and stared curiously at him and was beyond him.

He watched the meat moving about, an old bull and young bull and five cows and four growing calves. He saw the strong limbs that could outrun any man no matter how long his legs. He saw the power that, aroused to anger, could sweep a man down like a weed stem snapping and trample him into a red muddy smudge on the ground. He saw the sharp horns that could thrust into the body of a man like a lance entering and toss him lifeless twenty feet away.

He gathered all of his leather, what remained of his leggings with the widening flap down the sides that had waved as he walked and of his tattered shirt that had reached halfway to his knees and had a big double piece across the back over the shoulders and hanging down. He sliced all of this leather into thin strips. Knotted and braided together, these strips would make a good rope, a rough and bumpy rope but a strong one.

All day he worked on the rope. He saved the last strips for another purpose. With them he lashed the knife by its handle to the end of his stout walking stick, pulling them very tight and knotting and reknotting them so they they would not slip. By the time the dusk shadows came he had a rope nearly forty feet long, three thicknesses braided, and he had a lance taller than himself, pointed and edged with an iron blade.

In the morning he went downstream, hopping with aid of the lance and carrying the rope coiled about his waist. Midway down the canyon he stopped. He knew the place. He had watched the buffalo many days from his boulder top and knew their habits. They slept by the rock wall at the lower end of the canyon. In the morning hours they grazed slowly up in the open of the canyon floor. Near noontime they collected by the stream to drink and wade into the water where many bushes ringed a pool deep enough for them to splash the coolness over them. They had a path through the bushes to the pool. They had another leading out to the grasses again and farther up. When they were finished at the pool they came along this second path. Where this second path emerged into open land the bushes were thick and arched over so that it was like a tunnel opening and there was a good tree close by.

That was where Little Bear stopped. He made a very small loop in one end of his rope and passed the other end through it. He had a running slip noose. Carefully he hung the noose in the tunnel bushes so that it framed the opening. Carefully he set the rope so that leaves hid it on the sides and over the top and he heaped dust over it where it ran across the path on the ground. Carefully he led the loose end away through the bushes and tied it around the base of the tree. Carefully he laid himself down behind the tree and a little to one side so that he could see past it. He was hidden from the path by the bushes. He could see the tunnel opening and a few feet down it and that was all but that was enough. He lay still and the iron-pointed lance lay beside him.

He was very patient. He waited and the morning passed and the sun was high overhead. He heard the buffalo going to the water. He heard them on the other path, first one, then another, then more. He heard them splashing in the pool. He waited and he heard them coming up the second path. The old bull would be first, then the young bull, then the four cows with their calves. They would come single file because of the bushes. They would pass right through the loop. The one cow with no calf would be last, lingering behind the others. He would wait for her.

They stopped. One after another down the line they stopped and stood motionless. He could not see them through the bushes and he could hear no sound. He waited. He did not hear but sensed movement and the head and forequarters of the old bull appeared in the bush-tunnel opening. He saw the massive head with its wide snout and long chin hairs like a beard shading back into mane and small eyes and sharp horns and the thick short neck that was hardly a neck at all and the beginning of the great humped shoulders behind. The bull stood still, searching the open grassland ahead. It smelled the man-scent where there had been no man-scent before and was troubled. That did not mean danger to it, not an enemy to flee or to fight, not yet, but it was cautious and would not move forward. It took a step backward. Another and it would be out of the noose. Once turned away it would not lead its small herd along that path again.

Little Bear dared not wait any longer. Swiftly he reached past the tree trunk and took hold of the rope and pulled back and up and the noose ripped out of the bushes and up from the path and was a loose circlet about the massive head back of the horns above and under the chin below. The old bull leaped crashing in the bushes to swing around and away and the rope tightened and slid to grip around the short neck and Little Bear seized his lance and rolled over and over on the ground away from the tree heedless of the bushes tearing at him. He heard the other buffalo stampeding through the brush and splashing through the stream in head-long rush toward the far side of the canyon. He stopped rolling and pushed up onto his left leg, holding to the walking stick that was his lance.

Beyond the tree the old bull battered the bushes into the ground. It struggled back and the rope tightened around its thick neck. It leaped and plunged sideways and with each leap and plunge the rope worked deeper through the coarse hair of its mane and closed tighter, pressing upon the windpipe. It pawed furrows in the ground and its bellowing was a fearful sound. The rope was taut as a stretched bowstring and the noose bit deep into the neck. The bellowing died away to a hoarse gurgling in the throat. The small eyes, bloodshot and red-rimmed, glazed over. The bull fell to its knees, stumbling forward and to the ground. But as the weight eased forward in this way, the noose relaxed. The great ribs heaved and breath whistled in through the nostrils. The bull staggered to its feet and stood with head swaying and breath whistled in and out of the lungs. The eyes brightened and it reared upward and struggled back and leaped and plunged from side to side again and the noose bit deep.

Little Bear watched. He felt a fear. It was not the fear that sometimes came upon a hunter and made him turn aside from the chase. It was a fear that the rope would not endure such repeated battles. Hopping with the aid of his lance, he circled around until he was behind the bull. He waited until it stood up again with head swaying and breath whistling past the slightly eased noose. He hopped forward swiftly and a little to one side. When he was close and his weight was on his left foot and swinging ahead, he shifted his hands on the lance to lift and point it forward and held it firm and drove it into the side of the bull just back of the big shoulder with all of his weight bearing solidly upon it. The bull reared in one great shudder-ing movement and the rope snapped and Little Bear was flung into the air clinging to the lance and his grasp broke and he fell and rolled and the thought of the hard hooves and the sharp horns burned in his mind. There were no hooves trampling him. There were no horns thrusting into his body. He sat up and looked. The old bull lay on the ground and a bloody froth bubbled from its nostrils. He had planted the lance as a good hunter should, firmly and deep in the flesh. When the rope snapped suddenly, the bull, rearing high, had fallen back and sideways and the end of the lance had hit on the ground and the bull with its own weight had driven the edged point tearing deeper inward.

The fire was a brave brightness. It threw its light upward into the darkness in flickering happy flames. The carcass of the bull was a black humped shape on the ground. Little Bear sat between the fire and the carcass and watched the flames rising. He was very full. His right leg held an ache from the strains upon it, but the short bound sticks had held firm and he was very full. His stomach bulged with the strong food of a man. He had feasted on the first of the delicacies, the tongue and the nose. He sat in the firelight and his head nodded in drowsiness and the fire threw its light upward in joy at its own feasting on old dry wood.

Winds of night wandered over the plateau. They sent their exploring streamers through the cracks along the rock-wall rim and these chuckled one to the other with their hollow sounding. And the Maiyun of the canyon rocks floated out like a mist in the night. They took no form and they floated above the firelight and they laughed. They filled the upper air with their presence and they laughed but they did not mock him. Their laughter was a soft sound and pleasant in the hearing. "This is the one," they said, "who has killed the mighty buffalo. With one leg of bone and one leg of wood he fought. With the cunning of his mind and the courage of his heart he killed the leader of the herd." They floated higher and drifted away down the canyon and the echo of their laughter came back faint and fading. "Little brother. Live well. Live long. . . ."

3

The carcass of a full-grown buffalo contains nearly two thousand pounds of bone and flesh and hide and entrails. It seems smaller in bulk now that it lies on the ground and the strength and power of movement are gone. The senses are stilled. The intricate workings of the living organism have ceased. Already, following fast on the fact of death, the subtle degeneration of decay is beginning in some of the once vital organs. A man can kick it, cut it, climb over it, do what he wills with it, but it cannot retaliate. It is a heap of carrion lying on the earth from which all that is in it once came.

No. It is life and a way of life.

It is food. If a man knows how to prepare and to cook it, every part can be eaten except the bones and the hooves and even these, crushed and boiled during a hard winter of privation, will yield a grease that can sustain him. The blood, cooked until it is a hard jelly, is very good. The lungs, dried and roasted, have a delicate flavor. The liver is well liked, especially when sprinkled with gall. The small intestine, filled with chopped meat, makes a fine sausage to be boiled or roasted. The hide. cooked long with proper application of green leaves, is tender and good. The flesh-meat and the fat, when fresh, are excellent. Cut into strips and smoked or sun-dried, they will keep for a long time. All of the animal is food.

It is clothing. The hide, scraped clean and tanned with a mixture of the brains and liver and bone grease and the easily found soapweed, makes a fine leather, tough and durable. It can be left thick for warm wrapping robes and long-wearing moccasins or chipped to a more flexible thinness for breechclouts and leggings and hunting shirts. For extra warmth in winter the hair can be left on and the hair-side turned inward.

It is shelter. The tanned skin, stretched over lodge poles, makes a habitation for any weather. It is waterproof. It is windproof. It sheds the rain and the wind and the sun. In summer, when the lodge flap is open, the air moves in and up and out through the smoke hole at the top and the lodge is cooled. In winter, when the flap is closed and the fire burns, the warmth is held by the circling and sloping sides.

It is many things. The hair of the head and mane can be twisted into very strong rope. The great sinews lying either side of the dorsal spines, dried and split into strands, provide excellent threads for sewing. Water skins can be made from the bladder and heart sac. Cups and pots and kettles can be fashioned from the strong lining of the paunch. Knives and root diggers and hide scrapers and awls for punching holes in sewing and many other tools come from the many-shaped bones. Spoons and ladles come from the horns, steamed soft and bent into shape and dried. A single horn, hollowed and plugged with a tiny air hole left, can carry fire from place to place and for many hours and even days in the form of smoldering punk. Straight pieces of horn, glued together and wrapped with sinew, form a stout bow. The big tendon found under the shoulder blade is a bowstring that the strongest arm cannot break. The shoulder blade itself has a natural hole that can be used in softening the freshly tanned hide. The hide is pulled through again and again and the hole edges break the stiffness and a smooth softness develops. Drums can be made of the sounding rawhide, best from the neck where it is thickest, and rattles of skin bags with stones in them, and flutes from the marrow-bones.

It is all these things and many more. It is a basis for a way of life for a man, a tribe, a people.

That is what Little Bear had.

He is there with the carcass of an old bull buffalo in his canyon in the high border country. His leg is healing. He has food. He has material with which he can fashion for himself clothing and shelter and tools and weapons. He has long hours in which to work and to think and to dream while the days and the nights of summer drift over the hills. . . .

The timeless sun shone into the canyon, holding back the edge of autumn. It shone warm on the dark straight hair of Little Bear as he sat cross-legged on the ground making a bow out of pieces of horn. He fastened them together with a warm jelly-like glue made of rawhide chips boiled in water that would set firm when it cooled and hardened. He wrapped them with strips of sinew, moistened by long soaking so that they would shrink tighter when they dried. This would be a better bow than the one of juniper wood that lay beside him. He finished and laid the new bow on the ground to dry.

He stood up and stretched. His right leg was healed. There was a slight ridge around the bone where the break had been that he could feel through the flesh with his fingers. But the leg bore his weight well and full strength was returning to the muscles long cramped by the splint of short sticks. He wore a new shirt and new leggings and new moccasins, double thickness on the bottoms. He did not need the clothing yet for protection against the weather but it was still new and he was proud of it.

He looked out over his canyon. It was a good place. Berries were ripe on the bushes, late raspberries and some currants and many sarvissberries, enough for good eating now and for drying for good eating later. The wild grapes and two trees of wild plums would be ripe in a few weeks. Farther down the canyon the buffalo grazed, the young bull, the five cows, and three calves. The fourth calf he had taken. Its skin, softer and finer than that of the old bull, was in the new shirt and the leggings. He counted those remaining. Nine. They were his buffalo. It was a good place. Why was he restless in the warm afternoon sun?

He walked toward the upper corner of the canyon to the left of the waterfall where the raspberry bushes grew among many stones thrusting up above the soil. He limped a little, favoring his right leg. He moved slowly, eating the biggest of the berries, the choicest and ripest. He came around a clump of bushes and saw the badger. Its short-legged broad body was stretched out on a low flat stone. It was sleeping in the sun.

That was very strange. There had been no badger in the canyon and no sign of one. Rabbits, yes, and field mice and a few rock squirrels. But no badger. Perhaps it had fallen over the high rock edge and survived the falling, for a badger was the hardiest of all animals and could be beaten many times with a big club and still live and still try to fight the one beating. Perhaps it had come there by some magic of its own, for a badger had many powers and strong medicine. Little Bear stood still and bowed his head once in respect. Badgers were sometimes friendly with the Cheyenne people. They were wise and knew much. They had been known to talk to men and tell them what to do and how to live. He would not offend the sleeping one.

Quietly he sat down cross-legged on the ground. Time passed and the badger opened its eyes. It saw him. It did not leap up startled. It looked at him with its black shining eyes. "Oh badger," he said. "Speak to me." It jumped from the stone and was gone.

He sat still and thought long about this. He had been wrong. A man should not speak to a badger. It knew what was in his mind without his speaking. He should wait for it to speak. And this badger seemed to be very thin. It seemed to be very tired. Perhaps it would not like being in the canyon and would go as it had come. Meat was its food, the gophers and prairie dogs and other small animals which it could overtake in their burrows, digging much faster than they could with its great claws on its powerful forefeet. There were no gophers or prairie dogs in the canyon. The few field mice would not be much for such a badger and they had many rock cracks in which to hide.

He rose and went back to his camp by the stream where it emerged from the pool under the waterfall. He went to his storehouse, the big crack in the base of the rock wall to the right that extended in nearly six feet. He moved the stones away from the opening. He took a piece of dried meat out of the container made of the heavy bull rawhide. He went again among the raspberry bushes and the upthrust rocks. He laid the piece of meat on the low flat stone.

In the morning it was gone.

Each day for three days he put a piece of meat on the stone and waited a long time. Each morning following each day the meat was gone. But he did not see the badger. That was not strange. Badgers were not seen often even when there were many about. They kept to themselves. They could hide where another animal might think there was no place to hide. They could dig themselves out of sight in the ground so fast that they were gone before they were seen.

On the fourth day he laid a piece of meat on the stone and waited. He sat cross-legged twenty feet away and watched the stone. Time passed. The dark brown head of the badger with its long white stripe down the middle to the nose appeared over the stone. The badger saw him. It looked at him for many moments. It moved and the whole of the wide grizzled gray-brown body appeared on the stone. It ate the meat. It watched him while it ate and when it was finished eating it lay stretched out on the stone and watched him. He was very still.

The sun was warm on Little Bear and the badger watching each other. His mind was filled with many thoughts and many questions but he did not speak. He sat still and the movements of his mind slowed and the sun was warm on him and his head dropped forward in drowsiness. The badger looked at him and its eyes became very bright. It spoke. "Big brother," it said, "why do you feel that this canyon is a cage?" The eyes of the badger dimmed and closed and after a time they opened again and were very bright. "All men live in cages," it said. "They are shut in on all sides by rock walls of custom and the desire for the good opinion of their neighbors. They are bound by the need to provide food for their families." The eyes of the badger dimmed and its head rose and the eyes were very bright. It stood up on its short bowed legs and turned to go. It swung its head back for a last look at him. "There is a way," it said. "Stones piled upon stones rise upward. Rock striking on rock chips away small pieces. . . ."

Little Bear walked along the base of the near rock wall looking upward. He saw the place that he had not seen before. He saw the place where successive ledges topped each other at fifteen- to twenty-foot intervals. There were four, each wide enough for a man to find firm foothold upon it. On the ground at the base all around were many stones. Some were very big.

Others were small enough for a man to lift and carry them. He began to pile the stones one upon another in a solid heap that leaned against the rock wall and sloped upward toward the first ledge twenty feet above the ground. . . .

The sun shown into the canyon. It shone bravely but it could not hold back the edge of autumn. The air was chill. The rock was cold under the hands of Little Bear. He was pressed close against the rock wall above the first ledge. His feet were firm on a niche cut into the rock. His body was tight against the wall. His left hand gripped the edge of another niche a little below his shoulder height. His right hand held a piece of the hard flint stone that was found at the lower end of the canyon near the stream fissure where the freezings and thawings of endless seasons had split chunks off a vein of it running through the other rock. A pile of other pieces of the flint stone lay ready on the ledge below him. He reached with his right hand and struck the piece it held against the rock wall above him. He struck again and again and the tiny chips danced.

His right arm was tired. He leaned tighter against the wall and shifted his hands. His right hand now gripped the niche below his shoulder. His left hand held the piece of flint stone and struck at the rock above him.

Warning twinges ran down the backs of his legs, the first signs of the cramps that could come. He dropped the flint stone to the pile of others on the ledge. He climbed down and sat quietly on the ledge with his feet hanging over and his back against the rock wall. He rested. The strength of good meat was in him. He rose and climbed again to the niches. Again the flint stone struck against the rock wall.

Three days the storm lasted. Three days the snow fell, sometimes thick and big-flaked, sometimes light and floating in the air. Winds of winter whistled over the plateau and out over the open space of the canyon. They swept across and did not drop to the canyon floor, but they whipped the snow over the far rock edge and piled it in a twenty-foot drift along the base of the wall.

There was no more snow to fall. The sky cleared and the sun peered through the running clouds and smiled on the white shining beauty of the canyon.

Little Bear sat in his shelter that was built as he had heard old men say his people built their shelters when they lived in villages along the big river. His was small but it was built the same way, of poles close-set in the ground with their tops brought together and the space between filled with bunches of twisted long grasses woven in and out and a layer of rooted sod over all. A hole in the top center let out the smoke of the fire of buffalo chips and wood that burned all day and smoldered through the night. A flap of skin covered the small outside opening through which he crawled to come in or to go out. The covering could be fastened tight when the wind blew the wrong way. The shelter was not like a neat rising buffalo-skin lodge. But it was warm. It was his lodge.

In such weather he could not work on the niches in the rock wall which were up past the third ledge now. That did not trouble him. There was always much to be done. It was pleasant working in his shelter when a storm strode over the land.

He was finishing a pair of snowshoes. They were of willow wood bent into shape and tied and laced crisscross with rawhide strips. They had thongs to fasten them to his feet. He noticed that the light coming through the smoke hole was brighter. No more snowflakes drifted through to be met by the warmth of the fire and driven back out in the form of vapor. He loosened the small door covering and stooped to peer out and saw the white beauty of the snow.

He crawled through the doorway. He pulled the ankle flaps of his new winter mocassins up and tied them tightly. He fastened the thongs of the snowshoes firmly around his toes and around his ankles. He moved out on the snow with wide swinging steps and flapped his arms to make his blood flow fast and warm. It was good to be out in the open again, not just to push to the stream for water or to the storehouse for food, but out in the open and free to swing anywhere throughout his canyon.

Already some of his neighbors were about. Where the snow was thin on top of a stone a bird had landed and walked around. Each tiny footprint was clear and precise. Nearby were signs that a rabbit had left its storm hole and ventured into the new white world. Foolish rabbit. The snow was still light and unpacked. The natural snowshoes of the rabbit were not broad enough. His own snowshoes sank six or eight inches before they held. The rabbit had floundered even where the snow was not deep. The print of its belly was plain over the prints of its feet. The tracks stopped in deeper snow. The rabbit had burrowed down through the whiteness to wait in a cozy pocket warmed by its body heat until the snow would be better packed and a light crust formed.

A foolish rabbit. Very foolish. Rabbit fur was soft and had many uses. It made excellent mittens. He jumped headlong into the snow, diving into it, and his hands found the soft furry body. He struggled to his feet on the clumsy snowshoes. He held the rabbit by the ears with his left hand and with the edge of his right hand struck it at the base of the skull on the neck and it hung limp and lifeless. "Oh rabbit," he said. "I grieve for you, but I need your fur." He shook the snow out of his hair and swung on his new snowshoes over where the upthrust rocks marked the summer raspberry patch.

He found the flat stone under the snow. He brushed away the white covering and the piece of meat put there four days ago was still there. That was not strange. The badger slept most of the winter in some secret place deep in the ground. It came out only when there was a stretch of fairly warm days. It would not be out in weather like this. "Oh, badger," he said to the rocks around, "food is here. It is waiting."

He moved along by the near rock wall past the place where the rough slanting walkway of piled stones led up to the first ledge and the niches above. He did not look up. He was looking toward the lower end of the canyon. The buffalo were there. They were working out of the pocket-corner where they waited patiently with heads down through the worst of the storms. They were pawing down through the snow to the clumps of winter-cured grass. They were chewing on the smaller shoots of the aspen along the lower stretch of the stream. He counted them: the young bull, the three growing calves, and four cows. Eight in all. He had taken the fifth cow when the first winds of winter gave warning. Her skin was his sleeping robe. Her meat, some dried and some smoked, was in his storehouse. There was plenty of meat in the storehouse. Even some of the meat of the old bull was still there, and the meat of the calf. Perhaps he should not have taken the cow too. But he needed her hide.

This was a good place for the buffalo. They had fine food in summer. They had enough food in winter. They had water always near. It was running water and never froze over completely. They had bushy brier thickets in which to scrape away the gnats in summer. They had the high closing-in, overhanging rock walls of the corner-pocket to protect them from the storms in winter. It was a good place for them.

Already the dusk shadows were creeping forth. He returned to his shelter and skinned the rabbit. The fresh meat, not full of strength but savory, was very good. He ate all of it at the one meal. His stomach bulged over the breechclout string. That was a good feeling. He lay wrapped in the robe of the skin of the fifth cow and watched the smoke of the smouldering fire spiral upward and out through the roof hole. The canyon was a good place for him too.

Winds of winter night whistled over the high plateau. They did not drop down to disturb the peace of the canyon. And the Maiyun of the rock walls were there, riding the winds and laughing to themselves. They looked down as they raced high above. "Little brother. Are you warm? Are you well fed?"

In the wilderness all that has life must fight for that life. The rule is unchanging and eternal.

Dark shapes moved in the night on the plateau by the far side of the canyon. A small herd of wapiti had come down from the high ridges, a seven-point bull and six cows, creatures of the mountain forests and the upland glades. They seemed taller than buffalo because they carried their heads arching up when they moved, but they were smaller in bulk, finer-limbed, lighter in weight. They sought the open level of the plateau now where the winds had whipped the snow along leaving almost bare patches between the drifts. They did not often seek food here or in the night hours when darkness could cloak danger. Usually they fed in the early morning and in the late afternoon. But the storm had lasted a long time. They were very hungry.

Another dark shape moved in the night, creeping belly to the ground, using the drifts for cover; a great cat, a puma, the lion of the mountains. It was an old male, nearly eight feet from the blunted nose to the black tail tip, two hundred pounds of lean hunger. It crept close to the wapiti, upwind, silent and immaterial as a shadow in the half-light of the lonely stars on the snow. One of the cows moved near. The puma flowed forward and leaped for the neck, for the staggering impact of its weight on the head and the great crunching power of its jaws on the vertebrae just back of the skull.

The snow was soft. The footing was insecure. The puma missed its mark by inches and struck on the shoulder of the cow. Its claws sank through the hide and it clung, reaching now with its fanged jaws for the underside of the neck and the big vein pulsing there. The cow leaped ahead in terror. It drove through the drifts in great bounds. It saw the blackness of open space ahead and wrenched sideways to turn and the puma was torn loose and thrown scrambling and sliding into the snow on the edge of the high rock wall. Its claws bit down through the snow and into the sod but the soil was thin and the claws ripped through. It fell into the blackness, plummeting down and down and into the twenty-foot depth of the big drift below. . . .

It was the bellowing that woke Little Bear. He slept late because his stomach had been full of the good fresh meat of the rabbit. The sun was already more than an hour high when he started awake at the hoarse terrified bellowing from the lower end of the canyon. He sat up and listened and there was no sound. Then he heard the buffalo moving outside, close by, breathing heavily and floundering in the snow. He scrambled to the doorway and lifted the skin-flap and crawled through. The buffalo were running along the base of the near rock wall. They leaped and struggled where the snow was deep and drove on. They ran in among the upthrust rocks where the summer raspberry bushes grew and reached the wall of the upper end of the canyon and stopped. They stood in a compact bunch and stared back down the way they had come and their muscles jumped and twitched with a fear. It was very strange.

He put on his snowshoes and went toward them. They were afraid of him. They had been afraid of him since the killing of the old bull. Always they ran from him. But now they did not run. They pushed back until their rumps were against the rock wall and stared at him and stared past him down the canyon and their muscles twitched in a terror.

He stopped. He counted them. Seven. One was not there. One of the growing calves was not with them.

The young bull stood out in front of the others. It pawed the snow under its front feet. It lowered its big head and blew through its nostrils. It might rush at him. He turned and swung swiftly on the snowshoes down the canyon. He did not go far before he saw the tracks.

They were almost round tracks more than four inches across. Each had the imprint of the pad and of the four toes and the marks of the tips of the sheathed claws too were plain in the snow.

That could not be. The puma, the blood-drinking one that moved as a shadow no hunter could overtake and that killed horses in the dark of the night, could not be in his canyon. It was not there yesterday when he caught the rabbit. It was not there any of the days stretching back before. Yet the tracks were plain and there were many of them. Some evil spirit had taken its form and come to rob him of his buffalo. His own muscles twitched in a strange fear.

He hurried back to his shelter. He hung his quiver of bullhide on his left side with the carrying band over his right shoulder. He took his five arrows and rubbed their flint-stone points with a leaf of the white sage from the small pile of the leaves in a corner of the shelter. He did this to purify them and to remove any bad omens that might be clinging to them. He put the arrows in the quiver and took the bow of buffalo horn and strung it with the bowstring made from the great shoulder tendon of the old bull. He took the knife from the sheath fastened to his leggings on his right thigh and rubbed the blade with another leaf of the white sage and put it again in the sheath. He was sad now that he had not made a stout tomahawk or strong stone axe. He started down the canyon with wide swinging steps on the snowshoes.

The snow was better packed now and he could move swiftly but he did not. He moved slowly, looking hard all around and ahead. When he came to the tracks he took an arrow from the quiver and notched it on the bow-string and followed the tracks. They led back and forth and always worked farther down the canyon. He saw where the puma had scented the buffalo and slipped belly-low forward, leaving a mark like a great snake. He saw this mark lead twisting through thick-set clumps of bushes that blocked vision ahead. He stopped. He tried to remember what old hunters had told of the ways of the puma. When it killed it did not eat in the open. It dragged its kill beneath overhanging rocks or a low-limbed tree. There were no such rocks near. But there was a bushy pine a long bow shot ahead and to the right. And there was good bush cover about forty feet from it.

He moved very slowly. He was careful not to let the snowshoes bump together and to press each down gently at first before putting his weight on it so that there would be no crunching of the snow. He circled to the right and after many long moments he was behind the cover bushes. He moved even more slowly. He parted the bushes with infinite care and eased his way between them. At last he could see through those remaining.

The puma was there.

It was crouched under the bushy pine feeding on the carcass of the growing calf that would grow no more. Its back was towards him, turned a bit to one side. He could see the black tail tip waving from side to side as it fed. He could see the white insides of the ears when it lifted its head to let the fresh meat juices trickle down its throat. All of it except the tail tip and the ears was a deep reddish brown. It was a big puma, very big.

Carefully he drew the arrow back until the flint-stone point almost touched the bow. He aimed up along the side where the arrow could drive forward behind the ribs to the heart. He loosened his grip on the arrow and it sprang from the bow humming its low death song and it swerved in flight and struck, not in the side where it could drive forward to the heart, but in the flank where it sank into the big muscle there and hit bone.

The big cat leaped twisting in the air and in the leaping saw him and landed scrambling and was away in huge bounds scattering the snow and the second arrow that he had notched before the first hit sprang after it and went high and was buried in a drift beyond.

He was very sad. His arrows were poor arrows. They were not quite straight. They did not fly true. He was not a good arrow maker. Only a few men were and they made all the arrows for their villages and other men gave presents for them. Yet these were the only arrows he had. The puma had carried one of them away and he would have to hunt for another in the deep snow.

All the rest of the morning he followed the tracks of the puma and long into the afternoon. There were blood drippings with them for a time then these stopped. It moved like a shadow, slipping away before he was near or even knew he was near. He found the place where it had tried to draw the arrow out of its flank and had bitten the shaft through so that the shattered wood lay on the ground. Most of the day he followed the tracks and three times only he saw the puma. Once he was close enough to shoot another arrow and this went wide. He was afraid. The fear that had twitched his muscles in the early morning grew in him. Perhaps his arrows were good arrows after all. They would not fly true because the evil spirit in the puma was too powerful for them. It turned them aside. Then he became aware that the puma was not just running to get away from him and trying to hide and then running again when he unraveled the increasing maze of tracks and came near. He could not see it as it slipped from cover to cover but he could sense that it was watching him. It knew there was no way out of the canyon. It was watching him and moving as he moved. It did not go into the narrow upper end of the canyon. His scent was too strong there because his camp was there. It circled in the wide lower end and watched him and it was learning that he could not move as fast as it moved and the medicine of his arrows was weak. He remembered that old hunters said a puma never attacked a grown man except when it was caught where there was no escape. But that did not help much. Everything old hunters said was not always the exact truth.

He stopped following the tracks. He could not get near the puma, not while it was watching him. Darkness would be coming soon. He would fight another way. He would not let the puma have the meat it had killed. He went back to the carcass of the calf. He tried to drag it. It slid on the snow but it was too heavy. He cut it in two pieces, slicing through just behind the ribs and parting the vertebrae. In two trips he dragged it to his storehouse. When he returned for the second piece there were new tracks in the snow. He did not see the puma but he knew it was watching and he dragged the meat as fast as he could. He pushed the two pieces into the rock-crevice storehouse and piled the stones in front again. He hunted through the snow to find more stones, as big stones as he could move. He piled very many and wedged them tightly together.

The buffalo were still among the upthrust rock by the upper-end rock wall. There was little more for them to eat in that place but they did not venture down the canyon. He tramped back and forth across the canyon between them and the lower end. He made a path, at first with his snowshoes and then without them in just his moccasins. Perhaps his scent would keep the puma away. . . .

That was a long night. In his shelter he slept only in snatches, dozing and waking suddenly with a cold sweat on his face. Each time he waked he put more wood on the fire. There would be long stretches with no sound. No winds moved. Even the Maiyun remained deep in their rock homes. Then the silence would be shattered by a fearful sound. Five times in the night the puma screamed, a fearful sound that wailed and echoed through the canyon, sometimes like a woman in an agony, sometimes like an evil spirit tormenting helpless people. Each time he listened and his muscles twitched and the fear grew. . . .

In the morning the sun was high before he crawled out of the shelter. Twice he started and held back and the third time he went out. The bow was always in his left hand now.

The buffalo were there among the upthrust rocks. They were moving a little out but not far. There were no four-toed tracks at the upper end of the canyon. He felt much better. Perhaps his medicine was strong too.

He started down the canyon, moving slowly, watching all around. He saw many new tracks overlaying the old. He saw where the puma had lapped away every sign of blood where the carcass of the calf had been. He saw where it had killed a rabbit. A few small tufts of fur were all that remained. It was very hungry. A small rock rabbit was not much food for a puma as big as that one. And the appetite of an animal that held an evil spirit was always very strong.

Suddenly he knew that it was watching him. He turned. It was there, beyond bow shot, watching him with eyes that burned in the sunlight. It did not like having its meat taken away. It did not like having his scent between it and the buffalo. It was not running from him. It knew he could not overtake it. Only when he shouted and started toward it did it move. It slipped away like a shadow, disappearing so swiftly that he was not certain where it had gone. It was out of sight but he knew it was watching him. He hurried back to the upper end of the canyon.

All day he stayed in the open there. Much of the time he stood on top of a big stone and looked down the canyon. Sometimes he saw the puma. It moved restlessly, covering the entire area, searching for food. It was lean and very hungry. It did not seem to care that he could see it.

The buffalo knew it was there. They searched for food too and pawed through the snow for the scanty grass. Often they stared down the canyon

and snorted and trembled. But they did not snort or tremble when Little
Bear came near. They seemed to know that they were safer with him
between them and the puma.

Everything in the canyon knew it was there. Not a rabbit moved out of
its burrow, not a rock squirrel, not a fieldmouse even under the snow.
There were only the buffalo and Little Bear at the upper end of the
canyon and the puma searching and prowling at the lower end and creeping ever closer in its wide ranging from rock wall to rock wall.

Dusk shadows came. He stayed on the big stone watching the whiteness
of the snow with the bow ready in his hand. Darkness came and clouds
with it and the snow was only a vague grayness all around. He felt and
was not sure and felt again that the puma was watching him. It was near.
He could not tell where it was, on what side, in front of him or behind
him. The fear was too strong. He hurried to his shelter and fastened the
skinflap tight and nursed the fire into good burning. . . .

He sat crouched with the fire between him and the doorway. The flames
were low and would not leap up. The smoke rose slowly as if it were reluctant to drift out the smoke hole into the outer darkness. There was no
sound except the small whisperings of the fire yet his muscles twitched and
an awareness grew in him and suddenly there was a rushing of sounds.
The buffalo were snorting and whistling through their nostrils and they
were running. They were ploughing through the snow along the rock wall
down the canyon. The sounds faded and the silence returned yet the
awareness was still strong within him. The puma was there. It had not
followed the buffalo. It was outside and it was very near.

He listened. Drops of cold sweat dripped from his chin as he listened.
He heard the sound of claws on rock. It was trying to rip the stones away
from his storehouse. He shouted. He stirred the fire so that sparks flew
upward. He thumped the ground and screamed and screeched wordless
sounds. He seized a stick from the fire and thrust the burning end up
through the smoke hole in the roof and jumped over the fire and as he
jumped pushed his hand with the burning stick up through the hole and
flung it so that it fell outside hissing in the snow.

He crouched on the ground inside with the bow in his hand and an
arrow notched and listened. There was no sound. The immediate awareness died away within him. He put more wood on the fire and crouched
by it and gradually his muscles ceased twitching. The canyon outside was
a big bowl filled with a dark silence. He crouched by the fire and dark
shadows filled his mind.

Then the bellowing began. It was deep and rumbling. It rose and fell and
rose again. It stopped and it began again and it stopped again and began
yet again. There was silence and then there was bellowing and once the
great cat screamed, a high climbing scream that held a fearful fierceness
and a fearful fury. And the hours passed, slow and dragging, and he
crouched by the fire and the dark shadows whirled in his mind. . . .

It was morning. Mists floated over the hills. The sun beat upon them and drove them away and shone upon the plateau. But in the canyon the mists still clung.

Little Bear woke from the half-sleep of a gripping weariness. The fire was a few last embers. The light through the smoke hole told him it was day. He stretched his cramped muscles and suddenly he jerked upright and to his feet. The bellowing was beginning again. It was a hoarse and strained bellowing far off at the lower end of the canyon. It stopped and he stood shivering with the fear.

He moved. That was very hard but he moved. He unfastened the skin-flap and crawled out and tied on the snowshoes. The knife was in its sheath on his right leg. The quiver was by his left side with three arrows in it and in his hands was the bow with the fourth arrow ready notched. He looked down the canyon but he could see only here and there in patches because of the trailing mists. Carefully he went along his path and in among the upthrust rocks. Tracks were there, the four-toed tracks of the big puma. They led to the flat stone that belonged to the badger. The piece of meat was gone. They led around and along the base of the rock wall down the canyon the way the buffalo had run. He started along the wall following the tracks.

He moved slowly. The farther he went the slower became his movements. The fear had hold of him and gripped and pressed tight. He breathed in short gasps. He felt that this ribs were bound inward and that he would choke. At last he stopped. He could go no farther.

He stood still. He was unable to go forward and he was unable to go back. As he stood, the sun beat down upon the mists and the breezes came and moved them and he saw. Before him at the lower end of the canyon in the corner-pocket he saw the buffalo. They were crowded into the very corner. They were pressed close together and they stared outward with a fixed stare. Fifty feet in front of them the big puma crouched low in the snow. The black tip of the tail of the big puma waved gently from side to side as it watched them. And between them and the big puma stood the young bull. It breathed heavily and its head hung low with the horns pointing outward. The snow was packed hard where it had worn a broad path from closing-in rock wall to closing-in rock wall between them and the big puma. There was blood on the path and blood dripped from the big head of the young bull where claws had ripped downward. But the blood was not all its own. There was dark red drying on one horn.

Little Bear saw. He saw the puma turn its head to lick the gash along its side. He saw it rise and slide like a shadow to the right and the young bull swing to face it there. He saw it shift and slide to the left and the young bull swing again. He saw it leap forward and the young bull jump with feet braced and head lowered to meet it and he saw it dodge and dash to get around and scatter the other buffalo and the young bull spring with desperate speed to intercept it.

Little Bear stood taller. The fear snapped from around him like an old rotted rope. The air of his canyon rushed into his lungs until he thought that his ribs would burst outward. His voice rose in a mighty shout, "Oh buffalo! Fight well! I am coming!"

His short legs swept the snowshoes in powerful arcs over the snow. He swooped forward swiftly and the notched arrow was drawn back until the flint-stone head almost touched the bow. But the great cat heard him and leaped around snarling and was away in huge bounds.

He stopped where it had crouched low to the ground. He looked at the young bull and saw the big gashes that dripped blood. Yet the young bull pawed on its path and snorted at him. "Come forward," it seemed to say. "I will fight you too." He looked at it and his heart was big within him. "Oh buffalo," he said. "You have shamed me."

He swung about and followed the new tracks away. He moved swiftly over the snow. A mighty strength filled his muscles. He saw the blood drippings of the puma along the way and he was glad. The bounds were not as long between as they had been before. The puma was weakened. It had a stone arrowhead deep in the muscle of one flank. It had a long rip in the flesh of one side.

He saw the tracks leading on ahead. They led to a thickset pine. They did not lead away from the pine. The wounds were making the puma foolish. It was in the tree. It would be within reach of his arrows.

Carefully he moved close to the pine. The branches were very thick. He was almost under them before he could see the puma. It was nearly twenty feet up lying flat along a branch. It snarled and spat at him. He pulled the notched arrow back and released it and the low humming sounded. As he shot, the puma leaped out from the branch. It wanted to leap far out and over his head and away but the branch was springy under its weight and its muscles were stiffened from the wounds. It fell short. It came crashing through the ends of the branches above him. He saw it coming. He saw the gaping jaws and the long stretching unsheathed claws. He dropped the bow and his left hand reached grasping for the neck beneath the jaws and his right hand took the knife, the iron-bladed knife with an edge keener and harder than any stone. He fell backward with the weight of the puma upon him and the long claws tearing at him and he drove the knife deep into its body behind the shoulder. He held the foaming jaws from him with his left hand and wrenched with the knife and plunged it deeper. He struggled to roll and break free from the tearing claws. He let go the handle of the knife and with both hands heaved against the body of the puma and flung it away and was free. He staggered to his feet and the puma lay writhing on the ground. Its claws ripped into the snow and the grasses beneath. Its movements slowed and it became limp. Its eyes filmed over. It twitched and was still.

He stood swaying and gasping for breath. His clothing was slashed and torn. Blood streamed down his chest and down his thighs. He stooped and took handfuls of snow and rubbed these over the gashes. The stinging was sharp but the blood-flow slowed. And the stinging was good. It told him what it was that he had done.

He pulled the knife from the body of the puma and cleaned it. He unstrung the bow and looped the bowstring around the front paws of the puma and began to drag the carcass up the canyon. He left it near the doorway of his shelter where he would work upon it. He went inside and took a piece of dried meat from the supply there. He went among the upthrust rocks where the summer raspberry bushes grew. He laid the meat on the flat stone. "Oh badger," he said to the rocks. "The evil one that took your meat is dead."

He looked down his canyon. His buffalo were there. They were out of the corner-pocket. They were pawing through the snow to the dried clumps of the good grasses that grew all through the lower portion of his canyon. The wounds of the young bull would heal quickly. It would live to be the father of many calves. They would be good calves with the brave heart and the strong muscles of the father. They would make good meat. Their strength would become his strength.

The sun was bright on the near rock wall and on the snow. It had conquered the mists. The four-toed tracks would soon disappear. The sun would melt them away and other snow would cover where they had been and in the spring the grasses would grow green as if they had not been there at all. He spoke to the rocks all around. "Oh badger. It is a good cage. . . ."

The new green of the renewed grasses was bright and clear. The new green of the fresh young leaves of the long-bare trees was light and brilliant against the dark old green of the pines. The sun rose higher overhead and shone more hours into the canyon. It sparkled on the leaping spray of the waterfall and the running ripples of the stream. It shone warm and friendly on Little Bear as he crawled from his shelter and stripped off his leggings and breechclout, leaving only the manhood string around his waist, and ran and plunged into the pool for the splashing and the washing that was the first morning activity of every male Cheyenne when he was near water.

This water was cold, still tangy from the still melting snows that fed it far on up the hills that were not hills but mountains. It made him splutter and catch his breath in short puffs. It made him climb out quickly and jump and run to have his blood leap and flow with good warmth.

He dressed and ate. He took a piece of meat to the flat stone among the upthrust rocks. The piece left there yesterday was gone. The badger had not been sleeping in the sun-hours for many days now.

He started down the canyon. Every morning he made this circuit. He passed by the slanting walkway of piled rocks leading up to the first ledge and the niches that were up past the third ledge above and he did not look up. He could be hammering more niches in weather like this but he did not look up. There were always so many things to be done. There was no hurry for the niches. There was no need for them.

He saw the buffalo grazing on the renewed grasses. He counted them. There was the young bull that must be called the old bull now because he was the oldest male among them. The healed scars on his great head were badges that showed his right to be leader of the herd. There were the two growing calves that were not calves any more but yearlings, a young bull and a slenderer young cow. There were three of the old cows with their three little calves beside them, old enough now to walk almost steadily and butt against each other. But where was the fourth old cow that had produced no calf though she was very big and heavy? She was off by herself near the rock wall muzzling something on the ground.

He went closer but not so close that he would alarm her. Two some-things were on the ground and she was licking them, first one and then the other. They were two calves, smaller than the others were when first born but sturdily built and trying already to struggle up on wobbly legs. They would soon catch up to the others in growing. Twin calves were almost always healthy calves and grew fast. Their mother was a good mother. She had waited longer than the other mothers and for a good reason. She was the best of the mothers. She would have to eat plenty of good grass to have milk enough for those two lively calves. . . .

The grasses and the leaves were fresh green and the sun was warm and the rains were soft and did not last long and food was various and good and the days drifted and there was always so much to be done and so many hours to be sepnt in the warm sun watching the endlessly changing life of his canyon and so many more hours to be passed lying outside the shelter in the gentle nights and waiting until the moon climbed over the canyon wall and shone softly into his eyes. . . .

And then the dreams began.

He was nervous and for no reason. He was restless and did not know why. He was irritable and sudden angers flared in him when there was nothing at which to be angry. He ate little because he had no appetite and became thinner in the body. He ate more and stuffed himself and the food did him little good. It did not put strong flesh on him as the grasses were putting strong flesh on the buffalo. This was the season of fattening with the good living of late spring and he did not fatten. He slept little and when he slept he dreamed.

The dreams were formless and when he woke he could not remember them. Sometimes he woke more tired than when he went to sleep and he lay quiet and a strange lassitude held him. Sometimes he woke tense and disturbed and jumped up and walked around with hard hurried steps angry at all things. He strove to remember the dreams and he could not. They were elusive and he almost had them and they were gone. And then one came clearly and remained.

It was the dream he had before during the starving. He was walking in a good land and he knew this time it was his canyon and a fine well-sewn lodge of buffalo skins was before him and he knew it was his and by the entrance was a woman. It was the same woman and he could see her plainly and she was young and yet womanly and she was not beautiful but there was a warm wisdom and an understanding on her face and she was beckoning to him. He went toward her and she was gone and somehow he was gone too and he woke shaking as if with a strong fever. . . .

He sat cross-legged on the ground. He watched the flat stone and the piece of meat upon it. The dark brown head of the badger with its long white stripe appeared over the stone. It saw him. There was recognition in the small black eyes with the tiny flashes of light deep in them. It moved and the whole broad gray-brown body was on the stone. It ate the meat, it was thin and tired. It looked as if it had wandered far and had little to eat. Yet it did not finish the meat. It lay on the stone and looked at him.

He sat very still and the sun was warm upon them both and at last his head dropped forward in drowsiness. The badger looked at him and its eyes became very bright. It spoke and its voice was low and mournful. "There is much," it said. "But there is something lacking. There is no warmth of body to body in the shelter at night. . . ."

The rays of the late afternoon sun found Little Bear far up the near rock wall above the third ledge. His feet were set firmly into a niche. His left hand gripped the edge of the niche under his shoulder. His right hand held a piece of flint stone and struck against the rock above his head. The blows were hard and the tiny chips danced. . . .

## 4

The life of a Cheyenne of the high border country is given meaning by customs and the rituals of daily living. In that he and his people are no different from any other people, anywhere, anytime. The customs and the rituals alone are different.

Cheyenne customs and rituals change, but they change slowly. It is more accurate to say that they grow, that traditions encrust them ever more deeply, that the changing is a gradual adaptation of the old under the influence of the new. They are changing very slowly right now, so slowly that the people of the tribe do not know they are changing and think they are changeless. The wrenching impact of the whitemen and their ruthless overriding ways is still to come.

In nothing are these customs and rituals stronger and more carefully observed than in marriage and all that pertains to the mating cycle. On that rests the ultimate welfare of the tribe. That is what will keep it a social order, a loose social order but a social order nonetheless, of healthy and homogeneous people properly trained in the customs and the rituals that give their life meaning. . . .

The women of the tribe are as important as the men. They are the real rulers in the camp and the village as the men are the rulers in the chase and in war. Even in these latter things the women often advise the men and restrain the men from being hasty and overzealous and the men listen to them. The women own property and retain that property in marriage. They have their own societies and guilds. A woman who can make a fine lodge is as important as a man who is a good hunter. No woman is given in marriage without her consent. Strong persuasions may be spoken by her parents or by the brother or uncle who may "own" her in the sense that he is in charge of her disposal in marriage, but she will not be forced. Her person will be respected by all men at all times and in all places as long as she respects it. She is not a drudge, a chattel, a slave. She is a Cheyenne woman.

The young man who seeks to marry a Cheyenne woman will have a hard time if he cannot offer many presents for her father to distribute among her family and her near relatives. These show that the young man is a man able to take care of her and that he regards her highly and that he comes of a good family whose members have helped him gather together the presents. If he is accepted, the presents given in return to be distributed to his family and his relatives may match or overmatch those he has offered. But without his presents he will have a hard time. Without them he must be one who bears an important name and has counted many bold coups or she will not look with favor upon him. And if he is such a one, he is almost certain to have presents to offer. It is a difficult situation for a man who has no important name and no coups counted and few presents to speak for him in their place. He may be a good man and she may look upon him with eyes soft and regretful. But she is a Cheyenne woman. As a girl she has been trained more carefully than has been any boy for she will be a mother of the tribe and she is mindful of her responsibilities. . . .

All loyal Cheyennes respected by the tribe regard that procedure as the right and the normal procedure. Good marriages are built by it, good marriages that endure so that there are many old men whose favorite companions in all things are the old women who accepted them when they were young and full of life and have kept clean lodges for them and borne their children and winnowed the good out of the long drifting years together with them. There are exceptions, marriages made otherwise without careful observance of the customs, made sometimes in violation of them. But these are not often good marriages. . . .

That is the situation which confronted Little Bear.

He is there. He has finished his niches and is out on the open plain. He is Little Bear, onetime foster son of Strong Left Hand, now the strange one, the wanderer, who will not speak of his starving and what came of it in the four long seasons he was gone or of the scars he bears on his breast and thighs and will not dwell in any village but wanders from one to the other on a painted pony, wearing a shirt made from the skin of the puma and carrying a lance with an iron-bladed knife for a headpoint. He hunts with a mighty courage to bring meat to the lodge of the man with whom he stays for a brief time and he wanders on searching and searching for something that is no more substantial than a woman seen in a dream. . . .

There was silence in the lodge. All the family slept. But Little Bear did not sleep. He lay on the couch made soft by the robe for visitors that was unpacked and put upon it for him and he did not sleep. She was not in this village. Perhaps she was not in any village. Almost four full seasons he had searched and she was not in any village. He had been at the Medicine Lodge of the western villages and she was not there. He had been at the Medicine Lodge of the southern villages near the river called Niobrara and she was not there. Villages to the eastward remained and he must go among them. But sometimes families changed from village to village and how could a man be certain she was not now in some village where he had already been? How could he be certain she was in any village anywhere?

The soft light of the late spring moon sifted through the lodge entrance and called to him. Quietly he rose and went out and through the village and on to the open plain. He sat cross-legged in the long grasses and the night sounds murmured around him. And the Maiyun of that place whispered through the grasses and they knew him. The Maiyun of all places were kindred and they spoke to each other in the depths of the earth and shared their knowledge. And these Maiyun knew him and they spoke to him. "Little brother," they said, "have you found her?" He lowered his head forward until his chin rested upon his chest and he was very sad. The breezes rustled more strongly in the grasses and the Maiyun spoke chiding him. "Little brother, have you forgotten the old one?"

He raised his head and he looked at the moon. "The old one is dead," he said. "The old one has departed on the trail where all footprints point the same way and he dwells now with the spirits of the friends of his youth in the camp among the far stars." The head of Little Bear sank forward again and he was very sad. But the breezes rustled even more strongly and the Maiyun spoke and they were angry. "Did the old one fail you when your laughing father who did not laugh then spoke his name for the piercing of your ears? Did he fail you when he fought for the last breaths that would keep him living for your sake and he forced his spirit out into the night and across the dark plain and into the hills when you were afraid and would have fled from your starving?" The Maiyun spoke and they were angry with him and they raced rustling away through the grasses and it was still.

He pondered this a long time. He rose and went back through the village to the lodge. Quietly he took the lance with the iron-bladed knife as its head-point and slipped again through the village and out to where the horses grazed in the moonlight. He mounted the painted pony and rode eastward.

All night he rode and well into the next day. In the late afternoon he came to the place. The village was there. It had not been moved. But the lodge with the painted symbols was gone. It was two miles away, folded in fashion for traveling, resting beside the favorite weapons and the favorite pipes upon the burial platform in a grove of small trees where the old bones and the last fragments of flesh that had clung to them of the old one, the great one, Standing All Night, slept forever in a wrapping of buffalo robe.

He knew it would be so yet his heart was heavy to see that it was so.

With the old one gone, why would this village be different from any other?

He rode forward and at the first lodge a man stepped forward, a man not young and with a withered left arm but with strong eyes and a strong face. The man held up his right hand. He spoke. He spoke as one Cheyenne to another, direct and with courtesy. "My friend. I am called White Wolf."

"My friend. I am called Little Bear."

"You are welcome, Little Bear. How can I help you?"

"It is in my mind to stay with this village for a time."

"That is good. You will share my lodge."

"That is very good. I will hunt for you. I will bring you much meat."

"There is no need for meat. You will honor my lodge."

They sat together cross-legged on the ground. They smoked a pipe and passed it between them according to custom. The feeling of a man for a man was between them. White Wolf puffed on the good pipe. He held it from his mouth. "My friend. Word of your wandering has come even here. Why do you move from village to village?"

Little Bear took the pipe. He puffed on it in silence. He sought for words that would answer without answering because he could not speak to another what was in his heart. He sought for words and then he forgot to seek them.

The women of the village were going to the stream nearby for water for the cooking of the evening meal. They carried bowls and they laughed and talked together. And one among them was young and yet womanly and she was not beautiful but there was a warm wisdom and an understanding on her face. The heart of Little Bear leaped within him and his breath quickened. "My friend. Who is that one?"

The eyes of White Wolf became very bright. His question was answered by another question that yet was an answer. He took the pipe and drew in smoke from it. He let the smoke drift out through his nostrils. "She is called Spotted Turtle."

"She is unmarried?"

"She lives in the lodge of Yellow Moon."

The heart of Little Bear sank down within him. His head sank forward until his chin rested upon his chest. But the eyes of White Wolf were brighter even than before. "My friend. Yellow Moon is her brother."

There was much meat in the lodge of White Wolf. Even when his left arm was good and the great storm had not frozen it, there had not been so much meat in his lodge. There was meat to be given to those who always gave him of their own when they returned from a hunt because they knew he could no longer kill his own food. There was meat for feasting and the inviting of friends to the feasting. He was proud to have Little Bear, the strange one, the different one, but a mighty hunter, sharing his lodge. Three buffalo had Little Bear killed on this day, three in the one riding, and with no arrows but with the lance, and those who had hunted too said a laughter was in his mouth as he leaned from the painted pony and drove the lance straight into the life-center of the buffalo.

The old crier of the village called the names. The friends of White Wolf came to the feasting. But when the talking was loud and the food was being eaten, Little Bear was not in the lodge. He was standing in the dusk near the lodge of Yellow Moon. He was waiting as young men waited for the young women they wished to court to come out to fetch wood or to carry water so that they could pluck at the robes of the young women to attract their attention and see if the young women would speak to them. He was afraid. Little Bear, the mighty hunter, was afraid. He was shy and he knew that he was a strange one, a different one, and he was afraid.

A woman came out of the lodge. It was the wife of Yellow Moon. She saw him waiting in the dusk. Perhaps she smiled to herself remembering when young men waited in the dusk for her. She went past him without seeming to notice him and down the path to the stream. She returned and entered the lodge. He waited and was more afraid. Another woman came out of the lodge, a younger woman, in years not much more than a girl yet very womanly. It was Spotted Turtle. She did not look his way. She looked the other way. But when she moved towards the stream she passed very close to him. He reached and plucked at her robe.

She stopped and turned towards him. He strove hard to speak. "Spotted Turtle," he said. "Oh Spotted Turtle."

She saw that he was afraid and she smiled at him. "I am the one called Spotted Turtle."

"I am the one called Little Bear."

"I have heard. I have seen."

Then she looked closer at him in the deepening dusk and she stared at him and her eyes became wide in wonder. "You are the small one who had the moon in his eyes." He could not speak for the surprise and the wonder her words brought and she saw this in his face and smiled again at him. "I saw you. You saw me and did not see me. You had eyes only for the old one. I heard what you spoke and what he spoke. I was the great-granddaughter who prepared the soups for him." Still the wonder held him. Her face became sad and she spoke again. "Seven days after you left he died. He started up in the night and cried out. He was very troubled. He had failed you. He fell back and there was no life in him."

Little Bear was no longer afraid. He was a man and he could speak. "Oh Spotted Turtle. He did not fail me. Not in anything did he fail me." And then the words came rushing from him. "I saw you. I did not know it but I saw you. You leaped through my eyes into my heart. You have lived in my mind. You have beckoned to me in dreams in the night—"

Now she was afraid. Young men who waited for young women in the dusk did not speak in that way, not even after many evenings of talking. They observed the customs. They spoke only as friends, of impersonal topics, things that had happened in the village or in the hunt. They let any feeling between them and the young women grow slowly, unspoken, through many weeks and perhaps many months. She turned to go to the lodge. But Little Bear clutched at her robe and held it. The revelation of the wonder that the old one had wrought even after death was strong in him and the words rushed forth. "I am not a boy to stand around waiting evening after evening and let the things in my heart go unsaid. Four seasons I have searched for you through all the tribe and the place that is my own waits for us."

She pulled the robe from his hand and returned to the lodge. She paused in the entrance to look back. Her face, half lit from the fire within, was not angry. It was soft and womanly and a little afraid.

Little Bear stood in the dropping darkness and was ashamed. It was late in the night when he slipped quietly to his place in the lodge of White Wolf. . . .

Customs. There are customs binding all things, always and everywhere. There are customs for eating and sleeping and the dressing of one's body, for the hunt and the war trail, for the speaking of man to man and man to woman, for the making of a marriage and the merging of two into one and the beginning of a new family. They are good. They give texture to living and meaning to life. But sometimes they do not make sense to a strange one, a different one. Who is he to think that he can decide which are good and which are foolish? Who is he to think that they should be set aside to match his wishes and to soothe his conscience?

"My friend. Will you go to the lodge of Yellow Moon and speak for me according to custom? Will you say that I wish his sister for my wife?"

"What presents would you have me take? Yellow Moon is a mighty warrior. His sister is close to his heart. She has had many young men wait for her in the dusk of the evening but she has not looked with favor upon them."

"I have no presents."

"Have you no family, have you no relatives, to gather presents together for you?"

—To the westward is a small village and in that village is a man called Strong Left Hand. He will strip himself of many horses and many good weapons and many fine robes in behalf of a foster son as in behalf of his own sons, for he is a fair man in all his dealings with those who have lived in his lodge as a family. He has two sons who are brave warriors. They will go on the war trail, untiring in travel, to take horses for a foster brother who has been a boy together with them and shared the same heat from the same fire in the same lodge. But Strong Left Hand is not the true father. His sons are not the true brothers. And why should a man take from others what he cannot give in return when a need comes?—

"It is the same. I have no presents."

"There must be presents. I will give you what I can. I will speak to my relatives."

"That is good. But it cannot be. You are not my father. My father is dead. I would take only from the true father."

"But there must be presents. There must be things to serve as a sign."

"I have a painted pony. I have a lance whose death-point is an iron-bladed knife that has known the hand of the old one, her great-grandfather, Standing All Night."

"It would be better not to go at all than to go with one pony and one lance, even such a lance."

"My friend, I asked it as one man asks another whose lodge he has shared."

"Have you counted many coups?"

"With no horse and with the bone of my right leg broken and using my lance as a staff, I have killed an old bull, the leader of a herd."

"That is good."

"Rolling on the ground with my knife in my hand and with the great claws tearing at me, I have killed the puma, the blood-drinking one of the mountains."

"That is very good. But have you counted coups on the enemies of your people."

"I have not counted coups."

—This is certainly a strange one, a different one, a wanderer with a purpose yet without the means of grasping the purpose. He does not seek honor as all men should seek honor. He should stay here and acquire wealth. The women of my family will make robes for him of the hides of the buffalo he kills. He should go on the war trail and take horses. There is time for all things. Why must he be in a hurry? . . . And yet . . . He is a mighty hunter. There is meat in the lodge, more meat than ever before. It has been freely given. And he has a drawing quietness in him. When he smokes and passes the pipe a strong feeling of a man to a man goes with it. The woman has looked with some favor on him. All the village knows, as all the village always knows everything, that four times he has plucked at her robe and four times she has stopped for a brief time to talk to him. Perhaps for a strange one strange things can happen—

"My friend. I will go. I will speak for you."

White Wolf led the painted pony. In his withered left hand he carried the lance. He tied the pony in front of the lodge of Yellow Moon. He stuck the point of the lance in the ground so that it stood upright. He entered the lodge.

The wife of Yellow Moon stood in the lodge entrance. She called and children came running. She spoke to them and they scattered to run to other lodges and some ran out of the village to find men who were not in their lodges. She built a fire in front of the lodge and to one side and began to prepare food.

The relatives of Yellow Moon and his wife gathered in the lodge. They ate and they talked and they thought and they talked again. All the rest of the day they ate and thought and talked together. At last Yellow Moon spoke and the others were silent and listened.

He finished. The father of his wife rose and went out of the lodge. He untied the painted pony. He pulled the lance from the ground. He drove the pony before him to the lodge of White Wolf. He laid the lance on the ground. He turned and went away. The message was delivered. There would be no marriage.

The father of the wife of Yellow Moon stopped and turned again. He walked through the village as a man walked to enjoy the evening air. He passed near the lodge of White Wolf. He turned toward it like a man who had just remembered that a friend lived in that lodge. He entered the lodge and stepped to the right. He was not a messenger now. He was a visitor stopping to talk to a friend and exchange news of the village.

White Wolf sat on his couch at the rear of the lodge. Little Bear sat on his couch to the right and his head was forward and down so that his chin rested on his chest. The father-in-law of Yellow Moon did not look at Little Bear. He waited and sat at the place to the left where White Wolf pointed. And White Wolf filled a pipe and lit it and puffed upon it and passed it to him. And the visitor smoked the pipe and spoke.

"The man called Yellow Moon, who happens to be the husband of my daughter and the brother of the one called Spotted Turtle, has said many things in his lodge today. Since the death of his father two springs ago, he has been alone responsible for his sister. Even before that he was responsible for her giving in marriage because his father gave her to him in that manner in praise according to custom when he counted his first coup. He has seen the one called Little Bear in the hunt. He bows his head in honor of such hunting. But he would not shame his sister by giving her in marriage without presents to be laid before those who are close to her by blood and by marriage for their choosing."

And the visitor lit the pipe again and smoked. Again he spoke. "There is more. A man who has not yet counted coups on the enemies of his people is not yet really a man. He is still a boy and the years that have passed over him make no difference. That is an old saying of the tribe. It is a good saying. He who is a friend to the one called Little Bear would tell him to go forth on the war trail and count many coups and take many horses and be a man. . . ."

Is it the counting of coups on the enemies of his people even when they are not near and a danger to the tribe that makes a man? Is it the taking of horses that turns a boy into a warrior able to maintain a lodge of his own and a woman living in it? Must a man go against what is in his heart to obtain the other thing dwelling there too?

He sat cross-legged in the grasses and the moon was in his eyes. His mind wrestled with itself and beat against the bones of his forehead and he was very sad. Breezes rustled in the grasses and the Maiyun of the place whispered through them. He did not hear. They hummed louder and they made him listen. "Little brother. Your eyes have looked upon the mother of Spotted Turtle when she has gone forth to gather wood. Yet you have not really seen her. . . ."

"My friend. Why does the mother of Spotted Turtle keep her hair cut short and walk bare-legged in the open air and there are ever fresh gashes on her legs? Twice the four seasons have passed since the father of Spotted

Turtle found the trail where all footprints point the same way and still she mourns."

"She mourns because the spirit of her man has not found the trail. It wanders lost in a far country held there by the bones that lie unburied."

"He was taken by enemies?"

"He was not. He would have died in honor then and Heammawihio would have shown him the way. Enemies wounded him but evil spirits took him. He was with a war party that went into the land of the Crows. They went far and found many horses. They were discovered and in the fighting there were too many enemies. They fled with only the horses they rode. The enemies were between them and the way back to our own lands. They fled north and the enemies followed. They came to an evil place where the ground rises high and rough and broken into strange shapes that frighten the mind and where spirits evil beyond all others dwell. They must walk and lead the horses. He had an arrow in his thigh and could not walk well. The demons of that place marked him. They made him stumble and they seized him and dragged him over the edge of a cliff and threw him on the rocks below. The others called and he did not answer. Only the demons howled at them and the enemies were close. They fled. They slipped around the enemies and led them far away and escaped. Now his bones lie there unburied. There was not even a one to lay the body straight with the head to the east and fold the arms and cover it with a robe so that his spirit could have peace and find the right way."

"No one has gone to get the bones?"

"No one has gone."

"Yellow Moon is a great warrior. Has not Yellow Moon gone?"

"No man will go. It is beyond doing. The way lies through the land of many enemies. The bones lie where evil spirits guard them and would keep them."

"My friend. How would one know the place?"

He carried the lance and a pouch of pemmican and a bag, empty, made of old lodge skins. He moved on foot. A horse was heavy and had sharp hooves and its tracks could not be hidden except on hard rock or in the bed of a stream but a man could pick his way on foot and his tracks would be swallowed by the springy sod. Three days he was in the land of the Crows, moving through, and they did not know it. He kept to the low levels between the rolling ridges of the plain and when he must cross over the high levels he went slowly and slipped along often like a snake on his belly. He avoided the buffalo whenever he saw them, for hunting parties might be near them. Twice he circled to avoid small villages. On the fourth day he saw, rising ahead, rising abruptly out of the plain in strange twisting monstrous-shaped buttes, weather-carved and grotesque, the place where spirits evil beyond all others were said to dwell. And on the fourth day too a hunting party of Crows saw him.

There were nine of them, mounted on swift ponies. They were spread out scouting for buffalo. The first of them, the nearest, saw him against the sky when he paused on top of the last and highest ridge and his eyes looked for the first time on the evil place ahead of him and he forgot caution and stood straight staring at it. This one swung his horse and rode quickly to tell the others. Little Bear heard the sound of the hooves borne to him on the wind and he bent low from the skyline and ran. Straight for the evil place he ran, where men could not follow on horses and a lone man could dodge and twist among the strange-shaped rising rocks and find many a hollow in which to hide.

He had a long way to go, almost a mile, but the Crows were very cautious and did not hurry after him. They did not know that he was alone. They did not know that he was not a scout for some daring war party. They came slowly, ready to flee or to attack as judgment might tell them, and they watched carefully all around. When they came to where he had been, he was ahead and they could not see him. He had found and dropped into a narrow gulch that led twisting to the right and forward and he held his body low to hide his head and hurried along it. They searched over the ground. They found his tracks for in running he could not pick his way. Here and there between the grass clumps was the faint print of his moccasins. They searched and found no other tracks. They looked into the distance all around. From that high place they could see far in all directions. There was no war party. There was only the trace left by one man. They dashed forward following the faint trace of his tracks. They lost time again at the gulch. In their hurry they went past it, their horses taking it almost in stride.

They stopped and searched again over the ground. One dismounted and dropped into the gulch and saw the tracks there in the bottom sand. They shouted and dashed along the edge of the twisting way. But by then Little Bear was again far ahead. He was out of the gulch and creeping through the grasses towards the evil place that was now only a quarter of a mile ahead. He heard the shouts coming to him on the wind. He crept along like a snake and lay flat in the grasses and was very still and they rushed past behind him following the gulch. They dropped out of sight where the ground rolled downward and he jumped to his feet and ran forward. He ran leaping and striving with his breath fighting in long gasps and he was filled with a sadness for the shortness of his legs.

The rocks were ahead of him, rising in their strange and fearful formations, and behind him he heard new shouts. The Crows had swung back and now they saw him and they knew for certain that he was an enemy and that he was alone. They kicked with their heels on the sides of their ponies and leaned forward along the necks of their ponies and shouted. They raced after him and he leaped and strove with his short legs and he reached the rocks and leaped climbing and twisting upward among them and moved through the maze of their strange fearful shadows and he could leap no more and he stopped with his back against a weather-carved column of stone and held the lance ready and there was no one among the rocks with him. There was no sound of enemies climbing after him. There was only the low moaning that never ceased of the wind that blew above the plains and gnawed endlessly at the high rocks.

He crept to a jutting point of carved stone and looked back down the way he had come. He saw them. They were on the plain near the base of the rising rocks. They circled their ponies and looked up at the strange swooping heights and they talked together. They held back. They would not leave their ponies and enter the evil place. They circled and rode away over the plain. They reached the rolling ridge where they had seen him. They went out of sight down the other side.

A long time he watched from his high point and they did not appear. Not anywhere on the whole plain did they appear again, or anyone else or any living thing. They were gone and it was a vast and empty space before him and behind him climbed the strange and fearful formations of the place that must be very evil because even those in whose land it rose were afraid to enter it.

The sun was slanting down the sky. He must hurry or the night and the unnamed things that lived in the dark of such a place would have him. He must be near the spot he sought because the father of Spotted Turtle and his war party had come this way and they had not gone far into the rocks. Slowly he moved, working upward, and to the left he saw the two tall columns of stone, thick at the base and tapering and pointed and slightly curved like the horns of a giant buffalo. He moved closer and beyond was the rounded mass of rock that was like the hump of the same giant buffalo. It was as he had been told. Between the horns and the hump was where the demons had seized the wounded warrior and dragged him over the edge of a cliff and thrown him on the stones below.

In the light of the late slanting sun slicing across the strange formations and their long shadows it was not a hard way to go. Past the horns the path was rough and fell away swiftly on one side and a great crevice opened and dropped down. A man could stumble easily here and in the dark he would have no chance against the demons and the slipperiness they could put under his feet.

He crept down the swiftly falling slope to the edge of the crevice. He lay flat and peered over. It was not deep, no more than thirty feet, and the sides were jagged with many small edges and other good footholds. Compared to his canyon it was as nothing. And it was not closed in like his canyon because one end opened on through the rock and connected with another and larger crevice. But the bottom was broken by many cracks running in weird zigzags and covered by small bushes and thorny scrub growth. He lay still and studied the whole area. Nowhere could he see a sign of torn clothing or the whiteness of weather-washed bone. He laid the lance and the pouch of pemmican on the cliff top and climbed down, dropping easily from ledge to ledge. Quickly he began to search over the bottom, from crack to crack and among the bushes along the base of the cliff. There was nothing. He hurried, moving through the deepening shadows over all the bottom, and the sun sank below the horizon and it was dusk out on the plain but here in this strange and evil place it was night in the sudden swift cloaking rush of dark.

In the first moment he was afraid. Fear started him up the cliff. Fear stopped him midway where there was a ledge wide enough for a man to sit or lie without danger of falling. Here was the safest spot. It would be hard for anything or anyone to get at him from below or from above. And the demons of the place, coming forth to drink the dark night air, might not see him as he crouched close to the cliff-wall. He sat cross-legged on stone and his back rested against stone and he sat still and fought with the fear. . . .

The wind that blew above the plain moaned unceasing and grew stronger. It sent streamers through the cracks in the high rocks and these chuckled to each other with a hollow sounding. And the spirits of the place emerged like mist from their rock homes and floated in the air drinking its cool darkness and took hold of the wind and raced with it. They were not demons. They were Maiyun and their voices were like the voices of the Maiyun of the rock walls of his own canyon and they knew he was there and they knew him. "Little brother," they said, "have you found the bones of the warrior you seek?" They raced off, holding to the wind, and swirled in a mystic dance and raced back. "Little brother. Wait until the moon talks to you. . . ."

The moon was golden but its light was silver. Its light silvered the opposite edge of the crevice and crept downward. The soft luminance moved down the stone and fingered gently into a hollowed recess at the base. It was a recess that could not be seen from the cliff top because of the overhanging rock. It was recess that could not be seen from the floor of the crevice because of the clumped thick bushes in front. It could be seen from the ledge midway on the cliff as the slanting light of the moon slipped in. It was a hidden recess into which a wolf could drag the body of a dead warrior for a feasting on the flesh. And the light of the moon, slipping in, shone softly on the pale wan whiteness of bones. . . .

In the darkness after moonset Little Bear, the strange one, the different one, moved out from the base of the climbing rocks on to the open plain. He carried the lance and the pemmican pouch and the bag made of old lodge skins. The pemmican pouch was almost empty but the lodge-skin bag was heavy with the bones of a Cheyenne warrior that had lain unburied in the land of the Crows. He moved cautiously for this was where the hunting party had pursued him and the Crows were clever and relentless enemies. He moved a short distance and waited and listened. He moved again and he waited again and listened. There was no sound. He found a small stone the size of his fist and threw it as far as he could to one side and heard it land thumping softly on the sod. He listened. He heard a prairie owl hoot not far from where the stone had fallen and another answer on the other side and another in the distance and yet another. Instantly he turned and ran. He ran straight again for the climbing rocks and behind him and gathering to come after him he heard other feet running, many of them. He reached the rocks and leaped and strove up among them and this time he heard the feet following on the hard footing. They were close behind him. They would not let him escape now that they were so near. The bag was heavy and he groaned at the shortness of his legs and they were gaining. Desperately he leaped and he stumbled and fell and the bag slipped from his grasp and the lance went clattering and he rolled and caught himself and crawled quickly into a deeper pocket of darkness among the rocks.

He heard them searching. He heard them poking into the black pockets with their lances and working toward him. He remembered. A Cheyenne did not die like a prairie dog crouched in terror in its hole. A Cheyenne died fighting and his face was toward the enemies he fought. And he remembered again. He had done as his father had told him. His legs were short like the legs of the badger and not for fast running. But in his arms was the strength of the grizzly from many long weeks of climbing a rock wall and chipping hard stone upon stone.

They were almost upon him. He sprang forth to meet them. In his arms was the strength of the great grizzly bear and the laughter of his brave father was in his mouth. "Oh Maiyun of these rocks," he cried, "let us fight!" He brushed aside the lance of the first of the enemies as if it were the play fire-stick of a child. He seized the first of the enemies in his arms and he raised that one off the ground and threw him mightily among the others and they scattered and he sprang among them and struck one to the right of him and one to the left of him and he sprang back and waited for them to come.

But they did not come.

They were confused in the dark and afraid. They spoke to one another and the fear was plain in their voices. "This is one," they said, "who laughs when he is alone against many." They stepped backward. "This is one," they said, "who calls upon the spirits to fight with him." They stepped back farther and were more afraid. "This is a demon," they said, "who has taken the form of an enemy to draw us into the evil place to our deaths." They turned and ran. They did not stop until they reached their horses tied to pegs in a hollow of the plain. They mounted and rode swiftly away and the tale they would tell grew large in their minds as they rode. . . .

Little Bear came to the village from the west. The sun was settling toward the horizon behind him. He was tired and the lodge-skin bag was very heavy. He did not go around the village to come in through the entrance on the east. He went straight between two lodges on the west and into the open space of the central circle. He did not look to one side or the other. He went past the lodge of Yellow Moon and did not turn his head to see Spotted Turtle in the entrance watching him. He went past the sacred lodges of the medicine arrows and of the buffalo hat. He went straight to the lodge of White Wolf.

There was silence in the lodge when he entered. He hung the lance by a leather thong on a lodgepole. He laid the bag on the ground. The wife of White Wolf took her cooking things and left the lodge. White Wolf had seen him coming and the pipe was ready. They sat side by side on the couch of White Wolf. They passed the pipe.

"My friend. Will you speak for me once more? In the bag are my presents?"

A great wailing came from the lodge of Yellow Moon. The mother of Yellow Moon and of Spotted Turtle mourned over the bones of her man and women came from other lodges and wailed with her. As they wailed they made the burial preparations. They laid the bones out in correct order on a fine buffalo robe. They laid over them the finest of clothing. They folded the robe over from both sides until it was a long bundle and they wrapped ropes around it. They carried the bundle out of the lodge and fastened it on a travois of poles behind a fine horse.

The procession moved out of the village in the evening dusk and everyone who could walk moved with it. The mother of Yellow Moon and of Spotted Turtle led the fine horse pulling the travois. Yellow Moon walked behind the travois carrying weapons that had been favorites of his father. Spotted Turtle walked beside him carrying the pipes her father had liked best and a pouch of fragrant tobacco well mixed with powdered bark of the red willow. Behind him came the people of the village and among them, already saying the words over in his mind, was the old man who had been named to sing the death song. It would be one of the ancient death songs handed down from the forefathers and he would add special mention of the man being buried. And behind all these walked Little Bear, holding back a bit as a visitor should. He walked solemnly carrying the lance upright as a warrior should walk to the burial of another brave warrior.

All morning and most of the afternoon the women of the lodge of Yellow Moon worked with their sewing things. All morning and most of the afternoon the wife of White Wolf and her married daughter and the members of her sewing guild worked in the lodge of White Wolf. They worked hard for the time was short. One night had passed since the presents, strange presents from the strange one but presents that made a mighty tale for the village to claim, had been taken to the lodge of Yellow Moon. The answer must be given before another night passed for that was the custom. There could be no question what the answer would be. The presents had been accepted.

White Wolf and Little Bear sat cross-legged in front of the lodge they shared and passed the pipe. There was a great commotion in the village, people moving about and horses being led here and there and much shouting and laughter, but they paid no attention to all this. They passed the pipe and the feeling of a man for a man was between them.

The commotion increased and the shouts rose higher and then there was quiet. A procession moved across the center circle of the village. It started by the lodge of Yellow Moon where Yellow Moon himself sat alone on his couch with his breast full of peace that the spirit of his father was treading the path where all footprints point the same way and his mind full of pride at what he was having done for the sister who was close to his heart. It was a big procession. In the lead was the father-in-law of Yellow Moon. He walked with head high for he had fine words to speak. Behind him was Spotted Turtle. She was dressed in new clothes of soft deerskin well decorated with beads made of the bright stones found along the river called Niobrara and with quills of the porcupine stained with many colors. She rode on a fine horse led as was right by a woman who was not related to her. Behind her came other women carrying armloads of well-worked buffalo robes and stout weapons. And behind them came yet more women leading many fine horses, fifteen of them, black and bay and chestnut and white-spotted, and all of these wore bridles of strong braided rawhide. And behind again came the other people of the village and they spread out fanlike around the procession as it stopped in front of White Wolf and Little Bear. And among the people thus spread out was the mother of Spotted Turtle. Her legs were no longer bare. There were no new gashes on them under the leggings. She did not push forward among the people. She wore a robe and held it up so that it covered her face all but her eyes. It was not right that a new son-in-law should look upon the mother of his wife face-to-face or speak to her until time had passed and they had exchanged special gifts after the marriage. That too was according to custom.

The father-in-law of Yellow Moon stepped forward. He did not speak to Little Bear. He addressed himself only to White Wolf.

"It is Yellow Moon who speaks. Not if he sent all the horses that roam the wide plains to the edges of the earth, not if he sent weapons and robes to fill a big lodge, could he match the presents he has received. But he does what it is his to do. When the sun has risen tomorrow a lodge made of new skins of the cow buffalo will be raised for the man called Little Bear and the woman who is his wife. It will contain all things needful. She is here to be given to him. With her are these robes and these weapons and these horses. Yellow Moon has spoken."

The wife of White Wolf and her married daughter came out of the lodge and spread a robe upon the ground. They lifted Spotted Turtle from the fine horse and placed her so that she sat in the middle of the robe. Young men of the village pushed forward. They jostled each other for the honor of taking hold of the robe. They lifted it and Spotted Turtle upon it and carried it into the lodge and lowered it carefully to the ground. They came out laughing and looking at Little Bear with sidelong glances and the feeling of young men for another young man was in their glances. And the wife of White Wolf and her daughter went back into the lodge and took Spotted Turtle by the hands and lifted her to her feet and led her to the rear of the lodge. She stood quietly while they took from her the clothing that she wore. They dressed her in the new clothing they too had made. They unbraided her hair and combed it and rebraided it. They put upon her new ornaments, rings for her fingers and beaded hoops for her ears.

Outside the lodge the young men leaped and laughed and made jokes.

The older people watched and wondered what Little Bear would do with the fine gifts spread before him. He rose and stood as tall as he could on his short legs like the legs of a badger. He looked at the gifts and he was very proud. He looked at White Wolf. He spoke. "My friend. You have been to me as a father in this. Your wife has been as a mother. Your daughter has been as a sister. The gifts are yours." And there was much shouting among the people. What Little Bear had done was right because White Wolf had been as a father. It was generous too because White Wolf was not the real father. And White Wolf called his wife and daughter out of the lodge and the husband of his daughter from among the people and the parents of the husband of his daughter and the old man who was his cousin. He told them to choose and they divided the presents according to custom. And inside the lodge Spotted Turtle heard and her heart was filled with a happiness that her man was generous as well as brave. . . .

The food had been prepared. Spotted Turtle still sat at the rear of the lodge and Little Bear sat beside her. The wife of White Wolf put food in bowls for them. She cut the food for Spotted Turtle in small pieces so that Spotted Turtle would need to make no effort in eating. This night she must do no work.

Much food had been prepared. There was need for that.

The young men of the village came visiting. One came and another and then more and the lodge was crowded. They ate the food. They laughed and made jokes and talked in loud voices. They were showing Little Bear that they were his friends and they were glad he had obtained the woman he wanted. Some of them might even stay the whole night and sleep there in the lodge. But White Wolf was a man of experience. When the food was gone and the talking was not so loud, he rose to his feet. "My friends," he said. "It grieves me that my lodge is small. I have no couches to offer you." His face was sad but his eyes were bright and twinkling and the young men understood. They could stay and sleep on the ground and be there for the morning meal which would be the first meal Spotted Turtle would prepare as a wife and that would be in accord with a custom. But they understood. They rose too. They laughed more and jostled one another with their elbows and looked sidelong at Little Bear and Spotted Turtle. They left the lodge still laughing and jostling. They were good young men. They were fine friends.

White Wolf spoke then to his wife. "My woman," he said. "It is long since we walked together in the night and remembered when we were young and my left arm was as the arm of other men." He went to the lodge entrance and looked back. Words rushed to the lips of Little Bear. "Oh White Wolf. I must hunt now for the lodge of Yellow Moon and for the lodge that will be my own. But one quarter of each buffalo I kill will be yours." And White Wolf spoke. "There is no need of meat. You have honored my lodge." He went out into the night and his wife went after him and she paused in the entrance to look back and to unfasten the door-skin so that it fell and covered the opening.

Little Bear and Spotted Turtle were alone in the lodge. They could not look at one another. They tried and always their eyes turned away. He rose to his feet and stirred the fire with a small stick. He was shy and afraid again and he did not know what to say. He lay down on the couch that had a new covering spread over it. When he turned his head he could see her at the rear of the lodge. She was standing up and laying aside her robe. She was shy too and afraid and could not speak. She was very beautiful to him in the firelight and his heart beat in a strong rhythm in his breast. He looked at her and she was wearing a protective rope, the rope that all unmarried women wore at night and when they went abroad, the rope that all decent women wore when their men were away from the home village, the rope that meant no man worthy of being in the tribe would approach them in the way he should not. It was a small woven rope that went around the waist and was knotted in front and the two ends were carried down and passed between the thighs and wound around them to the knees. A newly married woman could wear such a rope even with her husband for ten days after the marriage and the husband, if he were a good husband, would respect it for that long. Spotted Turtle was wearing such a rope. Her hands rested on the knot and were still. She looked at him and her thoughts were plain on her face. It was her right for now to decide what would be done. Yet she would not claim that right. She was shy and she was afraid and yet she would let him decide. She was very beautiful to him and he could speak. "Oh Spotted Turtle, I am afraid of the newness as you are afraid. It is enough that you lie on the couch with me and we grow accustomed to being together in the night." She came to the couch and lay beside him and he pulled the new covering over them. He put his arms about her and was still. Slowly the stiffness went out of her body and she was quiet and relaxed beside him. Their voices were low as they talked in the darkness and the newness of being together. . . .

It was the third night in their own lodge, the fourth night of their marriage. He had hunted well and sent much meat to his mother-in-law and to the wife of White Wolf. He lay on the couch and watched his woman. She had cooked a big stew of meat and of *pommes blanches* and of turnips and Yellow Moon had eaten with them and pronounced it good. She was preparing now for the sleeping. She held the protective rope in her hand. She let it slip through her fingers and fall to the ground. She came and stood by the couch. "It is my wish," she said.

He hunted. Never was such hunting known in that village. He laughed and he shouted. Never did a man laugh better or shout louder at the life leaping in his blood. He wrestled with the other men and as he stood firmly on his short legs and strove with the strength in his arms no man could throw him. He rode the painted pony in the village races. Never did a man ride more recklessly and care less whether he lost or won as long as there was the wind of the running in his face and his woman was watching him ride. He hunted and laughed and played and loved and life was very good. . . .

Life is not all hunting and laughing and playing and loving. . . .

The old crier called out the names. The name of Little Bear was among them. At the appointed time he entered the lodge of Yellow Moon. He wore the fine robe that the mother of Yellow Moon, who was his mother-in-law, had made for him and that he had accepted in the ceremony of the purifying smoke of the sweet grasses. There was no laughter in his mouth. He sat in the place pointed out to him. It was first at the left of Yellow Moon, the place of most honor. Food was offered him and he ate as all the men in the lodge ate. He finished and they finished and they all wiped their hands.

Yellow Moon brought forth his ceremonial pipe. He filled it with tobacco well mixed with powdered red willow bark. He placed a pinch of powdered buffalo chip on top of the tobacco in the pipe for that was the custom of his tribal division. He held the pipe vertical, stem up, before him. "My friends. My father died in the land of the Crows. The war party he led there brought back no horses. It is in my mind now to lead a war party against the Crows and take many horses. I ask if you will go with me."

Yellow Moon pointed with the pipestem to the sky above where He-ammawihio dwells and to the earth beneath where the Maiyun move and to the four cardinal directions around. He lit the pipe and smoked. He passed the pipe to Little Bear in the place of most honor at his left.

Little Bear held the pipe upright in his hand according to custom. He sat still and looked at the ground. He had not raised his eyes since the pipe was brought forth. He did not raise them now. He was filled with a great sadness. His breath left his chest in what might have been a sigh. He passed the pipe unsmoked. . . .

—He is a strange one, a different one, and I do not like the strangeness and the difference. He is my brother-in-law and I grieve for what I have done to my sister. He is the reason that I have few horses, that my lodge is bare of many things that before were in it. Yet that could be changed. He is a mighty hunter. He is a good warrior. He can slip through the land of enemies like a shadow that is not seen. He can fight like the great grizzly when there is need. He could smoke and the others would see and would smoke after him. Yet he passes the pipe unsmoked. He is only the half of a man. I will not enter his lodge again—What shall we believe? He says that he crossed the land of the Crows, that he entered the evil place, that the bones are the bones of the father of Yellow Moon. He told this to White Wolf and the tale belongs to White Wolf and White Wolf has told it to us many times. It is a good tale that brings honor to our village. When he told it to White Wolf, he rubbed his hand over the pipe as he talked. He pointed to the lodge of the medicine arrows. He said: "Oh arrows, you hear me; I did these things." A man who does that cannot lie. And yet . . . And yet he passes the war pipe unsmoked. We will listen to the tale no more—

"Oh badger of my far canyon, I have not forgotten you. . . . Oh Maiyun of the walls of the cage that is a good cage, you call to me out of the hills over the wide plain. . . . Oh young bull now the old bull eating the good grasses by our stream, there is peace in that place that is ours where no man would know to follow. . . ."

". . . But Yellow Moon is my brother. He is your brother-in-law. There was between you the feeling of a man for a man and you have killed it."

"Oh my woman, you heard. You were by the lodge of the old one preparing soups and you heard him speak. It is not right that a man do what his heart tells him is wrong."

"I heard but I do not understand. Why must your heart tell you to go crosswise to the customs of your people? To go forth with a war party is hard. But it is the way a man wins honor for himself and for his family?"

"It is not my way. My heart speaks and I do not have words to say why. But one man cannot change a tribe or even a village. I will leave this village. I will go."

"And where will you go? Always there are villages. Always they are the same. A foolishness has taken you. It is the moon that has shone too long in your eyes and your mind has—"

"Stop, my woman, I grieve as you grieve. But I will go to a place that is mine, that the spirit of the old one who was your great-grandfather led me to in the time of my starving. There is food enough in that place and for always. There is a fine stream that does not wither away in the warm weather. There is shelter from the storms of winter. It is a place where no enemies can come to harm one or to take what is not theirs. It is a good place. It is my place and I will go. But there will be no light in my life if you do not go with me."

"Will that put laughter again in the mouth of my husband?"

"It will put laughter in my mouth."

"Will it make his eyes bright again and shining on me and all about him?"

"It will make them bright and shining."

"Will it keep him always reaching for me with eagerness and the crushing strength of his arms in the night?"

"It will do that."

"I will go. . . ."

5

The high border country endures. It endures the slow creeping change of geologic time and the cluttering surface change of man's calendared time. It rests remote and untroubled in itself, the land of high plains and high mountains that nourish the long reaching rivers which unite their waters to form the wide Missouri. There is the trail that Little Bear followed, westward along the Cheyenne River and swinging north and still west along the north fork that is known as La Belle Fourche. The trail strikes southward along one of the feeding streams and climbs up its course into the Black Hills that are not black and are not hills but sturdy mountains. It leads to the rock lip of his canyon.

The canyon was a good place then. It is a good place now. It is out of the way of the roads cutting through the hills and the towns hugging the low levels or hanging on the high hillsides. It is little changed. It rests quietly under the same sky and the four seasons pass over it in the same unending cycle.

It was not entered by the Sioux and their allies of other tribes when they retreated into these hills before the encroaching whitemen. It would have been a trap for them caught there under the searching guns of any enemies who might come.

It was not troubled by the miners when they came back into these hills. It does not show the terrible scars of the earth digging and the rock blasting they brought with them. Its stream, where easily accessible above and below, showed no traces and they passed by it.

No buffalo are there now. The last of them were killed long ago by the hide hunters, the whitemen hunters who erased the myriad-hoofed herds of the plains for the hides alone and left the carcasses to rot, who followed the remnants into the hills and who shot those in the canyon from the rock lip for the simple sport of the shooting and did not even take the hides because to get to them down the rock wall even with ropes and many men helping was not to them worth the trouble.

The long blunted triangle of the canyon endures. It can be seen in clear outline from the rock lip where the niches in the rock wall that the hide hunters did not see lead upward—and lead downward. It is a good place. The stream drops into the pool below through a rainbowed halo of mist and runs cold and clear to its fissure at the lower end. Trees group in groves in the lee of the high cliffs. Elders make a brave showing along the stream and aspen grows there too. Berry bushes nod their long briared stems among upthrust rocks. And everywhere in the open the good grasses grow. It is a good place for a man whose needs are simple, for a man who is like his fellows yet not like them, who would live apart from them because he differs in vision of purpose for the brief mystery of the life that is his. . . .

That is where Little Bear and Spotted Turtle were.

They are there. They are standing on the rock lip where the niches lead downward. They have turned loose into the freedom of the hills and the plains beyond the painted pony that has pulled a travois with their things upon it all the long way through many days. They are wrapping their things into a bundle in their lodge skins and trying this with a rope so that it can be let down from ledge to ledge. He is tying another rope around her waist and holding the other end so that she can go down the same way and be kept safe by the strength in his arms. . . .

He helped her with the lodge. She was a woman and she would do nothing else until the home was up and ready for the first night's sleeping. He cut new poles, long and strong because their lodge was large. They set these firmly for the conical structure that was not quite a cone because the poles on the westward curve opposite the entrance always leaned less and stood straighter so that they could brace against the others and withstand the winds of the plains that always blew hardest on that side. They stretched the skins and fastened them firmly. But she would not let him help her with the inside work. It was a woman's right to have things placed in the lodge as she wished within the limits of tribal custom. She would not even let him make the fire. It was a woman's right to kindle the flames that would cook the food and warm the lodge.

He watched his woman bustling in and out as she pinned up the softer skins of the lodge lining and stood with puckered lips wondering where to put this and where to hang that. She was not beautiful but there was a warm wisdom and an understanding on her face and she was beautiful to him and she was very womanly. He watched her and the clean air of his canyon filled his lungs and he turned and walked down along the stream. There were still fish in the clear water where it deepened and slowed in shallow pools. If a man were not greedy in catching them, there would always be fish in his stream.

The tracks of the buffalo were many among the bushes around their pool-for-splashing. And there were the buffalo themselves, farther down where the good grasses grew best. He counted them. The old bull that had been the young bull; the young bull that had been a yearling; two old cows; one young cow that had been a yearling; the five calves that had been small and were now growing yearlings and four new calves, small and frisky and pestering their mothers for milk. Thirteen in all. Those that had been there when he left were all there except two of the old cows. They had been very old. The winter must have been too hard and too long for them. And yet four calves jumped stiff-legged and butted each other and ran about. The young cow had one. It was her first and not very big but she would do better. One of the old cows had another. And the second old cow had two. It was the same old cow as before. She was a very good cow.

The old bull who had been the young bull was bigger than before. It had its full growth now. Its hump was a mighty hump. Its mane that covered its neck and shoulders and front legs was thick and long. The scars on its head were almost hidden by the hairs. It was a good leader for a good herd. And the young bull who had been a yearling was bigger too. It was growing fast on the strength of the good grasses. There would be a battle one day when it felt it was big enough to challenge the old bull. It would lose, but it would challenge again and yet again as it grew and a day would come when it would not lose. Perhaps before that day came the old bull should be taken for meat. It would never have to know then the feeling of being beaten by age and a younger bull. And its meat would be better if it were not too old. A man and his woman could live well around the four seasons taking no more than four buffalo and perhaps five and there would always be buffalo in their canyon.

He came back along the base of the near rock wall. He went in among the berry bushes where the upthrust rocks were. He found the flat stone and sat cross-legged in front of it. "Oh badger," he said. "I have come home." He waited and there was nothing. He waited and suddenly out of nowhere the dark brown head with its long white stripe appeared over the stone. The badger climbed on the stone and looked at him and it was angry. It was very thin and tired. It was an old badger and life was hard for an old badger caged in a canyon with no fat easily caught gophers and prairie dogs for fine meals. It must hunt long for the field mice that were difficult to catch and perhaps once in a long time a rabbit foolishly hiding in a burrow and once in a very long time a rock squirrel that found a way down the rock walls. It must even eat beetles and other insects and gnaw on roots and the bark of trees. It looked at him and was angry. There was no meat on the stone. It flirked its broad flat body and was gone. But he was happy. The badger was still there in his canyon. "Oh badger," he said. "There will be meat. Every day there will be meat. You will forget to be angry with me and you will talk to me again."

He stood up. Over the bushes he saw smoke rising by the stream. His woman was there and his lodge. She was cooking food that he had provided. And around them rose the high rock walls that set their canyon apart and made a shield and a protection. He was filled with a great peace. The clean air swelled his breast almost to bursting.

He hurried to the place where he had piled the stones in a rough steep-slanting walkway up to the first ledge. That was the connection between the floor of the canyon and the ladder of niches above. That was what made the place a way for one to climb up or to climb down. He started at the top of the slant and began to work downward, throwing and heaving the stones to the one side and to the other side. They bounced and rolled this way and that way and the slanting walkway began to dwindle and drop away under his feet. The smooth rock wall with no niches from the floor of the canyon to the ledge rose behind him.

He heard his woman calling to him. When food was ready she would not wait as most women waited for their men to come when they wished to come and eat. When food was ready, she called and he came. He had seen the smoke of the fire that would be a cooking fire and had known that the food would be ready soon. But he had waited for her to call. He liked to hear her call him. And he liked to go to her when she called. After they had eaten he would take her by the hand and walk with her and show her this cage that was a good cage.

"Is this where you killed the old bull? Is this the tree where you tied the rope made of strips of your shirt and your leggings? Do not tell me of it again now. I do not like to think of you hopping on one foot with the bone of your right leg broken. . . ."

"Is this where the young bull who is the old bull now fought the big puma all through the night and long into the morning? He is a brave bull. The scars on his head are signs of honor. He is our bull. But do not say that he shamed you. You were afraid yet you were out on the snow with your bow and your knife and you were not too late. . . ."

"Is this the shelter where you slept alone? It is the shelter a man would make, small and dark inside, out of the sun, with no things of comfort in it."

"It is the shelter where I slept but I was not alone. It is where you came to me in my dream."

"That is foolish talk. I did not come. I was far away in the village. . . . But it is good talk and I like to hear it. And it is a good shelter for even in its dimness I can see your eyes bright again and shining on me. . . ."

The quiet dark was over the canyon. In the lodge the firelight flickered low. He lay on the couch and watched his woman. She finished placing their things for the third time. She looked at him and away and a smile was on her lips. She came to the couch and lay beside him. He took her in his arms gently and then fiercely and it was good for them both. They lay still. The winds of night lifted out of the hills and blew over the high plateau. They sent exploring streamers through the cracks along the rock edges and these chuckled to one another with a soft hollow sounding. And the Maiyun of the rocks floated out like a mist and took hold of the winds and rode laughing through the upper air and he heard them and lay still and he laughed with them, soft and deep in his throat and with the same tone.

"Oh my Spotted Turtle. Listen. The Maiyun are talking."

"It is only the wind that I hear. But it is good to have laughter again in the mouth of my husband."

"Listen. They are talking to me."

"I hear what could be voices but I do not understand them. What are they saying?"

"They say: Little brother, you are home again. You have brought us a little sister. It is well."

And the Maiyun raced on the winds down the canyon and danced in the upper air and raced back and laughed softly among themselves.

"I hear the voices again but still I do not understand. What is it they say now?"

"They say: Little brother, the woman who is your woman is better than any woman in a dream. She is lovely as the light that slips over the edge of the world in the first glow of morning. She is warm as the summer sun when it is full overhead. She is comforting as the good sleep that comes in the night after a hard day of hunting."

"That is foolish talk. They would not say that. . . . But it is good talk. Tell me more of what you say they say. . . ."

It was autumn. He picked the wild plums and she stoned and dried them for the winter. He gathered quantities of the plentiful chokeberries and sarvissberries and she pounded them fine on a hollowed stone and made them into flat cakes and dried these for the cold weather. He gathered buffalo berries, which were not so many, and the wild grapes, which were few, and she prepared them too. These and other things helped fill the storehouse, which already held much meat from the old cow, not the cow that had twins, and one of the yearlings, a small bull, which he had taken from the herd. She worked on the hides, which was woman's work and which she would not let him do now that she was there, and he walked his canyon and sat cross-legged in the sun and the badger talked to him.

He sat quiet on this day and she left her work and came to him. The badger would stay when she came if she moved slowly, but it would not talk when she was there. She came slowly on this day and she had a small secret smile on her lips. "Oh Little Bear, my husband with the strong arms, you must take for us one of the calves, one of the very young spring calves."

"Why must I do that? We have meat. The calf will grow and be stronger and heavier when more seasons have passed."

"That is no matter now. I must make a small robe of the young tender skin. I am certain at last. We will have a child when the winter snows have melted and the trees begin to bud." She stood straight and proud for within her she was doing what a woman alone could do and what made her as important as a man in the home circle of the lodge.

He leaped to his feet and the badger flicked its broad flat body and was gone in a flickering of gray-brown fur. He leaped upon the flat stone. He laughed and shouted. "It will be a boy! It will have long legs and strong for fast running! It will be a son and I will be a father and there will be fine feeling between us!" He stood on the flat stone and looked at her. "Perhaps it will be a girl. It will be light and dainty on its feet as a young deer. It will grow warm and womanly like the mother. . . ."

The winter was kind. Snow fell and dwindled slowly on the ground and fell again. It was never so deep and hard-crusted that the buffalo could not feed. Storms passed overhead. They whipped through the hills but they did not whip down into the canyon. It was warm in the lodge with the snow banked outside and the slow fire always burning inside. He gathered buffalo chips when the ground was almost bare and fallen branches of the trees when the snow was there. That was woman's work but he would not let her do it. And when she had difficult times because she was carrying her first child, he did other work of a woman too. He cooked food, stews and soups made of nourishing meat and other things from their storehouse. He cleaned the bowls after the eating. But when he tried to put things back in their right places and to sweep the floor, she laughed at him and chased him outside with his snowshoes and did these herself. And sometimes at night when she could not sleep he leaned up beside her on one elbow and passed his other hand softly over her forehead again and again and told her what the Maiyun were saying high overhead in the upper air. And she was proud of it all, of the difficult times as of the easy times, for it was all part of what she was doing.

Yet when the winter was old and the snow dwindled on the ground and did not fall again and the first faint flush of green ran tracing along the bushes, she became very quiet. This was the time when she should be talking long with the old women of the village and there were no old women for any talking. This was the time when she should be asking the younger women of her choice to be ready to help her when the child came and there were no younger women to be asked. She was very quiet and there were long periods when she would not speak and when she did speak she was irritable and her voice snapped. Sometimes she shut her face against him as if he were not there. He saw all this and was troubled. He did even more of a woman's work and that was wrong because it made her remember that there was no mother or mother-in-law or woman cousin to help her do her work in her home at this time and she was even more irritable and spoke sharply to him.

He made a cradle, padded with moss under the lining, and she looked at it and looked away and said nothing. A cradle should be made by a woman who has had children, by a woman relative of the father-to-be or, if not, by a woman relative of the mother.

He made all things ready and kept them ready; the bowl in which the child would be washed and beside it the knife to cut the cord, the small soft robe in which the child would be wrapped and the pouch of powder from the prairie puffball which would be used to keep the tender skin of the inside of its small legs from chafing. She saw him arranging and constantly rearranging the things and her face opened and she smiled at him and told him how to find the right bark and to make the medicine that would ease the delivery for her. But when he did this her face closed again, for she remembered that such medicine made by a man was not as strong as that made by a woman who had borne children.

Yet when her time came, he was the one who was afraid and she was the one who spoke the cheerful words. The sweat ran down his face as if the pains were his and she had to tell him what to do and he was so startled at the first cries of the small one that he fumbled when he tried to wrap it in the soft robe and she had to make him lay it beside her so she could do the wrapping and it was a boy-child, small and well formed with legs that would be long and strong for fast running. . . .

The spring was not kind. It was chill and damp. Rain fell and did not stop for many days. The stream swelled and the ground was very wet. Only by making a ditch around the lodge and leading away could Little Bear keep the water from working under the lodge skins. When there was no rain, fog rolled down the mountains at night and into the canyon and fought long with the sun in the mornings. The smoke of the fire in the lodge would not rise as it should out the smoke hole. Only by hanging their robes on ropes close to the fire could Spotted Turtle keep the dampness out of them. And then their little-slim-person, their small-fuzzy-one, their Little Fox, caught a cough that would not leave him.

Spotted Turtle gave him tiny drops of tea made from the elk mint that was said to be good for lungs sore from much coughing. That did not help. She hurried all through the canyon and at last found a plant of the red medicine weed and rubbed the leaves to a powder and boiled this in water for many hours to make the thin syrup that was said to loosen and drive away a cough that lasted long. She gave him tiny drops of the thin syrup and it did not help. She did not know what else to do and Little Bear too did not know. She kept the small one warm and nursed him when he would eat but he would eat only a little and after a time none at all. He was very weak and very sick.

She would not leave the small one for a moment. She held him in her arms and rocked him in them and leaned her head over him and nothing would stop the coughing. It was a small sound with no strength in it yet it filled the lodge with a big fear. It beat at the ears of Little Bear and he did what he could. He put more wood on the fire and blew upon it and forced it to burn better and send its warmth through the lodge. He made a soup, strong and savory, and took some to her and she would not eat. He put some in his own mouth and it was good soup but the taste was bitter in his mouth and he too could not eat. The coughing was very feeble and still it beat at his ears and he stepped out of the lodge into the night. Clouds covered the ragged crescent of the halfmoon and the night was very dark. He stared into the blackness and then he walked. Back and forth he walked in front of the lodge and black thoughts whirled in his mind. If he could see this sickness, then he could fight it. He would let it tear at his own body with coughings worse than the tearings of the claws of the big puma so that he could be close to it and drive the knife into its evil life-center. How could a man fight what he could not see? Back and forth he walked and the black thoughts whirled in his mind.

He stopped. There was no sound anywhere. He stepped into the lodge. In the dimness of the fading fire he saw her sitting as she had been sitting. She was not rocking the small bundle in her arms. There was no sound of coughing, of a small throat struggling for breath. There was no sound at all.

He tried to speak and he could not. There were no words. He went to her and sat beside her and she rose and went with her still bundle to the other side of the lodge and sat there. He did not follow. He sat still. He was empty of words and it was as if he was empty of all feeling. His head sank down as hers was down and they sat very still and the fire faded to embers and these flickered out and it was as dark in the lodge as in the night outside. . . .

In the first light of the dawning he lifted his head. His neck was stiff but he did not notice that because his mind was stiff too with strange thoughts and these hurt him. Across the lodge she sat as before but her head too was up and she was looking at him. Her face was closed against him. It was a mask that meant nothing and she was withdrawn behind it. She looked away. She rose to her knees and laid the small bundle on the ground before her and began to prepare it for burial. She acted as if he were not there in the lodge with her. He went to her to help and she turned from him and there was nothing that he could do but stand and watch her.

When she finished and stood upright with the small bundle ready in her arms, it was still as if she were alone in the lodge and he was not there. He stepped in front of her. "I am the father." Her face closed but she looked at him and after a moment she reached and laid her small burden in his arms. He waited while she gathered together the things that had been for the small one and he led the way out. He stood in front of the lodge and she stood behind him and he looked about. All around his canyon he looked and chose the place. On the far rock wall at about the height of a man's head was a short ledge with a depression behind it forming a shallow cave. It was a good place and the right size. He went there and she followed. He laid the small bundle on the ledge, inside the cave. Carefully he pointed it eastward towards the rising sun. He took the things that had been the things of the small one from her and laid them about the bundle. And a fresh sadness gripped him. There was no painted pony to be killed by the grave so that the spirit of the small one could ride the spirit of the pony and travel fast along the path where all footprints go the same way. There was no old man of the tribe to sing a death song passed down from the forefathers to cheer the small spirit on the path. There was only a grieving father who could not speak and behind him yet not with him a grieving mother who could not speak. . . .

He sat cross-legged on the ground before the lodge and smoked the pipe and it brought no peace. The grief was great in him but there were no words for it. She was in the lodge and her face was closed against him and he could not be where she was. He heard her moving about. She came out and went past him and it was as if he were not there. She was looking for something. She found it, his axe, the axe with the sharpened stone head and the stout wooden handle, where he had left it when he had broken branches for the fire. She went past him again with it in her hand and into the lodge. And yet another sadness was upon him for he knew what she would do and he could not stop her. He could take the axe from her and she would find another way and wait until he was not near and watching. And he must not stop her, for it was according to custom.

He waited. He heard the dull sound of the axe falling and cutting and hitting against stone. He waited. She did not want him near. But he could not wait longer. He stood in the lodge entrance. She had stopped the blood and was bandaging the stump of the middle finger of her left hand which was cut off now at the first joint. The grief and the many sadnesses swelled in him but her face was a mask, hard against him, and he could not go to her. A man must not cut off a finger to show his grief. A man needed strong hands for hunting and fighting. He ripped off his shirt. His right hand took the knife from the sheath on his thigh. He drew the blade across his chest once and then twice, cutting through the skin and into the flesh. The bright blood ran in rivulets downward.

She saw his blood running in bright rivulets downward. Her face opened toward him.

He could not speak. It was not his grief he spoke. The running blood spoke that for him. It was the bitterness growing from his thoughts. "If there had been other women here, they would have known what to do." It was the bitterness and the sadness. "If there had been a man skilled in medicines, he would have known what to do. . . ."

And Little Bear, the strange one, the different one, went forth into his canyon. He walked along his stream and saw his fish in the shallow pools. He saw his buffalo eating the good grasses. He saw the high protective rock walls of his canyon marching around him. "My mind has lived too long in the light of the moon of the night. Let it be in the light of the sun of the day."

—A man comes into a canyon and makes it his own. With the cunning of his mind and the courage of his heart he makes it his own. With one leg of bone and one leg of wood he kills the mighty buffalo and he has what he needs for food and clothing and shelter. He keeps the canyon his own when he kills the evil one that would despoil it, the blood-drinking one of the mountains. It is his and he has made it so. But he has not done this alone. . . . In his hand is a knife that was made far away by another man, a knife that was given to him by an old one, a great one. In his mind is the knowledge to make fire and weapons and clothing and to find food and to provide shelter, knowledge given to him by those who taught him when he was a boy and those who showed him by their own doing when he lived among them. By himself he is nothing. Only the courage is his alone. All of those others are with him, even in his canyon, and he cannot ever be free of them for what they have given is with him and is part of him and without them he could not have made the canyon his own—

—A man brings a woman into his canyon. That is good. That is what makes complete the goodness of the place for him. She misses the talking with other women, the gossip of the village, the dances of the younger people, the advice and storytelling of the older people, the companionship of the relatives who are close to her heart. For him she will miss those things. She will not talk about the missing and she will try not to let him know about the missing. But it is there. . . . She has a child. She has it alone with only a fumbling man to help her. The child is taken with a sickness. It does not have the care that old women of experience or an old man skilled in medicines could give. It dies. Perhaps that is as Heammawihio, the Wise One Above, meant it should be and no care could save the child. But how can one be certain of such a thing? . . . There can be another child. It can live and be healthy and grow. It is a boy. Who is there to count a coup for it and pierce its ears? It has long legs and strong for fast running. Where are the other boys with whom it will play? Where are the old men to tell it tales of the old days of the tribe and the things it is needful to do? It grows and is troubled in its mind. Where is an old one, a great one, who can direct it in the test of a starving? It grows and the urging of a man begins in it. Where is a maiden who will look with favor on it when it waits in the dusk of the evening and plucks at her robe? . . . It is a girl. Where is the grandmother or other old woman to take the place of the grandmother and teach it the things a girl-child must be taught? Where are the other girls with whom it will play and make the endless girl-talk and practice the cutting of moccasins and the sewing of beads and of quills? Where is the young man on whom she will look with favor and for whom she will sit quiet and speak no objections while the father considers the presents the young man has sent and what is good for the daughter who is close to his heart?—

—What was it the old one meant with his words? A man must be certain that his heart speaks truth to him. . . . One man cannot change a tribe. But one man can live with a tribe and not let it change him too much—

And Little Bear, the strange one, the different one, the son of a laughing father and a soft-voiced mother, the small-fat-person with short legs whose ears were pierced by Standing All Night, went straight across his canyon to where the stones that had been piled into a slanting walkway lay heaved and thrown to both sides and the rock wall rose smooth with no niches up to the first ledge. He bent over and picked up a stone. He began to pile the stones one upon the other.

And Spotted Turtle, the great-granddaughter of Standing All Night, the sister of Yellow Moon and the wife of Little Bear, stood in the lodge entrance and saw him. She went to him.

"Why do you do that?"

"We are going back to our people."

The happiness of the words leaped in her and shone in her eyes and he saw that he was certain that his heart spoke the truth to him. Yet the sadness was a great sadness in him. It swelled until he thought his chest would burst. He turned away and went among the tall hiding berry bushes where the rocks thrust up from the ground and she remained and watched him go.

The badger was not there by the flat stone. There had been no meat for several days. It was off on its own secret ways hunting food. That was no matter now. He spoke to the rocks about him. "Oh badger, farewell. The blood of my breast runs downward with a new grief and I alone can see it."

But she was coming through the bushes to him. "Oh my husband. It is bad. But I am young. I am strong. I will have another child. And another. I will not let them die." She was very tired and her face was drawn from the pain of losing the little one and the pain of the cutting of the finger. But she was beautiful to him. "Oh my husband. I am not a silly woman who must have others clacking about her. It is enough that you are here. I would not take you from the place that is yours."

His voice was harsh and it grated in his throat. It was the voice of the man of the lodge speaking what was in his mind and what would not be changed. "You are not taking me out of this place. I am taking myself and my woman where we belong as a man must."

He left her. He returned to the stones by the near rock wall. He began to pile one stone upon another stone in the steep slanting walkway that would lead up to the ledge and the ladder of niches above. She came out of the bushes and stood still and watched him. On her face was a warm wisdom and an understanding. She moved forward to go to him and to help him.

# EUGENE MANLOVE RHODES

## *Pasó por Aquí*

### I

EXCEPTIONS ARE SO INEVITABLE that no rule is without them—except the one just stated. Neglecting fractions, then, not to insult intelligence by specifying the obvious, trained nurses are efficient, skillful, devoted. It is a noble calling.

Nevertheless, it is notorious that the official uniform is of reprehensible charm. This regulation is variously explained by men, women and doctors. "No fripperies, curlicues and didos—bully!" say the men. "Ah! Yes! But why? Artful minxes!" say the women, who should know best. "Cheerful influence in the sickroom," say the doctors.

Be that as it may, such uniform Jay wore, spotless and starched, crisp and cool; Jay Hollister, now seated on the wide portico of the Alamogordo Hospital; not chief nurse, but chief ornament, according to many, not only of that hospital but of the great railroad which maintained it. Alamogordo was a railroad town, a new town, a ready-made and highly painted town, direct from Toyland.

Ben Griggs was also a study in white—flannels, oxfords and panama; a privileged visitor who rather overstepped his privileges; almost a fixture in that pleasant colonnade.

"Lamp of life," said Ben, "let's get down to brass tacks. You're home-sick!"

"Homesick!" said Jay scornfully. "Homesick! I'm heartsick, bankrupt, shipwrecked, lost, forlorn—here in this terrible country, among these dreadful people. Homesick? Why, Ben, I'm just damned!"

"Never mind, heart's delight," said Ben the privileged. "You've got me."

Miss Hollister seemed in no way soothed by this reassuring statement. "Your precious New Mexico! Sand!" she said. "Sand, snakes, scorpions; wind, dust, glare and heat; lonely, desolate and forlorn!"

"Under the circumstances," said Ben, "you could hardly pay me a greater compliment. 'Whither thou goest, I will go,' and all that. Good girl! This unsolicited tribute—"

"Don't be a poor simpleton," advised the good girl. "I shall stick it out for my year, of course, since I was foolish enough to undertake it. That is all. Don't you make any mistakes. These people shall never be my people."

---

"*Pasó por Aquí*" *is reprinted from* THE BEST SHORT STORIES AND NOVELS OF EUGENE MANLOVE RHODES. *edited by Frank Dearing, with the permission of Houghton Mifflin Company, publisher.*

"No better people on earth. In all the essentials—"

"Oh, who cares anything about essentials?" cried Jay impatiently—voicing, perhaps, more than she knew. "A tin plate will do well enough to eat out of, certainly, if that is what you mean. I prefer china, myself. I'm going back where I can see flowers and green grass, old gardens and sundials."

"I know not what others may say," observed Ben grandly, "but as for me, you take the sundials and give me the sun. Right here, too, where they climb for water and dig for wood. Peevish, my fellow townsman, peevish, waspy, crabbed. You haven't half enough to do. In this beastly climate people simply will not stay sick. They take up their bed and beat it, and you can't help yourself. Nursing is a mere sinecure." His hands were clasped behind his head, his slim length reclined in a steamer chair, feet crossed, eyes half closed, luxurious. "Ah, idleness!" he murmured. "Too bad, too bad! You never were a grouch back home. Rather good company, if anything."

Ben's eyes were blue and dreamy. They opened a trifle wider now, and rolled slowly till they fell upon Miss Hollister, bolt upright and haughty in her chair, her lips pressed in a straight line. She regarded him sternly. He blinked, his hands came from behind his head, he straightened up and adjusted his finger tips to meet with delicate precision. "But the main trouble, the fount and origin of your disappointing conduct is, as hereinbefore said, homesickness. It is, as has been observed, a nobler pang than indigestion, though the symptoms are of striking similarity. But nostalgia, more than any other feeling, is fatal to the judicial faculties, and I think, my dear towny, that when you look at this fair land, your future home, you regard all things with a jaundiced eye."

"Oh-h!" gasped Jay, hotly indignant. "Look at it yourself! Look at it!"

The hospital was guarded and overhung by an outer colonnade of cottonwoods; she looked through a green archway across the leagues of shimmering desert, somber, wavering and dim; she saw the long bleak range beyond, saw-toothed and gray; saw in the midway levels the unbearable brilliance of the White Sands, a wild dazzle and tumult of light, a blinding mirror with two score miles for diameter.

But Ben's eyes widened with delight, their blue darkened to a deeper blue of exultation, not to be feigned.

"More than beautiful—fascinating," he said.

"Repulsive, hateful, malignant, appalling!" cried Jay Hollister bitterly. "The starved, withered grass, the parched earth, the stunted bushes—miserable, hideous—the abomination of desolation!"

"Girl, by all good rights I ought to shut your wild, wild mouth with kisses four—that's what I orter do—elocutin' that way. But you mean it, I guess." Ben nodded his head sagely. "I get your idea. Blotched and leprous, eh? Thin, starved soil, poisoned and mildewed patches—thorns and dwarfed scrub, red leer of the sun. Oh, *si!* Like that bird in Browning? Hills like giants at a huntin' lay—the round squat turret—all the lost adventures, my peers—the Dark Tower, weird noises just offstage, increasin' like a bill, I mean a bell—increasin' like a bell, fiddles a-moanin', 'O-o-o-h-h-h! What did you do-o-o with your summer's wa-a-a-ges? So this is Paris!' Yes, yes, but why not shed the second-hand stuff and come down to workaday?"

"Ben Griggs," said Miss Hollister with quiet and deadly conviction, "you are absolutely the most blasphemous wretch that ever walked in shoe leather. You haven't anything even remotely corresponding to a soul."

"When we are married," said Ben, and paused, reflecting. "That is, if I don't change my mind—"

"Married!" said Miss Hollister derisively. "When! You!" Her eyes scorned him.

"Woman," said Ben, "beware! You make utter confusion with the parts of speech. You make mere interjections of pronouns, prepositions and verbs and everything. You use too many shockers. More than that—mark me, my lass—isn't it curious that no one has ever thought to furnish printed words with every phonograph record of a song? Just a sheet of paper— why, it needn't cost more than a penny apiece at the outside. Then we could know what it was all about."

"The way you hop from conversational crag to crag," said Jay, "is beyond all praise."

"Oh, well, if you insist, we can go back to our marriage again."

"My poor misguided young friend," said Jay, "make no mistakes. I put up with you because we played together when we were kids, and because we are strangers here in a strange land, townies together—"

Ben interrupted her. "Two tawny townies twisting twill together!" he chanted happily, beating slow time with a gentle finger. "Twin turtles twitter tender twilight twaddle. Twice twenty travelers—"

"Preposterous imbecile!" said Jay, dimpling nevertheless adorably. "Here is something to put in your little book. Jay Hollister will never marry an idler and a wastrel. Why, you're not even a ne'er-do-well. You're a do-nothing, yet."

"All the world loves a loafer," Ben protested. "Still, as Alice remarked, if circumstances were different they would be quite otherwise. If frugal industry—"

"There comes your gambler friend," said Jay coldly.

"Who, Monte? Where?" Ben turned eagerly.

"Across the street. No, the other way." Though she fervently disapproved of Monte, Jay was not sorry for the diversion. It was daily more difficult to keep Ben in his proper place, and she had no desire to discuss frugal industry.

"Picturesque rascal, what? Looking real pleased about something too. Say, girl, you've made me forget something I was going to tell you."

"He is laughing to himself," said Jay.

"I believe he is, at that." Ben raised his voice. "Hi, Monte! Come over and tell us the joke."

2

Monte's mother had known him as Rosalio Marquez. The overname was professional. He dealt Monte wisely but not too well. He was nearing thirty-five, the easiest age of all; he was slender and graceful; he wore blue serge and a soft black hat, low crowned and wide brimmed. He carried that hat in his hand as he came up the steps. He bowed courteously to Jay, with murmured greetings in Spanish, soft syllables of lingering caress; he waved a friendly salute to Ben.

"Yes, indeed," said Ben. "With all my heart. Your statement as to the beauty of the day is correct in every particular, and it affords me great pleasure to indorse an opinion so just. But, after all, dear heart, that is hardly the point, is it? The giddy jest, the merry chuckles—those are the points on which we greatly desire information."

Monte hesitated almost imperceptibly, a shrewd questioning in his eyes.

"Yes, have a chair," said Jay, "and tell us the joke."

"Thees is good, here, thank you," said Monte. He sat on the top step and hung the black hat on his knee; his face lit up with soft low laughter. "The joke? Oh, eet ees upon the sheriff, Jeem Hunter. I weel tell eet."

He paused to consider. In his own tongue Monte's speech sounded uncommonly like a pack of firecrackers lit at both ends. In English it was leisured, low and thoughtful. The unslurred vowels, stressed and piquant, the crisp consonants, the tongue-tip accents—these things combined to make the slow caressing words into something rich and colorful and strange, all unlike our own smudged and neutral speech. The customary medium of the Southwest between the two races is a weird and lawless hodge-podge of the two tongues—a barbarous lingua franca.

As Miss Hollister had no Spanish, Monte drew only from his slender stock of English; and all unconsciously he acted the story as he told it.

"When Jeem was a leetle, small boy," said Monte, his hand knee-high to show the size in question, "he dream manee times that he find thoss marbles—oh, many marbles! That mek heem ver' glad, thees nize dream. Then he get older"—Monte's hand rose with the sheriff's maturity—"and sometime he dream of find money lak thoss marble. And now Jeem ees grown and sheriff—an' las' night he come home, ver' late, ver' esleepy. I weel tell you now how eet ees, but Jeem he did not know eet. You see, Melquiades, he have a leetle, litla game." He glanced obliquely at Miss Hollister, his shoulders and down-drawn lips expressed apology for the little game, and tolerance for it. "Just neeckels and dimes. An' some fellow he go home weener, and there ees hole een hees pocket. But Jeem he do not know. *Bueno*, Jeem has been to Tularosa, Mescalero, Fresnal, all places, to leef word to look out for thees fellow las' week that rob the bank at Belen, and he arrive back on a freight train las' night, mebbe so about three in the morning—oh, veree tired, ver' esleepy. So when he go up the street een the moonlight he see there a long streeng of neeckels and dimes under hees feet." Without moving, Monte showed the homeward progress of that drowsy man and his faint surprise. "So Jeem, he laugh and say, 'There ees that dream again.'" And he go on. But bimeby he steel see thoss neeckels, and he peench heemself, so—and he feel eet." Monte's eyes grew round with astonishment. "And he bend heemself to peek eet, and eet ees true money, and not dreaming at all! Yais. He go not back, but on ahead he peek up one dollar seexty-five cents of thees neeckels and dimes."

"I hadn't heard of any robbery, Monte," said Ben. "What about it?"

"Yes, and where is Belen?" said Jay. "Not around here, surely. I've never heard of the place."

"Oh, no—*muy lejos*—a long ways. Belen, what you call Bethlehem, ees yonder this side of Albuquerque, a leetle. I have been there manee times, but not estraight—round about." He made a looping motion of his hand to illustrate. "Las Vegas, and then down, or by Las Cruces, and then up. Eet is hundred feefty, two hundred miles in estraight line—I do not know."

"Anybody hurt?" asked Ben.

"Oh, no—no fuss! Eet ees veree funnee. Don Numa Frenger and Don Nestor Trujillo, they have there beeg estore to sell all theengs, leetle bank, farms, esheep ranch, freighting for thoss mines, buy wool and hides—all theengs for get the monee what ees there een thees place. And las' week, maybe Friday, Saturday, Nestor he ees go to deenair, and Numa Frenger ees in the estore, *solito*.

"Comes een a customer, *un colorado*—es-scusa me, a redhead. He buy tomatoes, cheese, crackers, sardines, sooch things, and a nose bag, and he ask to see shotgun. Don Numa, he exheebit two, three, and thees red he peek out nize shotgun. So he ask for shells, bird-eshot, buck-eshot, and he open the buck-eshot and sleep two shells een barrel, and break eet to throw out thoss shell weeth extractor, and sleep them again. 'Eet work fine!' he say. 'Have you canteen?'

"Then Numa Frenger he tek long pole weeth hook to get thoss canteen where eet hang from the *viga*, the r-rafter, the beams. And when he get eet, he turn around an' thees estranger ees present thees shotgun at hees meedle.

"'Have you money een your esafe?' say the *estranjero*, the estr-ranger. And Numa ees bite hees mouth. 'Of your kindness,' say the customer, 'weel you get heem? I weel go weeth you.'

"So they get thees money from the esafe. And thees one weel not tek onlee the paper money. 'Thees gold an' seelver ees so heav-ee,' he tell Numa Frenger. 'I weel not bozzer.' Then he pay for those theengs of which he mek purchase an' correc' Don Numa when he mek meestake in the *adición*, and get hees change back. And then he say to Numa, 'Weel you not be so good to come to eshow me wheech ees best road out from thees town to the ford of the reever?' And Numa, he ees ge-nash hees teeth, but there ees no *remedio*.

"And so they go walking along thees lane between the orchards, these two togezzer, and the leetle bir-rds esing een the *árboles*—thees red fellow laughing and talkin' weeth Numa, ver' gay—leading hees horse by the bridle, and weeth the shotgun een the crook of hees arm. So the people loog out from the doors of their house and say, 'Ah! Don Numa ees diverrt heemself weeth hees friend.'

"And when they have come beyond the town, thees fellow ees mount hees horse. 'For your courtesy,' he say, 'I thank you. At your feet,' he say. 'Weeth God!' And he ride off laughing, and een a leetle way he toss shotgun een a bush, and he ride on to cross the reever eslow. But when Numa Frenger sees thees, he run queeckly, although he ees a ver' fat man, an' not young; he grab thees gun, he point heem, he pull the triggle—Nozzing! He break open the gun to look wizzen side—Nozzing! *'O caballeros y conciudadanos!'* Monte threw down the gun; both hands grabbed his black locks and tugged with the ferocity of despair.

"Ah-h! What a lovely cuss word," cried Jay. "How trippingly it goes upon the tongue. I must learn that. Say it again!"

"But eet ees not a bad word, that," said Monte sheepishly. "Eet ees onlee idle word, to feel up. When thees politocos go up an' down, talking nonsense een the nose, when they weesh to theenk of more, then they say with *emoción*, 'O caballeros y conciudadanos'; that ees, 'gentlemen and fellow ceetizens.' No more."

"Well, now, the story?" said Ben. "He crossed the river, going east—was that it?"

"Oh, yes. Well, when Numa Frenger see that thees gun ees emptee, he ees ver' angree man. He ees mos enr-rage heemself for that than for all what gone befor-re. He ees arrouse all Belen, he ees send telegraph to Sabinal, La Joya, Socorro, San Marcial, ever wheech way, to mek queek the posse, to send queek to the mesa to catch thees man, to mek *proclamación* to pay for heem three thousand dollar of rewar-rd. 'Do not keel heem, I entr-reat you,' say Don Numa. 'Breeng heem back. I want to fry heem.'"

"Now isn't that New Mexico for you?" demanded Jay. "A man commits a barefaced robbery, and you make a joke of it."

Monte pressed the middle finger of his right hand firmly into the palm of his left, pressed as if to hold something there, and looked up under his brows at Miss Hollister.

"Then why do you laugh?" said Monte.

"You win," said Jay. "Go on with the story."

"Well, then," said Monte, "thees fellow he go up on the high plain on thees side of the reever, and he ride east and south by Sierra Montoso, and over the mountains of Los Pinos, and he mek to go over Chupadero Mesa to thoss ruins of Gran Quivira. But he ride onlee *poco á poco*, easalee. And already as posse from La Joya, San Acacia is ride up the Alamillo Cañon, and across the plain." His swift hands fashioned horseman, mountain, mesa and plain. "Page Otero and six, five other men. And they ride veree fast so that already they pass in front of heem to the south, and are now before heem on Chupadero, and there they see heem. Eet ess almost sundown.

"*Immediatamente* he turn and go back. And their horses are not so tired lak hees horse, and they spread out and ride fast, and soon they are about to come weethen gunshot weeth the rifle. And when he see eet, thees *colorado* ees ride oopon a reedge that all may see, and he tek that paper money from the nose bag at the head of the saddle and he toss eet up—pouf! The weend is blow gentle and thees money it go joomp, joomp, here, there, een the booshes. Agan he ride a leetle way, and again he scatter thees money lak a man to feed the hen een hees yard. So then he go on away, thees red one. And when thees posse come to that place, thees nize money is go hop, hop, along the ground and over the booshes. There ees feefty-dollar beel een the mesquite, there ees twenty-dollar beel een the tar-bush, there ees beels blow by, roll by, slide by. So thees posse ees deesmount heemself to peek heem, *muy enérgico*—lively. And the weend ees come up faster at sundown, *como siempre*. 'Come on!' says Page Otero. 'Come on, thees fellow weel to escape!' Then the posse loog up surprise, and say, 'Who, me?' and they go on to peek up thees monee. So that redhead get clear away thees time."

"Did they get all the money?" asked Ben.

"Numa he say yes. He do not know just how mooch thees bandit ees take, but he theenk they breeng back all, or most nearly all."

"Do they know who he was?" asked Jay.

"*Por cierto*, no. But from the deescreepcion and hees horse and saddle, they theenk eet ees a cowboy from Quemado, name—I cannot to prronounce thees name, Meester Ben. You say heem. I have eet here een *La Voz del Pueblo*." From a hip pocket he produced a folded newspaper printed in Spanish, and showed Ben the place.

"Ross McEwen—about twenty-five or older, red hair, gray eyes, five feet nine inches—humph!" he returned the paper. "Will they catch him, do you think?"

Monte considered. He looked slowly at the far dim hills; he bent over to watch an inch-high horseman at his feet, toiling through painful immensities.

"The world ees ver' beeg een thees country," he said at last. "I theenk most mebbe not. *Quién sabe?* Onlee thees fellow must have water—and there ees not much water. Numa Frenger ees send now to all places, to Leencoln County, to Jeem Hunter here, and he meks everyone to loog out, to Pat Garrett in Doña Ana Countee, and Pat watches by Parker Lake and the pass of San Agustin; to El Paso, and they watch there most of all that he pass not to Mexico Viejo. Eet may be at some water place they get heem. Or that he get them. He seem lak a man of some enterpr-rize, no?" He rose to go. "But I have talk too much. I mus' go now to my beesness."

"A poor business for a man as bright as you are," said Jay, and sniffed.

"But I geeve a square deal," said Monte serenely. "At you feet, senorita! Unteel then, Meester Ben."

"Isn't he a duck? I declare, it's a shame to laugh at his English," said Jay.

"Don't worry. He gets to hear our Spanish, even if he is too polite to laugh."

"I hate to think of that man being chased for blood money," said Jay. "Hunter and that Pat Garrett you think so much of are keen after that reward, it seems. It is dreadful the way these people here make heroes out of their killers and man hunters."

"Let's get this straight," said Ben. "You're down on the criminal for robbing and down on the sheriff for catching him. Does that sound like sense? If there was no reward offered, it's the sheriff's duty to catch him, isn't it? And if there is a reward, it's still his duty. The reward doesn't make him a man hunter. Woman, you ain't right in your head. And as for Pat Garrett and some of these other old-timers—they're enjoying temporary immortality right now. They've become a tradition while they still live. Do you notice how all these honest-to-goodness old-timers talk? All the world is divided into three parts. One part is old-timers and other two are not. The most clannish people on earth. And that brings us, by graceful and easy stages, to the main consideration, which I want to have settled before I go. And when I say settled I mean that nothing is ever settled till it is settled right—get me?" He stood up; as Jay rose he took her hands. "If circumstances were otherwise, Jay?"

She avoided his eyes. "Don't ask me now. I don't know, Ben—honest, I don't. You mustn't pester me now. It isn't fair when I'm so miserable." She pulled her hands away.

"Gawd help all poor sailors on a night like this!" said Ben fervently. "Listen, sister, I'm going to work, see? Goin' to fill your plans and specifications, every one, or bust a tug."

"I see you at it," jeered Jay, with an unpleasant laugh. "Work? You?"

"Me. I, myself. A faint heart never filled a spade flush," said Ben. "Going to get me a job and keep it. Lick any man that tries to fire me. Put that in your hope chest. Bye-bye. At your feet!"

As he went down the street his voice floated back to her:

> *But now my hair is falling out,*
> *And down the hill we'll go,*
> *And sleep together at the foot—*
> *John Barleycorn, my Jo!*

### 3

A high broad tableland lies east of the Rio Grande, and mountains make a long unbroken wall to it, with cliffs that front the west. This mesa is known locally as El Corredor. It is a pleasing and wholesome country. Zacatón and salt grass are gray green upon the level plain, checkered with patches of bare ground, white and glaring. On those bare patches, when the last rains fell, weeks, months, or years ago, an oozy paste filmed over the glossy levels, glazed by later suns, cracking at last to shards like pottery. But in broken country, on ridges and slopes, was a thin turf of buffalo and mesquite grass, curly, yellow and low. There was iron beneath this place and the sand of it was red, the soil was ruddy white, the ridges and the lower hill slopes were granite red, yellowed over with grass. Even the high crowning cliffs were faintly cream, not gray, as limestone is elsewhere. Sunlight was soft and mellow there, sunset was red upon these cliffs. And Ross McEwen fled down that golden corridor.

If he had ridden straight south he might have been far ahead by this time, well on the road to Mexico. But his plan had been to reach the Panhandle of Texas; he had tried easting and failed. Three times he had sought to work through the mountain barrier to the salt plains—a bitter country of lava flow and sinks, of alkali springs, salt springs, magnesia springs, soda springs; of soda lakes, salt lakes, salt marshes, salt creeks; of rotten and crumbling ground, of greasy sand, of chalk that powdered and rose on the lightest airs, to leave no trace that a fugitive had passed this way.

He had been driven back once by posse on Chupadero. Again at night he had been forced back by men who did not see him. He had tried to steal through by the old stage road over the Oscuro, and found the pass guarded; and the last time, today, had been turned back by men that he did not even see. In the mouth of Mockingbird Pass he had found fresh-shod tracks of many horses going east. Mockingbird was held against him.

He could see distinctly, and in one eye-flight, every feature of a country larger than all England. He could look north to beyond Albuquerque, past the long ranges of Manzano, Montoso, Sandia, Oscuro; southward, between his horse's ears, the northern end of the San Andrés was high and startling before him, blue black with cedar brake and piñon, except for the granite-gold top of Salinas Peak, the great valley of the Jornado del Muerto, the Journey of the Dead, which lay between the San Andrés and the Rio Grande.

And beyond the river was a bright enormous expanse, bounded only by the crest of the dozen ranges that made the crest of the Continental Divide—Dátil, Magdalena, San Mateo, the Black Range, the Mimbres, Florida.

Between, bordering the midway river, other mountain ranges lay tangled: Cuchillo Negro, Critobál, Sierra de los Caballos, Doña Ana, Robelero. It was over the summits of these ranges that he saw the Continental Divide.

Here was irony indeed. With that stupendous panorama outspread before him, he was being headed off, driven, herded! He cocked an eyebrow aslant at the thought, and spoke of it to his horse, who pricked back an ear in attention. He was a honey-colored horse, and his name was Miél, which is, by interpretation, Honey.

"Wouldn't you almost think, sweetness," said Ross McEwen in a plaintive drawl, "that there was enough elbow-room here to satisfy every reasonable man? And yet these lads are crowdin' me like a cop after an alley cat."

He sensed that an unusual effort was being made to take him, and he smiled—a little ruefully—at the reflection that the people at Mockingbird might well have been mere chance comers upon their lawful occasions, and with no designs upon him, no knowledge of him. Every man was a possible enemy. He was out of law.

This was the third day of his flight. The man was still brisk and bold, the honey-colored horse was still sturdy, but both lacked something of the sprightly resilience they had brought to the fords of Belen. There had been brief grazing and scant sleep, night riding, doubling and twisting to slip into lonely water holes. McEwen had chosen, as the lesser risk, to ride openly to Prairie Springs. He had found no one there and had borrowed grub for himself and several feeds of corn for the Honey horse. There had been no fast riding, except for the one brief spurt with the posse at Chupadero. But it had been a steady grind, doubly tiresome that they might not keep to the beaten trails. Cross-country traveling on soft ground is rough on horseflesh.

And now they left the plain and turned through tar-bush up the long slope to the San Andrés. A thousand ridges and hollows came plunging and headlong against them. And suddenly the tough little horse was tiring, failing.

Halfway to the hill foot they paused for a brief rest. High on their slim lances, banners of yucca blossoms were white and waxen, and wild bees hummed to their homes in the flower stalks of last year; flaunting afar, cactus flowers flamed crimson or scarlet through the black tar-bush.

Long since, McEwen had given up the Panhandle. He planned now to bear far to the southeast, crossing the salt plains below the White Sands to the Guadalupe Mountains, straddling the boundary between the territory and Texas, and so east to the Staked Plains. He knew the country ahead, or had known it ten years before. But there would be changes. There was a new railroad, so he had heard, from El Paso to Tularosa, and so working north toward the states. There would be other things, too— new ranches, and all that. For sample, behind him, just where this long slope merged with the flats, three unexpected windmills, each five miles from the other, had made a line across his path; he had made a weary detour to pass unseen.

The San Andrés made here a twenty-mile offset where they joined the Oscuro, with the huge round mass of Salinas Peak as their mutual corner. Lava Gap, the meeting place of the two ranges, was now directly at his left and ten miles away. The bleak and mile-high walls of it made a frame for the tremendous picture of Sierra Blanca, sixty long miles to the east, with a gulf of nothingness between. Below that nothingness, as McEwen knew, lay the black lava river of the Mal Pais. But Lava Gap was not for him. Unless pursuit was quite abandoned, Lava Gap and Dripping Springs would be watched and guarded. He was fenced in by probabilities.

But the fugitive was confident yet, and by no means at the end of his resources. He knew a dim old Indian trail over a high pass beyond Salinas Peak. It started at Grapevine Spring, Captain Jack Crawford's ranch.

"And at Grapevine," said Ross aloud, "I'll have to buy, beg, borrow or get me a horse. Hope there's nobody at home. If there's anyone there I'll have to get his gun first and trade afterwards. Borrowing horses is not highly recommended, but it beats killing 'em."

To the right and before him the Jornado was hazy, vast and mysterious. To the right and behind him, the lava flow of Pascual sprawled black and sinister in the lowlands; and behind him—far behind him, far below him, a low line of dust was just leaving the central windmill of those three new ranches, a dozen miles away. McEwen watched this dust with some interest while he rolled and lit a cigarette. He drank the last water from his canteen.

"Come on, me bold outlaw," he said, "keep moving. You've done made your bed, but these hellhounds won't let you sleep in it." He put foot to stirrup; he stroked the Honey horse.

"Miél, old man, you tough it out four or five miles more, and your troubles will be over. Me for a fresh horse at Grapevine, come hell or high water. Take it easy. No hurry. Just shuffle along."

The pursuing dust did not come fast, but it came straight his way. "I'll bet a cooky," said Ross sagely, "that some of these gay bucks have got a spyglass. I wonder if that ain't against the rules? And new men throwin' in with them at every ranch. I reckon I would, too, if it wasn't for this red topknot of mine. Why couldn't they meet up with some other red-headed hellion and take him back? Wouldn't that be just spiffin'? One good thing, anyway—I didn't go back to the Quemado country. Some of the boys would sure have got in Dutch, hidin' me out. This is better."

He crossed the old military road that had once gone through Lava Gap to Fort Stanton; he smiled at the shod tracks there; he came to the first hills, pleasingly decorated with bunches of mares—American mares, gentle mares—Corporal Tanner's mares. He picked a bunch with four or five saddle horses in it and drove them slowly up Grapevine Canon. The Miél horse held up his head and freshened visibly. He knew what this meant. The sun dropped behind the hills. It was cool and fresh in Grapevine. The outlaw took his time. He had an hour or more. He turned for a last look at the north and the cliffs of Oscuro Mountain blazing in the low sun to fiery streamers of red light. You would have seen, perhaps, only a howling wilderness, but this man was to look back, waking and in dream, and to remember that brooding and sunlit silence as the glowing heart of the world. From this place alone he was to be an exile.

"Nice a piece of country as ever laid outdoors," said Ross McEwen. "I've seen some several places where it would be right pleasant to have a job along with a bunch of decent punchers—good grub and all that, mouth organ by the firelight after supper—Or herding sheep."

Grapevine Spring is at the very head of the cañon. To east, south and west the hills rise directly from the corral fences. McEwen drove the mares into the water pen and called loudly to the house. The hail went unanswered. Eagles screamed back from a cliff above him.

"A fool for luck," said McEwen.

He closed the bars, he gave Miél his first installment of water. Then he went to the house. It was unlocked and there was no one there. The ashes on the hearth were cold. He borrowed two cans of beans and some bacon. There was a slender store of corn, and he borrowed one feed of this to make tomorrow's breakfast for the new horse he was soon to acquire. He found an old saddle and he borrowed that, with an old bridle as well; he brought his own to replace them; he lit the little lamp on the table and grinned happily.

"They'll find Miél and my saddle and the light," he said, "and they'll make sure I've taken to the brush."

He went back to the pen; he roped and saddled a saddle-marked brown, broad chested and short coupled, unshod. Shod tracks are too easily followed. Then he scratched his red head and grinned again. The pen was built of poles laid in panels, except at the front; the cedar brake grew to the very sides of it. He went to the back and took down two panels, laying the poles aside; he let the mares drift out there, seeing to it that some of them went around by the house, and the rest on the other side of the pen. It was almost dark by now.

"There," he said triumphantly. "The boys will drive in a bunch of stock when they come, for remounts, and they'll go right on through. Fine mess in the dark. And it'll puzzle them to find which way I went with all these tracks. Time I was gone."

He came back to the watering trough; he washed his hands and face and filled his canteen; he went on where Miél stood weary and huddled in the dusk. His hand was gentle on that drooping neck.

"Miél, old fellow," he said, "you've been one good little horse. *Bueno suerte.*" He led the brown to the bars. "I hate a fool," said Ross McEwen.

He took down the bars and rode into the cedar brush at right angles to the cañon, climbing steadily from the first. It was a high and desperate pass, and branches had grown across the unused trail; long before he had won halfway to the summit he heard, far below him, the crashing of horses in the brush, the sound of curses and laughter. The pursuit had arrived at Grapevine.

He topped the summit of that nameless pass an hour later, and turned down the dark cañon to the east—to meet grief at once. Since his time a cloud-burst had been this way. Where there had once been fair footing the flood had cut deep and wide, and every semblance of soil had washed away, leaving only a wild moraine, a loose rubble of rocks and tumbled boulders. But it was the only way. The hillsides were impossibly steep and sidelong, glassy granite and gneiss, or treacherous slides of porphyry. Ross led his horse. Every step was a hazard in that narrow and darkened place, with crumbling ridge and pit and jump off, with windrows of smooth round rock to roll and turn under their feet. It took the better part of two hours to win through the narrows, perhaps two miles. The cañon widened then, the hillsides were lower and Ross could ride again, picking his doubtful way in the starlight. He turned on a stepladder of hills to the north, and came about midnight to Dripstone, high in a secret hollow of the hills. The prodigious bulk of Salinas loomed mysterious and incredible above him in the starlight.

He tied the brown horse securely and named him Porch Climber. He built a tiny fire and toasted strips of bacon on the coals. Then he spread out his saddle blankets with hat and saddle for pillow, and so lay down to untroubled sleep.

## 4

He awoke in that quiet place before the first stirring of dawn. A low thin moon was in the sky and the mountains were dim across the east. He washed his eyes out with water from the canteen. He made a nose bag from the corn sack and hung it on Porch Climber's brown head. The Belen nose bag had gone into the discard days before. He built a fire of twigs and hovered over it while his precious coffee came to a boil; his coat was thin and the night air was fresh, almost chilly. He smacked his lips over the coffee; he saddled and watered Porch Climber at Dripstone and refilled his canteen there. The horse drank sparingly.

"Better fill up, old-timer," Ross advised him. "You're sure going to need it."

Knuckled ridges led away from Salinas like fingers of a hand. The eastern flat was some large fraction of a mile nearer to sea level than the high plain west of the mountain, and these ridges were massive and steep accordingly. He made his way down one of them. The plain was dark and cold below him; the mountains took shape and grew, the front range of the Rockies—Capitán, Carrizo, Sierra Blanca, Sacramento, with Guadalupe low and dim in the south; the White Sands were dull and lifeless in the midway plain. Bird twitter was in the air. Rabbits scurried through the brush, a quail whirred by and sent back a startled call; crimson streaks shot up the sky, and day grew broad across the silent levels. The cut banks of Salt Creek appeared, wandering away southwest toward the marshes. Low and far against the black base of the Sacramento, white feathers lifted and fluffed, the smoke of the first fires at Tularosa, fifty miles away. Flame tipped the far-off crests, the sun leaped up from behind the mountain wall, the level light struck on the White Sands, glanced from those burnished bevels and splashed on the western cliffs; the desert day blazed over this new half-world.

He had passed a few cows on the ridges, but now, as he came close to the flats, he was suddenly aware of many cattle before him, midges upon the vast plain; more cattle than he had found on the western side of the mountains. He drew rein, instantly on the alert, and began to quarter the scene with a keen scrutiny. At once a silver twinkling showed to northward—the steel fans of a windmill, perhaps six miles out from the foot of the main mountain. His eye moved slowly across the plain. He was shocked to find a second windmill tower six or eight miles south of the first, keeping at the same distance from the hills, and when he made out the faint glimmer of a third, far in the south, he gave way to indignation. It was a bald plain with no cover for the quietly disposed, except a few clumps of soapweed here and there. And this line of windmills was precisely the line of the road to El Paso. Where he had expected smooth going he would have to keep to the roughs; to venture into the open was to court discovery. He turned south across the ridges.

He had talked freely to Miél, but until now he had been reticent with Porch Climber, who had not yet won his confidence. At this unexpected reverse he opened his heart.

"Another good land gone wrong," he said. "I might have known it. This side of Salt Creek is only half-bad cow country, so of course it's all settled up, right where we want to go. No one lives east of Salt Creek, not even sheep herders. And we couldn't possibly make it, goin' on the other side of Salt Creek with all that marsh country and the hell of the White Sands. Why, this is plumb ridiculous!"

He meditated for a while upon his wrongs and then broke out afresh: "When I was here, the only water east of the mountains was the Wildy Well at the corner of the damn White Sands. Folks drove along the road, and when they wanted water they went up in the hills. It's no use to cross over to Tularosa. They'll be waiting for us there. No, sir, we've pointedly got to skulk down through the brush. And you'll find it heavy going, up one ridge and down another, like a flea on a washboard."

Topping the next ridge, he reined back swiftly into a hollow place. He dismounted and peered through a mesquite bush, putting the branches aside to look. A mile to the south two horsemen paced soberly down a ridge—and it was a ridge which came directly from the pass to Grapevine.

"Now ain't them the bright lads?" said the runaway, divided between chagrin and admiration. "What are you going to do with fellows like that? I ask you. I left plain word that I done took to the hills afoot, without the shadow of a doubt. Therefore they reasoned I hadn't. They've coppered every bet. Now that's what I call clear thinkin'. I reckon some of 'em did stay there, but these two crossed over that hell gate at night, just in case.

"I'll tell a man they had a ride where that cloud-burst was. Say, they'll tell their grandchildren about that—if they live that long, which I misdoubt, the way they're carryin' on. This gives me what is technically known as the willies. Hawse," said McEwen, "let's us tarry a spell and see what these hirelin' bandogs are goin' to do now."

He took off the bridle and saddle, he staked Porch Climber to rest and graze while he watched. What the bandogs did was to ride straight to the central windmill, where smoke showed from the house. McEwen awaited developments. Purely from a sense of duty he ate the other can of beans while he waited.

"They'll take word to every ranch," he prophesied gloomily. "Leave a man to watch where there isn't anyone there—take more men along when they find more than one at a well. Wish I was a drummer."

His prognostications were verified. After a long wait, which meant breakfast, a midget horesman rode slowly north toward the first windmill. A little later two men rode slowly south toward the third ranch.

"That's right, spread the news, dammit, and make everybody hate you," said Ross. He saddled and followed them, paralleling their course, but keeping to the cover of the brush.

It was heavy and toilsome going, boulders and rocks alternating with soft ground where Porch Climber's feet went through; gravel, coarse sand or piled rocks in the washes; tedious twisting in the brush and wearisome windings where a bay of open country forced a detour. He passed by the mouths of Good Fortune, Antelope and Cottonwood cañons, struggling through their dry deltas; he drew abreast of the northern corner of the White Sands. The reflection of it was blinding, yet he found it hard to hold his eyes away. The sun rode high and hot. McEwen consulted his canteen.

More than once or twice came the unwelcome thought that he might take to the hill country, discard Porch Climber and hide by some inaccessible seep or pothole until pursuit died down. But he was a stubborn man, and his heart was set upon Guadalupe; he had an inborn distaste for a diet of chance rabbit and tuna fruit—or, perhaps, slow deer without salt. A stronger factor in his decision—although he hardly realized it—was the horseman's hatred for being set afoot. He could hole in safely; there was little doubt of that. But when he came out of the hole, how then? A man from nowhere, on foot, with no past and no name and a long red beard— that would excite remark. He fingered the stubble on his cheeks with that reflection. Yes, such a man would be put to it to account for himself—and he would have to show up sometime, somewhere. The green cottonwood of Independent Spring showed high on the hill to his right. He held on to the south.

And now he came to the mouth of Sulphur Springs Cañon. Beyond here a great bay of open plain flowed into the hill foot under Kaylor Mountain; and midmost of that bay was another windmill, a long low house, spacious corrals. McEwen was sick of windmills. But this one was close under the mountain, far west of the line of the other ranches and of the El Paso road; McEwen saw with lively interest that his pursuers left the road and angled across the open to this ranch. That meant dinner.

"Honesty," said McEwen with conviction, "is the best policy. Dinnertime for some people, but only noon for me. . . . Early for grub too. . . . And how can these interprisin' chaps be pursuin' me when they're in front?

That isn't reasonable. Who ever heard of deputies goin' ahead and the bandit taggin' along behind. That's not right. It's not moral. I'm goin' around. Besides, if I don't this thing is liable to go on always, just windmills and windmills—to Mexico City—Peru—Chile. I'm plumb tired of windmills. Porch Climber," said McEwen, "have you got any gift of speed? Because, just as soon as these two sheriff men get to that ranch and have time to go in the house, you and me are going to drift out quiet and unostentatious across the open country till we hit the banks of the Salt Marsh. And if these fellows look out and see us you've just got to run for it. And they can maybe get fresh horses too. But if they don't see us we'll be right. We'll drift south under cover of the bank and get ahead of 'em while they stuff their paunches."

Half an hour later he turned Porch Climber's head to the east, and rode sedately across the smooth plain, desiring to raise no dust. Some three miles away, near where he crossed the El Paso road, grew a vigorous motte of mesquite trees. Once beyond that motte, he kept it lined up between him and the ranch; and so came unseen to where the plain broke away to the great marsh which rimmed the basin of the White Sands.

In the east the White Sands billowed in great dry dunes above the level of the plain, but the western half was far below that level, and waterbound. This was the home of mirages; they spread now all their pomp of palm and crystal lake and fairy hill. McEwen turned south along the margin. Here, just under the bank, the ground was moist, almost wet, and yet firm footing, like a road of hard rubber. He brought Porch Climber to a long-reaching trot, steady and smooth; he leaned forward in his stirrups and an old song came to his lips, unsummoned. He sang it with loving mockery, in a nasal but not unpleasing baritone:

> *They give him his orders at Monroe, Virginia,*
> *Sayin', "Pete, you're way behind ti-ime"—*

"Gosh, it does seem natural to sing when a good horse is putting the miles behind him," said McEwen. "This little old brown pony is holdin' up right well, too, after all the grief in the roughs this mawnin'."

> *He looked round then to his black, greasy fireman,*
> *"Just shovel in a little more co-o-oal,*
> *And when we cross that wide old maounting,*
> *You can watch old Ninety-Seven roll!"*

"Hey, Porch Climber! You ain't hardly keepin' time. Peart up a little! Now, lemme see. Must be about twenty mile to the old Wildy Well. Wonder if I'll find any more new ranches between here and there? Likely. Hell of a country, all cluttered up like this!"

> *It's a mighty rough road from Lynchburg to Danville,*
> *And a line on a three-mile gra-ade;*
> *It was on that grade that he lo'ost his av'rage,*
> *And you see what a jump he made!*

He rejoined the wagon road where the White Sands thrust a long and narrow arm far to the west. The old road crossed this arm at the shoulder, a three-mile speedway. Out on the sands magic islands came and went and rose and sank in a misty sea. But in the south, where the road climbed again to the plain, was the inevitable windmill—reality and no mirage.

McEwen followed the road in the posture of a man who had nothing to fear. He had outridden the rumor of his flight; he could come to this ranch with a good face. But he reined down to a comfortable jog. Those behind might overtake him close enough to spy him here in this naked place. Jaunting easily, nearing the ranch where he belonged, a horseman was no object of suspicion, but a man in haste was a different matter.

There was no one at the ranch. The water was brackish and flat, but the two wayfarers drank thankfully. He could see no signs that any horses were watering there; he made a shrewd guess that the boys had taken the horses and gone up into the mountains for better grass and sweet water, or perhaps to get out of sight of the White Sands, leaving the flats to the cattle.

"Probably they just ride down every so often to oil the windmill," he said. "Leastways, I would. Four hundred square miles of lookin'-glass, three hundred and sixty-four days a year—no, thank you! My eyes are most out now."

J.B. was branded on the gate posts of the corral, and on the door. There was canned stuff on a shelf and a few baking-powder biscuits, old and dry. He took a can of salmon and filed it for future reference.

"No time for gormandizin' now," he said. He stuffed the stale biscuits into his pockets to eat on the road. "There's this much about bread," said McEwen, "I can take it or I can leave it alone. And I've been leaving it alone for several days now."

A pencil and a tablet lay on the table. His gray eyes went suddenly a-dance with impish light. He tore out a page and wrote a few words of counsel and advice.

> Hey, you J.B. waddies: Look out for a fellow with red hair and gray eyes. Medium-sized man. He robbed the bank at Belen, and they think he came this way. Big reward offered for him. Two thousand, I hear. But I don't know for certain. Send word to the ranches up north. I will tell them as far south as Organ.
>
> JIM HUNTLEY

He hung this news-letter on a nail above the stove.

"There!" he said. "If them gay jaspers that are after me had any sense at all, they'd see it was no use to go any further, and they'd stay right here and rest up. But they won't. They'll say, 'Hey, this is the way he went—here's some more of the same old guff! But how ever did that feller get down here without us finding any tracks? You can see what a jump he made.' I don't want to be ugly," said McEwen, "but I've got to cipher up some way to shake loose from these fellows. I want to go to sleep. Now who in hell is Jim Huntley?"

Time for concealment was past. From now on he must set his hope on speed. He rode down the big road boldly and, for a time, at a brisk pace; he munched the dry biscuits and washed them down with warm and salty water from his canteen.

There was no room for another ranch between here and Wildy's Well. Wildy's was an old established ranch. It was among the possibilities that he might hit here upon some old acquaintance whose failing sight would not note his passing, and who would give him a fresh horse. He was now needing urge of voice and spur for Porch Climber's lagging feet. It sat in his mind that Wildy was dead. His brows knitted with the effort to remember. Yes, Wildy had been killed by a falling horse. Most likely, though, he would find no one living at the well. Not too bad, the water of Wildy's Well—but they would be in the hills with the good grass.

The brown horse was streaked with salt and sweat; he dragged in the slow sand. Here was a narrow broken country of rushing slopes, pinched between the White Sands and the mountains. The road wound up and down in the crowding brush; the footing was a coarse pebbly sand of broken granite from the crumbling hills. Heat waves rose quivering, the White Sands lifted and shuddered to a blinding shimmer, the dream islands were wavering, shifting and indistinct, astir with rumor. McEwen's eyes were dull for sleep, red rimmed and swollen from glare and alkali dust. The salt water was bitter in his belly. The stubble on his face was gray with powdered dust and furrowed with sweat stains; dust was in his nostrils and his ears, and the taste of dust was in his mouth. Porch Climber plowed heavily. And all at once McEwen felt a sudden distaste for his affair.

He had a searching mind and it was not long before he found a cause. That damn song. Dance music. There were places where people danced, where they would dance tonight. There was a garden in Rutherford—

## 5

There was no one at Wildy's Well, no horses there and no sign that any horses were using there. McEwen drank deep of the cool sweet water. When Porch Climber had his fill, McEwen plunged arms and head into the trough. Horse and man sighed together; their eyes met in comfortable understanding.

"Feller," said McEwen, "it was that salt water, much as anything else, that slowed you up, I reckon. Yuh was sure sluggish. And yuh just ought to see yourself now! Nemmine, that's over." He took down his rope, and cut off a length, the spread of his arms. He untwisted this length to three strands, soaked these strands in the trough, wrung them out and knotted them around his waist. He eyed the cattle that had been watering here. They had retreated to the far side at his coming and were now waiting impatiently. "Been many a long year since I've seen any Durham cattle," said McEwen. "Everybody's got white-face stuff now. Reckon they raise these for El Paso market. No feeder will buy 'em, unless with a heavy cut in the price."

He hobbled over and closed the corral gate. Every bone of him was a separate ache. A faint breeze stirred; the mill sails turned lazily; the gears squeaked a protest. Ross looked up with interest.

"That was right good water," he said. "Guess you've earned a greasing." He climbed the tall tower. Wildy's Well dated from before the steel windmill; this was massive and cumbersome, a wooden tower, and the wheel itself was of wood. After his oiling Ross scanned the north with an anxious eye. There was no dust. South by east, far in the central plain, dim hills swam indeterminate through the heat haze—Las Cornudas and Heuco. South by west, gold and rose, the peaks of the Organs peered from behind the last corner of the San Andrés. He searched the north again. He could see no dust—but he could almost see a dust.

He shook his head. "Them guys are real intelligent," he said. "I'm losin' my av'rage." He clambered down with some celerity, and set about what he had to do.

He tied the severed end of his rope to the saddle horn, tightened the cinches, swung into the saddle and shook out a loop. Hugging the fence, the cattle tore madly around the corral in a wild cloud of dust. McEwen rode with them on an inner circle, his eye on a big roan steer, his rope whirling in slow and measured rhythms. For a moment the roan steer darted to the lead; the loop shot out, curled over and tightened on both forefeet; Porch Climber whirled smartly to the left; the steer fell heavily. Ross swung off; as he ran, he tugged at the hogging string around his waist. Porch Climber dragged valiantly, Ross ran down the rope, pounced on the struggling steer, gathered three feet together and tied them with the hogging string. These events were practically simultaneous.

McEwen unsaddled the horse. "I guess you can call it a day," he said. He opened the gate and let the frightened cattle run out. "Here," he said, "is where I make a spoon or spoil a horn." He cut a thong from a saddle string and tied his old plow handle .45 so that it should not jolt from the scabbard. He made a tight roll of the folded bridle, that lonely can of salmon and his coat, with his saddle blanket wrapped around all; he tied these worldly goods securely behind the cantle. He uncoupled the cinches and let out the quarter straps to the last hole.

The tied steer threshed his head madly, bellowing wild threats of vengeance. McEwen carried the saddle and placed it at the steer's back, where he lay. He found a short and narrow strip of board, like a batten, under the tower; and with this, as the frantic roan steer heaved and threshed in vain efforts to rise, he poked the front cinch under the struggling body, inches at a time until at last he could reach over and hook his fingers into the cinch ring. Before he could do this he was forced to tie the free foot to the three that were first tied; it had been kicking with so much fury and determination that the task could not be accomplished. Into the cinch ring he tied the free end of his rope, bringing it up between body and tied feet; he took a double of loose rope around his hips, dug his heels into the sand and pulled manfully every time the steer floundered; and so, at last and painfully, drew the cinch under until the saddle was on the steer's back and approximately where it should be. Then he put in the latigo strap, taking two turns, and tugged at the latigo till the saddle was pulled to its rightful place. At every tug the roan steer let out an agonized bawl. Then he passed the hind cinch behind the steer's hips and under the tail, drawing it up tightly so that the saddle could not slip over the steer's withers during the subsequent proceedings.

McEwen stood up and mopped the muddy sweat from his face; he rubbed his aching back. He filled his canteen at the trough, drank again and washed himself. He rolled a smoke; he lashed the canteen firmly to the saddle forks. Porch Climber was rolling in the sand. McEwen took him by the forelock and led him through the open gate.

"If you should ask me," he said, "this corral is a spot where there is going to be trouble, and no place at all for you." He looked up the north road. Nothing in sight.

He went back to the steer. He hitched up his faded blue overalls, tightened his belt and squinted at the sun; he loosened the last-tied foot and coiled the rope at the saddle horn. Then he eased gingerly into the saddle. The steer made lamentable outcry, twisting his neck in a creditable attempt to hook his tormentor; the free foot lashed out madly. But McEwen flattened himself and crouched safely, with a full inch of margin; the steer was near to hooking his own leg and kicking his own face and he subsided with a groan. McEwen settled himself in the saddle.

"Are ye ready?" said McEwen.

"Oi am!" said McEwen.

"Thin go!" said McEwen, and pulled the hogging string.

The steer lurched sideways to his feet, paused for one second of amazement, and left the ground. He pitched, he plunged, he kicked at the stirrups, he hooked at the rider's legs, he leaped, he ran, bawling his terror and fury to the sky; weaving, lunging, twisting, he crashed sidelong into the fence, fell, scrambled up in an instant. The shimmy was not yet invented. But the roan steer shimmied, and he did it nobly; man and saddle rocked and reeled. Then, for the first time, he saw the open gate and thundered through it, abandoning all thought except flight.

Shaken and battered, McEwen was master. The man was a rider. To use the words of a later day, he was "a little warm, but not at all astonished." Yet he had not come off scot-free. When they crashed into the fence he had pulled up his leg, but had taken an ugly bruise upon the hip. The whole performance, and more particularly the shimmy feature, had been a poor poultice for aching bones.

Worse than all, the canteen had been crushed between fence and saddle. The priceless water was lost.

His hand still clutched the hogging string; he had no wish to leave that behind for curious minds to ponder upon. Until his mount slowed from a run to a pounding trot, he made no effort to guide him, the more because the steer's chosen course was not far from the direction in which McEwen wished to go. Wildy's Well lay at the extreme southwestern corner of the White Sands, and McEwen's thought was to turn eastward. He meant to try for Luna's Wells, the old stage station in the middle of the desert, on the road which ran obliquely from Organ to Tularosa.

When time was ripe McEwen leaned over and slapped his hat into the steer's face, on the right side, to turn him to the left and to the east.

The first attempt at guidance, and the fourth attempt, brought on new bucking spells. McEwen gave him time between lessons; what he most feared was that the roan would "sull," or balk, refusing to go farther. When the steer stopped, McEwen waited until he went on of his own accord; when his progress led approximately toward McEwen's goal, he was allowed to go his own way unmolested. McEwen was bethorned, dragged through mesquite bushes, raked under branches; his shirt was beribboned and torn. But he had his way at last. With danger, with infinite patience and with good judgment, he forced his refractory mount to the left and ever to the left, and so came at last into a deep trail which led due east. Muttering and grumbling, the steer followed the trail.

All this had taken time, but speed had also been a factor. When McEwen felt free to turn his head only a half circle of the windmill fans showed above the brush. Wildy's Well was miles behind them.

"Boys," said McEwen, "if you follow me this time, I'll say you're good!"

The steer scuffed and shambled, taking his own gait; he stopped often to rest, his tongue hung out, foam dripped from his mouth. McEwen did not urge him. The way led now through rotten ground and alkali, now through chalk that powdered and billowed in dust; deep trails, channeled by winds at war. As old trails grew too deep for comfort the stock had made new ones to parallel the old; a hundred paths lay side by side.

McEwen was a hard case. A smother of dust was about him, thirst tormented him, his lips were cracked and bleeding, his eyes sunken, his face fallen in; and weariness folded him like a garment.

"Slate water is the best water," said McEwen.

They came from chalk and brush into a better country; poor indeed, and starved, but the air of it was breathable. The sun was low and the long shadows of the hills reached out into the plain. And now he saw, dead in front, the gleaming vane and sails of a windmill. Only the top— the fans seemed to touch the ground—and yet it was clear to see. McEwen plucked up heart. This was not Luna's. Luna's was far beyond. This was a new one. If it stood in a hollow place—and it did—it could not be far away. Water!

For the first time McEwen urged his mount, gently, and only with the loose and raveled tie string. Once was enough. The roan steer stopped, pawed the ground and proclaimed flat rebellion. For ten minutes, perhaps, McEwen sought to overrule him. It was no use. The roan steer was done. He took down his rope. With a little loop he snared a pawing and rebellious forefoot. He pulled up rope and foot with all his failing strength, and took a quick turn on the saddle horn. The roan made one hop and fell flat-long. McEwen tied three feet, though there was scant need for it. He took off the saddle, carried it to the nearest thicket and raised it, with pain, into the forks of a high soapweed, tucking up latigos and cinches. With pain; McEwen, also, was nearly done.

"My horse gave out on me. I toted my saddle a ways, but it was too heavy, and I hung it up so the cows couldn't eat it," he said, in the tone of one who recites a lesson.

He untied the steer, then came back hotfoot to his soapweed, thinking the roan might be in a fighting humor. But the roan was done. He got unsteadily to his feet, with hanging head and slavering jaws; he waited for a little and moved slowly away.

"Glad he didn't get on the prod," said McEwen. "I sure expected it. That was one tired steer. He sure done me a good turn. Guess I'd better be strollin' into camp."

It was a sorry strolling. A hundred yards—a quarter—a half—a mile. The windmill grew taller; the first night breeze was stirring, he could see the fans whirl in the sun. A hundred yards—a quarter—a mile! An hour was gone. The shadows overtook him, passed him; the hills were suddenly very close and near, notched black against a crimson sky. Thirst tortured him, the windmill beckoned, sunset winds urged him on. He came to the brow of the shallow dip in which the ranch lay, he saw a little corral, a water pen, a long dark house beyond; he climbed into the water pen and plunged his face into the trough.

The windmill groaned and whined with a dismal clank and grinding of dry gears. Yet there was a low smoke over the chimney. How was this? The door stood open. Except for the creaking plaint of the windmill, a dead quiet hung about the place, a hint of something ominous and sinister. Stumbling, bruised and outworn, McEwen came to that low dark door. He heard a choking cough, a child's wailing cry. His foot was on the threshold.

"What wrong? *Qué es?*" he called.

A cracked and feeble voice made an answer that he could not hear. Then a man appeared at the inner door; an old man, a Mexican, clutching at the wall for support.

"*El garrotillo,*" said the cracked voice. "The strangler—diphtheria."

"I am here to help you," said McEwen.

## 6

Of what took place that night McEwen had never afterward any clear remembrance, except of the first hour or two. The drone of bees was in his ears, and a whir of wings. He moved in a thin, unreal mist, giddy and light-headed, undone by thirst, weariness, loss of sleep—most of all by alkaline and poisonous dust, deep in his lungs. In the weary time that followed, though he daily fell more and more behind on sleep and rest, he was never so near to utter collapse as on this first interminable night. It remained for him a blurred and distorted vision of the dreadful offices of the sickroom; of sickening odors; of stumbling from bed to bed as one sufferer or another shook with paroxysms of choking.

Of a voice, now far off and now clear, insistent with counsel and question, direction and appeal; of lamplight that waned and flared and dwindled again; of creak and clank and pounding of iron on iron in horrible rhythm, endless, slow, intolerable. That would be the windmill. Yes, but where? And what windmill?

Of terror, and weeping, and a young child that screamed. That woman —why, they had always told him grown people didn't take diphtheria. But she had it, all right. Had it as bad as the two youngsters, too. She was the mother, it seemed. Yes, Florencio had told him that. Too bad for the children to die. . . . But who the devil was Florencio? The windmill turned dismally—clank and rattle and groan.

That was the least one choking now—Felix. Swab out his throat again. Hold the light. Careful. That's it. Burn it up. More cloth, old man. Hold the light this way. There, there, *pobrecito!* All right now. . . . Something was lurking in the corners, in the shadows. Must go see. Drive it away. What's that? What say? Make coffee? Sure. Coffee. Good idea. Salty coffee. Windmill pumpin' salt water. Batter and pound and squeal. Round and round. Round and round. Round and round. . . . Tell you what. Goin' to grease that damn windmill. Right now. . . . Huh? What's that? Wait till morning? All right. All ri'. Sure.

His feet were leaden. His arms minded well enough, but his hands were simply wonderful. Surprisin' skillful, those hands. How steady they were to clean membranes from little throats. Clever hands! They could bring water to these people, too, lift them up and hold the cup and not spill a drop. They could sponge off hot little bodies when the children cried out in delirium. Wring out rag, too! Wonnerful hands! Mus' call people's 'tention to these hands sometime. There, there, let me wash you some more with the nice cool water. Now, now—nothing will hurt you. Uncle Happy's goin' to be right here, takin' care of you. Now, now—go to sleep —go-o to sleep!

But his feet were so big, so heavy and so clumsy, and his legs were insubordinate. Specially the calves. The calf of each leg, where there had once been good muscles of braided steel, was now filled with sluggish water of inferior quality. That wasn't the worst either. There was a distinct blank space, a vacuum, something like the bead in a spirit level, and it shifted here and there as the water sloshed about. Wonder nobody had ever noticed that.

Must be edgin' on toward morning. Sick people are worst between two and four, they say. And they're all easier now, every one. Both kids asleep —tossin' about. And now the mother was droppin' off. Yes, sir—she's goin' to sleep. What did the old man call her? Estefanía. Yes—Est'fa'—

He woke with sunlight in his eyes. His arm sprawled before him on a pine table and his head lay on his arm. He raised up, blinking, and looked around. This was the kitchen, a sorry spectacle. The sickroom lay beyond an open door. He sat by that door, where he could see into the sickroom.

They were all asleep. The woman stirred uneasily and threw out an arm. The old man lay huddled on a couch beyond the table.

McEwen stared. The fever had passed and his head was reasonably clear. He frowned, piecing together remembered scraps from the night before. The old man was Florencio Telles, the woman was the wife of his dead son, these were his grandchildren. Felix was one. Forget the other name. They had come back from a trip to El Paso a week ago, or some such matter, and must have brought the contagion with them. First one came down with the strangler, then another. Well poisoned with it, likely. Have to boil the drinking water. This was called Rancho Perdido—the Lost Ranch. Well named. The old fellow spoke good English.

McEwen was at home in Spanish, and, from what he remembered of last night, the talk had been carried on in either tongue indifferently. What a night!

He rose and tiptoed out with infinite precaution. The wind was dead. He went to the well and found the oil; he climbed up and drenched the bearings and gears. He was surprised to see how weak he was and how sore; and for the first time in his life he knew the feeling of giddiness and was forced to keep one hand clutched tightly to some support as he moved around the platform—he, Ross McEwen.

When he came back the old man met him with finger on lip. They sat on the warm ground, where they could keep watch upon the sickroom, obliquely, through two doors; just far enough away for quiet speech to be unheard.

"Let them sleep. Every minute of sleep for them is so much coined gold. We won't make a move to wake them. And how is it with you, my son, how is it with you?"

"Fine and fancy. When I came here last night I had a thousand aches, and now I've only got one."

"And that one is all over?"

"That's the place. Never mind me. I'll be all right. How long has this been going on?"

"This is the fifth day for the oldest boy, I think. He came down with it first, Demetrio. We thought it was only a sore throat at first. Maybe six days. I am a little mixed up."

"Should think you would be. Now listen. I know something about diphtheria. Not much, but this for certain. Here's what you've got to do, old man: Quick as they wake up in there, you go to bed and stay in bed. You totter around much more and you're going to die. There's your fortune told, and no charge for it."

"Oh, I'm not bad. I do not cough hard. The strangler never hurts old people much." So he said, but every word was an effort.

"Hell, no, you're not bad. Just a walkin' corpse, tha's all. You get to bed and save your strength. When any two of 'em are chokin' to death at once that'll be time enough for you to hobble out and take one of them off my hands. Do they sleep this long, often?"

"Oh, no. This is the first time. They are always better when morning comes, but they have not all slept at the same time, never before. My daughter, you might say, has not slept at all. It has been grief and anxiety with her as much as the sickness. They will all feel encouraged now, since you've come. If it please God, we'll pull them all through."

"Look here!" said McEwen. "It can't be far to Luna's Well. Can't I catch up a horse and lope over there after a while—bring help and send for a doctor?"

"There's no one there. Francisco Luna and Casimiro both have driven their stock to the Guadalupe Mountains, weeks ago. It has been too dry. And no one uses the old road now. All travel goes by the new way, beyond the new railroad.

"I found no one at the western ranches yesterday," said McEwen.

"No. Everyone is in the hills. The drought is too bad. There is no one but you. The nearest help is Alamogordo—thirty-five miles. And if you go there some will surely die before you get back. I have no more strength. I will be flat on my back this day."

"That's where you belong. I'll be nurse and cook for this family. Got anything to cook?"

"Not much. Frijoles, jerky, bacon, flour, a little canned stuff and dried peaches."

McEwen frowned. "It is my mind they ought to have eggs and milk."

"When the cattle come to water you can shut up a cow and a calf—or two of them—and we can have a little milk tonight. I'll show you which ones. As I told you last night, I turned out the cow I was keeping up, for fear I'd get down and she would die here in the pen."

"Don Florencio, I'm afraid I didn't get all you told me last night," said McEwen thoughtfully. "I was wild as a hawk, I reckon. Thought that windmill would certainly drive me crazy. Fever."

The old man nodded. "I knew, my son. It galled my heart to make demands on you, but there was no remedy. It had to be done. I was at the end of my strength. Little Felix, if not the other, would surely have been dead by now except for the mercy of God which sent you here."

McEwen seemed much struck by this last remark. He cocked his head a little to one side painfully, for his neck was stiff; he pursed his lip and held it between finger and thumb for a monent of meditation.

"So that was it!" he said. "I see! Always heard tell that God moves in a mysterious way His wonders to perform. I'll tell a man He does!"

A scanty breakfast, not without gratitude; a pitiful attempt at redding up the hopeless confusion and disorder. The sick woman's eyes followed McEwen as he worked. A good strangling spell all around, including the old man, then a period of respite. McEwen buckled on his gun and brought a hammer and a lard pail to Florencio's bed.

"If you need me, hammer on this, and I'll come a-running. I'm going out to the corral and shoot some beef tea. You tell me about what milk cows to shut up."

Don Florencio described several milk cows. "Any of them. Not all are in to water any one day. Stock generally come in every other day, because they get better grass at a distance. And my brand is TT—for my son Timoteo, who is dead. You will find the cattle in poor shape, but if you wait awhile you may get a smooth one."

McEwen nodded. "I was thinking that," he said. "I want some flour sacks. I'll hang some of the best up under the platform on the windmill tower, where the flies won't bother it."

They heard a shot later. A long time afterward he came in with a good chunk of meat, and set about preparing beef tea. "I shut up a cow to milk," he said. "A lot of saddle horses came in and I shut them up. Not any too much water in the tank. After while the cattle will begin bawling and milling around if the water's low. That will distress our family. Can't have that. So I'll just harness one onto the sweep of the horse power, slip on a blindfold and let him pump. You tell me which ones will work."

The old man described several horses.

"That's O.K." said McEwen. "I've got two of them in the pen. Your woodpile is played out. Had to chop down some of your back pen for firewood."

He departed to start the horsepower. Later, when beef tea had been served all around, he came over and sat by Florencio's bed.

"You have no drop or grain of medicine of any kind," he said, "and our milk won't be very good when we get it, from the looks of the cows—not for sick people. So, everything being just as it is, I didn't look for brands. I beefed the best one I could find, and hung the hide on the fence. Beef tea, right this very now, may make all the difference with our family. Me, I don't believe there's a man in New Mexico mean enough to make a fuss about it under the circumstances. But if there's any kick, there's the hide and I stand back of it. So that'll be all right. The brand was DW."

"It is my very good friend, Dave Woods, at San Nicolas. That will be all right. Don David is *muy simpático*. Sleep now, my son, sleep a little while you may. It will not be long. You have a hard night before you."

"I'm going up on the rising ground and set a couple of soapweeds afire," said McEwen at dark. "They'll make a big blaze and somebody might take notice. I'll hurry right back. Then I'll light some more about ten o'clock and do it again tomorrow night. Someone will be sure to see it. Just once, they might not think anything. But if they see a light in the same place three or four times, they might look down their nose and scratch their old hard heads—a smart man might. Don't you think so?"

"Why, yes," said Florencio; "it's worth trying."

"Those boys are not a bit better than they was. And your daughter is worse. We don't want to miss a bet. Yes, and I'll hold a blanket before the fire and take it away and put it back, over and over. That ought to help people guess that it is a signal. Only—they may guess that it was meant for someone else."

"Try it," said Florencio. "It may work. But I am not sure that our sick people are not holding their own. They are no better, certainly, even with your beef-tea medicine. But we can't expect to see a gain, if there is a gain, for days yet. And so far, they seem worse every night and then better every morning. The sunlight cheers them up at first, and then the day gets hot and they seem worse again. Try your signals, by all means. We need all the help there is. But if you could only guess how much less alone I feel now than before you came, good friend!"

"It must have been plain hell—" said the good friend.

"Isn't there any other one thing we can do?" demanded McEwen the next day, cudgeling his brains. It had been a terrible night. The little lives fluttered up and down; Estefanía was certainly worse; Florencio, though he had but few strangling spells, was very weak—the aftermath of his earlier labors.

"Not one thing. My poor ghost, no man could have done more. There is no more to do."

"But there is!" McEwen fairly sprang up, wearied as he was. "We have every handicap in the world, and only one advantage. And we don't use that one advantage. The sun has a feud with all the damn germs there is; your house is built for shade in this hot country. I'm going to tote all of you out in the sun with your bedding, and keep you there a spell. And while you're there I'll tear out a hole in the south end of your little old adobe wall and let more sunlight in. After the dust settles enough I'll bring you back. Then we'll shovel on a little more coal, and study up something else. And tonight we'll light up our signal fires again. Surely someone will be just fool enough to come out and see what the hell it's all about."

Hours later, after this program had been carried out, McEwen roused from a ten-minute sleep and rubbed his fists in his eyes.

"Are you awake, Don Florencio?" he called softly.

"Yes, my son. What is it?"

"It runs in my mind," said McEwen, "that they burn sulphur in diphtheria cases. Now, if I was to take the powder out of my cartridges and wet it down, let it get partly dry and make a smudge with it—a little at a time—There's sulphur in gunpowder. We'll try that little thing." He was already at work with horsesehoe pincers, twisting out the bullet. He looked up eagerly. "Haven't any tar, have you? To stop holes in your watering troughs."

"*Hijo*, you shame me. There is a can of piñon pitch, that I use for my troughs, under the second trough at the upper end. I never once thought of that."

"We're getting better every day," said McEwen joyfully. "We'll make a smoke with some of that piñon wax, and we'll steep some of it in boiling water and breathe the steam of it; we'll burn my wet powder, and when that's done, we'll think of something else; and we'll make old bones yet, every damn one of us! By gollies, tomorrow between times I'm goin' to take your little old rifle and shoot some quail."

"Between times? Oh, Happy!"

"Oh, well, you know what I mean—just shovel on a little more coal—better brag than whine. Hi, Estafanía—hear that? We've dug up some medicine. Yes, we have. Ask Don Florencio if we haven't. I'm going after it."

But as he limped past the window on his way to the corral he heard the sound of a sob. He paused midstep, thinking it was little Felix. But it was Estafanía.

*"Madre de Dios, ayudale su enviado!"*

He tiptoed away, shamefaced.

## 7

Sleeping on a very thin bed behind a very large boulder, two men camped at the pass of San Agustin; a tall young man and a taller man who was not so young. The very tall man was Pat Garrett, sheriff of Doña Ana, sometimes sheriff of other counties.

The younger man was Clint Llewllyn, his deputy, and their camp was official in character. They were keeping an eye out for that Belen bandit, after prolonged search elsewhere.

"Not but what he's got away long ago," said Pat, in his quiet drawling speech, "but just in case he might possibly double back this way."

It was near ten at night when Pat saw the light on the desert. He pointed it out to Clint. "See that fire out there? Your eyes are younger than mine. Isn't it sinking down and then flaring up again?"

"Looks like it is," said Clint. "I saw a fire there—or two of 'em, rather—just about dark, while you took the horses down to water."

"Did you?" said Pat. He stroked his mustache with a large slow hand. "Looks to me like someone was trying to attract attention."

"It does, at that," said Clint. "Don't suppose somebody's had a horse fall with him and got smashed, do you?"

"Do you know," said Pat slowly, "that idea makes me ache, sort of? One thing pretty clear. Somebody wants someone to do something for somebody. Reckon that's us. Looks like a long ride, and maybe for nothing. Yes. But then we're two long men. Where do you place that fire, Clint?"

"Hard to tell. Close to Luna's Wells, maybe."

"Too far west for that," said Garrett. "I'd say it was Lost Ranch. We'll go ask questions anyway. If we was layin' out there with our ribs caved in or our leg broke—Let's go!"

That is how they came to Lost Ranch between three and four the next morning. A feeble light shone in the window. Clint took the horses to water, while Garrett went to the house. He stopped at the outer door. A man lay on a couch within, a man Garrett knew—old Florencio. Folded quilts made a pallett on the floor, and on the quilts lay another man, a man with red hair and a red stubble of beard. Both were asleep. Florencio's hand hung over the couch, and the stranger's hand held to it in a tight straining clasp. Garrett stroked his chin, frowning.

Sudden and startling, a burst of strangled coughing came from the room beyond and a woman's sharp call.

"*Hijo!*" cried Florencio feebly, and pulled the hand he held. "Happy! Wake up!" The stranger lurched to his feet and staggered through the door. "Yes, Felix, I'm coming. All right, boy! All right now! Let me see. It won't hurt. Just a minute, now."

Garrett went into the house.

"Clint," said Pat Garrett, "there's folks dyin' in there, and a dead man doin' for them. You take both horses and light a rag for the Alamogordo Hospital. Diphtheria. Get a doctor and nurses out here just as quick as God will let them come." Garrett was pulling the saddle from his horse as he spoke. "Have 'em bring grub and everything. Ridin' turn about, you ought to make it tolerable quick. I'm stayin' here, but there's no use of your comin' back. You might take a look around Jarilla if you want to, but use your own judgment. Drag it, now. Every minute counts."

A specter came to the doorway. "Better send a wagonload of water," it said as Clint turned to go. "This well is maybe poisoned. Germs and such."

"Yes, and bedding, too," said Clint. I'll get everything and tobacco. So long!"

"Friend," said Pat, "you get yourself to bed. I'm takin' on your job. Your part is to sleep."

"Yes, son," Florencio's thin voice quavered joyously. "*Duerme y descansa.* Sleep and rest. Don Patricio will do everything."

McEwen swayed uncertainly. He looked at Garrett with stupid and heavy eyes. "He called you Patricio. You're not Pat Nunn, by any chance?"

"Why not?" said Garrett.

McEwen's voice was lifeless. "My father used to know you," he said drowsily. He slumped over his bed.

"Who was your father?" said Garrett.

McEwen's dull and glassy eyes opened to look at his questioner. "I'm no credit to him," he said. His eyes closed again.

"Boil the water!" said McEwen.

"He's asleep already!" said Pat Garrett. "The man's dead on his feet."

"Oh, Pat, there was never one like him!" said Florencio. He struggled to his elbow, and looked down with pride and affection at the sprawling shape on the pallet. "Don Patricio, I have a son in my old age, like Abrahán!"

"I'll pull off his boots," said Pat Garrett.

Garrett knelt over McEwen and shook him vigorously. "Hey, fellow, wake up. You, Happy—come alive! Snap out of it! Most sundown, and time you undressed and went to bed."

McEwen sat up at last rubbing his eyes. He looked at the big, kindly face for a little in some puzzlement. Then he nodded.

"I remember you now. You sent your pardner for the doctor. How's the sick folks?"

"I do believe," said Pat, "that we're going to pull 'em through—every one. You sure had a tough lay."

"Yes. Doctor come?"

"He's in sight now—him and the nurses. That's how come me to rouse you up. Fellow, I hated to wake you when you was going so good. But with the ladies comin', you want to spruce yourself up a bit. You look like the wrath of God!"

McEwen got painfully to his feet and wriggled his arms experimentally.

"I'm just one big ache," he admitted. "Who's them fellows?" he demanded. Two men were industriously cleaning up the house; two men he had never seen.

"Them boys? Monte, the Mexican, he's old Florencio's nephew. Heard the news this mawnin', and comes boilin' out here hell-for-leather. Been here for hours. The other young fellow came with him. Eastern lad. Don't know him, or why he came. Say, Mr. Happy, you want to bathe those two eyes of yours with cold water, or hot water, or both. They look like two holes burned in a blanket. Doc will have to give you a good jolt of whisky too. Man, you're pretty nigh ruined!"

"I knew there was something," said Mr. Happy. "Got to get me a name. And gosh, I'm tired! I'm a good plausible liar, most times, but I'll have to ask you to help out. Andy Hightower—how'd that do? Knew a man named Alan Hightower once, over on the Mangas.

"Does he run cattle over there now somewhere about Quemado?"

"Yes," said McEwen.

"I wouldn't advise Hightower," said Garrett.

"My name," said McEwen, "is Henry Clay."

Doctor Lamb, himself the driver of the covered spring wagon reached Lost Ranch at sundown. He brought with him two nurses, Miss Mason and Miss Hollister, with Lida Hopper, who was to be cook; also, many hampers and much bedding. Dad Lucas was coming behind, the doctor explained, with a heavy wagon loaded with water and necessaries. Garrett led the way to the sickroom.

Monte helped Garrett unload the wagon and care for the team; Lida Hopper prepared supper in the kitchen.

Mr. Clay had discreetly withdrawn, together with the other man. They were out in the corral now, getting acquainted. The other man, it may be mentioned, was none other than Ben Griggs; and his discretion was such that Miss Hollister knew nothing of his presence until the next morning.

Mr. Clay, still wearied, bedded down under the stars, Monte rustling the credentials for him. When Dad Lucas rolled in, the men made camp by the wagon.

"Well, doctor," said Garrett, "how about the sick? They going to make it?"

"I think the chances are excellent," said the doctor. "Barring relapse, we should save every one. But it was a narrow squeak. That young man who nursed them through—why, Mr. Garrett, no one on earth could have done better, considering what he had to do with. Nothing, practically, but his two hands."

"You're all wrong there, doc. He had a backbone all the way from his neck to the seat of his pants. That man," said Garrett, "will do to take along."

"Where is he, Mr. Garrett? And what's his name? The old man calls him 'son,' all the boys call him 'Uncle Happy.' What's his right name?"

"Clay," said Garrett. "He's dead to the world. You won't see much of him. A week of sleep is what he needs. But you remind me of something. If you will allow it I would like to speak to all of you together. Just a second. Would you mind asking the nurses to step in for a minute or two, while I bring the cook?

"Certainly," said Doctor Lamb.

"I want to ask a favor of all of you," said Garrett, when the doctor had ushered in the nurses. "I won't keep you. I just want to declare myself. Some of you know me, and some don't. My name is Pat Garrett, and I am the sheriff of Doña Ana County, over west. But for reasons that are entirely satisfactory to myself, I would like to be known as Pat Nunn, for the present. That's all. I thank you.

"Of course," said Doctor Lamb, "if it is to serve the purpose of the law—"

"I would not go so far," said Garrett. "If you put it that my purpose is served, you will be quite within the truth. Besides, this is not official. I am not sheriff here. This ranch is just cleverly over the line and in Otero County. Old Florencio pays taxes in Otero. I am asking this as a personal favor, and only for a few days. Perfectly simple. That's all. Thank you."

"Did you ask the men outside?"

"No. I just told them," said Mr. Pat Nunn. "It would be dishonorable for a lady to tip my hand; for a man it would be plumb indiscreet."

"Dad Lucas," said the doctor, "is a cynical old scoundrel, and a man without principle, and swivel tongued besides."

"He is all that you say, and a lot more that you would never guess," said Garrett, "but if I claimed to be Humpty Dumpty, Dad Lucas would swear that he saw me fall off of the wall." He held up his two index fingers, side by side. "Dad and me, we're like that. We've seen trouble together—and there is no bond so close. Again, one and all, I thank you. Meetin's adjourned."

Lost Ranch was a busy scene on the following day. A cheerful scene, too, despite the blazing sun, the parched desert and the scarred old house. Reports from the sickroom were hopeful. The men had spread a tarpaulin by the wagon, electing Dad Lucas for cook. They had salvaged a razor of Florencio's and were now doing mightily with it. Monte and Ben Griggs, after dinner, were to take Dad's team and Florencio's wagon to draw up a jag of mesquite roots. In the meantime Monte dragged up stopgap firewood by the saddlehorn, and Ben kept the horse power running in the water pen. Keeping him company, Pat Garrett washed Henry Clay's clothes. More accurately, it was Pat Nunn who did this needed work with grave and conscientious thoroughness.

"Henry Clay and me, after bein' in the house so long," said Mr. Nunn, "why, we'll have to boil up our clothes before we leave, or we might go scattering diphtheria hither and yonder and elsewhere."

"But how if you take it yourselves?"

"Then we'll either die or get well," said Mr. Nunn slowly. "In either case, things will keep juneing along just the same. Henry Clay ain't going to take it, or he'd have it now. It takes three days after you're exposed. Something like that. We'll stick around a little before we go, just in case."

"Which way are you going, Mr. Nunn?" asked Ben.

"Well, I'm going to Tularosa. Old Florencio will have to loan me a horse. Clay too. He's afoot. Don't know where he's going. Haven't asked him. He's too worn out to talk much. His horse played out on him out on the flat somewheres and he had to hang up his saddle and walk in. So Florencio told me. He's goin' back and get his saddle tomorrow."

Miss Mason being on duty, Jay Hollister, having picked up a bite of breakfast, was minded to get a breath of fresh air; and at this juncture she tripped into the water pen where Mr. Nunn and Ben plied their labors.

"And how is the workingman's bride this morning?" asked Ben brightly.

"Great Caesar's ghost! Ben Griggs, what in the world are you doing here?" demanded Jay with a heightened color.

"Workin'," said Ben, and fingered his blue overalls proudly. "Told you I was goin' to work. Right here is where I'm needed. Why, there are only four of us, not counting you three girls and the doctor, to do what Clay was doing. You should have seen Monte and me cleaning house yesterday."

"Yes?" Jay smiled sweetly. "What house was that?"

"Woman!" said Ben, touched in his workman's pride. "If you feel that way now, you should have seen this house when we got here."

"You're part fool. You'll catch diphtheria."

"Well, what about you? The diphtheria part, I mean. What's the matter with you gettin' diphtheria?"

"That's different. That's a trade risk. That's my business."

"You're my business," said Ben.

Jay shot a startled glance at Mr. Nunn, and shook her head.

"Oh, yes!" said Ben. "Young woman, have you met Mr. Nunn?"

Soap in hand, Mr. Nunn looked up from his task. "Good morning, miss. Don't mind me," he said. "Go right on with the butchery."

"Good morning, Mr. Nunn. Please excuse us. I was startled at finding this poor simpleton out here where he has no business to be. Have I met Mr. Nunn? Oh, yes, I've met him twice. The doctor introduced him once, and he introduced himself once."

Mr. Nunn acknowledged this gibe with twinkling eye. Miss Hollister looked around her, and shivered in the sun. "What a ghastly place!" she cried. "I can't for the life of me understand why anybody should live here. We came through some horrible country yesterday, but this is the worst yet. Honestly, Mr. Nunn, isn't this absolutely the most God-forsaken spot on earth?"

Mr. Nunn abandoned his work for the moment and stood up, smiling. So this was Pat Garrett of whom she had heard so much; the man who killed Billy the Kid. Well, he had a way with him. Jay could not but admire the big square head, the broad spread of his shoulders and a certain untroubled serenity in his quiet face.

"Oh, I don't know," said Mr. Nunn. "Look there!"

"Where? I don't see anything," said Jay. "Look at what?"

"Why, the bees," said Pat. "The wild bees. They make honey here. Little family of 'em in every sotol stalk; and that old house up there with the end broken in—No, Miss Hollister, I've seen worse places than this."

## 8

The patients were improving. Old Florencio, who had been but lightly touched, mended apace. He had suffered from exhaustion and distress quite as much as from disease itself. Demetrio and little Felix gained more slowly, and Estefanía was weakest of all.

The last was contrary to expectation. As a usual thing, diphtheria goes hardest with the young. But all were in a fair way to recover. Doctor Lamb and Dad Lucas had gone back to town. Dad had returned with certain comforts and luxuries for the convalescents.

Jay Hollister, on the morning watch, was slightly annoyed. Mr. Pat Garrett and the man Clay were leaving, it seemed, and nothing would do but that Clay must come to the sickroom for leave-taking. Quite naturally, Jay had not wished her charges disturbed. Peace and quiet were what they needed. But Garrett had been insistent, and he had a way with him. Oh, well! The farewell was quiet enough and brief enough on Clay's part, goodness knows, but rather fervent from old Florencio and his daughter-in-law. That was the Spanish of it, Jay supposed. Anyhow, that was all over and the disturbers were on their way to Tularosa.

Relieved by Miss Mason, Jay went in search of Ben Griggs to impart her grievance, conscious that she would get no sympathy there, and queerly unresentful of that lack. He was not to be seen. She went to the kitchen.

"Where's that trifling Ben, Lida?"

"Him? I'm sure I don't know, Miss Jay. That Mexican went up on top of the house just now. He'll know, likely."

Jay climbed the rickety ladder, stepped on the adobe parapet and so down to the flat roof. Monte sat on the farther wall, looking out across the plain so intently that he did not hear her coming.

"Do you know where Ben is?" said Jay.

Monte came to his feet. "Oh, yais! He is weeth the Señor Lucas to haul wood, Mees Hollister. Is there what I can do?"

"What are we going to do about water?" said Jay. "There's only one barrel left. Of course we can boil the well water, but its horrible stuff."

"*Prontamente*—queekly. All set. Ben weel be soon back, and here we go, Ben and me, to the spreeng of San Nicolas." He pointed to a granite peak of the San Andrés. "There at thees peenk hill yonder."

"What, from way over there?"

"Eet ees closest, and ver' sweet water, ver' good."

Jay looked and wondered, tried to estimate the void that lay between, and could not even guess. "What a dreadful country! How far is it?"

"Oh, twent-ee miles. *Es nada.* We feel up by sundown and come back in the cool stars."

"Oh, do sit down," said Jay, "and put on your hat. You're so polite you make me nervous. I shouldn't think you'd care much about the cool," said Jay, "the way you sit up here, for pleasure, in the broiling sun.

"Plezzer? Oh, no!" said Monte. "Look!" He turned and pointed. "No, not here, not close by. Mebbe four, three miles. Look across thees bare spot an' thees streep of mesquite to thees long chalk reedge; and now, beyond thees row and bunches of yuccas. You see them now?"

Jay followed his hand and saw, small and remote, two horsemen creeping black and small against the infinite recession of desert. She nodded.

"Eet ees with no joy," said Monte, "that I am to see the las' of *un caballero valiente*—how do you say heem?—of a gallan' gentleman—thees redhead."

"You are not very complimentary to Mr. Garrett," said Jay.

"Oh, no, no, no—you do not unnerstand!" Monte's eyes narrowed with both pity and puzzlement. He groped visibly for words. "*Seguramente, siempre,* een all ways Pat Garrett ees a man complete. Eet is known. But thees young fellow—he ees play out the streeng—*pobrecito!* Oh, Mees Jay, eet ees a bad spread! Es-scusame, please, Mees Hollister. I have not the good words—onlee the man talk."

"Oh, he did well enough—but why not?" said Jay. "What else could he do? There has been something all the time that I don't understand. Danger from diphtheria? Nonsense. I am not a bit partial to you people out here. Perhaps you know that. But I must admit that danger doesn't turn you from anything you have set your silly heads to do. Of course Mr. Clay had to work uncommonly hard, all alone here. But he had no choice. No; it's something else, something you have kept hidden from me all along. Why all the conspiracy and the pussyfoot mystery?"

"Eet was not jus' lak that, mees. Not *conjuración* exactlee. But everee man feel for heemself eet ees ver' good to mek no talk of thees theeng." For once Monte's hands were still. He looked off silently at the great bare plain and the little horsemen dwindling in the distance. "I weel tell you, then," he said at last. "Thees *cosa* are bes' not spoken, and yet eet ees right for you shall know. Onlee I have not those right words. Ben, he shall tell you when he come.

"Eet ees lak thees, Mees Jay. Ver' long ago—yais, before not any of your people is cross over the Atlantic Ocean—my people they are here een thees country and they go up and down to all places—yais, to *las playas de mar*, to the shores of the sea by California. And when they go by Zuñi and by thees rock El Morro, wheech your people call—I have forget that name. You have heard heem?"

"Yes," said Jay. "Inscription Rock. I've read about it."

"*Si, si!* That ees the name. Well, eet ees good camp ground, El Morro, wood and water, and thees gr-reat cleef for shade and for shelter een estr-rong winds. And here some fellow he come and he cry out, '*Adios, el mundo!* What lar-rge weelderness ees thees! And me, I go now eento thees beeg lonesome, and perhaps I shall not to r-return! *Bueno, pues,* I mek now for me a gravestone!' And so he mek on that beeg rock weeth hees dagger, '*Pasó por aquí, Don Fulano de Tal*'—passed by here, Meester So-and-So—weeth the year of eet. And after heem come others to El Morro—so few, so far from Spain. They see what he ees write there, and they say, '*Con razón!*'—eet ees weeth reason to do thees. An' they also mek eenscreepción, '*Pasó por aquí*'—and their names, and the year of eet."

His hand carved slow letters in the air. His eye was proud.

"I would not push my leetleness upon thees so lar-rge world, but one of thees, Mees Hollister—oh, not of the great, not of the first—he was of mine, my ver' great, great papa. So long ago! And he mek also '*Pasó por aquí*, Salvador Holguin.' I hear thees een the firelight when I am small fellow. And when I am man-high I mek veesit to thees place and see heem."

His eyes followed the far horsemen, now barely to be seen, a faint moving blur along the north.

"And thees fellow, too, thees redhead, he pass this way, *Pasó por aquí*"—again the brown hand wrote in the air—"and he mek here good and not weeked. But, before that—I am not God!" Lips, shoulders, hands, every line of his face disclaimed that responsibility. "But he is thief, I theenk," said Monte. "Yais, he ees thees one—Mack-Yune?—who rob the bank of Numa Frenger las' week at Belen. I theenk so."

Jay's eyes grew round with horror, her hand went to her throat. "Not arrested?"

For once Monte's serene composure was shaken. His eyes narrowed, his words came headlong.

"Oh, no, no, no! You do not unnerstan'. Ees eemposevilly, what you say! Pat Garrett ees know nozzing, he ees fir-rm r-resolve to know nozzing. An' thees Mack Yune, he ees theenk *por verdad* eet ees Pat Nunn who ride weeth heem to Tularosa. He guess no one theeng that eet ees the sheriff. Pat Garrett he go that none may deesturb or moless' heem. Becows, thees young fellow ees tek eshame for thees bad life, an' he say to heemself, 'I weel arize and go to my papa.'"

She began to understand. She looked out across the desert and the thorn, the white chalk and the sand. Sun dazzle was in her eyes. These people! Peasant, gambler, killer, thief—she felt the pulse pound in her throat.

"And een Tularosa, all old-timers, everee man he know Pat Garrett. Not lak thees Alamogordo, new peoples. And when thees old ones een Tularosa see Meester Pat Garrett mek good-by weeth hees friend at the tr-rain, they well theenk nozzing, say nozzing. *Adiós!*"

He sat sidewise upon the parapet and waved his hand to the nothingness where the two horsemen had been swallowed up at last.

"And him the sheriff!" said Jay. "Why, they could impeach him for that. They could throw him out of office."

He looked up, smiling. "But who weel tell?" said Monte. His outspread hands were triumphant. "We are all decent people."

# WALTER VAN TILBURG CLARK

## *The Watchful Gods*

### I

**B**UCK WOKE when the first gray light stole in at the window over his bed. His mind grabbed back after a last, small, elusive dream, like a hand trying to catch a lizard by the tail. He felt happy and excited, and almost as if he hadn't been asleep at all, so he believed that the dream might have been a good dream about Janet Haley, in which case he wanted to keep it. It skittered out from under his memory, however, and vanished completely.

He turned his head on the pillow and looked up through the window at where the big, brown hill should have been, with the grove of white-stemmed eucalyptus trees high and faraway on top of it. The hill wasn't

*From* THE WATCHFUL GODS AND OTHER STORIES *by Walter Van Tilburg Clark. Reprinted by permission of International Famous Agency, Inc. Copyright © 1950 by Walter Van Tilburg Clark*

there at all, though, and only a little of the eucalyptus grove showed in each of two places, up on the right shoulder of the hill. The fog drifted among the gently bowing, dark plumes, and across them, changing the shapes of the two openings, and everywhere else there was only fog moving across fog or turning slowly within fog. Still higher, above where the top of the hill would have been, it was all one pale, pearly color, and motionless, so that it might have been, except for the visibly moving fog below, just the clear sky of so early in the morning that there was no blue in it yet.

The black edge of the eucalyptus grove in the fog reminded Buck of the Japanese prints his mother liked so much, the ones that showed just the fuzzy, black edges of mountains standing up out of a gray mist that covered the rest of the paper, and was soft and pleasant because the paper was rice paper, and soft and pleasant itself. The Japanese mountains reminded him of others that he liked better himself, the craggy, storms and light-covered highlands in the engravings in his father's big, green edition of the works of Sir Walter Scott. It was easy, looking up at where the hill ought to be, and seeing only the black plumes of the eucalyptus, to imagine a much higher mountain with black crags and cliffs. Because this was an old exercise for Buck in the summer mornings, when there was usually fog over the hill, and because the fog always started in him the same searching and heroic sadness the engravings started, he began to arrange the characters for another version of *The Lady of the Lake*, which was his favorite theme, next after the Tristram story. He didn't even get into the action this time, however. He established Janet Haley as the lady of the lake at once, and passed over the details of her age and costume to settle first the always-perplexing problem of whether he himself should be the successful lowland prince, attractive in his lone daring, or the dour, short-spoken highland chieftain, whose long history of wrongs to be avenged and of rigorous, hungry living fitted in so much better with the engravings and with the fog outside the window.

It was at this point that he recognized what his eyes were looking at. They were looking at the wooden gun with a red-painted stock, and an old window-latch for a combination trigger and hammer, which his father had given him on his sixth birthday. The wooden gun was supported by two nails fixed in the redwood wall beyond the foot of his bed. It wasn't fastened diagonally and permanently, as an ornament, but lay free across the nails, ready to be taken down and used at any time.

At once, when he recognized the wooden gun, Buck remembered what day it was, and understood, though with a slight leavening of guilt at his disloyalty, that it wasn't because of Janet Haley that he was awake so early and so expectantly. It was because this was his twelfth birthday, and when, at the proper time, he went out through the living room and into the dining room, he might find, lying across his chair, with HAPPY BIRTHDAY, BUCK on the tag tied to the trigger guard, the real twenty-two rifle that always rested on the bottom pegs of the gun-rack in his father's study.

There would be other presents on the chair too, of course, probably all in different-shaped boxes wrapped in paper with different-colored pictures, but for the moment he thought of them as all of one lightness and inconsequence, unless there were among them the small, very heavy boxes that meant ammunition for the twenty-two. The thing was to see the twenty-two, which couldn't very well be wrapped, lying there across the chair in the middle of the nearly invisible other presents, with the morning light shining in a long, ruler-straight line on the oily barrel.

At the thought of the twenty-two, and of how short the time must be now, the small, contained excitement which he had misunderstood a moment before, rose up in him quickly, and swelled to such dimensions that it threatened to burst into a thousand glittering fragments. In this great column of joy he saw, like motes turning in a shaft of light, many of the minute, shining activities of the world which always created the same kind of excitement in him: gulls playing in the wind over the surf, with the morning sunlight dazzling on their breasts and underwings, the jewel-like sparkling of the far-out Pacific on a clear, breezy afternoon, the serpents of light that went slithering up across the wild wheat on the hills, and the tiny, multiple flashings of minnows in the waters of the marsh that was cut off from the ocean by the long, flying curve of empty beach between the cliff, where his house stood, and the village over on South Point, where Janet Haley lived. Behind these quick visions, just glimpsed in passing because they were all allied, because they all had their small, brilliant parts in the glad meaning of life, he perceived quieter things: the grains of beach sand, which contained even more light, for their size, than a flight of gulls, drops of the radiant mist that hung over the breakers when there was a shore wind blowing, even the tiny, conical shells, light as paper, abandoned by their inhabitants in a dark tangle of sea-weed on the beach, the empty, leopard-spotted half-shell of an egg no bigger than a fingernail lying under a black sweet-bush on the canyon wall, and the delicately grooved armor of a beetle, half sunk in red earth, with the beetle all eaten out of it by the enterprising ants. Even such inanimate things as these, or such cast-off husks of life, had the glad spirit of sparkle in them, the sprites that were Buck's innumerable friends, and so could not be dead. The great, swelling happiness that rose from any considerable gathering of the sprites, when quickened by the union of warm sunlight and cool sea-wind on Buck's naked body, could make him strut and sing loudly, if the surf was heavy enough to hide his voice, and then suddenly break into a wild run or a leaping, circling dance that he kept up until the excitement burst and suddenly sent him sprinting down the slope of the beach, to dive with a shout over the first wave and under the second. Such ecstasy, which was to Buck the very proof of being alive and goal of living, invariably swept all being up into one golden, weightless suspension, leaving no important difference between the living and the dead, or the great and the small, or the past and the present and the future. And this ecstasy could be approximated in memory.

This time, however, Buck had seen, in the same vision, the village over on South Point, with its miniature red roofs going up like stairs among the trees, from the seaward rocks, with the white border of surf among them, almost to the top of the mountain. It was inevitable, then, that all the winking sprites who were the companions of his daily solitude, should give way almost at once to the more fortunate sprites who inhabited the regions immediately surrounding Janet Haley, or, even better, dwelt in the very parts of her. For a moment he gazed upon Janet Haley as when he had first seen her, almost two months before.

Janet—he hadn't known her name then, of course—was sitting across the center tennis court from him, with her father beside her, as Buck's father was beside him. Two big, enviable men, somewhere between seventeen and twenty-five, were playing on the court. They were playing very well, dancing on their toes, with their elbows up and their rackets ready before them, each in the center of his base-line, darting from there first to the right and then to the left to hit swift, low shots, now down the line, now across to the farther corner, every shot making that convincing, firm pop on the strings of the racket, and the points continuing, one little explosion after another, with the light rushing of feet between, to sometimes as many as ten or twelve pops. The brown faces and necks and arms and legs of the men were shining like armor from their sweating, and they were panting audibly, and grinning all the time, showing their white teeth, and sometimes shouting suddenly when a point was all at once ended by a quick, hard shot in an unexpected direction. Until Janet Haley, with her father behind her, had come in and sat down across the court, Buck had been watching, with his fists closed, every whispering passage of the ball, every move of each player in turn as he received it, thinking himself hard into first one of them and then the other, so that he was able to make every stroke for both of them, and to feel himself getting bigger and swifter and more powerful all the time. A kind of golden haze, made up of millions of the sprites of joy, and just a trifle brighter than the sunlight itself, hung over the court where such magnificent action was going on. Because there was a fascinating point in play at the time, with the shorter, stockier man making one nearly impossible get after another, Buck didn't really see Janet and her father come in, but only in one corner of his mind, and through one corner of his eye, knew that somebody had come in and sat down on the gray bench opposite. But finally one of the stocky man's lobs was too short, and the taller, black-haired man moved in with two or three long, confident strides and leapt into the air and smashed the ball away into the corner farthest from the stocky man. The spell was broken then, and Buck was not only able to look away, but almost had to, in order to rest from the excitement and be ready to participate in the next point. So he looked across the court to see who had come in, and saw Janet Haley. She wasn't returning his look, but only watching the stocky man go back to the fence to pick up the ball, but immediately the golden haze from all over the court flowed together and was concentrated about her, so that her father sat nearly invisible in a separate and shadowy realm beside her. It was as if, suddenly, all the splendor had drained out of the sweating, brown, young men and entered her, although she was just sitting there, very upright, with her feet together so the pale blue ankle socks touched, and her racket across her lap on the starched, white skirt, with her hands folded over each other on the throat of it.

After that, Buck looked across at her frequently, sometimes even when the ball was in play, so that her face was turning rhythmically from side to side to follow its flight. Always he found her within that swarming, radiant nimbus, so that her father not only never emerged from the shadow of inconsequence that must lie, like a dimness of life, a half-being, upon any mortal in the immediate neighborhood of an immortal, but seemed even to recede in time also, toward becoming only the memory of a mortal. Buck looked at Janet more and more and at the magnificent young men less and less, until he was looking at Janet so continuously that he became unaware of looking at her at all, and found himself, without even knowing how he had got into it, engaged in playing a strangely sensible but unorthodox, and therefore difficult, Tristram, who was gently but masterfully in love with a Janet Haley—Isolt of Brittany, and seeking to escape from the dangerous toils of an Isolt of Ireland who was a good deal like Alice Gladding, who had sat in the row beside him, but two seats ahead, during the last school year, and been an orthodox Isolt of Ireland for eight months and a half out of the nine. Time and place were reversed, so that the brown, young men could be seen only dimly, like spirits in a mist, moving soundlessly and without meaning, far behind the distinct, audible and contemporary figures of the tragedy.

It was while the taller young man was walking slowly out to the side of the court to pick up a ball that the ages were again transposed. Tristram, in royal-blue velvet, sewn with golden lions, stood by the fair Isolt on the beach of Brittany. The sun was setting ominously in a mountain range of fog across the sea and over invisible Cornwall, where the dark Isolt sat with her mind coiled against them like a serpent. Tristram's eyes gazed, sad with this knowledge, down into the blue eyes of Isolt of Brittany, and the blue eyes, in return, gave up to him a whole and trusting love. Despite the evils he foresaw, Buck-Tristram was about to make his final and irrevocable vow, when Buck-not-Tristram saw that the blue eyes of Janet Haley were actually gazing across the center court into his own. For a moment the confusion of time and place and degree of acquaintance caused a panic in Buck compared with which the bewilderment of Tristram was a happy clarity. He was shocked by the discovery of Janet Haley's eyes looking into his own. He was unable to look away or to think or to breathe, and he was aware of no other part of Janet Haley but her eyes. So it was Janet who looked away first, and let him return to the present entirely and with a rush. He became abysmally conscious of how long and intently he must have been staring. The distance across the tennis court became greater than that to the sands of Brittany in exactly the proportion the embarrassed Janet Haley, seeing him for the first time in her life, could not be expected to share the feelings of Janet-Isolt. Buck experienced a ferocious shame that had in it not the least remnant of the pleasurable sorrows of Tristram. Despite this shame, however, he continued to stare, and finally, with the pair of practically invisible young men still hurling themselves about the court between, Janet Haley's blue eyes, though not straight on, but a little sideways, looked into his once more. They looked away again at once, but only shyly, and the determined unconsciousness with which Janet Haley was then following the foolish ball, could not wholly deceive even Buck. The flush which arose along her very white throat and then bloomed upon her equally white and only faintly freckled cheeks, could not be mistaken for an effect of sun, either on her skin or in his eyes. It was at this moment, naturally, that Buck, as if himself newly possessed of immortal particularity of vision, recognized the most fortunate sprites of all, those which lived always touching her, twinkling in her blue eyes, gleaming upon the delicate lower lip which at that instant she moistened with just the tip of an uneasy tongue, and shining in joyous, stirring thousands in the thick, red-gold hair which hung down almost to her waist behind, and was bound away from her face by a ribbon of pale blue silk.

Janet Haley, just as he had beheld her at that moment, always returned as the reigning goddess, the center, if not the veritable source, of Buck's moments of ecstatic union. Yet now above all times, when he was so close, perhaps, to possessing the twenty-two, he must conceal every token of celebration. There was another force in the world besides the tiny gods of light, a force with none of their bright affection or infinitely divided smallness. Rather, this force moved, when it moved at all, as one, though it was capable of spreading its influence almost without limit, of reaching with its shadowing malice and jealousy into every act and every revealed hope of one's life, as the fog out there was now reaching into every canyon of the brown hills. Buck did not exactly confuse them, of course, for the presence and power of the fog god could only be felt, single, oppressive and inattentive, as the sprites, in sufficient numbers, were light and uplifting, but the fog god seemed to him akin to many of the manifestations of the God in the thin, blue book of Old Testament stories, the one with all the colored pictures in it, that was lying over there on his bureau now, under the small, black New Testament.

If compelled to discuss God, Buck would have spoken in the standard Protestant-go-to-Sunday-school terms used in his presence by adults who also wished to veil their reservations. He would have spoken as if there were one God, continuous through the Old Testament and the New. Often, even when thinking about the matter by himself, and feeling the immediate force of the fog god upon the side of evil and a vaguely conceived death, and of the little, twinkling gods upon the side of good and life, he would nonetheless place this God that was still only a word with a capital letter, vastly above and beyond them, as a kind of single, ultimate, unimaginable head-God, to whom all the rest were subordinate. He could not, however, establish any direct contact with such a God. All the quick fluctuations of his internal life moved in accord with the dictates of the deputies, joy producing at once that all-embracing, the universe-is-one adoration of the sprites, and worry, or mischance, or the dark stroke of conscience, in particular the stroke of conscience, at once bringing the single, shadowing, malicious force very near to him, and making it terribly perceptive. Indeed, if Buck had been able to explain really what he felt, he must have confessed that for him the Jehova of the Old Testament and the God of Jesus were two quite different head Gods, the former akin to the fog god and the latter a fit master of the sprites. He must also have confessed that the Jehova of the Old Testament was not by any means always the same Jehova, or that, if He was, He was dangerously and incalculably whimsical. Certainly there was not all the same intention operating in the deity which chose, simply because they were devoted to Him, a ribald, drunken, fleshy outfit like Noah and his family, to save the creatures of the world, and in the deity which quietly and gently walked with the good Ruth at sunset, and put her life all in order again. It was still a different God, for that matter, or God in a very different mood, Who amused Himself by giving Adam his beloved companion Eve, and then, just when everything should have been happiest, doomed them with the smiling little apple trick, as if their tranquil drama bored Him. No, when you came right down to it, the Jehovas of the Old Testament seemed almost as many and as various as their worshippers.

Even so, Buck found the activities of the Old Testament, dark and uncertain though they were, much more convincing than those of the New Testament, which stirred in him only an exalted and insubstantial urge to be pure, an urge which could be induced, actually, more quickly and more completely just by touching the little black book and thinking about it in a vague and general way, than by reading in it. Indeed, this hunger for Godliness, which arose much more vigorously when he read one of the stories in his *Book of Saints and Friendly Beasts,* and lasted longer afterwards, too, was often lost when he really tried to read in the New Testament. It was so hard to believe some of the things that happened in it, and so hard to understand much that was said, that the willing, hopeful awe with which he usually opened the book, the eagerness of one in great need of an answer, was almost always transformed, after a page or two, into a discouraging perplexity and wish to escape. The fog god gained strength from the Jehova of the Old Testament. They were alike jealous, capricious, frequently angry and totally selfish, and they both existed as single and separate powers, somehow wholly believable, if not admirable. The God of the New Testament, on the contrary, became real only in the moments of ecstasy which arose from the union of the small, glad spirits of the outside world. He could not, therefore, be remembered and thought about. He had simply to be celebrated, as with trumpets and harps and gay, unquenchable dancing, during the brief time of His presence. The best that could be done beyond that was to keep the moments themselves, more in the flesh and the feelings than in the mind, as tokens of the one truly desirable state of the self, a state light as air, warm and single as sunlight, clean as a naked swim in the sea. And since even this representation of the bright god could not be long sustained, the dark god had a considerable advantage in their struggle for Buck's soul.

The nature of the fog god, however, gave Buck one useful power against him, quite apart from ecstasy. Since that deity chose to act upon the level of malice and deception, it was also permissible to deceive him in turn, as, for instance, David had deceived Jehova by pretending to renounce a Bathsheba of whom he was already weary. Buck had heard his father say something like that once, and it had immediately struck him as the explanation of his uneasiness about David's penance, besides, of course, the obvious fact that the penance had come too late to do any real good. It was possible, then, to oppose the fog god by oneself if only one concealed all outward signs, not only of the opposition, but also of any hopes or expectations which might arouse his envy. It followed, of course, that to reveal such hopes might well be fatal to them. This explosive excitement about the twenty-two was very dangerous.

Actually the excitement had not produced a single movement of Buck's body or a single sound from his swelling breast. The contest between him and the fog god was an old one, and his defense, a kind of rabbit's immobility, had been mounted at once when he remembered the day and the twenty-two. He lay perfectly still now, stretched out naked—he never wore pajamas in the summer—and straight under the blankets. He felt like the stone effigy of some medieval knight on the lid of a sarcophagus. His feet were together and his arms down straight along his sides. His careful breathing scarcely moved the covers. He continued to stare at the wooden gun with a face completely expressionless, save for a slight narrowing of his eyes and the least possible, scornful down-curving of his mouth. This contempt was not directed at the wooden gun, however, but at the thought of the twenty-two. It was designed to convince the fog god that a twenty-two was about the last thing in the world that mattered to Buck.

Thus concealed from the enemy, he listened attentively for any sound in those regions of the house beyond the closed door of his bedroom. His father always got up early, somewhere between five o'clock and six-thirty, and got breakfast for everybody, and then, when he'd finished his own, sat there at the table drinking coffee and smoking cigarettes and reading, or working out a chess problem, or thinking and sometimes quickly scribbling a line or two. He liked to have the house to himself for an hour before he began his work. This morning he would certainly be up early. Everybody got up early on birthdays. But there wasn't a sound in the house yet. Buck listened for a long time, and heard only the far-away, fog-softened breaking and whispering of the surf. It must be very early then. Maybe there was as much as an hour to wait still.

At the thought of waiting another hour, Buck felt a strong impulse to rise and sneak out into his father's study, and see if the twenty-two was still there on the bottom pegs of the gun-rack. For more than two years now, such visits had been almost as important to him, although he didn't make them nearly so often, as his constant revisions, with himself in the leads, of the adventures of Tristram and Roderick Dhu and Robin Hood, of Robinson Crusoe or the Swiss family Robinson, and sometimes, for greater variety in time and personality, of Theseus or Perseus or Kit Carson, or even of one of the saints with friendly beasts, in particular Saint Francis. He didn't use the saints very often, though, because it was almost impossible to work a heroine in with a saint in a manner that was at all satisfying and still keep the saint much of a saint. It had seemed diplomatic to stay out of the study entirely during the last couple of weeks, even as he had avoided heroes who used firearms, but he could imagine the twenty-two in there as clearly as ever, lying, lithe and real and full of its fatal promise, across its two pegs under the four bigger guns, the two shotguns, the Springfield and the old Winchester carbine with the brass-colored housing and butt-plate. He could see it as if he were in there now, feeling the rough, woolly, Navajo rug under his bare feet, and the austere presence of his father's big, flat desk behind him, with all the papers and books that mustn't be touched laid out on it, just where his father would want them. The shelves of books that went clear up to the raftered ceiling on both sides of the gun-rack were visible only in a general and collective sense, and even the four bigger guns, still more dreadful than desirable, were a little vague also, but the twenty-two was visible in every detail. It held the eye of his memory, as it did his real gaze when he went in there, as if it were a living thing, beautiful and unreasonably attractive, but not wholly to be trusted, a creature a little of the same nature as the big rattlesnake he had almost stepped on two or three weeks ago, when he was running down the canyon trail to his secret, and, for that matter, forbidden beach. At times, to be sure, the gleaming barrel and polished stock of the twenty-two were clearly inhabited by the little shining gods, but so were the eyes and the softly colored scales of a snake, if it was far enough away, and minding its own business. The major allegiance of both was clearly to the fog god.

Most things made by people, especially those used indoors, didn't interest Buck, since they were devoid of both the haunting power of the fog god and the ecstatic magic of the sprites. This had not always been so, for he could still remember, though not without shame, a time when he had held conversations with the one-eyed teddy-bear which was now hidden at the back of his closet shelf, and almost nightly had watched his bureau come to threatening life. But now there were only a few objects left in that category of the possessed, and those subject to limiting conditions. His mother's piano, when he thought clearly of the sound of her playing a particular composition on it, especially one of the short Chopin or Debussy pieces she played most often, or Beethoven's *Moonlight Sonata*, seemed full of the little gods, though in a queer, sad way that enlarged one more slowly and enduringly, as the engravings in the green Scott did. His own violin, a good deal when he was playing it by himself, inventing melodies that had in them little pieces of things he'd heard on the phonograph, especially from the Symphony Pathetique, and a little even when it was just lying shining at him in its case, was infused with their vitality, and often the phonograph was too, and his sister Evelyn's oil paints, when they were spread out in a row in their silver tubes with labels of the colors that were inside, or when they were squirted around in little puddles of pure color on her big, leaf-shaped palette. The memory of their presence remained in some of the books in his room, and out in the living room too, the ones he could just look at and remember scenes and people moving in them. But that was about all; nothing else that people made had them, or even had any of the fog god. And things without either, just didn't matter. They were practically invisible and stirred nothing inside but an occasional memory which seemed to come out of another age or world. Nor were the gods in even such things as the violin and the books in the same way they were outdoors, either. There were practically only the sprites, though quiet sprites, in Evelyn's paints, but in the sad, big music, and so in the instruments which made it, there was a good deal of the dark god as well, and in the twenty-two the dark god was more active than latent, and the residence of any gods of sunlight and air was most precarious.

For this very reason, of course, because the darkly, mysteriously desirable twenty-two was its particular, most concentrated symbol and token, the fog god was unusually concerned about it. He was likely to sense at once any long thoughts or strong feelings about the twenty-two. Once it was possessed, once it was seen lying upon the chair and had been picked up and held with both hands as one's own, then the envious spirit would be helpless to act against the giving, and would even, to some extent, fall into the power of the possessor, though never to a degree to be traded upon. But until that had happened, the envy had most particularly to be fended off.

So the instant Buck realized that he was imagining himself into the study and worshipping the twenty-two, he gave up the notion of such a venture, all the more dangerous because his father might be getting up at any minute anyway. Instead, he set about creating a sound humility within himself, by means of examining his conduct, both internal and external, during the critical period leading up to this twelfth birthday. He had long felt such documented humility to be the best defense against the fog god, whose natural contempt for such a poor, unprovoking spirit was bound to relax his attention.

2

The diplomacy of the last few weeks had been most difficult, for it had entailed a constant propitiation of two, separate powers, his parents, in particular his father, and the fog god, and this double propitiation had, moreover, to be carried on by exactly opposed methods, since it was necessary to convince the hostile spirit of his indifference to the twenty-two, while the very heart of his purpose was to demonstrate to his father that there was nothing in the world he wanted so much, and that he was now of a maturity to be trusted with it. For several days, just as many days, to be exact, as he had been carefully hinting to his father about the gun, he had also, in order to mislead the fog god, been practicing an attitude of body which was the upright and active counterpart of his present prone immobility and scorn. His mother had said, more than once, "My, but a boy grows up fast when he gets to be almost twelve," and he had caught his father smiling now and then when he passed through the room in this nonchalant but guarded manner, which approximated, he believed, the relaxed and confident advance of a skilled boxer from his corner, a boxer who revealed to his opponent nothing whatever of his feelings or intentions, but was nonetheless ready to move like a flash in reaction to any threat. His sister Evelyn, who was fifteen, and a junior in high school, and even had dates with a letter-man, was always looking at him and smiling in that infuriating, superior way she had, as if she could guess everything he was thinking and trying to do, and found it all pretty silly and childish. In the present review, however, Evelyn's smile didn't matter because, for all her thinking she was so important, she had no power either to give or to deny, or even to influence the decision. When his mother joked about him, though, and his father tried not to smile, Buck felt his defenses inadequate, and the independence of twelve dangerously diminished. Nevertheless, he had maintained his disguise stubbornly, and even, once he was alone, convinced himself that it had achieved the perfect balance, since it had misled the fog god, without in the least deceiving his parents.

He had the same feeling about the hints he had made. The hints were of two kinds. First, there were the occasional direct hints, such as saying, while he was cleaning the twenty-two after target practice, "How much oil should you leave on the barrel, Dad, to keep it from rusting?" or, at meal times, and as if coming out of a long reverie, "I guess a twenty-two would be pretty expensive for just a kid's birthday present," and, later, lest that be taken as suggesting that only a new rifle would be acceptable ,"I don't think I'd like any other twenty-two as much as the one you have. I don't think they make them as well now as they used to. Do you?" Then there were the much more numerous indirect hints, the carefully enacted proofs, without a word about the gun, that he was now an alert and responsible being, such as shooting his bow and arrow, when his father could see him, with perfect correctness and with a clearly harmless background for the target, or emptying the garbage or bringing in the firewood for his mother without being asked to, or even offering to take his little brother, Arthur, who was only five, out hunting on the beach, and watching him all the time, and letting him carry the wooden gun with the window-latch trigger.

That last he had felt to be a particularly fine stroke, since it exhibited not only his own trustworthiness, but also the shortcomings of a wooden gun for a twelve-year-old.

Now, however, after glancing over the record, he strove only to find the flaws in this campaign, and thereby, as they accumulated, to convince himself that his chances of being given the twenty-two were few and shaky. When he had succeeded in creating something very near real apprehension, a sad, heavy premonition of loss in his middle, he went on to maintain that salutary condition by examining in detail certain less directly related instances of misconduct which might, nonetheless, be construed by his penetrating elders as departures from the necessary discretion. After minor successes with incidents somewhat spuriously sinful, he suddenly remembered the last time he had come back from his secret beach, and was invaded by a misgiving that was not in the least invented.

He had been foolish that day. He was playing on the secret beach, building a pueblo out of wet sand, with ladders made of small fragments of the driftwood that was always strewn in wave-rows along the foot of the great sandstone cliff. When he had completed the pueblo, even to making a shade place in its plaza out of four upright twigs, with supporting twigs laid across and thatched with bits of the black, small-leafed, seaweed, he stood up to survey it whole. He was pleased with its completeness and with the verisimilitude the sun gave it by casting shadows of the buildings and the ladders and the well-like khiva mouths.

Feeling the pleasure grow in him, he looked up from the pueblo and quickly all around, taking in the high, sun-warmed cliff, the one, shadowy ravine, opening several feet above the beach, the creamy surf and the glitter of the rollers beyond it, the long, black, whaleshaped rocks that closed off the beach to the south, and the great, brown blocks of stone, like the tumbled masonry of some anciently industrious giant, that closed it off to the north. He felt himself wonderfully alone and in possession within these four barriers, the sea and the cliff and the two walls of rock. Thus fortified, he looked still farther north, miles farther, at the great, sun-smitten headland, wreathed about the base with surf and faintly misted over with spindrift. He often thought of this point as the shore throne of Poseidon, for there was room in his flexible universe for a small, not altogether serious classical pantheon somewhere between the primitive sprites and fog spirit and the latter day Jehova and God. He saw Poseidon as enormous and statuesque, like a Michelangelo Moses or Blake's God, lying all relaxed and mighty among the tidal boulders, his flesh still shining with sea-wet, his beard moving against his shoulder in the sea-wind, and his great eyes fixed dreamily upon the sparkling distances of his domain. Suddenly enlarged by distance and the magnificent, drowsy god, his pleasure about the pueblo leapt up like a surf and spread violently into the great, shining joy that at once destroyed his identity and made him one with the redoubled glow of sun and cliff that hung over the beach and was the afternoon celebration of incalculable billions of the sprites.

The transportation was even more than commonly explosive, catching him quite off guard after his long, selfless preoccupation with the pueblo. He stretched up his arms to the sky and made a great shout that was to be the beginning of a very loud, operatic-sounding song of praise, but even this gesture was insufficient, and before he could phrase the first bar of the chant, he had to turn and sprint down the steep beach, shouting a brassy challenge, and launch himself, spread like a bird, out into the surf. Even then he would have been secure in the practice of his rites, if only he hadn't been thinking about the pueblo on the canyon trail, so that he had started to build it at once when he reached the beach, without even stopping to take off the old pair of blue jeans, cut half way between his knees and his hips, that he wore for shorts. Usually he took the shorts off first thing, and threw them over onto the whale rock, for one of the important pleasures of his worship on the secret beach was going naked.

Almost nobody else ever came there, for the rocks that made both sheltering wings were all but impassable save at low tide, and the canyon trail was long and steep, and hot if the sun had been out any length of time. Moreover, nakedness was not only condoned, but actively approved by the presiding spirit in the cliff, a vague but warm, enormous and beneficent being, and by all the associated sprites, and even by the great, inconceivable, Master-God, Who, from somewhere clear above the blue sky and out of touch, presumably governed all that went on through these deputies. To be naked hastened, by the increased influence of all the sprites of sea, sun, wind and sand upon him, the ascension into ecstasy. It also preserved, later on, and no matter what he was doing, building pueblos, lying on his stomach peering into the shadowy and pastel wonderlands of the tide-pools, or playing seal in the surf, a steady, happy aliveness that was just comfortably below ecstasy, and sometimes seemed to him even better than ecstasy, because it felt like a state that might become permanent. It was possible, of course, that the fog god disapproved of such nakedness. It was even probable, for he disapproved, to begin with, of the exhilaration that came with it. But the fog god almost never visited the secret beach at the same time Buck did. It was not his temple, and when he did come, either by way of guilt in Buck or quite literally, in a low, gray cloud from the sea, he was an unmannerly intruder, and the warm spirit of the cliff and the gay sprites of the sun and spindrift simply withdrew and awaited his departure. It was inconceivable that he should really dispossess them.

It might be said, then, that it was just because Buck had not strictly observed the ritual forms of the secret beach, but had built the pueblo with his shorts on, that he found himself contemplating a really threatening sin. He had started home for lunch late, and scrambled right up the side of the ravine, through the black, aromatic brush, to save time, so that when he got home the shorts were not only wet, but also a little muddy from the canyon dust. His mother looked at them when he came into the kitchen, and he was sure she guessed, for her mouth set a little, the way it did when she was experiencing a disapproval too strong for mere passing rebuke. But she saved him from telling a useless lie by saying, "I was down on the beach nearly all morning, with Arthur and Connie. We looked for you."

She meant the long, safe beach between the beginning of the cliffs and the village point, where a good many people, sometimes even strangers, often came. So his lie, at least, might now be fitted into possible fact, and so be reduced to a half-lie.

"I was up the other side of the pier," he said, trusting that his mother had not departed from her custom of taking little Arthur, and Connie, who was only three, in the other direction, onto the widest, white-sand part of the beach. "I was looking for ink-fish in the tide-pools," he explained, and then added, because of the mud on his shorts, "And then I went up the ravine to get some rocks to make houses." If he had actually been just north of the pier, instead of way north on the secret beach, he would have meant the little ravine that came down past the house, which was permitted territory, just as the first rocks north of the pier were.

His mother looked at him again in that same tight, hurt way that hurt him too, because of her big worry about the secret beach, but all she said was, "Get into some dry pants. Lunch is all ready."

So the half-lie stood, for he had been north of the pier, of course, and he had climbed up into a canyon to get some stones, and he had even, after he came out of the surf, spent a few minutes of half-looking for ink fish in the pools of the whale rocks.

But now he suspected, looking back, that his mother had understood only too well the device of the half-truth, and had refrained from pressing him merely to keep him from telling a complete lie. He suspected also that some time during the day she had passed on her doubts to his father, though probably guardedly, for she feared his fathers' anger against him at least as much as he did, for at supper his father had told about a man from the village, a big, young man who was a strong swimmer, who had gone to the secret beach to dive for abalone and had never been seen again. His father had put the lesson of the story into an unmistakable remark at the end, too.

"Even if nothing had happened to him," he had said, "a man who would swim alone in a place like that hasn't sense enough to be trusted with anything." The "anything," of course, translated specifically into "twenty-two."

Evelyn had understood then what Buck was just now seeing fully for the first time. While the father was telling the story, she had kept glancing up from her plate and across the table at Buck, with that infernal, superior smile of hers, and after the father's last remark, she had kept on smiling while she ate, in a way that was even worse, as if she were continuing to discover ever profounder implications. But at least she hadn't said anything out loud, and so forced the application of the parable. That was something; that was a good deal, from Evelyn.

No, that whole guarded response to the wet shorts had been no accident,

and his parents' fear of the secret beach was great enough to make his disobedience serious. Most grown-ups feared the secret beach. They said it
was dangerous because it was so steep it had a bad undertow, and even
rip-tides, and because, when the tide was high, it was completely cut off
and the waves broke clear up against the cliff. There was no more use
trying to tell them why he felt safe there than there would have been
trying to talk to them about God in terms of sprites and fog. Indeed, Buck
could not himself have put into words, or into a clear thought, his feeling
of the goodness of the sprites and the kind, warm guardianship of the spirit
in the cliff. There was no way to oppose adult reason except in adult
terms, something about watching to see the tide didn't catch him, and
being able to get up into the mouth of the canyon in spite of waves, and
such things, and he knew better than to try to argue with adults in adult
terms, clear aside from the implication there would be, in this particular
case, that he still cherished the secret beach, and that, probably, since he
could argue from its natural features so glibly, he still went there. No,
that had been a truly dangerous error, and beyond mitigation by anything
but silence and time.

For a moment or two Buck, still lying there looking at the wooden gun,
calculated the time since his mother had observed the wet shorts, and
coming out at almost two weeks, decided that it was enough, perhaps, to
mean that punishment would not now be forthcoming, at least not in any
such drastic form as that of a chair with only boxes in colored papers on it.
The very fact, however, that he had, in the presence of the dark god,
switched over to the optimistic side in his self-searching, was evidence of
how far he had come from having to pretend uneasiness and humility. It
was perfectly certain, he understood, that if his father had intended physical punishment, it would have been administered at once. It was not nearly
so certain, since he had made no promise, that he would not consider even
a suspicion that Buck was still visiting the secret beach as reason enough
to make him wait another year for the twenty-two.

Hoping not only further to soften the jealous god, but perhaps even to
enlist the aid of some kindlier force, Buck examined the half-lie he had told
his mother, and silently confessed that it was a complete lie in intention
and, moreover, that he would probably have made it a complete lie in fact,
if his mother had pressed her suspicion. Then he decided, as a kind of
offering in propitiation, that if the twenty-two were on his chair at the
end of this everlasting hour, he would give the wooden gun with the red
stock and the window-latch trigger to Arthur. He even considered, in
addition, pledging himself right now, never again to go alone to the secret
beach, but this impulse he had to abandon, despite a feeling of weakness,
of softness, almost of moral stinginess, for there was clearly nothing good
to be gained by betraying the gods of life merely because his parents didn't
understand. Finally he set himself to re-examine, in order to increase the
weight of his father's judgment and strengthen his own humility, the one
time the ocean had really almost trapped him at the secret beach.

It was a very windy day, and the Pacific was heaped up into dark, saw-toothed ranges against the horizon, ranges that foamed and chattered as they came rolling in. There were seven or eight ranks of surf instead of the usual three or four, and as each rank leaned and broke, it boomed up along the shore like a thumping upon hundreds of huge, empty barrels. The spray leapt high in the air above the whale rocks, and the white, in-pouring smother flowed smoothly and rapidly over them, waist deep on Buck and deeper, and leapt again on the base of the cliff. The tumultuous back-wash was almost as strong as the surf. Buck was washed off the whale rocks four times, and then dragged back and forth by the deep water on the beach, being turned under and knocked against the rocks by the surf, and then hustled back down by the undertow and scoured along the sand when the water thinned away in its final, hissing rush. Even then he wasn't really afraid, but only a little worried and excited because he could no longer figure out how he was going to make his escape from this huge and active power of water. It kept crowding him so, with no time between waves, the backwash taking up all the time until the next giant wave came trembling and cracking in, high over him. That there would be a chance, however, that an escape finally would take place, he never doubted. It was not a dark afternoon. Whatever the storm was like out in the great central meadows of the Pacific, where it must have started, it was only wind here. The sunlight lay warm and orange on the cliff, even as it did on any quiet summer afternoon, and the benevolent deity of the place was in it.

Before the waves had trapped him, he had thought several times, looking north toward the ghost of the headland that showed through miles of spindrift, of the great, easy-going Poseidon sprawled against his throne and drenched by the spray. His beard was flying like a flag and his eyes were narrowed against the wind, but on his full-lipped mouth there was a smile of profound pleasure for all the uproar of water and air. And Buck had seen for a long time, with the accustomed lift of the heart going even higher and bolder than usual, the running shoreward of the white crests that were the horses of the sea, and the dazzling of the sprites of spray and ripple, and even, occasionally, dark, graceful shadows rising within the waves as they prepared to break, and then, with a quick flip of the tail, shooting up through the green, translucent curves to escape the crash by vanishing into light. They were shadows that might very well have been mermaids. He had imagined several times, with particular delight, one singularly graceful and playful mermaid among them all so graceful and playful, a mermaid with a very white body and arms and small, not yet womanly breasts, and with blue eyes and streaming, red-gold hair, the very color of the mist of sun-sprites that hung all that afternoon over the beach. How, on such a day and in such a place and such company, could anything happen under the sign of the dark god?

And sure enough, the chance came. One of the back-waves finally thinned away to a sliding sheet of water before the next incoming wave could cover it. He struggled to his feet and it pulled at him only up to his knees, instead of up to his waist or shoulders, and seemed to glide out under him more smoothly and slowly than any before it. He stood there, bracing himself and feeling the sand sucked away from under his feet, until the back-wash was clear down around his shins, and then sprinted up the beach ahead of the next breaker, and scrambled, by toe-holds and finger-holds, up the sandstone wall toward the high mouth of the ravine. Before the slow, pursuing wave struck the cliff, he had climbed high enough so it could only shower him and drag at his legs. He hung on, and when it receded, roaring, to meet and check the next wave, he worked carefully up the rest of the way and drew himself into the mouth of the ravine and altogether out of reach.

He stood in the mouth of the ravine for a long time, resting and catching his breath in the very warm, sunny, windy center of the benevolent god of the cliff, who was also smiling about the lively escape. He watched the magnificent battle of the waves under him, and felt the cliffs tremble when they were struck. He beheld the sprites out on the deep sea in such numbers that he had to squint against them, and stood in a pale radiance they made around him in the ravine. He had never before, that he could remember, felt so strong and confident and happy, or so much alive. He experienced one unification after another with the whole dazzling, wonderful world, so that, at moments, he even felt he could launch himself out from the canyon mouth, like a gull, and play with the wind over the surf in great, imaginative curves and swoops, and slow, feathery risings. Because of these bird thoughts, he finally, despite the weariness of struggle and repeated ecstasy, climbed up the north wall of the ravine to his lookout, almost at the top, and squatted there until just a little before the sun went down, watching the new, vast regions of glitter and height opened toward the ocean horizon.

The recollection of this glad triumph completely destroyed the remorse which Buck, lying straight out in his bed, like the effigy of a dead knight, had desired. Rather it exalted him toward celebration with such rapidity that he just caught himself in time. He promptly gave up trying to think of the secret beach as a place of sin, and listened again to the house beyond his bedroom, and glanced up toward the place where the hill should have been in his window. But there was not a sound in the house yet, and there was only a very little more of the eucalyptus crown of the hill showing, with everywhere below it the moving fog and above it the unmoving fog like a colorless sky. He could only conclude that the seeming hours of agitated, far-flung activity since his waking were actually, in the sluggish time kept by the thin, gold watch on his father's bedside table, no more than as many minutes, if that long.

Having failed so dangerously to procure directly the desired moral depression, he set himself to win at least a trustworthy sorrow by fiction. He considered first an adventure for a Buck-Kit Carson, in which Janet Haley, he could dimly see in prospect, would be rescued, in the depths of red, labyrinthine canyons, from the justly embittered but too personally and indiscriminately vindictive Navajos, but abandoned the theme before the outline was even completed, sensing immediately the twin dangers of such a rifle as Carson must use and of the concluding triumph. He scanned a number of safely tragic themes from older sources, but could not be quickly or wholly enough convinced by them this morning. He also passed over the return of Buck-Ulysses, despite the temptations of the butchery-of-the-suitors scene, because he felt impatient about its incurable moral and temporal difficulties. How, for instance, could Ulysses return as a worthy lover after such dubiously prolonged and explained visits with such women as Circe and Calypso? And how, even if he managed to fuse a Janet who could not be, at the most, more than eighteen, with a Penelope who had been waiting twenty years, and was no girl when she started, how, even then, was he to make a reunion with a wife of such long standing very exciting? And if he made her not yet a wife, but only a faithful lover, how was he to justify shooting all those suitors?

Because these several rejections had suddenly produced one of those rare, realistic moments in which he was forced to admit that he had never even spoken one word to the real Janet Haley, and probably never would, he settled at last into one of the few contemporary pieces in his repertoire, a piece which went back hopefully, as if in search of a new and more promising beginning, to the very center court where he had first seen Janet. In this tale he was always himself, though possessed of the physical attributes of a fine athlete of perhaps seventeen or eighteen, with moments of the worldly independence of twenty-one. In this form he saved Janet, who had moments of a marriageable eighteen, from the decadent intentions of a tennis player of national ranking and of thirty or even more sinister years, who was almost exclusively given, aside from tennis and seduction, to alcohol, cheating at poker, and miscalling his opponent's winning shots. He managed this rescue with something like the visible activities of the most inspired passages between the two brown, young men on that memorable afternoon, and with the third-set climax produced in point-by-point detail, by defeating the licentious old expert in an exhausting, five-set final before such a multitude as probably only the Rose Bowl could have seated, with Janet, by an evil, pre-match agreement into which Buck had somehow been trapped, as the real trophy. Janet sat in the front row center of the center box, with her shadowy father somewhere near her, and twisted her hands and prayed all through the six-hour feud, and covered her eyes each time Buck fell or crashed into the barrier while making a nearly impossible get, and flushed each time Buck was insulted by the sneering veteran. That turned out to be a good many times, since Buck lost the first two sets, though only at 9–7 and 15–13, and then went down 4–1 in the third before he pulled himself together and lifted his game to new heights by virtue of his cleaner living and more suitable youth, and by the greatness of his love, for which his opponent's mere ugly and perverse desire was no match. Even then the outcome was long in doubt, for the veteran had a great store of questionable resources with which to oppose the revival. Buck finally saved the crucial third set at 21–19 and four hours and twenty minutes.

He was about to undergo a similar harrowing in the fourth, which he expected to take at 12–10, when, at six all, he became aware that his father and mother had been moving around, and even speaking to each other, in the kitchen and dining room for some time, and that the smells of coffee and of bacon frying gave dependable evidence that the presents, whatever they might be, were already safe upon his chair. At this point the drenched and weary Buck on the center court, which was already in shadow, looked over at the prayerful Janet and received from her eyes, despite the watchfulness of both the vicious veteran and the shadowy father, who were, for financial reasons, allied, the first direct and passionate appeal she had made.

The effect was magical. Of a sudden Buck felt his weariness not at all, but bounded upon the green turf—the center court in the village was actually concrete, and Buck had never seen a turf court except in photographs and the movies, but turf was only fitting, as at Wimbledon or Forest Hills, for such important and masterful play—bounded upon the green turf like a hungry panther, volleying the hardest drives as he ran in, leaping at midcourt to put away terrific, untouchable smashes, serving booming ace after ace, and meeting his opponent's most desperate serves with crowding pick-up shots, almost contemptuous, and of deadly accuracy. The dismayed veteran had no further resources of any sort to oppose such an improbable renaissance. The grueling ten- and twelve-shot rallies fell away to explosive one- and two-shot points, the fourth set, in a matter of seconds, was gone at 8–6, and the final set, which had earlier promised the most desperate conflict of all, was put away at a stunning 6–0, with four love games and two games-fifteen. But then, just when the unforeseen seemed complete came the most astonishing move of all. The flushed and radiant Janet was just left sitting there in her front-row seat, with nothing in the way of reassurance from the new champion but the most perfunctory glance and wave of the racket, and the silver tournament trophy, huge and cumbersome as a coffee urn, likewise remained, unclaimed and desolate, on its table beside the referee's stand.

Buck jumped out of bed and stood, naked and skinny and nearly black all over from the sun of the secret beach, and propelled an unexplicit prayer upward toward, perhaps, the inconceivable head God beyond the blue. That is, he stood rigid and motionless for almost a minute, containing a tremendous upheaval of the spirit, half exaltation and half strenuous propitiation, which erased Janet, the center court, the despicable opponent, the conniving father, the wildly cheering multitude and the gigantic trophy all at once and in its first instant.

With the prayer stopped off just short of betraying incandescence, Buck quickly drew on, instead of the tight, blue-jean shorts, a pair of regular tan shorts which were distractingly long, coming clear down to his knees, so that he felt like the photographs of English explorers and army officers and tennis stars, who always looked as if something had slipped, but which did

have nice, baggy pockets, for carrying such things as, perhaps, twenty-
two cartridges. With the shorts, he assumed the expressionless face and
deceptive carriage of the prize fighter. Thus prepared, within and without,
he opened the bedroom door, paused in the doorway for a final moment
of token prayer, much more specific than any he had ventured before, and
stalked slowly out into the living room.

This morning the living room was at once familiar and disturbingly
unfamiliar The gray sea-light shone softly, with an odd, exciting significance, upon everything in it, the piano, his violin case on top of the piano,
his father's favorite, high-backed Spanish chair by the west window, and
the gilt titles of the many familiar books, now become all containers of a
single lore and meaning, quite strange and unsettling. Still cautiously erect
and ready, but with a violent, breathless tumbling going on under his ribs,
he passed among these reborn beings and entered the dining room.

### 3

The terrible tennis final must have taken longer than he had realized,
for his father had already finished eating, and was sitting at his place with
his book and cigarette and coffee. When Buck stopped on the other side
of the table from him, he read a few words more, perhaps finishing a paragraph, and looked up. At first his gaze was that of a preoccupied, though
kindly, stranger, one who was not really looking. Then his mind came
gradually up out of what the book had been saying to him, or what he
had been thinking about it, and he himself was present in his eyes and regarding Buck quizzically. He made a little grin, and Buck gave him back
almost exactly the same grin. Buck had the feeling he so often had when
he and his father grinned at each other, a feeling that, save for the first
gray at his father's temples, and the difference in time it indicated, he was
practically grinning at his own image in a mirror which made it larger.

"How does it feel to be twelve?" his father asked.

"Not much different, I guess," Buck said, and the mirror likeness diminished, because his father was maintaining the grin more easily than he could.

"No," his father agreed. "It's too gradual."

"Maybe if I was fifteen, it would feel different," Buck said.

"No," his father said, and the meaning of the grin was in his eyes too,
now. "It would still be too gradual. It's always too gradual, thank God."
He grinned a little more, and continued. "If you live to be as old as Me-
thuselah, it will still be too gradual. You'll never know the difference. The
ancient believeth himself one with the babe he was. It's a comfortable
arrangement."

This was a complicated thought, and even in his present expectancy, it
distracted Buck. He couldn't quite get hold of what he had to know in
order to begin straightening it out.

His father's grin became the teasing one to which Buck could not respond. "It is also an arrangement amazingly influential in even the most

consequential matters," he said. "One could do worse than to regard it as the key to an understanding of all human activity. All by itself, for instance, it has been sufficient to convince the learned Mr. Toynbee—" he tapped the open book upon his knee "—that, because he himself has the habit of it, the frail and imitative offspring of a moribund European dogma is sufficiently dynamic to become the fusing faith of a new world."

Buck understood, after a few words, that this second statement was not intended to mean anything to him, so he let it pass in order not to lose his hold on the first. He believed he could get the first all straight in time, except for that "thank God." Why thank God because you never felt any older? His father was always putting in little things like that "thank God," things that changed the whole feeling of what he was saying, and charged his most casual remark with hidden meanings almost certainly more important than those which appeared at once.

Buck had intended to explain that he meant there would be a difference if he somehow, and suddenly, became fifteen on the day when he should have been twelve, but now he let that go too, in order to store the complications of Methuselah and thank God for a future turning over. It might not have been wise to explain about fifteen anyhow. His father had a dangerous way of thinking right into one's mind. He was just as likely as not to ask, "Why fifteen in particular?" and there was no dignified way of explaining to anyone as old as his father that fifteen had become a kind of goal in time, as the ecstatic union was a goal in feeling. Fifteen, for instance, might easily be the point of maturity at which one could really speak, without fear of being ridiculous, to a girl like Janet Haley. It would probably be an age at which one would be big enough and far enough along in school to go out for the real teams in football and basketball, and experienced enough to play tennis that men would have to respect. It would certainly be an age at which he could go alone to the secret beach, and at which his sister Evelyn would have to quit her superior smiling.

"Or did you mean if you were fifteen this morning, although you were only eleven and three hundred and sixty-four days last night?" his father asked.

There it was, the mirror thought, like the mirror grin. Still, there was a kind of pleasure, a slight touch of the little gods, in such an understanding.

"Yes," Buck said, really grinning again. He shifted his weight to one foot, stood with the other foot clenched across it, and glanced away from his father's eyes at the back of his own chair where it showed above the table. He couldn't see what was on the chair. Because of his father's manner, the joking he didn't understand, and this stringing the talk out, that he knew was mostly teasing, he was greatly reassured. Nonetheless, even if everything had gone well as far as his father was concerned, the shadowy god of mischance was still near, and the act of possession, the holding in the hands, was yet to be accomplished. Also, they had gone far enough about fifteen.

His father refused to take the hint. "And why fifteen in particular?" he asked.

The face in the mirror was there again, and it was now exactly Buck's own, feature for feature. He unfolded his feet and folded them the other way, and replied with an entirely false vagueness to cover his deliberate selection of the one most public reason. "Oh, I don't know. I ought to be big enough to play football by then."

Because the quizzical look and the grin remained, and because there was a little pause, with nothing said at all, during which he heard his mother come in behind him from the kitchen, he knew that his father understood perfectly that football wasn't the only reason or the most important. The big face in the mirror carried the inquisition no further, however. There was an undefined but profound and trustworthy agreement between him and his father on what could and what could not be discussed or joked about in front of the mother or Evelyn.

"Well," his father said, laying his book down and settling back with his thumbs in his belt, prepared to watch, "there may even be compensations at twelve."

That was very good of him. That was the double reassurance, the fresh seal upon their enduring covenant. The fresh seal was required every now and then, for often, especially when he was in the grim or faraway state before he began to write something new, the father would go for hours, and even for days, without appearing to know that Buck existed, or at least without remembering that he was alive and had feelings.

His mother was standing there smiling at him, in quite a different way from the way the father smiled, a way that was like soft finger-tips moving out to touch his face, and made him afraid a hug was coming on. Right now, though, she was just wiping her hands on a dish towel with a border of bright blue and yellow stripes. Things like the bright stripes in the dish towel were almost painfully noticeable this morning. The gleaming in the diamond of his mother's engagement ring, although it came from the soft fog light in the windows, almost hurt his eyes, and the colors in it were too distinctly different. Also, he heard too distinctly the rubbing of the towel in her hands, and felt, in tiring detail, and then in an oppressive unity, so that the effect was of being for a moment with strangers, her presence before him and his father's behind him. It was like the strangeness that had been in the living room when he came through it. He was seeing and hearing and feeling everything too much. Probably that was just because he was excited, and maybe a little because he hadn't slept as long as usual, but he didn't like the feeling. It was as if he had carried across into the real world one of the most fully experienced scenes from a legend. The Tristram legend in particular, often developed that intensity, because the sadness of its final tragedy was in it from the start. Buck-Tristram would be looking at Isolt, for instance, standing outside her and seeing every last thing about her with the fierce clarity of expected loss, the blue light on her hair, the reflections of himself in her eyes, the burning color of every gem she wore, yet he wouldn't, as story-teller, just be making her say what she had to, but would actually be thinking it in her head and feeling it as if her breast were his. At the same time he would hear, as if he were there also, old Mark mumbling in another room, and would feel with him the dark, baffled rage against Tristram because Tristram made him feel like a coward and, in the weakness of his betrayed age, he could do nothing manly about it. Such painful omniscience belonged, really, only to the world of the tragic legends, in which it was mitigated by the pleasure of making things happen and making the people move and speak. The fear of death, either for one's self or for one very bitterly beloved, was what produced it, and when it happened really, among living people, like this, it brought a little of the fear of death and the shadows and stained-glass colors of the legends into the everyday world. Buck had come to think of the sensation as being dead but knowing. It was alarming in the dining room in the morning, and he wanted to get rid of it.

His mother stopped wiping her hands. She was anxious to see him get his presents. If he didn't begin, she would hug him yet. The melting promise of that indignity was growing in her eyes.

Arthur and Connie, still in their cotton pajamas that had been washed so often you could nearly see through them, were standing one at each side of her, half-protected by her skirt. Connie appeared to be busy with some long dream of her own and quite separated from the event, but Arthur was very much in this place and at this moment and practically bursting with information. Buck turned away from the three of them and moved around the table. His mother said something but he heard only her voice, and his whispered "Gee," was not a reply to her.

The twenty-two was there, lying across his chair in the middle of the unimportant packages in colored paper, and there was the tag tied to the trigger-guard, with "Happy Birthday, Buck, from Dad," on it in his father's bold, neat printing. Everything was as he had been seeing it for weeks, yet he was not pretending the awe in his "Gee," for the rifle, in its heavy, cold reality, lying there to be touched and picked up, was vital so far beyond his every imagination of it as to be a wholly new and un-expected creature. It had been oiled and polished until it really looked brand new anyway, and the long, tapered, blue-black barrel, set with its neat little sights, and shining full length with a thin line of window light, was beautifully and fatefully alive. The forbidden power, the one thing more, dwelt in the long tunnel of that barrel; that was the narrow re-pository of the secret of the fog god that made him fearful. The lovely, dark pattern in the grain of the polished stock, like ripple marks on the beach, was even more beautiful in itself, but the fascinated reluctance which was the chief ingredient of Buck's awe did not arise from the stock.

He came beside his chair and stared directly down at the twenty-two, but still did not touch it. He was no longer guarding his expression, how-ever, and when he looked up, he found his father grinning a little at him again, but now not at all in the teasing, delaying way. Their understanding of that moment was the most complete of all their many understandings.

He became aware of his mother waiting attentively behind him for the decisive words or act. He could feel that she did not understand about the twenty-two, that she was afraid without being fascinated, that she could not, in any part of her, touch the desire that was in the dread. He was sorry she felt that way, but his concern for her had to remain small and outside the understanding between him and his father.

"It's yours, son," his father said, and the deterring spell was broken.

"Gee, thanks," Buck said, and picked up the twenty-two and held it in his hands, by the narrow throat of the stock in his right hand and by the grooved, walnut grip of the pump action in his left. He had held it in this manner a hundred times before, yet this was the first time. Through his hands, by the weight of the rifle, always so surprising compared to its size, and by its smooth, slippery feel, and also by its smell of cold metal and oil in his nostrils, possession was consummated. The need for deception and propitiation was at an end. The dark, stolen power of the twenty-two entered into him, adult and self-sufficient among the innumerable brighter, more familiar, less consequential spirits of his twelve years of worship.

"Golly," he said softly, turning the twenty-two on its side and gazing down at the paler, oil-streaked steel of the ejection chamber, where also each new, living bullet must rise into the barrel. This was the small, sufficient gate of the dark power.

"Golly," he said again. "Thanks, Dad."

"You're welcome, Buck," his father said gravely, and then went on in another of his own ways of speaking, the way that sounded as if he weren't speaking of anyone in particular, but just stating a general principle. "It has always seemed to me," he said, "that when a boy is old enough to own a gun, he is also old enough to know how to handle it, and should be allowed to take it out alone."

"All by himself?" Arthur cried. He was impressed.

His father nodded without looking away from Buck. "All by himself," he said. "How else would he know it's his?"

Which again was exactly what Buck had been feeling all the time. He smiled quickly at his father, and then looked down at the twenty-two again, and slowly caressed the stock with his hand. He didn't want to do this with the others watching, but he must show his father that this understanding was complete also, and he couldn't think of any words that would tell him.

"Breakfast," Connie said suddenly. "Want breakfast."

This seemed like a very good way out of the difficult silence, but then his mother spoke.

"Just a minute, darling," she said, and drew Connie's small head, with its curly, golden hair, against her thigh with one hand. "How about a birthday kiss, twelve-year-old?" she asked, and the distance between them, the misunderstanding, even something more uncomfortable, as if he had hurt her feelings by caring so much for the twenty-two, was in her voice. He believed, unhappily, that he should be particularly kind to her at this moment, but that there was nothing he could say without weakening the power he had just won. So he didn't try to say anything, but only raised his face and allowed her to kiss him. The twenty-two lay cross-ways between them, and she took hold of his shoulders as she bent over it and kissed him, first on one cheek and then on the other. That wasn't at all the way she usually kissed him. It reminded him, especially because he was holding the twenty-two that way, of French generals kissing war heroes in the movies, after the medals had been pinned on. When she let go of his shoulders, he bent his head again at once to look down at the twenty-two, and closed his hands upon it very tightly. He had a feeling that her unseemly insistence might somehow have transformed the twenty-two, degraded it toward the nature of some foolish toy like the wooden gun with the red stock. It hadn't, though. The twenty-two lay there, beautiful and real as ever in his hands, steel-heavy and full of its sinister genius. Suddenly he was ashamed to be holding it so, between him and his mother, making so much of it while she was looking at him. The shame became resentment almost at once. Why can't she let me alone? he thought. Why can't she stop acting like I was a baby, or something? Or like I was going to murder somebody?

He heard Evelyn's voice coming from the living-room side of the table. "Aren't you even going to look at your other presents, Bucky?" she asked.

He didn't know when she had come into the dining room, but there she was, standing behind her chair and smiling at him as if she understood something he didn't, as if he were making a fool of himself in some way which she particularly, if silently, enjoyed. His resentment was at once turned against her, and considerably strengthened. No doubt she had entered just in time to see him being kissed. She never missed anything, the old nosey, not anything at all that would help to tease him. She knew he hated to be called Bucky, as if he were still Arthur's size. Even the mother had practically quit calling him Bucky. At the same time he felt what he had learned only by repeated shameful, angry experience, that it was no good trying to answer her. It would only spoil everything even more than her just being there spoiled it. The only thing to do with Evelyn was just never to tell her anything. There were some things, of course, like the secret beach, and singing and dancing on it, and telling himself stories about Janet Haley, that he couldn't tell anyone, but they weren't really keeping secrets. It just happened that way about them. You had to keep things secret from Evelyn on purpose. The only thing to do with Evelyn was just look right back at her, dead-pan, like the fighter coming out of his corner, and not say anything. Everything she got to know about, she spoiled.

What was more, on this particular morning she had undoubtedly given him a present herself. It would also spoil things to show ingratitude or indifference, even to Evelyn. He wondered, for a wavering instant, if she wasn't making fun of him because he had hurt her feelings by paying no attention to her present. And his mother had given him a present also, maybe even two or three presents, and Arthur had given him a present, and so had Connie, although his mother must have chosen the present for Connie, and maybe even for Arthur. They would all be hurt because he wasn't looking at their presents and being pleased about them, and anything slighting said to Evelyn would hurt their feelings a lot more than hers. It would hurt the mother's, anyway. Connie probably didn't even know what she was giving him; all she was interested in was her breakfast. And Arthur, small as he was, understood as well as Buck did that the twenty-two was the most important present. It was the presence of the twenty-two which had nearly split him with silence. He must remember to give Arthur the wooden gun.

It was all very complicated and uncomfortable, making him feel hemmed in and pushed around, even though he already had the twenty-two. The importance of everything he said and did was enlarged this morning, and intensified. He was the person they all waited for and watched and listened to. He was the public figure, and it was up to him to get it all over with.

"Gee, yes," he exclaimed, answering Evelyn just as if she had asked an honest, interested question, and being much heartier than he had been about the twenty-two.

Carefully he stood the twenty-two up against the table beside his chair, and looked at the other presents, trying to make it appear that he just couldn't decide, in his excitement, which one to start on. Finally he picked up the cylinder wrapped in paper with little red and blue tennis rackets and bathing suits and sun shades all over it, because he saw Evelyn's name on the card, and wanted to get that over with first. The rest would be easier. He knew perfectly well, from the shape of the package, and then from its hardness through the paper and the tiny clink and soft, inside thud it made when he picked it up, what it was. It was a can of tennis balls. That was a good present, though, a fine present. It would have been really exciting, if the twenty-two hadn't come first. He began to unwrap it, and at the same time to prepare himself to make a natural-sounding, astonished thank-you. Evelyn came around the table to watch him, and his father leaned forward to see better. Connie was saying something about breakfast again, and trying to climb into her high-chair, but the other four were all there, close around him and watching. The mother was helping Connie into her high-chair, so she wouldn't fall and start squalling, but she was helping only with her hands. Otherwise she was watching the most of all.

"Gee," he exclaimed, as soon as enough of the can showed. "Gee whiz, brand-new tennis balls. Gee, thanks ever so much, Evelyn. I can sure use those."

"My, aren't we surprised," Evelyn said, as if she were as old as the mother. He didn't even have to look at her to know just how she was smiling. "You could never have guessed what was in it, of course."

Still Buck fought resolutely against letting her spoil things. It was up to him to get through all this so everybody would feel good about it, and the quicker the better, so he could get by himself with the twenty-two.

Maybe Evelyn was just talking like that because she was embarrassed too.

"Just the same," he said, "they're swell. Just what I needed. Those old balls I been using are getting so light they practically float." And to show he meant all this pleasure, he even went so far as to open the can and pour the three balls out, releasing their fresh, inky-woolly, closed-in smell, and then to hold them up for the father to look at, and to bounce one of them, although he would much rather have kept them sealed in the can until right before he was going to use them.

He went even further for his mother. She had given him a pair of dark-blue bathing trunks with white stripes down the sides and a white belt, and a white sea-gull on one leg, and then, in a separate package, another big book about the knights of the round table, called *Sir Lancelot and His Knights Companion*, to go with the three books of the same set that he already had. They were very good presents too, and he religiously made them more important by giving each of them a particular thought about how he would enjoy it most. He thought of wearing the trunks over on the village beach, where lots of people went every afternoon, and where even Janet Haley might come, and he thought of lying on the couch in the corner of the sun porch, with his knees up and *Sir Lancelot* on them, and a couple of big pillows behind him. There would be nobody else out there, and he could hear the ocean all the time, and even look out at it once in a while, getting himself more into the story, feeling what Lancelot felt, which for the moment, remained a good deal like what Tristram felt, and making additions of his own for Buck-Lancelot to say or do. He thought of the day as a foggy one, like this morning, or maybe even rainy, with the rain beating on the porch roof and sometimes blowing against the windows, and water from the roof running gurgling down the drainpipe, which was in that same corner, and gushing out onto the rocks. Fog or rain made reading much cosier and more satisfying, because there was nothing else you wanted to do in them, and because they made you feel so much more alone and inside the story. They were particularly well suited to the mood of King Arthur stories anyway. With each of these quick little visions, especially that of himself reading *Lancelot*, barefooted and burrowed into the pillows, Buck conjured up a small but real flight of ecstasy, and so was able to make his thank-yous sound better, and even to bring himself, after opening each present, to kiss his mother with some show of spontaneity.

With the last presents, it was easier. Connie's name was on a package that had another book in it, a book about how to play tennis, with lots of photographs of the big stars running and jumping on the courts, so it wasn't hard to be glad about, and besides, all he had to do was wave the book at Connie and say thanks, it was swell, and scratch the top of her head. It was all much easier to act when you were older than the person who gave the present. Everybody laughed this time too, because, when he tickled Connie in her curls, she pointed at the book and said, "Bucky got book," which was close enough to saying she'd never seen it before, but not so close that it needed explaining. There wasn't anything very hard, either, about thanking his father for the queer-looking package that turned out to have a cleaning rod and a can of gun oil in it, or about thanking Arthur for the little package shaped like two steps, and wrapped in old red Christmas tissue, which turned out, as he had guessed at first glance, to be three boxes of cartridges. He was so glad to have the cartridges, especially since they were all long-rifles, that he almost promised Arthur the wooden gun right there, but a moment of his old affection for it, which produced such memories as stalking tigers in the tall, pale wild wheat, and holding off a thin, yelling Confederate line from his entrenchment at the edge of the eucalyptus grove on top of the hill, and riding on a stick horse beside Kit Carson into the ominous, red-templed land of the Navajos, prevented the immediate gesture, and the moment was lost.

By the time he had closed the box of cartridges he had opened to let Arthur look at them and touch them, his mother had gathered up the pile of wrappings and ribbons and tags from beside his chair, Connie was eating her cereal, and Evelyn had put bacon and eggs and toast on the table for the rest of them, and was filling the father's coffee cup again.

Buck wished to eat breakfast with the twenty-two across his lap, but he understood how much that notion lacked of manly restraint, and, again wearing the face of the watchful boxer, he walked over and stood it carefully in the corner. He consoled himself by leaving the opened box of cartridges beside his plate, and then, as an afterthought, because it would divert attention from his preoccupation, the tennis book also. The rest of his presents, he carefully arranged on the bench under the east window.

He made himself eat some of his breakfast, meanwhile, to keep from having to look at anybody, turning over, backward and forward, from picture to picture, the pages of the tennis book, and pretending to examine the leaping, white-clad figures against the black turf and crowd. He didn't want food. He was already filled with prevision, a kind of dark power of prophecy. Food was repugnant to him, as to one of the dedicated for the first time setting foot on the steps of the temple he has dreamed of during a lifetime and trudged hundreds of miles to pray in. When he had managed to swallow the last mouthful of fried egg and to break up his toast enough to conceal how much of it he hadn't eaten, he drank a sip or two of milk to make his mouth feel clean, wiped his lips hard, and looked at his father. His father, however, was deep in his book again, and didn't see the look or say anything to help. Buck returned to flipping the pages of the tennis book, and again thought about giving Arthur the wooden gun. The good moment having passed, the decision was now difficult. The old gun tugged at his affections like a long-time friend he was betraying. On the other hand, not to give Arthur the gun now would be almost like breaking an oath, besides being miserly. He tried to tell himself that there were many games he would still want to play with the wooden gun, because he couldn't use a real gun for games, but something small but adamant within him refused to break under this casuistry. Now, having accomplished the pilgrimage, having arrived at the threshold of the temple of the power and the fear, he would never again take the wooden gun off its pegs, unless it were, in a final act of traitorous condescension, to stand it in the corner or put it in the closet or under his bed to make room for the twenty-two on the pegs.

Throughout this brief trial, he kept looking back at his father, but still the father remained beyond reach in his book. Failing of intervention, Buck hit upon a logical, saving compromise, which had, for its instant, the brilliance of inspiration. He couldn't give Arthur the wooden gun right now, because if he did Arthur, beyond question, would beg to go with him, and that would make an unpleasant scene. Fortunately it was not only Buck who wouldn't want him to go. The parents would never consent to letting Arthur go, all excited by the wooden gun, when there was a real gun around. He would wait until he returned to give Arthur the wooden gun.

Strengthened by this apparent decision, Buck looked once more at his father, closed the tennis book, and said, "Well," as a preliminary to the escape, and stood up. Pushing his chair in carefully, he said, "If you'll excuse me, I guess I'll give her a try."

He at once reinforced this declaration and covered himself from the suddenly focused attention by slowly, right before them all, drawing the first two of the closely marshalled cartridges, the tiny troopers of the fog god in their lead helmets and copper caps, out of the box, and then shaking about half of them from the loosened end into his hand, and slipping them into the right pocket of his shorts.

"I want to go too," Arthur cried, letting his fork clatter down on his plate. "Can I go too, Buck?"

So it was coming anyway. Buck closed the box, and held it in his hand, and looked at his father.

"I don't really think," the mother began, but the father, who was looking at Arthur, not Buck, said, "No," just that, and because of the way he was looking, Arthur didn't say anything more.

The father slowly transferred his gaze to Buck and nodded.

The excitement leapt up in Buck again. His hand was on the barred gate and the gate was unlocked. But in order not to expose himself before Evelyn, and also a little because of Arthur's expression, he restrained himself once more.

"I better get these things out of the way, I guess," he said, and gathered up the tennis book and the presents from the window bench and carried them all into his bedroom. While he was in there, putting the boxed cartridges under the socks in his top bureau drawer, his mother called, "Put on a warm sweater or jacket, Bucky. The fog's cold, and it's hanging on this morning."

"My lord, old softy women," Buck muttered, but when he went to the closet to put the tennis balls and cleaning rod and oil up on the shelf, where Arthur couldn't reach them, he took down his oldest sweat shirt, the red one that was washed and bleached to a streaky pink and had only the ghost of a mounted Red Ryder on the front of it and holes in both elbows. There were certain realms in which his mother's gentle indecision could not be depended upon. He put the sweat shirt on, pushed the sleeves up above his elbows, and returned to the dining room, walking like the fighter coming out of his corner. It felt different this time, though, exactly the opposite of the way it had been before. It was against his mother and Evelyn and Arthur that the attentive dead-pan was turned now, not against the jealous god. Rather, he was allied with the jealous god; the jealous god, at last won over, or forced over, was awaiting him out there where his moving fog still covered the hills and filled the ravines. In this venture the fog god, for the first time, and however reluctantly, would be a kind of partner.

He picked up the twenty-two and looked at his father again. His father, grinning a very little, nodded.

Perhaps his mother was only dreamy from getting up so early, but she made him uneasy because she was staring at the gun with wide-open, half-seeing eyes. He felt almost that she was looking the gun away from him. Whatever she was day-dreaming about, it wasn't happy, either. As he was going past her, out of her gaze toward the kitchen, she woke up suddenly and looked at him again, making herself smile, and put a hand very lightly on his arm, almost as if she were afraid to touch him.

"Bucky, do be careful, won't you?" she said.

Again she was making everything wrong. She seemed to be trying to draw him to her, though she didn't, actually, not with her hand. It was as if she thought he was going a lot farther away than just out on the hill; as if she thought he might not come back. And calling him Bucky, though he had the twenty-two in his hand.

This time his father helped at once. "Buck will be all right, Mother," he said impatiently. "Stop fussing at him."

The mother took her hand off his arm, but she was still smiling at him that way. She still sounded just as wrong, too, although she said, "Of course he'll be all right. I'm just a nervous old hen." He still felt, as he went on toward the kitchen, that he was doing her a wrong, and that the whole hunt was going to be ruined because she couldn't understand.

"Don't forget you birthday dinner's at noon, Bucky," she called after him.

"And leave something for the other hunters, Bucky," Evelyn called, making fun of both him and the mother with her "Bucky."

But he was almost free now. He was pulling away from the hold of the mother's gentle, foolish concern, and away from Evelyn's superiority too. He could afford, though not altogether with an easy conscience about his mother, to be supremely contemptuous of them both, too contemptuous even to show it.

"Sure," he said casually, without turning his head, and went on only a little more quickly through the kitchen, padding softly on his bare feet, and went out onto the latticed porch, and closed first the door and then the screen door so carefully they scarcely made a sound.

## 4

The moment his feet touched the hard earth of the yard, however, he began to run. He carried the twenty-two balanced by the pump grip in his right hand and ran as hard as he could up the narrow dirt road that climbed around the base of the hill and vanished into the first ravine. He was running himself free of the hold they had on him down there in the house, of what he suspected Evelyn would be saying and his mother feeling. He was pulling straight all the little kinks and snarls they had made inside him, so that the threads could be drawn right out, leaving nothing at all attaching him to the house, nothing to hold him back.

The fog had lifted and thinned a good deal since he'd first looked out at it through his bedroom window. The whole big, rounded, lower part of the hill was revealed more distinctly in the darkened air than it ever was in sunlight, and even the eucalyptus grove on the summit was faintly but entirely visible. The eucalyptus, the laurel, the sweet grass, even the earth and stones, had strong, damp smells after the fog, and everything was so quiet that his own panting and the quick, rhythmic patting of his bare feet became disconcertingly loud. There was no wind at all; not even the wild wheat was moving. It was the interval of perfect balance between earth and ocean, when the land wind had died away to nothing, and the sea wind couldn't quite begin. The whole world of hills and ravines was waiting for the change, silent, motionless and attentive.

Buck stopped running as soon as he was around the big curve into the ravine, and out of sight from the house. Then, with only the fog above him and the brush-grown slopes of the ravine going up on each side, he could pretend that the family no longer had any hold on him at all. He turned his attention outward to the motionless world of the fog god, who was in his ascendency at this hour, and to the twenty-two that was a passport into that world as a new and considerable being. He cradled the twenty-two in his left arm, the way the mountain men had carried their guns, and climbed as swiftly and softly as an Indian, walking a little pigeon-toed, as they did, to keep a better grip on the path. Sternly he repressed each of the repeated little uprisings of excitement in himself that were too dangerously reminiscent of the ecstasies in sun and wind to be permitted their courses in this watchful silence.

Toward the top of the ravine, he turned off into a narrow branch trail that climbed more steeply and closed in upon him until dark brush often scraped lightly but sharply across his bare legs. Here he became Kit Carson, acting as scout for a cumbersome military expedition which was, at present, coming along slowly, far below and behind him, because he was hunting fresh meat for the noon halt. With the weight of the real twenty-two in his arm, he felt much more convincing as Carson than he had ever felt before, yet he felt himself drawn out of the part too often to follow it consistently, or shape the action to come, or select the rest of the cast, except, of course, for Janet Haley, who would be in it somewhere.

For one thing, the scraping brush kept distracting him. He liked the scraping, and the fine, white traceries it drew on his brown legs. It made his body feel awake and alive, a proper, mobile, alert explorer of the ravines and the hillsides under the low sky. It made him like the chill of the air and the drench that shook off the leaves onto his shorts and bare calves and feet. It made him feel careless and bold. But also, it kept drawing him back out of Kit Carson's mountains and Kit Carson's unmoved, familiar assurance with a rifle, into these real hills and the struggle against his childish delight about the twenty-two. Moreover, every time he was drawn back from Kit Carson's world into his own, he would remember that he was not just pretending to hunt something big, like an antelope or a deer, but was really hunting something much smaller, a ground-squirrel or a cotton-tail. Then he would be peeved because he had been dreaming, and would make his mind and his eyes and his feelings pay close attention to what he was doing, so that he caught the first movement of each small bird that started up near him and flitted away over the bushes. For a moment, as each flight began, he would think of shooting, and then, briefly, he would become the hunted, knowing exactly, as he stood still to watch, how much the bird wanted to go a safe distance and be hidden again to watch him, so that it was only the danger of breaking silence that kept him from calling out to reassure it.

The narrow, dramatic weight of the twenty-two in his arm also, of itself, made everything more real, with that intense reality of legend, so that legend, for once, was thinner than actuality, and it was more exciting to be himself than to be Kit Carson. He became constantly himself the hunter and himself the hunted, and as he climbed closer to the fog the bursts of happy excitement became fewer and fewer, until at last, he was feeling all the time, with oppressive reality, the kind of tragic fore-knowledge that was only enjoyably sad in the legends. The dark spirit became present everywhere and became, also, allied with what drew him back toward the house. It was secretly and maliciously grinning at him, with a kind of infinitely enlarged, demoniac version of Evelyn's smile, because it had tricked him into coming up here where it was all-powerful.

The twenty-two was not, after all, a sufficient token of the fog power to protect him. He felt the presence of the fog god directly with his body in the damp air, which was chilling him even through the old red sweat shirt, and on the damp earth and the black, shot-like pebbles under his feet. The little drops the fog had left clung at the points of leaves all around him and swelled and suddenly let go, falling with a sound like faint, scattered rain. He listened to this pattering always with a feeling that he was listening for something far more important behind it, and the hunter in him made the hunted fearful and cautious. Because of this slow transformation and the confusion made by the quality of legend in reality, he was very quiet and widely attentive when he came up around the hill onto a wide, sloping bench-land.

This region, covered with dark brush and cut across by ravines reaching down toward the ocean, extended north as far as he could see and the fog hung low over it, like the curtain of an enormous stage, just beginning to rise. This vast reach, after the small hills so close about him, added intolerably to his sense of seeing and feeling too clearly. He believed also that he could feel his ears stretching up and twisting forward, straining their gristle into the cupped, tapered shape of a rabbit's ears, for the silence on the bench-land was so great that the sounds of his own movements, reassuring within the confines of the pass, dwindled almost to nothing, and seemed not to come from him. Yet the sounds his body made by itself were alarming. The faint whispering of the surf, diminished by distance and height and fog, was less important than the sigh of his own breathing and the portentous pounding of blood in his head. The most insistent sound of all was a faint, soprano tocsin, which he knew must be in his own ears, but which nevertheless seemed to be ringing in the air itself, intent upon warning every living creature of the coming of this armed deputy of darkness.

Buck had run many times, and often singing, too, along these same narrow paths through the brush, but now the bench-land was as unfamiliar and hostile as the great plateau of Tibet. He had never been on it before, and the path was strange and possibly misleading. Against his uneasiness, he clenched his hand upon the stock of the twenty-two and declared, in bold words in his mind, that he would conquer this unknown, that, with this new power he had, he would make the whole region his in one journey across it. The exultation which followed this challenge and hastened the drumming of his blood, concealed from him the fact that at the moment he had come onto the bench-land and gazed so far and so much too clearly north along it, the fog spirit had separated itself into innumerable tiny parts, the very counterparts of the sprites, each alive and malicious with the original nature, and that these innumerable parts had scattered at once into their thousands of hiding places around him. They were no longer fragments of his own hunted self in all the bushes, but clever, vindictive little enemies, concealed and cowering for the moment, because he had the potent twenty-two, but only awaiting the instant when he should lay it down or misuse it.

Although he believed that it was because of his glee of anticipated conquest, and would have said, inscrutably, to any dull adult question, that he was far enough from the house now so he could really begin to hunt, it was actually because of this new enemy surveillance that Buck stopped walking, and looked all around him, first in one sweeping survey of the distance, and then more particularly at each near bush and open patch, before he lowered the twenty-two and began to load it. He slid up the loading tube until the small, arched doorway at which the emissaries of death went in showed dark and open. Then, drawing nearly all the cartridges from his pocket, he inserted them one by one, until twelve of them were lying concealed in close file within, ready to sally forth at his least touch. He closed the tube upon them, returned the disappointed unchosen to his pocket, and, with ceremonious care and firmness, only increased by the shockingly loud double-click of the action, pumped the first cartridge into the barrel. Then, with the twenty-two cradled again in his left arm, now the very instant, living, impatient instrument of the fog god, he moved forward upon the strange plateau.

He moved firmly and proudly, but also slowly, taking great care to be quiet, and watching every opening in the brush before him and beside him, for the first suitable token of life, the first moving target—he did not think of it more particularly—upon which to test his prowess. He felt exceedingly alert, but also exceedingly alone. He was too completely occupied with the task he had set his eyes, however, and too accustomed to feeling himself accompanied by swarms of the friendly little beings of light and wind, to know that he was alone. He knew only that he was so tense that any discernible movement, however distant or trivial, halted him if it didn't occur exactly where he was looking. Sometimes, if a movement were very quick and close, it would startle him so much he would even tremble afterwards, so that when he went on he was forced to swagger a little and assume the mask of the emerging fighter. Each time, however, the movement would prove to be just another of the little, dark birds making its sudden escape, leaping up and flitting and dipping away. Some of them, once they were hidden at a safer distance, chirped for a long time, adding another alarm to the tocsin of silence. Life on the plateau was not deceived about which power he was representing now. It knew he had gone over to the enemy. Gradually, because of these bird warnings, he began to realize that the multitudes that watched him were no longer sprites or the hunted parts of himself, but traitorous outposts of his new party, hostile, perhaps, to the brightness he had deserted, but also suspicious and envious of any new power among themselves.

Thus, tiringly alert, yet not in full possession of himself either, he went very slowly north over what seemed a long way, without seeing a single proper target. He passed inland around the washed sandstone heads of two ravines, through which the faraway talking of the surf came up to him distinctly. Gradually he became so nervously anxious to try the trigger that he had several times to repress an angry impulse to shoot at the sentinel birds. A few times he even started to raise the twenty-two, but he never quite gave in to the impulse, and each success in restraint left him with a pleasing sense of having conserved his power for a greater purpose.

At last he came to a place where the bench-land was severed by a ravine much longer and deeper than those before it. The trail he had been following dipped into the ravine and went down under him toward the head of it. Small, separate clouds of fog still clung here and there to the sides of the ravine, as if caught in the dark brush, or swam free in the great air between its walls, making the dark bottom crevice and the visible bits of sandy path going down toward the ocean on the other side appear very far below him. The sound of the surf came up the ravine like soft, gigantic sighing. For Buck, to whom any sound of ocean was always a profoundly suggestive, if mysterious, speaking, the ravine appeared at once an awful and exciting depth, a part of the geography of another world. As he gazed down into it, the wakefulness he had been so long striving to maintain was forgotten. He even forgot, for a moment, that the twenty-two lay in his arm. His attention, exhausted by long straining after particulars, drowsed out of touch, and formless, cosmic wonderings stirred slowly in him.

Yet it was out of this very instant of beginning to expand and lose himself that he was quickened for the first time by a really promising movement, a tiny, groundfast leaping on the far side of the ravine, a twitch like an illusion created by his own pulse, which was altogether different from the aerial tossing and dipping of the birds. He struggled against the other-worldliness in his eyes, but then, in hunting out the movement, moved himself. At once the tiny pulsing way across there in the pale grass between the dark bushes ceased. It was only by a long, careful searching that he discovered the rabbit sitting there, scarcely darker than the grass it sat in, yet unquestionably, once he found it, a rabbit, bolt upright and with its ears erect and attentive.

Buck forgot his awe of the big ravine and swept out of mind with one kingly gesture all the wearying confusions of his first expedition in the new alliance. All the while watching the rabbit, without, he believed, once blinking, he very slowly raised the twenty-two to his shoulder and sought to steady it and take precise aim. This was a long-familiar exercise, but the first time he had applied it to a living target, and that, he discovered, made a difference. Old warnings and instructions came up, but as if into airy spaces in his mind, floating free, like the fog clouds in the ravine, and with a voice of their own, or a voice like his father's, save for the unwonted urgency. Among them entered observations drawn from the particular moment, and much longer and more emotional than the instructions.

"A gully is always wider than it looks," the voice like his father's reminded him. "It must be an awful big rabbit to show that clearly across such a big gully," the voice of the moment put in, and added, getting clear down into his belly, "which is practically a crack in the globe, which is twenty-five thousand miles around—" "So aim a little high," the voice like his father's went on. "Now take a full breath, let half of it out, hold it." "—and floating free in space," put in the new, excited voice, "belted with cloud and spinning so that it must hum like a top and everything on it be fearfully and perpetually dizzy and clinging, and yet it is actually but a motionless, soundless speck in the dark abyss of eternity, too faintly lighted even to show among the other stars, and what does that make you, who are less upon it, far, far, less upon it, and as brief of being too, compared with it, than those tiny, practically invisible red spiders you saw climbing in and out of the craters in the skin of that orange in the copper bowl in the middle of the table Sunday."

"Squeeze the trigger; don't jerk it," admonished the calm, familiar voice.

"My God, what a canyon," cried the other, "opening right under your feet like the dark abyss of eternity."

Buck tried to shut it out in order to hear the final admonition of the practical voice before the rabbit over there, which must be as big as an elephant to appear so distinctly upon the far side of the abyss of eternity, decided to hop again and go off with his chance, with the very proof of his right to the new trust.

"You can't hold a sight steadily when you're standing up," said the practical voice. "Don't try to. Put it into slow motion. Sight below the target and squeeze as you come up. Only come up smoothly, and remember, you have to aim high, so leave the last little squeeze till just the top of the bull's-eye or even a hair above it."

The twenty-two, all by itself, so that it startled Buck, made a sound that was scarcely more than a sharp, short crackle above the gulf of the ravine and under the wide pall of the rising fog. It seemed to Buck, however, after his long silence, to make an indecent and violent uproar, a kind of sacrilege against the stillness of the bench-land and the ravine. The report was followed almost at once by a second report in the depths below, not nearly so sharp, but deeper, heavier and more protracted, like the distant firing of a much heavier weapon. Then, quickly, there came a second echo, shorter and fainter. It was as if two enemies were firing at each other across a considerable distance, down in the bottom of the ravine and toward the ocean.

Buck was astounded, when he lowered the twenty-two after these three reports, to discover the rabbit still sitting there, unchanged except that its right ear was no longer erect. For an instant he was chiefly, within the confusion left by the two voices, vexed because he had missed. Then it occurred to him that perhaps his eyes had deceived him, that perhaps he was seeing a rabbit only because he had been so long expecting to see a rabbit, where actually there was only a dead root or a small bush or grass clump that had, at that distance, something the shape of a rabbit. Peer as he would, however, it remained a rabbit to his eyes.

Quickly he ejected the empty shell and took aim again, very carefully. The voices resumed their opposed monologues in his head, but now he was hardly aware of them, save as a small panic of haste which he had to control in order to shoot well. He separated them from the act, leaving them to argue with each other, while he, quite alone, did the shooting, reminding himself of the necessary steps in a third voice, which was his own. This time, as he heard the crack of the real report, and then the soft, separated roars of the two echoes, he also saw, right through the notch of the rear sight and over the little point of the front sight, the rabbit's left ear drop. It dropped suddenly, not as if the rabbit had lowered it, but like a semaphore arm abruptly deprived of the current which had held it aloft. Yet the rabbit again just continued to sit there. The ear dropped by itself, and the rabbit didn't move.

For the first time there occurred in Buck a sudden and profound feeling for the rabbit as a rabbit, rather than as a target, an abstract object of his aim. It took the form of a violent revulsion in his middle, during which he was divided into two beings, as he had been previously divided between himself walking with the gun and himself watching from behind every bush and sharing the consternation of the birds. One part of him was still the hunter upon the south rim of the ravine, disturbed by his ineptitude, but the other part of him entered into the rabbit upon the north rim, patiently and inexplicably awaiting a third shot, and perhaps even, if that also proved a bad shot, the Lord only knew how many more for the Lord only knew what reason, if any. The hunter part of him was filled with a kind of desperation at the thought of the protracted cruelty. The two voices clamored incomprehensibly in his head, but he didn't even hear them. The third voice was unable to say a thing; the third speaker was choked up and very near to crying, and hadn't a single suggestion to make if he had been able to speak. For a moment Buck, the body, longed to throw the vicious twenty-two into the brush and run away, as far as he could, from the place where he had done such a thing. He didn't, though. Instead, without the least feeling that he had decided to do so, he shucked out the second shell and automatically, hastily, almost blindly, lifted the twenty-two and fired at the rabbit a third time. He didn't even hear the report and its sunken echoes this time, and he was more bewildered than anything else, to see the rabbit slump a little, as if it had gone soft and boneless, then leap feebly upon its side, twice, and stretch out slowly and lie still. Its stillness became a very important fact, the single most important fact in the universe, around which all other being and meaning, like an enormous, concerned audience, was gathered without motion and without sense of self.

At that instant a hawk rose out of the bench-land, two, or perhaps even three, ravines farther north, but almost directly above the rabbit. In the moment it required to rise against the sea-wind that was beginning now, and then curve back on rigid wings and sink away inland to vanish against the dark brush of the hills, it seemed, so tiny, quick-rising and unexpected, to be ominously related to the rabbit, to have risen, indeed, directly out of it, and so to be the other, the enduring, portion of the creature against whom the crime of murder, in a peculiarly lengthy, deliberate and despicable form, had been committed. It went up toward God with word of an unforgivable sin.

Then, in a typhoon of emotion within which thoughts were innumerable but none of them decipherable or important, Buck was running down the trail into the ravine. When he reached a point below where the rabbit should be, he scrambled, in the same panting, driven confusion, as nearly straight up as he could go among the bushes and through the dry, rustling grass. The steep slope and the weight of the twenty-two, however, slowed him down in spite of all he could do, and as he slowed down, the whirling confusion in his mind slowed down too, and he recognized among his feelings a surprising eagerness to lay hands upon his first kill. Because of the visions of abysses, inter-stellar loneliness and a small, hawk-shaped soul rising straight up, but then curving away and downward out of sight, as if it too, even it, had somehow been mortally wounded, he was very glad of this eagerness. He strove to give it strength. He fed it with fragments of worldly maxim and bits of thick-skinned, male, public attitude, hoping it would grow big enough to defend him. The result was not altogether satisfactory. Instead of pushing out the many disturbing notions, the eagerness first, though it seemed to become much larger, was transformed into a mere hollow imitation of experienced indifference, a sensation akin to the one that went with coming out like a prize-fighter. This, in turn, still didn't push out the disturbing notions, but rather blended with them to make an all-pervading, uneasy defiance against glimpses of souls of any kind, all transient ecstasies, the regrets of mothers, the silent disapproval of fathers, the superior smiling of sisters, the unimpeachable delicacy of red-headed loves and in particular against gods of every category, inherent, mythical and metaphysical.

When finally he came up to the rabbit and stood there, staring down at it, this too-widespread defiance was no longer able to sustain him at all. It vanished, leaving him empty and incredulous while, all unknown to him, the enormous, primal chaos engendered by his act slowly shrank and was reshaped toward reality.

It was not a big rabbit at all, not by any means the elephant-sized, well, at least large dog-sized, creature he had been rushing up to see. On the contrary, it was a very small rabbit, a baby cottontail. Slowly, as he gazed down upon it, he was informed, in the reasonable marksman's voice of another, that it was not the wideness of the ravine that had made the rabbit seem small, but the smallness of the rabbit which had made the ravine seem wide.

The small rabbit lay flat upon its side, extended in a grotesque, straining arc, the motionless imitation of a desperate leap. Only its downy fur stirred a little when the sea-wind lightly, tenderly caressed it. At each touch of the sea-wind, also, the nearby grasses bowed a little in suppressed agony, and the topmost leaves and twigs of the bush close above trembled stiffly in unison. There was no confusion any more, and no haste. The world was its own size again, its own tangible self, everything in it real and believable, if holding a little aloof from Buck. Time had stopped, and in its fixity there was no progression, no change, no possible escape. This dead creature, not as large as his own two hands, capable, with room to spare, of being cradled in his own two hands, which lay there soft upon the harsh grass of almost the same color, had only begun to savor the ecstasy and dread and infinite, curious variety of life. He had been able to kill it only because it was so young and it simply couldn't move when it was scared. It was so very young, indeed, that it had not learned even that first of all lessons very well, for it had forgotten to lower its ears.

One black-rimmed bullet hole, with only a very little blood seeping up around the edges of it, showed just above and in front of the alarmed, protuberant eye. It was a neat, exact orifice, a most improbably tiny entrance for death, yet the eye was already losing its alarm, closing out the last look at the world with a filmy shutter being let down just inside, between the eye and the mind.

Buck knelt and lifted one of the leaf-shaped ears upon his fingers. The ear was disturbingly warm and soft, and when thus extended, it revealed just what Buck had most hoped not to see. There was another little, neat, dark-rimmed hole through the base of the ear, not half an inch above the head. Through this hole Buck could see the color of his own finger. The delicate whorl of the fingertip was made distinct by gun oil and a little blood in its grooves. He wished desperately to end his examination with this one ear, but was unable to do so. As if by itself, while something tiny and important in his mind raced toward the back of his skull, away from where he could find it, his hands reached farther under and lifted the other ear, still not by pinching it between thumb and finger, but upon the flat of the palm, as if the ear might be reassured by such gentle handling, and feel able to rest in such a position. The tiny hole, which he could feel now as if it were pierced in himself, was in this ear also, though a little farther up from the head. The dark awe again moved faintly but fearfully within him, as at the first glimpse of the rising hawk.

The hole in front of the eye became almost a comfort. At the same time, Buck felt the power of the twenty-two as never before, and with loathing. A rebellion within the congress of his insides sought to place the whole blame upon the cold, slick, heavy, sharp-working twenty-two, as if it might by itself not only have sent forth the three tiny monsters of doom, but also made the fatal decision, so empty of understanding and so criminally stupid about visible sizes and distances. The twenty-two was easily able, without a sound or a movement, just by lying there across his thigh, to turn this false accusation and put it home where it belonged.

Then Buck was compelled to go even farther, to lift the small rabbit by its wounded ears, in the full grip of his fist, and turn it. He must see all that had happened. The hole in the other side of the head was not nearly so neat. Most of the eye was gone, and on the yellow grass where the head had been lying, there were clots and streaks of shiny, new red. Buck was not sick, not from the belly and out at the mouth sick, anyway. He hardened his middle and benumbed his mind; that was all. He felt only the warm, short-furred, gristly ears in the clutch of his fist, and considered only the surprising heaviness of the small rabbit hanging from them.

Death is awful heavy, he thought, on the surface of his mind, not letting the notion in where it would stir feelings. That's all it is, just heavy. It's all there, but it's done, so it's just heavy.

But then he saw again, upon the small, traitorous screen of his memory, the sudden ascent of the hawk, and could not help wondering if the thing which made lightness and ecstatic loveliness in life had fled up out of the rabbit by way of the hole made by the third bullet. His mind began to open and let the feelings up. He closed them under again, resolutely. He thought, like someone else, like his father's voice arguing with him, that he should stand up, make himself expressionless, and attentive to nothing going on inside himself, but only to the safe, fixed things about him, and continue to hunt, carrying the small rabbit with him. At the same time deeper, if less orderly, counsel assured him that he would not do so. He looked around quickly, feeling that he wasn't alone in the ravine or on the bench-land, that somewhere, not very near, but near enough, certainly, to see him and be curious and perhaps even to guess, there was a man standing, a quiet, watchful, judging man, almost, but not quite, a stranger. There was no man, though. The watching was there, but not the man to do it. There was nothing in sight, really, but the fog, still lifting and thinning, and the withdrawn, silently lamenting bushes and grass of the ravine. He was free to retreat, to stand up and glide silently away from this place, leaving behind him, with the body of the small rabbit, the fear and shame of what he had done.

He stood up, holding himself dead-pan against this wish to run away. With the rabbit still in one hand, and the twenty-two in the other, he looked for the first time at the ravine whole, and all at once knew where he was. The world had changed, but not in appearance. It had changed only because it was dead inside, and because it had shut him out, because it was no longer unceasingly quivering and shimmering with the multitude of invisible lives. Outwardly it was the same as ever, and he was not upon the edge of an abyss in the plateau of Tibet, but at the head of his own particular ravine, the ravine by which another Buck, back in another life, had usually gone down to the secret beach which had been the chosen resort of sprites and the charge of the benevolent spirit of the cliffs.

The outlaw Buck knew then what he wanted to do, and felt a relief at the knowledge, though a grave and somewhat dreamy relief, composed of a decision, with a trace of penitential eagerness, at the center, surrounded by a great holding-off of questions and feelings. Now that he had thought of it, indeed, it was not even what he wanted to do, but convincingly, blessedly, what he had to do, as if someone else, a trusted and much older and wiser someone, had ordered him to do it. He had to go swimming at the secret beach.

Still carrying the rabbit by its ears in one hand, and the twenty-two in the other, so that he had to go very slowly, balancing himself, and testing each foothold, he descended the steep side of the ravine. When he reached the trail, he turned down toward the beach. The smell of the sea was strong in the ravine, and the quiet seemed thickened and closed in, only the more complete for the pulsing whisper of the surf, which sent small, communicative ghosts of itself up along the brushy slopes above, and among the shelves and caves of bare sandstone in the chasm below. When he had gone a short way along the trail, Buck lifted the small rabbit against his sweat shirt and worked his hand around under it, until he could carry it safely upon his forearm. This relieved him greatly, removing a painful strain from his own ears.

## 5

It occurred to Buck, after a time, that he should be running. He always ran on the canyon trail, once he was out of sight from the top. Farther down, when he was running so fast that it was like half flying, and his barefeet seemed to have eyes of their own to sail him over reaching bushes and to pick the clear spots among the black pebbles that rolled like shot, he should begin to sing in the high, quick way that went with downhill running. When he came hurtling around the last big bend and saw, all at once, between the high wings of the canyon-mouth, the whole blue dome of ocean swelling away into the west and sparkling everywhere, and felt the cool breeze straight in his face, there should arise in his breast, whatever sound actually came out, a great, martial delight of brass and drum, equal to the near crashing of the surf, and sufficient to lift him instantly into the god that could not be reasoned about. It made him uneasy that the running and the martial music now seemed a far-back, improbable conduct. He felt as if he were already late coming down to the beach, too, because here he was still walking, when usually he began to run just a few yards down from the very top of the trail, where the last vestige of authority, the last thread to the house, let go, and the ravine became his own, a kind of extension of the secret beach and its guardian portal. The will of the benign spirit of the cliffs prevailed in it also, and its lesser deities had much the same meanings as those of the beach.

Even this remembered security and the nudge of time, however, could not start Buck flying now. He continued to feel behind time, but that only gave the greater power to the forces which restrained him, forces alien here, but so wholly in control this morning, and because of his deed, that the native spirits had withdrawn, and even the will of their benign chief seemed only doubtfully in force. It was steadily growing lighter in the ravine, but the fog had not broken overhead, and it was only a cold, gray, wet kind of lightness. There was no question, in the extreme silence between the dark walls and under the fog, that the god of conscience had taken over, and that Buck was being kept under observation.

The same spy who had stood on the other edge of the ravine and watched him, with anything but approval, while he examined the little rabbit, was now moving down invisibly along the walls of the ravine, first upon one side and then the other, keeping Buck always in sight. It was evident that this spy was a deputy of the fog god, and that Buck was not trusted. It even seemed as if the whole business of getting the twenty-two for his own had been a trick. He had lost the bright gods; he had even made himself their enemy, a result he had not foreseen, though it now appeared perfectly logical. And hadn't he even been warned of just this result, before he ever saw the rabbit? When he first gave up trying to be Kit Carson, and became a real hunter, with a real, loaded rifle in his arm, hadn't he seen only dark, frightened birds, birds ominous as legendary warnings, and nowhere any sprites? And hadn't he felt innumerable bits of himself hiding along the hillsides, filling the places of the betrayed beings of light and exultation?

He had lost the bright gods, and he had not been accepted by the dark. He was in no soul's land, and in its isolation his own soul was withdrawn, small and heavy as a stone within him, and closed about his evil deed. No wonder it could not take wing and make the heralding music. That was the whole of reality now, the little stone inside, and outside the cold, dark ravine and the inescapable watcher. His knees felt weak and his body deeply chilled, even with the red sweat shirt on, and the twenty-two and the rabbit were beginning to feel so heavy that he knew he couldn't have run with them even if his heart had been light and quick. Several times, when he felt himself most closely watched, as if for an immediate purpose, he looked up quickly, thinking, "There's really somebody in here watching me." He could never discover the watcher where he believed him to be, however, and each time, when he went on, after the first quick look, to search the side of the canyon, there would be only the still, black bushes and the narrow side-washes coming down into the ravine, and the sky of fog beginning to move and take shapes above the rim. Then he would realize that the watcher had slipped over onto the other side.

The rabbit, small though it was, became the particular burden. All the other impressions of his plight were fleeting as compared with his concentration upon the rabbit, and at times it seemed as if the rabbit and the small, inactive stone of his soul were the same thing. He wished very much that the rabbit were alive on his arm, nestling there of its own choice, like a pet cat. Several times he thought, with a small, imitation leap of ecstasy, of a miraculous resurrection of the rabbit. It would move on his hand and gather itself together, and then, when he knelt down to bring it closer to the earth, its small, strong hind legs would propel it out of his arm. Not at all afraid of him, but only glad to be back to what it knew, it would hop slowly away, sitting up now and then to look around or pull at a leaf and chew it. When it chewed it would work its mouth and nose the way rabbits always did, in both directions, side to side and up and down. At last, after he had watched it a long time, it would hop out of sight among the dark bushes, removing with itself all that Buck had done to transform the world so miserably.

None of these minor resurrections, however, helped against the unquestionable death that became heavier and heavier on his arm. The rabbit would not really draw itself warmly together and snuggle. On the contrary, it kept growing cooler and stretching out more, and now and then it rolled limply, as flexible but uncontrolled as jelly, and threatened to fall off. Each of these loose shifts within the rabbit weakened Buck like a failure of his own muscles. When he came around the third turn, where the ravine widened and the sound of surf was noticeably louder, Buck stopped and leaned the twenty-two against the wall of the trail and used both hands to arrange the small rabbit more compactly in the hollow of his arm. Despite his wish to close his eyes against the bullet holes in them, he also tenderly and painstakingly arranged the rabbit's ears to lie flat along its back. The act comforted him somewhat. It made, to the knowledge of his arm and hand, and his breast under the red sweat shirt, a considerable decrease in the difference between the living and the dead. The small stone of his soul enlarged and softened somewhat, and began to move within, so that it felt more like a stubborn egg, nearly ready to hatch. Something unknown, but of great importance because it was alive, could be felt pecking at the thick shell of self-accusation. Very gently he stroked the undamaged forehead of the small rabbit, and back along its ears, and still farther, smoothing the fur over its hind quarters. He became intensely aware, though for the first time, of the silky fluff of the tail, scarcely more substantial than air, against his hand.

"Poor damn little old rabbit," he murmured. "What did you ever do to anybody?"

The unexpected sound of his own voice suddenly brought tears to his eyes, and the rabbit dissolved and spread and contracted and solidified ridiculously, like something seen through heat waves. It was a queer, amusing movement, as if the rabbit were trying to dance on his hand, and Buck made a short laugh and sniffled. It frightened him, then, to realize that he was standing alone on the trail in the very quiet ravine, with the watcher somewhere above him, and laughing and sniffling out loud. He wouldn't look for the watcher this time, but he spoke for the ears of the watcher, defiantly, and more loudly than he had spoken to the rabbit.

"Well, there's no use crying about it, baby. It ain't gonna help the poor damn rabbit any for you to cry about it, is it?"

The "ain't gonna," which was no part of his usual way of speaking, was as useful, at the moment, as the "damn." Both of them, and the accusation as well, went a good way to make him someone who was not Buck. His body felt less numb and useless, and the stirring within the egg increased. He picked up the twenty-two again, and started on down.

Having broken the barrier of silence, he was a little less alone, and the world was a little less remote and sterile. He went on talking to the rabbit. He argued to it that the shooting had not been in any way personal. He also assured it of his affection and regard, and confessed to it that he had been a fool not to see how small a rabbit it was, and also that he was a damned poor shot, and should never be allowed to touch a gun again. Finally there were moments when the rabbit replied in a small voice in the back of Buck's mind. He could not yet exactly hear the words of the replies, but he believed that the rabbit, in its separated, still perceptive part, was moved toward forgiveness.

In the intervals of his conversation with the rabbit, he began to consider the practical implications of the murder. They resolved themselves eventually into two opposed views, which he argued out alternately with the points of his confession to the rabbit, so that sometimes the two discourses became one, as when he told the rabbit, "I guess maybe I should bury you and say a prayer."

When he thought of the prayer, he saw himself upon his knees beside a very small grave with a pile of stones on it and a little cross standing up out of the stones, and he thought of the prayer as being offered up for the undying, miniature-hawk part of the rabbit. Buck seldom prayed upon his knees. He felt, with a quick wing-beating of the prisoner in the egg, that to pray openly, upon his knees, for the hawk-soul of the rabbit, would be to act in a manner that would go very far, nearly all the way, to satisfying the rabbit part of the rabbit.

The flutter in the egg was quickly stilled, however, by the dry-voiced counsel for the opposition, who chose to regard rabbits as of so little consequence that it made no difference whether they were dead or alive, and who pointed out a variety of unfortunate events which might be anticipated in the future of a Buck who sniffled over a dead rabbit and gave serious consideration to the notion of burying it with religious ceremony. Such a burial, he suggested, leering, would actually be a little difficult to tell from concealing evidence. The counsel for the opposition did not speak with Buck's voice at all, but with the voice of the world, and that fact gave him an undue influence in the court, so that his specious, when not downright cowardly, arguments stood up against those of counsel for atonement far better than they should have. Nonetheless, here in the silent ravine, with the rabbit still upon his arm, Buck was so ashamed of this half of the debate that during it he sat, so to speak, flushed and with his head bowed before a judge who seemed likely to regard rabbits and men as having many characteristics, and many rights, in common.

Gradually, since the argument remained short of settlement, the audible plea to the rabbit ceased, and its intentions became insensibly fused with the case of the counsel for burial and prayer. Buck went on down the trail, but even more slowly now than at first, and almost as silently, as if the prolonged indecision had affected his body also. Only once did any part of the struggle come out for his actual ears to hear.

"Lordy," he said, "would Evelyn ever give me a rough time if I came home without anything."

It helped only a very little to increase the moral stature of this revelation, that behind the smugly smiling face of Evelyn, he saw also the gaze of his father, silent, speculative and inscrutable.

Thus, with his head bent and the rabbit reduced to a point of contention within him, he followed the trail down and around two more buttresses of the ravine wall, passing, between the two buttresses, a sandstone shelf across the gorge below, that made a jumping off place, and in the spring a muddy, frothing waterfall. Beyond the second buttress he found himself in a wide passage almost on the level of the stream-bed. Here the black, sweet brush grew larger and closer together, and crowded down against the path on both sides, like a hostile multitude waiting for him to run the gauntlet. Buck emerged at once from the monotony of the court room, where the case had fallen entirely into circling repetitions, and saw the hollow before him with shocking clarity. He stopped abruptly, and stood there, looking around. After a moment he remembered the waterfall ledge he had passed above, and saw how, at the lower side of the hollow, the water course vanished over another sandstone ledge and the trail bent right and steeply downward and went along the cliff again. Then he understood why he had stopped. This was where he had almost stepped on the rattlesnake, and he had stopped here every time since, and each time he had got across to where the trail went down along the cliff again, he had felt tremendously relieved. He had considered, every time, going high up around the side of the hollow instead of through it, though he had never permitted himself to do so. The hollow had become, especially its farther edge, the very spot, a kind of dangerous watch-gate, to be entered in the spirit of Bunyan's Pilgrim. Each time he came around the bend and saw the hollow now, he felt how vulnerable bare feet were, and how defenseless a body with nothing on it but a pair of shorts, and the feeling made him live the escape over again.

He had been running so fast down the steep pitch above the hollow that he could hardly keep his legs under him and the quick singing was reduced to broken, breathless snatches. He came around the buttress preparing himself joyously and with complete concentration to let his feet and legs dodge through the closing bushes like those of a clever broken-field runner. Indeed, he stopped the chanting entirely in order to grit his teeth, narrow his eyes and become Christman, State College's star sprinter and tailback, darting upfield from the kickoff among the huge, fierce, Western U tacklers. He curled his left hand tensely over the nose of the ball—it would never do to fumble when he was running away from the blockers like this—held his right hand a little forward and out to the side, preparing, the instant he must swing left, to extend it in a jolting straight-arm. So intent was he, as he came racing down among them, on transforming each outstanding bush into a giant tackler, and so exultant did he become as he avoided each of them with full Christman virtuosity and approached the goal line, which was the lower edge of the hollow, with the screams of the multitude beating upon him from the slopes of the ravine, that he forgot to look where his feet were going. It was only because his right foot rolled on a loose pebble, so that he had to glance down as he writhed to keep his balance, that he saw the snake at all. His eyes saw the snake, and his body responded at once, though his mind was so far gone in triumph that it was quite incredulous, and wanted more time to make sure. It was a large, heavy rattlesnake, and it was already prepared for his coming, lying coiled on the right edge of the path, half under the bush that an instant before had been Western's number 39, a stocky, wily quarter-back, and the last man to be passed. The snake's head lay balanced with purposeful lightness upon the drawn spring of its neck. Its chin just touched the dusty scales of the uppermost coil, and its square nose was aimed directly at Buck's bare legs. There, too close to be dodged, and in the only opening, and with the treacherous pebble and the sharp dip and turn of the path just beyond it furnishing problem enough without it, the snake appeared to be of mythical proportions and wholly unavoidable. Buck felt that it was not even a natural rattlesnake, for it was as silent as it was motionless. Only its black tongue flickered in and out of the stony head like a small, separate life. It was the coiled spring of evil, the agent of the dark meaning, the very perfect, appointed conductor in the gateway to the other side.

All this came to Buck in the time of a single stride, and despair came with it. His bare right foot and the calf of his right leg could already feel, as if they had a separate and mordant imagination of their own, the fat, cold body sinking under them, and the impact of the horny nose, followed instantly by the tiny double-burning of the fangs. His mind heightened the effect by choosing that moment to remember the big, graying man, a friend of his father's, who had walked in the brown hills with them, stooped to pick up a stone which interested him, and then suddenly straightened up with a brief exclamation and held out his right arm, regarding it as if it didn't belong to him, and revealing the rattlesnake hanging from it, an incongruous, scarf-like ornament of doom. In his one gasping glimpse of this memory, Buck was again most impressed by the expression on the man's big, adult face, with its heavy, black brows, the expression of a startled child who needs only a moment more to begin weeping. Buck's right leg at once expected to lunge on down the path with the fangs jerking in its calf and the long weight of the snake thumping and coiling about it. It cried its fear to the left leg, which had not stumbled, and together they took desperate action while Buck's mind was still staring at the face of his father's visitor, and still seeing through it a phantom of the 39 on the broad chest of the bush. The right leg, foreseeing that its foot would otherwise be plunged directly into the entangling coil, made a stride only inches long, just touched its toes down, uncertain upon what in that blind rush, and threw the whole duty over to the left leg, which launched Buck upward and forward in the longest, highest leap it could possibly manage alone.

Even as he leapt, Buck's mind was cleared at a single wipe of the big face and the last vestige of the ghostly 39. He saw only that the enormous snake was striking. As it passed from sight under him, he believed that he felt his right ankle brushed, almost tripped, by the harsh, sedentary body, and a small, quick stab just where the muscles of his calf began to bulge. Then the right leg was forced into action again. There was a wild flurry of half-steps, which still could not quite support him or turn him back into the path. Under the impetus of the swerving straight-arm, the rolling pebble and the lopsided leaped all at once, he careened off to the left just where the path swung the other way, and crashed headlong into a laurel bush. The whole thing happened so quickly that it was only as he began to dive that his left hand and arm stopped hugging the imaginary football and reached to break the tumble. As his body struck, feeling everywhere the digging and scratching of the laurel twigs, and the tiny, cool hands of the leaves making mock comfort, he even had a last impression of the fumbled ball flying on over the bush ahead of him.

Then the game was entirely gone, from his muscles as well as his mind.

The laurel bush had stopped him, but he was lying deeply imbedded in it, half over on his belly, and he had come so close to diving clear through it that he was looking down over the waterfall ledge into the basin of sand twenty feet below. He was not even aware of this height, however. He was concerned entirely with the enemy in the rear. His mind gave a dozen confused and hasty orders at once, so that the moment he stopped falling, he began a struggle to extricate himself, flailing out like a panic-stricken swimmer in a rip-tide, and at the same time trying to double himself up into the heart of the bush, pull all his extremities out of reach, turn over onto his back and free his hands and feet. Above all, though, he wanted to pull himself out of reach and turn over and be able to see the rattlesnake, which he believed to be only inches behind him, tossed there by his own foot, and coiling to strike again, into his leg or his buttocks, or even, for such a reach was not beyond it, into the naked, cringing small of his back. A series of chills coursed through him from each of those vulnerable points, but with his intentions thus simplified, he began to succeed. He turned onto his back, drew his knees up to his chest, got his arms free and rolled into a crouch, suspended precariously in the swinging heart of the laurel bush.

The snake, large enough still, Lord knows, but of less than mythological proportions after all, was coiled once more, sure enough, with its head aimed in his direction, and the little serpent-soul of the tongue flickering at him, but it was out in the middle of the path, and eight or ten feet away. In fact it was still right beside bush number 39, farther away than the length of Buck's body, or even its own. To Buck, with the branches swaying under him and the wiry fingers of the twigs still clutching him, this was not a safe distance, but it was promising. It was a distance which created great hope.

At once the haste of the frenzied swimmer was transformed into slow, searching withdrawals of one hand and one foot at a time. The caution of these maneuvers was increased by a sound which renewed the chills just as they had begun to pass off. Whether or not the snake had been rattling before, it was certainly rattling now. The small, dry, multiple percussions of its challenge were so exceedingly rapid as almost to blend into a single, shrill whining. They filled the ears and occupied, with tremendous import, the whole width and depth of the ravine.

Never looking away from the snake, Buck felt his way slowly sideward until one hand reached into the free air. Then, risking a single quick glance down, to make sure that he wouldn't be setting foot on another snake—it had become possible during the retreat to conceive of the whole laurel as underlain by a squirming carpet of snakes—he stepped gingerly out of the bush and onto the edge of the path, just where it turned and went down. One final, widespread chill passed over him, and the goose-pimples began to diminish behind it. Retreat was now possible along an open and visible route. Also, the guardian of the gate was no longer in a position to surprise him or take advantage of the insidious co-operation of the laurel bush.

The snake had not moved, save for its tongue and the small, frenetic gourds of its tail, and now the rattling was subsiding. It no longer screamed in the ears. It rose again, slightly, when Buck straightened up in the path, but only into a blurred buzzing, and then, since Buck stood still, it dropped away into a soft, slow, final shaking, in which it seemed almost impossible to hear each separate seed in its papery shell.

Gradually Buck's mind resumed full charge of his doing. By means of quick glances away from the snake, he made sure that there were not two tiny drops or ribbons of blood under his right calf. There were moments of doubt during this examination, because he had been scratched in so many places by the laurel bush, but he was able to reassure himself concerning each suggestive mark.

After that, he was too much relieved to be very angry at the snake, but it seemed necessary to drive it out of the path, if only to give the incident a tolerable conclusion. Making sure it was still coiled and safely distant, he stooped and picked up a pebble, and then, with rapidly increasing confidence, half a dozen more. Before he could straighten up again with his ammunition, however, the snake, as if warned of the intended indignity, relaxed slowly out of its coils, almost melting into extension. Holding itself ready to recoil, its head lifted toward Buck and its tongue working rapidly and unceasingly, it began to slither away at an angle, up-trail and toward bush 39. So Buck just stood there watching, after all, with the first insulting pebble still held in his right hand. Smoothly and silently the snake gathered speed, and finally, turning its head away for the first time, it glided under the bush. Imperceptibly, like the blending into silence of a final, diminishing violin note, its tail shrank out of sight. Only then, and simply to relieve the long-pent impulse, Buck tossed the one pebble idly in the general direction of the disappearance.

Now, as Buck stood above the scene of this adventure, with the small rabbit in his arms, he was assailed by a conviction that the snake and the rabbit were related within the intentions of the gods concerning himself. In one motion of his mind and spirit, released, for the time being, from their conscientious squabble, he felt the rabbit to have been a ward, if not a companion, of the forces of light and air and life, as the rattlesnake had been a servant of the fog god. Yet the rattlesnake had been set against him, who had proven the enemy of the rabbit. It had made this place of the waiting bushes an arena of repeated trial. Its nature lay always coiled in wait for him here, to break his running celebration and bring him chastened to the sacred beach. The snake was the defender of the rabbit. It followed that the powers of light and darkness were not wholly and always opposed to one another.

Buck, however, was unable to grasp so momentous a union all at once. It rather appeared to him, alone in the foggy ravine and struggling for his first hold of idea upon the feeling of unity, to have resulted from an absorbing victory for darkness. His sensation of guilt increased proportionately with this increase in the hostile power. He felt the need of appeasement.

"It should have got me," he said aloud, and then, looking down upon the huddle of fur in his arm, added bitterly, the connection now clear to his own mind, "Poor damn little rabbit. What did you ever do?"

This confession, accompanied by his first full recognition of the fact that the rabbit was incurably dead, gained him time, but he understood that the deed was required to prove the word.

"The hell with what they think," he said stoutly, and against his entire family. He buckled his determination against the ghost of the snake and advanced among the waiting bushes. Several times his eyes and his conscience together made a serpent where there was none, but each time he stared the vengeance out of being without even breaking his slow, processional walk. When he came at last to the turn and onto the clear trail along the wall of the ravine, his relief was like forgiveness, or at least like a seal of approval upon his intention.

"Don't worry," he said to the rabbit. "We'll find you a good place. We'll find you the best place there is," and he began to walk a little faster because of the weight that had been lifted from him and because of his eagerness to commence the penitential act.

At first he thought he would just go down the trail far enough to get into the stream-bed easily, and then work back up the sandy bottom and bury the rabbit under the second fall. The gesture, however, didn't seem adequate. There were four such falls in the ravine, with little save their order to distinguish them one from another. Besides, the narrow, year-long darkness below any of the walls was all wrong for this once gay, hopping, nibbling creature with a milkweed tail and a soul like a bug-sized hawk. The thought of the darkness under the falls, reminded him of how the brown torrent poured, slick as grease, over those ledges in the spring rains, and churned and lathered in the basins.

"Wouldn't anything stay buried there for a minute," he said aloud, and grimaced because he could see the little rabbit churned and lifted out of its quiet sand, and borne, tossing and bumping, down the narrows and over two falls, and at last rolled down the final incline to the beach. There it would lie in the wet channel in the sand, all sodden and disarranged, with the muddy water still splattering down on it, or it might even be rolled and nudged on down the channel until the sea got hold of it and unrelentingly dragged it up and down the beach and slowly southward toward the whale rocks. More than once, in the spring floods, he had run down the trail, the mud splattering at every step onto his bare legs, to follow some floating bit of wood or small, uprooted bush down, and he could picture clearly what would happen to the rabbit.

His mind, having rejected the basin below the fall, began to hunt at random along the high slopes of the ravine for a suitable burial spot. Having started in the mouth of the ravine, after following the rabbit down, it discovered the look-out almost at once.

"That's the place, rabbit," Buck said aloud, and almost joyously. "I wouldn't mind being buried there myself. It's way up, nearly to the top; a swell place. You can see everything from there. You can see the village over on the point, and the long beach, and part of my beach, and the pier, and you can see the sun the longest of any place."

Once more, stimulated by his own generosity, he had increased his pace.

"The sea-gulls go by there all the time too," he told the rabbit, "and the pelicans, only the pelicans are always way down, sort of sliding along practically right on the water. Sometimes you even can see a school of porpoises. It's a swell place; the best place there is."

This inspiration, which brought with it the memory of the lookout on a sunny, windy day, and which entailed much labor, and a gift that was a personal sacrifice, so much further lightened his burden that his legs took upon themselves to skip twice, preparatory to running, and his chest and throat and mouth felt a strong urge to start a song. He barely remembered in time the solemnity of his mission and the crime which made it necessary. He held himself down again, under the somewhat relenting gaze of the watcher, to merely walking quickly, and instead of singing, said, "And I'll come up there to see you pretty near every time I come down to my beach."

He conceived a necessary final touch. "And I'll make a prayer for you every time," he promised.

It was thus, half floating in golden expectancy, and wanting very much to run, that he went down past the third fall and started around the last blind buttress onto the point of the trail from which the whole blue, sparkling Pacific would open before him and the music like cymbals and trumpets burst forth.

What actually opened before him, then, was like a vast and dignified rebuke to his backsliding. There, almost immediately below him, was the last of the four falls, the one so narrowly enclosed and so high that someone had stood a notched driftwood timber up in one corner as a kind of ladder, and below it was the biggest sandstone basin of all, swept clean of sand by the ultimate force of the floods. And there, going up clear to the sky on both sides, were the great, angled walls of the ravine. But across this familiar and inspiriting V there stretched a completely strange ocean of slow, black, oily swells, an ocean which receded, before the eye had even begun to reach, into a lingering fog, which gradually veiled it from sight. The wind was not strong and clear, either, but slow and chill and heavy. Buck thought, one after another, of four of the darkest, deepest, least populous Doré prints in his father's copy of the *Inferno,* and at once perceived his secondary sin and the great distance between the actual present and the imagined past. He stood there on the point of the trail for a full minute, staring out of this indifferent, underworld sea, while the anticipatory glow faded within him and the funeral of the rabbit became a grim, necessary and inadequate penance.

## 6

He turned aside at the notched timber and climbed diagonally toward the lookout. The track was very steep, and with the dissolution of his forgiveness, excitement and lack of sleep began to have their effect. The rabbit and the twenty-two became heavier than ever, and because they kept him from using either hand to catch bushes or act as a third leg, he often wavered and stumbled and even slid back, so that he had to stand still to get his breath and his balance. Despite the fog and the strengthening wind, he began to sweat before he was half-way up the slope. He thought yearningly of sitting, or even lying down to rest, and began to consider a swim as an active and soothing pleasure rather than as a cleansing duty not altogether pleasant in the darkness and chill of the fog. By the time he finally reached the lookout, after a dozen panting halts, he no longer had any feeling whatever about the burial, or even about the vast change in the world which had occurred while he stood remembering the snake. He wanted only to be done with this necessary-because-promised act, and to rest. The nature of the world could take care of itself, and as to what it made of him, he was completely indifferent.

He stood for some time in the center of the lookout, panting and with his head bowed, waiting for the pounding of his heart to soften and slow down, and the swimming, circling motes to go out of his eyes. He could feel the sweat trickling down the sides of his jaw from his hair, and down his ribs and the channel of his back under the sweat shirt. When he could open his eyes and see the lookout clearly, the gentle slope of cratered sand with the ring of reddish-black rocks around it and the three clumps of black brush above it, he straightened himself and gazed up at the silhouettes of the bushes on the rim of the canyon, against the sky, and then at the edge of the cliff to his left, with the great gulf of air beyond it, and then, so far below that it seemed hardly to wrinkle or stir, the dark ocean. Always before, merely to come up to the lookout had been a joy to make him hug himself and invent fragmentary poems of praise. To see so far had been to possess the world, to become capable of embracing it before the obliterating ecstasy, so that memories remained that might be used to beget ecstasy in lesser places. It was something to celebrate that the great pier, nearly two miles south, was tiny and frail as a spider-web ladder, and a source of heroic legend that he could look straight across the bay at the village on the point, with the narrow, white rim of surf around it, and consider it only as a kind of tropical garden for the delight of Janet Haley. He always felt, squatting in the lookout, with the sea a great swoop below and the point a clean, arrowy flight across, that he was akin to the cormorants that nested on the high, shadowy ledges of the village cliffs, where the rollers boomed in caves under them, and to the white gulls in their shining play with wind and light. Now, for the first time, it was not so. He felt a little uneasy to be so near the edge of the cliff, and when he looked down beyond it, he wanted to draw back and hold onto something.

"For God's sake," he muttered against this fear. "Like some scaredy-cat girl."

He considered, just to try himself, going out to the very edge, so that he could look straight down at the toy rubble of the giant's building stones, with the edge of the sea foaming softly among them. His whole body resisted the test, and complained desperately of the encumbering rabbit and twenty-two. He excused himself aloud.

"You're all pooped out, that's all," he said, and turned around and sat down carefully in the center of the lookout, with the rabbit across his lap and the twenty-two propped against his shoulder. Thus secured, he looked down into the ravine and out at the whale rocks, like small, black fingers in the surf, and felt nothing about them, and south at the spider-web pier, and felt nothing, and across at the point, still dim with a mist of fog, and with a great nothingness of fog beyond it, and felt only that it was lonesome, and that it was improbable that Janet Haley, somewhere in it, was anything but a figure from one of his own less convincing tales. Later, for no reason at all, and out of a blank mind, he remembered his father saying, "Thank God," and "if you live to be as old as Methuselah." For a moment it seemed as if the full meaning behind those expressions was about to be unfolded within him, but when, with an effort, he sought to drive his mind to the understanding, the moment passed. Finally, when he was quite steady, and the edge of the cliff didn't seem so dangerously near, he began to feel that he was malingering, and again that it was necessary to propitiate the enormous dark power.

Because of the malingering, he said aloud, "Well you can't sit here all your life," and because of the dark reminder he spoke defiantly, and then added, in full Promethean resentment, "Bury the damn rabbit, if you're going to."

The counsel for burial and prayer revived sufficiently to point out to him both the blasphemy of this utterance, and its profound unfairness to the rabbit. He looked down quickly, and stroked the rabbit's head and ears. They were quite cold now.

"It's all right, rabbit," he said. "I didn't mean it."

There returned a sufficient sense of his crime against the rabbit to set him in motion. He drew off the old, red sweat shirt, pulling it carefully out from under the barrel of the twenty-two, and spread it on the sand beside him. He laid the small rabbit gently on its side in the middle of the sweat shirt, and straightened its ears and smoothed its fur. The dimly outlined arm of Red Ryder was raised in salute from behind the rabbit's head. With the sweat shirt off, the gray wind felt very cold on Buck's wet ribs. It put life into him, and he got up and leaned the twenty-two into one of the bushes above the lookout, and returned. He knelt beside the rabbit and looked at it, and touched its shoulder.

"We'll fix you up pretty quick now, rabbit," he said.

He began to dig a hole in the sand beside the red sweat shirt. The sand, however, proved to be only three or four inches deep. He would have to pile it up to cover the rabbit, and then the first rain or wind that came along would uncover it again. Under the sand, there was the solid sandstone of the ledges. He sat back on his heels and thought for a moment. Then he got up and went slowly around the ring of stones until he found one stone that had something like a point on it, and wasn't too heavy to use. With this he came back and knelt again, and began to chip at the sandstone, pausing every few minutes to clear out the loosened pieces with his hands. He had it in mind to make the grave big and deep compared to the rabbit. Every once in a while he paused and looked across at the rabbit, to measure his work by it.

It was during one of these pauses that he became aware that the watcher was present once more, standing up on the edge of the sky and looking down at him. Again it seemed to Buck that he was not violently hostile, or altogether a henchman of darkness, but that, like the detestable counsel for the opposition, he was more amused than anything else. It seemed to the watcher a little ridiculous that a boy of twelve, who had just inherited a twenty-two, presumably because he was near enough to a man to be trusted with it, should be spending all this labor and planning all this ceremony just to bury a rabbit. Since this attitude made him no more than a condescending intruder into matters wholly private to Buck and the rabbit, Buck wouldn't even give him the satisfaction of looking up.

When this contemptuous resistance had continued for several minutes, however, counsel for the opposition spoke again, in his dry, belittling voice. At first Buck replied for himself, as angrily and stubbornly as he continued to dig. But when, after rehearsing once more Buck's empty-handed entrance into the kitchen, and his passage under the eyes of his mother and sister, counsel for the opposition removed his pince-nez, and with a smile not unlike Evelyn's, and in a voice smoothly derisive, brought up the father for the first time, Buck was forced to withdraw and turn his case over once more to the counsel for burial and prayer. He stopped digging and sat back on his heels, staring into the little grave and feeling his face burn, while counsel for the opposition, now quite clearly representing the interests of worldly opinion, drew a picture, wonderfully visible in its every detail, of Buck entering the living room and finding his father there, as he often was, sitting in the chair by the ocean window and working on a writing board. The father looked up, with that wholly enigmatic attentiveness in his eyes that had been there ever since the death of the rabbit. He put his hand with the pen in it on the arm of the chair, as if preparing for a considerable discussion, and asked, in that casual manner proper to men, as if there were nothing in the world worth any particular fuss or attention, "Well, how did it go the first time out?"

At this point, counsel for the world leaned over toward Buck in the most ingratiating manner, and inquired gently, "And just how is the prisoner going to reply to that? Is he going to say, perhaps, 'I killed a rabbit, but I was sorry, so I buried it, and,' he added with particular emphasis, 'prayed over it'?"

He doesn't have to say anything," began the defender of the rabbit. "All he has to do is . . ."

"Or," interrupted counsel for the opposition, in the same politic tone, "is he simply going to lie, and maintain, before the quite penetrating, I assure you, gaze of his father, that he saw no rabbit whatever? Obviously not. His only possible seemly reply is to hold up the rabbit to be seen, saying not a word, and revealing not a thing by his expression. Am I right, Buck?"

And Buck had to admit he was right.

At so great a disadvantage, and already put out by the interruption, counsel for burial replied more angrily than convincingly, and the whole interminable argument was on again. Apparently the period of seeming agreement under the influence of the rattlesnake spirit had been merely a truce or a recess. Buck could only sit helpless under the contention, as he had before. Gradually, however, he became aware of an important difference in the proceedings. The nameless, inscrutable judge seemed to be paying no attention whatever to the bickering counsels, but to be keeping his gaze, enigmatic and attentive, constantly upon Buck himself. As time passed and this gaze did not waver or vary, Buck became uncomfortably aware also that the arguments of the counsel for burial, ill-tempered and faulty though they were, nonetheless represented quite fairly an obscure but vital truth within himself, and that they were being seriously weakened by his passivity and his tendency to hope, even, that he might be permitted to act by the cowardly but superficially more logical code of the opposition. Worst of all, he was sure that the judge understood all this.

After a time, however, since the debate produced little that was new, he began to chip fitfully at the sandstone of the grave again. Without his even knowing it, the grave became a good deal deeper and wider one than the small rabbit needed. Meanwhile the debate, through mere exhaustion, had thinned away nearly out of his hearing, when suddenly it ended in a most unexpected move by the counsel for burial, who made a point so simple and final that it seemed at once the first thing that should have been said.

"Even allowing the worthy opposition's argument for the necessity of bearing home some token of prowess," he said, adopting a manner disturbingly like that of counsel for the world, "is the defendant's manliness to be demonstrated to women in the eyeless corpse of a rabbit no bigger than his two hands? Or his skill demonstrated to his father, unquestionably an excellent marksman, by exhibiting in the ears of that tiny rabbit, the holes made by two cruel and clumsy shots which failed to kill?"

This argument was recognized at once as a basis for agreement and a means to action. The two counselors shook hands and departed, blending, at the door of Buck's soul, into something disquietingly near one being, and that one a good deal more like counsel for the world than like the advocate of burial, whose previous appearance had been much like that of one of the bearded prophets in robe and sandals in the blue book of Old Testament stories.

Only the judge made no move, but continued, on his high, fog-borne bench, to lean forward upon his folded hands and gaze down at Buck with that enigmatic attentiveness, so disturbingly familiar. He said nothing, but Buck was unable to deny, under the burden of his eyes, that the agreement, though it permitted the better action, had been arrived at by the most despicable means.

He attempted to conciliate the judge by exhibiting a busy devotion to the interests of the rabbit. He worked energetically for a few minutes longer at enlarging the grave still further beyond need. Then he cleaned it out to bare, hard sandstone walls and floor, and crumbled the last fragments as he piled them on the mound between his knees and the grave. This done, he paused for a minute, keeping a busy, preoccupied expression, and considered the matter of protection for the rabbit in its grave. He could bring down aromatic leaves from the bushes, and sheaves of the dry grass, and mold them into a nest in the hole. That would probably be a good deal like the rabbit's natural home. On the other hand, a covering of grass and leaves wouldn't keep out the dirt he'd have to pile on top. He looked at the rabbit, as if it might express a preference, and immediately, because of the renewed need for atonement, experienced a minor inspiration.

"I'll give you my sweat shirt, rabbit," he said. "It'll keep the dirt out, and keep you nice and warm, too."

He worked over on his knees until he was kneeling before the rabbit, and began to fold the sweat-shirt over it and tuck it together. A voice, certainly his own, which was some relief, but also certainly out of the nature of counsel for the opposition, spoke in his mind.

"What will your mother say if you come home without that sweatshirt?" it asked.

He ignored the question for the moment, because it had just occurred to him that he should put grass and sweet leaves into the sweat-shirt with the rabbit, both for hominess and incense. He clambered up onto the headland and gathered them, bruising the leaves with his fingers as he picked them, to make them smell stronger. Then he returned, undid the sweat shirt and slipped the grasses under the rabbit and scattered the leaves over it. When the sweat shirt had been folded closed once more, and bound around by its sleeves, he answered the question.

"I'll say I got too hot and took it off, and then I couldn't find it when I came back."

"But that is obviously untrue."

"I gotta say something," Buck said truculently. He was encouraged to this boldness because the lie, being made for the rabbit, seemed no lie at all, but only the final ornament to the final sacrifice of the sweat shirt.

"You'll have to wait till the sun comes out to make that excuse work."

"So I'll wait till the sun comes out."

"That may be a long time, my young friend. You've already been out a long time, and so far there's not the slightest sign of the sun coming out. Are you going to be late for your own birthday dinner after all, and that to support a lie?"

Buck looked up uneasily at the sky. It was still gray everywhere, though lifted well above the headland now, and thinned a good deal too, he thought. He looked out at the ocean, and saw that it was not quite so dark now, only slaty gray, and that real waves were beginning to move on it, and that it was visible all the way to the horizon, or at least to so far west that he couldn't be sure it wasn't the horizon.

"It'll come out," he said boldly, but then added, because of his doubt, "And I can't help it if it doesn't. Rabbit needs the sweat shirt more than I do."

This reply, like all his present attitude and activity, seemed a little faked, intended more to influence the judge than to please the rabbit.

"I'm sorry, rabbit," he said aloud, "but this is about as good as I can do."

He laid the sweat shirt, with the small, limp weight in it, gently in the grave, paused for an instant to give the moment its proper dignity, though with no specific thought or word, and began to fill the grave. First, in order not to disturb the rabbit, he carefully filled all around the sweat shirt with fragments of sandstone. Then, a little at a time and lightly, he sifted on the first covering of sand. Only when no part of the sweat shirt was any longer visible did he begin to take big handfuls and pour them in more boldly. He piled the sand on until it made a rectangular mound, and patted it down as firmly as he could with his hands. After another pause, he brought rocks from around the lookout and piled them against one another up the two sides of the mound, so that they made a kind of black, stone tent over it. It seemed to him that already the judge was relenting a little.

"You gotta have a cross, rabbit," he said aloud.

He thought about that for a while too, and then climbed up onto the headland once more, and searched in the black brush until he found two branches long enough and nearly enough straight to suit him. He broke them off, stripped them of twigs, and tried them across each other, held high in front of him. They made a pleasing, narrow, black cross against the gray sky. There came then, however, the problem of binding them together. First he tried several stalks of the yellow grass, twisted together, but even wet with the fog as they were, they proved too brittle. He considered pulling threads out of his shorts, but gave that up without a trial because he knew he couldn't get them out long enough. Finally he tried to peel strips of bark from one of the bushes, but they wouldn't come off long enough either, and they tore when he tried to knot them. Reluctantly he abandoned the idea of a wooden cross.

"You gotta have some kind of marker, though," he said, and then, after a moment, "It'll have to be a stone, I guess. I can make a cross on the stone."

He went back down to the lookout and worked his way slowly around it, trying the remaining stones in his mind. None of them was really good, with flat sides and a rounded top, but he selected the one that came nearest to that shape. It was longer than any of the others, so it would stand up above the stones on the grave, and it came to a kind of point and had one nearly flat side. He laid it flat side up in the sand beside the grave, worked it down in until it was quite firm, and began to scratch a cross on the upper half of it, using his digging stone as a chisel. While he worked, he thought of also scratching a name and the date below the cross.

"Peter Rabbit," he said to himself, but discarded it at once. It was too childish, a kind of insult to a real rabbit who had really died. He tried others in his mind, but they all seemed false. He decided, at last, that just Rabbit would have to do.

However, when he had done as well as he could with the cross, and still had only a wavering, scarcely visible figure on the black stone, it was evident that he could never write the whole of even Rabbit. He worked for a long time more, digging down and scraping with all his weight, until his hands were sore and his arms weary, and produced, at last, a single, scratchy R under the cross. He gave up the idea of the date, and set the headstone at the top of the grave, working it into the sand until it was steady. Finally he got slowly to his feet and stood looking down at the grave and the stone. He felt better about it then. It looked like a real grave, and a pretty special one, with that stone tent, and it stood out darkly against the sand. Also, looked down on from above, the gray scratches of the cross and the R showed quite clearly. He looked around, desiring to establish a suitable order all about the grave. The gaps in the ring of stones disturbed him, and he shifted those that were left until their intervals, though a little too wide, maybe, were regular. When this was done, he smoothed the sand of the whole lookout circle the best he could, and stood up, in the top of the grave, like the tin cans holding flowers he had seen in cemeteries, a single sprig of the sweet-brush.

There remained, then, only the prayer.

This final ceremony, however, didn't turn out to be so easy, after all. He stood up beside the grave and bowed his head and clasped his hands together, but then discovered that all truly prayerful feeling about the rabbit was gone. He had used everything up making the grave, or in the long argument with the bad ending. He tried to make himself feel something by thinking of the rabbit as he had first seen it, sitting up across the ravine from him, and as he had knelt beside it, feeling the bullet holes in the ears with his fingers, and as it was now, so alone in the red sweat shirt under the sand, but it remained quite separate from him. A small motion occurred within him at the memory of the hawk-soul, but it turned out to be nothing but a weak imitation of the ascent and falling away of the real hawk, and when he tried to stimulate it into something more inclusive, even the motion ceased. Then, because he had remembered kneeling beside the dead rabbit, he was reminded of his promise to kneel when he prayed for it. The idea of kneeling was now repulsive to him, but nevertheless he forced himself down. It made no difference. Everything inside him was dead, or anxious to escape. After a minute or two of this dull struggle on his knees, he was still further weakened because a notion he had been repressing ever since the end of the trial, just by keeping busy, spoke itself clearly in his mind. "You aren't going home without anything to show them, are you? There's still plenty of time to hunt before dinner. You could probably get a real, full-grown rabbit, just on the way home, if you kept your eyes open. And this time you wouldn't make any mistake. You'd take your time and make one clean shot."

He rejected the suggestion violently, but he knew perfectly well that all he was really trying to do was keep such ideas out of the little rabbit's funeral. He wasn't really promising he wouldn't hunt again. And he knew that he was simply avoiding the real point when he made it all a matter of the size of the rabbit and the skill of the shooting. He was doing all over again, just what he had done to end the trial.

It was clear, after that, that real prayer would not happen. He decided at least to speak a prayer of words, to complete the ceremony, if nothing better. There was no being to whom a prayer in words could be made except the inconceivable head-god, from whom no response was to be expected. For once, though, since his relations with the lesser deities had become so confused, he found a kind of comfort in this separation. It came to him, as he began to select the words of the prayer, that there might even be some understanding of his difficulty and some tolerance for his shortcomings in this most impalpable of gods, who had to supervise the activities of the gods of both light and darkness, and at this thought, the head-god moved in him toward reality, borrowing from Poseidon and the god of the cliff, who looked a good deal alike, something of the appearance of Michelangelo's Moses or Blake's God, but assuming a nature of his own, very close to that of the judge. The indignity of kneeling increased before such a god. It seemed that he must regard self-abasement as cowardice, and perhaps even as an affront to himself, as if the petitioner hoped to use him as David had used Jehova. Buck stood up and went around to the other side of the grave in order to face the ocean across it. He stood with his arms straight at his sides and lifted his face to the sky. He prayed aloud.

"O Lord and Father, take this little rabbit unto You. Give him back, O Father, the life that I have taken away. Make him forget how it hurt, and keep him with You forever and ever. Amen."

He looked down at the grave. It was not a good prayer. He understood that. It had a borrowed, church-going flavor quite unsuited to this high headland over the gray sea in the enormous, gray morning. It was almost as bad, in its inconsequence, as the talk of some men he had heard on the village beach in the early afternoon, when everybody came down, and the sand was crowded and unclean, men with too much stomach and clumsy walks, who would rub themselves all over with smelly oil and put on dark glasses and then sit there, with the salt wind in their faces and the whole blue bay sparkling before them and the magnificent sun freely making them warm and good-feeling and brown, and talk the whole time about business and taxes and politics. He was not in the least moved by the words himself, except perhaps a little when he said "how it hurt." It was not even faintly a prayer for which the god of light would have granted ecstasy, or the god of conscience some ease from the strain of having done wrong. There was, nevertheless, a comforting hope possible that an attentive and two-sided thinker like the judge-god would take account of its one small virtue of begging only for the rabbit. He had no sooner thought of this, however, than even that virtue was lost in the discovery that only the words had been for the rabbit, while actually, as in his first, too-busy digging of the grave, the real intention had been to influence the judge-god in his own favor. The faint mockery which was sometimes to be felt in his father's look before he said something distracting and incomprehensible was now in the judge-god's eyes, along with the enigmatic attentiveness.

Buck stood there for a minute, staring down at the grave, but not seeing it. He felt quite unhappy about this puny and dismal conclusion, but there seemed to be no way to improve on it without just getting himself in deeper. He turned and climbed out of the circle of the lookout, walking carefully, in order not to disturb the smoothed sand any more than he had to. He picked up the twenty-two out of the bush, cradled it in his arm, and started down the slope, going around outside the lookout, which now seemed to belong entirely to the rabbit. A few yards below the lookout, he stopped and turned around. He couldn't bear this emptiness and incompleteness. He looked back up at the small grave, with the pointed, black headstone standing at the top of it, and saw suddenly, as if his eyes had cleared and his vision opened out, how small and real it was on the great slope of the ravine, with the pale sky over it and the dark ocean filling the west. The bushes above the grave were jerking nervously in the wind, as the bushes had jerked above the rabbit when it died.

"Well, so long, Rabbit," he said. "I'm sorry I did it. Honest to God, I am."

Suddenly he was filled with a great sense of loss. The tears sprang to his eyes, blurring the black stone, so that it did a little, ridiculous dance, like the dance the rabbit had done.

"Well," he said, blinking hard, "there's not much I can do about it now, but I'll be up to see you again tomorrow."

He turned away and started down again, rubbing angrily at his eyes, and resolutely refusing to look back even once more. For a brief time the ceremony seemed at least a little cleaner and more honest. Even before he reached the bottom of the ravine, however, the calculating voice spoke again, just as he had known it would. "You aren't going home without anything at all to show them, are you?" it began. By the time he was working his way down the last ledges onto the wave-row of driftwood and black kelp, a second debate, desperately like every instalment of the first, was going on full voice within him. He sought now only to quell it, to put off deciding.

"Oh, forget it," he said aloud.

His first look around at the secret beach furnished a kind of reply in itself. The tide had gone down until nearly all the rocks stood out of the water, but the long incline of the sand was still dark and wet from the fog. He always felt the unimaginable age of the ocean and its shore much more profoundly on foggy days, but this was the first time he had seen the secret beach that way. The kind of sea-weed that had antlered heads and long, anchor-like tails with little, clutching hands at the ends of them, lay scattered along the shore like prehistoric monsters that had crept up into the present to rest. The cliff above him seemed much higher and more forbidding than usual, and was only pale and cool, giving off no glow and holding none. It was not impossible that in the cliffs farther north, beyond the giant's stones, tooth-billed pterodactyls perched and stared down soullessly, awaiting the passage of equally soulless serpent fish through the underworld sea below them. There were no presences of any sort to be named or greeted over the whole beach, but only one sad, indefinable something, a kind of gentle but limitless reprimand. The wind was moving the sea a little, but still it wasn't really attacking the shore, but only approaching it in slow, melancholy rollers and breaking weakly at the last possible moment, with a soft, prolonged sound like the tearing of paper. The whale rocks lay black and indolent above its farthest reach.

Buck went across to the nearest of them and leaned the twenty-two against it, and took off his shorts. He folded them as carefully as if he had to wear them to an uninteresting party later, and laid them on the rock beside the barrel of the twenty-two. Then he walked slowly down the beach until the last turning edge of the waves would cover his feet, and stood there, motionless, for several minutes, staring down at the foam sliding around his ankles, and not thinking or feeling anything in particular that he could have discovered. He knew without looking that there was no benign overseer in the cliff behind him, no far-looking Poseidon on the last point in the north, no single mermaid of any kind, let alone a red-headed one, riding up in those melancholy rollers. The new presence was greater and more inclusive, perhaps, than all his old friends put together, but it was a stranger, and not in the least interested in him, or in any single being, probably.

At last, however, he felt the coldness of the water around his ankles, and then the timid, used-up feeling of his whole body, within which some great change was rolling and growing by itself, silently as a new fog bank rises from the ocean horizon, and no more comfortingly.

"Golly, I'm pooped," he said aloud.

He looked down at his chest and belly and thighs, and then held out his arms and looked at them also, hunting for the faint traceries that were left from the scratches the laurel bush had made on him. Because he had done the same thing in the same way the morning he had escaped the snake, and because that now seemed like this morning too, or rather because it seemed that he had shot and buried the rabbit on the same morning, a long time ago, he thought of the same thing he had thought of then, when the scratches were still red and some of them bleeding. He thought of the colored plates his father had of some of the Spanish and Mexican Christos, the very thin wooden ones that were painted chalky white with heavy blue veins and scarlet lines of blood as regularly spaced as the arms of a candelabra or the branches of childish tree without leaves. Also he remembered his father's incomprehensible but obscurely moving remark about them, "The Christian idols are at once the most beautiful and the most terrible of all. The old ones, that is. The things they make these days are door-stops." The remark had not been made to him. It seemed important now, for some reason, that the remark had been made to the big man with the heavy eyebrows on the same day he was bitten by the rattlesnake, only before he was bitten, of course. It was the words "beauti-ful" and "terrible" together that hadn't seemed right, but now, remember-ing the pictures and his own newly scratched body and the same colored blood of the little rabbit on the bleached grass, he felt that he nearly under-stood. But no, when he began to try to get it in words even the feeling escaped him again, as it had in the matter of "Thank God," and "Me-thuselah." He felt merely sad and tired and lonely. He let his arms down to his sides again, remembering that when the scratches were fresh, he had felt ashamed because such unimportant injuries, and on himself, had re-minded him of the Christos.

The treacherous voice spoke unexpectedly in his mind. "You aren't going home without anything at all . . ." it said, before he could stop it.

Aloud and defiantly he said, "I gotta remember to give Arthur the red gun, first thing when I get home."

He looked out at the dark ocean under the low, gray sky. He was more than ever reluctant to enter it. His body had grown cold standing there in the increasing wind, and now it felt narrow and stiff and unusable. He began to tell himself the Kit Carson story again, but still the people would not speak their own words, and their faces, even Janet's, kept changing into the faces of others or bleaching out into white, dead faces that were all the same and a little like the faces of the Spanish Christos. After four failures, he abandoned the chronicle, saying, "Oh, the hell with it. Always thinking about some old girl."

At the very sound of that denial, however, he was more deeply moved than ever before, so that it hurt as if his insides were being twisted, by remembering as if she stood before him, as if he might reach out and touch her, the proud, cool beauty of the real Janet to whom he could not speak.

It was at this point that he noticed that everything was turning bright around him, with a faint, diffused shining that came from nowhere in particular. He looked north along the coastline and saw that way up, beyond the cliffs and almost to Poseidon's headland, the sun had broken through the fog and was reaching out to sea in a long, slanting column of white light. He was searched by this surprising magnificence in a way that was like the new feeling about Janet, only more so. It made him at the same time wish to weep and to burst out into triumphant song. He closed his hands into tight fists and pressed the fists into his ribs to stop the pain.

"O God, God," he cried out in a shrill voice that was quite strange to him.

He was shamed by the vehemence of this outburst. He looked away from the shaft of light in the north, to the ocean right in front of him. After a moment he assumed the expressionless countenance of the fighter advancing from his corner, and began to wade slowly out into the dark water, which was now faintly brightened upon all its ripples by the distant splendor.

The betraying voice spoke again in his mind. "You aren't going home . . . " it began, but he cut it off there.

Dorothy M. Johnson  *The Hanging Tree* (New York: Ballantine Books, 1957).

Frederick Manfred  *Arrow of Love* (Denver: Alan Swallow, 1961).

Katherine Anne Porter  *Pale Horse, Pale Rider* (New York: Harcourt, Brace and Company, 1939).

Conrad Richter  *The Sea of Grass* (New York: Alfred A. Knopf, Inc., 1936).

Mari Sandoz  *The Horsecatcher* (Philadelphia: Westminster Press, 1957).

Jack Schaefer  *The Short Novels of Jack Schaefer* (Boston: Houghton Mifflin Co., 1967).

Wallace Stegner  "The Whitemud River Range," *Wolf Willow* (New York: The Viking Press, Inc., 1962).

John Steinbeck  *The Red Pony* (New York: The Viking Press, Inc., 1938).

Stewart Edward White  "The Rawhide," (1907), *Great Short Novels of the American West*, edited by Don Ward. (New York: Collier Books, 1962).

# THREE

## The Short Story

T HE ELEVEN SHORT STORIES in this section, written over a period of more than a century, represent a wide variety of themes as well as of tones and techniques. Bret Harte's *The Right Eye of the Commander* is quite different from his predominantly sentimental tales. It is actually based on an old California legend, recounted in one form by Charles M. Skinner in Part Eight of this book. (See *The Governor's Right Eye,* p. 570). The two stories by Mark Twain show him at the pinnacle of his humorous style.

The Adams, Crane, and White stories emphasize the camaraderie, calm courage, and the wit and cleverness widely attributed to cowboys. *Love of Life,* with its Alaskan setting, is one of Jack London's most starkly naturalistic stories. *Mountain Medicine* is based on Colter's historic run in the Three Forks area after leaving the Lewis and Clark expedition.

The final three stories represent family life on western farms and ranches surprisingly well. I have long held that Rosicky is one of the most charming immigrants in American literature. With its shifting point of view, stream of consciousness, and spare use of dialogue, *The Peach Stone* is subtle and compelling in its revelation of the stresses going on in the minds of the four people in the tiny microcosm of the car. *The Leader of the People* is likely the most impressive evocation of the westward movement in a short story. The crass impiety of Tiflin is sketched in unforgettable contrast to the dignity of Jody's grandfather.

# BRET HARTE

## The Right Eye of the Commander

THE YEAR OF GRACE 1797 passed away on the coast of California in a southwesterly gale. The little bay of San Carlos, albeit sheltered by the headlands of the Blessed Trinity, was rough and turbulent; its foam clung quivering to the seaward wall of the mission garden; the air was filled with flying sand and spume, and as the Senor Comandante, Hermenegildo Salvatierra, looked from the deep embrasured window of the presidio guardroom, he felt the salt breath of the distant sea buffet a color into his smoke-dried cheeks.

The commander, I have said, was gazing thoughtfully from the window of the guardroom. He may have been reviewing the events of the year now about to pass away. But, like the garrison at the presidio, there was little to review. The year, like its predecessors, had been uneventful—the days had slipped by in a delicious monotony of simple duties, unbroken by incident or interruption. The regularly recurring feasts and saints' days, the half-yearly courier from San Diego, the rare transport ship and rarer foreign vessel, were the mere details of his patriarchal life. If there was no achievement, there was certainly no failure. Abundant harvests and patient industry amply supplied the wants of presidio and mission. Isolated from the family of nations, the wars which shook the world concerned them not so much as the last earthquake; the struggle that emancipated their sister colonies on the other side of the continent to them had no suggestiveness. In short, it was that glorious Indian summer of Californian history around which so much poetical haze still lingers—that bland, indolent autumn of Spanish rule, so soon to be followed by the wintry storms of Mexican independence and the reviving spring of American conquest.

The commander turned from the window and walked toward the fire that burned brightly on the deep ovenlike hearth. A pile of copybooks, the work of the presidio school, lay on the table. As he turned over the leaves with a paternal interest and surveyed the fair round Scripture text, the first pious pothooks of the pupils of San Carlos, an audible commentary fell from his lips: " 'Abimelech took her from Abraham'—ah, little one, excellent!—'Jacob sent to see his brother'—body of Christ! that upstroke of thine, Paquita, is marvelous; the governor shall see it!" A film of honest pride dimmed the commander's left eye—the right, alas! twenty years before had been sealed by an Indian arrow. He rubbed it softly with the sleeve of his leather jacket, and continued, " 'The Ishmaelites having arrived—' "

He stopped, for there was a step in the courtyard, a foot upon the threshold, and a stranger entered. With the instinct of an old soldier, the commander, after one glance at the intruder, turned quickly toward the wall, where his trusty Toledo hung, or should have been hanging. But it was not there, and as he recalled that the last time he had seen that weapon it was being ridden up and down the gallery by Pepito, the infant son of Bautista, the tortilio-maker, he blushed, and then contented himself with frowning upon the intruder.

But the stranger's air, though irreverent, was decidedly peaceful. He was unarmed, and wore the ordinary cape of tarpaulin and sea-boots of a mariner. Except a villainous smell of codfish, there was little about him that was peculiar.

His name, as he informed the commander in Spanish that was more fluent than elegant or precise—his name was Peleg Scudder. He was master of the schooner General Court, of the port of Salem, in Massachusetts, on a trading voyage to the South Seas, but now driven by stress of weather into the bay of San Carlos. He begged permission to ride out the gale under the headlands of the Blessed Trinity, and no more. Water he did not need, having taken in a supply at Bodega. He knew the strict surveillance of the Spanish port regulations in regard to foreign vessels, and would do nothing against the severe discipline and good order of the settlement. There was a slight tinge of sarcasm in his tone as he glanced toward the desolate parade ground of the presidio and the open unguarded gate. The fact was that the sentry, Felipe Gomez, had discreetly retired to shelter at the beginning of the storm, and was then sound asleep in the corridor.

The commander hesitated. The port regulations were severe, but he was accustomed to exercise individual authority, and beyond an old order issued ten years before, regarding the American ship Columbia, there was no precedent to guide him. The storm was severe, and a sentiment of humanity urged him to grant the stranger's request. It is but just to the commander to say that his inability to enforce a refusal did not weigh with his decision. He would have denied with equal disregard of consequences that right of a seventy-four-gun ship which he now yielded so gracefully to this Yankee trading schooner. He stipulated only that there should be no communication between the ship and shore. "For yourself, Senor Captain," he continued, "accept my hospitality. The fort is yours as long as you shall grace it with your distinguished presence," and with old-fashioned courtesy he made the semblance of withdrawing from the guardroom.

Master Peleg Scudder smiled as he thought of the half-dismantled fort, the two moldy brass cannon, cast in Manila a century previous, and the shiftless garrison. A wild thought of accepting the commander's offer literally, conceived in the reckless spirit of a man who never let slip an offer for trade, for a moment filled his brain, but a timely reflection of the commercial unimportance of the transaction checked him. He only took a capacious quid of tobacco, as the commander gravely drew a settle before the fire, and in honor of his guest untied the black silk handkerchief that bound his grizzled brows.

What passed between Salvatierra and his guest that night it becomes me not, as a grave chronicler of the salient points of history, to relate. I have said that Master Peleg Scudder was a fluent talker, and under the influence of divers strong waters, furnished by his host, he became still more loquacious. And think of a man with a twenty years' budget of gossip! The commander learned for the first time, how Great Britain lost her colonies; of the French Revolution; of the great Napoleon, whose achievements, perhaps, Peleg colored more highly than the commander's superiors would have liked. And when Peleg turned questioner, the commander was at his mercy. He gradually made himself master of the gossip of the mission and presidio, the "small beer" chronicles of that pastoral age, the conversions of the heathen, the presidio schools, and even asked the commander how he had lost his eye. It is said that at this point of the conversation Master Peleg produced from about his person diverse small trinkets, kickshaws and new-fangled trifles, and even forced some of them upon his host. It is further alleged that under the malign influence of Peleg and several glasses of aguardiente the commander lost somewhat of his decorum, and behaved in a manner unseemly for one in his position, reciting high-flown Spanish poetry, and even piping in a thin high voice diverse madrigals and heathen canzonets of an amorous complexion, chiefly in regard to a "little one" who was his, the commander's "soul." These allegations, perhaps unworthy the notice of a serious chronicler, should be received with great caution, and are introduced here as simple hearsay. That the commander, however, took a handkerchief and attempted to show his guest the mysteries of the sembi cuacua, capering in an agile but indecorous manner about the apartment, has been denied. Enough for the purposes of this narrative, that at midnight Peleg assisted his host to bed with many protestations of undying friendship, and then, as the gale had abated, took his leave of the presidio, and hurried aboard the General Court. When the day broke the ship was gone.

I know not if Peleg kept his word with his host. It is said that the holy Fathers at the mission that night heard a loud chanting in the plaza, as of the heathens singing psalms through their noses; that for many days after an odor of salt codfish prevailed in the settlement; that a dozen hard nutmegs, which were unfit for spice or seed, were found in the possession of the wife of the baker, and that several bushels of shoe-pegs, which bore a pleasing resemblance to oats, but were quite inadequate to the purposes of provender, were discovered in the stable of the blacksmith. But when the reader reflects upon the sacredness of a Yankee trader's word, the stringent discipline of the Spanish port regulations, and the proverbial indisposition of my countrymen to impose upon the confidence of a simple people, he will at once reject this part of the story.

A roll of drums, ushering in the year 1798, awoke the commander. The sun was shining brightly, and the storm had ceased. He sat up in bed, and through the force of habit rubbed his left eye. As the remembrance of the previous night came back to him, he jumped from his couch and ran to the window. There was no ship in the bay. A sudden thought seemed to strike him, and he rubbed both of his eyes. Not content with this, he consulted the metallic mirror which hung beside his crucifix. There was no mistake; the commander had a visible second eye—a right one—as good, save for the purposes of vision, as the left.

Whatever might have been the true secret of this transformation, but one opinion prevailed at San Carlos. It was one of those rare miracles vouchsafed a pious Catholic community as an evidence to the heathen, through the intercession of the blessed San Carlos himself. That their beloved commander, the temporal defender of the Faith, should be the recipient of this miraculous manifestation was most fit and seemly. The commander himself was reticent; he could not tell a falsehood—he dared not tell the truth. After all, if the good folk of San Carlos believed that the powers of his right eye were actually restored, was it wise and discreet for him to undeceive them? For the first time in his life the commander thought of policy—for the first time he quoted that text which has been the lure of so many well-meaning but easy Christians, of being "all things to all men." Infeliz Hermenegildo Salvatierra!

For by degrees an ominous whisper crept through the little settlement. The right eye of the commander, although miraculous, seemed to exercise a baleful effect upon the beholder. No one could look at it without winking. It was cold, hard, relentless, and unflinching. More than that, it seemed to be endowed with a dreadful prescience—a faculty of seeing through and into the inarticulate thoughts of those it looked upon. The soldiers of the garrison obeyed the eye rather than the voice of their commander, and answered his glance rather than his lips in questioning. The servants could not evade the ever-watchful but cold attention that seemed to pursue them. The children of the presidio school smirched their copybooks under the awful supervision, and poor Paquita, the prize pupil, failed utterly in that marvelous upstroke when her patron stood beside her. Gradually distrust, suspicion, self-accusation, and timidity took the place of trust, confidence, and security throughout San Carlos. Wherever the right eye of the commander fell, a shadow fell with it.

Nor was Salvatierra entirely free from the baleful influence of his miraculous acquisition. Unconscious of its effect upon others, he only saw in their actions evidence of certain things that the crafty Peleg had hinted on that eventful New Year's Eve. His most trusty retainers stammered, blushed, and faltered before him. Self-accusations, confessions of minor faults and delinquencies, or extravagant excuses and apologies met his mildest inquiries. The very children that he loved—his pet pupil, Paquita—seemed to be conscious of some hidden sin. The result of this constant irritation showed itself more plainly. For the first half-year the commander's voice and eye were at variance. He was still kind, tender, and thoughtful in speech. Gradually, however, his voice took upon itself the hardness of his glance and its skeptical, impassive quality, and as the year again neared its close it was plain that the commander had fitted himself to the eye, and not the eye to the commander.

It may be surmised that these changes did not escape the watchful solicitude of the Fathers. Indeed, the few who were first to ascribe the right eye of Salvatierra to miraculous origin and the special grace of the blessed San Carlos now talked openly of witchcraft and the agency of Luzbel, the evil one. It would have fared ill with Hermenegildo Salvatierra had he been aught but commander or amenable to local authority. But the reverend Father, Friar Manuel de Cortes, had no power over the political executive, and all attempts at spiritual advice failed signally. He retired baffled and confused from his first interview with the commander, who seemed now to take a grim satisfaction in the fateful power of his glance. The holy Father contradicted himself, exposed the fallacies of his own arguments, and even, it is asserted, committed himself to several undoubted heresies. When the commander stood up at mass, if the officiating priest caught that skeptical and searching eye, the service was inevitably ruined. Even the power of the Holy Church seemed to be lost, and the last hold upon the affections of the people and the good order of the settlement departed from San Carlos.

As the long dry summer passed, the low hills that surrounded the white walls of the presidio grew more and more to resemble in hue the leathern jacket of the commander, and Nature herself seemed to have borrowed his dry, hard glare. The earth was cracked and seamed with drought; a blight had fallen upon the orchards and vineyards, and the rain, long delayed and ardently prayed for, came not. The sky was as tearless as the right eye of the commander. Murmurs of discontent, insubordination, and plotting among the Indians reached his ear; he only set his teeth the more firmly, tightened the knot of his black silk handkerchief, and looked up his Toledo.

The last day of the year 1798 found the commander sitting, at the hour of evening prayers, alone in the guardroom. He no longer attended the services of the Holy Church, but crept away at such times to some solitary spot, where he spent the interval in silent meditation. The firelight played upon the low beams and rafters, but left the bowed figure of Salvatierra in darkness. Sitting thus, he felt a small hand touch his arm, and looking down, saw the figure of Paquita, his little Indian pupil, at his knee. "Ah! littlest of all," said the commander, with something of his old tenderness, lingering over the endearing dimunitives of his native speech—"sweet one, what does thou here? Art thou not afraid of him whom everyone shuns and fears?"

"No," said the little Indian readily, "not in the dark. I hear your voice—the old voice; I feel your touch—the old touch; but I see not your eye, Senor Comandante. That only I fear—and that, O senor, O my father," said the child, lifting her little arms towards his—"that I know is not thine own!"

The commander shuddered and turned away. Then, recovering himself, he kissed Paquita gravely on the forehead and bade her retire. A few hours later, when silence had fallen upon the presidio, he sought his own couch and slept peacefully.

At about the middle watch of the night a dusky figure crept through the low embrasure of the commander's apartment. Other figures were flitting through the parade ground, which the commander might have seen had he not slept so quietly. The intruder stepped noiselessly to the couch and listened to the sleeper's deep-drawn respiration. Something glittered in the firelight as the savage lifted his arm; another moment and the sore perplexities of Hermenegildo Salvatierra would have been over, when suddenly the savage started and fell back in a paroxysm of terror. The commander slept peacefully, but his right eye, widely opened, fixed and unaltered, glared coldly on the would-be assassin. The man fell to the earth in a fit, and the noise awoke the sleeper.

To rise to his feet, grasp his sword, and deal blows thick and fast upon the mutinous savages who now thronged the room, was the work of a moment. Help opportunely arrived, and the undisciplined Indians were speedily driven beyond the walls; but in the scuffle the commander received a blow upon his right eye, and lifting his hand to that mysterious organ, it was gone. Never again was it found, and never again, for bale or bliss, did it adorn the right orbit of the commander.

With it passed away the spell that had fallen upon San Carlos. The rain returned to invigorate the languid soil, harmony was restored between priest and soldier, the green grass presently waved over the sere hillsides, the children flocked again to the side of their martial preceptor, a *Te Deum* was sung in the mission church, and pastoral content once more smiled upon the gentle valleys of San Carlos. And far southward crept the General Court with its master, Peleg Scudder, trafficking in beads and peltries with the Indians, and offering glass eyes, wooden legs, and other Boston notions to the chiefs.

# MARK TWAIN

## *Baker's Bluejay Yarn*

ANIMALS TALK TO EACH OTHER, of course. There can be no question about that; but I suppose there are very few people who can understand them. I never knew but one man who could. I knew he could, however, because he told me so himself. He was a middle-aged, simple-hearted miner who had lived in a lonely corner of California, among the woods and mountains, a good many years, and had studied the ways of his only neighbors, the beasts and the birds, until he believed he could accurately translate any remark which they made. This was Jim Baker. According to Jim Baker, some animals have only a limited education, and use only

*"Baker's Bluejay Yarn" from* A TRAMP ABROAD
*by Mark Twain. Reprinted by permission of*
*Harper & Row, Publishers, Inc.*

very simple words, and scarcely ever a comparison or a flowery figure; whereas, certain other animals have a large vocabulary, a fine command of language and a ready and fluent delivery; consequently these latter talk a great deal; they like it; they are conscious of their talent, and they enjoy "showing off." Baker said, that after long and careful observation, he had come to the conclusion that the bluejays were the best talkers he had found among birds and beasts. Said he:

"There's more *to* a bluejay than any other creature. He has got more moods, and more different kinds of feelings than other creatures; and, mind you, whatever a bluejay feels, he can put it into language. And no mere commonplace language, either, but rattling, out-and-out book-talk—and bristling with metaphor, too—just bristling! And as for command of language—why *you* never see a bluejay get stuck for a word. No man ever did. They just boil out of him! And another thing: I've noticed a good deal, and there's no bird, or cow, or anything that uses as good grammar as a bluejay. You might say a cat uses good grammar. Well, a cat does—but you let a cat get excited once; you let a cat get to pulling fur with another cat on a shed, nights, and you'll hear grammar that will give you the lockjaw. Ignorant people think it's the *noise* which fighting cats make that is so aggravating, but it ain't so; it's the sickening grammar they use. Now I've never heard a jay use bad grammar but very seldom; and when they do, they are as ashamed as a human; they shut right down and leave.

"You may call a jay a bird. Well, so he is, in a measure—because he's got feathers on him, and don't belong to no church, perhaps; but otherwise he is just as much a human as you be. And I'll tell you for why. A jay's gifts, and instincts, and feelings, and interests, cover the whole ground. A jay hasn't got any more principle than a Congressman. A jay will lie, a a jay will steal, a jay will deceive, a jay will betray; and four times out of five, a jay will go back on his solemnest promise. The sacredness of an obligation is a thing which you can't cram into no bluejay's head. Now, on top of all this, there's another thing; a jay can out-swear any gentleman in the mines. You think a cat can swear. Well a cat can; but you give a bluejay a subject that calls for his reserve-powers, and where is your cat? Don't talk to *me*—I know too much about this thing. And there's yet another thing; in the one little particular of scolding—just good, clean, out-and-out scolding—a bluejay can lay over anything, a human or divine. Yes, sir, a jay is everything that a man is. A jay can cry, a jay can laugh, a jay can feel shame, a jay can reason and plan and discuss, a jay likes gossip and scandal, a jay has got a sense of humor, a jay knows when he is an ass just as well as you do—maybe better. If a jay ain't human, he better take in his sign, that's all. Now I'm going to tell you a perfectly true fact about some bluejays."

"When I first begun to understand jay language correctly, there was a little incident happened here. Seven years ago, the last man in this region but me moved away. There stands his house—been empty ever since; a log house, with a plank roof—just one big room, and no more; no ceiling—

nothing between the rafters and the floor. Well, one Sunday morning I was sitting out here in front of my cabin, with my cat, taking the sun, and looking at the blue hills, and listening to the leaves rustling so lonely in the trees, and thinking of the home away yonder in the states, that I hadn't heard from in thirteen years, when a bluejay lit on that house, with an acorn in his mouth, and says, 'Hello, I reckon I've struck something.' When he spoke, the acorn dropped out of his mouth and rolled down the roof, of course, but he didn't care; his mind was all on the thing he had struck. It was a knot-hole in the roof. He cocked his head to one side, shut one eye and put the other one to the hole, like a possum looking down a jug; then he glanced up with his bright eyes, gave a wink or two with his wings —which signifies gratification, you understand—and says, 'It looks like a hole, it's located like a hole—blamed if I don't believe it *is* a hole!'

"Then he cocked his head down and took another look; he glances up perfectly joyful, this time; winks his wings and his tail both, and says, 'Oh, no, this ain't no fat thing, I reckon! If I ain't in luck!—why its a perfectly elegant hole!' So he flew down and got that acorn, and fetched it up and dropped it in, and was just tilting his head back, with the heavenliest smile on his face, when all of a sudden he was paralyzed into a listening attitude and that smile faded gradually out of his countenance like a breath off'n a razor, and the queerest look of surprise took its place. Then he says, 'Why I didn't hear it fall!' He cocked his eye at the hole again, and took a long look; raised up and shook his head; stepped around to the other side of the hole and took another look from that side; shook his head again. He studied a while, then he just went into the *details*— walked round and round the hole and spied into it from every point of the compass. No use. Now he took a thinking attitude on the comb of the roof and scratched the back of his head with his right foot a minute, and finally says, 'Well, it's too many for *me*, that's certain; must be a mighty long hole; however, I ain't got no time to fool around here, I got to 'tend to business; I reckon it's all right—chance it, anyway.'

"So he flew off and fetched another acorn and dropped it in, and tried to flirt his eye to the hole quick enough to see what become of it, but he was too late. He held his eye there as much as a minute; then he raised up and sighed, and says, 'Confound it, I don't seem to understand this thing, no way; however, I'll tackle her again.' He fetched another acorn, and done his level best to see what become of it, but he couldn't. He says, 'Well, *I* never struck no such hole as this before; I'm of the opinion it's a totally new kind of a hole.' Then he begun to get mad. He held in for a spell, walking up and down the comb of the roof and shaking his head and muttering to himself; but his feelings got the upper hand of him, presently, and he broke loose and cussed himself black in the face. I never see a bird take on so about a little thing. When he got through he walks to the hole and looks in again for half a minute; then he says, 'Well, you're a long hole, and a deep hole, and a mighty singular hole altogether—but I've started in to fill you, and I'm d—d if I *don't* fill you, if it takes a hundred years!'

"And with that, away he went. You never see a bird work so since you was born. He laid into his work like a nigger, and the way he hove acorns into that hole for about two hours and a half was one of the most exciting and astonishing spectacles I ever struck. He never stopped to take a look any more—he just hove 'em in and went for more. Well, at last he could hardly flop his wings, he was so tuckered out. He comes a-drooping down, once more, sweating like an ice-pitcher, drops his acorn in and says, '*Now* I guess I've got the bulge on you by this time!' So he bent down for a look. If you'll believe me, when his head come up again he was just pale with rage. He says, 'I've shoveled acorns enough in there to keep the family thirty years, and if I can see a sign of one of 'em I wish I may land in a museum with a belly full of sawdust in two minutes!'

"He just had strength enough to crawl up on to the comb and lean his back agin the chimbly, and then he collected his impressions and begun to free his mind. I see in a second that what I had mistook for profanity in the mines was only just the rudiments, as you may say.

"Another jay was going by, and heard him doing his devotions, and stops to inquire what was up. The sufferer told him the whole circumstance, and says, 'Now yonder's the hole, and if you don't believe me, go and look for yourself.' So this fellow went and looked, and comes back and says, 'How many did you say you put in there?' 'Not any less than two tons,' says the sufferer. The other jay went and looked again. He couldn't seem to make it out, so he raised a yell, and three more jays come. They all made the sufferer tell it over again, then they all discussed it, and got off as many leather-headed opinions about it as an average crowd of humans could have done.

"They called in more jays; then more and more, till pretty soon this whole region 'peared to have a blue flush about it. There must have been five thousand of them; and such another jawing and disputing and ripping and cussing, you never heard. Every jay in the whole lot put his eye to the hole and delivered a more chuckle-headed opinion about the mystery than the jay that went there before him. They examined the house all over, too. The door was standing half open, and at last one old jay happened to go and light on it and look in. Of course, that knocked the mystery galley-west in a second. There lay the acorns, scattered all over the floor. He flopped his wings and raised a whoop. 'Come here!' he says, 'Come here, everybody; hang'd if this fool hasn't been trying to fill up a house with acorns!' They all came a-swooping down like a blue cloud, and as each fellow lit on the door and took a glance, the whole absurdity of the contract that that first jay had tackled hit him home and he fell over backward suffocating with laughter, and the next jay took his place and done the same.

"Well, sir, they roosted around here on the housetops and the trees for an hour, and guffawed over that thing like human beings. It ain't any use to tell me a bluejay hasn't got a sense of humor, because I know better. And memory, too. They brought jays here from all over the United States to look at that hole, every summer for three years. Other birds, too. And they could all see the point, except an owl that come from Nova Scotia to visit the Yo Semite, and he took this thing in on his way back. He said he couldn't see anything funny in it. But then he was a good deal disappointed about Yo Semite, too."

# The Celebrated Jumping Frog
## of Calaveras County

IN COMPLIANCE WITH THE REQUEST of a friend of mine, who wrote me from the East, I called on good-natured, garrulous old Simon Wheeler, and inquired after my friend's friend, *Leonidas W*. Smiley, as requested to do, and I hereunto append the result. I have a lurking suspicion that *Leonidas W*. Smiley is a myth; that my friend never knew such a personage; and that he only conjectured that, if I asked old Wheeler about him, it would remind him of his infamous *Jim* Smiley, and he would go to work and bore me nearly to death with some exasperating reminiscence of him as long and tedious as it should be useless to me. If that was the design, it succeeded.

I found Simon Wheeler dozing comfortably by the bar-room stove of the dilapidated tavern in the decayed mining camp of Angel's, and I noticed that he was fat and bald-headed, and had an expression of winning gentleness and simplicity upon his tranquil countenance. He roused up and gave me good-day. I told him a friend of mine had commissioned me to make some inquiries about a cherished companion of his boyhood named *Leonidas W*. Smiley—*Rev. Leonidas W*. Smiley—a young minister of the Gospel, who he had heard was at one time a resident of Angel's Camp. I added that, if Mr. Wheeler could tell me anything about this Rev. Leonidas W. Smiley, I would feel under many obligations to him.

Simon Wheeler backed me into a corner and blockaded me there with his chair, and then sat me down and reeled off the monotonous narrative which follows this paragraph. He never smiled, he never frowned, he never changed his voice from the gentle-flowing key to which he tuned the initial sentence, he never betrayed the slightest suspicion of enthusiasm; but all through the interminable narrative there ran a vein of impressive earnestness and sincerity, which showed me plainly that, so far from his imagining that there was anything ridiculous or funny about his story, he regarded it as a really important matter, and admired its two heroes as men of transcendent genius in *finesse*. I let him go on in his own way, and never interrupted him once:

"Rev. Leonidas W. H'm, Reverend Le—well, there was a feller here

*"The Celebrated Jumping Frog of Calaveras County" from*
A TRAMP ABROAD *by Mark Twain. Reprinted by permission
of Harper & Row, Publishers, Inc.*

once by the name of *Jim* Smiley, in the winter of '49—or maybe it was the spring of '50—I don't recollect exactly, somehow, though what makes me think it was one or the other is because I remember the big flume wasn't finished when he first came to the camp; but any way, he was the curiosest man about always betting on any thing that turned up you ever see, if he could get any body to bet on the other side; and if he couldn't, he'd change sides. Any way that suited the other man would suit him—any way just so's he got a bet, *he* was satisfied. But still he was lucky, uncommon lucky; he most always come out winner. He was always ready and laying for a chance; there couldn't be no solit'ry thing mentioned but that feller'd offer to bet on it, and take any side you please, as I was just telling you. If there was a horse-race, you'd find him flush, or you'd find him busted at the end of it; if there was a dog-fight, he'd bet on it; if there was a cat-fight, he'd bet on it; if there was a chicken-fight, he'd bet on it; why, if there was two birds setting on a fence, he would bet you which one would fly first; or if there was a camp-meeting, he would be there reg'lar, to bet on Parson Walker, which he judged to be the best exhorter about there, and so he was, too, and a good man. If he even seen a straddle-bug start to go any-wheres, he would bet you how long it would take him to get wherever he was going to, and if you took him up, he would foller that straddle-bug to Mexico but what he would find out where he was bound for and how long he was on the road. Lots of the boys here has seen that Smiley, and can tell you about him. Why, it never made no difference to *him*—he would bet on *any* thing—the dangdest feller. Parson Walker's wife laid very sick once, for a good while, and it seemed as if they warn't going to save her; but one morning he come in, and Smiley asked how she was, and he said she was considerable better—thank the Lord for his inf'nite mercy—and coming on so smart that, with the blessing of Prov'dence, she'd get well yet; and Smiley, before he thought, says, "Well, I'll resk two-and-a-half that she don't, anyway."

Thish-yer Smiley had a mare—the boys called her the fifteen-minute nag, but that was only in fun, you know, because, of course, she was faster than that—and he used to win money on that horse, for all she was so slow and always had the asthma, or the distemper, or the consumption, or something of that kind. They used to give her two or three hundred yards start, and then pass her under way; but always at the fag-end of the race she'd get excited and desperate-like, and come cavorting and straddling up, and scattering her legs around limber, sometimes in the air, and sometimes out to one side amongst the fences, and kicking up m-o-r-e dust, and raising m-o-r-e racket with her coughing and sneezing and blowing her nose—and always fetch up at the stand just about a neck ahead, as near as you could cipher it down.

And he had a little small bull pup, that to look at him you'd think he wa'nt worth a cent, but to set around and look ornery, and lay for a chance to steal something. But as soon as money was up on him, he was a different dog; his under-jaw'd begin to stick out like the fo'castle of a steamboat, and his teeth would uncover, and shine savage like the furnaces. And a dog might tackle him, and bully-rag him, and bite him, and throw him over his shoulder two or three times, and Andrew Jackson—which was the name of the pup—Andrew Jackson would never let on but what *he* was satisfied, and hadn't expected nothing else—and the bets being doubled and doubled on the other side all the time, till the money was all up; and then all of a sudden he would grab that other dog jest by the j'int of his hind leg and freeze to it—not chaw, you understand, but only jest grip and hang on till they throwed up the sponge, if it was a year. Smiley always come out winner on that pup, till he harnessed a dog once that didn't have no hind legs, because they'd been sawed off by a circular saw, and when the thing had gone along far enough, and the money was all up, and he come to make a snatch for his pet holt, he saw in a minute how he'd been imposed on, and how the other dog had him in the door, so to speak, and he 'peared surprised, and then he looked sorter discouraged-like, and didn't try no more to win the fight, and so he got shucked out bad. He give Smiley a look, as much as to say his heart was broke, and it was *his* fault, for putting up a dog that hadn't no hind legs for him to take holt of, which was his main dependence in a fight, and then he limped off a piece and laid down and died. It was a good pup, was that Andrew Jackson, and would have made a name for hisself if he'd lived, for the stuff was in him, and he had genius—I know it, because he hadn't had no opportunities to speak of, and it don't stand to reason that a dog could make such a fight as he could under them circumstances, if he hadn't no talent. It always makes me feel sorry when I think of that last fight of his'n, and the way it turned out.

Well, thish-yer Smiley had rat-tarriers, and chicken cocks, and tom-cats, and all them kind of things, till you couldn't rest, and you couldn't fetch nothing for him to bet on but he'd match you. He ketched a frog one day, and took him home, and said he calk'lated to edercate him; and so he never done nothing for three months but set in his back yard and learn that frog to jump. And you bet he *did* learn him, too. He'd give him a little punch behind, and the next minute you'd see that frog whirling in the air like a doughnut—see him turn one summerset, or may be a couple, if he got a good start, and come down flat-footed and all right, like a cat. He got him up so in the matter of catching flies, and kept him in practice so constant, that he'd nail a fly every time as far as he could see him. Smiley said all a frog wanted was education, and he could do most anything—and I believe him. Why, I've seen him set Dan'l Webster down here on this floor—Dan'l Webster was the name of the frog—and sing out, "Flies, Dan'l, flies!" and quicker'n you could wink, he'd spring straight up, and snake a fly off'n the counter there, and flop down on the floor again as solid as a gob of mud, and fall to scratching the side of his head with his hind foot as indifferent as if he hadn't no idea he'd been doin' any more'n any frog might do. You never see a frog so modest and straightfor'ard as he was, for all he was so gifted. And when it come to fair and square jumping on a dead level, he could get over more ground at one straddle than any animal of his breed you ever see. Jumping on a dead level was his strong suit, you understand; and when it come to that, Smiley would ante up money on him as long as he had a red. Smiley was monstrous proud of his frog, and well he might be, for fellers that had been everywheres, all said he laid over any frog that ever *they* see.

Well, Smiley kept the beast in a little lattice box, and he used to fetch him down town sometimes and lay for a bet. One day a feller—a stranger in the camp, he was—come across him with his box, and says:

"What might it be that you've got in that box?"

And Smiley says, sorter indifferent like, "It might be a parrot, or it might be a canary, may be, but it ain't—it's only a frog."

And the feller took it, and looked at it careful, and turned it round this way and that, and says, "H'm—so 'tis. Well, what's *he* good for?"

"Well," Smiley says, easy and careless, "he's good enough for *one* thing, I should judge—he can outjump any frog in Calaveras county."

The feller took the box again, and took another long, particular look, and give it back to Smiley, and says, very deliberate, "Well, I don't see no p'ints about that frog that's any better'n any other frog."

"May be you don't," Smiley says. "May be you understand frogs, and maybe you don't understand 'em; may be you've had experience, and may be you ain't only a amature, as it were. Anyways I've got *my* opinion, and I'll risk forty dollars he can outjump any frog in Calaveras county."

And the feller studied a minute, and then says, kinder sad like, "Well, I'm only a stranger here, and I ain't got no frog; but if I had a frog, I'd bet you."

And the Smiley says, "That's all right—that's all right—if you'll hold my box a minute, I'll go and get you a frog." And so the feller took the box, and put up his forty dollars along with Smiley's, and set down to wait.

So he set there a good while thinking and thinking to hisself, and then he got the frog out and prized his mouth open and took a teaspoon and filled him full of quail shot—filled him pretty near up to his chin—and set him on the floor. Smiley he went to the swamp and slopped around in the mud for a long time, and finally he ketched a frog, and fetched it in, and give him to this feller, and says:

"Now, if you're ready, set him along side of Dan'l, with his fore-paws just even with Dan'l, and I'll give the word." Then he says, "One—two—three—jump!" and him and the feller touched up the frogs from behind, and the new frog hopped off, but Dan'l give a heave, and hysted up his shoulders—so—like a Frenchman, but it wan't no use—he couldn't budge; he was planted as solid as an anvil, and he couldn't no more stir than if he was anchored out. Smiley was a good deal surprised, and he was disgusted too, but he didn't have no idea what the matter was, of course.

The feller took the money and started away; and when he was going out at the door, he sorter jerked his thumb over his shoulders—this way—at Dan'l, and says again, very deliberate, "Well, *I* don't see no p'ints about that frog that's any better'n any other frog."

Smiley he stood scratching his head and looking down at Dan'l a long time, and at last he says, "I do wonder what in the nation that frog throw'd off for—I wonder if there ain't something the matter with him—he 'pears to look mighty baggy, somehow." And he ketched Dan'l by the nap of the neck, and lifted him up and says, "Why, blame my cats, if he don't weigh five pound!" and turned him upside down, and he belched out a double handful of shot. And then he see how it was, and he was the maddest man—he set the frog down and took out after that feller, but he never ketched him. And—

(Here Simon Wheeler heard his name called from the front yard, and got up to see what was wanted.) And turning to me as he moved away, he said: "Just set where you are, stranger, and rest easy—I ain't going to be gone a second."

But, by your leave, I did not think that a continuation of the history of the enterprising vagabond *Jim* Smiley would be likely to afford me much information concerning the Rev. *Leonidas W.* Smiley, and so I started away.

At the door I met the sociable Wheeler returning, and he buttonholed me and recommenced:

"Well, thish-yer Smiley had a yeller one-eyed cow that didn't have no tail, only jest a short stump like a bannanner, and—"

"Oh! hang Smiley and his afflicted cow!" I muttered, good-naturedly, and bidding the old gentleman good-day, I departed.

# ANDY ADAMS

## *In the Hands of His Friends*

THERE WAS A PAINTING at the World's Fair at Chicago named "The Reply," in which the lines of two contending armies were distinctly outlined. One of these armies had demanded the surrender of the other. The reply was being written by a little fellow, surrounded by grim veterans of war. He was not even a soldier. But in this little fellow's countenance shone a supreme contempt for the enemy's demand. His patriotism beamed out as plainly as did that of the officer dictating to him. Physically he was debarred from being a soldier; still there was a place where he could be useful.

So with Little Jack Martin. He was a cripple and could not ride, but he could cook. If the way to rule men is through the stomach, Jack was a general who never knew defeat. The "J + H" camp, where he presided over the kitchen, was noted for good living. Jack's domestic tastes followed him wherever he went, so that he surrounded himself at this camp with chickens, and a few cows for milk. During the spring months, when the boys were away on the various round-ups, he planted and raised a fine garden. Men returning from a hard month's work would brace themselves against fried chicken, eggs, milk, and fresh vegetables. After drinking alkali water for a month and living out of tin cans, who wouldn't love Jack? In addition to his garden, he always raised a fine patch of watermelons. This camp was an oasis in the desert. Every man was Jack's friend, and an enemy was an unknown personage. The peculiarity about him, aside from his deformity, was his ability to act so much better than he could talk. In fact he could barely express his simplest wants in words.

Cripples are usually cross, irritable, and unpleasant companions. Jack was the reverse. His best qualities shone their brightest when there were a dozen men around to cook for. When they ate heartily he felt he was useful. If a boy was sick, Jack could make a broth, or fix a cup of beef tea like a mother or sister. When he went out with the wagon during beef-shipping season, a pot of coffee simmered over the fire all night for the boys on night herd. Men going or returning on guard liked to eat. The bread and meat left over from the meals of the day were always left convenient for the boys. It was the many little things that he thought of which made him such a general favorite with every one.

Little Jack was middle-age when the proclamation of the President opening the original Oklahoma was issued. This land was to be thrown open in April. It was not a cow-country then, though it had been once. There was a warning in this that the Strip would be next. The dominion of the cowman was giving way to the homesteader. One day Jack found opportunity to take Miller, our foreman, into his confidence. They had been together five or six years. Jack had coveted a spot in the section which was to be thrown open, and he asked the foreman to help him get it. He had been all over the country when it was part of the range, and had picked out a spot on Big Turkey Creek, ten miles south of the Strip line. It gradually passed from one to another of us what Jack wanted. At first we felt blue about it, but Miller, who could see farther than the rest of us, dispelled the gloom by announcing at dinner, "Jack is going to take a claim if this outfit has a horse in it and a man to ride him. It is only a question of a year or two at the farthest until the rest of us will be guiding a white mule between two corn rows, and glad of the chance. If Jack goes now, he will have just that many years the start of the rest of us."

We nerved ourselves and tried to appear jolly after this talk of the foreman. We entered into quite a discussion as to which horse would be the best to make the ride with. The ranch had several specially good saddle animals. In chasing gray wolves in the winter those qualities of endurance which long races developed in hunting these enemies of cattle, pointed out a certain coyote-colored horse, whose color marks and "Dead Tree" brand indicated that he was of Spanish extraction. Intelligently ridden with a light rider he was First Choice on which to make this run. That was finally agreed to by all. There was no trouble selecting the rider for this horse with the zebra marks. The lightest weight was Billy Edwards. This qualification gave him the preference over us all.

Jack described the spot he desired to claim by an old branding-pen which had been built there when it had been part of the range. Billy had ironed up many a calf in those same pens himself. "Well, Jack," said Billy, "if this outfit don't put you on the best quarter section around that old corral, you'll know that they have throwed off on you."

It was two weeks before the opening day. The coyote horse was given special care from this time forward. He feasted on corn, while others had to be content with grass. In spite of all the bravado that was being thrown into these preparations, there was noticeable a deep under current of regret. Jack was going from us. Every one wanted him to go, still these dissolving ties moved the simple men to acts of boyish kindness. Each tried to outdo the others, in the matter of a parting present to Jack. He could have robbed us then. It was as bad as a funeral. Once before we felt similarly when one of the boys died at camp. It was like an only sister leaving the family circle.

Miller seemed to enjoy the discomfiture of the rest of us. This creedless old Christian had fine strata in his make-up. He and Jack planned continually for the future. In fact they didn't live in the present like the rest of us. Two days before the opening, we loaded up a wagon with Jack's effects. Every man but the newly installed cook went along. It was too early in the spring for work to commence. We all dubbed Jack a boomer from this time forward. The horse so much depended on was led behind the wagon.

On the border we found a motley crowd of people. Soldiers had gathered them into camps along the line to prevent "sooners" from entering before the appointed time. We stopped in a camp directly north of the claim our little boomer wanted. One thing was certain, it would take a better horse than ours to win the claim away from us. No sooner could take it. That and other things were what all of us were going along for.

The next day when the word was given that made the land public domain, Billy was in line on the coyote. He held his place to the front with the best of them. After the first few miles, the others followed the valley of Turkey Creek, but he maintained his course like wild fowl, skirting the timber which covered the first range of hills back from the creek. Jack followed with the wagon, while the rest of us rode leisurely, after the first mile or so. When we saw Edwards bear straight ahead from the others, we argued that a sooner only could beat us for the claim. If he tried to out-hold us, it would be six to one, as we noticed the leaders closely when we slacked up. By not following the valley, Billy would cut off two miles. Any man who could ride twelve miles to the coyote's ten with Billy Edwards in the saddle was welcome to the earth. That was the way we felt. We rode together, expecting to make the claim three quarters of an hour behind our man. When near enough to sight it, we could see Billy and another horseman apparently protesting with one another. A loud yell from one of us attracted our man's attention. He mounted his horse and rode out and met us. "Well, fellows, it's the expected that's happened this time," said he. "Yes, there's a sooner on it, and he puts up a fine bluff of having ridden from the line; but he's a liar by the watch, for there isn't a wet hair on his horse, while the sweat was dripping from the fetlocks of this one."

"If you are satisfied that he is a sooner," said Miller, "he has to go."

"Well, he is a lying sooner," said Edwards.

We reined in our horses and held a short parley. After a brief discussion of the situation, Miller said to us: "You boys go down to him,—don't hurt him or get hurt, but make out that you're going to hang him. Put plenty of reality into it, and I'll come in in time to save him and give him a chance to run for his life."

We all rode down towards him, Miller bearing off towards the right of the old corral,—rode out over the claim noticing the rich soil thrown up by the mole-hills. When we came up to our sooner, all of us dismounted. Edwards confronted him and said, "Do you contest my right to this claim?"

"I certainly do," was the reply.

"Well, you won't do so for long," said Edwards. Quick as a flash Mouse prodded the cold steel muzzle of a six-shooter against his ear. As the sooner turned his head and looked into Mouse's stern countenance, one of the boys relieved him of an ugly gun and knife that dangled from his belt. "Get on your horse," said Mouse, emphasizing his demand with an oath, while the muzzle of a forty-five in his ear made the order undebatable. Edwards took the horse by the bit and started for a large black-jack tree which stood near by. Reaching it, Edwards said, "Better use Coon's rope; it's manilla and stronger. Can any of you boys tie a hangman's knot?" he inquired when the rope was handed him.

"Yes, let me," responded several.

"Which limb will be best?" inquired Mouse.

"Take this horse by the bit," said Edwards to one of the boys, "till I look." He coiled the rope sailor fashion, and made an ineffectual attempt to throw it over a large limb which hung out like a yard-arm, but the small branches intervening defeated his throw. While he was coiling the rope to make a second throw, some one said, "Mebby so he'd like to pray."

"What! him pray?" said Edwards. "Any prayer that he might offer couldn't get a hearing amongst men, let alone above, where liars are forbidden."

"Try that other limb," said Coon to Edwards; "there's not so much brush in the way; we want to get this job done sometime today." As Edwards made a successful throw, he said, "Bring that horse directly underneath." At this moment Miller dashed up and demanded, "What in hell are you trying to do?"

"This sheep-thief of a sooner contests my right to this claim," snapped

Edwards, "and he has played his last cards on this earth. Lead that horse under here."

"Just one moment," said Miller. "I think I know this man—think he worked for me once in New Mexico." The sooner looked at Miller appealingly, his face blanched to whiteness. Miller took the bridle reins out of the hands of the boy who was holding the horse, and whispering something to the sooner said to us, "Are you all ready?"

"Just waiting on you," said Edwards. The sooner gathered up the reins. Miller turned the horse halfway round as though he was going to lead him under the tree, gave him a slap in the flank with his hand, and the sooner, throwing the rowels of his spurs into the horse, shot out from us like a startled deer. We called to him to halt, as half a dozen six-shooters encouraged him to go by opening a fusillade on the fleeing horseman, who only hit the high places while going. Nor did we let up fogging him until we emptied our guns and he entered the timber. There was plenty of zeal in this latter part, as the lead must have zipped and cried near enough to give it reality. Our object was to shoot as near as possible without hitting.

Other horsemen put in an appearance as we were unsaddling and preparing to camp, for we had come to stay a week if necessary. In about an hour Jack joined us, speechless as usual, his face wreathed in smiles. The first step toward a home he could call his own had been taken. We told him about the trouble we had had with the sooner, a story which he seemed to question, until Miller confirmed it. We put up a tent among the black-jacks, as the nights were cool, and were soon at peace with all the world.

At supper that evening Edwards said: "When the old settlers hold their reunions in the next generation, they'll say, 'Thirty years ago Uncle Jack Martin settled over there on Big Turkey,' and point him out to their children as one of the pioneer fathers."

No one found trouble in getting to sleep that night, and the next day arts long forgotten by most of us were revived. Some plowed up the old branding-pen for a garden. Others cut logs for a cabin. Every one did two ordinary days' work. The getting of the logs together was the hardest. We sawed and chopped and hewed for dear life. The first few days Jack and one of the boys planted a fine big garden. On the fourth day we gave up the tent, as the smoke curled upward from our own chimney, in the way that it does in well-told stories. The last night we spent with Jack was one long to be remembered. A bright fire snapped and crackled in the ample fireplace. Every one told stories. Several of the boys could sing "The Lone Star Cow-trail," while "Sam Bass" and "Bonnie Black Bess" were given with a vim.

The next morning we were to leave for camp. One of the boys who would work for us that summer, but whose name was not on the pay-roll until the round-up, stayed with Jack. We all went home feeling fine, and leaving Jack happy as a bird in his new possession. As we were saddling up to leave, Miller said to Jack ,"Now if you're any good, you'll delude some girl to keep house for you 'twixt now and fall. Remember what the Holy Book says about it being hard luck for man to be alone. You notice all your boomer neighbors have wives. That's a hint to you to do likewise."

We were on the point of mounting, when the coyote horse began to act up in great shape. Some one said to Edwards, "Loosen your cinches!" "Oh, it's nothing but the corn he's been eating and a few days' rest," said Miller. "He's just running a little bluff on Billy." As Edwards went to put his foot in the stirrup a second time, the coyote reared like a circus horse. "Now look here, colty," said Billy, speaking to the horse, "my daddy rode with Old John Morgan, the Confederate cavalry raider, and he'd be ashamed of any boy he ever raised that couldn't ride a bad horse like you. You're plum foolish to act this way. Do you think I'll walk and lead you home?" He led him out a few rods from the others and mounted him without any trouble. "He just wants to show Jack how it affects a cow-horse to graze a few days on a boomer's claim,—that's all," said Edwards, when he joined us.

"Now, Jack," said Miller, as a final parting, "if you want a cow, I'll send one down, or if you need anything, let us know and we'll come a-running. It's a bad example you've set us to go booming this way, but we want to make a howling success out of you, so we can visit you next winter. And mind what I told you about getting married," he called back as he rode away.

We reached camp by late noon. Miller kept up his talk about what a fine move Jack had made; said that we must get him a stray beef for his next winter's meat; kept figuring constantly what else he could do for Jack. "You come around in a few years and you'll find him as cosy as a coon, and better off than any of us," said Miller, when we were talking about his farming. "I've slept under wet blankets with him, and watched him kindle a fire in the snow, too often not to know what he's made of. There's good stuff in that little rascal."

About the ranch it seemed lonesome without Jack. It was like coming home from school when we were kids and finding mother gone to the neighbor's. We always liked to find her at home. We busied ourselves re-pairing fences, putting in flood-gates on the river, doing anything to keep away from camp. Miller himself went back to see Jack within ten days, remaining a week. None of us stayed at the home ranch any more than we could help. We visited other camps on hatched excuses, until the home round-ups began. When any one else asked us about Jack, we would blow about what a fine claim he had, and what a boost we had given him. When we buckled down to the summer's work the gloom gradually left us. There were men to be sent on the eastern, western, and middle divisions of the general round-up of the Strip. Two men were sent south into the Cheyenne country to catch anything that had winter-drifted. Our range lay in the middle division. Miller and one man looked after it on the general round-up.

It was a busy year with us. Our range was full stocked, and by early fall was rich with fat cattle. We lived with the wagon after the shipping season commenced. Then we missed Jack, although the new cook did the best he knew how. Train after train went out of our pasture, yet the cattle were never missed. We never went to camp now; only the wagon went in after supplies, though we often came within sight of the stabling and corrals in our work.

One day, late in the season, we were getting out a train load of "Barb Wire" cattle, when who should come toddling along on a plow nag but Jack himself. Busy as we were, we held quite a levee, though he didn't give down much news, nor have anything to say about himself or the crops. That night at camp, while the rest of us were arranging the guards for the night, Miller and Jack prowled off in an opposite direction from the beef herd, possibly half a mile, and afoot, too. We could all see that something was working. Some trouble was bothering Jack, and he had come to a friend in need, so we thought. They did not come back to camp until the moon was up and the second guard had gone out to relieve the first. When they came back not a word was spoken. They unrolled Miller's bed and slept together.

The next morning as Jack was leaving us to return to his claim, we overheard him say to Miller, "I'll write you." As he faded from our sight, Miller smiled to himself, as though he was tickled about something. Finally Billy Edwards brought things to a head by asking bluntly, "What's up with Jack? We want to know."

"Oh, it's too good," said Miller. "If that little game-legged rooster hasn't gone and deluded some girl back in the State into marrying him, I'm a horse-thief. You fellows are all in the play, too. Came here special to see when we could best get away. Wants every one of us to come. He's built another end to his house, double log style, floored both rooms and the middle. Says he will have two fiddlers, and promises us the hog killingest time of our lives. I've accepted the invitation on behalf of the 'J + H's' without consulting any one."

"But supposing we are busy when it takes place," said Mouse, "then what?"

"But we won't be," answered Miller. "It isn't every day that we have a chance at a wedding in our little family, and when we get the word, this outfit quits then and there. Ordinary callings in life, like cattle matters, must go to the rear until important things are attended to. Every man is expected to don his best togs, and dance to the centre on the word. If it takes a week to turn the trick properly, good enough. Jack and his bride must have a blow-out right. This outfit must do themselves proud. It will be our night to howl, and every man will be a woolly wolf."

We loaded the beeves out the next day, going back after two trains of "Turkey Track" cattle. While we were getting these out, Miller cut out two strays and a cow or two, and sent them to the horse pasture at the home camp. It was getting late in the fall, and we figured that a few more shipments would end it. Miller told the owners to load out what they wanted while the weather was fit, as our saddle horses were getting worn out fast. As we were loading out the last shipment of mixed cattle of our own, the letter came to Miller. Jack would return with his bride on a date only two days off, and the festivities were set for one day later. We pulled into headquarters that night, the first time in six weeks, and turned everything loose. The next morning we overhauled our Sunday bests, and worried around trying to pick out something for a wedding present.

Miller gave the happy pair a little "Flower Pot" cow, which he had rustled in the Cheyenne country on the round-up a few years before. Edwards presented him with a log chain that a bone-picker had lost in our pasture. Mouse gave Jack a four-tined fork which the hay outfit had forgotten when they left. Coon Floyd's compliments went with five cowbells, which we always thought he rustled from a boomer's wagon that broke down over on the Reno trail. It bothered some of us to rustle something for a present, for you know we couldn't buy anything. We managed to get some deer's antlers, a gray wolf's skin for the bride's tootsies, and several colored sheepskins, which we had bought from a Mexican horse herd going up the trail that spring. We killed a nice fat little beef, the evening before we started, hanging it out overnight to harden. None of the boys knew the brand; in fact, it's bad taste to remember the brand on anything you've beefed. No one troubles himself to notice it carefully. That night a messenger brought a letter to Miller, ordering him to ship out the remnant of "Diamond Tail" cattle as soon as possible. They belonged to a northwest Texas outfit, and we were maturing them. The messenger stayed all night, and in the morning asked, "Shall I order cars for you?"

"No, I have a few other things to attend to first," answered Miller.

We took the wagon with us to carry our bedding and the other plunder, driving along with us a cow and a calf of Jack's, the little "Flower Pot" cow, and a beef. Our outfit reached Jack's house by the middle of the afternoon. The first thing was to be introduced to the bride. Jack did the honors himself, presenting each of us, and seemed just as proud as a little boy with new boots. Then we were given introductions to several good-looking neighbor girls. We began to feel our own inferiority.

While we were hanging up the quarters of beef on some pegs on the north side of the cabin, Edwards said, whispering, "Jack must have pictured this claim mighty hifalutin to that gal, for she's a way up goodlooker. Another thing, watch me build to the one inside with the black eyes. I claimed her first, remember. As soon as we get this beef hung up I'm going in and sidle up to her."

"We won't differ with you on that point," remarked Mouse, "but if she takes any special shine to a runt like you, when there's boys like the rest of us standing around, all I've got to say is, her tastes must be a heap sight sorry and depraved. I expect to dance with the bride—in the head set—a whirl or two myself."

"If I'd only thought," chimed in Coon, "I'd sent up to the State and got me a white shirt and a standing collar and a red necktie. You galoots out-hold me on togs. But where I was raised, back down in Palo Pinto County, Texas, I was some punkins as a ladies' man myself—you hear me."

"Oh, you look all right," said Edwards. "You would look all right with only a cotton string around your neck."

After tending to our horses, we all went into the house. There sat Miller talking to the bride just as if he had known her always, with Jack standing with his back to the fire, grinning like a cat eating paste. The neighbor girls fell to getting supper, and our cook turned to and helped. We managed to get fairly well acquainted with the company by the time the meal was over. The fiddlers came early, in fact, dined with us. Jack said if there were enough girls, we could run three sets, and he thought there would be, as he had asked every one both sides of the creek for five miles. The beds were taken down and stowed away, as there would be no use for them that night.

The company came early. Most of the young fellows brought their best girls seated beside them on saddle horses. This manner gave the girl a chance to show her trustful, clinging nature. A horse that would carry double was a prize animal. In setting up a new country, primitive methods crop out as a matter of necessity.

Ben Thorn, an old-timer in the Strip, called off. While the company was gathering, the fiddlers began to tune up, which sent a thrill through us. When Ben gave the word, "Secure your pardners for the first quadrille," Miller led out the bride to the first position in the best room, Jack's short leg barring him as a participant. This was the signal for the rest of us, and we fell in promptly. The fiddles struck up "Hounds in the Woods," the prompter's voice rang out "Honors to your pardner," and the dance was on.

Edwards close-herded the black-eyed girl till supper time. Not a one of us got a dance with her even. Mouse admitted next day, as we rode home, that he squeezed her hand several times in the grand right and left, just to show her that she had other admirers, that she needn't throw herself away on any one fellow, but it was no go. After supper Billy corralled her in a corner, she seeming willing, and stuck to her until her brother took her home nigh daylight.

Jack got us boys pardners for every dance. He proved himself clean strain that night, the whitest little Injun on the reservation. We knocked off dancing about midnight and had supper,—good coffee with no end of way-up fine chuck. We ate as we danced, heartily. Supper over, the dance went on full blast. About two o'clock in the morning, the wire edge was well worn off the revelers, and they showed signs of weariness. Miller, noticing it, ordered the Indian war-dance as given by the Cheyennes. That aroused every one and filled the sets instantly. The fiddlers caught the inspiration and struck into "Sift the Meal and save the Bran." In every grand right and left, we ki-yied as we had witnessed Lo in the dance on festive occasions. At the end of every change, we gave a war-whoop, some of the girls joining in, that would have put to shame any son of the Cheyennes.

It was daybreak when the dance ended and the guests departed. Though we had brought our blankets with us, no one thought of sleeping. Our cook and one of the girls got breakfast. The bride offered to help, but we wouldn't let her turn her hand. At breakfast we discussed the incidents of the night previous, and we all felt that we had done the occasion justice.

# STEPHEN CRANE

## *The Bride Comes to Yellow Sky*

THE GREAT PULLMAN was whirling onward with such dignity of motion that a glance from the window seemed simply to prove that the plains of Texas were pouring eastward. Vast flats of green grass, dull-hued spaces of mesquite and cactus, little groups of frame houses, woods of light and tender trees, all were sweeping into the east, sweeping over the horizon, a precipice.

A newly married pair had boarded this coach at San Antonio. The man's face was reddened from many days in the wind and sun, and a direct result of his new black clothes was that his brick-colored hands were constantly performing in a most conscious fashion. From time to time he looked down respectfully at his attire. He sat with a hand on each knee, like a man waiting in a barber's shop. The glances he devoted to other passengers were furtive and shy.

The bride was not pretty, nor was she very young. She wore a dress of blue cashmere, with small reservations of velvet here and there, and with steel buttons abounding. She continually twisted her head to regard her puff sleeves, very stiff, straight, and high. They embarrassed her. It was quite apparent that she had cooked, and that she expected to cook, dutifully. The blushes caused by the careless scrutiny of some passengers as she had entered the car were strange to see upon this plain, underclass countenance, which was drawn in placid, almost emotionless lines.

They were evidently very happy. "Ever been in a parlor-car before?" he asked, smiling with delight.

"No," she answered; "I never was. It's fine, ain't it?"

"Great! And then after a while we'll go forward to the diner, and get a big lay-out. Finest meal in the world. Charge a dollar."

"Oh, do they?" cried the bride. "Charge a dollar? Why, that's too much —for us—ain't it, Jack?"

"Not this trip, anyhow," he answered bravely. "We're going to go the whole thing."

Later he explained to her about the trains. "You see, its a thousand miles from one end of Texas to the other; and this train runs right across it, and never stops but four times." He had the pride of an owner. He pointed out to her the dazzling fittings of the coach; and in truth her eyes opened wider as she contemplated the sea-green figured velvet, the shining brass, silver, and glass, the wood that gleamed as darkly brilliant as the surface of a pool of oil. At one end a bronze figure sturdily held a support for a separated chamber, and at convenient places on the ceiling were frescos in olive and silver.

To the minds of the pair, their surroundings reflected the glory of their marriage that morning in San Antonio; this was the environment of their new estate; and the man's face in particular beamed with an elation that made him appear ridiculous to the Negro porter. This individual at times surveyed them from afar with an amused and superior grin. On other occasions he bullied them with skill in ways that did not make it exactly plain to them that they were being bullied. He subtly used all the manners of the most unconquerable kind of snobbery. He oppressed them; but of this oppression they had small knowledge, and they speedily forgot that infrequently a number of travellers covered them with stares of derisive enjoyment. Historically there was supposed to be something infinitely humorous in their situation.

"We are due in Yellow Sky at 3:42," he said, looking tenderly into her eyes.

"Oh, are we?" she said, as if she had not been aware of it. To evince surprise at her husband's statement was part of her wifely amiability. She took from her pocket a little silver watch; and as she held it before her, and stared at it with a frown of attention, the new husband's face shone.

"I bought it in San Anton' from a friend of mine," he told her gleefully.

"It's seventeen minutes past twelve," she said, looking up at him with a kind of shy and clumsy coquetry. A passenger, noting this play, grew excessively sardonic, and winked at himself in one of the numerous mirrors.

At last they went to the dining-car. Two rows of Negro waiters, in glowing white suits, surveyed their entrance with interest, and also the equanimity, of men who had been forewarned. The pair fell to the lot of a waiter who happened to feel pleasure in steering them through their meal. He viewed them with the manner of a fatherly pilot, his countenance radiant with benevolence. The patronage, entwined with the ordinary deference, was not plain to them. And yet, as they returned to their coach, they showed in their faces a sense of escape.

To the left, miles down a long purple slope, was a little ribbon of mist where moved the keening Rio Grande. The train was approaching it at an angle, and the apex was Yellow Sky. Presently it was apparent that, as the distance from Yellow Sky grew shorter, the husband became commensurately restless. His brick-red hands were more insistent in their prominence. Occasionally he was even rather absent-minded and far-away when the bride leaned forward and addressed him.

As a matter of truth, Jack Potter was beginning to find the shadow of a deed weigh upon him like a leaden slab. He, the town marshal of Yellow Sky, a man known, liked, and feared in his corner, a prominent person, had gone to San Antonio to meet a girl he believed he loved, and there, after the usual prayers, had actually induced her to marry him, without consulting Yellow Sky for any part of the transaction. He was now bringing his bride before an innocent and unsuspecting community.

Of course people in Yellow Sky married as it pleased them, in accordance with a general custom; but such was Potter's thought of his duty to his friends, or of their idea of his duty, or of an unspoken form which does not control men in these matters, that he felt he was heinous. He had committed an extraordinary crime. Face to face with this girl in San Antonio, and spurred by his sharp impulse, he had gone headlong over all the social hedges. At San Antonio he was like a man hidden in the dark. A knife to sever any friendly duty, any form, was easy to his hand in that remote city. But the hour of Yellow Sky—the hour of daylight— was approaching.

He knew full well that his marriage was an important thing to his town. It could only be exceeded by the burning of the new hotel. His friends could not forgive him. Frequently he had reflected on the advisability of telling them by telegraph, but a new cowardice had been upon him. He feared to do it. And now the train was hurrying him toward a scene of amazement, glee, and reproach. He glanced out of the window at the line of haze swinging slowly in toward the train.

Yellow Sky had a kind brass band, which played painfully, to the delight of the populace. He laughed without heart as he thought of it. If the citizens could dream of his prospective arrival with his bride, they would parade the band at the station and escort them, amid cheers and laughing congratulations, to his adobe home.

He resolved that he would use all the devices of speed and plainscraft in making the journey from the station to his house. Once within that safe citadel, he could issue some sort of vocal bulletin, and then not go among the citizens until they had time to wear off a little of their enthusiasm.

The bride looked anxiously at him. "What's worrying you, Jack?"

He laughed again. "I'm not worrying, girl; I'm only thinking of Yellow Sky."

She flushed in comprehension.

A sense of mutual guilt invaded their minds and developed a finer tenderness. They looked at each other with eyes softly aglow. But Potter often laughed the same nervous laugh; the flush upon the bride's face seemed quite permanent.

The traitor to the feelings of Yellow Sky narrowly watched the speeding landscape. "We're nearly there," he said.

Presently the porter came and announced the proximity of Potter's home. He held a brush in his hand, and, with all his airy superiority gone, he brushed Potter's new clothes as the latter slowly turned this way and that way. Potter fumbled out a coin and gave it to the porter, as he had seen others do. It was a heavy and muscle-bound business, as that of a man shoeing his first horse.

The porter took their bag, and as the train began to slow they moved forward to the hooded platform of the car. Presently the two engines and their long string of coaches rushed into the station of Yellow Sky.

"They have to take water here," said Potter, from a constricted throat and in mournful cadence, as one announcing death. Before the train stopped his eye had swept the length of the platform, and he was glad and astonished to see there was none upon it but the station-agent, who, with a slightly hurried and anxious air, was walking toward the water-tanks. When the train had halted, the porter alighted first, and placed in position a little temporary step.

"Come on, girl," said Potter, hoarsely. As he helped her down they each laughed on a false note. He took the bag from the Negro, and bade his wife cling to his arm. As they slunk rapidly away, his hang-dog glance perceived that they were unloading the two trunks, and also that the station-agent, far ahead near the baggage car, had turned and was running toward him, making gestures. He laughed, and groaned as he laughed, when he noted the first effect of his marital bliss upon Yellow Sky. He gripped his wife's arm firmly to his side, and they fled. Behind them the porter stood, chuckling fatuously.

## II

The California express on the Southern Railway was due at Yellow Sky in twenty-one minutes. There were six men at the bar of the Weary Gentleman saloon. One was a drummer who talked a great deal and rapidly; three were Texans who did not care to talk at that time; and two were Mexican sheepherders, who did not talk as a general practice in the Weary Gentleman saloon. The barkeeper's dog lay on the board walk that crossed in front of the door. His head was on his paws, and he glanced drowsily here and there with the constant vigilance of a dog that is kicked on occasion. Across the sandy street were some vivid green grass-plots, so wonderful in appearance, amid the sands that burned near them in a blazing sun, that they caused a doubt in the mind. They exactly resembled the grass mats used to represent lawns on the stage. At the cooler end of the railway station, a man without a coat sat in a tilted chair and smoked his pipe. The fresh-cut bank of the Rio Grande circled near the town, and there could be seen beyond it a great plum-colored plain of mesquite.

Save for the busy drummer and his companions in the saloon, Yellow Sky was dozing. The new-comer leaned gracefully upon the bar, and recited many tales with the confidence of a bard who has come upon a new field.

"—and at the moment that the old man fell downstairs with the bureau in his arms, the old woman was coming up with two scuttles of coal, and of course—"

The drummer's tale was interrupted by a young man who suddenly appeared in the open door. He cried: "Scratchy Wilson's drunk, and has turned loose with both hands." The two Mexicans at once set down their glasses and faded out of the rear entrance of the saloon.

The drummer, innocent and jocular, answered: "All right, old man. S'pose he has? Come in and have a drink, anyhow."

But the information had made such an obvious cleft in every skull in the room that the drummer was obliged to see its importance. All had become instantly solemn. "Say," said he, mystified, "what is this?" His three companions made the introductory gesture of eloquent speech; but the young man at the door forestalled them.

"It means, my friend," he answered, as he came into the saloon, "that for the next two hours this town won't be a health resort."

The barkeeper went to the door, and locked and barred it; reaching out of the window, he pulled in heavy wooden shutters, and barred them. Immediately a solemn, chapel-like gloom was upon the place. The drummer was looking from one to another.

"But say," he cried, "what is this, anyhow? You don't mean there is going to be a gun-fight?"

"Don't know whether there'll be a fight or not," answered one man, grimly; "but there'll be some shootin'—some good shootin'."

The young man who had warned them waved his hand. "Oh, there'll be a fight fast enough, if any one wants it. Anybody can get a fight out there in the street. There's a fight just waiting."

The drummer seemed to be swayed between the interest of a foreigner and a perception of personal danger.

"What did you say his name was?" he asked.

"Scratchy Wilson," they answered in chorus.

"And will he kill anybody? What are you going to do? Does this happen often? Does he rampage around like this once a week or so? Can he break in that door?"

"No; he can't break down that door," replied the barkeeper. "He's tried it three times. But when he comes you'd better lay down on the floor, stranger. He's dead sure to shoot at it, and a bullet may come through."

Thereafter the drummer kept a strict eye upon the door. The time had not yet been called for him to hug the floor, but, as a minor precaution, he sidled near to the wall. "Will he kill anybody?" he said again.

The men laughed low and scornfully at the question.

"He's out to shoot, and he's out for trouble. Don't see any good in experimentin' with him."

"But what do you do in a case like this? What do you do?"

A man responded: "Why, he and Jack Potter—"

"But," in chorus the other men interrupted, "Jack Potter's in San Anton'."

"Well, who is he? What's he go to do with it?"

"Oh, he's the town marshal. He goes out and fights Scratchy when he gets on one of these tears."

"Wow!" said the drummer, mopping his brow. "Nice job he's got."

The voices had toned away to mere whisperings. The drummer wished to ask further questions, which were born of an increasing anxiety and bewilderment; but when he attempted them, the men merely looked at him in irritation and motioned him to remain silent. A tense waiting hush was upon them. In the deep shadows of the room their eyes shone as they listened for sounds from the street. One man made three gestures at the barkeeper; and the latter, moving like a ghost, handed him a glass and a bottle. The man poured a full glass of whisky, and set down the bottle noiselessly. He gulped the whisky in a swallow, and turned again toward the door in immovable silence. The drummer saw that the barkeeper, without a sound, had taken a Winchester from beneath the bar. Later he saw this individual beckoning to him, so he tiptoed across the room.

"You better come with me back of the bar."

"No, thanks," said the drummer, perspiring; "I'd rather be where I can make a break for the back door."

Whereupon the man of bottles made a kindly but peremptory gesture. The drummer obeyed it, and, finding himself seated on a box with his head below the level of the bar, balm was laid upon his soul at sight of various zinc and copper fittings that bore a resemblance to armor-plate. The barkeeper took a seat comfortably upon an adjacent box.

"You see," he whispered, "this here Scratchy Wilson is a wonder with a gun—a perfect wonder; and when he goes on the war-trail, we hunt our holes—naturally. He's about the last one of the old gang that used to hang out along the river here. He's a terror when he's drunk. When he's sober he's all right—kind of simple—wouldn't hurt a fly—nicest fellow in town. But when he's drunk—whoo!"

There were periods of stillness. "I wish Jack Potter was back from San Anton'," said the barkeeper. "He shot Wilson up once—in the leg—and he would sail in and pull out the kinks in this thing."

Presently they heard from a distance the sound of a shot, followed by three wild yowls. It instantly removed a bond from the men in the darkened saloon. There was a shuffling of feet. They looked at each other. "Here he comes," they said.

### III

A man in a maroon-colored flannel shirt, which had been purchased for purposes of decoration, and made principally by some Jewish women on the East Side of New York, rounded a corner and walked into the middle of the main street of Yellow Sky. In either hand the man held a long, heavy, blue-black revolver. Often he yelled, and these cries rang through a semblance of a deserted village, shrilly flying over the rooms in a volume that seemed to have no relation to the ordinary vocal strength of a man. It was as if the surrounding stillness formed the arch of a tomb over him. These cries of ferocious challenge rang against the walls of silence. And his boots had red tops with gilded imprints, of the kind beloved in winter by little sledding boys on the hillsides of New England.

The man's face flamed in a rage begot of whiskey. His eyes, rolling, and yet keen for ambush, hunted the still doorways and windows. He walked with the creeping movement of the midnight cat. As it occurred to him, he roared menacing information. The long revolvers in his hands were as easy as straws; they were moved with an electric swiftness. The little fingers of each hand played sometimes in a musician's way. Plain from the low collar of the shirt, the cords of his neck straightened and sank, straightened and sank, as passion moved him. The only sounds were his terrible invitations. The calm adobes preserved their demeanor at the passing of this small thing in the middle of the street.

There was no offer of fight—no offer of fight. The man called to the sky. There were no attractions. He bellowed and fumed and swayed his revolvers here and everywhere.

The dog of the barkeeper of the Weary Gentleman saloon had not appreciated the advance of events. He yet lay dozing in front of his master's door. At sight of the dog, the man paused and raised his revolver humorously. At sight of the man, the dog sprang up and walked diagonally away, with a sullen head, and growling. The man yelled, and the dog broke into a gallop. As it was about to enter an alley, there was a loud noise, a whistling, and something spat the ground directly before it. The dog screamed, and, wheeling in terror, galloped headlong in a new direction. Again there was a noise, a whistling, and sand was kicked viciously before it. Fear-stricken, the dog turned and flurried like an animal in a pen. The man stood laughing, his weapons at his hips.

Ultimately the man was attracted by the closed door of the Weary Gentleman saloon. He went to it and, hammering with a revolver, demanded drink.

The door remaining imperturbable, he picked a bit of paper from the walk, and nailed it to the framework with a knife. He then turned his back contemptuously upon this popular resort and, walking to the opposite side of the street and spinning there on his heel quickly and lithely, fired at the bit of paper. He missed it by a half-inch. He swore at himself, and went away. Later he comfortably fusilladed the windows of his most intimate friend. The man was playing with this town; it was a toy for him.

But still there was no offer of fight. The name of Jack Potter, his ancient antagonist, entered his mind, and he concluded that it would be a glad thing if he should go to Potter's house, and by bombardment induce him to come out and fight. He moved in the direction of his desire, chanting Apache scalp-music.

When he arrived at it, Potter's house presented the same still front as had the other adobes. Taking up a strategic position, the man howled a challenge. But the house regarded him as might a great stone god. It gave no sight. After a decent wait, the man howled further challenges, mingling with them wonderful epithets.

Presently there came the spectacle of a man churning himself into deepest rage over the immobility of a house. He fumed at it as the winter wind attacks a prairie cabin in the North. To the distance there should have gone the sound of a tumult like the fighting of two hundred Mexicans. As necessity bade him, he paused for breath or to reload his revolvers.

**IV**

Potter and his bride walked sheepishly and with speed. Sometimes they laughed together shamefacedly and low.

"Next corner, dear," he said finally.

They put forth the efforts of a pair walking bowed against a strong wind. Potter was about to raise a finger to point the first appearance of the new home when, as they circled the corner, they came face to face with a man in a maroon-colored shirt, who was feverishly pushing cartridges into a large revolver. Upon the instant the man dropped his revolver to the ground and, like lightning, whipped another from its holster. The second weapon was aimed at the bridegroom's chest.

There was a silence. Potter's mouth seemed to be merely a grave for his tongue. He exhibited an instinct to at once loosen his arm from the woman's grip, and he dropped the bag to the sand. As for the bride, her face had gone as yellow as old cloth. She was a slave to hideous rites, gazing at the apparitional snake.

The two men faced each other at a distance of three paces. He of the revolver smiled with a new and quiet ferocity.

"Tried to sneak up on me," he said. "Tried to sneak up on me;" His eyes grew more baleful. As Potter made a slight movement, the man thrust his revolver venomously forward. "No; don't you do it, Jack Potter. Don't you move a finger toward a gun just yet. Don't you move an eyelash. The time has come for me to settle with you, and I'm goin' to do it my own way, and loaf along with no interferin'. So if you don't want a gun bent on you, just mind what I tell you."

Potter looked at his enemy. "I ain't got a gun on me, Scratchy," he said. "Honest, I ain't." He was stiffening and steadying, but yet somewhere at the back of his mind a vision of the Pullman floated: the sea-green figured velvet, the shining brass, silver, and glass, the wood that gleamed as darkly brilliant as the surface of a pool of oil—all the glory of the marriage, the environment of the new estate. "You know I fight when it comes to fighting, Scratchy Wilson; but I ain't got a gun on me. You'll have to do all the shootin' yourself."

His enemy's face went livid. He stepped forward, and lashed his weapon to and fro before Potter's chest. "Don't you tell me you ain't got no gun on you, you whelp. Don't tell me no lie like that. There ain't a man in Texas ever seen you without no gun. Don't take me for no kid." His eyes blazed with light, and his throat worked like a pump.

"I ain't takin' you for no kid," answered Potter. His heels had not moved an inch backward. "I'm takin' you for a damn fool. I tell you I ain't got a gun, and I ain't. If you're goin' to shoot me up, you better begin now; you'll never get a chance like this again."

So much enforced reasoning had told on Wilson's rage; he was calmer. "If you ain't got a gun, why ain't you got a gun?" he sneered. "Been to Sunday-school?"

"I ain't got a gun because I've just come from San Anton' with my wife. I'm married," said Potter. "And if I'd thought there was going to be any galoots like you prowling around when I brought my wife home, I'd had a gun, and don't you forget it."

"Married!" said Scratchy, not at all comprehending.

"Yes, married. I'm married," said Potter, distinctly.

"Married?" said Scratchy. Seemingly for the first time, he saw the drooping, drowning woman at the other man's side. "No!" he said. He was like a creature allowed a glimpse of another world. He moved a pace backward, and his arm, with the revolver, dropped to his side. "Is this the lady?" he asked.

"Yes; this is the lady." answered Potter.

There was another period of silence.

"Well," said Wilson at last, slowly, "I s'pose it's all off now."

"It's all off if you say so, Scratchy. You know I dind't make the trouble." Potter lifted his valise.

"Well, I 'low it's off, Jack," said Wilson. He was looking at the ground. "Married!" He was not a student of chivalry; it was merely that in the presence of this foreign condition he was a simple child of the earlier plains. He picked up his starboard revolver, and, placing both weapons in their holsters, he went away. His feet made funnel-shaped tracks in the heavy sand.

# STEWART EDWARD WHITE

## *A Corner in Horses*

IT WAS DARK NIGHT. The stray-herd bellowed frantically from one of the big corrals; the cow-and-calf-herd from a second. Already the remuda, driven in from the open plains, scattered about the thousand acres of pasture. Away from the conveniences of fence and corral, men would have had to patrol all night. Now, however, everyone was gathered about the camp fire.

Probably forty cowboys were in the group, representing all types, from old John, who had been in the business forty years, and had punched from the Rio Grande to the Pacific, to the Kid, who would have given his chance of salvation if he could have been taken for ten years older than he was. At the moment Jed Parker was holding forth to his friend Johnny Stone in reference to another old crony who had that evening joined the round-up.

"Johnny," inquired Jed with elaborate gravity, and entirely ignoring the presence of the subject of conversation, "what is that thing just beyond the fire, and where did it come from?"

Johnny Stone squinted to make sure.

"That?" he replied. "Oh, this evenin' the dogs see something run down a hole, and they dug it out, and that's what they got."

The newcomer grinned.

"The trouble with you fellows," he proffered, "is that you're so plumb alkalied you don't know the real thing when you see it."

"That's right," supplemented Windy Bill drily. "He come from New York."

"No," cried Jed. "You don't say so? Did he come in one box or in two?"

Under cover of the laugh, the newcomer made a raid on the Dutch ovens and pails. Having filled his plate, he squatted on his heels and fell to his belated meal. He was a tall, slab-sided individual, with a lean, leathery face, a sweeping white mustache, and a grave and sardonic eye. His leather chaps were plain and worn, and his hat had been fashioned by time and wear into much individuality. I was not surprised to hear him nicknamed Sacatone Bill.

"Just ask him how he got that game foot," suggested Johnny Stone to me in an undertone, so, of course, I did not.

Later someone told me that the lameness resulted from his refusal of an urgent invitation to return across a river. Mr. Sacatone Bill happened not to be riding his own horse at the time.

The Cattleman dropped down beside me a moment later.

"I wish," said he in a low voice, "we could get that fellow talking. He is a queer one. Pretty well educated apparently. Claims to be writing a book of memoirs. Sometimes he will open up in good shape, and sometimes he will not. It does no good to ask him direct, and he is as shy as an old crow when you try to lead him up to a subject. We must just lie low and trust to Providence."

A man was playing on the mouth organ. He played excellently well, with all sorts of variations and frills. We smoked in silence. The deep rumble of the cattle filled the air with its diapason. Always the shrill coyotes raved out in the mesquite. Sacatone Bill had finished his meal, and had gone to sit by Jed Parker, his old friend. They talked together low-voiced. The evening grew, and the eastern sky silvered over the mountains in anticipation of the moon.

Sacatone Bill suddenly threw back his head and laughed.

"Reminds me of the time I went to Colorado!" he cried.

"He's off!" whispered the Cattleman.

A dead silence fell on the circle. Everybody shifted position the better to listen to the story of Sacatone Bill.

About ten years ago I got plumb sick of punchin' cows around my part of the country. She hadn't rained since Noah, and I'd forgot what water outside a pail or a trough looked like. So I scouted around inside of me to see what part of the world I'd jump to, and as I seemed to know as little of Colorado and minin' as anything else, I made up the pint of bean soup I call my brains to go there. So I catches me a buyer at Benson and turns over my pore little bunch of cattle and prepared to fly. The last day I hauled up about twenty good buckets of water and threw her up against the cabin. My buyer was settin' his hoss waitin' for me to get ready. He didn't say nothin' until we'd got down about ten mile or so.

"Mr. Hicks," says he, hesitatin' like, "I find it a good rule in this country not to overlook other folks' plays, but I'd take it mighty kind if you'd explain those actions of yours with the pails of water."

"Mr. Jones," says I, "it's very simple. I built that shack five year ago, and it's never rained since. I just wanted to settle in my mind whether or not that damn roof leaked."

So I quit Arizona, and in about a week I see my reflection in the winders of a little place called Cyanide in the Colorado mountains.

Fellows, she was a bird. They wasn't a pony in sight, nor a squar' foot of land that wasn't either street or straight up. It made me plumb lonesome for a country where you could see a long ways even if you didn't see much. And this early in the evenin' they wasn't hardly anybody in the streets at all.

I took a look at them dark, gloomy old mountains, and a sniff at the breeze that would have frozen the whiskers of hope, and I made a dive for the nearest lit winder. They was a sign over it that just said:

THIS IS A SALOON

I was glad they labeled her. I'd never have known it. They had a fifteen-year-old kid tendin' bar, no games goin', and not a soul in the place.

"Sorry to disturb your repose, bub," says I, "but see if you can sort out any rye among them collections of sassapariller of yours."

I took a drink, and then another to keep it company—I was beginnin' to sympathize with anythin' lonesome. Then I kind of sauntered out to the back room where the hurdy-gurdy ought to be. Sure enough, there was a girl settin' on the pianner stool, another in a chair, and a nice shiny drummer danglin' his feet from a table. They looked up when they see me come in, and went right on talkin'.

"Hello, girls!" says I.

At that they stopped talkin' complete.

"How's tricks?" says I.

"Who's your woolly friend?" the drummer asks of the girls.

I looked at him a minute, but I see he'd been raised a pet, and then, too, I was so hungry for sassiety I was willin' to pass a bet or two.

"Don't you admire these cow gents?" snickers one of the girls.

"Play somethin', sister," says I to the one at the pianner.

She just grinned at me.

"Interdooce me," says the drummer in a kind of a way that made them all laugh a heap.

"Give us a tune," I begs, tryin' to be jolly, too.

"She don't know any pieces," says the salesman.

"Don't you?" I asks pretty sharp.

"No," says she.

"Well, I do," says I.

I walked up to her, jerked out my guns, and reached around both sides of her to the pianner. I ran the muzzles up and down the keyboard two or three times, and then shot out half a dozen keys.

"That's the piece I know," says I.

But the other girl and the drummer had punched the breeze.

The girl at the pianner just grinned, and pointed to the winder where they was some ragged glass hangin'. She was dead game.

"Say, Susie," says I, "you're all right, but your friends is tur'ble. I may be rough, and I ain't never been curried below the knees, but I'm better to tie to than them sons of guns."

"I believe it," says she.

So we had a drink at the bar, and started out to investigate the wonders of Cyanide.

Say, that night was a wonder. Susie faded after about three drinks, but I didn't seem to mind that. I hooked up to another saloon kept by a thin Dutchman. A fat Dutchman is stupid, but a thin one is all right.

In ten minutes I had more friends in Cyanide than they is fiddlers in hell. I begun to conclude Cyanide wasn't so lonesome. About four o'clock in comes a little Irishman about four foot high, with more upper lip than a muley cow, and enough red hair to make an artificial aurorer borealis. He had big red hands with freckles pasted onto them, and stiff red hairs standin' up separate and lonesome like signal stations. Also his legs was bowed.

He gets a drink at the bar, and stands back and yells:

"God bless the Irish and let the Dutch rustle!"

Now, this was none of my town, so I just stepped back of the end of the bar quick where I wouldn't stop no lead. The shootin' didn't begin.

"Probably Dutchy didn't take no note of what the locoed little dogie did say," thinks I to myself.

The Irishman bellied up to the bar again, and pounded on it with his fist.

"Look here!" he yells. "Listen to what I'm tellin' ye! God bless the Irish and let the Dutch rustle! Do ye hear me?"

"Sure, I hear ye," says Dutchy, and goes on swabbin' his bar with a towel.

At that my soul just grew sick. I asked the man next to me why Dutchy didn't kill the little fellow.

"Kill him!" says this man. "What for?"

"For insultin' of him, of course."

"Oh, he's drunk," says the man, as if that explained anythin'.

That settled it with me. I left that place, and went home, and it wasn't more than four o'clock, neither. No, I don't call four o'clock late. It may be a little late for night before last, but it's just the shank of the evenin' for to-night.

Well, it took me six weeks and two days to go broke. I didn't know sic 'em about minin'; and before long I knew that I didn't know sic 'em. Most all day I poked around them mountains—not like our'n—too much timber to be comfortable. At night I got to droppin' in at Dutchy's. He had a couple of quiet games goin', and they was one fellow among that lot of grubbin' prairie dogs that had heerd tell that cows had horns. He was the wisest of the bunch on the cattle business. So I stowed away my consolation, and made out to forget comparing Colorado with God's country.

About three times a week this Irishman I told you of—name O'Toole— comes bulgin' in. When he was sober he talked minin' high, wide, and handsome. When he was drunk he pounded both fists on the bar and yelled for action, tryin' to get Dutchy on the peck.

"God bless the Irish and let the Dutch rustle!" he yells about six times. "Say, do you hear?"

"Sure," says Dutchy, calm as a milk cow, "sure, I hear ye!"

I was plumb sorry for O'Toole. I'd like to have given him a run; but, of course, I couldn't take it up without makin' myself out a friend of this Dutchy party, and I couldn't stand for that. But I did tackle Dutchy about it one night when they wasn't nobody else there.

"Dutchy," says I, "what makes you let that bow-legged cross between a bulldog and a flamin' red sunset tromp on you so? It looks to me like you're plumb spiritless."

Dutchy stopped wipin' glasses for a minute.

"Just you hold on," says he. "I ain't ready yet. Bimeby I make him sick; also those others who laugh with him."

He had a little grey flicker in his eye, and I thinks to myself that maybe they'd get Dutchy on the peck yet.

As I said, I went broke in just six weeks and two days. And I was broke a plenty. No hold-outs anywhere. It was a heap long ways to cows; and I'd be teetotally chawed up and spit out if I was goin' to join these minin' terrapins defacin' the bosom of nature. It sure looked to me like hard work.

While I was figurin' what next, Dutchy came in. Which I was tur'ble surprised at that, but I said good-mornin' and would he rest his poor feet.

"You like to make some money?" he asks.

"That depends," says I, "on how easy it is."

"It is easy," says he. "I want you to buy hosses for me."

"Hosses! Sure!" I yells, jumpin' up. "You bet you! Why, hosses is where I live! What hosses do you want?"

"All hosses," says he, calm as a faro dealer.

"What?" says I. "Elucidate, my bucko. I don't take no such blanket order. Spread your cards."

"I mean just that," says he. "I want you to buy all the hosses in this camp, and in the mountains. Every one."

"Whew!" I whistles. "That's a large order. But I'm your meat."

"Come with me, then," says he. I hadn't but just got up, but I went with him to his little old poison factory. Of course, I hadn't had no breakfast; but he staked me to a Kentucky breakfast. What's a Kentucky breakfast? Why, a Kentucky breakfast is a three-pound steak, a bottle of whisky, and a setter dog. What's the dog for? Why, to eat the steak, of course.

We come to an agreement. I was to get two-fifty a head commission. So I started out. There wasn't many hosses in that country, and what there was the owners hadn't much use for unless it was to work a whim. I picked up about a hundred head quick enough, and reported to Dutchy.

"How about burros and mules?" I asks Dutchy.

"They goes," says he. "Mules same as hosses; burros four bits a head to you."

At the end of a week I had a remuda of probably two hundred animals. We kept them over the hills in some "parks," as these sots call meadows in that country. I rode into town and told Dutchy.

"Get them all?" he asks.

"All but a cross-eyed buckskin that's mean, and the bay mare that Noah bred to."

"Get them," says he.

"The bandits want too much," I explains.

"Get them anyway," says he.

I went away and got them. It was scand'lous; such prices.

When I hit Cyanide again I ran into scenes of wild excitement. The whole passel of them was on that one street of their'n, talkin' sixteen ounces to the pound. In the middle was Dutchy, drunk as a soldier—just plain foolish drunk.

"Good Lord!" thinks I to myself, "he ain't celebratin' gettin' that bunch of buzzards, is he?"

But I found he wasn't that bad. When he caught sight of me, he fell on me drivelin'.

"Look there!" he weeps, showin' me a letter.

I was the last to come in; so I kept that letter—here she is. I'll read her.

Dear Dutchy:—I suppose you thought I'd flew the coop, but I haven't and this is to prove it. Pack up your outfit and hit the trail. I've made the biggest free gold strike you ever see. I'm sending you specimens. There's tons just like it, tons and tons. I got all the claims I can hold myself; but there's heaps more. I've writ to Johnny and Ed at Denver to come on. Don't give this away. Make tracks. Come in to Buck Cañon in the Whetsones and oblige.

Yours truly,<br>HENRY SMITH.

Somebody showed me a handful of white rock with yeller streaks in it. His eyes was bulgin' until you could have hung your hat on them. That O'Toole party was walkin' around, wettin' his lips with his tongue and swearin' soft.

"God bless the Irish and let the Dutch rustle!" says he. "And the fool had to get drunk and give it away!"

The excitement was just started, but it didn't last long. The crowd got the same notion at the same time, and it just melted. Me and Dutchy was left alone.

I went home. Pretty soon a fellow named Jimmy Tack came around a little out of breath.

"Say, you know that buckskin you bought off'n me?" says he, "I want to buy him back."

"Oh, you do," says I.

"Yes," says he. "I've got to leave town for a couple of days, and I got to have somethin' to pack."

"Wait and I'll see," says I.

Outside the door I met another fellow.

"Look here," he stops me with. "How about that bay mare I sold you? Can you call that sale off? I got to leave town for a day or two and—"

"Wait," says I. "I'll see."

By the gate was another hurryin' up.

"Oh, yes," says I when he opens his mouth. "I know all your troubles. You have to leave town for a couple of days, and you want back that lizard you sold me. Well, wait."

After that I had to quit the main street and dodge back of the hog ranch. They was all headed my way. I was as popular as a snake in a prohibition town.

I hit Dutchy's by the back door.

"Do you want to sell hosses?" I asks. "Everyone in town wants to buy." Dutchy looked hurt.

"I wanted to keep them for the valley market," says he, "but . . . How much did you give Jimmy Tack for his buckskin?"

"Twenty," says I.

"Well, let him have it for eighty," says Dutchy; "and the other in proportion."

I lay back and breathed hard.

"Sell them all, but the one best hoss," says he—"no, the two best."

"Holy smoke!" says I, gettin' my breath. "If you mean that, Dutchy, you lend me another gun and give me a drink."

He done so, and I went back home to where the whole camp of Cyanide was waitin'.

I got up and made them a speech and told them I'd sell them hosses all right, and to come back. Then I got an Injin boy to help, and we rustled over the remuda and held them in a blind cañon. Then I called up these miners one at a time, and made bargains with them. Roar! Well, you could hear them at Denver, they tell me, and the weather reports said, "Thunder in the mountains." But it was cash on delivery, and they all paid up. They had seen that white quartz with the gold stickin' into it, and that's the same as a dose of loco to miner gents.

Why didn't I take a hoss and start first? I did think of it—for about one second. I wouldn't stay in that country then for a million dollars a minute. I was plumb sick and loathin' it, and just waitin' to make high jumps back to Arizona. So I wasn't aimin' to join this stampede, and didn't have no vivid emotions.

They got to fightin' on which should get the first hoss; so I bent my gun on them and made them draw lots. They roared some more, but done so; and as fast as each one handed over his dust or dinero he made a rush for his cabin, piled on his saddle and pack, and pulled his freight in a cloud of dust. It was sure a grand stampede, and I enjoyed it no limit.

So by sundown I was alone with the Injin. Those two hundred head brought in about twenty thousand dollars. It was heavy, but I could carry it. I was about alone in the landscape; and there were the two best hosses I had saved out for Dutchy. I was sure some tempted. But I had enough to get home on anyway; and I never yet drank behind the bar, even if I might hold up the saloon from the floor. So I grieved some inside that I was so tur'ble conscientious, shouldered the sacks, and went down to find Dutchy.

I met him headed his way, and carryin' of a sheet of paper.

"Here's your dinero," says I, dumpin' the four big sacks on the ground.

He stooped over and hefted them. Then he passed one over to me.

"What's that for?" I asks.

"For you," says he.

"My commission ain't that much," I objects.

"You've earned it," says he, "and you might have skipped with the whole wad."

"How did you know I wouldn't?" I asks.

"Well," says he, and I noted that jag of his had flew. "You see, I was behind that rock up there, and I had you covered."

I saw; and I began to feel better about bein' so tur'ble conscientious.

We walked a little ways without sayin' nothin'.

"But ain't you goin' to join the game?" I asks.

"Guess not," says he, jinglin' of his gold. "I'm satisfied."

"But if you don't get a wiggle on you, you are sure goin' to get left on those gold claims," says I.

"There ain't no gold claims," says he.

"But Henry Smith—" I cries.

"There ain't no Henry Smith," says he.

I let that soak in about six inches.

"But there's a Buck Cañon," I pleads. "Please say there's a Buck Cañon."

"Oh, yes, there's a Buck Cañon," he allows. "Nice limestone formation— makes good hard water."

"Well, you're a marvel," says I.

We walked on together down to Dutchy's saloon. We stopped outside.

"Now," says he, "I'm goin' to take one of those hosses and go some-wheres else. Maybe you'd better do likewise on the other."

"You bet I will," says I.

He turned around and tacked up the paper he was carryin'. It was a sign. I read:

### THE DUTCH HAS RUSTLED

"Nice sentiment," says I. "It will be appreciated when the crowd comes back from that little pasear into Buck Cañon. But why not tack her up where the trail hits the camp? Why on this particular door?"

"Well," said Dutchy, squintin' at the sign sideways, "you see I sold this place day before yesterday—to Mike O'Toole."

# JACK LONDON

## *Love of Life*

"*This out of all will remain—*
*They have lived and have tossed:*
*So much of the game will be gain,*
*Though the gold of the dice has been lost.*"

THEY LIMPED PAINFULLY down the bank, and once the foremost of the two men staggered among the rough-strewn rocks. They were tired and weak, and their faces had the drawn expression of patience which comes of hardship long endured. They were heavily burdened with blanket packs which were strapped to their shoulders. Head-straps, passing across the forehead, helped support these packs. Each man carried a rifle. They walked in a stooped posture, the shoulders well forward, the head still farther forward, the eyes bent upon the ground.

"I wish we had just about two of them cartridges that's layin' in that cache of ourn," said the second man.

His voice was utterly and drearily expressionless. He spoke without enthusiasm; but the first man, limping into the milky stream that foamed over the rocks, vouchsafed no reply.

The other man followed at his heels. They did not remove their foot-gear, though the water was icy cold—so cold that their ankles ached and their feet went numb. In places the water dashed against their knees, and both men staggered for footing.

The man who followed slipped on a smooth boulder, nearly fell, but recovered himself with a violent effort, at the same time uttering a sharp exclamation of pain. He seemed faint and dizzy, and put out his free hand while he reeled, as though seeking support against the air. When he had steadied himself he stepped forward, but reeled again and nearly fell. Then he stood still and looked at the other man, who had never turned his head.

The man stood still for fully a minute, as though debating with himself. Then he called out:

"I say, Bill, I've sprained my ankle."

Bill staggered on through the milky water. He did not look around. The man watched him go, and though his face was expressionless as ever, his eyes were like the eyes of a wounded deer.

The other man limped up the farther bank and continued straight on without looking back. The man in the stream watched him. His lips trembled a little, so that the rough thatch of brown hair which covered them was visibly agitated. His tongue even strayed out to moisten them.

"Bill!" he cried out.

It was the pleading cry of a strong man in distress, but Bill's head did not turn. The man watched him go, limping grotesquely and lurching forward with stammering gait up the slow slope toward the soft sky-line of the low-lying hill. He watched him go till he passed over the crest and disappeared. Then he turned his gaze and slowly took in the circle of the world that remained to him now that Bill was gone.

Near the horizon the sun was smoldering dimly, almost obscured by formless mists and vapors, which gave an impression of mass and density without outline or tangibility. The man pulled out his watch, the while resting his weight on one leg. It was four o'clock, and as the season was near the last of July or first of August—he did not know the precise date within a week or two—he knew that the sun roughly marked the north-west. He looked to the south and knew that somewhere beyond those bleak hills lay the Great Bear Lake; also, he knew that in that direction the Arctic Circle cut its forbidding way across the Canadian Barrens. This stream in which he stood was a feeder to the Coppermine River, which in turn flowed north and emptied into Coronation Gulf and the Arctic Ocean. He had never been there, but he had seen it, once, on a Hudson Bay Company chart.

Again his gaze completed the circle of the world about him. It was not a heartening spectacle. Everywhere was soft sky-line. The hills were all low-lying. There were no trees, no shrubs, no grasses—naught but a tremendous and terrible desolation that sent fear swiftly dawning into his eyes.

"Bill!" he whispered, once and twice; "Bill!"

He cowered in the midst of the milky water, as though the vastness were pressing in upon him with overwhelming force, brutally crushing him with its complacent awfulness. He began to shake as with an ague-fit, till the gun fell from his hand with a splash. This served to rouse him. He fought with his fear and pulled himself together, groping in the water and recovering the weapon. He hitched his pack farther over on his left shoulder, so as to take a portion of its weight from off the injured ankle. Then he proceeded, slowly and carefully, wincing with pain, to the bank.

He did not stop. With a desperation that was madness, unmindful of the pain, he hurried up the slope to the crest of the hill over which his comrade had disappeared—more grotesque and comical by far than that limping, jerking comrade. But at the crest he saw a shallow valley, empty of life. He fought with his fear again, overcame it, hitched the pack still farther over on his left shoulder, and lurched on down the slope.

The bottom of the valley was soggy with water, which the thick moss held, sponge-like, close to the surface. This water squirted out from under his feet at every step, and each time he lifted a foot the action culminated in a sucking sound as the wet moss reluctantly released its grip. He picked his way from muskeg to muskeg, and followed the other man's footsteps along and across the rocky ledges which thrust like islets through the sea of moss.

Though alone he was not lost. Farther on he knew he would come to where dead spruce and fir, very small and weazened, bordered the shore of a little lake, the *tit-chinnichilie*—in the tongue of the country, the "land of little sticks." And into that lake flowed a small stream, the water of which was not milky. There was rush-grass on that steram—this he remembered well—but no timber, and he would follow it till its first trickle ceased at a divide. He would cross this divide to the first trickle of another stream, flowing to the west, which he would follow until it emptied into the River Dease, and here he would find a cache under an upturned canoe and piled over with many rocks. And in this cache would be ammunition for his empty gun, fish-hooks and lines, a small net—all the utilities for the killing and snaring of food. Also, he would find flour—not much—a piece of bacon and some beans.

Bill would be waiting for him there, and they would paddle away south down the Dease to the Great Bear Lake. And south across the lake they would go, ever south, till they gained the Mackenzie. And south, still south, they would go, while the winter raced vainly after them, and the ice formed in the eddies, and the days grew chill and crisp, south to some warm Hudson Bay Company post, where timber grew tall and generous and there was grub without end.

These were the thoughts of the man as he strove onward. But hard as he strove with his body, he strove equally hard with his mind, trying to think that Bill had not deserted him, that Bill would surely wait for him at the cache. He was compelled to think this thought, or else there would not be any use to strive, and he would have lain down and died. And as the dim ball of the sun sank slowly into the northwest he covered every inch, and many times, of his and Bill's flight south before the downcoming winter. And he conned the grub of the cache and the grub of the Hudson Bay Company post over and over again. He had not eaten for two days; for a far longer time he had not had all he wanted to eat. Often he stooped and picked pale muskeg berries, put them into his mouth and chewed and swallowed them. A muskeg berry is a bit of seed enclosed in a bit of water. In the mouth the water melts away and the seed chews sharp and bitter. The man knew there was no nourishment in the berries, but he chewed them patiently with a hope greater than knowledge and defying experience.

At nine o'clock he stubbed his toe on a rocky ledge, and from sheer weariness and weakness staggered and fell. He lay for some time, without movement, on his side. Then he slipped out of the pack-straps and clumsily dragged himself into a sitting posture. It was not yet dark, and in the lingering twilight he groped about among the rocks for shreds of dry moss. When he had gathered a heap he built a fire—a smoldering, smudgy fire—and put a tin pot of water on to boil.

He unwrapped his pack, and the first thing he did was to count his matches. There were sixty-seven. He counted them three times to make sure. He divided them into several portions, wrapping them in oil paper, disposing of one bunch in his empty tobacco pouch, of another bunch in the inside band of his battered hat, of a third bunch under his shirt on the chest. This accomplished, a panic came upon him and he unwrapped them all and counted them again. There were still sixty-seven.

He dried his wet footgear by the fire. The moccasins were in soggy shreds. The blanket socks were worn through in places, and his feet were raw and bleeding. His ankle was throbbing and he gave it an examination. It had swollen to the size of his knee. He tore a long strip from one of his two blankets and bound the ankle tightly. He tore other strips and bound them about his feet to serve for both moccasins and socks. Then he drank the pot of water, steaming hot, wound his watch, and crawled between his blankets.

He slept like a dead man. The brief darkness around midnight came and went. The sun arose in the northeast—at least the day dawned in that quarter, for the sun was hidden by gray clouds.

At six o'clock he awoke, quietly lying on his back. He gazed straight up into the gray sky and knew that he was hungry. As he rolled over on his elbow he was startled by a loud snort, and saw a bull caribou regarding him with alert curiosity. The animal was not more than fifty feet away, and instantly into the man's mind leaped the vision and the savor of a caribou steak sizzling and frying over a fire. Mechanically he reached for the empty gun, drew a bead, and pulled the trigger. The bull snorted and leaped away, his hoofs rattling and clattering as he fled across the ledges.

The man cursed and flung the empty gun from him. He groaned aloud as he started to drag himself to his feet. It was a slow and arduous task. His joints were like rusty hinges. They worked harshly in their sockets, with much friction, and each bending or unbending was accomplished only through a sheer exertion of will. When he finally gained his feet, another minute or so was consumed in straightening up, so that he could stand erect as a man should stand.

He crawled up a small knoll and surveyed the prospect. There were no trees, no bushes, nothing but a gray sea of moss scarcely diversified by gray rocks, gray-colored lakelets, and gray streamlets. The sky was gray. There was no sun or hint of sun. He had no idea of north, and he had forgotten the way he had come to this spot the night before. But he was not lost. He knew that. Soon he would come to the land of the little sticks. He felt that it lay off to the left somewhere, not far—possibly just over the next low hill.

He went back to put his pack into shape for traveling. He assured himself of the existence of his three separate parcels of matches, though he did not stop to count them. But he did linger, debating, over a squat moose-hide sack. It was not large. He could hide it under his two hands. He knew that it weighed fifteen pounds—as much as all the rest of the pack—and it worried him. He finally set it to one side and proceeded to roll the pack. He paused to gaze at the squat moose-hide sack. He picked it up hastily with a defiant glance about him, as though the desolation were trying to rob him of it; and when he rose to his feet to stagger on into the day, it was included in the pack on his back.

He bore away to the left, stopping now and again to eat muskeg berries. His ankle had stiffened, his limp was more pronounced, but the pain of it was as nothing compared with the pain of his stomach. The hunger pangs were sharp. They gnawed and gnawed until he could not keep his mind steady on the course he must pursue to gain the land of little sticks. The muskeg berries did not allay this gnawing, while they made his tongue and the roof of his mouth sore with their irritating bite.

He came upon a valley where rock ptarmigan rose on whirring wings from the ledges and muskegs. *Ker—ker—ker* was the cry they made. He threw stones at them, but could not hit them. He placed his pack on the ground and stalked them as a cat stalks a sparrow. The sharp rocks cut through his pants' legs till his knees left a trail of blood; but the hurt was lost in the hurt of his hunger. He squirmed over the wet moss, saturating his clothes and chilling his body; but he was not aware of it, so great was his fever for food. And always the ptarmigan rose, whirring, before him, till their *ker—ker—ker* became a mock to him, and he cursed them and cried aloud at them with their own cry.

Once he crawled upon one that must have been asleep. He did not see it till it shot up in his face from its rocky nook. He made a clutch as startled as was the rise of the ptarmigan, and there remained in his hand three tail-feathers. As he watched its flight he hated it, as though it had done him some terrible wrong. Then he returned and shouldered his pack.

As the day wore along he came into valleys or swales where game was more plentiful. A band of caribou passed by, twenty and odd animals, tantalizingly within rifle range. He felt a wild desire to run after them, a certitude that he could run them down. A black fox came toward him, carrying a ptarmigan in his mouth. The man shouted. It was a fearful cry, but the fox leaping away in fright did not drop the ptarmigan.

Late in the afternoon he followed a stream, milky with lime, which ran through sparse patches of rush-grass. Grasping these rushes firmly near the root, he pulled up what resembled a young onion-sprout no larger than a shingle-nail. It was tender and his teeth sank into it with a crunch that promised deliciously of food. But its fibers were tough. It was composed of stringy filaments saturated with water, like the berries, and devoid of nourishment. But he threw off his pack and went into the rush-grass on hands and knees, crunching and munching, like some bovine creature.

He was very weary and often wished to rest—to lie down and sleep; but he was continually driven on—not so much by his desire to gain the land of little sticks as by his hunger. He searched little ponds for frogs and dug up the earth with his nails for worms, though he knew in spite that neither frogs nor worms existed so far north.

He looked into every pool of water vainly, until, as the long twilight came on, he discovered a solitary fish, the size of a minnow, in such a pool. He plunged his arm in up to the shoulder, but it eluded him. He reached for it with both hands and stirred up the milky mud at the bottom. In his excitement he fell in, wetting himself to the waist. Then the water was too muddy to admit of his seeing the fish, and he was compelled to wait until the sediment had settled.

The pursuit was renewed, till the water was again muddied. But he could not wait. He unstrapped the tin bucket and began to bale the pool. He baled wildly at first, splashing himself and flinging the water so short a distance that it ran back into the pool. He worked more carefully, striving to be cool, though his heart was pounding against his chest and his hands were trembling. At the end of half an hour the pool was nearly dry. Not a cupful of water remained. And there was no fish. He found a hidden crevice among the stones through which it had escaped to the adjoining and larger pool—a pool which he could not empty in a night and a day. Had he known of the crevice, he could have closed it with a rock at the beginning and the fish would have been his.

Thus he thought, and crumpled up and sank down upon the wet earth. At first he cried softly to himself, then he cried loudly to the pitiless desolation that ringed him around; and for a long time after he was shaken by great dry sobs.

He built a fire and warmed himself by drinking quarts of hot water, and made camp on a rocky ledge in the same fashion he had the night before. The last thing he did was to see that his matches were dry and to wind his watch. The blankets were wet and clammy. His ankle pulsed with pain. But he knew only that he was hungry, and through his restless sleep he dreamed of feasts and banquets and of food served and spread in all imaginable ways.

He awoke chilled and sick. There was no sun. The gray of earth and sky had become deeper, more profound. A raw wind was blowing, and the first flurries of snow were whitening the hill-tops. The air about him thickened and grew white while he made a fire and boiled more water. It was wet snow, half rain, and the flakes were large and soggy. At first they melted as soon as they came in contact with the earth, but ever more fell, covering the ground, putting out the fire, spoiling his supply of moss-fuel.

This was the signal for him to strap on his pack and stumble onward he knew not where. He was not concerned with the land of little sticks, nor with Bill and the cache under the upturned canoe by the River Dease. He was mastered by the verb "to eat." He was hunger-mad. He took no heed of the course he pursued, so long as that course led him through the swale bottoms. He felt his way through the wet snow to the watery muskeg berries, and went by feel as he pulled up the rush-grass by the roots. But it was tasteless stuff and did not satisfy. He found a weed that tasted sour, and he ate all he could find of it, which was not much, for it was a creeping growth, easily hidden under the several inches of snow.

He had no fire that night nor hot water, and crawled under his blanket to sleep the broken hunger-sleep. The snow turned into a cold rain. He awakened many times to feel it falling on his upturned face. Day came— a gray day and no sun. It had ceased raining. The keenness of his hunger had departed. Sensibility, so far as concerned the yearning for food, had been exhausted. There was a dull, heavy ache in his stomach, but it did not bother him so much. He was more rational, and once more he was chiefly interested in the land of little sticks and the cache by the River Dease.

He ripped the remnant of one of his blankets into strips and bound his bleeding feet. Also, he recinched the injured ankle and prepared himself for a day of travel. When he came to his pack he paused long over the squat moosehide sack, but in the end it went with him.

The snow had melted under the rain and only the hilltops showed white. The sun came out, and he succeeded in locating the points of the compass, though he knew now that he was lost. Perhaps, in his previous days' wanderings, he had edged away too far to the left. He now bore off to the right to counteract the possible deviation from his true course.

Though the hunger pangs were no longer so exquisite, he realized that he was weak. He was compelled to pause for frequent rests when he attacked the muskeg berries and rush-grass patches. His tongue felt dry and large, as though covered with a fine hairy growth, and it tasted bitter in his mouth. His heart gave him a great deal of trouble. When he had traveled a few minutes it would begin a remorseless thump, thump, thump, and then leap up and away in a painful flutter of beats that choked him and made him go faint and dizzy.

In the middle of the day he found two minnows in a large pool. It was impossible to bale it, but he was calmer now and managed to catch them in his tin bucket. They were no longer than his little finger, but he was not particularly hungry. The dull ache in his stomach had been growing duller and fainter. It seemed almost that his stomach was dozing. He ate the fish raw, masticating with painstaking care, for the eating was an act of pure reason. While he had no desire to eat he knew that he must eat to live.

In the evening he caught three more minnows, eating two and saving the third for breakfast. The sun had dried stray shreds of moss, and he was able to warm himself with hot water. He had not covered more than ten miles that day, and the next day, traveling whenever his heart permitted him, he covered no more than five miles. But his stomach did not give him the slightest uneasiness. It had gone to sleep. He was in a strange country, too, and the caribou were growing more plentiful, also the wolves. Often their yelps drifted across the desolation, and once he saw three of them slinking away before his path.

Another night, and in the morning, being more rational, he untied the leather string that fastened the squat moosehide sack. From its open mouth poured a yellow stream of coarse gold-dust and nuggets. He roughly divided the gold in halves, caching one half on a prominent ledge, wrapped in a piece of blanket, and returning the other half to the sack. He also began to use strips of the one remaining blanket for his feet. He still clung to his gun, for there were cartridges in that cache by the River Dease.

This was a day of fog, and this day hunger awoke in him again. He was very weak and was afflicted with a giddiness which at times blinded him. It was no uncommon thing now for him to stumble and fall; and stumbling once, he fell squarely into a ptarmigan nest. There were four newly hatched chicks a day old—little specks of pulsating life no more than a mouthful; and he ate them ravenously, thrusting them alive into his mouth and crunching them like egg-shells between his teeth. The mother ptarmigan beat about him with great out-cry. He used his gun as a club with which to knock her over, but she dodged out of reach. He threw stones at her and with one chance shot broke a wing. Then she fluttered away, running, trailing the broken wing, with him in pursuit.

The little chicks had no more than whetted his appetite. He hopped and bobbed clumsily along on his injured ankle, throwing stones and screaming hoarsely at times; at other times hopping and bobbing silently along, picking himself up grimly and patiently when he fell, or rubbing his eyes with his hand when the giddiness threatened to overpower him.

The chase led him across swampy ground in the bottom of the valley, and he came upon footprints in the soggy moss. They were not his own—he could see that. They must be Bill's. But he could not stop, for the mother ptarmigan was running on. He would catch her first, then he would return and investigate.

He exhausted the mother ptarmigan; but he exhausted himself. She lay panting on her side. He lay panting on his side, a dozen feet away, unable to crawl to her. And as he recovered she recovered, fluttering out of reach as his hungry hand went out to her. The chase was resumed. Night settled down and she escaped. He stumbled from weakness and pitched head-fore-most on her face, cutting his cheek, his pack upon his back. He did not move for a long while; then he rolled over on his side, wound his watch, and lay there until morning.

Another day of fog. Half of his last blanket had gone into foot-wrap-pings. He failed to pick up Bill's trail. It did not matter. His hunger was driving him too compellingly—only—only he wondered if Bill, too, were lost. By mid-day the irk of his pack became too oppressive. Again he divided the gold, this time merely spilling half of it on the ground. In the afternoon he threw the rest of it away, there remaining to him only the half-blanket, the tin bucket, and the rifle.

An hallucination began to trouble him. He felt confident that one car-tridge remained to him. It was in the chamber of the rifle and he had overlooked it. On the other hand, he knew all the time that the chamber was empty. But the hallucination persisted. He fought it off for hours, then threw his rifle open and was confronted with emptiness. The disap-pointment was as bitter as though he had really expected to find the cartridge.

He plodded on for half an hour, when the hallucination arose again. Again he fought it and still it persisted, till for very relief he opened his rifle to unconvince himself. At times his mind wandered farther afield, and he plodded on, a mere automaton, strange conceits and whimsicalities gnawing at his brain like worms. But these excursions out of the real were of brief duration, for ever the pangs of the hunger-bite called him back. He was jerked back abruptly once from such an excursion by a sight that caused him nearly to faint. He reeled and swayed, doddering like a drunken man to keep from falling. Before him stood a horse. A horse! He could not believe his eyes. A thick mist was in them, intershot with sparkling points of light. He rubbed his eyes savagely to clear his vision, and beheld not a horse, but a great brown bear. The animal was studying him with bellicose curiosity.

The man had brought his gun halfway to his shoulder before he realized. He lowered it and drew his hunting-knife from its beaded sheath at his hip. Before him was meat and life. He ran his thumb along the edge of his knife. It was sharp. The point was sharp. He would fling himself upon the bear and kill it. But his heart began its warning thump, thump, thump. Then followed the wild upward leap and tattoo of flutters, the pressing as of an iron band about his forehead, the creeping of the dizziness into his brain.

His desperate courage was evicted by a great surge of fear. In his weak-ness, what if the animal attacked him! He drew himself up to his most imposing stature, gripping the knife and staring hard at the bear. The bear advanced clumsily a couple of steps, reared up and gave vent to a tentative growl. If the man ran he would run after him; but the man did not run. He was animated now with the courage of fear. He, too, growled, savagely, terribly, voicing the fear that is to life germane and that lies twisted about life's deepest roots.

The bear edged away to one side, growling menacingly, himself appalled by this mysterious creature that appeared upright and unafraid. But the man did not move. He stood like a statue till the danger was past, when he yielded to a fit of trembling and sank down into the wet moss.

He pulled himself together and went on, afraid now in a new way. It was not the fear that he should die passively from lack of food, but that he should be destroyed violently before starvation had exhausted the last particle of the endeavor in him that made toward surviving. There were the wolves. Back and forth across the desolation drifted their howls, weaving the very air into a fabric of menace that was so tangible that he found himself, arms in the air, pressing it back from him as it might be the walls of a wind-blown tent.

Now and again the wolves in packs of two and three crossed his path. But they sheered clear of him. They were not in sufficient numbers, and besides they were hunting the caribou which did not battle, while this strange creature that walked erect might scratch and bite.

In the late afternoon he came upon scattered bones where the wolves had made a kill. The débris had been a caribou calf an hour before, squawking and running and very much alive. He contemplated the bones, cleanpicked and polished, pink with the cell-life in them which had not yet died. Could it possibly be that he might be that ere the day was done! Such was life, eh? A vain and fleeting thing. It was only life that pained. There was no hurt in death. To die was to sleep. It meant cessation, rest. Then why was he not content to die?

But he did not moralize long. He was squatting in the moss, a bone in his mouth, sucking at the shreds of life that still dyed it faintly pink. The sweet meaty taste, thin and elusive almost as a memory, maddened him. He closed his jaws on the bones and crunched. Sometimes it was the bone that broke, sometimes his teeth. Then he crushed the bones between rocks, pounded them to a pulp and swallowed them. He pounded his fingers, too, in his haste, and yet found a moment in which to feel surprise at the fact that his fingers did not hurt much when caught under the descending rock.

Came frightful days of snow and rain. He did not know when he made camp, when he broke camp. He traveled in the night as much as in the day. He rested wherever he fell, crawled on whenever the dying life in him flickered up and burned less dimly. He as a man no longer strove. It was the life in him, unwilling to die, that drove him on. He did not suffer. His nerves had become blunted, numb, while his mind was filled with weird visions and delicious dreams.

But ever he sucked and chewed on the crushed bones of the caribou calf, the least remnants of which he had gathered up and carried with him. He crossed no more hills or divides, but automatically followed a large stream which flowed through a wide and shallow valley. He did not see this stream or this valley. He saw nothing save visions. Soul and body walked or crawled side by side, yet apart, so slender was the thread that bound them.

He awoke in his right mind, lying on his back on a rocky ledge. The sun was shining bright and warm. Afar off he heard the squawking of caribou calves. He was aware of vague memories of rain and wind and snow, but whether he had been beaten by the storm for two days or two weeks he did not know.

For some time he lay without movement, the genial sunshine pouring upon him and saturating his miserable body with its warmth. A fine day, he thought. Perhaps he could manage to locate himself. By a painful effort he rolled over on his side. Below him flowed a wide and sluggish river. Its unfamiliarity puzzled him. Slowly he followed it with his eyes, winding in wide sweeps among the bleak bare hills, bleaker and barer and lower-lying than any hills he had yet encountered. Slowly, deliberately, without excitement or more than the most casual interest, he followed the course of the strange stream toward the sky-line and saw it emptying into a bright and shining sea. He was still unexcited. Most unusual, he thought, a vision, or a mirage—more likely a vision, a trick of his disordered mind. He was confirmed in this by sight of a ship lying at anchor in the midst of the shining sea. He closed his eyes for a while, then opened them. Strange how the vision persisted! Yet not strange. He knew there were no seas or ships in the heart of the barren lands, just as he had known there was no cartridge in the empty rifle.

He heard a snuffle behind him—a half-choking gasp or cough. Very slowly, because of his exceeding weakness and stiffness, he rolled over on his other side. He could see nothing near at hand, but he waited patiently. Again came the snuffle and cough, and outlined between two jagged rocks not a score of feet away he made out the gray head of a wolf. The sharp ears were not pricked so sharply as he had seen them on other wolves; the eyes were bleared and blood-shot, the head seemed to droop limply and forlornly. The animal blinked continually in the sunshine. It seemed sick. As he looked it snuffled and coughed again.

This, at least, was real, he thought, and turned on the other side so that he might see the reality of the world which had been veiled from him before by the vision. But the sea still shone in the distance and the ship's spars were plainly discernible. Was it reality after all? He closed his eyes for a long while and thought, and then it came to him. He had been making north by east, away from the Dease Divide and into the Coppermine Valley. This wide and sluggish river was the Coppermine. That shining sea was the Arctic Ocean. That ship was a whaler, strayed east, far east, from the mouth of the Mackenzie, and it was lying at anchor in Coronation Gulf.

He remembered the Hudson Bay Company chart he had seen long ago, and it was all clear and reasonable to him.

He sat up and turned his attention to immediate affairs. He had worn through the blanket-wrappings, and his feet were like shapeless lumps of raw meat. His last blanket was gone. Rifle and knife were both missing. He had lost his hat somewhere, with the bunch of matches in the band, but the matches against his chest were safe and dry inside the tobacco pouch and oil-paper. He looked at his watch. It marked eleven o'clock and was still running. Evidently he had kept it wound.

He was calm and collected. Though extremely weak he had no sensation of pain. He was not hungry. The thought of food was not even pleasant to him, and whatever he did was done by his reason alone. He ripped off his pants' legs to the knees and bound them about his feet. Somehow he had succeeded in retaining the tin bucket. He would have some hot water before he began what he foresaw was to be a terrible journey to the ship.

His movements were slow. He shook as with a palsy. When he started to collect dry moss he found he could not rise to his feet. He tried again and again, then contented himself with crawling about on hands and knees. Once he crawled near to the sick wolf. The animal dragged itself reluctantly out of his way, licking its chops with a tongue which seemed hardly to have the strength to curl. The man noticed that the tongue was not the customary healthful red. It was a yellowish brown and seemed coated with a rough and half-dry mucus.

After he had drunk a quart of hot water the man found he was able to stand, and even to walk as well as a dying man might be supposed to walk. Every minute or so he was compelled to rest. His steps were feeble and uncertain, just as the wolf's that trailed him were feeble and uncertain; and that night, when the shining sea was blotted out by blackness, he knew he was nearer to it by no more than four miles.

Throughout the night he heard the cough of the sick wolf, and now and then the squawking of the caribou calves. There was life all around him, but it was strong life, very much alive and well, and he knew the sick wolf clung to the sick man's trail in the hope that the man would die first. In the morning, on opening his eyes, he beheld it regarding him with a wistful and hungry stare. It stood crouched, with tail between its legs, like a miserable and woe-begone dog. It shivered in the chill morning wind, and grinned dispiritedly when the man spoke to it in a voice which achieved no more than a hoarse whisper.

The sun rose brightly, and all morning the man tottered and fell toward the ship on the shining sea. The weather was perfect. It was the brief Indian summer of the high latitudes. It might last a week. To-morrow or next day it might be gone.

In the afternoon the man came upon a trail. It was of another man, who did not walk, but who dragged himself on all fours. The man thought it might be Bill, but he thought in a dull, uninterested way. He had no curiosity. In fact sensation and emotion had left him. He was no longer susceptible to pain. Stomach and nerves had gone to sleep. Yet the life that was in him drove him on. He was very weary, but it refused to die. It was because it refused to die that he still ate muskeg berries and minnows, drank his hot water, and kept a wary eye on the sick wolf.

He followed the trail of the other man who dragged himself along, and soon came to the end of it—a few fresh-picked bones where the soggy moss was marked by the foot-pads of many wolves. He saw a squat moose-hide sack, mate to his own, which had been torn by sharp teeth. He picked it up, though its weight was almost too much for his feeble fingers. Bill had carried it to the last. Ha! ha! He would have the laugh on Bill. He would survive and carry it to the ship in the shining sea. His mirth was hoarse and ghastly, like a raven's croak, and the sick wolf joined him, howling lugubriously. The man ceased suddenly. How could he have the laugh on Bill if that were Bill; if those bones, so pinky-white and clean, were Bill!

He turned away. Well, Bill had deserted him; but he would not take the gold, nor would he suck Bill's bones. Bill would have, though, had it been the other way around, he mused, as he staggered on.

He came to a pool of water. Stooping over in quest of minnows, he jerked his head back as though he had been stung. He had caught sight of his reflected face. So horrible was it that sensibility awoke long enough to be shocked. There were three minnows in the pool, which was too large to drain; and after several ineffectual attempts to catch them in the tin bucket he forbore. He was afraid, because of his great weakness, that he might fall in and drown. It was for this reason that he did not trust himself to the river astride one of the many drift-logs which lined its sand-pits.

That day he decreased the distance between him and the ship by three miles; the next day by two—for he was crawling now as Bill had crawled; and the end of the fifth day found the ship still seven miles away and him unable to make even a mile a day. Still the Indian summer held on, and he continued to crawl and faint, turn and turn about; and ever the sick wolf coughed and wheezed at his heels. His knees had become raw meat like his feet, and though he padded them with the shirt from his back it was a red track he left behind him on the moss and stones. Once glancing back he saw the wolf licking hungrily his bleeding trail, and he saw sharply what his own end might be—unless—unless he could get the wolf. Then began as grim a tragedy of existence as was ever played—a sick man that crawled, a sick wolf that limped, two creatures dragging their dying carcasses across the desolation and hunting each other's lives.

Had it been a well wolf, it would not have mattered so much to the man; but the thought of going to feed the maw of that loathsome and all but dead thing was repugnant to him. He was finicky. His mind had begun to wander again, and to be perplexed by hallucinations, while his lucid intervals grew rarer and shorter.

He was awakened once from a faint by a wheeze close in his ear. The wolf leaped lamely back, losing its footing and falling in its weakness. It was ludicrous, but he was not amused. Nor was he even afraid. He was too far gone for that. But his mind was for the moment clear, and he lay and considered. The ship was no more than four miles away. He could see it quite distinctly when he rubbed the mists out of his eyes, and he could see the white sail of a small boat cutting the water of the shining sea. But he could never crawl those four miles. He knew that, and was very calm in the knowledge. He knew that he could not crawl half a mile. And yet he wanted to live. It was unreasonable that he should die after all he had undergone. Fate asked too much of him. And, dying, he declined to die. It was stark madness, perhaps, but in the very grip of Death he defied Death and refused to die.

He closed his eyes and composed himself with infinite precaution. He steeled himself to keep above the suffocating languor that lapped like a rising tide through all the wells of his being. It was very like a sea, this deadly languor, that rose and rose and drowned his consciousness bit by bit. Sometimes he was all but submerged, swimming through oblivion with a faltering stroke; and again, by some strange alchemy of soul, he would find another shred of will and strike out more strongly.

Without movement he lay on his back, and he could hear slowly drawing near and nearer the wheezing intake and output of the sick wolf's breath. It drew closer, ever closer, through an infinitude of time, and he did not move. It was at his ear. The hard dry tongue grated like sandpaper against his cheek. His hands shot out—or at least he willed them to shoot out. The fingers were curved like talons, but they closed on empty air. Swiftness and certitude require strength, and the man had not this strength.

The patience of the wolf was terrible. The man's patience was no less terrible. For half a day he lay motionless, fighting off unconsciousness and waiting for the thing that was to feed upon him and upon which he wished to feed. Sometimes the languid sea rose over him and he dreamed long dreams; but ever through it all, waking and dreaming, he waited for the wheezing breath and the harsh caress of the tongue.

He did not hear the breath, and he slipped slowly from some dream to the feel of the tongue along his hand. He waited. The fangs pressed softly; the pressure increased; the wolf was exerting its last strength in an effort to sink teeth in the food for which it had waited so long. But the man had waited long, and the lacerated hand closed on the jaw. Slowly, while the wolf struggled feebly and the hand clutched feebly, the other hand crept across to a grip. Five minutes later the whole weight of the man's body was on top of the wolf. The hands had not sufficient strength to choke the animal, but the face of the man was pressed close to the throat of the wolf and the mouth was full of hair. At the end of half an hour the man was aware of a warm trickle in his throat. It was not pleasant. It was like molten lead being forced into his stomach, but it was forced by his will alone. Later the man rolled over on his back and slept.

There were some members of a scientific expedition on the whaleship Bedford. From the deck they remarked a strange object on the shore. It was moving down the beach toward the water. They were unable to classify it, and, being scientific men, they climbed into the whaleboat alongside and went ashore to see. And they saw something that was alive, but that could hardly be called a man. It was blind, unconscious. It squirmed along the ground like some monstrous worm. Most of its efforts were ineffectual, but it was persistent, and it writhed and twisted and went ahead perhaps a score of feet an hour.

Three weeks afterward the man lay in a bunk on the whaleship Bedford, and with tears streaming down his wasted cheeks told who he was and what he had undergone. He also babbled incoherently of his mother, of sunny Southern California, and a home among the orange groves and flowers.

The days were not many after that when he sat at table with the scientific men and ship's officers. He gloated over the spectacle of so much food, watching it anxiously as it went into the mouths of others. With the disappearance of each mouthful an expression of deep regret came into his eyes. He was quite sane, yet he hated those men at mealtime because they ate so much food. He was haunted by a fear that it would not last. He inquired of the cook, the cabin-boy, the captain, concerning the food stores. They reassured him countless times; but he could not believe them, and pried cunningly about the lazarette to see with his own eyes.

It was noticed that the man was getting fat. He grew stouter with each day. The scientific men shook their heads and theorized. They limited the man at his meals, but still his girth increased and his body swelled prodigiously under his shirt.

The sailors grinned. They knew. And when the scientific men set a watch on the man, they knew too. They saw him slouch for'ard after breakfast, and like a mendicant, with outstretched palm, accost a sailor. The sailor grinned and passed him a fragment of sea-biscuit. He clutched it avariciously, looked at it as a miser looks at gold, and thrust it into his shirt bosom. Similar were the donations from other grinning sailors.

The scientific men were discreet. They left him alone. But they privily examined his bunk. It was lined with hardtack; the mattress was stuffed with hardtack; every nook and cranny was filled with hardtack. Yet he was sane. He was taking precautions against another possible famine—that was all. He would recover from it, the scientific men said; and he did, ere the Bedford's anchor rumbled down in San Francisco Bay.

# A. B. GUTHRIE

## *Mountain Medicine*

THE MIST ALONG THE CREEK shone in the morning sun, which was coming up lazy and half-hearted, as if of a mind to turn back and let the spring season wait. The cottonwoods and quaking aspens were still bare and the needles of the pines old and dark with winter, but beaver were prime and beaver were plenty. John Clell made a lift and took the drowned animal quietly from the trap and stretched it in the dugout with three others.

Bill Potter said, "If 'tweren't for the Injuns! Or if 'tweren't for you and your notions!" For all his bluster, he still spoke soft, as if on the chance that there were other ears to hear.

Clell didn't answer. He reset the trap and pulled from the mud the twig that slanted over it and unstoppered his goathorn medicine bottle, dipped the twig in it and poked it back into the mud.

"Damn if I don't think sometimes you're scary," Potter went on, studying Clell out of eyes that were small and set close. "What kind of medicine is it makes you smell Injuns with nary one about?"

"Time you see as many of them as I have, you'll be scary too," Clell answered, slipping his paddle into the stream. He had a notion to get this greenhorn told off, but let it slide. What was the use? You couldn't put into a greenhorn's head what it was you felt. You couldn't give him the feel of distances and sky-high mountains and lonely winds and ideas spoken out of nowhere, ideas spoken into the head by medicines a man couldn't put a name to. Like now. Like here. Like this idea that there was brown skin about, and Blackfoot skin at that.

"I seen Blackfeet enough for both of us," he added. His mind ran back to Lewis and Clark and a time that seemed long ago because so much had come between; to days and nights and seasons of watching out, with just himself and the long silence for company; to last year and a hole that lay across the mountains to the south, where the Blackfeet and the Crows had fought, and he had sided with the Crows and got a wound in the leg that hurt sometimes yet. He could still see some of the Blackfeet faces. He would know them, and they would know him, being long-remembering.

He knew Blackfeet all right, but he couldn't tell Bill Potter why he thought some of them were close by. There wasn't any sign he could point to; the creek sang along and the breeze played in the trees, and overhead a big eagle was gliding low, and nowhere was there a footprint or a movement or a whiff of smoke. It was just a feeling he had, and

---

*"Mountain Medicine" is reprinted from* THE BIG IT AND OTHER STORIES *by A. B. Guthrie, with the permission of Houghton Mifflin Company, publisher.*

Potter wouldn't understand it, but would only look at him and maybe smile with one side of his mouth.

"Ain't anybody I knows of carried a two-shoot gun but you," Potter said, still talking as if Clell was scared over nothing.

Clell looked down at it, where he had it angled to his hand. It had two barrels, fixed on a swivel. When the top one was fired, you slipped a catch and turned the other up. One barrel was rifled, the other bigger and smooth-bored, and sometimes he loaded the big one with shot, for birds, and sometimes with a heavy ball, for bear or buffalo, or maybe with ball and buck both, just for what-the-hell. There was shot in it this morning, for he had thought maybe to take ducks or geese, and so refresh his taste for buffalo meat. The rifle shone in the morning sun. It was a nice piece, with a patch box a man wouldn't know to open until someone showed him the place to press his thumb. For no reason at all, Clell called his rifle Mule Ear.

He said, "You're a fool, Potter, more ways than one. Injuns'll raise your hair for sure, if it don't so happen I do it myself. As for this here two-shooter, I like it, and that's that."

Bill Potter always took low when a man dared him like that. Now all he said was "It's heavy as all hell."

Slipping along the stream, with the banks rising steep on both sides, Clell thought about beaver and Indians and all the country he had seen— high country, pretty as paint, wild as any animal and lonesome as time, and rivers unseen but by him, and holes and creeks without a name, and one place where water spouted hot and steaming and sometimes stinking from the earth, and another where a big spring flowed with pure tar; and no one believed him when he told of them, but called him the biggest liar yet. It was all right, though. He knew what he knew, and kept it to himself now, being tired of queer looks and smiles and words that made out he was half crazy.

Sometimes, remembering things, he didn't see what people did or hear what they said or think to speak when spoken to. It was all right. It didn't matter what was said about his sayings or his doings or his ways of thinking. A man long alone where no other white foot ever had stepped got different. He came to know what the Indians meant by medicine. He got to feeling like one with the mountains and the great sky and the lonesome winds and the animals and Indians, too, and it was a little as if he knew what they knew, a little as if there couldn't be a secret but was whispered to him, like the secret he kept hearing now.

"Let's cache," he said to Potter. The mist was gone from the river and the sun well up and decided on its course. It was time, and past time, to slide back to their hidden camp.

"Just got one more trap to lift," Porter argued.

"All right, then."

Overhead the eagle still soared close. Clell heard its long, high cry.

He heard something else, too, a muffled pounding of feet on the banks above. "Injuns!" he said, and bent the canoe into the cover of an over-hanging bush. "I told you."

Potter listened. "Buffalo is all. Buffalo trampin' around.

Clell couldn't be sure, except for the feeling in him. Down in this little canyon a man couldn't see to the banks above. It could be buffalo, all right, but something kept warning, "Injuns! Injuns!"

Potter said, "Let's git on. Can't be cachin' from every little noise. Even sparrers make noise."

"Wait a spell."

"Scary." Potter said just the one word, and he said it under his breath, but it was enough. Clell dipped his paddle. One day he would whip Potter, but right now he reckoned he had to go on.

It wasn't fear that came on him a shake later, but just the quick knowing he had been right all along, just the holding still, the waiting, the watching what to do, for the banks had broken out with Indians—Indians with feathers in their hair, and bows and war clubs and spears in their hands; Indians yelling and motioning and scrambling down to the shores on both sides and fitting arrows to their bow strings.

Potter's face had gone white and tight like rawhide drying. He grabbed at his rifle.

Clell said, "Steady!" and got the pipe that hung from around his neck and held it up, meaning he meant peace.

These were the Blackfeet sure enough. These were the meanest Indians living. He would know them from the Rees and Crows and Pierced Noses and any other. He would know them by their round heads and bent noses and their red-and-green leather shields and the moccasins mismatched in color, and their bows and robes not fancy, and no man naked in the bunch.

The Indians waved them in. Clell let go his pipe and stroked with his paddle. Potter's voice was shrill. "You fool! You gonna let 'em torment us to death?"

That was the way with a mouthy greenhorn—full of himself at first, and then wild and shaken. "Steady!" Clell said again. "I aim to pull to shore. Don't point that there rifle 'less you want a skinful of arrows."

There wasn't a gun among the Indians, not a decent gun, but only a few rusty trade muskets. They had battle axes, and bows taken from their cases, ready for business, and some had spears, and all looked itching for a white man's hair. They waited, their eyes bright as buttons, their faces and bare forearms and right shoulders shining brown in the sun. Only men were at the shore line, but Clell could see the faces of squaws and young ones looking down from the bank above.

An Indian splashed out and got hold of the prow of the canoe and pulled it in. Clell stepped ashore, holding up his pipe. He had to watch Potter. Potter stumbled out, his little eyes wide and his face white, and fear showing even for an Indian to see. When he stepped on the bank, one of the Indians grabbed his rifle and wrenched it from him, and Potter just stood like a scared rabbit, looking as if he might jump back in the dugout any minute.

Clell reached out and took a quick hold on the rifle and jerked it away and handed it back to Potter. There was a way to treat Indians. Act like a squaw and they treated you bad; act like a brave man and you might have a chance.

Potter snatched the gun and spun around and leaped. The force of the jump carried the canoe out. He made a splash with the paddle. An arrow whispered in the air and made a little thump when it hit. Clell saw the end of it, shaking from high in Potter's back.

Potter cried out, "I'm hit! I'm hit, Clell!"

"Come back! Easy! Can't get away!"

Instead, Potter swung around with the rifle. There were two sounds, the crack of the powder and the gunshot plunk of a ball. Clell caught a glimpse of an Indian going down, and then the air was full of the twang of bowstrings and the whispered flight of arrows, and Potter slumped slowly back in the canoe, his body stuck like a pincushion. An Indian splashed out to take the scalp. Two others carried the shot warrior up the bank. Already a squaw was beginning to keen.

Clell stood quiet as a stump, letting only his eyes move. It was so close now that his life was as good as gone. He could see it in the eyes around him, in the hungry faces, in the hands moving and the spears and the bows being raised. He stood straight, looking their eyes down, thinking the first arrow would come any time now, from anyplace, and then he heard the eagle scream. Its shadow lazed along the ground. His thumb slipped the barrel catch, his wrist twisted under side up. He shot without knowing he aimed. Two feathers puffed out of the bird. It went into a steep climb and faltered and turned head down and spun to the ground, making a thump when it hit.

The Indians' eyes switched back to him. Their mouths fell open, and slowly their hands came over the mouth holes in the sign of surprise. It was as he figured in that flash between life and death. They thought all guns fired a single ball. They thought he was big medicine as a marksman. One of them stepped out and laid his hand on Mule Ear, as if to draw some of its greatness into himself. A murmur started up, growing into an argument. They ordered Clell up the bank. When he got there, he saw one Indian high-tailing it for the eagle, and others following, so's to have plumes for their war bonnets, maybe, or to eat the raw flesh for the medicine it would give them.

There was a passel of Indians on the bank, three or four hundred, and more coming across from the other side. The man Clell took for the chief had mixed red earth with spit and dabbed it on his face. He carried a bird-wing fan in one hand and wore a half-sleeved hunting shirt made of big-horn skin and decorated with colored porcupine quills. His hair was a wild bush over his eyes and ears. At the back of it he had a tuft of owl feathers hanging. He yelled something and motioned with his hands, and the others began drifting back from the bank, except for a couple of dozen that Clell figured were head men. Mostly, they wore leggings and moccasins, and leather shirts or robes slung over the left shoulder. A few had scarlet trade blankets, which had come from God knew where. One didn't wear anything under his robe.

The squaws and the little squaws in their leather sacks of dresses, the naked boys with their potbellies and swollen navels, and the untried and middling warriors were all back now. The chief and the rest squatted down in a half circle, with Clell standing in front of them. They passed a pipe around. After a while they began to talk. He had some of the hang of Blackfoot, and he knew, even without their words, they were arguing what to do with him. One of them got up and came over and brought his face close to Clell's. His eyes picked at Clell's head and eyes and nose and mouth. Clell could smell grease on him and wood smoke and old sweat, but what came to his mind above all was that here was a man he had fought last season while siding with the Crows. He looked steadily into the black eyes and saw the knowing come into them, too, and watched the man turn back and take his place in the half circle and heard him telling what he knew.

They grunted like hogs, the Blackfeet did, like hogs about to be fed, while the one talked and pointed, arguing that here was a friend of their old enemies, the Crows. The man rubbed one palm over the other, saying in sign that Clell had to be rubbed out. Let them stand him up and use him for a target, the man said. The others said yes to that, not nodding their heads as white men would, but bowing forward and back from the waist.

Clell had just one trick left. He stepped over and showed his gun and pointed to the patch box and, waving one hand to catch their eyes, he sprang the cover with the other thumb. He closed the cover and handed the gun to the chief.

The chief's hands were red with the paint he had smeared on his face. Clell watched the long thumbnail, hooked like a bird claw, digging at the cover, watched the red fingers feeling for a latch or spring. While the others stretched their necks to see, the chief turned Mule Ear over, prying at it with his eyes. It wasn't any use. Unless he knew the hidden spot to press, he couldn't spring the lid. Clell took the piece back, opened the patch box again, closed it and sat down.

He couldn't make more medicine. He didn't have a glass to bring the sun down, and so to light a pipe, or even a trader's paper-backed mirror for the chief to see how pretty he was. All he had was the shot at the eagle and the patch box on Mule Ear, and he had used them both and had to take what came.

Maybe it was the eagle that did it, or the hidden cover, or maybe it was just the crazy way of Indians. The chief got up, and with his hands and with his tongue asked if the white hunter was a good runner.

Clell took his time answering, as a man did when making high palaver. He lighted his pipe. He said, "The white hunter is a bad runner. The other

Long Knives think he runs fast. Their legs are round from sitting on a horse. They cannot run."

The chief grunted, letting the sign talk and the slow words sink into him. "The Long Knife will run." He pointed to the south, away from the creek. "He will run for the trading house that the whiteface keeps among the Crows. He will go as far as three arrows will shoot, and then he will run. My brothers will run. If my brothers run faster—" The chief brought his hand to his scalp lock.

The other Indians had gathered around, even the squaws and the young ones. They were grunting with excitement. The chief took Mule Ear. Other hands stripped off Clell's hunting shirt, the red-checked woolen shirt underneath, his leggings, his moccasins, his smallclothes, until he stood white and naked in the sun, and the squaws and young ones came up close to see what white flesh looked like. The squaws made little noises in their throats. They poked at his bare hide. One of them grabbed the red-checked shirt from the hands of a man and ran off with it. The chief made the sign for "Go!"

Clell walked straight, quartering into the sun. He walked slow and solemn, like going to church. If he hurried, they would start the chase right off. If he lazed along, making out they could be damned for all he cared, they might give him more of a start.

He was two hundred yards away when the first whoop sounded, the first single whoop, and then all the voices yelling and making one great whoop. From the corner of his eye he saw their legs driving, saw the uncovered brown skins, the feathered hair, the bows and spears, and then he was running himself, seeing ahead of him the far tumble and roll of high plains and hills, with buffalo dotting the distances and a herd of prairie goats sliding like summer mist, and everywhere, so that not always could his feet miss them, the angry knobs of cactus. South and east, many a long camp away where the Bighorn joined the Roche Jaune, lay Lisa's Fort, the trading house among the Crows.

He ran so as to save himself for running, striding long and loose through the new-sprouting buffalo grass, around the cactus, around the pieces of sandstone where snakes were likely to lie. He made himself breathe easy, breathe deep, breathe full in his belly. Far off in his feelings he felt the cactus sting him and the spines pull off to sting again. The sun looked him in the face. It lay long and warm on the world. At the sky line the heat sent up a little shimmer. There wasn't a noise anywhere except the thump of his feet and his heart working in his chest and his breath sucking in and out and, behind him, a cry now and then from the Indians, seeming not closer or farther away than at first. He couldn't slow himself with a look. He began to sweat.

A man could run a mile, or two or three, and then his breath wheezed in him. It grew into a hard snore in the throat. The air came in, weak and dry, and burned his pipes and went out in one spent rush while his lungs sucked for more. He felt as if he had been running on forever. He felt strange and out of the world, a man running in a dream, except that the ache in his throat was real and the fire of cactus in his feet. The earth spread away forever, and he was lost in it and friendless, and not a proper part of it any more; and it served him right. When a man didn't pay any mind to his medicine, but went ahead regardless, as he had done, his medicine played out on him.

Clell looked back. He had gained, fifty yards, seventy-five, half a musket shot; he had gained on all the Indians except one, and that one ran as swift and high-headed as a prairie goat. He was close and coming closer.

Clell had a quick notion to stop and fight. He had an idea he might dodge the spear the Indian carried and come to grips with him. But the rest would be on him before he finished. It took time to kill a man just with the hands alone. Now was the time for the running he had saved himself for. There was strength in his legs yet, He made them reach out, farther, faster, farther. The pound of them came to be a sick jolting inside his skull. His whole chest fought for air through the hot, closed tunnel of his throat. His legs weren't a part of him; they were something to think about, but not to feel, something to watch and to wonder at. He saw them come out and go under him and come out again. He saw them weakening, the knees bending in a little as the weight came on them. He felt wetness on his face, and reached up and found his nose was streaming blood.

He looked over his shoulder again. The main body of Indians had fallen farther back, but the prairie goat had gained. Through a fog he saw the man's face, the chin set high and hard, the black eyes gleaming. He heard the moccasins slapping in the grass.

Of a sudden, Clell made up his mind. Keep on running and he'd get a spear in the back. Let it come from the front. Let it come through the chest. Let him face up to death like a natural man and to hell with it. His feet jolted him to a halt. He swung around and threw up his hands as if to stop a brute.

The Indian wasn't ready for that. He tried to pull up quick. He made to lift his spear. And then he stumbled and fell ahead. The spear handle broke as the point dug in the ground. Clell grabbed at the shaft, wrenched the point from the earth and drove it through the man. The Indian bucked to his hands and knees and strained and sank back. It was as easy as that.

Bending over him, Clell let his chest drink, let his numb legs rest, until he heard the yells of the Indians and, looking up, saw them strung out in a long file, with the closest of them so close he could see the set of their faces. He turned and ran again, hearing a sudden, louder howling as the Indians came on the dead one, and then the howling dying again to single cries as they picked up the chase. They were too many for him, and too close. He didn't have a chance. He couldn't fort up and try to stand them off, not with his hands bare. There wasn't any place to hide. He should have listened to his medicine when it was talking to him back there on the creek.

Down the slope ahead of him a river ran—the Jefferson Fork of the

Missouri, he thought, while he made his legs drive him through a screen of brush. A beaver swam in the river, its moving head making a quiet V in the still water above a dam. As he pounded closer, its flat tail slapped the water like a pistol shot, the point of the V sank from sight, and the ripples spread out and lost themselves. He could still see the beaver, though, swimming under water, its legs moving and the black tail plain, like something to follow. It was a big beaver, and it was making for a beaver lodge at Clell's right.

Clell dived, came up gasping from the chill of mountain water, and started stroking for the other shore. Beaver lodge! Beaver lodge! It was as if something spoke to him, as if someone nudged him, as if the black tail pulled him around. It was a fool thing, swimming under water and feeling for the tunnel that led up into the lodge. A fool thing. A man got so winded and weak that he didn't know medicine from craziness. A fool thing. A man couldn't force his shoulders through a beaver hole. The point of his shoulder pushed into mud. A snag ripped his side. He clawed ahead, his lungs bursting. And then his head was out of water, in the dark, and his lungs pumped air.

He heard movement in the lodge and a soft churring, but his eyes couldn't see anything. He pulled himself up, still hearing the churring, expecting the quick slice of teeth in his flesh. There was a scramble. Something slid along his leg and made a splash in the water of the tunnel, and slid again and made another splash.

His hands felt sticks and smooth, dry mud and the softness of shed hair. He sat up. The roof of the lodge just cleared his head if he sat slouched. It was a big lodge, farther across than the span of his arms. And it was as dark, almost, as the inside of a plugged barrel. His hand crossing before his eyes was just a shapeless movement.

He sat still and listened. The voices of the Indians sounded far off. He heard their feet in the stream, heard the moccasins walking softly around the lodge, heard the crunch of dried grass under their steps. It was like something dreamed, this hiding and being able to listen and to move. It was like being a breath of air, and no one able to put a hand on it.

After a while the footsteps trailed off and the voices faded. Now Clell's eyes were used to blackness, the lodge was a dark dapple. From the shades he would know it was day, but that was all. He felt for the cactus spines in his feet. He had been cold and wet at first, but the wetness dried and the lodge warmed a little to his body. Shivering, he lay down, feeling the dried mud under his skin, and the soft fur. When he closed his eyes he could see the sweep of distances and the high climb of mountains, and himself all alone in all the world, and, closer up, he could see the beaver swimming under water and its flat tail beckoning. He could hear voices, the silent voices speaking to a lonesome man out of nowhere and out of everywhere, and the beaver speaking, too, the smack of its tail speaking.

He woke up later, quick with alarm, digging at his dream and the noise that had got mixed with it. It was night outside. Not even the dark dapple showed inside the lodge, but only such a blackness as made a man feel himself to make sure he was real. Then he heard a snuffling of the air, and the sound of little waves lapping in the tunnel, and he knew that a beaver had nosed up and smelled him and drawn back into the water.

When he figured it was day, he sat up slowly, easing his muscles into action. He knew, without seeing, that his feet were puffed with the poison of the cactus. He crawled to the tunnel and filled his lungs and squirmed into it. He came up easy, just letting his eyes and nose rise above the water. The sun had cleared the eastern sky line. Not a breath of air stirred; the earth lay still, flowing into spring. He could see where the Indians had flattened the grass and trampled an edging of rushes, but there were no Indians about, not on one side or the other, not from shore line to sky line. He struck out for the far shore.

Seven days later a hunter at Fort Lisa spotted a figure far off. He watched it for a long spell, until a mist came over his eyes, and then he called to the men inside the stockade. A half dozen came through the big gate, their rifles in the crooks of their arms, and stood outside and studied the figure too.

"Man, all right. Somep'n ails him. Look how he goes."

"Injun, I say. A Crow, maybe, with a Blackfoot arrer in him."

"Git the glass."

One of them went inside and came back and put the glass to his eye. "Naked as a damn jay bird."

"Injun, ain't it?"

"Got a crop of whiskers. Never seed a Injun with whiskers yet."

"Skin's black."

"Ain't a Injun, though."

They waited.

"It ain't! Yes, I do believe it's John Clell! It's John Clell or I'm a Blackfoot!"

They brought him in and put his great, raw swellings of feet in hot water and gave him brandy and doled out roast liver, and bit by bit, that day and the next, he told them what had happened.

They knew why he wouldn't eat prairie turnips afterward, seeing as he lived on raw ones all that time, but what they didn't understand, because he didn't try to tell them, was why he never would hunt beaver again.

# WILLA CATHER

## *Neighbour Rosicky*

WHEN DOCTOR BURLEIGH told neighbour Rosicky he had a bad heart, Rosicky protested.

"So? No, I guess my heart was always pretty good. I got a little asthma, maybe. Just a awful short breath when I was pitchin' hay last summer, dat's all."

"Well, now, Rosicky, if you know more about it than I do, what did you come to me for? It's your heart that makes you short of breath, I tell you. You're sixty-five years old, and you've always worked hard, and your heart's tired. You've got to be careful from now on, and you can't do heavy work any more. You've got five boys at home to do it for you."

The old farmer looked up at the Doctor with a gleam of amusement in his queer, triangular-shaped eyes. His eyes were large and lively, but the lids were caught up in the middle in a curious way, so that they formed a triangle. He did not look like a sick man. His brown face was creased but not wrinkled, he had a ruddy colour in his smooth-shaven cheeks and in his lips, under his long brown moustache. His hair was thin and ragged around his ears, but very little grey. His forehead, naturally high and crossed by deep parallel lines, now ran all the way up to his pointed crown. Rosicky's face had the habit of looking interested,—suggested a contented disposition and a reflective quality that was gay rather than grave. This gave him a certain detachment, the easy manner of an on-looker and observer.

"Well, I guess you ain't got no pills for a bad heart, Doctor Ed. I guess the only thing is fur me to git me a new one."

Doctor Burleigh swung round in his desk-chair and frowned at the old farmer. "I think if I were you I'd take a little care of the old one, Rosicky."

Rosicky shrugged. "Maybe I don't know how. I expect you mean fur me not to drink my coffee no more."

"I wouldn't, in your place. But you'll do as you choose about that. I've never yet been able to separate a Bohemian from his coffee or his pipe. I've quit trying. But the sure thing is you've got to cut out farm work. You can feed the stock and do chores about the barn, but you can't do anything in the fields that makes you short of breath."

"How about shelling corn?"

"Of course not!"

Rosicky considered with puckered brows.

---

"I can't make my heart go no longer'n it wants to, can I, Doctor Ed?

"I think it's good for five or six years yet, maybe more, if you'll take the strain off it. Sit around the house and help Mary. If I had a good wife like yours, I'd want to stay around the house."

His patient chuckled. "It ain't no place fur a man. I don't like no old man hanging round the kitchen too much. An' my wife, she's a awful hard worker her own self."

"That's it; you can help her a little. My Lord, Rosicky, you are one of the few men I know who has a family he can get some comfort out of; happy dispositions, never quarrel among themselves, and they treat you right. I want to see you live a few years and enjoy them."

"Oh, they're good kids, all right," Rosicky assented.

The Doctor wrote him a prescription and asked him how his oldest son, Rudolph, who had married in the spring, was getting on. Rudolph had struck out for himself, on rented land. "And how's Polly? I was afraid Mary mightn't like an American daughter-in-law, but it seems to be work-ing out all right."

"Yes, she's a fine girl. Dat widder woman bring her daughters up very nice. Polly got lots of spunk, an' she got some style, too. Da's nice, for young folks to have some style." Rosicky inclined his head gallantly. His voice and his twinkly smile were an affectionate compliment to his daughter-in-law.

"It looks like a storm, and you'd better be getting home before it comes. In town in the car?" Doctor Burleigh rose.

"No, I'm in de wagon. When you got five boys, you ain't got much chance to ride round in de Ford. I ain't much for cars, noway."

"Well, it's a good road out to your place; but I don't want you bumping around in a wagon much. And never again on a hay-rake, remember!"

Rosicky placed the Doctor's fee delicately behind the desk-telephone looking the other way, as if this were an absent-minded gesture. He put on his plush cap and his corduroy jacket with a sheepskin collar, and went out.

The Doctor picked up his stethoscope and frowned at it as if he were seriously annoyed with the instrument. He wished it had been telling tales about some other man's heart, some old man who didn't look the Doctor in the eye so knowingly, or hold out such a warm brown hand when he said good-bye. Doctor Burleigh had been a poor boy in the country before he went away to medical school; he had known Rosicky almost ever since he could remember, and he had a deep affection for Mrs. Rosicky.

Only last winter he had had such a good breakfast at Rosicky's, and that when he needed it. He had been out all night on a long, hard confine-ment case at Tom Marshall's—a big rich farm where there was plenty of stock and plenty of feed and a great deal of expensive farm machinery of the newest model, and no comfort whatever. The woman had too many children and too much work, and she was no manager. When the baby was born at last, and handed over to the assisting neighbour woman, and the mother was properly attended to, Burleigh refused any breakfast in that slovenly house, and drove his buggy—the snow was too deep for a car—eight miles to Anton Rosicky's place. He didn't know another farm-house where a man could get such a warm welcome, and such good strong coffee with rich cream. No wonder the old chap didn't want to give up his coffee!

He had driven in just when the boys had come back from the barn and were washing up for breakfast. The long table, covered with a bright oil-cloth, was set out with dishes waiting for them, and the warm kitchen was full of the smell of coffee and hot biscuit and sausage. Five big handsome boys, running from twenty to twelve, all with what Burleigh called natural good manners,—they hadn't a bit of the painful self-consciousness he himself had to struggle with when he was a lad. One ran to put his horse away, another helped him off with his fur coat and hung it up, and Josephine, the youngest child and the only daughter, quickly set another place under her mother's direction.

With Mary, to feed creatures was the natural expression of affection,—her chickens, the calves, her big hungry boys. It was a rare pleasure to feed a young man whom she seldom saw and of whom she was as proud as if he belonged to her. Some country housekeepers would have stopped to spread a white cloth over the oilcloth, to change the thick cups and plates for their best china, and the wooden-handled knives for plated ones. But not Mary.

"You must take us as you find us, Doctor Ed. I'd be glad to put out my good things for you if you was expected, but I'm glad to get you any way at all."

He knew she was glad,—she threw back her head and spoke out as if she were announcing him to the whole prairie. Rosicky hadn't said anything at all; he merely smiled his twinkling smile, put some more coal on the fire, and went into his own room to pour the Doctor a little drink in a medicine glass. When they were all seated, he watched his wife's face from his end of the table and spoke to her in Czech. Then, with the instinct of politeness which seldom failed him, he turned to the Doctor and said slyly, "I was just tellin' her not to ask you no questions about Mrs. Marshall till you eat some breakfast. My wife, she's terrible fur to ask questions."

The boys laughed, and so did Mary. She watched the Doctor devour her biscuit and sausage, too much excited to eat anything herself. She drank her coffee and sat taking in everything about her visitor. She had known him when he was a poor country boy, and was boastfully proud of his success, always saying: "What do people go to Omaha for, to see a doctor, when we got the best one in the State right here?" If Mary liked people at all, she felt physical pleasure in the sight of them, personal exultation in any good fortune that came to them. Burleigh didn't know many women like that, but he knew she was like that.

When his hunger was satisfied, he did, of course, have to tell them about Mrs. Marshall, and he noticed what a friendly interest the boys took in the matter.

Rudolph, the oldest one (he was still living at home then), said: "The last time I was over there, she was lifting them big heavy milk-cans, and I knew she ought not to be doing it."

"Yes, Rudolph told me about that when he come home, and I said it wasn't right," Mary put in warmly. "It was all right for me to do them things up to the last, for I was terrible strong, but that woman's weakly. And do you think she'll be able to nurse it, Ed?" She sometimes forgot to give him the title she was so proud of. "And to think of your being up all night and then not able to get a decent breakfast! I don't know what's the matter with such people."

"Why, mother," said one of the boys, "if Doctor Ed had got breakfast there, we wouldn't have him here. So you ought to be glad."

"He knows I'm glad to have him, John, any time. But I'm sorry for that poor woman, how bad she'll feel the Doctor had to go away in the cold without his breakfast."

"I wish I'd been in practice when these were getting born." The doctor looked down the row of close-clipped heads. "I missed some good breakfasts by not being."

The boys began to laugh at their mother because she flushed so red, but she stood her ground and threw up her head. "I don't care, you wouldn't have got away from this house without breakfast. No doctor ever did. I'd have had something ready fixed that Anton could warm up for you."

The boys laughed harder than ever, and exclaimed at her: "I'll bet you would!" "She would, that!"

"Father, did you get breakfast for the doctor when we were born?"

"Yes, and he used to bring me my breakfast, too, mighty nice. I was always awful hungry!" Mary admitted with a guilty laugh.

While the boys were getting the Doctor's horse, he went to the window to examine the house plants. "What do you do to your geraniums to keep them blooming all winter, Mary? I never pass this house that from the road I don't see your windows full of flowers."

She snapped off a dark red one, and a ruffled new green leaf, and put them in his buttonhole. "There, that looks better. You look too solemn for a young man, Ed. Why don't you git married? I'm worried about you. Settin' at breakfast, I looked at you real hard, and I seen you've got some grey hairs already."

"Oh, yes! They're coming. Maybe they'd come faster if I married."

"Don't talk so. You'll ruin your health eating at the hotel. I could send your wife a nice loaf of nut bread, if you only had one. I don't like to see a young man getting grey. I'll tell you something, Ed; you make some strong black tea and keep it handy in a bowl, and every morning just brush it into your hair, an' it'll keep the grey from showin' much. That's the way I do!"

Sometimes the Doctor heard the gossipers in the drugstore wondering why Rosicky didn't get on faster. He was industrious, and so were his boys, but they were rather free and easy, weren't pushers, and they didn't always show good judgment. They were comfortable, they were out of debt, but they didn't get much ahead. Maybe, Doctor Burleigh reflected, people as generous and warmhearted and affectionate as the Rosickys never got ahead much; maybe you could not enjoy your life and put it into the bank, too.

## II

When Rosicky left Doctor Burleigh's office, he went into the farm-implement store to light his pipe and put on his glasses and read over the list Mary had given him. Then he went into the general merchandise place next door and stood about until the pretty girl with the plucked eyebrows, who always waited on him, was free. Those eyebrows, two thin India-ink strokes, amused him, because he remembered how they used to be. Rosicky always prolonged his shopping by a little joking; the girl knew the old fellow admired her, and she liked to chaff with him.

"Seems to me about every other week you buy ticking, Mr. Rosicky, and always the best quality," she remarked as she measured off the heavy bolt with red stripes.

"You see, my wife is always makin' goose-fedder pillows, and de' thin stuff don't hold in dem little down-fedders."

"You must have lots of pillows at your house."

"Sure. She makes quilts of dem, too. We sleeps easy. Now she's makin' a fedder quilt for my son's wife. You know Polly, that married my Rudolph. How much my bill, Miss Pearl?"

"Eight eighty-five."

"Chust make it nine, and put in some candy fur de women."

"As usual. I never did see a man buy so much candy for his wife. First thing you know, she'll be getting too fat."

"I'd like dat. I ain't much fur all dem slim women like what de style is now."

"That's one for me, I suppose, Mr. Bohunk!" Pearl sniffed and elevated her India-ink strokes.

When Rosicky went out to his wagon, it was beginning to snow,—the first snow of the season, and he was glad to see it. He rattled out of town and along the highway through a wonderfully rich stretch of country, the finest farms in the county. He admired this High Prairie, as it was called, and always liked to drive through it. His own place lay in a rougher territory, where there was some clay in the soil and it was not so productive. When he bought his land, he hadn't the money to buy on High Prairie; so he told his boys, when they grumbled, that if their land hadn't some clay in it, they wouldn't own it at all. All the same, he enjoyed looking at these fine farms, as he enjoyed looking at a prize bull.

After he had gone eight miles, he came to the graveyard, which lay just at the edge of his own hay-land. There he stopped his horses and sat still on his wagon seat, looking about at the snowfall. Over yonder on the hill he could see his own house, crouching low, with the clump of orchard behind and the windmill before, and all down the gentle hill-slope the rows of pale gold cornstalks stood out against the white field. The snow was falling over the cornfield and the pasture and the hay-land, steadily, with very little wind,—a nice dry snow. The graveyard had only a light wire fence about it and was all overgrown with long red grass. The fine snow, settling into this red grass and upon the few little evergreens and the headstones, looked very pretty.

It was a nice graveyard, Rosicky reflected, sort of snug and homelike, not cramped or mournful,—a big sweep all around it. A man could lie down in the long grass and see the complete arch of the sky over him, hear the wagons go by; in summer the mowing-machine rattled right up to the wire fence. And it was so near home. Over there across the cornstalks his own roof and windmill looked so good to him that he promised himself to mind the Doctor and take care of himself. He was awful fond of his place, he admitted. He wasn't anxious to leave it. And it was a comfort to think that he would never have to go farther than the edge of his own hayfield. The snow, falling over his barnyard and the graveyard, seemed to draw things together like. And they were all old neighbours in the graveyard, most of them friends; there was nothing to feel awkward or embarrassed about. Embarrassment was the most disagreeable feeling Rosicky knew. He didn't often have it,—only with certain people whom he didn't understand at all.

Well, it was a nice snowstorm; a fine sight to see the snow falling so quietly and graciously over so much open country. On his cap and shoulders, on the horses' backs and manes, light, delicate, mysterious it fell; and with it a dry cool fragrance was released into the air. It meant rest for vegetation and men and beasts, for the ground itself; a season of long nights for sleep, leisurely breakfasts, peace by the fire. This and much more went through Rosicky's mind, but he merely told himself that winter was coming, clucked to his horses, and drove on.

When he reached home, John, the youngest boy, ran out to put away his team for him, and he met Mary coming up from the outside cellar with her apron full of carrots. They went into the house together. On the table, covered with oilcloth figured with clusters of blue grapes, a place was set, and he smelled hot coffeecake of some kind. Anton never lunched in town; he thought that extravagant, and anyhow he didn't like the food. So Mary always had something ready for him when he got home.

After he was settled in his chair, stirring his coffee in a big cup, Mary took out of the oven a pan of *kolache* stuffed with apricots, examined them anxiously to see whether they had got too dry, put them beside his plate, and then sat down opposite him.

Rosicky asked her in Czech if she wasn't going to have any coffee.

She replied in English, as being somehow the right language for transacting business: "Now what did Doctor Ed say, Anton? You tell me just what."

"He said I was to tell you some compliments, but I forgot 'em." Rosicky's eyes twinkled.

"About you, I mean. What did he say about your asthma?"

"He says I ain't got no asthma." Rosicky took one of the little rolls in his broad brown fingers. The thickened nail of his right thumb told the story of his past.

"Well, what is the matter? And don't try to put me off."

"He don't say nothing much, only I'm a little older, and my heart ain't so good like it used to be."

Mary started and brushed her hair back from her temples with both hands as if she were a little out of her mind. From the way she glared, she might have been in a rage with him.

"He says there's something the matter with your heart? Doctor Ed says so?"

"Now don't yell at me like I was a hog in de garden, Mary. You know I always did like to hear a woman talk soft. He didn't say anything de matter wid my heart, only it ain't so young like it used to be, an' he tell me not to pitch hay or run de corn-sheller."

Mary wanted to jump up, but she sat still. She admired the way he never under any circumstances raised his voice or spoke roughly. He was city-bred, and she was country-bred; she often said she wanted her boys to have their papa's nice ways.

"You never have no pain there, do you? It's your breathing and your stomach that's been wrong. I wouldn't believe nobody but Doctor Ed about it. I guess I'll go see him myself. Didn't he give you no advice?"

"Chust to take it easy like, an' stay round de house dis winter. I guess you got some carpenter work for me to do. I kin make some new shelves for you, and I want dis long time to build a closet in de boys' room and make dem two little fellers keep dere clo'es hung up."

Rosicky drank his coffee from time to time, while he considered. His moustache was of the soft long variety and came down over his mouth like the teeth of a buggy-rake over a bundle of hay. Each time he put down his cup, he ran his blue handkerchief over his lips. When he took a drink of water, he managed very neatly with the back of his hand.

Mary sat watching him intently, trying to find any change in his face. It is hard to see anyone who has become like your own body to you. Yes, his hair had got thin, and his high forehead had deep lines running from left to right. But his neck, always cleanshaved except in the busiest seasons, was not loose or baggy. It was burned a dark reddish brown, and there were deep creases in it, but it looked firm and full of blood. His cheeks had a good colour. On either side of his mouth there was a half-moon down the length of his cheek, not wrinkles, but two lines that had come there from his habitual expression. He was shorter and broader than when she married him; his back had grown broad and curved, a good deal like the shell of an old turtle, and his arms and legs were short.

He was fifteen years older than Mary, but she had hardly ever thought about it before. He was her man, and the kind of man she liked. She was rough, and he was gentle,—city-bred, as she always said. They had been shipmates on a rough voyage and had stood by each other in trying times. Life had gone well with them because, at bottom, they had the same ideas about life. They agreed, without discussion, as to what was most important and what was secondary. They didn't often exchange opinions, even in Czech,—it was as if they had thought the same thought together. A good deal had to be sacrificed and thrown overboard in a hard life like theirs, and they had never disagreed as to the things that could go. It had been a hard life, and a soft life, too. There wasn't anything brutal in the short, broad-backed man with the three-cornered eyes and the forehead that went on to the top of his skull. He was a city man, a gentle man, and though he had married a rough farm girl, he had never touched her without gentleness.

They had been at one accord not to hurry through life, not to be always skimping and saving. They saw their neighbours buy more land and feed more stock than they did, without discontent. Once when the creamery agent came to the Rosickys to persuade them to sell him their cream, he told them how much money the Fasslers, their nearest neighbours, had made on their cream last year.

"Yes," said Mary, "and look at them Fassler children! Pale, pinched little things, they look like skimmed milk. I had rather put some colour into my children's faces than put money into the bank."

The agent shrugged and turned to Anton.

"I guess we'll do like she says," said Rosicky.

### III

Mary very soon got into town to see Doctor Ed, and then she had a talk with her boys and set a guard over Rosicky. Even John, the youngest, had his father on his mind. If Rosicky went to throw hay down from the loft, one of the boys ran up the ladder and took the fork from him. He sometimes complained that though he was getting to be an old man, he wasn't an old woman yet.

That winter he stayed in the house in the afternoons and carpentered, or sat in the chair between the window full of plants and the wooden bench where the two pails of drinking-water stood. This spot was called "Father's corner," though it was not a corner at all. He had a shelf there, where he kept his Bohemian papers and his pipes and tobacco, and his shears and needles and thread and tailor's thimble. Having been a tailor in his youth, he couldn't bear to see a woman patching at his clothes, or at the boys'. He liked tailoring, and always patched all the overalls and jackets and work shirts. Occasionally he made over a pair of pants one of the older boys had outgrown, for the little fellow.

While he sewed, he let his mind run back over his life. He had a good deal to remember, really; life in three countries. The only part of his youth he didn't like to remember was the two years he had spent in London, in Cheapside, working for a German tailor who was wretchedly poor. Those days, when he was nearly always hungry, when his clothes were dropping off him for dirt, and the sound of a strange language kept him in continual bewilderment, had left a sore spot in his mind that wouldn't bear touching.

He was twenty when he landed at Castle Garden in New York, and he had a protector who got him work in a tailor shop in Vesey Street, down near a Washington Market. He looked upon that part of his life as very happy. He became a good workman, he was industrious, and his wages were increased from time to time. He minded his own business and envied nobody's good fortune. He went to night school and learned to read English. He often did overtime work and was well paid for it, but somehow he never saved anything. He couldn't refuse a loan to a friend, and he was self-indulgent. He liked a good dinner, and a little went for beer, a little for tobacco; a good deal went to the girls. He often stood through an opera on Saturday nights; he could get standing-room for a dollar. Those were the great days of opera in New York, and it gave a fellow something to think about for the rest of the week. Rosicky had a quick ear, and a childish love of all the stage splendour; the scenery, the costumes, the ballet. He usually went with a chum, and after the performance they had beer and maybe some oysters somewhere. It was a fine life; for the first five years or so it satisfied him completely. He was never hungry or cold or dirty, and everything amused him: a fire, a dog fight, a parade, a storm, a ferry ride. He thought New York the finest, richest, friendliest city in the world.

Moreover, he had what he called a happy home life. Very near the tailor shop was a small furniture-factory, where an old Austrian, Loeffler, employed a few skilled men and made unusual furniture, most of it to order, for the rich German housewives uptown. The top floor of Loeffler's five-story factory was a loft, where he kept his choice lumber and stored the odd pieces of furniture left on his hands. One of the young workmen he employed was a Czech, and he and Rosicky became fast friends. They persuaded Loeffler to let them have a sleeping-room in one corner of the loft. They bought good beds and bedding and had their pick of the furniture kept up there. The loft was low-pitched, but light and airy, full of windows, and good-smelling by reason of the fine lumber put up there to season. Old Loeffler used to go down to the docks and buy wood from South America and the East from the sea captains. The young men were as foolish about their house as a bridal pair. Zichec, the young cabinet-maker, devised every sort of convenience, and Rosicky kept their clothes in order. At night and on Sundays, when the quiver of machinery underneath was still, it was the quietest place in the world, and on summer nights all the sea winds blew in. Zichec often practiced on his flute in the evening. They were both fond of music and went to the opera together. Rosicky thought he wanted to live like that forever.

But as the years passed, all alike, he began to get a little restless. When spring came round, he would begin to feel fretted, and he got to drinking. He was likely to drink too much of a Saturday night. On Sunday he was languid and heavy, getting over his spree. On Monday he plunged into work again. So he never had time to figure out what ailed him, though he knew something did. When the grass turned green in Park Place, and the lilac hedge at the back of Trinity churchyard put out its blossoms, he was tormented by a longing to run away. That was why he drank too much; to get a temporary illusion of freedom and wide horizons.

Rosicky, the old Rosicky, could remember as if it were yesterday the day when the young Rosicky found out what was the matter with him. It was on a Fourth of July afternoon, and he was sitting in Park Place in the sun. The lower part of New York was empty. Wall Street, Liberty Street, Broadway, all empty. So much stone and asphalt with nothing going on, so many empty windows. The emptiness was intense, like the stillness in a great factory when the machinery stops and the belts and bands cease running. It was too great a change, it took all the strength out of one. Those blank buildings, without the stream of life pouring through them, were like empty jails. It struck young Rosicky that this was the trouble with big cities; they built you in from the earth itself, cemented you away from any contact with the ground. You lived in an unnatural world, like the fish in an aquarium, who were probably much more comfortable than they ever were in the sea.

On that very day he began to think seriously about the articles he had read in the Bohemian papers, describing prosperous Czech farming communities in the West. He believed he would like to go out there as a farm-hand; it was hardly possible that he could ever have land of his own. His people had always been workmen; his father and grandfather had worked in shops. His mother's parents had lived in the country, but they rented their farm and had a hard time to get along. Nobody in his family had ever owned any land,—that belonged to a different station of life altogether. Anton's mother died when he was little, and he was sent into the country to her parents. He stayed with them until he was twelve, and formed those ties with the earth and the farm animals and growing things which are never made at all unless they are made early. After his grandfather died, he went back to live with his father and stepmother, but she was very hard on him, and his father helped him to get passage to London.

After that Fourth of July day in Park Place, the desire to return to the country never left him. To work on another man's farm would be all he asked; to see the sun rise and set and to plant things and watch them grow. He was a very simple man. He was like a tree that has not many roots, but one tap-root that goes down deep. He subscribed for a Bohemian paper printed in Chicago, then for one printed in Omaha. His mind got farther and farther west. He began to save a little money to buy his liberty. When he was thirty-five, there was a great meeting in New York of Bohemian athletic societies, and Rosicky left the tailor shop and went home with the Omaha delegates to try his fortune in another part of the world.

## IV

Perhaps the fact that his own youth was well over before he began to have a family was one reason why Rosicky was so fond of his boys. He had almost a grandfather's indulgence for them. He had never had to worry about any of them—except, just now, a little about Rudolph.

On Saturday night the boys always piled into the Ford, took little Josephine, and went to town to the moving-picture show. One Saturday morning they were talking at the breakfast table about starting early that evening, so that they would have an hour or so to see the Christmas things in the stores before the show began. Rosicky looked down the table.

"I hope you boys ain't disappointed, but I want you to let me have de car tonight. Maybe some of you can go in with de neighbours."

Their faces fell. They worked hard all week, and they were still like children. A new jack-knife or a box of candy pleased the older ones as much as the little fellow.

"If you and Mother are going to town," Frank said, "maybe you could take a couple of us along with you, anyway."

"No, I want to take de car down to Rudolph's, and let him an' Polly go in to de show. She don't git into town enough, an' I'm afraid she's gittin' lonesome, an' he can't afford no car yet."

That settled it. The boys were a good deal dashed. Their father took another piece of apple-cake and went on: "Maybe next Saturday night de two little fellers can go along wid dem."

"Oh, is Rudolph going to have the car every Saturday night?"

Rosicky did not reply at once; then he began to speak seriously: "Listen, boys; Polly ain't lookin' so good. I don't like to see nobody lookin' sad. It comes hard fur a town girl to be a farmer's wife. I don't want no trouble to start in Rudolph's family. When it starts, it ain't so easy to stop. An American girl don't git used to our ways all at once. I like to tell Polly she and Rudolph can have the car every Saturday night till after New Year's, if it's all right with you boys."

"Sure it's all right, Papa," Mary cut in. "And it's good you thought about that. Town girls is used to more than country girls. I lay awake nights, scared she'll make Rudolph discontented with the farm."

The boys put as good a face on it as they could. They surely looked forward to their Saturday nights in town. That evening Rosicky drove the car the half-mile down the road to Rudolph's new, bare little house.

Polly was in a short-sleeved gingham dress, clearing away the supper dishes. She was a trim, slim little thing, with blue eyes and shingled yellow hair, and her eyebrows were reduced to a mere brush-stroke, like Miss Pearl's.

"Good-evening, Mr. Rosicky. Rudolph's at the barn, I guess." She never called him father, or Mary mother. She was sensitive about having married a foreigner. She never in the world would have done it if Rudolph hadn't been such a handsome, persuasive fellow and such a gallant lover. He had graduated in her class in the high school in town, and their friendship began in the ninth grade.

Rosicky went in, though he wasn't exactly asked. "My boys ain't goin' to town to-night, an' I brought de car over fur you two to go in to de picture show."

Polly, carrying dishes to the sink, looked over her shoulder at him. "Thank you. But I'm late with my work tonight, and pretty tired. Maybe Rudolph would like to go in with you."

"Oh, I don't go to de shows! I'm too old-fashioned. You won't feel so tired after you ride in de air a ways. It's a nice clear night, an' it ain't cold. You go an' fix yourself up, Polly, an' I'll wash de dishes an' leave everything nice fur you."

Polly blushed and tossed her bob. "I couldn't let you do that, Mr. Rosicky. I wouldn't think of it."

Rosicky said nothing. He found a bib apron on a nail behind the kitchen door. He slipped it over his head and then took Polly by her two elbows and pushed her gently toward the door of her own room. "I washed up de kitchen many times for my wife, when de babies was sick or somethin'. You go an' make yourself look nice. I like you to look prettier'n any of dem town girls when you go in. De young folks must have some fun, an' I'm goin' to look out fur you, Polly."

That kind, reassuring grip on her elbows, the old man's funny bright eyes, made Polly want to drop her head on his shoulder for a second. She restrained herself, but she lingered in his grasp at the door of her room, murmuring tearfully: "You always lived in the city when you were young, didn't you? Don't you ever get lonesome out here?"

As she turned round to him, her hand fell naturally into his, and he stood holding it and smiling into her face with his peculiar, knowing, indulgent smile without a shadow of reproach in it. "Dem big cities is all right fur de rich, but dey is terrible hard fur de poor."

"I don't know. Sometimes I think I'd like to take a chance. You lived in New York, didn't you?"

"An' London. Da's bigger still. I learned my trade dere. Here's Rudolph comin', you better hurry."

"Will you tell me about London sometime?'

"Maybe. Only I ain't no talker, Polly. Run an' dress yourself up."

The bedroom door closed behind her, and Rudolph came in from the outside, looking anxious. He had seen the car and was sorry any of his family should come just then. Supper hadn't been a very pleasant occasion. Halting in the doorway, he saw his father in a kitchen apron, carrying dishes to the sink. He flushed crimson and something flashed in his eye. Rosicky held up a warning finger.

"I brought de car over fur you an' Polly to go to de picture show, an' I made her let me finish here so you won't be late. You go put on a clean shirt, quick!"

"But don't the boys want the car, father?"

"Not tonight dey don't." Rosicky fumbled under his apron and found his pants pocket. He took out a silver dollar and said in a hurried whisper: "You go an' buy dat girl some ice cream an' candy tonight, like you was courtin'. She's awful good friends wid me."

Rudolph was very short of cash, but he took the money as if it hurt him. There had been a crop failure all over the country. He had more than once been sorry he'd married this year.

In a few minutes the young people came out, looking clean and a little stiff. Rosicky hurried them off, and then he took his own time with the dishes. He scoured the pots and pans and put away the milk and swept the kitchen. He put some coal in the stove and shut off the draughts, so the place would be warm for them when they got home late at night. Then he sat down and had a pipe and listened to the clock tick.

Generally speaking, marrying an American girl was certainly a risk. A Czech should marry a Czech. It was lucky that Polly was the daughter of a poor widow woman; Rudolph was proud, and if she had a prosperous family to throw up at him, they could never make it go. Polly was one of four sisters, and they all worked; one was book-keeper in the bank, one taught music, and Polly and her younger sister had been clerks, like Miss Pearl. All four of them were musical, had pretty voices, and sang in the Methodist choir, which the eldest sister directed.

Polly missed the sociability of a store position. She missed the choir, and the company of her sisters. She didn't dislike housework, but she disliked so much of it. Rosicky was a little anxious about this pair. He was afraid Polly would grow so discontented that Rudy would quit the farm and take a factory job in Omaha. He had worked for a winter up there, two years ago, to get money to marry on. He had done very well, and they would always take him back at the stockyards. But to Rosicky that meant the end of everything for his son. To be a landless man was to be a wage-earner, a slave, all your life; to have nothing, to be nothing.

Rosicky thought he would come over and do a little carpentering for Polly after the New Year. He guessed she needed jollying. Rudolph was a serious sort of chap, serious in love and serious about his work.

Rosicky shook out his pipe and walked home across the fields. Ahead of him the lamplight shone from his kitchen windows. Suppose he were still in a tailor shop on Vesey Street, with a bunch of pale, narrow-chested sons working on machines, all coming home tired and sullen to eat supper in a kitchen that was a parlour also; with another crowded, angry family quarrelling just across the dumb-waiter shaft, and squeaking pulleys at the windows where dirty washings hung on dirty lines above a court full of old brooms and mops and ashcans. . . .

He stopped by the windmill to look up at the frosty winter stars and draw a long breath before he went inside. That kitchen with the shining windows was dear to him; but the sleeping fields and bright stars and the noble darkness were dearer still.

V

On the day before Christmas the weather set in very cold; no snow, but a bitter, biting wind that whistled and sang over the flat land and lashed one's face like fine wires. There was baking going on in the Rosicky kitchen all day, and Rosicky sat inside, making over a coat that Albert had outgrown into an overcoat for John. Mary had a big red geranium in bloom for Christmas, and a row of Jerusalem cherry trees, full of berries. It was the first year she had ever grown these; Doctor Ed brought her the seeds from Omaha when he went to some medical convention. They reminded Rosicky of plants he had seen in England; and all afternoon, as he stitched, he sat thinking about those two years in London, which his mind usually shrank from even after all this while.

He was a lad of eighteen when he dropped down into London, with no money and no connexions except the address of a cousin who was supposed to be working at a confectioner's. When he went to the pastry shop, however, he found that the cousin had gone to America. Anton tramped the streets for several days, sleeping in doorways and on the Embankment, until he was in utter despair. He knew no English, and the sound of the strange language all about him confused him. By chance he met a poor German tailor who had learned his trade in Vienna, and could speak a little Czech. This tailor, Lifschnitz, kept a repair shop in a Cheapside basement, underneath a cobbler. He didn't much need an apprentice, but he was sorry for the boy and took him in for no wages but his keep and what he could pick up. The pickings were supposed to be coppers given you when you took work home to a customer. But most of the customers called for their clothes themselves, and the coppers that came Anton's way were very few. He had, however, a place to sleep. The tailor's family lived upstairs in three rooms; a kitchen, a bedroom, where Lifschnitz and his wife and five children slept, and a living-room. Two corners of this living-room were curtained off for lodgers; in one Rosicky slept on an old horsehair sofa, with a feather quilt to wrap himself in. The other corner was rented to a wretched, dirty boy, who was studying the violin. He actually practised there. Rosicky was dirty, too. There was no way to be anything else. Mrs. Lifschnitz got the water she cooked and washed with from a pump in a brick court, four flights down. There were bugs in the place, and multitudes of fleas, though the poor woman did the best she could. Rosicky knew she often went empty to give another potato or a spoonful of dripping to the two hungry, sad-eyed boys who lodged with her. He used to think he would never get out of there, never get a clean shirt to his back again. What would he do, he wondered, when his clothes actually dropped to pieces and the worn cloth wouldn't hold patches any longer?

It was still early when the old farmer put aside his sewing and his recollections. The sky had been a dark grey all day, with not a gleam of sun, and the light failed at four o'clock. He went to shave and change his shirt while the turkey was roasting. Rudolph and Polly were coming over for supper.

After supper they sat round in the kitchen, and the younger boys were saying how sorry they were it hadn't snowed. Everybody was sorry. They wanted a deep snow that would lie long and keep the wheat warm, and leave the ground soaked when it melted.

"Yes, sir," Rudolph broke out fiercely; "if we have another dry year like last year, there's going to be hard times in this country."

Rosicky filled his pipe. "You boys don't know what hard times is. You don't owe nobody, you got plenty to eat an' keep warm, an' plenty water to keep clean. When you got them, you can't have it very hard."

Rudolph frowned, opened and shut his big right hand, and dropped it clenched upon his knee. "I've got to have a good deal more than that, Father, or I'll quit this farming gamble. I can always make good wages railroading or at the packing house, and be sure of my money."

"Maybe so," his father answered dryly.

Mary, who had just come in from the pantry and was wiping her hands on the roller towel, thought Rudy and his father were getting too serious. She brought her darning-basket and sat down in the middle of the group.

"I ain't much afraid of hard times, Rudy," she said heartily. "We've had a plenty, but we've always come through. Your father wouldn't never take nothing very hard, not even hard times. I got a mind to tell you a story on him. Maybe you boys can't hardly remember the year we had that terrible hot wind, that burned everything up on the Fourth of July? All the corn an' the gardens. An' that was in the days when we didn't have alfalfa yet,—I guess it wasn't invented.

"Well, that very day your father was out cultivatin' corn, and I was here in the kitchen makin' plum preserves. We had bushels of plums that year. I noticed it was terrible hot, but it's always hot in the kitchen when you're preservin', an' I was too busy with my plums to mind. Anton come in from the field about three o'clock, an' I asked him what was the matter.

" 'Nothin',' he says, 'but it's pretty hot, an' I think I won't work no more today.' He stood round for a few minutes, an' then he says: 'Ain't you near through? I want you should git up a nice supper for us tonight. It's Fourth of July.'

"I told him to git along, that I was right in the middle of preservin', but the plums would taste good on hot biscuit. 'I'm goin' to have fried chicken, too,' he says, and he went off an' killed a couple. You three oldest boys was little fellers, playin' round outside, real hot an' sweaty, an' your father took you to the horse tank down by the windmill an' took off your clothes an' put you in. Them two box-elder trees was little then, but they made shade over the tank. Then he took off all his own clothes, an' got in with you. While he was playin' in the water with you, the Methodist preacher drove into our place to say how all the neighbors was goin' to meet at the schoolhouse that night, to pray for rain. He drove right to the windmill, of course, and there was your father and you three with no clothes on. I was in the kitchen door, an' I had to laugh, for the preacher acted like he ain't never seen a naked man before. He surely was embarrassed, an' your father couldn't git to his clothes; they was all hangin up on the windmill to let the sweat dry out of 'em. So he laid in the tank where he was, an' put one of you boys on top of him to cover him up a little, an' talked to the preacher.

"When you got through playin' in the water, he put clean clothes on you and a clean shirt on himself, and by that time I'd begun to get supper. He says: 'It's too hot in here to eat comfortable. Let's have a picnic in the orchard. We'll eat our supper behind the mulberry hedge, under them linden trees.'

"So he carried our supper down, an' a bottle of my wild-grape wine, an' everything tasted good, I can tell you. The wind got cooler as the sun was goin' down, and it turned out pleasant, only I noticed how the leaves was curled up on the linden trees. That made me think, an' I asked your father if that hot wind all day hadn't been terrible hard on the gardens an' the corn.

" 'Corn,' he says, 'there ain't no corn.'

" 'What you talkin' about?' I said. 'Ain't we got forty acres?'

" 'We ain't got an ear,' he says, 'nor nobody else ain't got none. All the corn in this country was cooked by three o'clock today, like you'd roasted it in an oven.'

" 'You mean you won't get no crop at all?' I asked him. I couldn't believe it, after he'd worked so hard.

" 'No crop this year,' he says. 'That's why we're havin' a picnic. We might as well enjoy what we got.'

"An' that's how your father behaved, when all the neighbours was so discouraged they couldn't look you in the face. An' we enjoyed ourselves that year, poor as we was, an' our neighbours wasn't a bit better off for bein' miserable. Some of 'em grieved till they got poor digestions and couldn't relish what they did have."

The younger boys said they thought their father had the best of it. But Rudolph was thinking that, all the same, the neighbours had managed to get ahead more, in the fifteen years since that time. There must be something wrong about his father's way of doing things. He wished he knew what was going on in the back of Polly's mind. He knew she liked his father, but he knew, too, that she was afraid of something. When his mother sent over coffee-cake or prune tarts or a loaf of fresh bread, Polly seemed to regard them with a certain suspicion. When she observed to him that his brothers had nice manners, her tone implied that it was remarkable they should have. With his mother she was stiff and on her guard. Mary's hearty frankness and gusts of good humour irritated her. Polly was afraid of being unusual or conspicuous in any way, of being "ordinary," as she said!

When Mary had finished her story, Rosicky laid aside his pipe.

"You boys like me to tell you about some of dem hard times I been through in London?" Warmly encouraged, he sat rubbing his forehead along the deep creases. It was bothersome to tell a long story in English (he nearly always talked to the boys in Czech), but he wanted Polly to hear this one.

"Well, you know about dat tailor shop I worked in in London? I had one Christmas dere I ain't never forgot. Times was awful bad before Christmas; de boss ain't got much work, an' have it awful hard to pay his rent. It ain't so much fun, bein' poor in a big city like London, I'll say! All de windows is full of good t'ings to eat, an' all de pushcarts in de streets is full, an' you smell 'em all de time, an' you ain't got no money,—not a damn bit. I didn't mind de cold so much, though I didn't have no overcoat, chust a short jacket I'd outgrowed so it wouldn't meet on me, an' my hands was chapped raw. But I always had a good appetite, like you all know, an' de sight of dem pork pies in de windows was awful fur me!

"Day before Christmas was terrible foggy dat year, an' dat fog gits into your bones and makes you all damp like. Mrs. Lifschnitz didn't give us nothin' but a little bread an' drippin' for supper, because she was savin' to try for to give us a good dinner on Christmas Day. After supper de boss say I can go an' enjoy myself, so I went into de streets to listen to de Christmas singers. Dey sing old songs an' make very nice music, an' I run round after dem a good ways, till I got awful hungry. I t'ink maybe if I go home, I can sleep till morning an' forgit my belly.

"I went into my corner real quiet, and roll up in my fedder quilt. But I ain't got my head down, till I smell somet'ing good. Seem like it git stronger an' stronger, an' I can't git to sleep noway. I can't understand dat smell. Dere was a gas light in a hall across de court, dat always shine in at my window a little. I got up an' look round. I got a little wooden box in my corner fur a stool, 'cause I ain't got no chair. I picks up dat box, and under it dere is a roast goose on a platter! I can't believe my eyes. I carry it to de window where de light comes in, an' touch it and smell it to find out, an' den I taste it to be sure. I say, I will eat chust one little bite of dat goose, so I can go to sleep, and tomorrow I won't eat none at all. But I tell you, boys, when I stop, one half of dat goose was gone!"

The narrator bowed his head, and the boys shouted. But little Josephine slipped behind his chair and kissed him on the neck beneath his ear.

"Poor little Papa, I don't want him to be hungry!"

"Da's long ago, child. I ain't never been hungry since I had your mudder to cook fur me."

"Go on and tell us the rest, please," said Polly.

"Well, when I come to realize what I done, of course, I felt terrible. I felt better in de stomach, but very bad in de heart. I set on my bed wid dat platter on my knees, an it all come to me; how hard dat poor woman save to buy dat goose, and how she get some neighbour to cook it dat got more fire, an' how she put it in my corner to keep it way from dem hungry children. Dey was an old carpet hung up to shut my corner off, an' de children wasn't allowed to go in dere. An' I know she put it in my corner because she trust me more'n she did de violin boy. I can't stand it to face her after I spoil de Christmas. So I put on my shoes and go out into de city. I tell myself I better throw myself in de river; but I guess I ain't dat kind of a boy.

"It was after twelve o'clock, an' terrible cold, an' I start out to walk about London all night. I walk along de river awhile, but dey was lots of drunks all along; men, and women too. I chust move along to keep away from the police. I git onto de Strand, an' den over to New Oxford Street, where dere was a big German restaurant on de ground floor, wid big big windows all fixed up fine, an' I could see de people havin' parties inside. While I was lookin' in, two men and two ladies come out, laughin' and talkin' and feelin' happy about all dey been eatin' an' drinkin', and dey was speakin' Czech,—not like de Austrians, but like de home folks talk it.

"I guess I went crazy, an' I done what I ain't never done before nor since. I went right up to dem gay people an' begun to beg dem: 'Fellow countrymen, for God's sake give me money enough to buy a goose!'"

"Dey laugh, of course, but de ladies speak awful kind to me an' dey take me back into de restaurant and give me hot coffee and cakes, an' make me tell all about how I happened to come to London, an' what I was doin' dere. Dey take my name and where I work down on paper, an' both of dem ladies give me ten shillings.

"De big market at Covent Garden ain't very far away, an' by dat time it was open. I go dere an' buy a big goose an' some pork pies, an' potatoes and onions, an' cakes an' oranges fur de children,—all I could carry! When I git home, everybody is still asleep. I pile all I bought on de kitchen table, an' go in an' lay down on my bed, an' I ain't waken up till I hear dat woman scream when she come out into her kitchen. My goodness, but she was surprise! She laugh an' cry at de same time, an' hug me and waken all de children. She ain't stop fur no breakfast; she git de Christmas dinner ready dat morning, and we all sit down an' eat all we can hold. I ain't never seen dat violin boy have all he can hold before.

"Two three days after dat, de two men come to hunt me up, an' dey ask my boss, and he give me a good report an' tell dem I was a steady boy all right. One of dem Bohemians was very smart an' run a Bohemian news-paper in New York, an' de odder was a rich man, in de importing business, an' dey been travelling togedder. Dey told me how t'ings was easier in New York, an' offered to pay my passage when dey was goin' home soon on a boat. My boss say to me: 'You go. You ain't got no chance here, an' I like to see you git ahead, fur you always been a good boy to my woman, and fur dat fine Christmas dinner you give us all.' An' da's how I got to New York."

That night when Rudolph and Polly, arm in arm, were running home across the fields with the bitter wind at their backs, his heart leaped for joy when she said she thought they might have his family come over for supper on New Year's Eve. "Let's get up a nice supper, and not let your mother help at all; make her be company for once."

"That would be lovely of you, Polly," he said humbly. He was a very simple, modest boy, and he, too, felt vaguely that Polly and her sisters were more experienced and worldly than his people.

## VI

The winter turned out badly for farmers. It was bitterly cold, and after the first light snows before Christmas there was no snow at all,—and no rain. March was as bitter as February. On those days when the wind fairly punished the country, Rosicky sat by his window. In the fall he and the boys had put in a big wheat planting, and now the seed had frozen in the ground. All that land would have to be ploughed up and planted over again, planted in corn. It had happened before, but he was younger then, and he never worried about what had to be. He was sure of himself and of Mary; he knew they could bear what they had to bear, that they would always pull through somehow. But he was not so sure about the young ones, and he felt troubled because Rudolph and Polly were having such a hard start.

Sitting beside his flowering window while the panes rattled and the wind blew in under the door, Rosicky gave himself to reflection as he had not done since those Sundays in the loft of the furniture-factory in New York, long ago. Then he was trying to find what he wanted in life for himself; now he was trying to find what he wanted for his boys, and why it was he so hungered to feel sure they would be here, working this very land, after he was gone.

They would have to work hard on the farm, and probably they would never do much more than make a living. But if he could think of them as staying here on the land, he wouldn't have to fear any great unkindness for them. Hardships, certainly; it was a hardship to have the wheat freeze in the ground when seed was so high; and to have to sell your stock be-cause you had no feed. But there would be other years when everything came along right, and you caught up. And what you had was your own. You didn't have to choose between bosses and strikers, and go wrong either way. You didn't have to do with dishonest and cruel people. They were the only things in his experience he had found terrifying and hor-rible; the look in the eyes of a dishonest and crafty man, of a scheming and rapacious woman.

In the country, if you had a mean neighbour, you could keep off his land and make him keep off yours. But in the city, all the foulness and misery and brutality of your neighbours was part of your life. The worst things he had come upon in his journey through the world were human, —depraved and poisonous specimens of man. To this day he could recall certain terrible faces in the London streets. There were mean people everywhere, to be sure, even in their own country town here. But they weren't tempered, hardened, sharpened, like the treacherous people in cities who live by grinding or cheating or poisoning their fellow-men. He had helped to bury two of his fellow-workmen in the tailoring trade, and he was distrustful of the organized industries that see one out of the world in big cities. Here, if you were sick, you had Doctor Ed to look after you; and if you died, fat Mr. Haycock, the kindest man in the world, buried you.

It seemed to Rosicky that for good, honest boys like his, the worst they could do on the farm was better than the best they would be likely to do in the city. If he'd had a mean boy, now, one who was crooked and sharp and tried to put anything over on his brothers, then town would be the place for him. But he had no such boy. As for Rudolph, the discontented one, he would give the shirt off his back to anyone who touched his heart. What Rosicky really hoped for his boys was that they could get through the world without ever knowing much about the cruelty of human beings. "Their mother an' me ain't prepared them for that," he sometimes said to himself.

These thoughts brought him back to a grateful consideration of his own case. What an escape he had had, to be sure! He, too, in his time, had had to take money for repair work from the hand of a hungry child who let it go so wistfully; because it was money due his boss. And now, in all these years, he had never had to take a cent from anyone in bitter need,— never had to look at the face of a woman become like a wolf's from struggle and famine. When he thought of these things, Rosicky would put on his cap and jacket and slip down to the barn and give his work-horses a little extra oats, letting them eat it out of his hand in their slobbery fashion. It was his way of expressing what he felt, and made him chuckle with pleasure.

The spring came warm, with blue skies,—but dry, dry as a bone. The boys began ploughing up the wheat-fields to plant them over in corn. Rosicky would stand at the fence corner and watch them, and the earth was so dry it blew up in clouds of brown dust that hid the horses and the sulky plough and the driver. It was a bad outlook.

The big alfalfa-field that lay between the home place and Rudolph's came up green, but Rosicky was worried because during that open windy winter a great many Russian thistle plants had blown in there and lodged. He kept asking the boys to rake them out; he was afraid that their seed would root and "take the alfalfa." Rudolph said that was nonsense. The boys were working so hard planting corn, their father felt he couldn't insist about the thistles, but he set great score by that big alfalfa field. It was a feed you could depend on,—and there was some deeper reason, vague, but strong. The peculiar green of that clover woke early memories in old Rosicky, went back to something in his childhood in the old world. When he was a little boy, he had played in fields of that strong blue-green colour.

One morning, when Rudolph had gone to town in the car, leaving a work-team idle in his barn, Rosicky went over to his son's place, put the horses to the buggy rake, and set about qiuetly raking up those thistles. He behaved with guilty caution, and rather enjoyed stealing a march on Doctor Ed, who was just then taking his first vacation in seven years of practice and was attending a clinic in Chicago. Rosicky got the thistles raked up, but did not stop to burn them. That would take some time, and his breath was pretty short, so he thought he had better get the horses back to the barn.

He got them into the barn and to their stalls, but the pain had come on so sharp in his chest that he didn't try to take the harness off. He started for the house, bending lower with every step. The cramp in his chest was shutting him up like a jackknife. When he reached the windmill, he swayed and caught at the ladder. He saw Polly coming down the hill, running with the swiftness of a slim greyhound. In a flash she had her shoulder under his armpit.

"Lean on me, Father, hard! Don't be afraid. We can get to the house all right."

Somehow they did, though Rosicky became blind with pain; he could keep on his legs, but he couldn't steer his course. The next thing he was conscious of was lying on Polly's bed, and Polly bending over him wringing out bath towels in hot water and putting them on his chest. She stopped only to throw coal into the stove, and she kept the tea-kettle and the black pot going. She put these hot applications on him for nearly an hour, she told him afterwards, and all that time he was drawn up stiff and blue, with the sweat pouring off him.

As the pain gradually loosed its grip, the stiffness went out of his jaws, the black circles round his eyes disappeared, and a little of his natural colour came back. When his daughter-in-law buttoned his shirt over his chest at last, he sighed.

"Da's fine, de way I feel now, Polly. It was a awful bad spell, an' I was so sorry it all come on you like it did."

Polly was flushed and excited. "Is the pain really gone? Can I leave you long enough to telephone over to your place?"

Rosicky's eyelids fluttered. "Don't telephone, Polly. It ain't no use to scare my wife. It's nice and quiet here, an' if I ain't too much trouble to you, just let me lay still till I feel like myself. I ain't got no pain now. It's nice here."

Polly bent over him and wiped the moisture from his face. "Oh, I'm so glad it's over!" she broke out impulsively. "It just broke my heart to see you suffer so, Father."

Rosicky motioned her to sit down on the chair where the tea-kettle had been, and looked up at her with that lively affectionate gleam in his eyes. "You was awful good to me, I won't ever forget dat. I hate it to be sick on you like dis. Down at de barn I say to myself, dat young girl ain't had much experience in sickness, I don't want to scare her, an' maybe she's got a baby comin' or somet'ing."

Polly took his hand. He was looking at her so intently and affectionately and confidingly; his eyes seemed to caress her face, to regard it with pleasure. She frowned with her funny streaks of eyebrows, and then smiled back at him.

"I guess maybe there is something of that kind going to happen. But I haven't told anyone yet, not my mother or Rudolph. You'll be the first to know."

His hand pressed hers. She noticed that it was warm again. The twinkle in his yellow-brown eyes seemed to come nearer.

"I like mighty well to see dat little child, Polly," was all he said. Then he closed his eyes and lay half-smiling. But Polly sat still, thinking hard. She had a sudden feeling that nobody in the world, not her mother, not Rudolph, or anyone, really loved her as much as old Rosicky did. It perplexed her. She sat frowning and trying to puzzle it out. It was as if Rosicky had a special gift for loving people, something that was like an ear for music or an eye for colour. It was quiet, unobtrusive; it was merely there. You saw it in his eyes,—perhaps that was why they were merry. You felt it in his hands, too. After he dropped off to sleep, she sat holding his warm, broad, flexible brown hand. She had never seen another in the least like it. She wondered if it wasn't a kind of gypsy hand, it was so alive and quick and light in its communications,—very strange in a farmer. Nearly all the farmers she knew had huge lumps of fists, like mauls, or they were knotty and bony and uncomfortable-looking, with stiff fingers. But Rosicky's hand was like quicksilver, flexible, muscular, about the colour of a pale cigar, with deep, deep creases across the palm. It wasn't nervous, it wasn't a stupid lump; it was a warm brown human hand, with some cleverness in it, a great deal of generosity, and something else which Polly could only call "gypsy-like,"—something nimble and lively and sure, in the way that animals are.

Polly remembered that hour long afterward; it had been like an awakening to her. It seemed to her that she had never learned so much about life from anything as from old Rosicky's hand. It brought her to herself; it communicated some direct and untranslatable message.

When she heard Rudolph coming in the car, she ran out to meet him.

"Oh, Rudy, your father's been awful sick! He raked up those thistles he's been worrying about, and afterwards he could hardly get to the house. He suffered so I was afraid he was going to die."

Rudolph jumped to the ground. "Where is he now?"

"On the bed. He's asleep. I was terribly scared, because, you know, I'm so fond of your father." She slipped her arm through his and they went into the house. That afternoon they took Rosicky home and put him to bed, though he protested that he was quite well again.

The next morning he got up and dressed and sat down to breakfast with his family. He told Mary that his coffee tasted better than usual to him, and he warned the boys not to bear any tales to Doctor Ed when he got home. After breakfast he sat down by his window to do some patching and asked Mary to thread several needles for him before she went to feed her chickens,—her eyes were better than his, and her hands steadier. He lit his pipe and took up John's overalls. Mary had been watching him anxiously all morning, and as she went out of the door with her bucket of scraps, she saw that he was smiling. He was thinking, indeed, about Polly, and how he might never have known what a tender heart she had if he hadn't got sick over there. Girls nowadays didn't wear their heart on their sleeve. But now he knew Polly would make a fine woman after the foolishness wore off. Either a woman had that sweetness at her heart or she hadn't. You could always tell by the look of them; but if they had that, everything came out right in the end.

After he had taken a few stitches, the cramp began in his chest, like yesterday. He put his pipe cautiously down on the window-sill and bent over to ease the pull. No use,—he had better try to get to his bed if he could. He rose and groped his way across the familiar floor, which was rising and falling like the deck of a ship. At the door he fell. When Mary came in, she found him lying there, and the moment she touched him she knew that he was gone.

Doctor Ed was away when Rosicky died, and for the first few weeks after he got home he was hard driven. Every day he said to himself that he must get out to see the family that had lost their father. One soft, warm moonlight night in early summer he started for the farm. His mind was on other things, and not until his road ran by the graveyard did he realize that Rosicky wasn't over there on the hill where the red lamplight shone, but here, in the moonlight. He stopped his car, shut off the engine, and sat there for a while.

A sudden hush had fallen on his soul. Everything here seemed strangely moving and significant, though signifying what, he did not know. Close by the wire fence stood Rosicky's mowing-machine, where one of his boys had been cutting hay that afternoon; his own work-horses had been going up and down there. The new-cut hay perfumed all the night air. The moonlight silvered the long, billowy grass that grew over the graves and hid the fence; the few little evergreens stood out black in it, like shadows in a pool. The sky was very blue and soft, the stars rather faint because the moon was full.

For the first time it struck Doctor Ed that this was really a beautiful graveyard. He thought of city cemeteries; acres of shrubbery and heavy stone, so arranged and lonely and unlike anything in the living world. Cities of the dead, indeed; cities of the forgotten, of the "put away." But this was open and free, this little square of long grass which the wind forever stirred. Nothing but the sky overhead, and the many-coloured fields running on until they met that sky. The horses worked here in summer;

the neighbours passed on their way to town; and over yonder, in the cornfield, Rosicky's own cattle would be eating fodder as winter came on. Nothing could be more undeathlike than this place; nothing could be more right for a man who had helped to do the work of great cities and had always longed for the open country and had got to it at last. Rosicky's life seemed to him complete and beautiful.

# PAUL HORGAN

## *The Peach Stone*

As they all knew, the drive would take them about four hours, all the way to Weed, where *she* came from. They knew the way from traveling it so often, first in the old car, and now in the new one; new to them, that is, for they'd bought it second-hand, last year, when they were down in Roswell to celebrate their tenth wedding anniversary. They still thought of themselves as a young couple, and *he* certainly did crazy things now and then, and always laughed her out of it when she was cross at the money going where it did, instead of where it ought to go. But there was so much droll orneriness in him when he did things like that that she couldn't stay mad, hadn't the heart, and the harder up they got, the more she loved him, and the little ranch he'd taken her to in the rolling plains just below the mountains.

This was a day in spring, rather hot, and the mountain was that melting blue that reminded you of something you could touch, like a china bowl. Over the sandy brown of the earth there was coming a green shadow. The air struck cool and deep in their breasts. *He* came from Texas, as a boy, and had lived here in New Mexico ever since. The word *home* always gave *her* a picture of unpainted, mouse-brown wooden houses in a little cluster by the rocky edge of the last mountain-step—the town of Weed, where Jodey Powers met and married her ten years ago.

They were heading back that way today.

Jodey was driving, squinting at the light. It never seemed so bright as now, before noon, as they went up the valley. He had a rangy look at the wheel of the light blue Chevvie—a bony man, but still fuzzed over with some look of a cub about him, perhaps the way he moved his limbs, a slight appealing clumsiness, that drew on thoughtless strength. On a rough road, he flopped and swayed at the wheel as if he were on a bony horse that galloped a little sidewise. His skin was red-brown from the sun. He had pale blue eyes, edged with dark lashes. *She* used to say he "turned them on" her, as if they were lights. He was wearing his suit, brown-striped, and a fresh blue shirt, too big at the neck. But he looked well dressed. But he would have looked that way naked, too, for he communicated his physical essence through any covering. It was what spoke out from him to anyone who encountered him. Until Cleotha married him, it had given him a time, all right, he used to reflect.

Next to him in the front seat of the sedan was Buddy, their nine-year-old boy, who turned his head to stare at them both, his father and mother.

She was in back.

On the seat beside her was a wooden box, sandpapered, but not painted. Over it lay a baby's coverlet of pale yellow flannel with cross-stitched flowers down the middle in a band of bright colors. The mother didn't touch the box except when the car lurched or the tires danced over corrugated places in the gravel highway. Then she steadied it, and kept it from creeping on the seat cushions. In the box was coffined the body of their dead child, a two-year-old girl. They were on their way to Weed to bury it there.

In the other corner of the back seat sat Miss Latcher, the teacher. They rode in silence, and Miss Latcher breathed deeply of the spring day, as they all did, and she kept summoning to her aid the fruits of her learning. She felt this was a time to be intelligent, and not to give way to feelings.

The child was burned to death yesterday, playing behind the adobe chickenhouse at the edge of the arroyo out back, where the fence always caught the tumbleweeds. Yesterday, in a twist of wind, a few sparks from the kitchen chimney fell in the dry tumbleweeds and set them ablaze. Jodey had always meant to clear the weeds out: never seemed to get to it: told Cleotha he'd get to it next Saturday morning, before going down to Roswell: but Saturdays went by, and the wind and the sand drove the weeds into a barrier at the fence, and they would look at it every day without noticing, so habitual had the sight become. And so for many a spring morning, the little girl had played out there, behind the gray stucco house, whose adobe bricks showed through in one or two places.

The car had something loose; they believed it was the left rear fender: it chattered and wrangled over the gravel road.

Last night Cleotha stopped her weeping.

Today something happened; it came over her as they started out of the ranch lane, which curved up toward the highway. She looked as if she were trying to see something beyond the edge of Jodey's head and past the windshield.

Of course, she had sight in her eyes; she could not refuse to look at the world. As the car drove up the valley that morning, she saw in two ways —one, as she remembered the familiar sights of this region where she lived; the other, as if for the first time she were really seeing, and not simply looking. Her heart began to beat faster as they drove. It seemed to knock at her breast as if to come forth and hurry ahead of her along the sunlighted lanes of the life after today. She remembered thinking that her head might be a little giddy, what with the sorrow in her eyes so bright and slowly shining. But it didn't matter what did it. Ready never to look at anyone or anything again, she kept still; and through the window, which had a meandering crack in it like a river on a map, all that she looked upon seemed dear to her. . . .

Jodey could only drive. He watched the road as if he expected it to rise up and smite them all over into the canyon, where the trees twinkled and flashed with bright drops of light on their new varnished leaves. Jodey watched the road and said to himself that if it thought it could turn him over or make him scrape the rocks along the near side of the hill they were going around, if it thought for one minute that he was not master of this car, this road, this journey, why, it was just crazy. The wheels spraying the gravel across the surface of the road traveled on outward from his legs; his muscles were tight and felt tired as if he were running instead of riding. He tried to *think*, but he could not; that is, nothing came about that he would speak to her of, and he believed that she sat there, leaning forward, waiting for him to say something to her.

But this he could not do, and he speeded up a little, and his jaw made hard knots where he bit on his own rage; and he saw a lump of something coming in the road, and it aroused a positive passion in him. He aimed directly for it, and charged it fast, and hit it. The car shuddered and skidded, jolting them. Miss Latcher took a sharp breath inward, and put out her hand to touch someone, but did not reach anyone. Jodey looked for a second into the rear-view mirror above him, expecting something; but his wife was looking out of the window beside her, and if he could believe his eyes, she was smiling, holding her mouth with her fingers pinched up in a little claw.

The blood came up from under his shirt, he turned dark, and a sting came across his eyes.

He couldn't explain why he had done a thing like that to her, as if it were she he was enraged with, instead of himself.

He wanted to stop the car and get out and go around to the back door on the other side, and open it, and take her hands, bring her out to stand before him in the road, and hang his arms around her until she would be locked upon him. This made a picture that he indulged like a dream, while the car ran on, and he made no change, but drove as before. . . .

The little boy, Buddy, regarded their faces, again, and again, as if to see in their eyes what had happened to them.

He felt the separateness of the three.

He was frightened by their appearance of indifference to each other. His father had a hot and drowsy look, as if he had just come out of bed. There was something in his father's face which made it impossible for Buddy to say anything. He turned around and looked at his mother, but she was gazing out the window, and did not see him; and until she should see him, he had no way of speaking to her, if not with his words, then with his eyes, but if she should happen to look at him, why he would wait to see what she looked *like*, and if she *did*, why, then he would smile at her, because he loved her, but he would have to know first if she was still his mother, and if everything was all right, and things weren't blown to smithereens—*bla-a-ash! wh-o-o-m!*—the way the dynamite did when the highway came past their ranch house, and the men worked out there for months, and whole hillsides came down at a time. All summer long, that was, always something to see. The world, the family, he, between his father and mother, was safe.

He silently begged her to face toward him. There was no security until she should do so.

"Mumma?"

But he said it to himself, and she did not hear him this time, and it seemed intelligent to him to turn around, make a game of it (the way things often were worked out), and face the front, watch the road, delay as long as he possibly could bear to, and *then* turn around again, and *this* time, why, she would probably be looking at him all the time, and it would *be:* it would simply *be.*

So he obediently watched the road, the white gravel ribbon passing under their wheels as steadily as time.

He was a sturdy little boy, and there was a silver nap of child's dust on his face, over his plum-red cheeks. He smelled something like a raw potato that has just been pared. The sun crowned him with a ring of light on his dark hair. . . .

What Cleotha was afraid to do was break the spell by saying anything or looking at any of them. This was *vision*, it was all she could think; never had anything looked so in all her life; everything made her heart lift, when she had believed this morning, after the night, that it would never lift again. There wasn't anything to compare her grief to. She couldn't think of anything to answer the death of her tiny child with. In her first hours of hardly believing what had happened, she had felt her own flesh and tried to imagine how it would have been if she could have borne the fire instead of the child. But all she got out of that was a longing avowal to herself of how gladly she would have borne it. Jodey had lain beside her, and she clung to his hand until she heard how he breathed off to sleep. Then she had let him go, and had wept at what seemed faithless in him. She had wanted his mind beside her then. It seemed to her that the last degree of her grief was the compassion she had had to bestow upon him while he slept.

But she had found this resource within her, and from that time on, her weeping had stopped.

It was like a wedding of pride and duty within her. There was nothing she could not find within herself, if she had to, now, she believed.

And so this morning, getting on toward noon, as they rode up the valley, climbing all the way, until they would find the road to turn off on, which would take them higher and higher before they dropped down toward Weed on the other side, she welcomed the sights of that dusty trip. Even if she had spoken her vision aloud, it would not have made sense to the others.

Look at that orchard of peach trees, she thought. I never saw such color as this year; the trees are like lamps, with the light coming from within. It must be the sunlight shining from the other side, and, of course, the petals are very thin, like the loveliest silk; so any light that shines upon them will pierce right through them and glow on the side. But they are so bright! When I was a girl at home, up to Weed, I remember we had an orchard of peach trees, but the blossoms were always a deeper pink than down here in the valley.

My! I used to catch them up by the handful, and I believed when I was a girl that if I crushed them and tied them in a handkerchief and carried the handkerchief in my bosom, I would come to smell like peach blossoms and have the same high pink in my face, and the girls I knew said that if I took a peach *stone* and held it *long enough* in my hand, it would *sprout;* and I dreamed of this one time, though, of course, I knew it was nonsense; but that was how children thought and talked in those days—we all used to pretend that *nothing* was impossible, if you simply did it hard enough and long enough.

But nobody wanted to hold a peach stone in their hand until it *sprouted,* to find out, and we used to laugh about it, but I think we believed it. I think I believed it.

It seemed to me, in between my *sensible* thoughts, a thing that any woman could probably do. It seemed to me like a parable in the Bible. I could preach you a sermon about it this day.

I believe I see a tree down there in that next orchard which is dead; it has old black sprigs, and it looks twisted by rheumatism. There is one little shoot of leaves up on the top branch, and that is all. No, it is not dead, it is aged, it can no longer put forth blossoms in a swarm like pink butterflies; but there is that one little swarm of green leaves—it is just about the prettiest thing I've seen all day, and I thank God for it, for if there's anything I love, it is to see something growing. . . .

Miss Latcher had on her cloth gloves now, which she had taken from her blue cloth bag a little while back. The little winds that tracked through the moving car sought her out and chilled her nose, and the tips of her ears, and her long fingers, about which she had several times gone to visit various doctors. They had always told her not to worry, if her fingers seemed cold, and her hands moist. It was just a nervous condition, nothing to take very seriously; a good hand lotion might help the sensation, and in any case, some kind of digital exercise was a good thing— did she perhaps play the piano. It always seemed to her that doctors never *paid any attention* to her.

Her first name was Arleen, and she always considered this a very pretty name, prettier than Cleotha; and she believed that there was such a thing as an *Arleen look,* and if you wanted to know what it was, simply look at her. She had a long face, and pale hair; her skin was white, and her eyes were light blue. She was wonderfully clean, and used no cosmetics. She was a girl from "around here," but she had gone away to college, to study for her career, and what she had known as a child was displaced by what she had heard in classrooms. And she had to admit it: people *here* and *away* were not much alike. The men were different. She couldn't imagine marrying a rancher and "sacrificing" everything she had learned in college.

This poor little thing in the other corner of the car, for instance: she seemed dazed by what had happened to her—all she could do evidently was sit and stare out the window. And that man in front, simply driving, without a word. What did they have? What was their life like? They hardly had good clothes to drive to Roswell in, when they had to go to the doctor, or on some social errand.

But I must not think uncharitably, she reflected, and sat in an attitude of sustained sympathy, with her face composed in Arleenish interest and tact. The assumption of a proper aspect of grief and feeling produced the most curious effect within her, and by her attitude of concern she was suddenly reminded of the thing that always made her feel like weeping, though of course, she never did, but when she stopped and *thought*—

Like that painting at college, in the long hallway leading from the Physical Education lecture hall to the stairway down to the girls' gym: an enormous picture depicting the Agony of the Christian Martyrs, in ancient Rome. There were some days when she simply couldn't look at it; and there were others when she would pause and see those maidens with their tearful faces raised in calm prowess, and in them, she would find herself—they were all Arleens; and after she would leave the picture she would proceed in her imagination to the arena, and there she would know with exquisite sorrow and pain the ordeals of two thousand years ago, instead of those of her own lifetime. She thought of the picture now, and traded its remote sorrows for those of today until she had sincerely forgotten the mother and the father and the little brother of the dead child with whom she was riding up the spring-turning valley, where noon was warming the dust that arose from the graveled highway. It was white dust, and it settled over them in an enriching film, ever so finely. . . .

Jodey Powers had a fantastic scheme that he used to think about for taking and baling tumbleweed and make a salable fuel out of it. First, you'd compress it—probably down at the cotton compress in Roswell—where a loose bale was wheeled in under the great power-drop, and when the nigger at the handle gave her a yank, down came the weight, and packed the bale into a little thing, and then they let the steam exhaust go, and the press sighed once or twice, and just seemed to *lie* there, while the men ran wires through the gratings of the press and tied them tight. Then up came the weight, and out came the bale.

If he did that to enough bales of tumbleweed, he believed he'd get rich. Burn? It burned like a house afire. It had oil in it, somehow, and the thing to do was to get it in shape for use as a fuel. Imagine all the tumbleweed that blew around the State of New Mexico in the fall, and sometimes all winter. In the winter, the weeds were black and brittle. They cracked when they blew against fence posts, and if one lodged there, then another one caught at its thorny lace; and the next time it blew, and the sand came trailing, and the tumbleweeds rolled, they'd pile up at the same fence and build out, locked together against the wires. The wind drew through them, and the sand dropped around them. Soon there was a solid-looking but airy bank of tumbleweeds built right to the top of the fence, in a long windward slope; and the next time the wind blew, and the weeds came, they would roll up the little hill of brittle twigs and leap off the other side of the fence, for all the world like horses taking a jump, and go galloping ahead of the wind across the next pasture on the plains, a black and witchy procession.

If there was an arroyo, they gathered there. They backed up in the miniature canyons of dirt-walled watercourses, which were dry except when it rained hard up in the hills. Out behind the house, the arroyo had filled up with tumbleweeds; and in November, when it blew so hard and so cold, but without bringing any snow, some of the tumbleweeds had climbed out and scattered, and a few had tangled at the back fence, looking like rusted barbed wire. Then there came a few more; all winter the bank grew. Many times he'd planned to get out back there and clear them away, just e-e-ease them off away from the fence posts, so's not to catch the wood up, and then set a match to the whole thing, and in five minutes, have it all cleared off. If he did like one thing, it was a neat place.

How Cleotha laughed at him sometimes when he said that, because she knew that as likely as not he would forget to clear the weeds away. And if he'd said it once he'd said it a thousand times, that he was going to gather up that pile of scrap iron from the front yard, and haul it to Roswell, and sell it—old car parts, and the fenders off a truck that had turned over up on the highway, which he'd salvaged with the aid of the driver.

But the rusting iron was still there, and he had actually come to have a feeling of fondness for it. If someone were to appear one night and silently make off with it, he'd be aroused the next day, and demand to know who had robbed him: for it was dear junk, just through lying around and belonging to him. What was his was part of him, even that heap of fenders that rubbed off on your clothes with a rusty powder, like a caterpillar fur.

But even by thinking hard about all such matters, treading upon the fringe of what had happened yesterday, he was unable to make it all seem long ago, and a matter of custom and even of indifference. There was no getting away from it—if anybody was to blame for the terrible moments of yesterday afternoon, when the wind scattered a few sparks from the chimney of the kitchen stove, why he was.

Jodey Powers never claimed to himself or anybody else that he was any *better* man than another. But everything he knew and hoped for, every reassurance his body had had from other people, and the children he had begotten, had been knowledge to him he was *as good* a man as any.

And of this knowledge he was now bereft.

If he had been alone in his barrenness, he could have solaced himself with heroic stupidities. He could have produced out of himself abominations, with the amplitude of biblical despair. But he wasn't alone; there they sat; there was Buddy beside him, and Clee in back, even the teacher, Arleen—even to her he owed some return of courage.

All he could do was drive the damned car, and keep *thinking* about it.

He wished he could think of something to say, or else that Clee would.

But they continued in silence, and he believed that it was one of his making. . . .

The reverie of Arleen Latcher made her almost ill, from the sad, sweet experiences she had entered into with those people so long ago. How wonderful it was to have such a rich life, just looking up things!—And the most wonderful thing of all was that even if they were beautiful, and wore semitransparent garments that fell to the ground in graceful folds, the maidens were all pure. It made her eyes swim to think how innocent they went to their death. Could anything be more beautiful, and reassuring, than this? Far, far better. Far better those hungry lions, than the touch of lustful men. Her breath left her for a moment, and she closed her eyes, and what threatened her with real feeling—the presence of the Powers family in the faded blue sedan climbing through the valley sunlight toward the turn-off that led to the mountain road—was gone. Life's breath on her cheek was not so close. Oh, others had suffered. She could suffer.

"All that pass by clap their hands at thee: they hiss and wag their heads at the daughter of Jerusalem—"

This image made her wince, as if she herself had been hissed and wagged at. Everything she knew made it possible for her to see herself as a proud and threatened virgin of Bible times, which were more real to her than many of the years she had lived through. Yet must not Jerusalem have sat in country like this with its sandy hills, the frosty stars that were so bright at night, the simple Mexicans riding their burros as if to the Holy Gates? We often do not see our very selves, she would reflect, gazing ardently at the unreal creature which the name Arleen brought to life in her mind.

On her cheeks there had appeared two islands of color, as if she had a fever. What she strove to save by her anguished retreats into the memories of the last days of the Roman Empire was surely crumbling away from her. She said to herself that she must not give way to it, and that she was just wrought up; the fact that she really *didn't* feel anything—in fact, it was a pity that she *couldn't* take that little Mrs. Powers in her arms, and comfort her, just *let* her go ahead and cry, and see if it wouldn't probably help some. But Miss Latcher was aware that she felt nothing that related to the Powers family and their trouble.

Anxiously she searched her heart again, and wooed back the sacrifice of the tribe of heavenly Arleens marching so certainly toward the lions. But they did not answer her call to mind, and she folded her cloth-gloved hands and pressed them together, and begged of herself that she might think of some way to comfort Mrs. Powers; for if she could do that, it might fill her own empty heart until it became a cup that would run over......

Cleotha knew Buddy wanted her to see him; but though her heart turned toward him, as it always must, no matter what he asked of her, she was this time afraid to do it because if she ever lost the serenity of her sight now she might never recover it this day; and the heaviest trouble was still before her.

So she contented herself with Buddy's look as it reached her from the side of her eye. She glimpsed his head and neck, like a young cat's, the wide bones behind the ears, and the smooth but visible cords of his nape, a sight of him that always made her want to laugh because it was so pathetic. When she caressed him she often fondled those strenuous hollows behind his ears. Heaven only knew, she would think, what went on within the shell of that topknot! She would pray between her words and feelings that those unseen thoughts in the boy's head were ones that would never trouble him. She was often amazed at things in him which she recognized as being like herself; and at those of Buddy's qualities which came from some alien source, she suffered pangs of doubt and fear. He was so young to be a stranger to her!

The car went around the curve that hugged the rocky fall of a hill; and on the other side of it, a green quilt of alfalfa lay sparkling darkly in the light. Beyond that, to the right of the road, the land leveled out, and on a sort of platform of swept earth stood a two-room hut of adobe. It had a few stones cemented against the near corner, to give it strength. Clee had seen it a hundred times—the place where that old man Melendez lived, and where his wife had died a few years ago. He was said to be simpleminded and claimed he was a hundred years old. In the past, riding by here, she had more or less delicately made a point of looking the other way. It often distressed her to think of such a helpless old man, too feeble to do anything but crawl out when the sun was bright and the wall was warm, and sit there, with his milky gaze resting on the hills he had known since he was born, and had never left. Somebody came to feed him once a day, and see if he was clean enough to keep his health. As long as she could remember, there'd been some kind of dog at the house. The old man had sons and grandsons and great-grandsons—you might say a whole orchard of them, sprung from this one tree that was dying, but that still held a handful of green days in its ancient veins.

Before the car had quite gone by, she had seen him. The sun was bright, and the wall must have been warm, warm enough to give his shoulders and back a reflection of the heat which was all he could feel. He sat there on his weathered board bench, his hands on his branch of apple tree that was smooth and shiny from use as a cane. His house door was open, and a deep tunnel of shade lay within the sagged box of the opening. Cleotha leaned forward to see him, as if to look at him were one of her duties today. She saw his jaw moving up and down, not chewing, but just opening and closing. In the wind and flash of the car going by, she could not hear him; but from his closed eyes, and his moving mouth, and the way his head was raised, she wouldn't have been surprised if she had heard him singing. He was singing some thread of song, and it made her smile to imagine what kind of noise it made, a wisp of voice.

She was perplexed by a feeling of joyful fullness in her breast, at the sight of the very same old witless sire from whom in the past she had turned away her eyes out of delicacy and disgust.

The last thing she saw as they went by was his dog, who came around the corner of the house with a caracole. He was a mongrel puppy, partly hound—a comedian by nature. He came prancing outrageously up to the old man's knees, and invited his responses, which he did not get. But as if his master were as great a wag as he, he hurled himself backward, pretending to throw himself recklessly into pieces. Everything on him flopped and was flung by his idiotic energy. It was easy to imagine, watching the puppy-fool, that the sunlight had entered him as it had entered the old man. Cleotha was reached by the hilarity of the hound, and when he tripped over himself and plowed the ground with his flapping jowls, she wanted to laugh out loud.

But they were past the place, and she winked back the merriment in her eyes, and she knew that it was something she could never have told the others about. What it stood for, in her, they would come to know in other ways, as she loved them. . . .

Jodey was glad of one thing. He had telephoned from Hondo last night, and everything was to be ready at Weed. They would drive right up the hill to the family burial ground. They wouldn't have to wait for anything. He was glad, too, that the wind wasn't blowing. It always made his heart sink when the wind rose on the plains and began to change the sky with the color of dust.

Yesterday: it was all he could see, however hard he was *thinking* about everything else.

He'd been on his horse, coming back down the pasture that rose up behind the house across the arroyo, nothing particular in mind—except to make a joke with himself about how far along the peaches would get before the frost killed them all, *snap*, in a single night, like that—when he saw the column of smoke rising from the tumbleweeds by the fence. Now who could've lighted them, he reflected, following the black smoke up on its billows into the sky. There was just enough wind idling across the long front of the hill to bend the smoke and trail it away at an angle, toward the blue.

The hillside, the fire, the wind, the column of smoke.

Oh my God! And the next minute he was tearing down the hill as fast as his horse could take him, and the fire—he could see the flames now—the fire was like a bank of yellow rags blowing violently and torn in the air, rag after rag tearing up from the ground. Cleotha was there, and in a moment, so was he, but they were too late. The baby was unconscious. They took her up and hurried to the house, the back way where the screen door was standing open with its spring trailing on the ground. When they got inside where it seemed so dark and cool, they held the child between them fearing to lay her down. They called for Buddy, but he was still at school up the road, and would not be home until the orange school bus stopped by their mailbox out front at the highway after four o'clock. The fire poured in cracking tumult through the weeds. In ten minutes they were only little airy lifts of ash off the ground. Everything was black. There were three fence posts still afire; the wires were hot. The child was dead. They let her down on their large bed.

He could remember every word Clee had said to him. They were not many, and they shamed him, in his heart, because he couldn't say a thing. He comforted her, and held her while she wept. But if he had spoken then, or now, riding in the car, all he could have talked about was the image of the blowing rags of yellow fire, and blue, blue, plaster blue behind and above, sky and mountains. But he believed that she knew why he seemed so short with her. He hoped earnestly that she knew. He might just be wrong. She might be blaming him, and keeping so still because it was more proper, now, to *be* still than full of reproaches.

But of the future, he was entirely uncertain; and he drove, and came to the turn-off, and they started winding in back among the sandhills that lifted them toward the rocky slopes of the mountains. Up and up they went; the air was so clear and thin that they felt transported, and across the valleys that dropped between the grand shoulders of the pine-haired slopes, the air looked as if it were blue breath from the trees. . . .

Cleotha was blinded by a dazzling light in the distance, ahead of them, on the road.

It was a ball of diamond-brilliant light.

It danced, and shook, and quivered above the road far, far ahead. It seemed to be traveling between the pine trees on either side of the road, and somewhat above the road, and it was like nothing she had ever seen before. It was the most magic and exquisite thing she had ever seen, and wildly, even hopefully as a child is hopeful when there is a chance and a need for something miraculous to happen, she tried to explain it to herself. It could be a star in the daytime, shaking and quivering and traveling ahead of them, as if to lead them. It was their guide. It was shaped like a small cloud, but it was made of shine, and dazzle, and quiver. She held her breath for fear it should vanish, but it did not, and she wondered if the others in the car were smitten with the glory of it as she was.

It was brighter than the sun, whiter; it challenged the daytime, and obscured everything near it by its blaze of flashing and dancing light.

It was almost as if she had approached perfect innocence through her misery, and were enabled to receive portents that might not be visible to anyone else. She closed her eyes for a moment.

But the road curved, and everything traveling on it took the curve too, and the trembling pool of diamond-light ahead lost its liquid splendor, and turned into the tin signs on the back of a huge oil truck which was toiling over the mountain, trailing its links of chain behind.

When Clee looked again, the star above the road was gone. The road and the angle of the sun to the mountaintop and the two cars climbing upward had lost their harmony to produce the miracle. She saw the red oil truck, and simply saw it, and said to herself that the sun might have reflected off the big tin signs on the back of it. But she didn't believe it, for she was not thinking, but rather dreaming; fearful of awakening. . . .

The high climb up this drive always made Miss Latcher's ears pop, and she had discovered once that to swallow often prevented the disagreeable sensation. So she swallowed. Nothing happened to her ears. But she continued to swallow, and feel her ears with her cloth-covered fingers, but what really troubled her now would not be downed, and it came into her mouth as a taste; she felt giddy—that was the altitude, of course—when they got down the other side, she would be all right.

What it was was perfectly clear to her, for that was part of having an education and a trained mind—the processes of thought often went right on once you started them going.

Below the facts of this small family, in the worst trouble it had ever known, lay the fact of envy in Arleen's breast.

It made her head swim to realize this. But she envied them their entanglement with one another, and the dues they paid each other in the humility of the duty they were performing on this ride, to the family burial ground at Weed. Here she sat riding with them, to come along and be of help to them, and she was no help. She was unable to swallow the lump of desire that rose in her throat, for life's uses, even such bitter ones as that of the Powers family today. It had been filling her gradually, all the way over on the trip, this feeling of jealousy and degradation.

Now it choked her and she knew she had tried too hard to put from her the thing that threatened her, which was the touch of life through anybody else. She said to herself that she must keep control of herself.

But Buddy turned around again, just then, slowly, as if he were a young male cat who just happened to be turning around to see what he could see, and he looked at his mother with his large eyes, so like his father's: pale petal-blue, with drops of light like the centers of cats' eyes, and dark lashes. He had a solemn look, when he saw his mother's face, and he prayed her silently to acknowledge him. If she didn't, why, he was still alone. He would never again feel safe about running off to the highway to watch the scrapers work, or the huge Diesel oil tankers go by, or the cars with strange license plates—of which he had already counted thirty-two different kinds, his collection, as he called it. So if she didn't see him, why, what might he find when he came back home at times like those, when he went off for a little while just to play?

They were climbing down the other side of the ridge now. In a few minutes they would be riding into Weed. The sights as they approached were like images of awakening to Cleotha. Her heart began to hurt when she saw them. She recognized the tall iron smokestack of the sawmill. It showed above the trees down on the slope ahead of them. There was a stone house which had been abandoned even when she was a girl at home here, and its windows and doors standing open always seemed to her to depict a face with an expression of dismay. The car dropped farther down—they were making that last long curve of the road to the left— and now the town stood visible, with the sunlight resting on so many of the unpainted houses and turning their weathered gray to a dark silver. Surely they must be ready for them, these houses: all had been talked over by now. They could all mention that they knew Cleotha as a little girl.

She lifted her head.

There were claims upon her.

Buddy was looking at her soberly, trying to predict to himself how she would *be*. He was ready to echo with his own small face whatever her face would show him.

Miss Latcher was watching the two of them. Her heart was racing in her breast.

The car slowed up. Now Cleotha could not look out the windows at the wandering earthen street, and the places alongside it. They would have to drive right through town, to the hillside on the other side.

"Mumma?" asked the boy softly.

Cleotha winked both her eyes at him, and smiled, and leaned toward him a trifle.

And then he blushed, his eyes swam with happiness, and he smiled back at her, and his face poured forth such radiance that Miss Latcher took one look at him, and with a choke, burst into tears.

She wept into her hands, her gloves were moistened, her square shoulders rose to her ears, and she was overwhelmed by what the mother had been able to do for the boy. She shook her head and made long gasping sobs. Her sense of betrayal was not lessened by the awareness that she was weeping for herself.

Cleotha leaned across to her, and took her hand, and murmured to her. She comforted her, gently.

"Hush, honey, you'll be all right. Don't you cry now. Don't you think about us. We're almost there, and it'll soon be over. God knows you were mighty sweet to come along and be with us. Hush, now, Arleen, you'll have Buddy crying too."

But the boy was simply watching the teacher, in whom the person he knew so well every day in school had broken up, leaving an unfamiliar likeness. It was like seeing a reflection in a pond, and then throwing a stone in. The reflection disappeared in ripples of something else.

Arleen could not stop.

The sound of her 'ooping made Jodey furious. He looked into the rear-view mirror and saw his wife patting her and comforting her. Cleotha looked so white and strained that he was frightened, and he said out, without turning around: "Arleen, you cut that out, you shut up, now. I won't have you wearin' down Cleo, God damn it, you quit it!"

But this rage, which arose from a sense of justice, made Arleen feel guiltier than ever; and she laid her head against the car window, and her sobs drummed her brow bitterly on the glass.

"Hush," whispered Cleotha, but she could do no more, for they were arriving at the hillside, and the car was coming to a stop. They must awaken from this journey, and come out onto the ground, and begin to toil their way up the yellow hill, where the people were waiting. Over the ground grew yellow grass that was turning to green. It was like velvet, showing dark or light, according to the breeze and the golden afternoon sunlight. It was a generous hill, curving easily and gradually as it rose. Beyond it was only the sky, for the mountains faced it from behind the road. It was called Schoolhouse Hill, and at one time, the whole thing had belonged to Cleotha's father; and before there was any schoolhouse crowning its noble swell of earth, the departed members of his family had been buried halfway up the gentle climb.

Jodey helped her out of the car, and he tried to talk to her with his holding fingers. He felt her trembling, and she shook her head at him. Then she began to walk up there, slowly. He leaned into the car and took the covered box in his arms, and followed her. Miss Latcher was out of the car on her side, hiding from them, her back turned, while she used her handkerchief and positively clenched herself back into control of her thoughts and sobs. When she saw that they weren't waiting for her, she hurried, and in humility, reached for Buddy's hand to hold it for him as they walked. He let her have it, and he marched, watching his father, whose hair was blowing in the wind and sunshine. From behind, Jodey looked like just a kid. . . .

And now for Cleotha her visions on the journey appeared to have some value, and for a little while longer, when she needed it most, the sense of being in blind communion with life was granted her, at the little grave-side where all those kind friends were gathered on the slow slope up of the hill on the summit of which was the schoolhouse of her girlhood.

It was afternoon, and they were all kneeling toward the upward rise, and Judge Crittenden was reading the prayer book.

Everything left them but a sense of their worship, in the present.

And a boy, a late scholar, is coming down the hill from the school, the sunlight edging him; and his wonder at what the people kneeling there are doing is, to Cleotha, the most memorable thing she is to look upon today; for she has resumed the life of her infant daughter, whom they are burying, and on whose behalf, something rejoices in life anyway, as if to ask the mother whether love itself is not ever-living. And she watches the boy come discreetly down the hill, trying to keep away from them, but large-eyed with a hunger *to know* which claims all acts of life, for him, and for those who will be with him later; and his respectful curiosity about those kneeling mourners, the edge of sunlight along him as he walks away from the sun and down the hill, is of all those things she saw and rejoiced in, the most beautiful; and at that, her breast is full, with the heaviness of a baby at it, and not for grief alone, but for praise.

"I believe, I believe!" her heart cries out in her, as if she were holding the peach stone of her eager girlhood in her woman's hand.

She puts her face into her hands, and weeps, and they all move closer to her. Familiar as it is, the spirit has had a new discovery. . . .

Jodey then felt that she had returned to them all; and he stopped seeing, and just remembered, what happened yesterday; and his love for his wife was confirmed as something he would never be able to measure for himself or prove to her in words.

# JOHN STEINBECK

## *The Leader of the People*

ON SATURDAY AFTERNOON Billy Buck, the ranch-hand, raked together the last of the old year's haystack and pitched small forkfuls over the wire fence to a few mildly interested cattle. High in the air small clouds like puffs of cannon smoke were driven eastward by the March wind. The wind could be heard whishing in the brush on the ridge crests, but no breath of it penetrated down into the ranch-cup.

The little boy, Jody, emerged from the house eating a thick piece of buttered bread. He saw Billy working on the last of the haystack. Jody tramped down scuffing his shoes in a way he had been told was destructive to good shoe-leather. A flock of white pigeons flew out of the black cypress tree as Jody passed, and circled the tree and landed again. A half-grown tortoise-shell cat leaped from the bunkhouse porch, galloped on stiff legs across the road, whirled and galloped back again. Jody picked up a stone to help the game along, but he was too late, for the cat was under the porch before the stone could be discharged. He threw the stone into the cypress tree and started the white pigeons on another whirling flight.

Arriving at the used-up haystack, the boy leaned against the barbed wire fence. "Will that be all of it, do you think?" he asked.

The middle-aged ranch-hand stopped his careful raking and stuck his fork into the ground. He took off his black hat and smoothed down his hair. "Nothing left of it that isn't soggy from ground moisture," he said. He replaced his hat and rubbed his dry leathery hands together.

"Ought to be plenty mice," Jody suggested.

"Lousy with them," said Billy. "Just crawling with mice."

"Well, maybe, when you get all through, I could call the dogs and hunt the mice."

"Sure, I guess you could," said Billy Buck. He lifted a forkful of the damp ground-hay and threw it into the air. Instantly three mice leaped out and burrowed frantically under the hay again.

Jody sighed with satisfaction. Those plump, sleek, arrogant mice were doomed. For eight months they had lived and multiplied in the haystack. They had been immune from cats, from traps, from poison and from Jody. They had grown smug in their security, overbearing and fat. Now the time of disaster had come; they would not survive another day.

Billy looked up at the top of the hills that surrounded the ranch. "Maybe you better ask your father before you do it," he suggested.

"Well, where is he? I'll ask him now."

"He rode up to the ridge ranch after dinner. He'll be back pretty soon."

Jody slumped against the fence post. "I don't think he'd care."

As Billy went back to his work he said ominously, "You better ask him anyway. You know how he is."

Jody did know. His father, Carl Tiflin, insisted upon giving permission for anything that was done on the ranch, whether it was important or not. Jody sagged farther against the post until he was sitting on the ground. He looked up at the little puffs of wind-driven cloud. "Is it like to rain, Billy?"

"It might. The wind's good for it, but not strong enough."

"Well, I hope it don't rain until after I kill those damn mice." He looked over his shoulder to see whether Billy had noticed the mature profanity. Billy worked on without comment.

Jody turned back and looked at the side-hill where the road from the outside world came down. The hill was washed with lean March sunshine. Silver thistles, blue lupins and a few poppies bloomed among the sage bushes. Halfway up the hill Jody could see Doubletree Mutt, the black dog, digging in a squirrel hole. He paddled for a while and then paused to kick bursts of dirt out between his hind legs, and he dug with an earnestness which belied the knowledge he must have had that no dog had ever caught a squirrel by digging in a hole.

Suddenly, while Jody watched, the black dog stiffened, and backed out of the hole and looked up the hill toward the cleft in the ridge where the road came through. Jody looked up too. For a moment Carl Tiflin on horseback stood out against the pale sky and then he moved down the road toward the house. He carried something white in his hand.

The boy started to his feet. "He's got a letter," Jody cried. He trotted away toward the ranch house, for the letter would probably be read aloud and he wanted to be there. He reached the house before his father did, and ran in. He heard Carl dismount from his creaking saddle and slap the horse on the side to send it to the barn where Billy would unsaddle it and turn it out.

Jody ran into the kitchen. "We got a letter!" he cried.

His mother looked up from a pan of beans. "Who has?"

"Father has. I saw it in his hand."

Carl strode into the kitchen then, and Jody's mother asked, "Who's the letter from, Carl?"

He frowned quickly. "How did you know there was a letter?"

She nodded her head in the boy's direction. "Big-Britches Jody told me."

Jody was embarrassed.

His father looked down at him contemptuously. "He is getting to be a Big-Britches," Carl said. "He's minding everybody's business but his own. Got his big nose into everything."

Mrs. Tiflin relented a little. "Well, he hasn't enough to keep him busy. Who's the letter from?"

Carl still frowned on Jody. "I'll keep him busy if he isn't careful." He held out a sealed letter. "I guess it's from your father."

Mrs. Tiflin took a hairpin from her head and slit open the flap. Her lips pursed judiciously. Jody saw her eyes snap back and forth over the lines. "He says," she translated, "he says he's going to drive out Saturday to stay for a little while. Why, this is Saturday. The letter must have been delayed." She looked at the postmark. "This was mailed day before yesterday. It should have been here yesterday." She looked up questioningly at her husband, and then her face darkened angrily. "Now what have you got that look on you for? He doesn't come often."

Carl turned his eyes away from her anger. He could be stern with her most of the time, but when occasionally her temper arose, he could not combat it.

"What's the matter with you?" she demanded again.

In his explanation there was a tone of apology Jody himself might have used. "It's just that he talks," Carl said lamely. "Just talks."

"Well, what of it? You talk yourself."

"Sure I do. But your father only talks about one thing."

"Indians!" Jody broke in excitedly. "Indians and crossing the plains!"

Carl turned fiercely on him. "You get out, Mr. Big-Britches! Go on, now! Get out!"

Jody went miserably out the back door and closed the screen with elaborate quietness. Under the kitchen window his shamed, downcast eyes fell upon a curiously shaped stone, a stone of such fascination that he squatted down and picked it up and turned it over in his hands.

The voices came clearly to him through the open kitchen window. "Jody's damn well right," he heard his father say. "Just Indians and crossing the plains. I've heard that story about how the horses got driven off about a thousand times. He just goes on and on, and he never changes a word in the things he tells."

When Mrs. Tiflin answered her tone was so changed that Jody, outside the window, looked up from his study of the stone. Her voice had become soft and explanatory. Jody knew how her face would have changed to match the tone. She said quietly, "Look at it this way, Carl. That was the big thing in my father's life. He led a wagon train clear across the plains to the coast, and when it was finished, his life was done. It was a big thing to do, but it didn't last long enough. Look!" she continued, "it's as though he was born to do that, and after he finished it, there wasn't anything more for him to do but think about it and talk about it. If there'd been any farther west to go, he'd have gone. He's told me so himself. But at last there was the ocean. He lives right by the ocean where he had to stop."

She had caught Carl, caught him and entangled him in her soft tone.

"I've seen him," he agreed quietly. "He goes down and stares off west over the ocean." His voice sharpened a little. "And then he goes up to the Horseshoe Club in Pacific Grove, and he tells people how the Indians drove off the horses."

She tried to catch him again. "Well, it's everything to him. You might be patient with him and pretend to listen."

Carl turned impatiently away. "Well, if it gets too bad, I can always go down to the bunkhouse and sit with Billy," he said irritably. He walked through the house and slammed the front door after him.

Jody ran to his chores. He dumped the grain to the chickens without chasing any of them. He gathered the eggs from the nests. He trotted into the house with the wood and interlaced it so carefully in the wood-box that two armloads seemed to fill it to overflowing.

His mother had finished the beans by now. She stirred up the fire and brushed off the stove-top with a turkey wing. Jody peered cautiously at her to see whether any rancor toward him remained. "Is he coming to-day?" Jody asked.

"That's what his letter said."

"Maybe I better walk up the road to meet him."

Mrs. Tiflin clanged the stove-lid shut. "That would be nice." she said. "He'd probably like to be met."

"I guess I'll just do it then."

Outside, Jody whistled shrilly to the dogs. "Come on up the hill," he commanded. The two dogs waved their tails and ran ahead. Along the roadside the sage had tender new tips. Jody tore off some pieces and rubbed them on his hands until the air was filled with the sharp wild smell. With a rush the dogs leaped from the road and yapped into the brush after a rabbit. That was the last Jody saw of them, for when they failed to catch the rabbit, they went back home.

Jody plodded on up the hill toward the ridge top. When he reached the little cleft where the road came through, the afternoon wind struck him and blew up his hair and ruffled his shirt. He looked down on the little hills and ridges below and then out at the huge green Salinas Valley. He could see the white town of Salinas far out in the flat and the flash of its windows under the waning sun. Directly below him, in an oak tree, a crow congress had convened. The tree was black with crows all cawing at once.

Then Jody's eyes followed the wagon road down from the ridge where he stood, and lost it behind a hill, and picked it up again on the other side. On that distant stretch he saw a cart slowly pulled by a bay horse. It disappeared behind the hill. Jody sat down on the ground and watched the place where the cart would reappear again. The wind sang on the hilltops and the puff-ball clouds hurried eastward.

Then the cart came into sight and stopped. A man dressed in black dismounted from the seat and walked to the horse's head. Although it was so far away, Jody knew he had unhooked the check-rein, for the horse's head dropped forward. The horse moved on, and the man walked slowly up the hill beside it. Jody gave a glad cry and ran down the road toward them. The squirrels bumped along off the road, and a road-runner flirted its tail and raced over the edge of the hill and sailed out like a glider.

Jody tried to leap into the middle of his shadow at every step. A stone rolled under his foot and he went down. Around a little bend he raced, and there, a short distance ahead, were his grandfather and the cart. The boy dropped from his unseemly running and approached at a dignified walk.

The horse plodded stumble-footedly up the hill and the old man walked beside it. In the lowering sun their giant shadows flickered darkly behind them. The grandfather was dressed in a black broadcloth suit and he wore kid congress gaiters and a black tie on a short, hard collar. He carried his black slouch hat in his hand. His white beard was cropped close and his white eyebrows overhung his eyes like moustaches. The blue eyes were sternly merry. About the whole face and figure there was a granite dignity, so that every motion seemed an impossible thing. Once at rest, it seemed the old man would be stone, would never move again. His steps were slow and certain. Once made, no step could ever be retraced; once headed in a direction, the path would never bend nor the pace increase nor slow.

When Jody appeared around the bend, Grandfather waved his hat slowly in welcome, and he called, "Why, Jody! Come down to meet me, have you?"

Jody sidled near and turned and matched his step to the old man's step and stiffened his body and dragged his heels a little. "Yes, sir," he said. "We got your letter only today."

"Should have been here yesterday," said Grandfather. "It certainly should. How are all the folks?"

"They're fine, sir." He hesitated and then suggested shyly, "Would you like to come on a mouse hunt tommorow, sir?"

"Mouse hunt, Jody?" Grandfather chuckled. "Have the people of this generation come down to hunting mice? They aren't very strong, the new people, but I hardly thought mice would be game for them."

"No, sir. It's just play. The haystack's gone. I'm going to drive out the mice to the dogs. And you can watch, or even beat the hay a little."

The stern, merry eyes turned down on him. "I see. You don't eat them, then. You haven't come to that yet."

Jody explained, "The dogs eat them, sir. It wouldn't be much like hunting Indians, I guess."

"No, not much—but then later, when the troops were hunting Indians and shooting children and burning teepees, it wasn't much different from your mouse hunt."

They topped the rise and started down into the ranch cup, and they lost the sun from their shoulders. "You've grown," Grandfather said. "Nearly an inch, I should say."

"More," Jody boasted. "Where they mark me on the door, I'm up more than an inch since Thanksgiving even."

Grandfather's rich throaty voice said, "Maybe you're getting too much water and turning to pitch and stalk. Wait until you head out, and then we'll see."

Jody looked quickly into the old man's face to see whether his feelings should be hurt, but there was no will to injure, no punishing nor putting-in-your-place light in the keen blue eyes. "We might kill a pig," Jody suggested.

"Oh, no! I couldn't let you do that. You're just humoring me. It isn't the time and you know it."

"You know Riley, the big boar, sir?"

"Yes. I remember Riley well."

"Well, Riley ate a hole into that same haystack, and it fell down on him and smothered him."

"Pigs do that when they can," said Grandfather.

"Riley was a nice pig, for a boar, sir. I rode him sometimes, and he didn't mind."

A door slammed at the house below them, and they saw Jody's mother standing on the porch waving her apron in welcome. And they saw Carl Tiflin walking up from the barn to be at the house for the arrival.

The sun had disappeared from the hills by now. The blue smoke from the house chimney hung in flat layers in the purpling ranch-cup. The puff-ball clouds, dropped by the falling wind, hung listlessly in the sky.

Billy Buck came out of the bunkhouse and flung a wash basin of soapy water on the ground. He had been shaving in mid-week, for Billy held Grandfather in reverence, and Grandfather said that Billy was one of the few men of the new generation who had not gone soft. Although Billy was in middle age, Grandfather considered him a boy. Now Billy was hurrying toward the house too.

When Jody and Grandfather arrived, the three were waiting for them in front of the yard gate.

Carl said, "Hello, sir. We've been looking for you."

Mrs. Tiflin kissed Grandfather on the side of his beard, and stood still while his big hand patted her shoulder. Billy shook hands solemnly, grinning under his straw moustache. "I'll put up your horse," said Billy, and he led the rig away.

Grandfather watched him go, and then, turning back to the group, he said as he had a hundred times before, "There's a good boy. I knew his father, old Mule-tail Buck. I never knew why they called him Mule-tail except he packed mules."

Mrs. Tiflin turned and led the way into the house. "How long are you going to stay, Father? Your letter didn't say."

"Well, I don't know. I thought I'd stay about two weeks. But I never stay as long as I think I'm going to."

In a short while they were sitting at the white oilcloth table eating their supper. The lamp with the tin reflector hung over the table. Outside the dining-room windows the big moths battered softly against the glass.

Grandfather cut his steak into tiny pieces and chewed slowly. "I'm hungry," he said. "Driving out here got my appetite up. It's like when we were crossing. We all got so hungry every night we could hardly wait to let the meat get done. I could eat about five pounds of buffalo meat every night."

"It's moving around does it," said Billy. My father was a government packer. I helped him when I was a kid. Just the two of us could about clean up a deer's ham."

"I knew your father, Billy," said Grandfather. "A fine man he was. They called him Mule-tail Buck. I don't know why except he packed mules."

"That was it," Billy agreed. "He packed mules."

Grandfather put down his knife and fork and looked around the table. "I remember one time we ran out of meat—" His voice dropped to a curious low sing-song, dropped into a tonal groove the story had worn for itself. "There was no buffalo, no antelope, not even rabbits. The hunters couldn't even shoot a coyote. That was the time for the leader to be on the watch. I was the leader, and I kept my eyes open. Know why? Well, just the minute the people began to get hungry, they'd start slaughtering the team oxen. Do you believe that? I've heard of parties that just ate up their draft cattle. Started from the middle and worked toward the ends. Finally they'd eat the lead pair, and then the wheelers. The leader of a party had to keep them from doing that."

In some manner a big moth got into the room and circled the hanging kerosene lamp. Billy got up and tried to clap it between his hands. Carl struck with a cupped palm and caught the moth and broke it. He walked to the window and dropped it out.

"As I was saying," Grandfather began again, but Carl interrupted him. "You'd better eat some more meat. All the rest of us are ready for our pudding."

Jody saw a flash of anger in his mother's eyes. Grandfather picked up his knife and fork. "I'm pretty hungry, all right," he said. "I'll tell you about that later."

When supper was over, when the family and Billy Buck sat in front of the fireplace in the other room, Jody anxiously watched Grandfather. He saw the signs he knew. The bearded head leaned forward; the eyes lost their sternness and looked wonderingly into the fire; the big lean fingers laced themselves on the black knees. "I wonder," he began, "I just wonder whether I ever told you how those thieving Piutes drove off thirty-five of our horses."

"I think you did," Carl interrupted. "Wasn't it just before you went up into the Tahoe country?"

Grandfather turned quickly toward his son-in-law. "That's right. I guess I must have told you that story."

"Lots of times," Carl said cruelly, and he avoided his wife's eyes. But he felt the angry eyes on him, and he said, " 'Course I'd like to hear it again."

Grandfather looked back at the fire. His fingers unlaced and laced again. Jody knew how he felt, how his insides were collapsed and empty. Hadn't Jody been called a Big-Britches that very afternoon? He arose to heroism and opened himself to the term Big-Britches again. "Tell about Indians," he said softly.

Grandfather's eyes grew stern again. "Boys always want to hear about Indians. It was a job for men, but boys want to hear about it. Well, let's see. Did I ever tell you how I wanted each wagon to carry a long iron plate?"

Everyone but Jody remained silent. Jody said, "No. You didn't."

"Well, when the Indians attacked, we always put the wagons in a circle and fought from between the wheels. I thought that if every wagon carried a long plate with rifle holes, the men could stand the plates on the outside of the wheels when the wagons were in the circle and they would be protected. It would save lives and that would make up for the extra weight of the iron. But of course the party wouldn't do it. No party had done it before and they couldn't see why they should go to the expense. They lived to regret it, too."

Jody looked at his mother, and knew from her expression that she was not listening at all. Carl picked at a callus on his thumb and Billy Buck watched a spider crawling up the wall.

Grandfather's tone dropped into its narrative groove again. Jody knew in advance exactly what words would fall. The story droned on, speeded up for the attack, grew sad over the wounds, struck a dirge at the burials on the great plains. Jody sat quietly watching Grandfather. The stern blue eyes were detached. He looked as though he were not very interested in the story himself.

When it was finished, when the pause had been politely respected as the frontier of the story, Billy Buck stood up and stretched and hitched his trousers. "I guess I'll turn in," he said. Then he faced Grandfather.

"I've got an old powder horn and a cap and ball pistol down to the bunk-house. Did I ever show them to you?"

Grandfather nodded slowly. "Yes, I think you did, Billy. Reminds me of a pistol I had when I was leading the people across. Billy stood politely until the little story was done, and then he said, "Good night," and went out of the house.

Carl Tiflin tried to turn the conversation then. "How's the country between here and Monterey? I've heard it's pretty dry."

"It is dry," said Grandfather. "There's not a drop of water in the Laguna Seca. But it's a long pull from '87. The whole country was powder then, and in '61 I believe all the coyotes starved to death. We had fifteen inches of rain this year."

"Yes, but it all came too early. We could do with some now." Carl's eye fell on Jody. "Hadn't you better be getting to bed?"

Jody stood up obediently. "Can I kill the mice in the old haystack, sir?"

"Mice? Oh! Sure, kill them all off. Billy said there isn't any good hay left."

Jody exchanged a secret and satisfying look with Grandfather. "I'll kill every one tomorrow," he promised.

Jody lay in his bed and thought of the impossible world of Indians and buffaloes, a world that had ceased to be forever. He wished he could have been living in the heroic time, but he knew he was not of heroic timber. No one living now, save possibly Billy Buck, was worthy to do the things that had been done. A race of giants had lived then, fearless men, men of a staunchness unknown in this day. Jody thought of the wide plains and of the wagons moving across like centipedes. He thought of Grandfather on a huge white horse, marshaling the people. Across his mind marched the great phantoms, and they marched off the earth and they were gone.

He came back to the ranch for a moment, then. He heard the dull rush-ing sound that space and silence make. He heard one of the dogs, out in the doghouse, scratching a flea and bumping his elbow against the floor with every stroke. Then the wind arose again and the black cypress groaned and Jody went to sleep.

He was up half an hour before the triangle sounded for breakfast. His mother was rattling the stove to make the flames roar when Jody went through the kitchen. "You're up early," she said. "Where are you going?"

"Out to get a good stick. We're going to kill the mice today."

"Who is 'we'?"

"Why, Grandfather and I."

"So you've got him in it. You always like to have someone in with you in case there's blame to share."

"I'll be right back," said Jody. "I just want to have a good stick ready for after breakfast."

He closed the screen door after him and went out into the cool blue morning. The birds were noisy in the dawn and the ranch cats came down from the hill like blunt snakes. They had been hunting gophers in the dark, and although the four cats were full of gopher meat, they sat in a semi-circle at the back door and mewed piteously for milk. Double-tree Mutt and Smasher moved sniffling along the edge of the brush, performing the duty with rigid ceremony, but when Jody whistled, their heads jerked up and their tails waved. They plunged down to him, wriggling their skins and yawning. Jody patted their heads seriously, and moved on to the weathered scrap pile. He selected an old broom handle and a short piece of inch-square scrap wood. From his pocket he took a shoelace and tied the ends of the sticks loosely together to make a flail. He whistled his new weapon through the air and struck the ground experimentally, while the dogs leaped aside and whined with apprehension.

Jody turned and started down past the house toward the old haystack ground to look over the field of slaughter, but Billy Buck, sitting patiently on the back steps, called to him, "You better come back. It's only a couple of minutes till breakfast."

Jody changed his course and moved toward the house. He leaned his flail against the steps. "That's to drive the mice out," he said. "I'll bet they're fat. I'll bet they don't know what's going to happen to them today."

"No, nor you either," Billy remarked philosophically, "nor me, nor anyone."

Jody was staggered by this thought. He knew it was true. His imagination twitched away from the mouse hunt. Then his mother came out on the back porch and struck the triangle, and all thoughts fell in a heap.

Grandfather hadn't appeared at the table when they sat down. Billy nodded at his empty chair. "He's all right? He isn't sick?"

"He takes a long time to dress," said Mrs. Tiflin. "He combs his whiskers and rubs up his shoes and brushes his clothes."

Carl scattered sugar on his mush. "A man that's led a wagon train across the plains has got to be pretty careful how he dresses."

Mrs. Tiflin turned on him. "Don't do that, Carl! Please don't!" There was more of threat than of request in her tone. And the threat irritated Carl.

"Well, how many times do I have to listen to the story of the iron plates, and the thirty-five horses? That time's done. Why can't he forget it, now it's done?" He grew angrier while he talked, and his voice rose. "Why does he have to tell them over and over? He came across the plains. All right! Now it's finished. Nobody wants to hear about it over and over."

The door into the kitchen closed softly. The four at the table sat frozen. Carl laid his mush spoon on the table and touched his chin with his fingers.

Then the kitchen door opened and Grandfather walked in. His mouth smiled tightly and his eyes were squinted. "Good morning," he said, and he sat down and looked at his mush dish.

Carl could not leave it there. "Did—did you hear what I said?"

Grandfather jerked a little nod.

"I don't know what got into me, sir. I didn't mean it. I was just being funny."

Jody glanced in shame at his mother, and he saw that she was looking at Carl, and that she wasn't breathing. It was an awful thing that he was doing. He was tearing himself to pieces to talk like that. It was a terrible thing to him to retract a word, but to retract it in shame was infinitely worse.

Grandfather looked sidewise. "I'm trying to get right side up," he said gently. "I'm not being mad. I don't mind what you said, but it might be true, and I would mind that."

"It isn't true," said Carl. "I'm not feeling well this morning. I'm sorry I said it."

"Don't be sorry, Carl. An old man doesn't see things sometimes. Maybe you're right. The crossing is finished. Maybe it should be forgotten, now it's done."

Carl got up from the table. "I've had enough to eat. I'm going to work. Take your time, Billy!" He walked quickly out of the dining-room. Billy gulped the rest of his food and followed soon after. But Jody could not leave his chair.

"Won't you tell any more stories?" Jody asked.

"Why, sure I'll tell them, but only when—I'm sure people want to hear them."

"I like to hear them, sir."

"Oh! Of course you do, but you're a little boy. It was a job for men, but only little boys like to hear about it."

Jody got up from his place. "I'll wait outside for you, sir. I've got a good stick for those mice."

He waited by the gate until the old man came out on the porch. "Let's go down and kill the mice now," Jody called.

"I think I'll just sit in the sun, Jody. You go kill the mice."

"You can use my stick if you like."

"No, I'll just sit here a while."

Jody turned disconsolately away, and walked down toward the old haystack. He tried to whip up his enthusiasm with thoughts of the fat juicy mice. He beat the ground with his flail. The dogs coaxed and whined about him, but he could not go. Back at the house he could see Grandfather sitting on the porch, looking small and thin and black.

Jody gave up and went to sit on the steps at the old man's feet.

"Back already? Did you kill the mice?"

"No, sir. I'll kill them some other day."

The morning flies buzzed close to the ground and the ants dashed about in front of the steps. The heavy smell of sage slipped down the hill. The porch boards grew warm in the sunshine.

Jody hardly knew when Grandfather started to talk. "I shouldn't stay here, feeling the way I do." He examined his strong old hands. "I feel as though the crossing wasn't worth doing." His eyes moved up the side-hill and stopped on a motionless hawk perched on a dead limb. "I tell those old stories, but they're not what I want to tell. I only know how I want people to feel when I tell them.

"It wasn't Indians that were important, nor adventures, nor even getting out here. It was a whole bunch of people made into one big crawling beast. And I was the head. It was westering and westering. Every man wanted something for himself, but the big beast that was all of them wanted only westering. I was the leader, but if I hadn't been there, someone else would have been the head. The thing had to have a head.

"Under the little bushes the shadows were black at white noonday. When we saw the mountains at last, we cried—all of us. But it wasn't getting here that mattered, it was movement and westering.

"We carried life out here and set it down the way those ants carry eggs. And I was the leader. The westering was as big as God, and the slow steps that made the movement piled up and piled up until the continent was crossed.

"Then we came down to the sea, and it was done." He stopped and wiped his eyes until the rims were red. "That's what I should be telling instead of stories."

When Jody spoke, Grandfather started and looked down at him. "Maybe I could lead the people some day," Jody said.

The old man smiled. "There's no place to go. There's the ocean to stop you. There's a line of old men along the shore hating the ocean because it stopped them."

"In boats I might, sir."

"No place to go, Jody. Every place is taken. But that's not the worst—no, not the worst. Westering has died out of the people. Westering isn't a hunger any more. It's all done. Your father is right. It is finished." He laced his fingers on his knee and looked at them.

Jody felt very sad. "If you'd like a glass of lemonade I could make it for you."

Grandfather was about to refuse, and then he saw Jody's face. "That would be nice," he said. "Yes, it would be nice to drink a lemonade."

Jody ran into the kitchen where his mother was wiping the last of the breakfast dishes. "Can I have a lemon to make a lemonade for Grandfather?"

His mother mimicked—"And another lemon to make a lemonade for you."

"No, ma'am. I don't want one."

"Jody! You're sick!" Then she stopped suddenly. "Take a lemon out of the cooler," she said softly. "Here, I'll reach the squeezer down to you."

# FURTHER READING

COLLECTIONS OF SHORT STORIES BY INDIVIDUAL AUTHORS

Willa Cather  *Obscure Destinies* (New York: Alfred A. Knopf, Inc., 1932).

Walter Van Tilburg Clark  *The Watchful Gods and Other Stories* (New York: Random House, Inc., 1950).

H. L. Davis  *Team Bells Woke Me* (New York: William Morrow and Company, Inc., 1953).

Vardis Fisher  *Love and Death, The Complete Stories* (New York: Doubleday & Company, Inc., 1959).

A. B. Guthrie  *Mountain Medicine* (and other stories) (New York: Pocket Books, Inc., 1961).

Bret Harte  *The Outcasts of Poker Flat and Other Tales* (New York: New American Library, 1961).

Paul Horgan  *The Peach Stone; Stories from Four Decades* (New York: Farrar, Straus and Giroux, 1967).

Dorothy M. Johnson  *Indian Country* (New York: Ballantine Books, 1953).

Jack London  *The Call of the Wild and Selected Stories* (New York: The New American Library, 1960).

Frederick Manfred  *Apples of Paradise and Other Stories* (New York: Trident Press, 1968).

Katherine Anne Porter  *Flowering Judas* (New York: Harcourt, Brace and Company, 1935).

Jack Schaefer  *The Collected Stories of Jack Schaefer* (Boston: Houghton Mifflin Co., 1966).

Wallace Stegner
*The City of the Living and Other Stories* (Boston: Houghton Mifflin Co., 1956).
*A Shooting Star* (New York: The Viking Press, Inc., 1961).
*Women on the Wall* (New York: The Viking Press, 1962).

John Steinbeck
*The Long Valley* (New York: The Viking Press, 1938).

ANTHOLOGIES

*El Espejo (The Mirror): Selected Mexican-American Literature.* Edited by Octavio Ignacio Romano-V (Berkeley, Calif.: Quinto Sol Publications, Inc., 1969).

   This anthology consists primarily of short stories but also includes a number of poems and a scenario for a screen play. One author is from Mexico and the others are from Texas, New Mexico, Arizona, and California. A number of the selections are in Spanish, some of which have English translations.

*Great Tales of the American West.* Edited by Harry E. Maule (New York: The Modern Library, Inc., 1945).

   There are 18 stories in this collection, mainly dealing with prospectors, cowboys, Indians, and outlaws.

*Great Western Short Stories.* Edited by J. Golden Taylor (Palo Alto: The American West Publishing Company, 1967).

   This collection has 30 stories, three in each of the following 10 categories:
   Indians
   Mountain Men and Troopers
   Treasure Seekers and Tricksters
   Entrepreneurs and Gamblers
   Outlaws and Lawmen
   Cowboys and Horsemen
   Ranchers and Homesteaders
   Farmers and Townspeople
   Hunters and Hunted
   Contemporary Westerners
   It also contains an introduction by Wallace Stegner on the western short story: "History, Myth, and the Western Writer."

# FOUR

## Poetry

THIS SECTION IS unofficially divided into four parts. First there is the work of three earlier poets: Harte's ironic humor from the gold camps of California, and the romantic, nostalgic poems of Miller and Whitman.

The second group includes poets of very considerable stature who have written primarily in the first half of the twentieth century. Jeffers is without any doubt the greatest poet who has lived and written in the West. Davis and Ferril have created significant evocations of life in, primarily, Oregon and Colorado. Though Frost was born in San Francisco, he, as well as Cummings and MacLeish, are Easterners who have used western history, scenes and themes in some of their poems.

There are samples of the writing of five contemporary poets from New Mexico, Minnesota, and California. They represent in their work a wide range of concerns: nature, history, legend, social conscience, sexuality, psychology.

Concluding this section are two essays about western poetry. Morton L. Ross describes Alan Swallow's efforts over thirty years to identify what is western in western poetry. The other essay analyzes the poetry of a prominent contemporary West Coast poet, William Stafford.

# BRET HARTE

## *Plain Language from Truthful James*

WHICH I WISH to remark,
    And my language is plain,
That for ways that are dark
    And for tricks that are vain,
The heathen Chinee is peculiar,
    Which the same I would rise to explain

Ah Sin was his name;
    And I shall not deny,
In regard to the same,
    What the name might imply;
But his smile it was pensive and child-like,
    As I frequent remarked to Bill Nye.

It was August the third,
    And quite soft was the skies;
Which it might be inferred
    That Ah Sin was likewise;
Yet he played it that day upon William
    And me in a way I despise.

Which we had a small game,
    And Ah Sin took a hand:
It was Euchre. The same
    He did not understand;
But he smiled as he sat by the table,
    With the smile that was child-like and bland.

Yet the cards they were stocked
    In the way that I grieve,
And my feelings were shocked
    At the state of Nye's sleeve,
Which was stuffed full of aces and bowers,
    And the same with intent to deceive.

But the hands that were played
    By that heathen Chinee,
And the points that he made,

*Published in* OVERLAND MONTHLY, *September, 1870.*

Were quite frightful to see,—
Till at last he put down a right bower,
    Which was the same Nye had dealt unto me.

Then I looked up at Nye
    And he gazed upon me;
And he rose with a sigh,
    And said, "Can this be?
We are ruined by Chinese cheap labor,"—
    And he went for that heathen Chinee.

In the scene that ensued
    I did not take a hand,
But the floor it was strewed
    Like the leaves on the strand
With the cards that Ah Sin had been hiding,
    In the game "he did not understand."

In his sleeves, which were long,
    He had twenty-four packs,—
Which was coming it strong,
    Yet I state but the facts;
And we found on his nails, which were taper,
    What is frequent in tapers,—that's wax.

Which is why I remark,
    And my language is plain,
That for ways that are dark
    And for tricks that are vain,
The heathen Chinee is peculiar,—
    Which the same I am free to maintain.


# JOAQUIN MILLER

## *The Missouri*

WHERE RANGED THEY, black-maned woolly bulls
    By millions, fat and unafraid;
Where gold, unclaimed in cradlefuls,
    Slept 'mid the grass roots, gorge, and glade;
Where peaks companioned with the stars,

And propped the blue with shining white.
With massive silver beams and bars,
    With copper bastions, height on height—
There was thou born, O lord of strength!
O yellow lion, leap and length
Of arm from out an Arctic chine
To far, fair Mexic seas are thine!

What colors? Copper, silver, gold
    With sudden sweep and fury blent,
Enwound, unwound, inrolled, unrolled,
    Mad molder of the continent!
What whirlpools and what choking cries
    From out the concave swirl and sweep
As when some god cries out and dies
    Ten fathoms down thy tawny deep!
Yet on, right on, no time for death,
No time to gasp a second breath!
You plow a pathway through the main
To Morro's castle, Cuba's plain.
Hoar sire of hot, sweet Cuban seas,
    Gray father of the continent,
Fierce fashioner of destinies,
    Of states thou has upreared or rent,
Thou know'st no limit; seas turn back,
    Bent, broken from the shaggy shore;
But thou, in thy resistless track,
    Art lord and master evermore.
Missouri, surge and sing and sweep!
Missouri, master of the deep,
From snow-reared Rockies to the sea
Sweep on, sweep on eternally!


# WALT WHITMAN

## *Pioneers! O Pioneers!*


COME MY tan-faced children,
    Follow well in order, get your weapons ready,
Have you your pistols? have you your sharp-edged axes?
    Pioneers! O pioneers!

     For we cannot tarry here,
We must march my darlings, we must bear the brunt of danger,
We the youthful sinewy races, all the rest on us depend,
         Pioneers! O pioneers!

     O you youths, Western youths,
So impatient, full of action, full of manly pride and friendship,
Plain I see you Western youths, see you tramping with the foremost,
         Pioneers! O pioneers!

     Have the elder races halted?
Do they droop and end their lesson, wearied over there beyond the seas?
We take up the task eternal, and the burden and the lesson,
         Pioneers! O pioneers!

     All the past we leave behind,
We debouch upon a newer mightier world, varied world,
Fresh and strong the world we seize, world of labor and the march,
         Pioneers! O pioneers!

     We detachments steady throwing,
Down the edges, through the passes, up the mountains steep,
Conquering, holding, daring, venturing as we go the unknown ways,
         Pioneers! O pioneers!

     We primeval forests felling,
We the rivers stemming, vexing we and piercing deep the mines within,
We the surface broad surveying, we the virgin soil upheaving,
         Pioneers! O pioneers!

     Colorado men are we,
From the peaks gigantic, from the great sierras and the high plateaus,
From the mine and from the gully, from the hunting trail we come,
         Pioneers! O pioneers!

     From Nebraska, from Arkansas,
Central inland race are we, from Missouri, with the continental blood
   intervein'd,
All the hands of comrades clasping, all the Southern, all the Northern,
         Pioneers! O pioneers!

     O resistless restless race!
O beloved race in all! O my breast aches with tender love for all!
O I mourn and yet exult, I am rapt with love for all,
         Pioneers! O pioneers!

Raise the mighty mother mistress,
Waving high the delicate mistress, over all the starry mistress, (bend your
    heads all,)
Raise the fang'd and warlike mistress, stern, impassive, weapon'd mistress,
        Pioneers! O pioneers!

See my children, resolute children,
By those swarms upon our rear we must never yield or falter,
Ages back in ghostly millions frowning there behind us urging,
        Pioneers! O pioneers!

On and on the compact ranks,
With accessions ever waiting, with the places of the dead quickly fill'd,
Through the battle, through defeat, moving yet and never stopping,
        Pioneers! O pioneers!

O to die advancing on!
Are there some of us to droop and die? has the hour come?
Then upon the march we fittest die, soon and sure the gap is fill'd,
        Pioneers! O pioneers!

All the pulses of the world,
Falling in they beat for us, with the Western movement beat,
Holding single or together, steady moving to the front, all for us,
        Pioneers! O pioneers!

Life's involv'd and varied pageants,
All the forms and shows, all the workmen at their work,
All the seamen and the landsmen, all the masters with their slaves,
        Pioneers! O pioneers!

All the hapless silent lovers,
All the prisoners in the prisons, all the righteous and the wicked,
All the joyous, all the sorrowing, all the living, all the dying,
        Pioneers! O pioneers!

I too with my soul and body,
We, a curious trio, picking, wandering on our way,
Through these shores amid the shadows, with the apparitions pressing,
        Pioneers! O pioneers!

Lo, the darting bowling orb!
Lo, the brother orbs around, all the clustering suns and planets,
All the dazzling days, all the mystic nights with dreams,
        Pioneers! O pioneers!

These are of us, they are with us,
All for primal needed work, while the followers there in embryo wait
   behind,
We to-day's procession heading, we the route for travel clearing,
     Pioneers! O pioneers!


     O you daughters of the West!
O you young and elder daughters! O you mothers and you wives!
Never must you be divided, in our ranks you move united,
     Pioneers! O pioneers!


     Minstrels latent on the prairies!
(Shrouded bards of other lands, you may rest, you have done your work,)
Soon I hear you coming warbling, soon you rise and tramp amid us,
     Pioneers! O pioneers!


     Not for delectations sweet,
Not the cushion and the slipper, not the peaceful and the studious,
Not the riches safe and palling, not for us the tame enjoyment,
     Pioneers! O pioneers!


     Do the feasters gluttonous feast?
Do the corpulent sleepers sleep? have they lock'd and bolted doors?
Still be ours the diet hard, and the blanket on the ground,
     Pioneers! O pioneers!


     Has the night descended?
Was the road of late so toilsome? did we stop discouraged nodding on our
   way?
Yet a passing hour I yield you in your tracks to pause oblivious,
     Pioneers! O pioneers!


     Till with sound of trumpet,
Far, far off the daybreak call—hark! how loud and clear I hear it wind,
Swift! to the head of the army!—swift! spring to your places,
     Pioneers! O pioneers!

# ROBINSON JEFFERS

## *Boats in a Fog*

SPORTS AND GALLANTRIES, the stage, the arts, the antics of dancers,
The exuberant voices of music,
Have charm for children but lack nobility; it is bitter earnestness
That makes beauty; the mind
Knows, grown adult.
   A sudden fog-drift muffled the ocean,
A throbbing of engines moved in it,
At length, a stone's throw out, between the rocks and the vapor,
One by one moved shadows
Out of the mystery, shadows, fishing-boats, trailing each other,
Following the cliff for guidance,
Holding a difficult path between the peril of the sea-fog
And the foam on the shore granite.
One by one, trailing their leader, six crept by me,
Out of the vapor and into it,
The throb of their engines subdued by the fog, patient and cautious.
Coasting all round the peninsula
Back to the buoys in Monterey harbor. A flight of pelicans
Is nothing lovelier to look at;
The flight of the planets is nothing nobler; all the arts lose virtue
Against the essential reality
Of creatures going about their business among the equally
Earnest elements of nature.

## *Shine, Perishing Republic*

WHILE THIS AMERICA settles in the mold of its vulgarity, heavily thickening to empire,
And protest, only a bubble in the molten mass, pops and sighs out, and the mass hardens,

I sadly smiling remember that the flower fades to make fruit, the fruit rots to make earth.

---

Out of the mother; and through the spring exultances, ripeness and decadence; and home to the mother.

You making haste haste on decay: not blameworthy; life is good, be it
stubbornly long or suddenly
A mortal splendor: meteors are not needed less than mountains: shine,
perishing republic.

But for my children, I would have them keep their distance from the
thickening center; corruption
Never has been compulsory, when the cities lie at the monster's feet there
are left the mountains.

And boys, be in nothing so moderate as in love of man, a clever servant,
insufferable master.
There is the trap that catches noblest spirits, that caught—they say—God,
when he walked on earth.

## Hurt Hawks

### I

THE BROKEN PILLAR of the wing jags from the clotted shoulder,
The wing trails like a banner in defeat,
No more to use the sky forever but live with famine
And pain a few days: cat nor coyote
Will shorten the week of waiting for death, there is game without talons.
He stands under the oak-bush and waits
The lame feet of salvation; at night he remembers freedom
And flies in a dream, the dawns ruin it.
He is strong and pain is worse to the strong, incapacity is worse.
The curs of the day come and torment him
At distance, no one but death the redeemer will humble that head,
The intrepid readiness, the terrible eyes.
The wild God of the world is sometimes merciful to those
That ask mercy, not often to the arrogant.
You do not know him, you communal people, or you have forgotten him;
Intemperate and savage, the hawk remembers him;
Beautiful and wild, the hawks, and men that are dying, remember him.

I'd sooner, except the penalties, kill a man than a hawk; but the great
  redtail
Had nothing left but unable misery
From the bone too shattered for mending, the wing that trailed under his
  talons when he moved.
We had fed him six weeks, I gave him freedom,
He wandered over the foreland hill and returned in the evening, asking
  for death,
Not like a beggar, still eyed with the old
Implacable arrogance. I gave him the lead gift in the twilight. What fell
  was relaxed,
Owl-downy, soft feminine feathers; but what
Soared: the fierce rush: the night-herons by the flooded river cried fear
  at its rising
Before it was quite unsheathed from reality.


## *Tor House*


IF YOU SHOULD LOOK for this place after a handful of lifetimes:
  Perhaps of my planted forest a few
May stand yet, dark-leaved Australians or the coast cypress, haggard
With storm-drift; but fire and the axe are devils.
Look for foundations of sea-worn granite, my fingers had the art
To make stone love stone, you will find some remnant.
But if you should look in your idleness after ten thousand years:
It is the granite knoll on the granite
And lava tongue in the midst of the bay, by the mouth of the Carmel
River-valley, these four will remain
In the change of names. You will know it by the wild sea-fragrance of
  wind
Though the ocean may have climbed or retired a little;
You will know it by the valley inland that our sun and our moon were
  born from
Before the poles changed; and Orion in December
Evenings was strung in the throat of the valley like a lamp-lighted bridge.
Come in the morning you will see white gulls
Weaving a dance over blue water, the wane of the moon
Their dance-companion, a ghost walking

By daylight, but wider and whiter than any bird in the world.
My ghost you needn't look for; it is probably
Here, but a dark one, deep in the granite, not dancing on wind
With the mad wings and the day moon.

# ARCHIBALD MACLEISH

## *Wildwest*[1]

THERE WERE NONE of my blood in this battle:
There were Minneconjous, San Arcs, Brules,
Many nations of Sioux: they were few men galloping.
This would have been in the long days in June:
They were galloping well deployed under the plum-trees:
They were driving riderless horses: themselves they were few.

Crazy Horse had done it with few numbers.
Crazy Horse was small for a Lakota.
He was riding always alone thinking of something:

He was standing alone by the picket lines by the ropes:
He was young then, he was thirty when he died:
Unless there were children to talk he took no notice.

When the soldiers came for him there on the other side
On the Greasy Grass in the villages we were shouting
"Hoka Hey! Crazy Horse will be riding!"

They fought in the water: horses and men were drowning:
They rode on the butte: dust settled in sunlight:
Hoka Hey! they lay on the bloody ground.

No one could tell of the dead which man was Custer . . .
That was the end of his luck: by that river.
The soldiers beat him at Slim Buttes once:

[1] Black Elk's memories of Crazy Horse recorded by Neihardt.

---

*"Wildwest"* is reprinted from COLLECTED POEMS 1917–1952
*by Archibald MacLeish with the permission of
Houghton Mifflin Company, publisher.*

They beat him at Willow Creek when the snow lifted:
The last time they beat him was the Tongue.
He had only the meat he had made and of that little.

Do you ask why he should fight? It was his country:
My God should he not fight? It was his.
But after the Tongue there were no herds to be hunting:

He cut the knots of the tails and he led them in:
He cried out "I am Crazy Horse! Do not touch me!"
There were many soldiers between and the gun glinting . . .

And a Mister Josiah Perham of Maine had much of the
land Mister Perham was building the Northern Pacific
railroad that is Mister Perham was saying at lunch that

forty say fifty millions of acres in gift and
government grant outright ought to be worth a
wide price on the Board at two-fifty and

later a Mister Cooke had relieved Mister Perham and
later a Mister Morgan relieved Mister Cooke:
Mister Morgan converted at prices current:

It was all prices to them: they never looked at it:
why should they look at the land? they were Empire Builders:
it was all in the bid and the asked and the ink on their books . . .

When Crazy Horse was there by the Black Hills
His heart would be big with the love he had for that country
And all the game he had seen and the mares he had ridden

And how it went out from you wide and clean in the sunlight


## Burying Ground by the Ties

AYEE! AI! This is heavy earth on our shoulders:
There were none of us born to be buried in this earth:
Niggers we were, Portuguese, Magyars, Polacks:

---

*"Burying Ground by the Ties" is reprinted from* COLLECTED
POEMS 1917–1952 *by Archibald MacLeish with the
permission of Houghton Mifflin Company, publisher.*

We were born to another look of the sky certainly.
Now we lie here in the river pastures:
We lie in the mowings under the thick turf:

We hear the earth and the all-day rasp of the grasshoppers.
It was we laid the steel to this land from ocean to ocean:
It was we (if you know) put the U.P. through the passes

Bringing her down into Laramie full load,
Eighteen mile on the granite anticlinal,
Forty-three foot to the mile and the grade holding:

It was we did it: hunkies of our kind.
It was we dug the caved-in holes for the cold water:
It was we built the gully spurs and the freight sidings:

Who would do it but we and the Irishmen bossing us?
It was all foreign-born men there were in this country:
It was Scotsmen, Englishmen, Chinese, Squareheads, Austrians . . .

Ayee! but there's weight to the earth under it.
Not for this did we come out—to be lying here
Nameless under the ties in the clay cuts:

There's nothing good in the world but the rich will buy it:
Everything sticks to the grease of a gold note—
Even a continent—even a new sky!

Do not pity us much for the strange grass over us:
We laid the steel to the stone stock of these mountains:
The place of our graves is marked by the telegraph poles!

It was not to lie in the bottoms we came out
And the trains going over us here in the dry hollows . . .

# Empire Builders

THE MUSEUM ATTENDANT:

This is *The Making of America in Five Panels:*

This is Mister Harriman making America:
Mister-Harriman-is-buying-the-Union-Pacific-at-Seventy:
The Santa Fe is shining on his hair.

This is Commodore Vanderbilt making America:
Mister-Vanderbilt-is-eliminating-the-short-interest-in-Hudson:
Observe the carving on the rocking chair.

This is J. P. Morgan making America:
(The Tennessee Coal is behind to the left of the Steel Company.)
Those in mauve are braces he is wearing.

This is Mister Mellon making America:
Mister-Mellon-is-represented-as-a-symbolical-figure-in-aluminum-
Strewing-bank-stocks-on-a-burnished-stair.

This is the Bruce is the Barton making America:
Mister-Barton-is-selling-us-Doctor's-Deliciousest-Dentifrice.
This is he in beige with the canary.

You have just beheld the Makers making America:
This is The Making of America in Five Panels:
America lies to the west-southwest of the switch-tower:
There is nothing to see of America but land.

THE ORIGINAL DOCUMENT
UNDER THE PANEL PAINT:

"To Thos. Jefferson Esq. his obd't serv't
M. Lewis: captain: detached:
                                        Sir:

Having in mind your repeated commands in this matter,
And the worst half of it done and the streams mapped,

---

*"Empire Builders"* is reprinted from COLLECTED POEMS 1917–1952
by Archibald MacLeish with the permission of
Houghton Mifflin Company, publisher.

And we here on the back of this beach beholding the
Other ocean—two years gone and the cold

Breaking with rain for the third spring since St. Louis,
The crows at the fishbones on the frozen dunes,

The first cranes going over from south north,
And the river down by a mark of the pole since the morning,

And time near to return, and a ship (Spanish)
Lying in for the salmon: and fearing chance or the

Drought or the Sioux should deprive you of these discoveries—
Therefore we send by sea in this writing.

                                               Above the
Platte there were long plains and a clay country:
Rim of the sky far off, grass under it,

Dung for the cook fires by the sulphur licks.
After that there were low hills and the sycamores,

And we poled up by the Great Bend in the skiffs:
The honey bees left us after the Osage River:

The wind was west in the evenings, and no dew and the
Morning Star larger and whiter than usual—

The winter rattling in the brittle haws.
The second year there was sage and the quail calling.

All that valley is good land by the river:
Three thousand miles and the clay cliffs and

Rue and beargrass by the water banks
And many birds and the brant going over and tracks of

Bear, elk, wolves, marten: the buffalo
Numberless so that the cloud of their dust covers them:

The antelope fording the fall creeks, and the mountains and
Grazing lands and the meadow lands and the ground

Sweet and open and well-drained.
                                 We advise you to
Settle troops at the forks and to issue licenses:

Many men will have living on these lands.
There is wealth in the earth for them all and the wood standing

And wild birds on the water where they sleep.
There is stone in the hills for the towns of a great people . . ."

You have just beheld the Makers Making America:

They screwed her scrawny and gaunt with their seven-year panics:
They bought her back on their mortgages old-whore-cheap:

They fattened their bonds at her breasts till the thin blood ran from
     them.
Men have forgotten how full clear and deep
The Yellowstone moved on the gravel and the grass grew
When the land lay waiting for her westward people!

# E. E. CUMMINGS

## *Buffalo Bill's*

BUFFALO BILL'S
           defunct
                    who used to
                    ride a watersmooth-silver
                                              stallion
              and break onetwothreefourfive pigeonsjustlikethat
                                                               Jesus
              he was a handsome man
                                    and what i want to know is
              how do you like your blueeyed boy
              Mister Death

---

# ROBERT FROST

## Once by the Pacific

THE SHATTERED WATER made a misty din.
Great waves looked over others coming in,
And thought of doing something to the shore
That water never did to land before.
The clouds were low and hairy in the skies,
Like locks blown forward in the gleam of eyes.
You could not tell, and yet it looked as if
The shore was lucky in being backed by cliff,
The cliff in being backed by continent;
It looked as if a night of dark intent
Was coming, and not only a night, an age.
Someone had better be prepared for rage.
There would be more than ocean-water broken
Before God's last *Put out the Light* was spoken.

## Desert Places

SNOW FALLING and night falling fast, oh, fast
In a field I looked into going past,
And the ground almost covered smooth in snow,
But a few weeds and stubble showing last.

The woods around it have it—it is theirs.
All animals are smothered in their lairs.
I am too absent-spirited to count;
The loneliness includes me unawares.

And lonely as it is, that loneliness
Will be more lonely ere it will be less—
A blanker whiteness of benighted snow
With no expression, nothing to express.

They cannot scare me with their empty spaces
Between stars—on stars where no human race is.
I have it in me so much nearer home
To scare myself with my own desert places.


# H. L. DAVIS

## *The Valley Harvest*


H**ONEY IN THE HORN**! I brought my horse from the water
And from the white grove of tall alders over the spring,
And brought him past a row of high hollyhocks
Which flew and tore their flowers thin as his mane.
And women there watched, with hair blown over their mouths;
Yet in watching the oat field they were quiet as the spring.

"Are the hollyhocks full bloomed? It is harvest then.
The hay falls like sand falling in a high wind
When the weeds blow and fly—but steady the sand falls.
It is harvest, harvest, and honey in the horn.
I would like to go out, in a few days, through the stubble field,
And to all the springs—yours too we have known for years—
And to the bearing vines, and clean the berries from them."

Call, women!—why do you stand if not for your pride's sake?

But the women would neither call to me nor speak,
Nor to any man not mowing during their harvest.
They watched with their hair blowing, near the stalks,
In the row of red hollyhocks.
                          Quiet as the spring.
What is by the spring? A bird, and a few old leaves.

---

# Baking Bread

RED BERRIES are on the bent stalks: these turn to the sky
That might be a pond of water. Geese come all day
In long squadrons which make no shadow, to the wild grass,
Silver-poplar leaf foxing in the frozen stalks,
A white blaze in this old garden, what poplar grove
Was that where the three women worked baking bread?
Where they began at morning, by their fire under the wet boughs
And laid the loaves in the sun?
                          So one of these women came
From the bread-board, and a little into the grass,
And braided her dark hair again with cold hands.
One came loaded with dead wood close to the fire
And leaned, pulling her dress tight at the breast, to warm.
One was laying out loaves—two women at the fire.
I saw between them the leaves start along the wind's lane.
And heard leaves like spray on the white trees, and saw the stems,
And low branches, which break in winter, bend and draw down.
Boughs drew between our eyes and the fire, eldest daughter.
That the blaze blew apart like leaves. She said: "Wind again,
To chill us, and to shake leaf-water over our bread.
This is our third month: and what have we to show
When the men brag that they have cleared so much ground?
The bread even tastes bitter of the poplar stems
That blow wild; look, this is spray from the river
On my hands and hair; the fire is blown out.
I am tired of cold and wind, and wild geese, and this field,
And of trimming fire and hair to suit the wind."

And said: "We'll have a house, and pleasure, when the grain's in,
And when all this has lost me the use of my pride."
And like river waves, heavy across the frozen beach,
The hair was heavy which her hands lifted; and her mouth
Had no color; and there was spray upon her face.
By now surely that woman is either old—
Or dead, more likely. Yet in pity of her pride
The mind stirs uneasy, as if she this day
Stood by the field's edge braiding her hair, and gazed
At the fire in wind, under wet poplar boughs.

---

"Baking Bread" originally appeared in POETRY.
© 1920 by The Modern Poetry Association. Reprinted by
permission of the editor of POETRY.

# The Rain-Crow

WHILE WOMEN WERE still talking near this dead friend,
I came out into a field where evergreen berry vines
Grew over an old fence, with rain on their leaves;
And would not have thought of her death, except for a few
Low sheltered berry leaves: I believed the rain
Could not reach them; but it rained on them every one.
So when we thought this friend safest and most kind,
Resetting young plants against winter, it was she
Must come to be a dead body. And to think
That she knew so much, and not that she would die!
Not that most simple thing—for her hands, or her eyes.

Dead. There were prints in the soft spaded ground
Which her knees made when she dug her tender plants.
Above the berry leaves the black garden and all the land
Steamed with rain like a winded horse, appeared strong.
And the rain-crow's voice, which we took for a sign of rain,
Began like a little bell striking in the leaves.
So I sat in the rain listening to this bird's voice,
And thought that our friend's mouth now, its "Dead, I am dead,"
Was like the rain-crow sounding during the rain:
And if rain were a thing none of us had ever seen.


# THOMAS HORNSBY FERRIL

## Time of Mountains

SO LONG AGO my father led me to
The dark impounded orders of this canyon,
I have confused these rocks and water with

---

My life, but not unclearly, for I know
What will be here when I am here no more.

I've moved in the terrible cries of the prisoned water,
And prodigious stillness where the water folds
Its terrible muscles over and under each other.
When you've walked a long time on the floor of a river,
And up the steps and into the different rooms,
You know where the hills are going, you can feel them,
The far blue hills dissolving in luminous water,
The solvent mountains going home to the oceans.
Even when the river is low and clear,
And the waters are going to sleep in the upper swales,
You can feel the particles of the shining mountains
Moping against your ankles toward the sea.

Forever the mountains are coming down and I stalk
Against them, cutting the channel with my shins,
With the lurch of the stiff spray cracking over my thighs;
I feel the bones of my back bracing my body,
And I push uphill behind the vertebrate fish
That lie uphill with their bony brains uphill
Meeting and splitting the mountains coming down.

I push uphill behind the vertebrate fish
That scurry uphill, ages ahead of me.
I stop to rest but the order still keeps moving:
I mark how long it takes an aspen leaf
To float in sight, pass me, and go downstream;
I watch a willow dipping and springing back
Like something that must be a water-clock,
Measuring mine against the end of mountains.

But if I go before these mountains go,
I'm unbewildered by the time of mountains,
I, who have followed life up from the sea
Into a black incision in this planet,
Can bring an end to stone infinitives.
I have held rivers to my eyes like lenses,
And rearranged the mountains at my pleasure,
As one might change the apples in a bowl,
And I have walked a dim unearthly prairie
From which these peaks have not yet blown away.

# Ghost Town

HERE WAS THE GLINT *of the blossom rock,*
*Here Colorado dug the gold*
*For a sealskin vest and a rope of pearl*
*And a garter jewel from Amsterdam*
*And a house of stone with a jig-saw porch*
*Over the hogbacks under the moon*
*Out where the prairies are.*

*Here's where the conifers long ago*
*When there were conifers cried to the lovers:*
    Dig in the earth for gold while you are young!
*Here's where they cut the conifers and ribbed*
*The mines with conifers that sang no more,*
*And here they dug the gold and went away,*
*Here are the empty houses, hollow mountains,*
*Even the rats, the beetles and the cattle*
*That used these houses after they were gone*
*Are gone; the gold is gone,*
*There's nothing here,*
*Only the deep mines crying to be filled.*

*You mines, you yellow throats,*
*You mountainsides of yellow throats*
*Where all the trees are gone,*
*You yellow throats crying canyon chant:*
    Fill what is hollow;
*Crying like thunder going home in summer:*
    Fill what is hollow in the earth;
*Crying deep like old trees long ago:*
    Fill what is hollow now the gold is gone;
*Crying deep like voices of the timbers,*
*Conifers blowing, feathered conifers,*
*Blowing the smell of resin into the rain,*
*Over the afternoons of timber cutters,*
*Over the silver axes long ago,*
*Over the mountains shining wet like whipsaws,*
*Crying like all the wind that goes away:*
    Fill what is hollow,
    Send something down to fill the pits
    Now that the gold is gone;

*Reprinted from* WESTERING *by Thomas Hornsby Ferril.*
*Copyright © 1934 by Yale University Press*

*You mines, you yellow throats,*
*Cry to the hills, be patient with the hills,*
*The hills will come, the houses do not answer.*

*These houses do not answer any cry.*
*I go from door to door, I wait an hour*
*Upon a ledge too high to be a street,*
*Saying from here a man could throw a rock*
*On any roof in town, but I will wait:*
*It's time the people came out of their houses*
*To show each other where the moon is rising;*
*Moon, do you hear the crying of the mines:*
  *Fill what is hollow,*
  *Send down the moonlight?*

*It's time the people kindled evening fires,*
*I'll watch the chimneys, then I will go down;*
*Steeple, why don't you ring a bell?*
*Why don't you ring a mad high silver bell*
*Against the crying of the yellow throats?*
*Wait for me, steeple, I will ring the bell.*
  Pull the rope,
  Drift, stope,
  Pull a fathom of rock
  And a cord of ore
  From the higher place to fill the lower,
  The Rocky Mountains are falling down,
  Go into any house in town,
  You can hear the dark in the kitchen sing,
  The kitchen floor is a bubbling spring,
  The mountains have sealed like the door of a tomb
  The sliding doors to the dining room;
  Then thump your hand on the parlor wall
  And hear the Rocky Mountains fall,
  Feel the plaster ribs and the paper skin
  Of the Rocky Mountains caving in;
  Pull the rope,
  Drift, stope,
  Pull down the birds out of the air,
  Pull down the dust that's floating where
  The conifers blew the resin rain,
  Pull all the mountains down again,
  Pull the steeple down
  And a cord of ore
  To fill the dark
  On the hollow floor.

*I am an animal, I enter houses.*
*Some of the animals have liked this house:*
*The first to come and go were men,*
*Men animals who dreamed of yellow gold,*
*Then small things came and the cattle came.*
*The cattle used this room for many years,*
*The floor is level with the baseboard now,*
*But probably the ants came first*
*Before the people went away;*
*Before the children wore the sill*
*With stepping in and out to die;*
*It may have been an afternoon*
*Before the conifers were dead,*
*An afternoon when the rain had fallen*
*And the children were going back to play.*
*You children going back to play,*
*Did you ask the things the animals can't ask?*
*Did you ask what made the mountains glisten blue?*
*Did you say:* "The great wet mountains shine like whipsaws"?
*Did you say:* "We're here and there's the sun"?
*Did you say:* "The golden mines are playing
Yellow leapfrog down the hills"?
*Did you say:* "Think what it would be like
To be way up on the mountain top
And see how beautiful it is
To be where we are now"?

*The children made this doorstone look*
*Like a whetstone worked too hard in the center,*
*And the ants went out and the wall went out,*
*And the rats went out and the cattle came,*
*But they're gone now, all the animals;*
*If they were here, and all of us together,*
*What could we say about the gold we dug,*
*What could we say about this house we used,*
*What could we say that we could understand?*

*You men and women, builders of these houses,*
*You lovers hearing the conifers at night,*
*You lovers making children for the houses,*
*Did you say to yourselves when reckoning*
*The yield of gold per cord of ore,*
*Running drifts per cord of ore,*
*Stoping per fathom per cord of ore,*
*Filling buckets per cord of ore,*

*Dressing tailings per cord of ore—*
*You lovers making children in these mountains,*
*Did you say something animals can't say?*
*Did you say:* "We know why we built these houses"?
*Did you say:* "We know what the gold is for"?

*I cannot tell: you and the gold are gone,*
*And nearly all the animals are gone;*
*It seems that after animals are gone,*
*The green things come to houses and stay longer;*
*The things with blossoms take an old house down*
*More quietly than wind, more slow than mountains.*
*I say I cannot tell, I am alone,*
*It is too much to the last one here,*
*For now I hear only the yellow throats*
*Of deep mines crying to be filled again*
*Even with little things like bones of birds,*
*But I can hear some of the houses crying:*

   "Which of the animals did use us better?"
*And I can hear the mountains falling down*
*Like thunder going home.*

## Something Starting Over

You DON'T SEE buffalo skulls very much any more
On the Chugwater buttes or down the Cheyenne plains,
And when you roll at twilight over a draw,
With ages in your heart and hills in your eyes,
You can get about as much from a Model-T,
Stripped and forgotten in a sage arroyo,
As you can from asking the blue peaks over and over:
   "Will something old come back again tonight?
   Send something back to tell me what I want."

I do not know how long forever is,
But today is going to be long long ago,
There will be flint to find, and chariot wheels,
And silver saxophones the angels played,

So I ask myself if I can still remember
How a myth began this morning and how the people
Seemed hardly to know that something was starting over.

Oh, I get along all right with the old old times,
I've seen them sifting the ages in Nebraska
On Signal Butte at the head of Kiowa creek.
   (You can drink from the spring where old man Roubadeau
   Had his forge and anvil up in Cedar Valley,
   You can look back down the valley toward Scottsbluff
   And still see dust clouds on the Oregon trail.)
I entered the trench they cut through Signal Butte,
And I pulled a buffalo bone from the eight-foot layer,
And I watched the jasper shards and arrowheads
Bounce in the jigging screen through which fell dust
Of antelope and pieces of the world
To small to have a meaning to the sifters.
One of them said, when I held the bone in my hand:
   "This may turn out to be the oldest bison
In North America," and I could have added:
   "How strange, for this is one of the youngest hands
That ever squeezed a rubber bulb to show
How helium particles shoot through water vapor."
And the dry wind out of Wyoming might have whispered:
   "Today is going to be long long ago."

I know how it smells and feels to sift the ages,
But something is starting over and I say
It's just as beautiful to see the yucca
And cactus blossoms rising out of a Ford
In a sage arroyo on the Chugwater flats,
And pretend you see the carbon dioxide slipping
Into the poverty weed, and pretend you see
The root hairs of the buffalo grass beginning
To suck the vanadium steel of an axle to pieces,
An axle that took somebody somewhere,
To moving picture theaters and banks,
Over the ranges, over the cattle-guards,
Took people to dance-halls and cemeteries—
I like to think of them that way together:
Dance-halls and cemeteries, bodies beginning
To come together in dance-halls where the people
Seem hardly to know that hymns are beginning too;
There's a hymn in the jerk of the sand-hill crawl of the dancers,
And all the gods are shining in their eyes;

Then bodies separating and going alone
Into the tilting uphill cemeteries,
Under the mesas, under the rimrock shadows.

I can look at an axle in a sage arroyo,
And hear them whispering, the back-seat lovers,
The old myth-makers, starting something over.


# WINFIELD TOWNLEY SCOTT

## *The Difference*


THE BUFFALO LOOMED at the far loop of the field:
Though mildly grazing in twilight, a thunderhead tethered.
Spectators—man and two children—some others—
Clutched tickets and kept their distance, regarding the rare beast.

We were—after all—suddenly there—there in the same grass
At the edge of our town: the familiar vacant lot
Usurped by the savage shape which grazed inattentive:
We grew—embarrassed, frightened—into shy invaders.

Staring and silent, we stood back. Though the crickets rang
And the evening star opened low over the western fence
The shadowy field was bisontine; the ground shook—
Once—with the thud of an absent-minded forefoot.

The little girl said to her father "I want to go see him";
But the boy dared not: he watched them hand in hand
Go slowly within the dusk to confront—quite close—
While he stayed alone among strangers—that hunching darkness.

Silhouette now: the buffalo: horned ghost
Of an ancient philosopher, bearded and ominous,
Transmigrated, neither free nor dead. Nothing occurred
To the father and sister. They returned safe. The three went home.

# Year of Drought

THE MAN AND WOMAN neither young nor old
  Walked the hot sand of the river bed.
The man kicked a bone like a giant phallus
Yellow as dirty bees-wax. Then he spoke.
"When the rain comes I will be strong enough
  To know again how to touch you." But the woman
Said nothing; her silent walking seemed a waiting.
Rocks caught fire while cactus shriveled thin
Along the parched route of the afternoon
In light too bright to see by. The man said
"I want you to cut a day off the end of my life
  And a day—and a day—and a day—so many more."
She walked silent with waiting. "Only," he said,
"By my desire can you conceive my deaths.
How can I raise it except if the rain comes?"
He moaned and shivered beneath the angry sun.
They bowed like two that had lost belief in rain
Even under a sky swollen with thunder.


# MAX JORDAN

## Conjugality

IN THE NINTH month
  Through scraggly stands of spruce and pine
Turning aspen and
Ripening chokecherries,
Savoring the astringent fruit
We climbed with packs
In evening
Up the winding gorge

---

To where it opened on
A park-fringed,
Dawn-like lake—
Made to rejuvenate
The Body and the Soul.

Soon at dusk
Reclining against her pack
Beside the steady pitch pine fire
She lay,
Relaxed
In her whole being,
Looking at the lake—
And like the lake—
The very cunt
Of contentment,
Calm with un-need,
Beautiful—
Passionless.

As the moon rose,
I mused, and smiling
Dwelt on silhouetted
Thrusting Long's Peak
Masculinely rising
Above the lake.
And there
In the silvered darkness
I, at thirty-two, replenished
And reflected on the fire—
The irony
Of insatiable fire
In a world of placid water.

## Envy in the Mountains

IN A mountain meadow
Above Santa Fe
I rested against my pack
One spring day at noon,

And looking up
I saw a chickadee,
Just a tiny damned ordinary
Chickadee, restlessly
Moving about beside his mate
On an eighth-inch twig
Of an arbor vitae—
Too preoccupied
To sing.

Suddenly
He mounted her
And flourished delicately but firmly—
And again—and again—and again.
Fascinated,
I began counting the seconds
Between these blissful devotions—
These mini prodigies of passion.
And I can now report
That these performances
Recurred at six- to ten-second
Intervals—
For some time.

Finally preening himself
He burst out in one shrill song,
And then they flew
Flirtingly off together—
But I had lost interest
In the brazen display
Of this miniature
Mountain show-off,
This exhibitionist
In his Edenic bower—
Now bragging
About his potency
On that precarious twig.

# GARY SNYDER

## *Rolling In at Twilight*

Rolling in at twilight—Newport Oregon—
cool of september ocean air, I
saw Phil Whalen with a load of groceries
   walking through a dirt lot full
   of logging trucks, cats
      and skidders
   looking at the ground.
I yelld as the bus wheeld by
   but he kept looking down.
   ten minutes later with my books and pack
      knockt at his door
"Thought you might be on that bus"
      he said, and
   showed me all the food.


## *Marin-An*

sun breaks over the eucalyptus
grove below the wet pasture,
water's about hot,
I sit in the open window
& roll a smoke.
distant dogs bark, a pair of
cawing crows; the twang
of a pygmy nuthatch high in a pine—
from behind the cypress windrow
the mare moves up, grazing.
a soft continuous roar
comes out of the far valley
of the six-lane highway—thousands
and thousands of cars
driving men to work.

# Nooksack Valley

FEBRUARY 1956

AT THE FAR END of a trip north
In a berry-pickers cabin
At the edge of a wide muddy field
Stretching to the woods and cloudy mountains,
Feeding the stove all afternoon with cedar,
watching the dark sky darken, a heron flap by,
A huge setter pup nap on the dusty cot.
High rotten stumps in the second-growth woods
Flat scattered farms in the bend of the Nooksack
River. Steelhead run now
      a week and I go back
Down 99, through towns, to San Francisco
                and Japan.
All America south and east,
Twenty-five years in it brought to a trip-stop
Mind-point, where I turn
Caught more on this land—rock tree and man,
Awake, than ever before, yet ready to leave.
      damned memories,
Whole wasted theories, failures and worse success,
Schools, girls, deals, try to get in
To make this poem a froth, a pity,
A dead fiddle for lost good jobs.
            the cedar walls
Smell of our farm-house, half built in '35.
Clouds sink down the hills
Coffee is hot again. The dog
Turns and turns about, stops and sleeps.

# Milton by Firelight

Piute Creek, August 1955

"O HELL, what do mine eyes
     with grief behold?"
Working with an old

---

*"Nooksack Valley" and "Milton by Firelight" are reprinted
from* RIPRAP *by Gary Snyder by permission of the author.*

Singlejack miner, who can sense
The vein and cleavage
In the very guts of rock, can
Blast granite, build
Switchbacks that last for years
Under the beat of snow, thaw, mule-hooves.
What use, Milton, a silly story
Of our lost general parents,
       eaters of fruit?
The Indian, the chainsaw boy,
And a string of six mules
Came riding down to camp
Hungry for tomatoes and green apples.
Sleeping in saddle-blankets
Under a bright night-sky
Han River slantwise by morning.
Jays squall
Coffee boils

In ten thousand years the Sierras
Will be dry and dead, home of the scorpion.
Ice-scratched slabs and bent trees.
No paradise, no fall,
Only the weathering land
The wheeling sky,
Man, with his Satan
Scouring the chaos of the mind.
Oh Hell!

Fire down
Too dark to read, miles from a road
The bell-mare clangs in the meadow
That packed dirt for a fill-in
Scrambling through loose rocks
On an old trail
All of a summer's day.

# ROBERT BLY

## *A Missouri Traveller Writes Home: 1846*

THE SPRING RIDES DOWN; from Judith and the Larb,
Straining and full, the choked Missouri, choked
With sticks and roots, and high with floating trees
Rides down, as my mind at this oakwood table.
For May unlocks the Crazy Hills
Pouring, as she has done before, the shattered snowfields down
Till the rumbling brown has burned the land away
A hundred feet below the plain
With spoils of snowfields from the Crazy Hills.
Day breaks, and the Pawnees on those cliffs
Above, shouting, keep pace with us;
The warrior trains like rocks against the sky:
At dawn we see the crumbling cliffs at first,
Then horse and rider, then the Western sky;
Those ash-grey horses black against the clouds!
Tall men, high, fierce, with shoulders as if brass
They lift long warbows made by the Dakotahs,
Above their Pawnee shields of black and white;
With cries and howls, all day they shriek on cliffs.
The buffalo, drinking at the shore, in herds
Hear, and shoulders humping, the buffalo stampede
Alarmed, up porch to porch, onto the plains of dust,
And I have heard the buffalo stampede
With muffled clatter of colliding horns.
On the whole, peril hangs above this land
Like smoke that floats at dawn above dead fires.

The Sioux believe all people, scalped or choked,
Are locked out of Paradise, yet I have seen
Small Sioux women hanging from scraggly trees;
On scaffolds stretch the acres of the dead,
Corroding in their sepulchres of air; at night
With cries, the Osage from their teepee doors,
Mourn the dead, cutting their arms, and screaming;
At dawn the buzzard flocks awake on trees, dew-damp,
And stretch their black wings toward the sun to dry.
Such are the few details that I have seen.

The River splits this country, and it seems
We see the Indians always walking Western banks,
Faced toward full sun, like nephews of the sun;
And there are signs of what will come: the whites,
With steel traps hanging, swung from saddle thongs,
Or flat Virginians, behind great round wheels:
All whites believe these Rees and Sioux and Kaws
And Mandans are not men, but damned as beasts:
Are damned; are held knit in damnation now
Like grasp of snakes, in Satan's grasp himself,
And like the serpent's hold, it is by death alone
To be released: The Sioux are still and silent
Generally, and I have watched them stand
By ones and twos upon the river's bank
As glum as Hudson's blankets winding them,
While shuttling steamboats smoke, labouring up
The breaking foam, beyond the cottonwoods,
Into the region of their dead and of their youth,
Pushed up, they say, by smoke; and they believe
The tribe of whites, like smoke, soon shall return
From whence it came: and therefore in both minds
The truth is absent; and the hands alone
Are like the willow trees, forever green
And undeceived: the hands continue killing,
The hands go on, the minds remain behind,
As if the concepts handled by the mind
Were lesser than the concepts of the hands,
As if a man achieves more than he knows;
Or if the pain of action were so great
And life so freezing and Medusa-faced,
That, like Medusa's head, it could be held
And not observed, lest eye's reward be stone.

The night grows old above this river boat.
Before I end, I shall include account
Of an incident tonight that moved my wonder.
At dusk we tied the boat to trees on shore;
No mortal boat in these night shoals can live.
At first I heard a cry: shuffling and cries
And muffled sounds on deckoak overhead
Drew me on deck, the air was chill, and there
I sensed, because these senses here are sharp
And must be, something living and unknown.
To night and North a crowd stared from the boatrail,
Upriver, nightward and North: a speck of white.
The thing was white: the resonance of night

Returned its grunts and whistlings on the air.
The frontier men swore in that river thicket
In ambush like the beasts they're modeled on,
Bristling for war, would be a thresh of Sioux;
The crew and gamblers nudged, to bait the settlers,
And arms nudged cry, "Along the river there's
Some settler's cows, Hereford or Poland China,
Some farmer could not nail tight enough in cribs,
And terrorizing frogs and catfish now."
But Mormons see some robe in that faint white,
In that dim white the angel of death, come
In cottonwoods to sign the Second Coming;
And on the river's border there they see
Some angel of Joseph upon the chill Missouri;
One man believed that there was nothing there,
As the moon too is false, and its white is false.
I sensed a fear, as if the wind protected it.
When the talk died, eight men, and I with them,
Set off, and moving overboard in dark,
With guns, protected by the thunder's noise,
Up the dark river, toward where the splashes rose,
So armed in case of Sioux, to our surprise
We found a white and wounded Northern Bear,
Shot in that day about the snout and head.
The pure-white bear, not native to these parts,
But to the Horns, or Ranges born, and shot
That morning, had turned downward South and East,
And had apparently through these dry plains
Passed South, to lay its burning paws and head
And lay its fever-proud and festered flesh
Within the cool Missouri's turbid bed.
Soon after, clouds of rain drove us indoors,
And lightning fell like sheets upon the sand,
Said to be sudden in these Western lands.
Minutes before it broke, a circling mass
Of split-tail swallows came and then were gone.
But now to bed. We disembark at dawn
And start to westward through the heavy grass.

# Hatred of Men with Black Hair

I HEAR VOICES praising Tshombe, and the Portuguese
In Angola, these are the men who skinned Little Crow!
We are all their sons, skulking
In back rooms, selling nails with trembling hands!

We distrust every person on earth with black hair;
We send teams to overthrow Chief Joseph's government;
We train natives to kill Presidents with blowdarts;
We have men loosening the nails on Noah's ark.

The State Department floats in the heavy jellies near the bottom
Like exhausted crustaceans, like squids who are confused,
Sending out beams of black light to the open sea,
Fighting their fraternal feeling for the great landlords.

We have violet rays that light up the jungles at night, showing
The friendly populations; we are teaching the children of ritual
To overcome their longing for life, and we send
Sparks of black light that fit the holes in the generals' eyes.

Underneath all the cement of the Pentagon
There is a drop of Indian blood preserved in snow:
Preserved from a trail of blood that once led away
From the stockade, over the snow, the trail now lost.

## COMMENTARY BY ROBERT BLY

"A Missouri Traveller Writes Home" was written while I was reading
many Western diaries, biographies of mountain men, and journals of Indian fighters. These restless explorers and settlers came through to me not
as the Americanized free spirits the history books taught me to expect, but
rather Europeans who have suffered some ghastly loss, men shot in the
snout, in Melville's words, "not so much bound to any haven ahead as
rushing from all havens astern."

"Hatred of Men with Black Hair" touches on events a hundred years
and more later: in the 1960's. By that time the United States had become an arrogant and independent nation, and then, abruptly, and to the
astonishment of many of its own citizens, began to commit suicide in Vietnam, a country about which it knew almost nothing. As I watched the

war develop, I thought the link between ourselves and Vietnam was not imperialist aggression, nor fear of communism, nor the military-industrial complex, but the American Indian.

The murder of the Indians by the early settlers and their children has left a wound in the American psyche which refuses to heal. Murder of a race is a deep crime. The Church in the Middle Ages provided ways of atonement—walks to Compostella, fasts, years of silence—to those who had committed crimes. Freud, more recently, noted that atonement was not the natural response to consciousness of crime, and suggested that the following three acts occur in a natural order: a man commits a crime, then he forgets it, then he repeats it. If we make war with Anglo-Saxons, we make moderately intelligent decisions, and give them the Marshall plan later. It is when we deal with the dark-haired people that we act irrationally. The Vietnamese have certain clear resemblances to American Indians: they have dark skins, they seem savage, their religion is alien to us, some of them hardly wear clothes, they refuse to fight like white men, some of them even use bows and arrows. Pilots over Hanoi used to exclaim: "Man, it was just like Custer among the Indians!" Indians came over the Bering Strait, so we know that the Vietnamese and the Chinese are in fact related to them. The war for us goes on in a psychic trance, and since it is a kind of ritual of repetition, no one is allowed to interrupt it. Because the Chinese also have black hair, we will be tempted in fifteen years to wipe them out with nuclear bombs. These were some of the things I was thinking about when I wrote "Hatred of Men with Black Hair." The Little Crow mentioned in the second line was Sioux leader who led the Sioux Rebellion in Minnesota in 1862. Defeated, he retreated into South Dakota. A couple of years later, he returned a few miles into Minnesota, with his young son, picking blueberries. He was surprised and shot by a white farmer, who had no idea of the Indian's identity. When the whites in the area discovered by markings that the body was Little Crow's, they did something interesting: they cut his head off, then skinned the body, and kept the skin; and gave it to the Historical Society.

# N. SCOTT MOMADAY

## Rainy Mountain Cemetery

MOST IS YOUR NAME the name of this dark stone.
 Deranged in death, the mind to be inheres
Forever in the nominal unknown,
The wake of nothing audible he hears
Who listens here and now to hear your name.

The early sun, red as a hunter's moon,
Runs in the plain. The mountain burns and shines;
And silence is the long approach of noon
Upon the shadow that your name defines—
And death this cold, black density of stone.

# MORTON L. ROSS

## Alan Swallow and Modern, Western American Poetry

THE SPAN OF Alan Swallow's attention to the nature and dimensions of
 modern, Western American poetry covers a thirty year period. The arc
of that span is particularly illuminating. Shortly before his nineteenth
birthday, he editorialized on "Regionalism" in the undergraduate magazine he had founded at the University of Wyoming. There he scored
H. G. Merriam's anthology, *Northwest Verse*, for expressing "merely the
outward signs and habits of the region," thereby neglecting the unique
contribution the region might make "to the national culture." The root
of that contribution, he insisted, was "the fundamental influence of environment that distinguishes the Northwest and its peoples from any other
region in the country."[1] This statement indicates one premise, one direction explored during his thirty-year, off and on, quest for that peculiar

[1] *Sage*, I (January, 1934), p. 1.

---

sensibility which might order the creation of poetry distinctive enough to be grouped and identified as "Western."

The present status of this search was announced by Swallow in an essay contributed to a 1964 symposium on Western literature. At the eminence of his career as a one-man, Rocky Mountain literary establishment—a career as publisher, editor, reviewer, critic, aesthetic theorist, literary historian, teacher, fictionist, and poet—Swallow again surveyed the "poetry of the West." He apologized twice in the essay, once for the persistent ambiguity of a topic which still requires careful definition and once again for listing "Western" poets in such amazing variety instead of drawing from them generalizations which would make the adjective meaningful. What the list does indicate is that he has been forced to abandon his original environmentalist premise: "It is clear from this recital that the West *as a place* has not been a determining factor upon these many poets." Yet if Swallow now believes that a sufficiently unique Western sensibility has not emerged from the massage of regional topography, he also believes that he has found that "significant common denominator which marks this as 'Western.'" After admitting that this quality may be "as much a well-known wish of mine as it is a possible reality," Swallow now gives a name to what he was only pointing toward in 1934. It is "rationality," "the overall attitude that poetry itself is responsible human behavior (most notably spelled out in the criticism of Yvor Winters.)"[2] What Swallow means by this and by what process he arrived here from the 1934 departure may be inferred from a review of his observations on the subject scattered over the thirty year interval.

While still a senior at Wyoming, and later as a graduate student at Louisiana State University, Swallow commented extensively on poetry in the pages of Ray B. West's *Intermountain Review*. In a 1937 review of the poetry of Robinson Jeffers, he had already moved a bit from his 1934 editorial position on the influence of environment, beginning with the observation that "a man's personal culture is not directly conditioned by his geographical environment." But the landscape is still relevant, for in the rugged California coast, "the poet has found the setting fit for his culture,"[3] a medium for the expression of that which Jeffers brought to it from elsewhere. Here the landscape has moved from the category of "inspiration" to that of "technique," two terms which Swallow had earlier used to divide the elements of poetry. In the next issue Swallow rejoiced that *Story* magazine had broken precedent by publishing poetry, and that the poems chosen belonged to a poet of the Rocky Mountain West, Brewster Ghiselin. But he used the occasion to lament the literary tradition hitherto dominant in the West which he labeled "romanticism" and saw as "a direct contradiction of the realism, the appropriation, the pragmatism which is

---

2 "Poetry of the West," *South Dakota Review*, II (Autumn, 1964), pp. 86–87.

3 "The Poetry of Robinson Jeffers," *Intermountain Review*, II (Fall, 1937), p. 8.

the tradition of practical life on the frontier and in the later West."[4] Swallow here implies yet a third role for the landscape in the creation of Western poetry—not direct influence or inspiration, not wholly medium or technique, but rather the locus for a distinctive set of habits requiring more consonant modes for their proper expression in poetry.

This role is further explored in what is probably Swallow's major statement on the problem during this early phase of his career. In a review titled "Two Rocky Mountain Poets," he begins by considering parts of Thomas Hornsby Ferril's essay on "Rocky Mountain Metaphysics." He then finds a corresponding cast of mind reflected in the poetry of his Wyoming contemporary, Ted Olson.

> He has met the problem suggested by Ferril by a philosophy natural to the Rocky Mountain region and the pioneer tradition. The poet has noted the impotence of man before the bigness, and the occasional cruelty, of nature. . . . Such a philosophy, or any philosophy for that matter, cannot of course solve the specific poetic problem. But it can provide the materials and the temper of a distinctive regional poetry.[5]

Swallow does not specify the promising "philosophy" exemplified in Olson's poetry further than to describe it—in a comparison with A. E. Housman—as a "more urgent, more impulsive, less tempered" pessimism. What this essay does indicate, at this stage in Swallow's continuing speculation about the problem, is an assumption different from, yet still related to his premise of 1934. This assumption is that the Western landscape, while perhaps not a direct influence or cause in the creation of a unique poetic sensibility, yet circumscribes a range of human attitudes "natural" to itself.

Swallow further refined this basic notion during the decade of the forties—a period which might be termed the second stage in his pursuit of an elusive "Western" poetry. This process of refining occurs, perhaps paradoxically, because Swallow's preoccupations now go well beyond the boundaries of regional verse. His activities as poetry editor (from 1942 to 1948) for the *New Mexico Quarterly Review* seem to have greatly enlarged his acquaintance with and interest in the whole spectrum of modern poetry. While he still commented sympathetically on regional poets, the category disappeared within his quarterly reviews of current poetry, covering "as many as eighty volumes a year."[6] But perhaps the major reason for Swallow's new direction was the work of Yvor Winters, an influence Swallow has acknowledged freely and often.

Swallow's first public response to Winters, in 1940, was praise and defense of "The Sage of Palo Alto." In that essay he approved Winters' famous temper by observing that "he has one of the most prized of

---

[4] "Brewster Ghiselin," *Intermountain Review*, II (Winter, 1938), p. 4.
[5] *Rocky Mountain Review*, III (Fall, 1938), p. 3.
[6] Swallow, *An Editor's Essays of Two Decades* (Denver, 1962), p. ii.

Western virtues, the determination to 'stick by his guns'."[7] This virtue, first identified as regional, is rephrased in 1944 to become "a sort of uncompromising determination and perhaps even arrogance," now identified only as "virtues of the creative intellect."[8] The same expansion occurs in Swallow's judgments of Winters' rank as a critic. In 1940, Winters is "among our four or five most stimulating and penetrating critics." In 1944, he became "the greatest critic of the recent critical renaissance."

Swallow's concern with both Winters' virtues and the deliberate calibration of his rank is consistent with his understanding of the critic's thought. In both essays Swallow took pains to explain, for those who allegedly misunderstood Winters, that the key to the critic's remarkably complete system was the concept of the "moral" artist. This centers on the obligation "to write as a full-bodied man, as a man of responsibility in possession of his faculties." To do so also demands a complete response, "the integration (if the author attains integration) of response by the author to the literary situation."[9] Swallow also singles out Winters' careful examinations of "the relation between ideas of art and technical methods used in the work," concluding that Winters' skill is perhaps most evident in his numerous demonstrations that "there is an exact relation between one's conception of art and the way he will write."[10]

This feature of Winters' practice, it seems to me, was especially attractive to Swallow because it focused the problems he had already encountered in his thinking about Western poetry. Winters' close attention to the degree of congruence necessary between a genuinely "moral" poetic sensibility and those techniques by which it is best embodied provided an alternative to the "romantic" tradition which Swallow had earlier stigmatized as false to Western life. In Winters, Swallow seems to have found a clear description of qualities of mind and imagination most appropriate to regional experience and a meaningful guide for a proper selection among available techniques. It is at least clear that this preoccupation with the exact relationship between aesthetic idea and practical technique shaped Swallow's own thinking in the decade of the forties. It informs, for example, his most ambitious attempts at systematic literary history, three essays, originally in the *New Mexico Quarterly Review*, exploring the links between "a general literary method" and "the intellectual climate of an age."[11] More importantly, and more practically, Winter's prescriptive preferences—particularly the pith of his strictures on "experimental" poetry—greatly influenced Swallow's choice of critical vocabulary in his

[7] *Rocky Mountain Review*, IV (Spring–Summer, 1940), p. 1.

[8] "An Examination of Modern Critics: Yvor Winters," *Rocky Mountain Review*, IX (Fall, 1944), pp. 32–33.

[9] "The Sage of Palo Alto," p. 3.

[10] "An Examination of Modern Critics: Yvor Winters," p. 36.

[11] *An Editor's Eassays of Two Decades*, p. 15; the essays "Allegory as Literary Method," "Induction as Poetic Method," "Subjectivism as Poetic Method" are collected in this volume.

reviews of current volumes. Some of Ted Olson's poems betray the faults of "prolixity and lack of tension," but his "phrasal shock and impact" are praiseworthy. Spender is guilty of "lack of control of rhythm and of image"; Coblentz of "easy phrasing"; John Frederick Nims of "strained images"; Winfield Townley Scott of "laxness of composition." Some of Mark Van Doren's poems seem "a little too soft" and some of Shapiro's display "obscurantism."

Typical of Swallow's judgments during the period, such phrasing suggests not only his debt to Winters, but also his relative indifference to the marks or merits of regional poetry. His only explicit reference to the matter in these reviews is an oblique notice of Ferril's use of "some private symbolism about the West." Swallow's practice as a reviewer during the forties demonstrates that he was working from assumptions which classified and graded poetry according to the degree in which its creation had been controlled and disciplined by what he had learned to prefer as the fully moral and fully responsible imagination.

What Winters means by the moral imagination and the range of poetic techniques congenial to it is beyond the scope of this essay. What Swallow came to mean by these things during the fifties is increasingly clear as the arc of his attention curved again to the specific problems of creating Western poetry. In 1957 he offered what he twice labels as the result of much speculation about the possibility of a unique Western literature. Recalling his acquaintance with "writers from all over the West, the famous and the struggling," he found it remarkable that:

> these people are in some way alike, in friendliness, in skepticism of the national trends, in doubt of the "official" attitudes of the Eastern intellectual circles. There is a common ground, even among persons of diverse beliefs.[12]

Here Swallow again, after a lapse of almost twenty years, defines a cast of mind peculiarly Western, but this time it is a temper conditioned not by topography, but by the group's shared isolation from and reaction to the Eastern literary establishment—the kind of reaction displayed, for example, in Wallace Stegner's recent blast, "Born a Square—The Westerner's Dilemma."[13] The pattern is continued in Swallow's 1959 essay which treats five Western writers under the title "The Mavericks," largely because of their common troubles with Eastern panjandrums. The maverick is "at odds with all the evidences of intellectual dominance of the past two decades. He is mostly on uneasy terms with the fashions of book publishing today. He is frequently berated or ignored in the reviews. He is not among the honored 'men of letters' who have risen to great recognition in this period."[14] Swallow has further documented the maverick syn-

---

[12] "A Magazine for the West?" *Inland*, I (Summer, 1957), p. 4.

[13] *Atlantic Monthly*, January, 1964, pp. 46–50.

[14] *Critique*, II (Winter, 1959), p. 76.

drome with his essays on the perils of an independent publisher in the West, and it is clear that his professional struggles against Eastern hegemony of the nation's taste inform these most recent efforts to delimit a common ground for Western poetry.

In the late fifties Swallow took the offensive, making explicit the claims of Western creativity in this regional power struggle. In 1957 he was specifically concerned with the necessary conditions for a Western magazine "which could achieve national influence upon the direction of people's thought." Such an organ is justified because he senses that a "creative flowering" may be on the West as it was on the South thirty years before. In the 1959 essay, he is even more aggressive, warning that this flowering "is not being recognized in those places which marshal our intellectual life, which create our literary fads, which make us think we are keeping up on cultural affairs." Swallow then predicts that the decades of the sixties and seventies "shall see a gradual dominance come to our intellectual life, and particularly to our poetry and our fiction, from the West." He ends this passage with a battle cry: "The movement is on."[15]

The militant tone of these maneuvers is indicative of an important change in Swallow's treatment of the category, "Western poetry." In his earlier efforts to define its common ingredients, he was guided by a rough empirical method, an inductive attempt to construct a genus precise, yet capacious enough to do justice to its individual members. Recently, however, he has resisted the method, scorning it in 1957 as "foolish," in 1959 as "silly," and in the 1964 essay contenting himself with that broad phylum which delimits Western poetry as "the poems written by persons who have spent much, even most, of their creative lives in the West."[16] What Swallow now prefers to descriptive classification is prescriptive recommendation. He now feels, as he phrased it in 1957, "that if there is to be a common ground among Western writers which can convey much to the national direction of our culture, it must be the rationalist spirit . . . ," a belief with which he also concludes the 1964 essay. Here the pattern of ideas which Swallow shares with Winters and terms "rationality" is adopted as an imperative for the Western writer. The exercise of the moral, responsible, integrated imagination—particularly as it disciplines the choice of poetic technique—has become a program for, rather than a description of, the Western poet. For the task of simply treating the subject, such a substitution has one distinct advantage. Whereas the construction of a descriptive genus strains to embrace the variety of those it would include, a prescriptive program allows the variety of deviating individuals as heretical. Swallow is edging in this direction when he notes, for example, that in Western writing "there is, indeed, a great deal of reliance on the anti-rational (an example: the so-called cultural renaissance of the San Francisco area); there is hearkening after the symbolist, or after

---

[15] *Ibid.*, pp. 74–75.
[16] Poetry of the West," p. 79.

the wayward, or after the anti-intellectual; and sometimes there is a decided interest in the mystic."[17]

Yet Swallow is understandably uneasy in this role of the prophetic commissar. His "rationalistic" program for Western poetry, despite its occasional militant note, has been offered not belligerently, but rather tentatively, most often labeled as his personal hope. His affirmation that "a common ground among Western writers . . . must be the rationalistic spirit" is less dogmatic than it might seem because it is so strongly qualified: "I do not think we are very near to it and may never achieve it."

This, then, is the present state of Swallow's thirty year quest for a uniquely Western poetic sensibility. It must be described, I think, as a stasis, created in part by the fact that his most recent speculations lead into paradox. Having largely abandoned the attempt to define Western poetry through descriptive classification, he has found in his critical preoccupations of the forties a prescription for a Western poetry which might have a significant national influence. But the authority of his impressions about those characteristics which Western writers actually have in common make it doubtful whether this, or any, prescription can ever shape the creative reality. Swallow's "mavericks," so skeptical of dictation from the East and so doggedly independent, seem as unlikely to be guided by a locally recommended formula as by an imported one.

It is, of course, much too early to determine whether Swallow is the Cassandra of Western poetry's future, and it is unfair to think of the sequence of his speculation as a simple case study, especially since it is only one aspect of his passionate commitment to the whole literary enterprise. Yet Swallow's struggles with the problem are instructive because they map both cul-de-sacs and promising access routes for those who share his interest in the possibilities of a uniquely Western creativity.

[17] "A Magazine for the West?" p. 5.

# J. RUSSELL ROBERTS, SR.

## *Listening to the Wilderness with William Stafford*

"I COULD HEAR the wilderness listen," wrote Stafford in the title poem of *Traveling Through the Dark*. Again and again in Stafford's poetry we hear the wilderness; though it utters no word to him, he feels its presence with eyes and ears specially attuned by sympathies, inherent and learned.

*Reprinted from* WESTERN AMERICAN LITERATURE, *Vol. III, No. 3 with the permission of the editor.*

To understand these sympathies with the wilderness in Stafford's verse, it is not enough to say that he is "Wordsworthian." We may question whether Wordsworth ever traveled through the dark, and if he did it was a different dark from Stafford's. Stafford's wilderness seizes us with wonder at the enigma, grim, not friendly, yet not always forbidding either, of something that is a presence, all encompassing, but unknowable.

Man's dependence upon some conception of a living wilderness from which he derives sustenance for his ego has long been recognized as one of the landmarks of the romantic view. How much of the affliction diagnosed as "alienation" or loss of personal identity in our present literary setting may be traced to our failure to recognize or to respond to the wilderness? Stafford expressed this predicament in "By the Snake River" in *West of Your City:*[1]

> Something sent me out in these desert places
> to this apparition river among the rocks
> because what I tried to carry in my hands
> was all spilled from jostling when I went
> among the people to be one of them.
> This river started among such mountains
> that I look up to find those valleys
> where intentions were before they flowed
> in the kind of course the people would allow
> where I was a teacher, a son, a father, a man.

For many people there is no wilderness left. It all but vanishes when the land becomes real estate. Stafford's poetry keeps reminding us of what we have lost. Particularly in the Pacific Northwest, what man has done to the natural setting by ignoring or by never knowing its inherent value is striking. Where there are mountains like Hood and Rainier dwarfing the skyscrapers of Seattle, Tacoma, and Portland, or where there are waterways like the Columbia river and Puget Sound—there the ugliness of what man has made contrasts ironically with the grandeur of the environment; and it is spread before all who have "view" windows. This contrast appears in many places in Stafford's poems: the sanitary, cautious, secure life of the suburbanite living perhaps in quiet desperation, the crass commercialism and ignorance of the memory of any wilderness seems to obsess us— all of this is limned with irony by Stafford when he writes, "Gasoline makes game scarce" and "it takes a lot of miles to equal one wildcat." The poem in which these lines appear carries the curious title, "Written on the Stub of the First Paycheck." It is printed in *West of Your City*.

The confrontation of the wilderness with the works of man often induces a questioning of accepted values. For example the setting of the Seattle Art Museum poses a kind of dilemma for a visitor. He admires the beautiful facade of the Museum and may be curious about the marble rams of ancient oriental breed and the Chinese warrior, invincible also in

[1] Poems quoted here from *West of Your City* are reprinted with the permission of the *Hudson Review*.

marble; but if he faces about he sees the Olympic mountains across the Sound spreading north whiter than the clouds: here is the city; there is the bay and the mountains; and the panorama, always impressive, presents him with a dramatic confrontation of the wilderness and civilization. The visitor's dilemma may be put in Stafford's words from "Doubt on the Great Divide" in *The Rescued Year*:[2]

> Mountains that thundered promises now say something small—

In Stafford's eyes this condition exists in Texas, in Kansas, in Oregon, in California; and he deals with it in his poetry by showing us how our humanness is affected by mountains, rivers, and prairies. With him it is an American wilderness with continental amplitude, energy, grimness and beauty. It is the dramatic essence of many of his poems. In some instances the men are absorbed into the living wilderness. Such is the case of the father and son in "Some Shadows" in *The Rescued Year*. More often, however, the people Stafford writes about are estranged from and ignorant of their dependence on natural phenomena. We may find an example in the second stanza of "Two Evenings" in *West of Your City:*

> Today toward night when bats came out—
> flyers so nervous they rest by turning
> and foreknow collision by calling out "Maybe!"—
> we anticipated something we did not expect.
> Counting the secretaries coming out of a building
> there were more people than purposes.
> We stared at the sidewalk looking for ourselves,
> like antelope fading into evening.

The wilderness has many voices in Stafford's poetry. He hears it in the big sky of the West, in the forested mountains, and on the untenanted prairie. It is the pulsing life within these forms that he is sensitive to. His intuition presses the symbolic meaning from a tumbleweed; he touches the head of a dead duck and feels "through the feathers all the dark." He imagines a panting lizard "waiting for history" at a bomb testing site. In "Listening" from *The Rescued Year* he explains that:

> My father heard so much that we still stand
> inviting the quiet by turning the face,
> waiting for a time when something in the night
> will touch us too from that other place.

The ecologist knows the cycles of life that tie together the creatures treading the forest floor and those that swim to the spawning headwaters of the rivers, but a poet like Stafford captures the meaning of the order and unity of nature and expresses it in a flash of insight: "they have killed the river and built a dam" and the fish counter numbers "So many Chinook souls, so many Silverside."

[2] Poems from *The Rescued Year* by William Stafford are reprinted by permission of Harper & Row, Publishers, Inc. Copyright © 1966 by William Stafford.

A student who heard Stafford read some of his poems observed that: "I felt just as if he were talking to me." His poems have an intimate appeal because, like the psalmist or Dante, he penetrates to the sources of poetic sensibility, to those themes which have been and are the ponderable themes: love and death, beauty and terror and the unknowable infinite. These ponderable themes are qualified in Stafford's verse by the haunting presence of the wilderness as if the poems had grown up with him. Starting with a homely, everyday chore like "Setting a trotline after sundown," to catch a channel cat, the action is prosaic enough, until, in the poet's vision, we see

> Eyes that were still eyes in the rush of darkness,
> flowing feelers noncommittal and black,

and we feel that there is here a perspective of the life of the river, not just the life of the fish but the "rush of darkness" and the feel of the "swerve and the deep current which tugged at the tree roots below the river." This observation is found in "In the Deep Channel" printed in *West of Your City*.

Like Whitman, Stafford, captures the untameable, the irreconcilable, the die-fighting fierceness of wild things. This last resort of the courageous spirit, where a man or animal cornered by enemies reverts to tooth and claw, suggests Robinson Jeffers' "Hurt Hawks," and Faulkner's short story "The Bear." Like Whitman, Stafford is "not a bit tamed" and because of this there is in his poetry a fresh perception of what we call "wild life" and its setting.

This perception is frequently not noticed by those who have never felt the stretching distances covered by the open sky of eastern Oregon. Such a wilderness does not give up its secrets casually to those who have never listened to its music nor been charmed by its spell. Its appreciation comes from a way of feeling about the land, as Whitman felt when he "walked with the tender and growing night."

The lasting spell of wilderness life, its effect on the family, and particularly on the son, grown to manhood and lecturing to a sophisticated audience, is the subject of "Some Shadows," one of the longer meditative poems in *The Rescued Year*. It is a dramatic monologue; the lecturer wishes to persuade the audience that they do not "want too reserved a speaker—that is a cold way to live."

He then tries to carry the audience back to "the barren lands," to the country that was shadowed by the Indians when his mother was a girl and she had to run "to school winter mornings with hot potatoes in her hands." "She could not hear very well," and though frightened,

> she loved, like everyone.
> A lean man, a cruel, took her.

Dramatically at this point the speaker announces:

> "I am his son."

and for this reason he could not be too reserved and he says:

> Forgive me these shadows I cling to, good people,
> trying to hold quiet in my prologue.
> Hawks cling the barrens wherever I live.
> The world says, "Dog eat dog."

And the town people had called his father *Hawk;*

> He lived by trapping and hunting
> wherever the old slough ran.

Are we justified in feeling that the poet had lived with the recognition of the contrasts between the "cold way to live" in an urban setting and the lean and cruel life of the pioneer? The wild life of the "old slough" and many places like it must have filled his mind with wonder, fed his imagination, and seeded his thinking with questions.

A number of questions stemming from prairie life emerge in another poem in *The Rescued Year*, "Uncle George." On Uncle George's farm "Only telephone poles remember the place" where the blizzards massacred the stock; nevertheless:

> Some catastrophes are better than others.

But it was here that the poet hunted through the snow for "furred things"; he watches spring birds "measuring" their nesting streams and he "flutters" like one driven on and "measures his stream" of memory. The images in the poem may be recondite at first. Why should one "live reluctantly one life at a time;"? The answer is not explicit but may be found in the way Uncle George and the farm are recalled as essences suggesting other perceptions and associations. First the savage ferocity of the blizzard is seen distanced by the wry comment that "Some catastrophes are better than others." In this setting the poet says "I plow and belong," progressing toward "ultimate identification." Ultimate identification is perceived intuitively as birds measure their nesting stream. And as the poet measures his stream, the memory of Uncle George comes flooding back to give us the most immediate drama of the poem. I plow and *belong;* belong to that day and that place and it leads us by its symbolic force to the abstraction called "ultimate identification." This abstraction may well be the theme of the poem.

If we regard the wilderness as comprehending something more than man, something man can not reproduce, but something of which he is a part, and yet is estranged from by a polarity between his mind and his instincts, this something becomes intelligible to us in Stafford's poetry through symbolic reference and dramatized moments of insight. The title poem of *Traveling Through the Dark*[3] will illustrate.

> Traveling through the dark I found a deer
> dead on the edge of the Wilson River road.
> It is usually best to roll them into the canyon:

[3] "Traveling Through the Dark" from *Traveling Through the Dark* (1962) by William Stafford. Copyright © 1960 by William Stafford. Reprinted by permission of Harper & Row, Publishers, Inc.

> that road is narrow; to swerve might make more dead.
> By glow of the tail-light I stumbled back of the car
> and stood by the heap, a doe, a recent killing;
> she had stiffened already, almost cold.
> I dragged her off; she was large in the belly.
> My fingers touching her side brought me the reason—
> her side was warm; her fawn lay there waiting,
> alive, still, never to be born.
> Beside that mountain road I hesitated.
> The car aimed ahead its lowered parking lights;
> under the hood purred the steady engine.
> I stood in the glare of the warm exhaust turning red;
> around our group I could hear the wilderness listen.
> I thought hard for us all—my only swerving—,
> then pushed her over the edge into the river.

"Her side was warm; her fawn lay there waiting, alive," while, "The car aimed ahead its lowered parking lights; under the hood purred the steady engine." The strict rhetorical economy of this passage only emphasizes the symbolic force of the contrast between the unborn fawn and the purring engine. But this contrast does not comprise the whole meaning. Between the two symbols stands the line:

> Beside that mountain road I hesitated.

In the words "I hesitated," the moment of insight is dramatized unhindered by superfluous exposition.

A freshman student who heard Stafford read this poem felt the cruel decision implied in "I hesitated." Angrily she exclaimed, "How could he do it? Push that deer over the bank!" Her spontaneous indignation, misguided though it be, is probably a valid test of the dramatic effect of the poem and the truth of its symbolism. A more sophisticated reader might not have reacted with such simplicity because, familiar with literary conventions, he stands at a distance from the immediate experience, and is impressed with the artistry of the poet. Yet the identification is there, essential to the poem. And the hard decision to push the doe over the bank points up man's predicament: his intellect versus his instinct.

This observation brings us to the paradox implied in the concepts of wilderness and civilization. Questions are raised: why does man want to conquer this wilderness and at the same time why does he crave renewal of primitive energies, of peace of mind, and finally, a renewal of self? These questions are all alive in Stafford's poetry. For example, we may find this paradox hinted by the tulip tree in his garden.

"Many a winter night" the tulip tree dramatically articulates the quizzical, low-keyed line " 'I am still here.' " And there it is, ghostly, by the evergreen, sustaining

> . . . what really belonged
> but would, if severely doubted,
> disappear.

This, by artful suggestion, raises the question and answers it—what is it that "really belonged" in this scene? What would return on "many a winter night" to live ". . . again among other trees"? The tree is a reminder of the sleeping life, present but unseen, and, if it is not severely doubted, it is a winter reminder of the green life that is waiting—one of the grand phenomena of nature, and one of the most thrilling expectations, deep in the consciousness of man, is expressed in his careful watch over trees and shrubs for the witness of the swelling leaf buds. Stafford's poem probes this consciousness; gives it a prod, as it were.

In some of his more recent poems, particularly those published under the collective title of "Poems of Earth and Air" in the *Hudson Review*, autumn 1967, Stafford has matured the wilderness theme by giving it a range of association derived from new experiences. But these new experiences are used to reinforce the doctrine that man's deepest urges, the springs of life are only unmasked when he faces the wilderness. "For a Colleague who Took His Life" affords an example in the lines

> . . . I read the news
> and felt the fox gnaw all day inside my coat.

This fox finds a congenial place among the animal images of Stafford. He is not the stereotyped fox of the Spartan legend. He is a pain in the gut, and more, he becomes the fanged wildness lurking in man's autonomic nervous system.

Glimpses of the wilderness flash momentarily in Stafford's verse like the revelations found in Joyce's epiphanies.

> We were back of three mountains called
> "Sisters" along the Green Lakes trail
> and had crossed a ridge when that
> one little puff of air touched us,
> hardly felt at all.

In this stanza from "Things that Happen" we should note that the place names are incidental and might be changed without altering the meaning of the experience which could happen to mountaineers anywhere in the world and that the "little puff of air" was the "greatest event of the day; it righted all wrong."

In "Farewell to Summer" man's activities are dwarfed by a kind of cosmic patience to be found in the "remote quiet areas" where the erosion of time is caught in the refrain:

> A wave, and a wave, and a wave—

This dwarfing of man and his institutions in the presence of natural processes occurs in many poems which suggest that the man's effort to construct his own world is ironic.

In one of his earlier poems ("Back Home" from *The Rescued Year* previously published in *Northwest Review*, Summer, 1959) Stafford expressed this irony thus:

the wild hills coming to drink at the river,
the church pondering its old meanings.
I believe the hills won;

While all poets draw upon nature, each in his own way and while English poets of the eighteenth and nineteenth century were dominated by the pastoral tradition of Milton and Shakespeare, Stafford's use of nature is uncolored by the tradition. He is not pretending to be a shepherd and his scenes are not the conventional pastoral pictures, but present a new vision of mountains and prairies. His animals are not the literary beasts bequeathed by Theocritus. They are American wild things: snakes, lizards, coyotes, and hawks.

It may be, however, that the relationship of Stafford's poetry to the wilderness is best defined in "Traveling Through the Dark" when he hesitated beside the mountain road and "thought hard for us all." It is the time and the place prompting the thought that are important. The thought itself is not articulated.

In "Father's Voice" he is definite; he says:

World, I am your slow guest,
one of the common things
that move in the sun and have
close, reliable friends
in the earth, in the air, in the rock.

Perhaps this stanza brings us as close as we can get to a definition of Stafford's role as a poet. He knows what he is, and his friends in the earth, in the air, in the rock determine his identity. Hence his role is in no way pompous but does exemplify the simplest and the toughest of virtues. This toughest of virtues may be simply the will to live in a world where

Our lives are an amnesty given us.

as intimated in "Our City is Guarded by Automatic Rockets" from *The Rescued Year*. In that poem an ultimate moral purpose welds the closing stanza:

There is a place behind our hill so real
it makes me turn my head, no matter. There
in the last thicket lies the cornered cat
saved by its claws, now ready to spend
all there is left of the wilderness, embracing
its blood. And that is the way that I will spit
life, at the end of any trail where I smell any hunter,
because I think our story should not end—
or go on in the dark with nobody listening.

"With nobody *listening*"—There is that word again, and again it raises a question: is there in man a primitive compulsion—"all that is left of the wilderness"? If there is, may it not save him from ultimate extinction?

Margot Astrov, ed. *American Indian Prose and Poetry: "The Winged Serpent," An Anthology* (New York: Capricorn Books, 1962).

Robert Bly
*Silence in the Snowy Fields* (Middletown, Conn.: Wesleyan University Press, 1962).
*The Light Around the Body* (New York: Harper & Row, 1967).

Thomas Hornsby Ferril
*Westering* (New Haven: Yale University Press, 1934).
*Trial by Time* (New York: Harper & Bros., 1944).
*Words for Denver and Other Poems* (New York: William Morrow & Co., Inc., 1966).

Robinson Jeffers
*The Double Axe* (New York: Random House, 1948).
*Roan Stallion, Tamar, and Other Poems* (New York: Random House, Inc., 1925).

Archibald MacLeish *Conquistador* (Boston: Houghton Mifflin Co., 1932).

John G. Neihardt *The Cycle of the West* (New York: The Macmillan Company, 1949).

Winfield Townley Scott *New and Selected Poems* (Garden City, N.J.: Doubleday & Co., 1967).

Gary Snyder
*The Back Country* (New York: New Directions Publishing Corp., 1968).
*Myths and Texts* (Sussex, England: Centaur Press, 1960).
*Riprap and Cold Mountain Poems* (San Francisco: Four Seasons Foundation, 1965).
*Six Sections from Mountains and Rivers Without End* (San Francisco: Four Seasons Foundation, 1965).

William E. Stafford
*West of Your City* (New York: Harper & Row, 1960).
*Traveling Through the Dark* (New York: Harper & Row, 1962).
*The Rescued Year* (New York: Harper & Row, 1966).

A. Wilbur Stevens, ed. *Poems Southwest* (Prescott, Ariz.: Prescott College Press, 1968).

CRITICAL ARTICLES ON WESTERN POETRY:

Jay Gurian    "The Possibility of a Western Poetics," *The Colorado Quarterly*, Vol. XV, No. 1 (Summer, 1966), 69–85.

Thomas J. Lyon
  "Gary Snyder, A Western Poet," *Western American Literature*, Vol. III, No. 3 (Fall, 1968), 207–216.
  "The Ecological Vision of Gary Snyder," *Kansas Quarterly*, Vol. II, No. 2 (Spring, 1970).

Robert F. Richards    "Thomas Hornsby Ferril and the Problems of the Poet in the West," *Kansas Quarterly*, Vol. II, No. 2 (Spring, 1970).

Kenneth S. Rothwell    "In Search of a Western Epic: Neihardt, Sandburg, and Jaffe as Regionalists and Astoriadists," *Kansas Quarterly*, Vol. II, No. 2 (Spring, 1970).

# FIVE

# The Essay of Social Criticism

THE AMERICAN WEST has been the scene of some of America's worst social injustices; discrimination since the Civil War against Negroes even in the United States Army; the rape of Indian land and destruction of much of their culture; the attempts of individuals, groups, and corporations to get possession of the public lands for private exploitation; and finally, the outrageous confinement of the Japanese Americans in concentration camps at the outbreak of World War II.

In twenty years of writing critical essays for *Harpers The Easy Chair*, Bernard DeVoto probably holds some kind of record as a western social critic; for, though he went East, his mind and heart remained in the West. Almost everything he wrote concerned the West, and he dealt with the land grabbers and their congressional collaborators with great finesse.

Deloria is a Sioux, and he brings to his Indian manifesto a thorough knowledge of American perfidy in its treaties with the Indians, but also gusto and a robust sense of humor in its remarkable chastisement of the whites.

Hosakawa deals with the worst outrage to occur in the American West in my lifetime—his is a quiet, eloquent account that will mortify anyone who was an adult when it happened, and said nothing.

Two of the most important contemporary social critics in the West are Eldridge Cleaver and Gary Snyder, both of the San Francisco Bay area. Cleaver, one of the founders of the controversial Black Panther Party for Self-Defense, advocates militancy in his book, *Soul On Ice* (1968). Snyder with his commitment to Zen has a mystical, ecological view of man's place in the world; and in *Earth House Hold* (1969) he describes both his ideal free life and what he considers sterile and worse in the establishment.

# BERNARD DeVOTO

## The Sturdy Corporate Homesteader

### (MAY 1953)

IN A HAPPIER TIME, so a U.S. Chamber of Commerce speaker tells us, the government used the public domain to "give every man a chance to earn land for himself through his own skill and hard work." This is the sturdy homemaker sob with which the air will presently resound when this gentleman's associates get to work on Congress. He may have been thinking of the California redwood forest. It was so attractive a part of the public domain that in this generation we have had to raise millions of dollars from rich men and school children to buy back a few acres of it here and there for the public.

Under a measure called the Timber and Stone Act, a homemaker who had his first citizenship papers could buy 160 acres of redwood forest from the government for $2.50 an acre, quite a bit less than a panel for your living room costs. Agents of a lumber company would go to a sailors' boardinghouse on the waterfront. They would press a gang of home-makers and lead them to a courthouse to take out first papers. Then they went to a land office and each filed claim to 160 acres of redwood: a quarter section whose number the lumber company had supplied. At a lawyer's office they transferred to the lumber company the homesteads they had earned by skill and hard work, received $50 for services rendered, and could go back to the boardinghouse. "Fifty dollars was the usual fee," a historian says, "although the amount soon fell to $10 or $5 and eventually to the price of a glass of beer."

Under this Act four million acres of publicly owned timber passed into corporate ownership at a small fraction of its value, and 95 per cent of it by fraud. Under other Acts supposed to "give every man a chance to earn land for himself," enormously greater acreages came to the same end with the sturdy homemaker's help.

The laws stipulated that the homemaker must be in good faith. Erecting a "habitable dwelling" on his claim would prove that he was. Or if it was irrigable land, he had to "bring water" to it, for a homemaker would need water. Under a couple of dozen aliases apiece, employees of land companies or cattle companies would file claim to as many quarter sections or half sections of the public domain and after six months would "commute" them, get title to them, at $1.25 per acre.

---

*Reprinted from* THE EASY CHAIR *by Bernard DeVoto with the permission of Houghton Mifflin Company, publisher.*

414

The sworn testimony of witnesses would prove that they had brought water to the claim; there was no reason for the witnesses to add they had brought it in a can. Or the witnesses swore that they had "seen water" on a homestead and so they had, having helped to throw it there cupful by cupful. Or to erect a "twelve by fourteen" cabin on a claim would prove good faith. Homemaker and witnesses neglected to mention that the size of this "habitable dwelling" was twelve by fourteen inches, not feet. Alternatively, a "shingled residence" established that the homemaker intended to live on his claim; one could be created by fastening a couple of shingles to each side of a tent below the ridgepole. Sometimes a scrupulous corporation would build a genuine log cabin twelve by fourteen feet, mount it on wagon wheels, and have the boys drive it from claim to claim, getting the homemaker a lot of public domain in a few hours. In a celebrated instance in Utah the efficiency of this device was increased by always pushing the truck over the corner where four quarter sections met.

In six months the homemakers, who meanwhile had been punching cows or clerking in town, commuted their two dozen parcels of the public domain. They transferred them to their employers and moved on to earn two dozen more quarter sections apiece by their skill and hard work. Many millions of acres of publicly owned farmland and grazing land thus passed economically into the possession of corporate homemakers. If the corporation was a land company it might get half a million acres convenient to a railroad right of way or within a proposed irrigation district. Or a cattle company could thus acquire ten thousand acres that monopolized the water supply for miles and so graze a hundred thousand acres of the public domain entirely free of charge.

Lumber companies could operate even more cheaply. Their employees need not pay $1.25 per acre or wait to commute their claims. They could pay a location fee, say $16 per 320 acres and the company could forthwith clear-cut the timber and let the claims lapse. At twenty cents an acre virgin stands of white or ponderosa pine, Douglas fir, or Norway or Colorado spruce were almost as good a buy as some of the damsites which, our propagandist hopes, will presently be offered to the power companies.

These are typical, routine, second-magnitude land frauds in the history of the public domain out West—to describe the bigger ones would require too much space. Enough that in the golden age of landgrabs the total area of the public domain proved up and lived on by actual homesteaders amounted to only a trivial fraction of the area fraudulently acquired by land companies, cattle companies, and lumber companies. Among the compelling reasons why the present public-land reserves had to be set aside was the headlong monopolization of the public domain that was threatening the West with peonage. Those reserves were also made to halt the waste of natural resources which the United States has dissipated more prodigally than any other nation. They had to be made so that a useful part of our national wealth could be preserved, developed, wisely managed, and intelligently used in future times. They had to be made so that the watersheds which control the destiny of the West could be safe-guarded. But no one should forget for a moment that they were, besides, necessary to prevent Eastern and foreign corporations from taking over the whole West by fraud, bribery, and engineered bankruptcy.

The land frauds and the landgrabs compose the shabbiest chapter in our history. We have had seventy-five years now of conservation as a govern-ment policy, of husbanding, developing, and using the publicly owned natural resources for the public benefit. So we have grown used to be-lieving that such corruption, such raids on the treasury, such blind im-becility were ended for all time. But at this moment some powerful interests are preaching that what was intolerable corruption on a scale of half a million acres becomes wise public policy if you up the scale to half a billion acres. They are calling on Congress to legalize a final, conclusive raid on the publicly owned resources of the United States.

This one would be for keeps and it would put the government itself into the land-fraud racket. Officials of the government, true enough, were sometimes in that racket in the past, from two-dollar-a-day deputy clerks in the General Land Office on up to Senators and Secretaries of the In-terior. Always before, however, the government regarded them as com-mon criminals. It threw them out, sent to jail those it could get the goods on, and did what it could to repair the damage. Now Congress is asked to legitimatize and legalize what it used to make them felons for trying to do. It is asked, with an effrontery so great that it has not yet been widely perceived, to perpetrate by its own deliberate act a land fraud beside which any in our shameful period would appear insignificant.

As I write this, at mid-March, we have not learned by what means the citizens of forty-five states will have their property alienated on behalf of three states. Senator Holland's bill to convey to Texas, Louisiana, and California the publicly owned oil under the marginal sea has had slow going. The Attorney General has perceived some impairments of sover-eignty and some administrative difficulties that were not visible when the tidelands were a bait for votes. There has arisen the interesting possi-bility that Rhode Island or some inland state which owns part of that oil may bring suit on the ground that Congress has no constitutional power to give it to any state. At least a part of the Administration is showing some regret for its campaign commitment. But it is committed and we may assume that the Supreme Court will find some opening through which it can follow the election returns.

So be it, but let's be clear about the tidelands episode. There has never been any doubt that the natural resources thus handed over to three states belong to the public, to the people of all the states. The Supreme Court has three times declared that they do; indeed in one of the cases which the Court was adjudicating, the State of Louisiana stipulated that they do. What we shall see, then, will be governmental conversion of public prop-erty. That the raiders were three sovereign states does not alter the fact that this is a successful raid on the public heritage.

So, with that precedent, what next? Senator Butler of Nebraska, the Chairman of the Senate Committee on Interior and Insular Affairs, has announced that when the tidelands business is finished his committee will take up proposals for still more important attacks on our property. First the Committee will deal with proposed measures to turn over the public lands to the states, then with similar measures to turn over the public power installations. This means, as the tidelands bills do not, the sale of public property to private corporations—the only reason for giving the public lands to the states is that the states will sell them. Unable to buy the public heritage from the federal government, corporations will be able to buy them at fire-sale prices from eleven Western states. They belong to the people of forty-eight states, the people of the eleven states have borne maybe two percent of the cost of protecting and developing them, patriotic private enterprise can bid them in cheap, and everybody should be happy, more or less.

Among those who testified on the tidelands questions before Senator Butler's committee was Mr. Oscar L. Chapman, lately Secretary of the Interior. He was afraid, he said, that the tidelands action would "establish the pattern for the greatest give-away program in the history of the world." He added, "For years powerful pressure groups have been attempting to raid various parts of the public domain. They are now redoubling their efforts." Mr. Chapman was entirely right. He mentioned the U.S. Chamber of Commerce. In 1947 it supported the notorious effort of stockgrowing interests to grab (at a few cents an acre) large areas of the national forests, the national parks, and other public reservations. Public opinion stopped the stockmen cold and scared the Chamber into reversing its stand for a while. Now it is again agitating for the sale of public lands to private (that is, corporate) parties and is broadcasting remarkably misleading propaganda. The National Association of Manufacturers has lined up beside it, with propaganda equally mendacious and much subtler. For the first time in a generation big lumber interests are supporting the raid. As always the stockmen are out in front, happily carrying the ball for stronger and cannier groups that happily let them carry it. Previously circumspect power companies have come out from behind their public relations programs and various granges and farm bureaus have signed up.

In short, desirous ears have heard the sound of a great Perhaps which they hope they can convert to the great Amen. The day of jubilo may be about to dawn. The federal government's seventy-five years of fidelity to the public interest, the millions of dollars of public money spent to maintain and develop the public lands, the long husbanding and use of them for the benefit of all the people—this is acknowledged to have been a memorable and splendid thing. For lo, this policy has multiplied the value of the public assets a thousandfold—and now the harvest can be reaped by those prepared to cash in on it. A business administration means business, doesn't it? Prolonging federal protection of this public interest would be bureaucratic tyranny and inefficiency, wouldn't it? There is so big a melon to be cut that not to cut it would be creeping socialism— let's go. Or, wheresoever the carcass is, there will the eagles be gathered together.

It is quite a carcass. Mr. Chapman told Senator Butler's committee that the public lands "contain an estimated 4 billion barrels of oil, enough oil shale to produce 130 billion barrels of crude oil, 111 trillion cubic feet of gas, and 324 billion tons of coal." These are sample figures; Mr. Chapman said nothing about timber, grass, electric power plants, sites for future ones, irrigation and other water potentials, precious metals, other minerals, and the rest of the miscellany now owned by the public—by everybody, including you. He said that a rough estimate of their value in the United States, not counting Alaska, made it "well over a trillion dollars." Nobody can think of a trillion dollars; the sum is only a symbol. But it gives the scale of the proposed operation of transferring publicly owned property to the states, so that whatever corporations may prove to be in the best position can buy it for a fraction of what it is worth. Every bill that Senator Butler's committee will proceed to take up could be titled, An Act to Enrich Stockholders at the Expense of Taxpayers.

In the cruder age there had to be a pretense that the homemaker was to benefit but there can't be now, for no land suitable for homesteading is left. Instead, the public lands are to be disposed of on the sound business principle that they are a storehouse of raw materials of value to corporations. The great stands of timber will go to Big Lumber, oil and oil shale to Big Oil, minerals and chemicals to Big Mining, public power plants and sites for future ones to Big Power. Nor is there any pretense that the desirous Western shibboleths will be regarded: the local enterprise and home rule that were to emancipate the plundered province from absentee ownership. The power company that is prepared to build an installation in Hell's Canyon which will generate 40 or maybe 60 per cent of the power the government planned to is not an Idaho corporation. It is not even a Western corporation: it is chartered in Maine and largely owned by investment trusts.

The landgrabbers of the golden age were small-time. A cattle company's two hundred thousand acres of public grazing land at $1.25, a lumber company's half-million acres of publicly owned Douglas fir at $2.50 and a glass of beer—they are police court stuff compared to a political job that undertakes to knock off half a billion acres of public land in a single session of Congress. This proposed steal is so large that its size is counted on to conceal it—like ultraviolet light and supersonic sound it is to escape attention. But it is under way. The bills are drawn, Congressmen have been found who will introduce them and direct their course, and Senator Butler has agreed to clear the decks.[1]

Mr. Chapman told the committee that the estimate of a trillion dollars

[1] As it turned out, the syndicate in part learned discretion and in part lost its nerve. Only a handful of the prepared bills were introduced in the 83rd Congress and of these only two were stubbornly pushed. Both were beaten.

was only a rough guess, was in fact much too low. And, he said, "if this Administration is intent upon following a give-away policy, the people are at least entitled to know what and how much is being given away." So he proposed that a commission be established to inventory and appraise the public property that is to become corporate assets. It is an excellent suggestion. We are being told every few minutes that business is on trial now, that this Administration will give business its chance to prove itself, and everything ought to be done on the best business principles. Establish the commission and have it hire Price, Waterhouse.

The trouble is that such a study would put an end to Operation Götterdämmerung on the public lands. Publication of its results would instantly blow this culminating land fraud sky high. As a matter of fact that is going to happen anyway. The script is OK but the casting is wrong: it calls for the public to be docile and for Congress to be fools.

A very distant association with the Credit Mobilier—railroad-land fraud—kept James G. Blaine, and it may be Schuyler Colfax too, out of the White House. There was William Lorimer of Illinois: expelled from the Senate for corrupt practices rooted in timber-land fraud. There was Senator John Mitchell of Oregon: found guilty of timber-land fraud but dying before he could serve his sentence. Albert B. Fall, Secretary of the Interior, went to jail—oil-land fraud. Richard A. Ballinger, Secretary of the Interior, left a blasted name to history—coal-land fraud. A lot of lesser names have disappeared from the newspapers but not from memory. When you hear them or look them up in books they give off, after all these years, the odor of corruption. Land fraud always did and it always will.

The redwood forest deals, the Oregon timber frauds, Teapot Dome— they were peanuts, birdseed, compared to what this crew of blue-sky pitchmen are asking Congress to slip over on us now. But the stench still rises from them and drifts down history and over Capitol Hill. Congress will sit this one out, the carefully planned agenda notwithstanding.

# VINE DELORIA, JR.

## *Indian Humor*

ONE OF THE BEST ways to understand a people is to know what makes them laugh. Laughter encompasses the limits of the soul. In humor life is redefined and accepted. Irony and satire provide much keener insights into a group's collective psyche and values than do years of research.

It has always been a great disappointment to Indian people that the humorous side of Indian life has not been mentioned by professed experts on Indian Affairs. Rather the image of the granite-faced grunting redskin has been perpetuated by American mythology.

People have little sympathy with stolid groups. Dick Gregory did much more than is believed when he introduced humor into the Civil Rights struggle. He enabled non-blacks to enter into the thought world of the black community and experience the hurt it suffered. When all people shared the humorous but ironic situation of the black, the urgency and morality of Civil Rights was communicated.

The Indian people are exactly opposite of the popular stereotype. I sometimes wonder how anything is accomplished by Indians because of the apparent overemphasis on humor within the Indian world. Indians have found a humorous side of nearly every problem and the experiences of life have generally been so well defined through jokes and stories that they have become a thing in themselves.

For centuries before the white invasion, teasing was a method of control of social situations by Indian people. Rather than embarrass members of the tribe publicly, people used to tease individuals they considered out of step with the concensus of tribal opinion. In this way egos were preserved and disputes within the tribe of a personal nature were held to a minimum.

Gradually people learned to anticipate teasing and began to tease themselves as a means of showing humility and at the same time advocating a course of action they deeply believed in. Men would depreciate their feats to show they were not trying to run roughshod over tribal desires. This method of behavior served to highlight their true virtues and gain them a place of influence in tribal policy-making circles.

Humor has come to occupy such a prominent place in national Indian affairs that any kind of movement is impossible without it. Tribes are being brought together by sharing humor of the past. Columbus jokes gain great sympathy among all tribes, yet there are no tribes extant who had anything to do with Columbus. But the fact of white invasion from which all tribes have suffered has created a common bond in relation to Columbus jokes that gives a solid feeling of unity and purpose to the tribes.

The more desperate the problem, the more humor is directed to describe it. Satirical remarks often circumscribe problems so that possible solutions are drawn from the circumstances that would not make sense if presented in other than a humorous form.

Often people are awakened and brought to a militant edge through funny remarks. I often counseled people to run for the Bureau of Indian Affairs in case of an earthquake because nothing could shake the BIA. And I would watch as younger Indians set their jaws, determined that they, if nobody else, would shake it. We also had a saying that in case of fire call the BIA and they would handle it because they put a wet blanket on everything. This also got a warm reception from people.

Columbus and Custer jokes are the best for penetration into the heart of the matter, however. Rumor has it that Columbus began his journey with four ships. But one went over the edge so he arrived in the new world with only three. Another version states that Columbus didn't know where he was going, didn't know where he had been, and did it all on someone else's money. And the white man has been following Columbus ever since.

It is said that when Columbus landed, one Indian turned to another and said, "Well, there goes the neighborhood." Another version has two Indians watching Columbus land and one saying to the other, "Maybe if we leave them alone they will go away." A favorite cartoon in Indian country a few years back showed a flying saucer landing while an Indian watched. The caption was "Oh, no, not again."

The most popular and enduring subject of Indian humor is, of course, General Custer. There are probably more jokes about Custer and the Indians than there were participants in the battle. All tribes, even those thousands of miles from Montana, feel a sense of accomplishment when thinking of Custer. Custer binds together implacable foes because he represented the Ugly American of the last century and he got what was coming to him.

Some years ago we put out a bumper sticker which read "Custer Died for Your Sins." It was originally meant as a dig at the National Council of Churches. But as it spread around the nation it took on additional meaning until everyone claimed to understand it and each interpretation was different.

Originally, the Custer bumper sticker referred to the Sioux Treaty of 1868 signed at Fort Laramie in which the United States pledged to give free and undisturbed use of the lands claimed by Red Cloud in return for peace. Under the covenants of the Old Testament, breaking a covenant called for a blood sacrifice for atonement. Custer was the blood sacrifice for the United States breaking the Sioux treaty. That, at least originally, was the meaning of the slogan.

Custer jokes, however, can barely be categorized, let alone sloganized. Indians say that Custer was well-dressed for the occasion. When the Sioux found his body after the battle, he had on an Arrow shirt.

Many stories are derived from the details of the battle itself. Custer is said to have boasted that he could ride through the entire Sioux nation with his Seventh Cavalry and he was half right. He got half-way through.

One story concerns the period immediately after Custer's contingent had been wiped out and the Sioux and Cheyennes were zeroing in on Major Reno and his troops several miles to the south of the Custer battle-field.

The Indians had Reno's troopers surrounded on a bluff. Water was scarce, ammunition was nearly exhausted, and it looked like the next attack would mean certain extinction.

One of the white soldiers quickly analyzed the situation and shed his clothes. He covered himself with mud, painted his face like an Indian, and began to creep toward the Indian lines.

A Cheyenne heard some rustling in the grass and was just about to shoot.

"Hey, chief," the soldier whispered, "don't shoot, I'm coming over to join you. I'm going to be on your side."

The warrior looked puzzled and asked the soldier why he wanted to change sides.

"Well," he replied, "better red than dead."

Custer's Last Words occupy a revered place in Indian humor. One source states that as he was falling mortally wounded he cried, "Take no prisoners!" Other versions, most of them off color, concentrate on where those **** Indians are coming from. My favorite last saying pictures Custer on top of the hill looking at a multitude of warriors charging up the slope at him. He turns resignedly to his aide and says, "Well it's better than going back to North Dakota."

Since the battle it has been a favorite technique to boost the numbers on the Indian side and reduce the numbers on the white side so that Custer stands out as a man fighting against insurmountable odds. One question no pseudo-historian has attempted to answer, when changing the odds to make the little boy in blue more heroic, is how what they say were twenty thousand Indians could be fed when gathered into one camp. What a tremendous pony herd must have been gathered there, what a fantastic herd of buffalo must have been nearby to feed that amount of Indians, what an incredible source of drinking water must have been available for fifty thousand animals and some twenty thousand Indians!

Just figuring water-needs to keep that many people and animals alive for a number of days must have been incredible. If you have estimated correctly, you will see that the Little Big Horn was the last great *naval* engagement of the Indian wars.

The Sioux tease other tribes a great deal for not having been at the Little Big Horn. The Crows, traditional enemies of the Sioux, explain their role as Custer's scouts as one of bringing Custer where the Sioux could get at him! Arapahos and Cheyennes, allies of the Sioux in that battle, refer to the time they "bailed the Sioux out" when they got in trouble with the cavalry.

Even today variations of the Custer legend are bywords in Indian country. When an Indian gets too old and becomes inactive, people say he is "too old to muss the Custer anymore."

The early reservation days were times when humorous incidents abounded as Indians tried to adapt to the strange new white ways and occasionally found themselves in great dilemmas.

At Fort Sisseton, in Dakota territory, Indians were encouraged to enlist as scouts for the Army after the Minnesota Wars. Among the requirements for enlistment were a working knowledge of English and having attained twenty-one years of age. But these requirements were rarely met. Scouts were scarce and the goal was to keep a company of scouts at full strength, not to follow regulations from Washington to the letter.

In a short time the Army had a company of scouts who were very efficient but didn't know enough English to understand a complete sentence. Washington, finding out about the situation, as bureaucracies do, sent an inspector to check on the situation. While he was en route, orders to disband the scouts arrived, and so his task became one of closing the unit and making the mustering-out payments.

The scouts had lined up outside the command officer's quarters and were interviewed one by one. They were given their choice of taking money, horses, or a combination of the two as their final severance pay from the Army. Those who could not speak English were severely reprimanded and tended to get poorer horses in payment because of their obvious disregard of the regulations.

One young scout, who was obviously in violation of both requirements, was very worried about his interview. He quizzed the scouts who came from the room about the interview. To a man they repeated the same story: "You will be asked three questions, how old you are, how long you have been with the scouts, and whether you want money or horses for your mustering-out pay."

The young scout memorized the appropriate answers and prepared himself for his turn with the inspector. When his turn came he entered the room, scared to death but determined to do his best. He stood at attention before the man from Washington, eager to give his answers and get out of there.

The inspector, tired after a number of interviews, wearily looked up and inquired:

"How long have you been in the scouts?"

"Twenty years," the Indian replied with a grin.

The inspector stopped short and looked at the young man. Here was a man who looked only eighteen or twenty, yet he had served some twenty years in the scouts. He must have been one of the earliest recruits. It just didn't seem possible. Yet, the inspector thought, you can't tell an Indian's age from the way he looks, they sure can fool you sometimes. Or was he losing his mind after interviewing so many people in so short a time? Perhaps it was the Dakota heat. At any rate, he continued the interview.

"How old are you?" he continued.

"Three years."

A look of shock rippled across the inspector's face. Could this be some mysterious Indian way of keeping time? Or was he now delirious?

"Am I crazy or are you?" he angrily asked the scout.

"Both" was the reply and the scout relaxed, smiled, and leaned over the desk, reaching out to receive his money.

The horrified inspector cleared the window in one leap. He was seen in Washington, D.C., the following morning, having run full speed during the night. It was the last time Indian scouts were required to know English and applications for interpreter were being taken the following morning.

The problems of the missionaries in the early days provided stories which have become classics in Indian country. They are retold over and over again wherever Indians gather.

One story concerns a very obnoxious missionary who delighted in scaring the people with tales of hell, eternal fires, and everlasting damnation. This man was very unpopular and people went out of their way to avoid him. But he persisted to contrast heaven and hell as a carrot-and-stick technique of conversion.

One Sunday after a particularly fearful description of hell he asked an old chief, the main holdout of the tribe against Christianity, where he wanted to go. The old chief asked the missionary where *he* was going. And the missionary replied that, of course, he as a missionary of the gospel was going to heaven.

"Then I'll go to hell," the old chief said, intent on having peace in the world to come if not in this world.

On the Standing Rock reservation in South Dakota my grandfather served as the Episcopal missionary for years after his conversion to Christianity. He spent a great deal of his time trying to convert old Chief Gall, one of the strategists of Custer's demise, and a very famous and influential member of the tribe.

My grandfather gave Gall every argument in the book and some outside the book but the old man was adamant in keeping his old Indian ways. Neither the joys of heaven nor the perils of hell would sway the old man. But finally, because he was fond of my grandfather, he decided to become an Episcopalian.

He was baptized and by Christmas of that year was ready to take his first communion. He fasted all day and attended the Christmas Eve services that evening.

The weather was bitterly cold and the little church was heated by an old wood stove placed in the center of the church. Gall, as the most respected member of the community, was given the seat of honor next to the stove where he could keep warm.

In deference to the old man, my grandfather offered him communion first. Gall took the chalice and drained the entire supply of wine before returning to his seat. The wine had been intended for the entire congregation and so the old man had a substantial amount of spiritual refreshment.

Upon returning to his warm seat by the stove, it was not long before the wine took its toll on the old man who by now had had nothing to eat for nearly a day.

"Grandson," he called to my grandfather, "now I see why you wanted me to become a Christian. I feel fine, so nice and warm and happy. Why didn't you tell me that Christians did this every Sunday. If you had told me about this, I would have joined your church years ago."

Needless to say, the service was concluded as rapidly as possible and attendance skyrocketed the following Sunday.

Another missionary was traveling from Gallup to Albuquerque in the early days. Along the way he offered a ride to an Indian who was walking to town. Feeling he had a captive audience, he began cautiously to promote his message, using a soft-sell approach.

"Do you realize," he said, "that you are going to a place where sinners abound?"

The Indian nodded his head in assent.

"And the wicked dwell in the depths of their iniquities?"

Again a nod.

"And sinful women who have lived a bad life go?"

A smile and then another nod.

"And no one who lives a good life goes there?"

A possible conversion, thought the missionary, and so he pulled out his punch line: "And do you know what we call that place?"

The Indian turned, looked the missionary in the eye, and said, "Albuquerque."

Times may have changed but difficulties in communications seem to remain the same. At Santee, Nebraska, the people tell of a full blood who had a great deal of trouble understanding English. He used the foreign tongue as little as possible and managed to get along. But he knew only phrases of broken English, which he used when bargaining for his necessities of life.

One day he approached a white farmer and began bargaining for a fine rooster that the farmer owned. The old timer had brought two large bags filled with new potatoes and he motioned to the farmer that he wanted to trade them for the rooster.

Pointing from one to the other, he anxiously inquired, "potato rooster, potato rooster?" Soon the white farmer got the message and decided that it would be a good trade.

"Sure, chief," he replied, "I'll trade you."

So the Indian picked up the rooster, looked at it with satisfaction, tucked the rooster under his arm, and started to walk away.

As he was leaving, the white farmer began to think about the exchange. Obviously the rooster would be of little value without some hens for it. The potatoes were more than adequate to pay for a number of chickens, so he called after the Indian:

"Chief, do you want a pullet?"

The Indian turned around, tucked the rooster tighter under his arm, and said, "No, I can carry it."

In the Southwest, Indians like to talk about a similar play on words. One favorite story concerns a time when the Apaches and the settlers were fighting it out for control of Arizona territory. The chief of one Apache band was the last one needed to sign the peace treaty. Scout after scout had urged him to sign so the territory could have peace. But to no avail.

One day the chief took sick and, because he realized his days were numbered, he called his three sons together and made them pledge not to make peace unless all three signed the treaty. Soon after that the old man died and his three sons, Deerfoot, Running Bear, and Falling Rocks, all left to seek their fortunes with portions of the original band.

Scouts quickly found Deerfoot and Running Bear and convinced them they should sign the treaty. But they were unable to find Falling Rocks. Years went by and everyone in the territory sought the missing band so the treaty could be concluded. Falling Rocks was not to be found.

Eventually everyone gave up except the state highway department. They continued looking for him. And that is why today as you drive through the mountain passes in Arizona you will see large signs that read, "Look out for Falling Rocks."

The years have not changed the basic convictions of the Indian people that they are still dealing with the United States as equals. At a hearing on Civil Rights in South Dakota a few years ago a white man asked a Sioux if they still considered themselves an independent nation, "Oh, yes," was the reply, "we could still declare war on you. We might lose but you'd know you'd been in a terrible fight. Remember the last time in Montana?"

During the 1964 elections Indians were talking in Arizona about the relative positions of the two candidates, Johnson and Goldwater. A white man told them to forget about domestic policies and concentrate on the foreign policies of the two men. One Indian looked at him coldly and said that from the Indian point of view it was all foreign policy.

The year 1964 also saw the emergence of the Indian vote on a national scale. Rumors reached us that on the Navajo reservation there was more enthusiasm than understanding of the political processes. Large signs announced, "All the Way with LBJ."

The current joke is that a survey was taken and only 15 percent of the Indians thought that the United States should get out of Vietnam. Eighty-five percent thought they should get out of America!

One of the most popular topics of Indian humor is the Bureau of Indian Affairs. When asked what was the biggest joke in Indian country, a man once said, "the BIA." During the years of termination, no matter how many tribes were being terminated the BIA kept adding employees. Since the thrust of termination was to cut government expenditures, the continual hiring of additional people led Indians to believe that such was not the real purpose. The rumor began that the BIA was phasing out Indians and would henceforth provide services only for its own employees.

A favorite story about the BIA concerns the time when Interior tried to merge the Standing Rock and Cheyenne River Sioux agencies in an economy move. A Sioux from Cheyenne River told an investigating committee the following story.

One day an Indian went to the Public Health Service because he had a bad headache. The PHS doctor decided to operate on him and he cut the Indian's head open and took out the brain to examine it.

Just then a man came in the door and shouted, "Joe, your house is on fire."

Joe, lying on the operating table, urged the doctor to sew up his head so that he could go and fight the fire. The doctor did as requested and Joe headed for the door.

"Wait, Joe," the doctor yelled, "you forgot your brain."

"I don't need any brain," Joe answered as he went out the door. "After I get the fire put out, I'm going to work for the BIA."

An additional story about the BIA concerns the Indian who wanted a new brain. He walked into the PHS clinic and asked for an operation whereby he could exchange his brain for a better one.

The doctor took him into a room that contained many shelves upon which were rows of jars containing brains. Each jar had a price tag on it. A doctor's brain sold for ten dollars an ounce, a professor's brain sold for fifteen dollars an ounce. Similar brains from professional people ranged higher and higher until, at the very end of the back row of jars, there was a jar marked one thousand dollars an ounce.

The Indian asked why that type of brain was so expensive and wanted to know what kind of brain it was. The doctor said that the jar contained brains of the BIA, and added, "You know, it takes so many of them to make an ounce."

In 1967 we had a conference on manpower at Kansas City. One panel on employment had a well-known BIA representative moderating it. He made an excellent presentation and then asked for questions. For a long time the assembled delegates just sat and looked at him. So again he asked for questions, mentioned a few things he thought were important, and waited for response from the audience. Nothing.

Finally he said, "I really didn't want any discussion. I just wanted to show that the BIA can come to a conference and stand here without saying anything."

"You proved that during your speech," one of the Indians retorted.

Perhaps the most disastrous policy, outside of termination, ever undertaken by the Bureau of Indian Affairs was a program called Relocation. It began as a policy of the Eisenhower administration as a means of getting Indians off the reservation and into the city slums where they could fade away.

Considerable pressure was put on reservation Indians to move into the cities. Reservation people were continually harassed by bureau officials until they agreed to enter the program. Sometimes the BIA relocation officer was so eager to get the Indians moved off the reservation that he would take the entire family into the city himself.

But the Indians came back to the reservation as soon as they learned what the city had to offer. Many is the story by BIA people of how Indians got back to the reservations before the BIA officials who had taken them to the city returned.

When the space program began, there was a great deal of talk about sending men to the moon. Discussion often centered about the difficulty of returning the men from the moon to earth, as reentry procedures were considered to be very tricky. One Indian suggested that they send an Indian to the moon on relocation. "He'll figure out some way to get back."

Chippewas always tease the Sioux about the old days when they ran the Sioux out of Minnesota. It was, they claim, the first successful relocation program. In turn, the tribes that were pushed aside by the Sioux when they invaded the plains are ribbed about the relocation program which the Sioux conducted.

One solution to the "Indian problem" advocated in the Eisenhower years was closing the rolls of Indians eligible to receive federal services. Instead of federal services, each Indian would receive a set per capita share of the total budget. As each Indian died off, the total budget would be reduced. When all of the eligible Indians died off, that would be the end of federal-Indian relationships.

This plan was the favorite solution of Commissioner Glenn Emmons, who was heading the bureau at that time. But try as he might, he couldn't sell the program to anyone.

An agency superintendent from the Rosebud Sioux reservation in South Dakota had to go to Washington on business and so he decided to drive. As long as he was going he decided to take an old full blood with him to let the old man see the nation's capital.

The old man was very excited to be going to Washington and he made up his mind to see the Commissioner when he arrived there. So the superintendent began to suggest that the old man might have some solution to the Indian problem that he could share with the Commissioner. The old Indian discussed several ideas but admitted that they would probably be rejected.

Finally the superintendent outlined Emmon's plan to distribute the federal budget being spent on Indians among those then eligible for services. The old man pondered the idea for some time. Then he said, "That's the craziest idea I ever heard of. If I said something like that to the Commissioner, he would have me thrown out of his office."

Later the superintendent said he had always wished that the old man had suggested the plan to Emmons. "I always wanted," he told me, "to see the look on Emmon's face when an uneducated full blood suggested his own plan to him. I'd bet my last dollar that things would have changed at the BIA."

Frequently, without intending any humor, Indians can create a situation that is so funny that it is nearly impossible to believe. At the Manpower Conference in Kansas City in 1967 a series of events set up a hilarious incident. At least, looking back at it, Indians still chuckle over the results of the conference.

In 1966, after Philleo Nash had been Commissioner and had been fired for protecting the tribes, Udall gathered all of his top people and began to plan for a massive new program for "his" Indians. The administration also planned a comprehensive survey of Indian problems, perhaps realizing that Interior would once again draw a blank.

All of 1966 a secret Presidential Task Force surveyed Indian Affairs. By late December of that year they had compiled their report which, among other things, advocated a transfer of the Bureau of Indian Affairs from Interior to Health, Education and Welfare. Rumors began to fly in

Indian country about the impending transfer and so the administration sent John Gardner, then Secretary of HEW, to Kansas City to present the idea to the assembled tribes.

In spite of all we could do to get HEW to advance the idea to a series of small conferences made up of influential tribal leaders, HEW insisted on presenting the idea to the entire group of assembled tribes—cold. So Gardner embarked for Kansas City with the usual entourage of high officialdom to present the message.

The tribal chairmen were greatly concerned about the possible loss of treaty rights which might occur during the transfer. When Gardner finished his presentation he opened the floor for questions, and the concerned chairmen began.

The first man wanted to know if all treaty rights would be protected by law. The Secretary of HEW assured him that treaty rights would be protected by law. The second man said that he had had such assurances before and now he wanted Gardner to give him his personal assurance so he could go back and talk with his people. Gardner gave him the personal assurances he wanted.

The next chairman wanted Gardner's assurance that nothing would be changed in the method of operations. The third wanted Gardner's assurance that no part of the existing structure would be changed, but that only the name plates would be different. The man following again wanted assurance that nothing would be changed, absolutely nothing. Wearily Gardner explained that *nothing* would be changed, everything would remain the same, all personnel would remain the same.

Eight straight chairmen questioned Gardner, asking for assurances that the basic structure would remain absolutely as it had been under Interior. Not a jot or tittle, according to Gardner, would be changed at all. There was no possible way that anything could be changed. Everything was to remain just as it was.

The ninth questioner brought down the house. "Why," he inquired, "if there are to be no changes at all, do you want to transfer the bureau to HEW? It would be the same as it is now," he concluded.

It suddenly occurred to everyone that the chairmen had successfully trapped Gardner in a neat box from which there was no escape. Suffice it to say, there was no transfer.

Not only the bureau, but other agencies, became the subject of Indian humor. When the War on Poverty was announced, Indians were justly skeptical about the extravagant promises of the bureaucrats. The private organizations in the Indian field, organized as the Council on Indian Affairs, sponsored a Capital Conference on Poverty in Washington in May of 1966 to ensure that Indian poverty would be highlighted just prior to the passage of the poverty program in Congress.

Tribes from all over the nation attended the conference to present papers on the poverty existing on their reservations. Two Indians from the plains area were asked about their feelings on the proposed program.

"Well," said one, "if they bring that War on Poverty to our reservation, they'll know they've been in a fight."

At the same conference, Alex Chasing Hawk, a nationally famous Indian leader from Cheyenne River and a classic storyteller, related the following tale about poverty.

It seemed that a white man was introduced to an old chief in New York City. Taking a liking to the old man, the white man invited him to dinner. The old chief hadn't eaten a good steak in a long time and eagerly accepted. He finished one steak in no time and still looked hungry. So the white man offered to buy him another steak.

As they were waiting for the steak, the white man said, "Chief, I sure wish I had your appetite."

"I don't doubt it, white man," the chief said. "You took my land, you took my mountains and streams, you took my salmon and my buffalo. You took everything I had except my appetite and now you want that. Aren't you ever going to be satisfied?"

At one conference on urban renewal, an Indian startled the audience when he endorsed the program. All day he had advocated using the poverty program to solve Indian problems on the reservation. Then, when the discussion got around to urban renewal, he abruptly supported the program.

He was asked why he wanted the program. It was, he was assured, perfectly natural for black and Mexican people to support urban renewal because so many of their people lived in the cities. But it didn't make sense to the conference participants what good an urban program would do for reservation Indians.

"I know," the Indian replied, "that a great many blacks and Mexicans want the program because so many of their people live in the cities and these cities must be rebuilt to give them a better life. But the program would also mean a better life for my people. You see, after the cities are rebuilt and everyone is settled there, we are going to fence them off and run our buffalo all over the country again."

People are always puzzled when they learn that Indians are not involved in the Civil Rights struggle. Many expect Indians to be marching up and down like other people, feeling that all problems of poor groups are basically the same.

But Indian people, having treaty rights of long standing, rightly feel that protection of existing rights is much more important to them. Yet intra-group jokes have been increasing since the beginning of the Civil Rights movement and few Indians do not wryly comment on movements among the other groups.

An Indian and a black man were in a bar one day talking about the problems of their respective groups. The black man reviewed all of the progress his people had made over the past decade and tried to get the Indian inspired to start a similar movement of activism among the tribes.

Finally the black man concluded, "Well, I guess you can't do much, there are so few of you."

"Yes," said the Indian, "and there won't be very many of you if they decide to play cowboys and blacks."

Another time, an Indian and a black man were talking about the respective races and how they had been treated by the white man. Each was trying to console the other about the problem and each felt the other group had been treated worse.

The Indian reminded the black man how his people had been slaves, how they had not had a chance to have a good family life, and how they were so persecuted in the South.

The black man admitted all of the sufferings of his people, but he was far more eloquent in reciting the wrongs against the Indians. He reviewed the broken treaties, the great land thefts, the smallpox infected blankets given to the tribes by the English, and the current movement to relocate all the Indians in the cities, far from their homelands.

Listening to the vivid description, the Indian got completely carried away in remorse. As each wrong was recited he nodded sorrowfully and was soon convinced that there was practically no hope at all for his people. Finally he could stand no more.

"And do you know," he told the black man, "there was a time in the history of this country when they used to shoot us *just to get the feathers!*"

During the riots, an Indian and a black man were talking about the terrible things going on. The black man said that the Indians could have prevented all of this grief if they had only stopped the white men at the Allegheny Mountains in the early days. Then there would have been no expansion of white influence and perhaps even slavery would not have been started. Why, the black man wanted to know, hadn't the Indians stopped the white man when it was possible for them to do so.

"I know, I know," the Indian answered, "but every time we tried to attack their forts, they had 'Soul Brother' painted on them, and so we never got the job done."

Because there is so little communication between minority communities, inter-group jokes always have the great danger of being misunderstood. In 1966, beside the Custer cards, we put out a card which read "We Shall Overrun," which, at least to us, harked to the scenes in Western movies where a small group of Indians mysteriously grows as it is outlined along the rim of a canyon until it appears as if several thousand warriors have sprung from the initial group of a dozen.

When we showed the card to various blacks in the Civil Rights movement, they didn't know how to take it and several times there was a tense situation until the card was explained.

Such is not the case when tribes tease each other. Then everything is up for grabs. Sioux announce that safe-conduct passes are available to Chippewas at the registration desk. Chippewas retort that if the Sioux don't behave they will relocate them again. Southwestern tribes innocently proclaim that their chili is very mild when in reality they are using asbestos pottery to serve it in. And the northern tribes seem always to take large helpings, which they somehow manage to get down amid tears and burnt mouths.

In the old days, after the buffalo were gone, the Sioux were reduced to eating dogs to keep alive. They had no meat of any kind and rabbits on the reservations were rare. Other tribes keep up the ribbing by announcing that the chef has prepared a special treat for the Sioux present at the annual banquet through the special cooperation of the local dog pound.

In 1964, Billy Mills, a Sioux from Pine Ridge, South Dakota, won the ten thousand meter run at the Olympics in Tokyo. Justly proud of Billy, the Sioux went all out to inform other tribes of his achievement. One day we were bragging about Billy's feat to the Coeur d'Alenes of Idaho, who politely nodded their heads in agreement.

Finally the wife of the chairman, Leona Garry, announced that Mills' running ability did not really surprise the Coeur d'Alenes. "After all," she said, "up here in Idaho, Sioux have to run far, fast, and often if they mean to stay alive." That ended the discussion of Sioux athletic ability for the evening.

Clyde Warrior, during his time, was perhaps the single greatest wit in Indian country. One day he announced that the bureau was preparing a special training program for the other tribes. When quizzed about how it differed from other programs in existence, he noted that it had a restriction of only a half-hour lunch period. "Otherwise," Clyde said, "they would have to be retrained after lunch."

Providing information to inquisitive whites has also proved humorous on occasion. At a night club in Washington, D.C., a group of Indians from North Dakota were gathered, taking the edge off their trip before returning home. One man, a very shy and handsome Chippewa, caught the eye of one of the entertainers. She began to talk with him about Indian life.

Did Indians still live in tents, she inquired. He admitted shyly that he sometimes lived in a tent in the summer time because it was cooler than a house. Question after question came and was answered by the same polite responses. The girl took quite a fancy to the Chippewa and he got more and more embarrassed at the attention.

Finally she wanted to know if Indians still raided wagon trains. He said no, they had stopped doing that a long time ago. She was heartbroken at hearing the news. "I sure would like to be raided by you," she said, and brought down the house.

Louie Sitting Crow, an old timer from Crow Creek, South Dakota, used to go into town and watch the tourists who traveled along Highway 16 in South Dakota to get to the Black Hills. One day at a filling station a car from New York pulled up and began filling its tank for the long drive.

A girl came over to talk with Louie. She asked him a great many questions about the Sioux and Louie answered as best he could. Yes, the Sioux were fierce warriors. Yes, the Sioux had once owned all of the state. Yes, they still wished for the old days.

Finally the girl asked if the Indians still scalped people. Louie, weary of the questions, replied, "Lady, remember, when you cross that river and head west, you will be in the land of the fiercest Indians on earth and you will be very lucky to get to the Black Hills alive. And you ask me if they still scalp. Let me tell you, it's worse than that. Now they take the whole head."

As Louie recalled, the car turned around and headed east after the tank was full of gas.

Southwestern Indians can get off a good one when they are inspired. A couple of years ago I was riding a bus from Santa Fe to Albuquerque late at night. The bus was late in leaving Santa Fe and seemed like it was taking forever to get on its way.

Two old men from one of the pueblos between the two cities were aboard and were obviously feeling contented after their night in town. They filled the time we were waiting for the bus to depart telling stories and as the bus got under way they began to make comments on its snail's pace.

The bus driver was in no humor to withstand a running commentary on the speed of the bus that night and so he turned around and said, "If you don't like the speed we're making, why don't you get out and walk?"

"Oh, we couldn't do that," one of the men said. "They don't expect us home until the bus gets in."

An Indian in Montana was arrested for driving while intoxicated and he was thrown in jail for the night. The following morning he was hauled before the judge for his hearing. Not knowing English very well, the Indian worried about the hearing, but he was determined to do the best he could.

The judge, accustomed to articulate, English-speaking people appearing before him, waited for the man to make his plea. The Indian stood silently waiting for the judge to say something. As the two looked at each other the silence began to become unbearable and the judge completely forgot what the man was being tried for.

Finally, he said, "Well, speak up, Indian, why are you here?"

The Indian, who had been planning to plead not guilty, was also completely off balance. He gulped, looked at the judge, and said, "Your honor, I was arrested for driving a drunken car."

One-line retorts are common in Indian country. Popovi Da, the great Pueblo artist, was quizzed one day on why the Indians were the first ones on this continent. "We had reservations," was his reply. Another time, when questioned by an anthropologist on what Indians called America before the white man came, an Indian said simply, *Ours.* A young Indian was asked one day at a conference what a peace treaty was. He replied, "That's when the white man wants a piece of your land."

The best example of Indian humor and militancy I have ever heard was

given by Clyde Warrior one day. He was talking with a group of people
about the National Indian Youth Council, of which he was then president,
and its program for a revitalization of Indian life. Several in the crowd
were skeptical about the idea of rebuilding Indian communities along traditional Indian lines.

"Do you realize," he said, "that when the United States was founded, it
was only 5 percent urban and 95 percent rural and now it is 70 percent
urban and 30 percent rural?"

His listeners nodded solemnly but didn't seem to understand what he
was driving at.

"Don't you realize what this means?" he rapidly continued. "It means
we are pushing them into the cities. Soon we will have the country back
again."

Whether Indian jokes will eventually come to have more significance
than that, I cannot speculate. Humor, all Indians will agree, is the cement
by which the coming Indian movement is held together. When a people
can laugh at themselves and laugh at others and hold all aspects of life together without letting anybody drive them to extremes, then it seems to me
that that people can survive.

# BILL  HOSOKAWA

## *The Unhappy Days*

NEWS OF THE PEARL HARBOR DISASTER hit official Washington that lazy
afternoon with stunning impact. Top government leaders rushed un-
bidden to their offices, doing what they knew had to be done, awaiting
instructions and leadership from President Roosevelt. Among the earliest
to react outside of the War and Navy Departments was Secretary of the
Treasury Henry Morgenthau, Jr. In his first official action after the attack
he ordered the Secret Service to double the guard at the White House.
In his second order Morgenthau closed the nation's borders to all Japanese
nationals and through his Foreign Funds Control Office, removed all
licenses under which Japanese firms and individuals were doing business.

Of the various civilian departments of the Federal Government, Justice
through the FBI had been the first to involve itself with the Japanese
American minority after Pearl Harbor. Under authority provided by a
Presidential proclamation, FBI Chief J. Edgar Hoover's office issued orders

*From* NISEI: THE QUIET AMERICANS *by Bill Hosokawa. Reprinted
by permission of William Morrow and Company, Inc.
Copyright © 1969 by William K. Hosokawa.*

to execute plans drawn up in anticipation of this unhappy day, and special agents fanned out swiftly to round up enemy aliens who had been under surveillance for many months. The Treasury Department was only a half step behind. Officials of both quickly became aware, if they hadn't been already, of the ancient, smouldering anti-Japanese emotionalism of the West Coast that had been fanned into instant life by the outbreak of hostilities. It did not take long for that emotionalism to be felt in Washington. In the book *Years of War*, the third volume of the Morgenthau diaries, we find this passage:

". . . deep-rooted hostility to the Japanese generated frequent rumors about espionage and subversion and frightened demands for repressive treatment not only of local Japanese residents but also of *Nisei*, American citizens of Japanese descent. On December 10 some of the staff of Foreign Funds Control urged Morgenthau to take over thousands of small businesses owned by Japanese and *Nisei* in the area between the Pacific Ocean and Utah."

Morgenthau apparently thought the proposal was important enough to summon the FBI's Hoover to his office that evening to discuss it with him and two Treasury officials. That same night, perhaps by coincidence, a Treasury Department agent told West Coast military authorities that some 20,000 Japanese in the San Francisco metropolitan area were "ready for organized action."

"Without checking the authenticity of the report," the Army admits in its official history, *Guarding the United States and Its Outposts*, "the Ninth Corps Area staff (in San Francisco) hurriedly completed a plan for their evacuation that was approved by the corps area commander."

The Ninth Corps Area staff, thoroughly spooked, was jumping at shadows. The 1940 census shows a total Japanese population—men, women and children; the senile and bedridden as well as infants—of 12,644 in San Francisco and nearby San Mateo, Alameda, Contra Costa and Marin counties. But apparently no one on the staff bothered to check with Army Intelligence. The so-called "evacuation plan," which has never been made public, to be effective had to call inevitably for clearing of entire blocks at bayonet point, with troops hammering at doors in the middle of the night and families being rousted out of bed and herded into concentration areas. Fortunately, the order to execute the plan was never given.

The Army's official history tells us: "The next morning the Army called the local FBI chief, who 'scoffed at the whole affair as the wild imaginings of a discharged former FBI man.' This stopped any further local action for the moment, but the corps area commander duly reported the incident to Washington and expressed the hope that 'it may have the effect of arousing the War Department to some action looking to the establishment of an area or areas for the detention of aliens.' "

In his meeting with Morgenthau that night of December 10, Hoover argued that no further action against Japanese Americans was required at the time since his agents had the situation well in hand with hundreds of aliens considered potentially dangerous already in custody. Later, Hoover wrote a memo about the meeting to his chief, Attorney General Francis Biddle, reporting that Morgenthau had been in telephone conversation with one of his representatives in San Francisco, and that: "It was the opinion of Mr. X that there should be a roundup of the Japanese in San Francisco, Los Angeles and the Bay Cities . . . as well as certain sections of the San Joaquin Valley."

Morgenthau did not make a decision that night, but by next morning he had decided the proposal "was not only hysterical but impractical." His basic position was that moves to counter subversion and espionage were the responsibility of the Justice Department, and it behooved Treasury to confine itself to an interest in the financial affairs of any aliens of any country who were doing business in the United States. Morgenthau continues in his memoirs:

"Someone with 'some horse sense,' moreover, had to be sure that the Treasury was not preventing Japanese farmers from providing food for Los Angeles markets. Californians, Morgenthau said, 'were so hysterical they wanted the Army to go out and work the truck farms while they put the Japanese into a concentration camp.' He would have no part of that: 'We have just got to keep our feet on the ground.' "

When Edward Foley, the Treasury's general counsel, objected that it was no time to be thinking about civil liberties when the country was in danger, Morgenthau by his own account replied:

"Listen, when it comes to suddenly mopping up 150,000 Japanese and putting them behind barbed wire, irrespective of their status, and consider doing the same with the Germans, I want at some time to have caught my breath . . . Anybody that wants to hurt this country or injure us, put him where he can't do it, but . . . indiscriminately, no."

The charred wreckage of Pearl Harbor was not even cool and all the facts had not been tallied, but already a member of President Roosevelt's Cabinet was being pressured to seize *Issei* and *Nisei* businesses and lock up their owner and their families in concentration camps. Early news dispatches from Honolulu had repeated hysterical rumors of widespread acts of sabotage by resident Japanese coordinated with the aerial attack. These rumors were categorically denied by military and civilian defense officials weeks and months later, but the truth did not always catch up with the lies. The point of view expressed by Edward Foley was espoused by many high officials and as we shall see, ultimately it was accepted by President Roosevelt. It is difficult to deny that this reflected unabashed racism. At best it was thoughtless racism. In retrospect, it seems likely that Foley and the other well-meaning individuals who thought as he did would not have been quite so willing to shelve civil rights had it meant restricting the freedoms of persons other than a faceless, powerless, relatively insignificant American minority which was of the same race as the enemy.

The *Nisei* were, of course, totally unaware of what was going on behind closed doors in Washington, but they were painfully cognizant of the need to improve their public relations. After the shock and numbness of December 7 had eased a bit—it was weeks before it could be said they had regained their emotional equilibrium—residents of the Japanese communities on the Pacific Coast hastened to repair their image scarred by a happening thousands of miles away. At this point the *Issei* were more realistic about their plight than the *Nisei*. The *Issei* could understand the inevitability of being treated as enemy aliens. But the *Nisei*, who had taken deep pride in their rights as citizens, were depressed and frustrated to find themselves being considered one with the enemy Jap. It was *their* country that had been attacked. It was *not* their country that had assaulted Pearl Harbor. Their experience having been what it was, they were realistic enough to see dark days ahead for themselves. Yet, not one in a thousand thought seriously that the time would come when their government would lock them up in concentration camps on the basis of race and race alone.

In seeking to analyze the reason why reaction against Japanese Americans was so intense, some observers have noted that Germany had Hitler and Italy had Mussolini, both figures that were easy to hate and easy to caricature. These caricatures could not be linked with German Americans or Italo Americans. But there were no such handy targets in Japan for America's patriotic ire. Tojo and Hirohito were virtually unknown to the American public. They had not appeared larger-than-life on American newsreel screens, ranting and posturing in front of phalanxes of uniformed henchmen. So an old stereotype was dusted off and the Japanese enemy pictured as a buck-toothed, bespectacled, monkey-faced sneak, a hateful racial canard that was easily applicable to the *Issei* and *Nisei*. Their racial homogeneity ("They all look alike to me," two generations of whites had complained without really trying to see individuals) made them perfect subjects for stereotyping. The physical characteristics of the Japanese made it simple to segregate them, just as with the Negroes. And in the stereotype mold, a *Nisei* instantly became "Jap," no matter how many generations his family had been separated from the old country, no matter how wide the cultural and ideological gap that had been opened between him and his ancestral land. The caricature of the Japanese enemy was identifiable as the schoolboy, the vegetable farmer, the gardener and corner grocer in military uniform. Not so with Germans and Italians. Like other elements of the racial potpourri that is America, they come in many shades of white, in many suit sizes, their noses hooked or straight with their hair ranging from blond to darkest brunette. In the melting pot they quickly became indistinguishable. Morton Grodzins points out additionally that the German enemy (Nazi) and Italian enemy (Fascist) would be distinguished verbally from Germans and Italians in the United States, "but no such convenient nomenclature existed for the Japanese. In most public discussions both citizens and enemies were 'Japs.' "

Caught napping and humiliated at Pearl Harbor, albeit by a dishonorable act, it was only human for Americans to point the finger of righteous anger at the treachery of the Jap in an effort to lighten the weight of their own culpability. And in an environment where anti-Oriental racism had been a seldom-questioned tradition—comparable to the Deep South's attitude toward Negroes—and a way of successful political life, it was inevitable that the racial stereotype should be projected onto the *Issei* and *Nisei* and their loyalty loudly challenged. On the West Coast this was as predictable as a knee-jerk is to the stimulus of a rap with a rubber hammer. There were whites who honestly believed they were helping to win the war by throwing a brick through the window of a Japanese grocery store or firing a shot from a speeding car into the home of a Japanese farmer; their mentality was little different from the sheeted and hooded night riders in the Deep South. After Pearl Harbor the *Issei* who had experienced the West Coast's racism feared the worst. The *Nisei*, too young as a group to be aware of the past, were less disturbed by the darkening clouds.

Their youth and immaturity was another key factor in the inability of the *Nisei* to stand up and be recognized as loyal Americans. Their parents for many reasons had kept largely to themselves and were little known outside their segregated communities. The *Nisei* had gone to school with white children, played ball with them, visited in their homes, but they were still strangers to the men in positions of authority and influence. There were too few *Nisei* like Tom Yatabe. Literally and figuratively, the *Nisei* had no Joe DiMaggio whose baseball brilliance all but obliterated the fact of his Italian immigrant heritage. No one would dream of suspecting Joe DiMaggio's father, much less the great Yankee Clipper himself, of disloyalty toward the United States even though the elder DiMaggio was an alien. (One small but significant point needs to be made: Unlike the *Issei*, the elder DiMaggio had the privilege of naturalization. Up to 1941 he had not chosen to exercise it.) Yet the vast preponderance of *Issei* and *Nisei* were no less loyal than the DiMaggios, father and son.

The *Nisei* needed no prompting to demonstrate their loyalty, and Kido's telegram to President Roosevelt was only the start of a spontaneous, uncoordinated series of actions that were more notable for their sincerity than their effectiveness. In Seattle the JACL chapter formed an Emergency Defense Committee. Jimmie Sakamoto headed it for the simple reason that he was the first to see a need for such an organization and all other potential leaders were too busy with their own affairs. The committee quickly sponsored a community-wide loyalty rally at the Buddhist church. Mayor Earl Millikin, still free of the hostile pressures that were to weigh heavily on him shortly, was happy to address a crowd that packed the gymnasium and overflowed into the basement rooms and out onto the sidewalk. His audience, apprehensive at first, was relieved to hear a flag-waving speech expressing his faith in the American democratic system, and promising fair play. But within two and a half months Mayor Millikin was to have second thoughts. Appearing before the Select Committee Investigating National Defense Migration, better known as the Tolan Committee for its chairman, Congressman John H. Tolan of California, Millikin demonstrated he had been swept along by the rising clamor for evacuation. The good mayor confessed it was "utterly impossible" to weed out the dangerous ones among the people he had addressed as "my fellow Americans." And because of this inability to distinguish the good from the bad, he offered as the city's contribution to the evacuation program the services of the 500 horsemen of Seattle's "Cavalry Brigade" to lead every last Japanese American into exile east of the Cascade mountains.

In San Francisco *Nisei* were urged by their leaders to support the Hearst newspapers—those antagonists of long ago—in their widely publicized but largely unfruitful campaign to collect money to buy "bombers for Tokyo," and were duly photographed making their contributions. In Los Angeles the JACL chapter called a special meeting at which everyone fervently pledged his loyalty to the United States. An "Anti-Axis Committee" was organized with Tokie Slocum as chairman to ferret out "subversive activity," and this development was duly reported by local papers and the wire services.

Someone suggested it would make good publicity to get the Los Angeles County Board of Supervisors to join their *Nisei* constituents in signing a loyalty pledge. Masao Satow, who had known Board Chairman John Anson Ford through YMCA activities, was named to head a committee of three to call on the officials. The supervisors were more embarrassed than honored. Ford, who had—and has—an excellent civil rights record, said he was happy to vouch for Satow's loyalty because they were old friends, but he declined to be associated with the other two *Nisei* members of the delegation whom he did not know. In community after community *Nisei* made belated efforts to advertise their loyalty with rallies to which civic dignitaries were invited, with purchases of war bonds and donations of blood, with newspaper publicity about the extent to which *Nisei* had become assimilated into American life (the intended implication being that they couldn't possibly be disloyal), with statements condemning Japanese militarists and pledging fealty for the United States even unto death. Scores of *Nisei* volunteered for military service but they discovered, as the Kuroki brothers did, that suddenly they had become unacceptable to their country.

In one particularly ingenious publicity ploy, Ham Fisher, creator of the then popular Joe Palooka comic strip, was asked to work a *Nisei* GI into his story. Palooka, a somewhat simpleminded but clean-living, patriotic American had given up his heavyweight championship of the world to join the Army and it would not have been illogical for him to meet a *Nisei* at his training camp. Fisher graciously found reasons why this could not be done, but he drew a single panel in which Palooka recognized the loyalty of *Nisei* in American Army uniform, and the Seattle *Times* published it. Such efforts, unfortunately, were too little by far and much too late to do a great deal toward swaying public opinion.

The Treasury Department's blanket crackdown on aliens immediately following the outbreak of war had been applied indiscriminately in the case of Japanese against citizens and aliens alike. *Nisei* who went to draw money from bank accounts found their funds blocked for the reason that they had Japanese names. Purchase of food and other necessities became a problem almost instantly. In San Francisco Annie Clo Watson summoned heads of welfare agencies, outlined the problem and demanded assistance. Mrs. Eleanor Roosevelt, the tireless First Lady who served unofficially as the President's eyes and ears, happened to be passing through San Francisco. Only three days before the Pearl Harbor attack, on December 4, the New York *Times* had published a statement from her about the possible effects of war which she pointedly said had been cleared with the Departments of State and Justice:

"I see absolutely no reason why anyone who has had a good record—that is, who has no criminal nor anti-American record—should have any anxiety about his position. This is equally applicable to the Japanese who cannot become citizens but have lived here for 30 or 40 years and to those newcomers who have not yet had time to become citizens."

Now a *Nisei* delegation called on her to ask her good offices in getting funds, at least those of citizens, released. She promised to see what could be done. But no action had been taken when Mike Masaoka finally made his way back to San Francisco on Thursday, December 11. At Kido's bidding he got on the telephone once more to Senator Thomas in Washington and explained the problem. Precisely what Thomas was able to accomplish is unknown. At any rate, in a short while the Treasury eased its orders so that both *Issei* and *Nisei* could draw up to $100 a month for living expenses and most of their businesses were permitted to resume normal operations. In many instances, however, the thaw came too late to avoid costly losses. *Issei-Nisei* flower growers in California, for example, found many of their long-time customers had switched to other suppliers. With the Christmas season approaching, they couldn't afford to take a chance on losing a source of supply, and who knew what the government would do next? Workmen who had been trained over the years left their Japanese employers in fear that they would not be paid. Similarly fearful, suppliers demanded cash from Japanese customers whose credit record had been impeccable.

Tom Sashihara's experience was not untypical. While bank accounts were frozen he took home receipts from his three stores in Los Angeles and hid the money. Soon he had much more cash around the house than he was comfortable with. But let him tell the story in his own words:

"One day during the first week two federal agents came unannounced to my drugstore No. 1 and ordered immediate closing. Upon my exhortations and after much telephoning with their superior, they allowed me to pay $50 cash to each of my employees. The rest of the cash and all valuables were put in the safe, on which was placed a government seal.

"The agents also closed my store No. 2 and went right down the street closing all larger stores in Little Tokyo, one by one. On the third day they were about to padlock Kimura Brothers. Then a special dispatch came from Washington ordering them not to close any more stores, so Kimura and a few other fortunate ones down the street escaped. We were informed that reopening applications might be filed at the Federal Reserve Bank. It took three days of waiting in the corridor of the bank to obtain an application blank. The filing required more time and figuring than it took to fill out an income tax return. I kept on calling every day until the permit was issued on December 21 and the government agents broke the seals on our doors. When the stores were reopened the stagnant air mixed with the nauseating odor of spoiled food in the fountain was unbearable. It took a full day to put the store in shape. But I was thankful that we were allowed to open before Christmas, even though only three days of shopping remained."

Meanwhile the well-publicized FBI roundups continued amid periodic reports of suspicious activity. The press was filled with sensational revelations about mysterious goings-on. A flaming arrow pointing toward Seattle was reportedly touched off by fifth columnists in the wooded hills above Port Angeles. Tomatoes had been planted, the press reported, so they formed an arrow showing the way to a Southern California aircraft plant. The truth was that the "flaming arrow" was brush being burned by forest workers, and the tomato plants, capped with paper to protect them against frost, were planted in a field that came to a point. If one looked far enough, there were numerous other such tomato field "markers" pointing in every direction, even straight out to sea. The logical explanations, alas, were never as exciting as the original alarms and never attracted quite the same attention.

Other published reports had more substance but were equally misleading. The FBI announced it had seized a total of 2,592 guns from enemy aliens, 199,000 rounds of ammunition, 1,652 sticks of dynamite, 1,458 radio receivers, 2,014 cameras and other contraband items. Enough material to launch and guide a major insurrection! What was not explained until considerably later was that most of the guns were sporting weapons owned by persons who had every right to possess them, that much of the ammunition was picked up in sporting goods stores, that it was normal for farmers to have dynamite to blow up stumps on land being cleared. Attorney General Biddle eventually admitted that his men had been making searches without warrants in pursuit of fifth columnists, but they had uncovered "no Japanese saboteurs . . . and no illegal radio transmitter was found at all." He went on to say:

"We have not uncovered through these searches any dangerous persons that we could not otherwise know about. We have not found among all the sticks of dynamite and gun powder any evidence that any of it was to be used in bombs. We have not found a single machine gun nor have we found any gun in any circumstances indicating that it was to be used in a manner helpful to our enemies. We have not found a camera which we have reason to believe was for use in espionage."

Biddle's report was intended as a tribute to the preparedness of the FBI, but in effect it also absolved the *Issei*. But his words were heard and heeded by few. It was easier to remember all those guns and ammunition and dynamite the FBI had seized from those treacherous Japs. The public's apprehensions were whipped up even further when Secretary of the Navy Frank Knox, after a hurried inspection of Pearl Harbor and Honolulu, issued a report on December 15 that most segments of the press promptly interpreted as confirming earlier accounts of fifth column treachery on the part of Hawaii's Japanese population. Knox's official report made no mention of fifth column activity. In fact he praised Hawaiian *Nisei* who had rushed to man guns against the enemy. But in a press conference in conjunction with the release of his report, he was quoted as saying: "I think the most effective fifth column work of the entire war was done in Hawaii, with the possible exception of Norway."

Did he mean to say espionage—the kind of diplomatic spying that is an accepted part of international relations? Was the mention of "fifth column work" an unconscious slip of the tongue? If so, why was not the error corrected? Or was it an intentional slip calculated to whip up war fever and stir the national anger? These are questions that cannot now be answered, but Knox's statement was to come back to haunt the *Nisei* time and again as the first isolated cries for evacuation became a frantic chorus.

In its zeal the FBI was guilty of picking up some rather unlikely suspects. Take the case of Mrs. Tora Miyake, arrested in Portland. She was a frail, shy, middle-aged widow who owned a debt-ridden weekly Japanese language newspaper she had inherited from her husband. It was edited for her by an employee and she had virtually no control over its content. What little money the paper made was through its printing shop which she operated. To supplement her income she gave piano lessons and taught young *Nisei* at a Japanese language school. Several years before the outbreak of war she had gone to Japan to visit sisters she hadn't seen for more than twenty-five years, but was so disillusioned by her experiences that she cut short her trip. She had two adult children, a married daughter and a son in college. This hardly seemed to be the kind of background that made it necessary to arrest her as an alien dangerous to the safety of the United States. Friends who could never understand why the FBI seized her wondered if the similarity of her name, Tora, to that of her late husband, Taro, hadn't resulted in a ghastly error. Soon after she was taken into custody her son, Kenneth, quit school and enlisted in the U.S. Army where he served with distinction.

(Another case of confused if not mistaken identity is related by Yas Abiko, the San Francisco newspaperman whose father Kyutaro Abiko, had published the *Nichi Bei*. Kyutaro died in 1936. By strange coincidence, a Japanese named Kyuta Abiko published a newspaper, also called the *Nichi Bei*, in New York City. Perhaps because the authorities could not figure out the relationship, Yas Abiko was denied permission to enter states under jurisdiction of the Eastern Defense Command during the war.)

Meanwhile, the patriotic determination to win the war and avenge the perfidy of Pearl Harbor was being expressed in strange ways. Some hotels and restaurants fired their *Issei* chefs. *Issei* janitors were told their services were no longer needed. Railroads discharged *Issei* section foremen with service records unblemished for twenty or thirty years. Many municipalities cancelled business licenses to operate grocery stores, beer halls and cleaning shops. Some hospitals refused to accept Japanese patients. Each of these acts of misguided patriotism created a hardship. Many of the families of men seized by the FBI found themselves without funds. Japanese communities that had taken pride in avoiding the welfare rolls even in the depths of the Depression suddenly found many of their people in want. With *Issei* organizations decimated, JACL chapters took over in community after community, accepting contributions to be distributed to the needy, serving as a buffer between government officials and the *Issei*, operating as a clearing house for information. The Federal Government's several departments had many things to say to the *Issei* and *Nisei* but it had no line of communication. Metropolitan newspaper coverage of federal pronouncements was spotty and confused. Here again JACL stepped in. In San Francisco Kido and Masaoka gathered what information they could from federal officials. With the help of volunteers they cut stencils and mimeographed bulletins which were airmailed to JACL chapter officials up and down the Pacific Coast. In Northern California the Japanese newspapers had been closed down. In Southern California they were permitted to operate under federal supervision. Where there were no newspapers, local JACL leaders copied the bulletins from headquarters, had some of the information translated into Japanese and ran off their own mimeographed newsletters which were distributed door to door by Boy Scouts. With rumors thick in the air, authoritative information was necessary to prevent panic.

One of the most persistent rumors had it that all Japanese nationals—the *Issei*—were to be interned in concentration camps for the duration. Although no one could confirm the report and no one could trace it to its origins, it did not seem especially outlandish. After all the *Issei* were enemy aliens, and a goodly number of them were already under detention.

Then one day late in December, Kido had a caller. He was Fred Nomura, who operated an insurance business in the East Bay area. Nomura seemed to be deeply agitated. "Sab," he said, "I hear they're going to put all the Japanese in concentration camps. Do you know anything about that?"

"Who says so?" Kido challenged. He thought it was another wild rumor and was anxious to quash it.

"The chief of police in Oakland told me," Nomura said. "He told me everybody—*Issei*, *Nisei*, even the little kids—are going to be interned."

"He's crazy," Kido replied. "They can't do that to us. We're American citizens. We've got our rights."

Vine Deloria, Jr. *Custer Died for Your Sins* (New York: The Macmillan Company, 1969).

Bernard DeVoto *The Easy Chair* (Boston: Houghton Mifflin Co., 1955).

Philip Durham and Everett L. Jones *The Negro Cowboys* (New York: Dodd, Mead & Company, 1965).

Audrie Girdner and Ann Loftis *The Great Betrayal* (New York: The Macmillan Company, 1969).

Nancie Gonzalez *The Spanish Americans of New Mexico: A Heritage of Pride* (Albuquerque: University of New Mexico Press, 1969).

Bill Hosokawa *Nisei* (New York: William Morrow & Company, Inc., 1969).

William H. Leckie *The Buffalo Soldiers* (Norman, Okla.: University of Oklahoma Press, 1967).

Charles F. Lummis *Bullying the Moqui* (Prescott, Ariz.: Prescott College Press, 1968).

Gene Marine *America the Raped: The Engineering Mentality and the Devastation of a Continent* (New York: Simon and Schuster, 1969).

Peter Nabokov *Tijerina and the Courthouse Raid* (Albuquerque: University of New Mexico Press, 1969).

George I. Sanchez *Forgotten People* (Albuquerque: Calvin Horn, Publisher, Inc., 1967).

Stan Steiner
    *La Raza:The Mexican-Americans* (New York: Harper & Row, 1970).
    *The New Indians* (New York: Dell Publishing Co., Inc., 1970).

# SIX

## The Nature Essay

MOST OF THE PUBLIC LAND—national parks, national forests, and wilderness areas—is in the West, so the struggle between the conservationists and the exploiters has found the West its main battleground.

Wallace Stegner has published at least eight essays on the enjoyment and conservation of nature. *Wilderness Letter* is one of the best statements in print on the philosophy of wilderness preservation. Mr. McKee describes New Mexico, the land and the culture in anomalous contrast.

Joseph Wood Krutch and David Ross Brower are noted nature writers, and some of their most impressive essays are reprinted here; each of these essays has been included in the magnificent Exhibit Format Series published by the Sierra Club.

# WALLACE STEGNER

## *Wilderness Letter*

Los Altos, Calif.
Dec. 3, 1960

DAVID E. PESONEN
Wildland Research Center
Agricultural Experiment Station
243 Mulford Hall
University of California
Berkeley 4, Calif.

Dear Mr. Pesonen:

I believe that you are working on the wilderness portion of the Outdoor Recreation Resources Review Commission's report. If I may, I should like to urge some arguments for wilderness preservation that involve recreation, as it is ordinarily conceived, hardly at all. Hunting, fishing, hiking, mountain-climbing, camping, photography, and the enjoyment of natural scenery will all, surely, figure in your report. So will the wilderness as a genetic reserve, a scientific yardstick by which we may measure the world in its natural balance against the world in its man-made imbalance. What I want to speak for is not so much the wilderness uses, valuable as those are, but the wilderness *idea*, which is a resource in itself. Being an intangible and spiritual resource, it will seem mystical to the practical-minded —but then anything that cannot be moved by a bulldozer is likely to seem mystical to them.

I want to speak for the wilderness idea as something that has helped form our character and that has certainly shaped our history as a people. It has no more to do with recreation than churches have to do with recreation, or than the strenuousness and optimism and expansiveness of what historians call the "American Dream" have to do with recreation. Nevertheless, since it is only in this recreation survey that the values of wilderness are being compiled, I hope you will permit me to insert this idea between the leaves, as it were, of the recreation report.

Something will have gone out of us as a people if we ever let the remaining wilderness be destroyed; if we permit the last virgin forests to be turned into comic books and plastic cigarette cases; if we drive the few remaining members of the wild species into zoos or to extinction; if we pollute the last clear air and dirty the last clean streams and push our paved roads through the last of the silence, so that never again will Americans be free in their own country from the noise, the exhausts, the stinks of human and automotive waste. And so that never again can we have the chance to see ourselves single, separate, vertical and individual in the world, part of the environment of trees and rocks and soil, brother to the other animals, part of the natural world and competent to belong in it. Without any remaining wilderness we are committed wholly, without chance for even momentary reflection and rest, to a headlong drive into our technological termite-life, the Brave New World of completely man-controlled environment. We need wilderness preserved—as much of it as is still left, and as many kinds—because it was the challenge against which our character as a people was formed. The reminder and the reassurance that it is still there is good for our spiritual health even if we never once in ten years set foot in it. It is good for us when we are young, because of the incomparable sanity it can bring briefly, as vacation and rest, into our insane lives. It is important to us when we are old simply because it is there—important, that is, simply as idea.

We are a wild species, as Darwin pointed out. Nobody ever tamed or domesticated or scientifically bred us. But for at least three millennia we have been engaged in a cumulative and ambitious race to modify and gain control of our environment, and in the process we have come close to domesticating ourselves. Not many people are likely, any more, to look upon what we call "progress" as an unmixed blessing. Just as surely as it has brought us increased comfort and more material goods, it has brought us spiritual losses, and it threatens now to become the Frankenstein that will destroy us. One means of sanity is to retain a hold on the natural world, to remain, insofar as we can, good animals. Americans still have that chance, more than many peoples; for while we were demonstrating ourselves the most efficient and ruthless environment-busters in history, and slashing and burning and cutting our way through a wilderness continent, the wilderness was working on us. It remains in us surely as Indian names remain on the land. If the abstract dream of human liberty and human dignity became, in America, something more than an abstract dream, mark it down at least partially to the fact that we were in subtle ways subdued by what we conquered.

The Connecticut Yankee, sending likely candidates from King Arthur's unjust kingdom to his Man Factory for rehabilitation, was over-optimistic, as he later admitted. These things cannot be forced, they have to grow. To make such a man, such a democrat, such a believer in human individual dignity, as Mark Twain himself, the frontier was necessary, Hannibal and the Mississippi and Virginia City, and reaching out from those the wilderness; the wilderness as opportunity and as idea, the thing that has helped to make an American different from and, until we forget it in the roar of our industrial cities, more fortunate than other men. For an American, insofar as he is new and different at all, is a civilized man who has renewed himself in the wild. The American experience has been the confrontation by old peoples and cultures of a world as new as if it had just risen from the sea. That gave us our hope and our excitement, and the hope and excitement can be passed on to newer Americans, Americans who never saw any phase of the frontier. But only so long as we keep the remainder of our wild as a reserve and a promise—a sort of wilderness bank.

As a novelist, I may perhaps be forgiven for taking literature as a reflection, indirect but profoundly true, of our national consciousness. And our literature, as perhaps you are aware, is sick, embittered, losing its mind, losing its faith. Our novelists are the declared enemies of their society. There has hardly been a serious or important novel in this century that did not repudiate in part or in whole American technological culture for its commercialism, its vulgarity, and the way in which it has dirtied a clean continent and a clean dream. I do not expect that the preservation of our remaining wilderness is going to cure this condition. But the mere example that we can as a nation apply some other criteria than commercial and exploitative considerations would be heartening to many Americans, novelists or otherwise. We need to demonstrate our acceptance of the natural world, including ourselves; we need the spiritual refreshment that being natural can produce. And one of the best places for us to get that is in the wilderness where the fun houses, the bulldozers, and the pavements of our civilization are shut out.

Sherwood Anderson, in a letter to Waldo Frank in the 1920's, said it better than I can. "Is it not likely that when the country was new and men were often alone in the fields and the forest they got a sense of bigness outside themselves that has now in some way been lost . . . Mystery whispered in the grass, played in the branches of trees overhead, was caught up and blown across the American line in clouds of dust at evening on the prairies . . . I am old enough to remember tales that strengthen my belief in a deep semi-religious influence that was formerly at work among our people. The flavor of it hangs over the best work of Mark Twain . . . I can remember old fellows in my home town speaking feelingly of an evening spent on the big empty plains. It had taken the shrillness out of them. They had learned the trick of quiet . . ."

We could learn it too, even yet; even our children and grandchildren could learn it. But only if we save, for just such absolutely non-recreational, impractical, and mystical uses as this, all the wild that still remains to us.

It seems to me significant that the distinct downturn in our literature from hope to bitterness took place almost at the precise time when the frontier officially came to an end, in 1890, and when the American way of life had begun to turn strongly urban and industrial. The more urban it has become, and the more frantic with technological change, the sicker and more embittered our literature, and I believe our people, have become. For myself, I grew up on the empty plains of Saskatchewan and Montana and in the mountains of Utah, and I put a very high valuation on what those places gave me. And if I had not been able periodically to renew myself in the mountains and deserts of western America I would be very nearly bughouse. Even when I can't get to the back country, the thought of the colored deserts of southern Utah, or the reassurance that there are still stretches of prairie where the world can be instantaneously perceived as disk and bowl, and where the little but intensely important human being is exposed to the five directions and the thirty-six winds, is a positive consolation. The idea alone can sustain me. But as the wilderness areas are progressively exploited or "improved," as the jeeps and bulldozers of uranium prospectors scar up the deserts and the roads are cut into the alpine timberlands, and as the remnants of the unspoiled and natural world are progressively eroded, every such loss is a little death in me. In us.

I am not moved by the argument that those wilderness areas which have already been exposed to grazing or mining are already deflowered, and so might as well be "harvested." For mining I cannot say much good except that its operations are generally short-lived. The extractable wealth is taken and the shafts, the tailings, and the ruins left, and in a dry country such as the American West the wounds men make in the earth do not quickly heal. Still, they are only wounds; they aren't absolutely mortal. Better a wounded wilderness than none at all. And as for grazing, if it is strictly controlled so that it does not destroy the ground cover, damage the ecology, or compete with the wildlife it is in itself nothing that need conflict with the wilderness feeling or the validity of the wilderness experience. I have known enough range cattle to recognize them as wild animals; and the people who herd them have, in the wilderness context, the dignity of rareness; they belong on the frontier, moreover, and have a look of rightness. The invasion they make on the virgin country is a sort of invasion that is as old as Neolithic man, and they can, in moderation, even emphasize a man's feeling of belonging to the natural world. Under surveillance, they can belong; under control, they need not deface or mar. I do not believe that in wilderness areas where grazing has never been permitted, it should be permitted; but I do not believe either that an otherwise untouched wilderness should be eliminated from the preservation plan because of limited existing uses such as grazing which are in consonance with the frontier condition and image.

Let me say something on the subject of the kinds of wilderness worth preserving. Most of those areas contemplated are in the national forests and in high mountain country. For all the usual recreational purposes, the alpine and forest wildernesses are obviously the most important, both as genetic banks and as beauty spots. But for the spiritual renewal, the recognition of identity, the birth of awe, other kinds will serve every bit as well. Perhaps, because they are less friendly to life, more abstractly non-human, they will serve even better. On our Saskatchewan prairie, the nearest neighbor was four miles away, and at night we saw only two lights on all the dark rounding earth. The earth was full of animals—field mice, ground squirrels, weasels, ferrets, badgers, coyotes, burrowing owls, snakes. I knew them as my little brothers, as fellow creatures, and I have never been able to look upon animals in any other way since. The sky in that country came clear down to the ground on every side, and it was full of great weathers, and clouds, and winds, and hawks. I hope I learned something from knowing intimately the creatures of the earth; I hope I learned something from looking a long way, from looking up, from being much alone. A prairie like that, one big enough to carry the eye clear to the sinking, rounding horizon, can be as lonely and grand and simple in its forms as the sea. It is as good a place as any for the wilderness experience to happen; the vanishing prairie is as worth preserving for the wilderness idea as the alpine forests.

So are great reaches of our western deserts, scarred somewhat by prospectors but otherwise open, beautiful, waiting, close to whatever God you want to see in them. Just as a sample, let me suggest the Robbers' Roost country in Wayne County, Utah, near the Capitol Reef National Monument. In that desert climate the dozer and jeep tracks will not soon melt back into the earth, but the country has a way of making the scars insignificant. It is a lovely and terrible wilderness, such a wilderness as Christ and the prophets went out into; harshly and beautifully colored, broken and worn until its bones are exposed, its great sky without a smudge or taint from Technocracy, and in hidden corners and pockets under its cliffs the sudden poetry of springs. Save a piece of country like that intact, and it does not matter in the slightest that only a few people every year will go into it. That is precisely its value. Roads would be a desecration, crowds would ruin it. But those who haven't the strength or youth to go into it and live can simply sit and look. They can look two hundred miles, clear into Colorado; and looking down over the cliffs and canyons of the San Rafael Swell and the Robbers' Roost they can also look as deeply into themselves as anywhere I know. And if they can't even get to the places on the Aquarius Plateau where the present roads will carry them, they can simply contemplate the *idea*, take pleasure in the fact that such a timeless and uncontrolled part of earth is still there.

These are some of the things wilderness can do for us. That is the reason we need to put into effect, for its preservation, some other principle than the principles of exploitation or "usefulness" or even recreation. We simply need that wild country available to us, even if we never do more than drive to its edge and look in. For it can be a means of reassuring ourselves of our sanity as creatures, a part of the geography of hope.

Very sincerely yours,
Wallace Stegner

# JOHN DeWITT McKEE

## *The Unrelenting Land*

NEW MEXICO ANSWERS no questions. It is as impersonal as an equation, as unpersonified as a law of physics, and more immutable. Yet not immutable at all, but ever-changing; set solid as a boulder, yet changing with the sun. The land itself sings no songs, tells no tales, will not be romanticized into prettiness. It does not give, nor does it ask.

Still we stand fascinated by the unanswered question, pulled like Ulysses to the unsung song, stretched tight to breaking toward the story that quivers forever on the brink of being. And if we are tuned, we vibrate to the unheard melody, we take the salt of wisdom from the words unspoken.

What is it then that holds us to this curious, raw, new, old and savage land? It is not love, for the land itself is too aloof for love. It is not land-scape, for there is no landscape here. There is only the land, which can no more be trapped for taming than can the fleeting watermelon color of the mountains, come and gone between one eye-blink and the next. Land-scapes can be whistled in and brought to heel, ordered and arranged in frames. But this! So seemingly inert, impassive, barren, this land will not submit to capture.

The land's alive. It has a tensile strength unknown in the matronly luxuriance of greener places. It has a thrusting power not found in the contented pregnancy of midland fields. This land is impassive, yes; but it is never passive. The land itself by slow degrees takes those who come to it and shapes them till they fit, till they take the color of the desert, till they can look almost unwaveringly at the sky. This is the land then. This it is that holds us, this and the paradox.

Consider the paradox. Here is a land uncompromising in its honesty, the naked geologic ribs of earth stripped for man to try to conquer. There is about this land an unrelenting clarity whose very air would seem to make a lie impossible.

Nevertheless, a shabby falseness walks upon this land, a movie-set un-reality which stems, perhaps, from insecurity and results in an intellectu-ally self-conscious insistence that the observer take for bed-rock reality what is instead either imported veneer or artificial and mechanical resurrection.

For the culture that exists here—as opposed to the Culture which is so hopefully advertised—is a colloidal compound of traditions. Some of the traditions were here from the beginning; they grew from the earth with the Indian. Some came from Spain or Mexico, some from the Midwest, some from the South, others from New England. This land, which is like a cat and belongs to no man, has taken to itself the traditions of all of Western man. There is no culture here. There are only cultures, swirled together like many oils of different weights, on water.

What stands for culture here, however, makes much of Culture. It shows off like a boy walking a board fence. It takes inordinate pride in its success in blending "three cultures," by which it means the Indian, the Spanish, and every other culture of which the New Mexican is compounded, which it lumps as "Anglo."

As for blending, we've taken the architecture of the Pueblo Indian, which grew out of earth and necessity and remained a part of the land, and we've built things of steel and hollow tile and cement blocks, adding useless mass because that mass is a part of the appearance of Pueblo architecture, and we've called it "modified Pueblo." We've hung dubious Navajo blankets in front of roadside "snake pits" to draw the tourist trade, and we've provided places where you can "watch the Indians work," like queer fish in a waterless aquarium, while they make for you "authentic" Indian jewelry.

Here society seems somehow transplanted, too—like an orchid in the desert—unreal, pretentious, self-conscious. Adolescent Albuquerque, the biggest city in New Mexico, its nerve center, its cultural hub, goes into the world of after-dark wearing green mascara and falsies and sophistication.

Here individuality has become a cult, demanding a sort of conformity in non-conformity. There is pride in being an artistic center, a literary center, a meeting place for intellectuals. But it is a defensive pride. New Mexico is not unique in this. It is, in fact, a national phenomenon which began in colonial days. But the poseur is the more obvious because the works of man, dabbed impertinently upon the face of agelessness, ephemeral everywhere, seem even more so here.

The organized individualists decry the decline of taste, and write and paint and think in circles, to be read and viewed and discussed in the closed circle of the organization, creating a sort of artistic and intellectual hoop snake with its tail in its mouth. Nothing can succeed, apparently, unless it is organized. One must "belong" to dance the square dance, to grow a beard, to appreciate poetry, to love horses, or to learn to unsex the Chinese elm. Recreation itself is organized and departmentalized and loaded with people who have been especially trained to organize it and departmentalize it.

Neither is this a provincial nor a regional matter. It is nationwide, and it goes beyond the arts and recreation. The plumbers, the morticians, the service station attendants, the bakers, the bottlers, the meat packers, the dry cleaners, the model builders, the philatelists, the hi-fi addicts—name your group. It *is* a group, complete with president, vice president, secretary and treasurer.

Perhaps no man can any longer face the immensity and complexity of the land alone. Perhaps the idea of "teamwork"—in medicine, in advertising, in religion, in nearly every human endeavor—is a necessary weapon with which to combat fear. And perhaps the very insistence on organization has generated a fear of being alone. If the soul needs solitude as the tree needs room to grow, we may be afraid to grow. For even if we pride ourselves on being different, we surround ourselves, for protection, with others who are being different in like manner.

The group is everywhere, but here it is more obvious, being naked. Against this land, beneath this sky, men gather under banners to give necessary meaning to themselves. Much is made of diversity, and there is diversity in plenty. But it is group, not individual, diversity. It is self-conscious diversity, supported by organization for its own sake. It does not have the integrity that makes differentness incidental. Only from an honest and unpretentious expression of self can grow, paradoxically, a fundamental unity. And from that unity can grow a culture that fits like a loose jacket, with no necessity to call attention to itself. The culture here, on the other hand, binds the swelling chest of its own self-consciousness.

There is a reason for this, too. American society has always been fluid, always moving, always looking for the new frontier. And here is the last of the frontiers. This land which is old is yet so new. What was a somnolent village yesterday may be a bursting city today, with the stink of boom about it. There is space to move here. The new frontiersmen see the space, the sky and the mesa, the desert and the forest, but they are baffled by the land that under-girds them. Or they ignore it.

The artist deprecates, and is deprecated by, the businessman; the scientist jostles the cattleman; the intellectual shouts baffled imprecations from his tower; and the features of the Indian become more and more blurred as he becomes more and more "assimilated" and helps the white man carry his burden. The dances, the legends, the art, and the religion of the Indian are already being mummified and preserved in the collection cases of the "tradition" hunters.

And here they place a tradition in an iron lung and will not let it die a decent death. They build an association around it to give pneumatic similitude of life to the tradition, and busyness to minds beseiged by boredom. They do not realize that when it is pumped up and preserved in associations and annual meetings, it is as false as the seeming blush of life on the rouged face of a corpse. They fail to see, for instance, that the strength of aesthetic pleasure in folk arts is rooted in the absolute material and spiritual necessity of those arts. They do not realize, for example, that the conglomeration which passes for Spanish Colonial or modified Pueblo, because it is cut off from the roots of aesthetic and pragmatic necessity, is bastard architecture. The fiesta dress, on the other hand, is in a tradition and is alive. It is alive because it is aesthetically pleasing, and it is practical. So far as architecture is concerned, a new tradition may arise in the Southwest out of the growing practicality of solar heating. These things can become and remain traditions because they grow out of the needs of the people on the land and out of the land itself.

It is fascinating, this New Mexico, and the paradox is no less fascinating than the land. But one can only explore. New Mexico gives no answers. It is a grinding, clashing, many-cornered conglomerate. It is cattle and oil and cotton; it is mines and pines and mountains. It has, in spite of all the unconscious attempts to spoil it, a fine, firm honesty, like the uncompromising, harsh beauty of the malpais. But it wears a coy curtain of posing, poster-paint culture, much like the flapping canvas come-on of a carnival sideshow. The backdrop is real; the show itself is not; for behind the curtain is still the same hula girl from Keokuk.

Yet the land holds us and shoves our roots hard and deep into the rock beneath the shifting sand. The sky holds us, curved tight above the land like the blue bubble of a bomber. And the scything wind-sweeps of the cattle-dotted grasslands; the dust-blown, curving plow tracks in the cotton fields in winter, and the nodding, waving whiteness of the same fields in the fall; the oil pumps, singly or in ranks, sucking nectar from the earth like metal mantises, living to devour—these hold us and mark this place as home. Rising out of long forgotten seas like a massive shrug of shoulders, the mountains stand firm and hold us. Volcanic cones against the sky, monuments to the grandeur of past violence, hold us, too, in something that approaches awe.

Man may scratch the past with his frail stick plow. He may fling himself into the future seeking limits to the limitless sky. He may strut upon a stage too vast for any drama he may make or comprehend. It does not matter. It is the land that holds us here. It is the unrelenting land, this great, fierce, challenging, canyon-gutted, mesa-muscled land, which holds us and which gives us space enough to write a life on—and leaves it to us whether we have courage enough and faith to fill the page.

# JOSEPH WOOD KRUTCH

## The Mystique of the Desert

To MOST LAYMEN as well as to many professionals the word "science" means "a collection of observable facts about the physical universe." And there are many who profess to believe that beyond such observable facts we should never allow our minds to wander.

Actually, however, no one ever did stop there. No human being is so completely unspeculative, so totally devoid of imagination, so incapable of drawing general conclusions, that he does not go on from observable facts to draw morals, to set up standards of value and to philosophize in one way or another. He does so even at the very moment when he is assuring himself that he will do nothing of the sort. Even to say that one has no philosophy is to have one.

More than two thousand years ago Aristotle coined the word "metaphysics"—which means "beyond physics"—in order to give a name to that whole realm of intellectual activity which begins where the observation and organization of physical facts leaves off. More recently, Bernard Shaw, half-jokingly, has coined on the same model another word, "metabiology." Time has not tested it so thoroughly as it has tested Aristotle's "metaphysics" but it may turn out to be useful by calling attention to an important fact.

Both words suggest that such subjects of inquiry as morals (or the nature of the good) and aesthetics (or the nature of the beautiful) lie beyond the reach of that kind of positive knowledge with which the physical sciences deal. But there is a difference between what Aristotle's word seems to imply and what Shaw's word is intended to suggest. Meta*physics* seems to accept the recent assumption that life itself is reducible to physical and chemical laws and to imply, therefore, that moral and aesthetic questions can best be answered by referring them to the laws of the physical universe. Meta*biology*, on the other hand, suggests that since life itself is not completely explainable in merely physical terms, moral and aesthetic questions should be discussed in connection with what we know about living creatures without any attempt to reduce such questions to merely physical terms. The difference, in other words, is the difference between the purely materialistic, mechanistic approach to such questions, which is favored by the so-called "positivists," and an approach which recognizes that living things, being radically different from inanimate objects, are capable of standards of value which correspond to nothing in the merely physical world.

If your ethics, your aesthetics, your epistomology even, are things which lie immediately beyond what you know or think you know about the phenomena associated with living creatures; if these seem to you a better taking-off place than facts about mechanics or even chemistry, then your metaphysical convictions will take on a color sufficiently distinctive to justify a distinctive name. And if you attempt, as Shaw did, to formulate these convictions into a consistent system, then you may quite properly call yourself not so much a "metaphysician" as a "metabiologist."

Shaw was, of course, thinking especially of what seemed to him to follow from his own belief that evolution is the most important of all observable facts and that what evolution reveals is not merely a Darwinian mechanism but the effectiveness, throughout all time, of the imagination which can dream of something better and the will which can make the dream come true. Upon that conviction he based his philosophy, his metaphysics, or, as he preferred to call it, his metabiology.

Whether one accepts Shaw's conviction or not—and most biologists will, I imagine, shake their heads—the fact remains that a great many of us are today "metabiologists" of one sort or another whether we realize it or not. And by that I mean simply that for us the most important of all the "collections of observable facts" which the centuries have accumulated are those which concern the behavior of living creatures. And it is "beyond" these facts that, for us, the most significant philosophy must lie.

People nowadays are less interested in theology than they were in times gone by. They are not interested because they do not believe that they have any facts about God upon which, or just beyond which, metaphysical convictions about Him could be based. Perhaps most people are, whether they know it or not, simple positivists in the sense that they believe that even man is a machine wholly explainable in physical terms. But there is an increasing number who feel that the attempt to account for life in purely physical terms has failed. They may continue to insist that no available evidence suggests the existence of any God. But they also insist that life is not demonstrably "merely chemical" and that biology must recognize realities not either physical or chemical.

For them, therefore, philosophy lies "beyond" biology, not beyond physics. For them the place to start that philosophy is not with physics or with chemistry but with life itself as a fact no less primary than the facts of physics and chemistry. Because I myself make that assumption, many of the speculations in which I have permitted myself to indulge in this book are heretical from the conventional biologist's point of view. But the heresy seems to me to have a desirable consequence—it redeems the universe from that deadness which mechanistic science has increasingly attributed to it.

Let us suppose that you are "interested in nature"—at least to the extent that anyone who has willingly read thus far in this book must be. If that means only that it somehow pleases you to know that road runners eat snakes, that Gila monsters are our sole poisonous lizards, or that the cacti are native to the New World only, then your interest is "scientific" in the most limited possible sense of the term. If you go beyond that to the extent of trying to learn how this scientific knowledge may be useful to man in his struggle to feed himself well or to preserve his health, then your interest is both scientific in the limited sense and also "technological." But as soon as you take the next step and begin to ask yourself not merely what immediate practical use can be made of known facts but also what they suggest to the speculative mind about the potentialities and limitations of living matter; as soon as you begin to find yourself thinking of what the human mind cannot help calling the "intentions" and "the standards of value" which nature pursues, then you have entered the realm of the metabiological.

Any consideration of evolution, for instance, becomes metabiological as soon as it abandons a mere description of the evolutionary process to permit itself to refer even cautiously to "higher" and "lower" forms of life, to celebrate "growth" and "change" and "survival value" as moral concepts; at that point the consideration has gone "beyond" the narrow limits of the science of biology and become metaphysical, or metabiological, no matter what you may prefer to call it. Similarly, ecology is narrowly scientific when it merely describes the interrelations of living things. It is narrowly technological when it seeks to learn only how forests can be preserved and farms kept fertile through the application of our knowledge. And so long as it is interested in nothing except "land management," for instance, it remains just technological and nothing more. But when it begins to develop what Aldo Leopold called a "land ethic," then it is "beyond" either science or technology because any sort of ethic is metaphysical and an ethic erected upon our knowledge of biology is specifically "metabiological."

I hope that when in this book I have described some aspect of desert life it has usually been clear that the metabiology of the desert is one of the things which has interested me most. If it had not interested me, I do not think that I would ever have concerned myself much with either science or technology. Moreover, having said that—and I realize that to say even so much is to condemn myself in the eyes of a certain class of scientist and technician—I must confess to something even worse. I must confess that there are moments when what seems most important of all is something of which the metabiologist may be almost as suspicious as the strict biologist is suspicious of the metabiological.

Just as the realm of speculative reason lies beyond the facts of science, so also, beyond the realm of speculative reason, lies the realm of emotion. To me that realm is no less important than the realm of fact or the realm of speculative thought, though to discuss what one experiences in the realm of emotion one must either depreciate it and explain it away, as the pure rationalist does, or one must accept what one can only call the *mystique* as opposed to the *rational* of the human being's intercourse with the universe around him.

Your Philistine never enters this realm of the mystical. When he has read the great poem, looked at the great picture, heard the great music, or even grasped the great theory, he always makes the same comments in words which lie halfway between exclamation and question: "So what?" Since neither music, nor poetry, nor pure theory has practical usefulness, and since the mystique of all three eludes him, his comment-question is perfectly proper. And the only—usually impossible—answer to him lies in the mystique itself.

Though in this book I have presented facts and, at moments, permitted myself metabiological speculations, neither the one nor the other really says all that I would like to be able to say. If Dipodomys never drinks; if the moth desires the candle; if the seed has learned to disregard the wetness of summer while waiting for the wetness of spring; if the cactus has learned to be at home where its ancestors would have perished; who cares? Why, having learned these things, did I not say, "So what" and pass on? The ultimate answer, I think, is to be found only by admitting the mystical element. The reason for my deepest caring does not lie within the scope of biology or even metabiology. One cannot recognize it without being to that extent a mystic.

Of the official mystical writers I am no great reader. The clarity of their visions, the overwhelming certainty of their conviction that ultimate truth has been revealed to them, is foreign to my own experience. At most I have "intimations," not assurances, and I doubt that I could ever go further in recommendation of the complete mystics than William James goes when he bids the ordinary mortal recognize the reality, in some realm, of the phenomena to which the mystics testify, no matter what interpretation we ordinary mortals put upon them. Yet I, and many whose temperaments are no more mystical than mine, do know moments when we draw courage and joy from experiences which lie outside the getting and spending of everyday life.

The occasions of such experiences are many. The commonest and perhaps the least obviously related are these: reading a poem and contemplating a child—human or animal. But the experiences come to different men in many different ways. Some are most likely to be aware of them in solitude, others in crowds; some while looking at the stars, some while watching the waves roll in upon a beach. And whether you call the experience infrarational or superrational, it involves the momentary acceptance of values not definable in terms of that common sense to which we ordinarily accord our first loyalty. And to all such experiences one thing is common. There is a sense of satisfaction which is not personal but impersonal. One no longer asks, "What's in it for me?" because one is no longer a separate selfish individual but part of the welfare and joy of the whole.

Those to whom such mystical experiences are habitual and hence more ordinary than what most people call ordinary life, can often call upon them at will as the religious mystics do by the repetition of a prayer. But to the majority there is no certain formula or ritual—not even a private, much less a communicable, one. At most we can only, for example, plunge into the crowd or retire into a solitude, knowing that sometimes in the one situation or the other we will glimpse out of the corner of our eyes what, if one may believe the true mystics, is usually at the very center of the true mystic's vision.

I happen to be one of those, and we are not a few, to whom the acute awareness of a natural phenomenon, especially of a phenomenon of the living world, is the thing most likely to open the door to that joy we cannot analyze. I have experienced it sometimes when a rabbit appeared suddenly from a bush to dash away to the safety which he values so much, or when, at night, a rustle in the leaves reminds me how many busy lives surround my own. It has also come as vividly when I suddenly saw a flower opening or a stem pushing out of the ground.

But what is the content of the experience? What is it that at such moments I seem to realize? Of what is my happiness compounded?

First of all, perhaps, there is the vivid assurance that these things, that the universe itself, really do exist, that life is not a dream; second, that the reality is pervasive and, it seems, unconquerable. The future of mankind is dubious. Perhaps the future of the whole earth is only somewhat less dubious. But one knows that all does not depend upon man, that possibly, even, it does not depend upon this earth. Should man disappear, rabbits may well still run and flowers may still open. If this globe itself should perish, then it seems not unreasonable to suppose that what inspires the stem and the flower may exist somewhere else. And I, it seems, am at least part of all this.

God looked upon the world and found that it was good. How great is the happiness of being able, even for a moment, to agree with Him! And how much easier that is if one is not committed to considering only some one section of the world or of the universe.

Long before I ever saw the desert I was aware of the mystical overtones which the observation of nature made audible to me. But I have never been more frequently or more vividly aware of them than in connection with the desert phenomena. And I have often wondered why.

Were I to believe what certain psychologists have been trying to tell me, the thing which I call a "mystique" and especially what I call "the mystique of the desert" is only the vague aura left behind by certain experiences of infancy and childhood. Should I search my memory of the latter I should certainly find there what nearly every other American or European would: a Christmas card showing Wise Men crossing the desert and also, in some school geography, another picture of rolling dunes, a camel and the caption, "Sahara Desert." Both seemed then to be things I should never see; both were remote from the scene of my sorrows—whatever at the moment I found my sorrows to be. "Poof!" say those psychologists. The "mystique" is mysterious no longer. To adjust yourself to your environment would have been a simple matter. Had you been so adjusted you would never have gone to live in the American Southwest. And you would not give a damn whether Dipodomys drinks or not.

If those psychologists are right, then I am glad that I, at least, was not "adjusted" to everything and hence incapable of giving a damn about anything whatsoever. But I am not sure that they *are* right. Curiosity is not always the result of conditioning and there are words at which most imaginations kindle. Among them are all those words which suggest the untamed extravagances or the ultimate limits of nature in any one of her moods. We may prefer to live amid hills and meadows, fields and wood-lots, or even, for that matter, surrounded by steel and concrete. But "wil-derness," "jungle," and "desert" are still stirring words, as even movie-makers know. And it is just possible that they will continue to be such after the last Christmas card having anything to do with Christmas has disappeared from the shops and after school geographies have consented to confine themselves exclusively to "things relevant to the child's daily life." Perhaps the mind is not merely a blank slate upon which anything may be written. Perhaps it reaches out spontaneously toward what can nourish either intelligence or imagination. Perhaps it is part of nature and, without being taught, shares nature's intentions.

Most of the phrases we use glibly to exorcise or explain away the reali-ties of our intimate experience are of quite recent origin—phrases like "emotional conditioning," "complex," "fixation," and even "reflex." But one of the most inclusive, and the most relevant here, is older. It was Ruskin, of all people, who invented the term "pathetic fallacy" to stigma-tize as in some sense unjustified our tendency to perceive a smiling land-cape as "happy," a somber one as "sad." But is it really a fallacy? Are we so separate from nature that our states are actually discontinuous with it? Is there nothing outside ourselves which is somehow glad or sad? Is it really a fallacy when we attribute to nature feelings analogous to our own?

Out of the very heart of the romantic feeling for nature the question arose. And it was Coleridge, again of all people, who gave the answer upon which the post-romantic "scientific" attitude rests: "Only in ourselves does nature live." But Wordsworth, who recorded Coleridge's dictum, was not himself always sure. When he was most himself it seemed to him that, on the contrary, the joy of nature was older than the joy of man and that what was transitory in the individual was permanent somewhere else. When the moment of happiness passed, it was not because the glory had faded but only because his own sight had grown dim.

> There was a time when meadow, grove, and stream,
> The earth, and every common sight,
> > To me did seem
> Apparelled in celestial light,
> The glory and the freshness of a dream.

> Oh joy! that in our embers
> Is something that doth live,
> That nature yet remembers
> What was so fugitive!

Something like this is what, in clumsy prose, I am trying to suggest. "Wilderness," "jungle," "desert," are not magic words because we have been "conditioned" to find them such but because they stand for things which only conditioning can make seem indifferent or alien. How could the part be greater than the whole? How can nature's meaning come wholly from man when he is only part of that meaning? "Only in ourselves does nature live" is less true than its opposite: "Only in nature do *we* have a being."

The most materialistic of historians do not deny the influence upon a people of the land on which they live. When they say, for instance, that the existence of a frontier was a dominant factor in shaping the character of the American people, they are not thinking only of a physical fact. They mean also that the idea of a frontier, the realization that space to be occupied lay beyond it, took its place in the American imagination and sparked the sense that there was "somewhere else to go" rather than that the solution of every problem, practical or spiritual, had to be found within the limits to which the man who faced them was confined.

In the history of many other peoples the character of their land, even the very look of the landscape itself, has powerfully influenced how they felt and what they thought about. They were woodsmen or plainsmen or mountaineers not only economically but spiritually also. And nothing, not even the sea, has seemed to affect men more profoundly than the desert, or seemed to incline them so powerfully toward great thoughts, perhaps because the desert itself seems to brood and to encourage brooding. To the Hebrews the desert spoke of God, and one of the most powerful of all religions was born. To the Arabs it spoke of the stars, and astronomy came into being.

Perhaps no fact about the American people is more important than the fact that the continent upon which they live is large enough and varied enough to speak with many different voices—of the mountains, of the plains, of the valleys and of the seashore—all clear voices that are distinct and strong. Because Americans listened to all these voices, the national character has had many aspects and developed in many different directions. But the voice of the desert is the one which has been least often heard. We came to it last, and when we did come, we came principally to exploit rather than to listen.

To those who do listen, the desert speaks of things with an emphasis quite different from that of the shore, the mountains, the valleys or the plains. Whereas they invite action and suggest limitless opportunity, exhaustless resources, the implications and the mood of the desert are something different. For one thing the desert is conservative, not radical. It is more likely to provoke awe than to invite conquest. It does not, like the plains, say, "Only turn the sod and uncountable riches will spring up." The heroism which it encourages is the heroism of endurance, not that of conquest.

Precisely what other things it says depends in part upon the person listening. To the biologist it speaks first of the remarkable flexibility of living things, of the processes of adaptation which are nowhere more remarkable than in the strange devices by which plants and animals have learned to conquer heat and dryness. To the practical-minded conservationist it speaks sternly of other things, because in the desert the problems created by erosion and overexploitation are plainer and more acute than anywhere else. But to the merely contemplative it speaks of courage and endurance of a special kind.

Here the thought of the contemplative crosses the thought of the conservationist, because the contemplative realizes that the desert is "the last frontier" in more senses than one. It is the last because it was the latest reached, but it is the last also because it is, in many ways, a frontier which *cannot* be crossed. It brings man up against his limitations, turns him in upon himself and suggests values which more indulgent regions minimize. Sometimes it inclines to contemplation men who have never contemplated before. And of all answers to the question "What is a desert good for?" "Contemplation" is perhaps the best.

The eighteenth century invented a useful distinction which we have almost lost, the distinction between the beautiful and the sublime. The first, even when it escapes being merely the pretty, is easy and reassuring. The sublime, on the other hand, is touched with something which inspires awe. It is large and powerful; it carries with it the suggestion that it might overwhelm us if it would. By these definitions there is no doubt which is the right word for the desert. In intimate details, as when its floor is covered after a spring rain with the delicate little ephemeral plants, it is pretty. But such embodiments of prettiness seem to be only tolerated with affectionate contempt by the region as a whole. As a whole the desert is, in the original sense of the word, "awful." Perhaps one feels a certain boldness in undertaking to live with it and a certain pride when one discovers that one can.

I am not suggesting that everyone should listen to the voice of the desert and listen to no other. For a nation which believes, perhaps rightly enough, that it has many more conquests yet to make, that voice preaches a doctrine too close to quietism. But I am suggesting that the voice of the desert might well be heard occasionally among the others. To go "up to the mountain" or "into the desert" has become part of the symbolical language. If it is good to make occasionally what the religious call a "retreat," there is no better place than the desert to make it. Here if anywhere the most familiar realities recede and others come into the foreground of the mind.

A world traveler once said that every man owed it to himself to see the tropics at least once in his life. Only there can he possibly realize how completely nature can fulfill certain potentialities and moods which the temperate regions only suggest. I have no doubt that he was right. Though

I have never got beyond the outer fringe of the tropical lands, I hope that some day I shall get into their heart. But I am sure that they are no more necessary than the desert to an adequate imaginative grasp of the world we live in. Those who have never known it are to be pitied, like a man who has never read *Hamlet* or heard the *Jupiter Symphony*. He has missed something which is unique. And there is nothing else which can give him more than a hint of what he has missed. To have experienced it is to be prepared to see other landscapes with new eyes and to participate with a fresh understanding in the life of other natural communities.

## Selections from *The Great Chain of Life, Grand Canyon* and *Human Nature and the Human Condition*

BELIEVING THAT EVERYTHING about him was alive, primitive man attributed a psychic life to mountains and winds, to rivers and stones. No doubt the distinction that was slowly made between the living and the inanimate was tremendously important in defining his own mental world, because it tended to draw him emotionally closer to other living things while it marked him off from whatever did not live. But it is a curious aspect of modern intellectual development that modern thought has, on the contrary, tended to obliterate again the distinction, to interpret life in mechanistic terms until, by now, it might almost be said to have come to a conclusion exactly opposite the assumption of primitive man. If the latter thought that everything in the universe was alive, the mechanist believes that nothing is, and the significance of even the word "organism" as distinguished from the word "machine" tends to disappear. Moreover, and as the result of a somewhat similar development, the medieval man who saw "purpose" everywhere and, for the most part, purpose directed toward him and his needs, has given way to the mechanist who sees purpose nowhere and rejects the assumption of even the most generalized "intention" in nature almost as vehemently as he rejects a naïve, man-centered teleology.

The discovery of America meant different things to different people. To some it meant only gold and the possibility of other plunder. To others less mean-spirited it meant a wilderness which might in time become another Europe. But there were also not a few whose imaginations were most profoundly stirred by what it *was* rather than by what it might become.

The wilderness and the idea of the wilderness is one of the permanent homes of the human spirit. Here, as many realized, had been miraculously preserved until the time when civilization could appreciate it, the richness and variety of a natural world which had disappeared unnoticed and little by little from Europe. America was a dream of something long past which had suddenly become a reality. It was what Thoreau called the great "poem" before many of its fairest pages had been ripped out and thrown away. The desire to experience that reality rather than to destroy it drew to our shores some of the best who have ever come to them.

If man has no true nature as distinguished from what his condition at a given time creates; if no persisting needs, tastes, preferences, and capacities are either met or frustrated by that condition; then there is no reason why he should not be as contentedly "adjusted" to the condition of what Johnson calls a "geometrician" exclusively. But if there *is* such a thing as human nature, and if both man's history and his literature give some clue as to what that nature is; if, indeed, they reveal it more surely than all the polls, questionnaires and tests which "geometry" has been able to devise; then Johnson may be right when he suggests that it is in man's nature to be moral and, perhaps, even religious; that it is, as a matter of fact, in accord with his nature to be a moralist perpetually and a geometer only by chance. And if you do believe this to be true, then it may also seem that the deepest cause of the anxiety which has given its name to our age; that the deepest cause of the fact that man is not so secure, so happy, and so content in his age of power and abundance as it would seem that he should be; that he is, indeed, so frequently forced to seek the aid of psychiatrists or those who can minister to a mind diseased that we are told it is impossible to train as many such ministers as are now needed—if all this is true then, it may be, I say, that the deepest reason is simply this: Man's condition as geometer and as the child of geometry is not harmonious with his nature.

Since the beginning of the scientific age, there have been differing conceptions of what science was "for." Quite properly it was sometimes regarded as "useful" and sometimes as valuable simply because it increased understanding. But though pure science is a legitimate pursuit, pure technology (i.e., technology regarded as an end in itself) is antihuman—and it is to that we have come. The machine rather than man has become the measure of all things and we regard the improvement, even the welfare, of man's tools as more important than man's own.

---

We are no longer much surprised when we hear, for example, that a rocket expert who designed weapons for one of our enemies shrugs his shoulders when asked to work for us instead. He is not interested, we say, in politics. But that is not quite adequate. Actually, he is simply not interested in what rockets are to be used for. He is interested simply in rockets—which is to say in machines (or power) for its own sake. And though this attitude is only occasionally so dramatically revealed, millions have unconsciously adopted it. If we worshiped only the machines which *make* things, we might say that we were materialists. But we are almost equally impressed by those which merely *do* things—which go faster, or higher, or farther. We do not, like a utilitarian, ask what good they are or, like a materialist, what we can get out of them. Like the members of many primitive religious cults, we are uncertain whether the powers we worship are evil or good; we are sure only that they are powerful and that, therefore, they should be worshiped.

Since man first recognized or suspected power outside himself, he has worshiped many strange gods, adored them in many strange rituals and sacrificed himself to them in many strange ways. He has slaughtered animals and maidens; he has whipped, starved, and mutilated himself. He has slept on nails, gazed at the sun until blind, and held his arms aloft until they withered. It was not himself but the god of his idolatry whom he was determined to serve. And so it is again with us. To Thoreau, the inhabitants of his own Concord "appeared to be doing penance in a thousand remarkable ways." What would he think of the new ways devised since his time?

Our prophets often describe the "new world" which lies just ahead when atomic power has been harnessed to peaceful uses; when we can travel across space instead of merely through air; or even when the work week has been reduced to twenty-five hours. But there is in actual fact nothing really *new* about this new world. It would be merely one which had taken another step in the direction which many previous steps had taken. New worlds never were and never will be created except by new ideas, or aims, or desires, or convictions. Christianity created a new world and so did the seventeenth century's new faith that a knowledge of the laws of nature could change rapidly and radically mankind's condition. To some slight extent our own age is still part of the new world Christianity created and it is still very much part of the new world which faith in science created. But there will be no newer world as long as there is no idea or ideal newer than that of the seventeenth century.

If we should ever decide that we do want a new world we shall have to find first the faith which could make it. As long as we believe that the only human reality is the human condition there will be no fundamental change in that condition. If we should become convinced again that man has a nature and that the greatest of his needs is to create a condition suited to it, then a really new world might come gradually into being.

# From *The Desert Year*

**T**HE FACT THAT I never had stayed long in any part of the monument country may be the consequence of a certain defensive reaction. There is a kind of beauty—and it is presumably the kind prevailing throughout most of the universe—of which man gets thrilling glimpses but which is fundamentally alien to him. It is well for him to glance occasionally at the stars or to think for a moment about eternity. But it is not well to be too continuously aware of such things, and we must take refuge from them with the small and the familiar . . . Wherever the earth is clothed with vegetation not too sparse to modify its essential outlines, it makes man feel to some extent at home because things which, like him, change and grow and die have asserted their importance. But wherever, as in this region of wind-eroded stone, living things are no longer common enough or conspicuous enough to seem more than trivial accidents, he feels something like terror . . . this is a country where the inanimate dominates and in which not only man but the very plants themselves seem intruders. We may look at it as we look at the moon, but we feel rejected. It is neither for us nor for our kind.

# DAVID ROSS BROWER

## From *Wilderness Alps*

**I**N THE NORTHERN CASCADES there is alpine wilderness that belongs to our national gallery. Such places are the last of our primeval landscapes, the few surviving samples of a natural world, to walk and rest in, to see, to listen to, to feel the mood of, to comprehend, to care about. There isn't much of it left. What there is is all all men will ever have, and all their children. It is only as safe as people, knowing about it, want it to be.

But do enough people know about it? We didn't, and went in to look it over. We had heard about the region, and about a conflict between those who wanted to use raw materials and those who wanted to preserve

---

*Selection from* THE DESERT YEAR *by Joseph Wood Krutch.
Published by William Sloane Associates, Inc. Reprinted by
permission of William Morrow and Company, Inc. Copyright
© 1951, 1952 by Joseph Wood Krutch.*

*Selection from* WILDERNESS ALPS *reprinted with permission
of the Sierra Club.*

natural beauty. We weren't prepared for what began to unfold—an amazing wilderness of rugged alps built in grand scale, unique, unsurpassed anywhere in the United States.

The Northern Cascades country was once, all of it, as wild as the sea—the wild, shining sea, shaping the earth through the ages, never the same, yet not to be changed by man, who long ago learned to accept it for what it is, even as we are now learning not to change some of the wild land, but to keep it natural, to seek from it answers to questions we may yet learn how to ask.

Can we set apart, unmanaged, unspoiled, enough of these places? Can we spare the stillness of a rain forest, where trees can live out their full span and return to the earth they came from? All that lives here repays in full for value received, nourishes as it has been nourished. Scores of centuries built this, a cool green world, hushed as a prayer. Man could wipe it out in a decade. Or consecrate it as a park, not to be impaired, a place where all generations could come to know the dignity of nature.

Our first trip in was a flight—too hurried, too cut off, too unreal for us to feel the country or remember the shape of the waves of the storm-tossed sea of peaks. We knew it was great country, big country. We also saw that its size alone could not protect it. On the west side men were already clearcutting the last virgin forests, getting timber and pulp from forested avenues of approach needed very much as primeval setting and living space to look at and to look from. Crossing Cascade Pass, in the heart of the wilderness, we were but a few minutes from other wild forests, also wanted for their timber, but needed as setting too.

Our trail climbed grassy canyonsides to a small shelter in its own private alp below the pass. We only had time that day to explore a lower side trail for a mile or two, to see what a wilderness forest is like when man leaves it to its own wondrous devices. We walked waist-deep in ferns, quietly, looking backward on the eternity that has made this forest what it is. We poked along the high trails, wandered through the grasslands, let the mountain wind blow away flat-land cares.

Everywhere there were wild gardens. And here, deep in the heart of the little-known alps, seemingly remote, we met at noon a friend who had left New York City late the night before, a whole continent away.

He came up through virgin forest with huge trees, almost a rain forest, still as a cathedral, in it a clear stream from an unscarred watershed, clear in spite of the northern weather. The northern traveler, we all knew, is seldom bored by blue skies. But then, monotonous fair weather can't build mountains like these, and their glaciers and forests and flowers. We liked the way the mountains looked and discovered how to like what made them that way—don't scurry for cover and miss the show. Stay out and be part of it! Not on a high peak, of course. But take a walk, down in the sheltered valley. So we walked out into it, heads up, and felt the freshness the rains bring, saw the new patterns, smelled the wet leaves, now washed and cool, and we looked up to see the old contest between the crags and the mists.

We were close to the pass, making camp, our own mountain world spread out around us, each clump of trees a timberline penthouse, each room perfectly air-conditioned. Then dawn brought a flush to Glacier Peak.

The sun would light all this mountain land soon, and we hope it will always reveal wilderness there—in the avenues of unspoiled forest, in the flashing waters of the sidestreams and the river, in the friendly lower gardens and grassy alplands, up at timberline and in tundra, on the glaciers and peaks.

Other people will want to be walking our trails, up where the tree reaches high for the cloud, up where the flower takes the summer wind with beauty, and the summer rain too. They will want to discover for themselves the wildness that the ages have made perfect.

They have a right to discover wild places. They can discover them, but only if we keep some wildness in between the shining seas; only if man remembers, in his rising tide, not to engulf his last islands of wilderness.

## Preface to *Not Man Apart*

THE JEFFERS COUNTRY is fully qualified, if any place is, to be a national seashore in perpetuity, but it never will be—not in the usual sense. The national approach that seems to be working along the Ocean Strip of the Olympic Peninsula, or at Point Reyes, or at Capes Cod and Hatteras, or on Fire Island, is not likely to work between Point Lobos and Piedras Blancas —the Big Sur Coast.

If the traditional approach to preservation won't work for this, one of the great meetings of wild ocean and almost-wild coast, then what can be done to make sure it will remain a great place? We need to find out and *Not Man Apart* may play a role in the search. We hope also that it will remind those who already know it how splendid a place it is, or will bring an intimation of that splendor to those who have never been there, encouraging them, not too many at a time, to seek it out.

If they do and their spirits are not moved by it, they cannot help. Those who are moved, we would like to think, will somehow see that the significant things on this coastline endure; it was John Muir's postulate

*Reprinted from* NOT MAN APART *with permission of the Sierra Club.*

seventy-three years ago that those who know a place well can defend it best and we still think so. In the Club he founded we still try to make as secure as we can—by enlisting public assistance—those exhibits of wildness where the evolutionary force, the life force, has come down through the ages unbroken in its essence by man and his technology. We are concerned about this continuity in areas already dedicated by various agencies of government. We are also concerned about places, growing ever rarer, that are still wilderness in fact even though the government has not yet been persuaded to set them aside.

We give high priority to wilderness because it is the most fragile resource: man can destroy but not create it. Whoever would rescue wilderness, we have also learned, must watch his point of view. The threshold he steps into wilderness from, or the frame he looks into it through, is also important, and we concern ourselves with both. We believe that neither will be safe unless it can be demonstrated that both will serve man. Other creatures have a right to a place in the sun, whether or not man be there, but they have no standing in court and no vote with which to defend themselves against technology. We try to vote in their behalf, now and then, and for the wildness that they cannot live without. We and several organizations like us welcome the assistance of citizens who, like Aldo Leopold, cannot live without wildness either.

What is wilder than the Pacific? An occasional ship passes by, but its wake closes quickly, emphasizing the wildness. The foreground, however, may do something else; it can destroy the mood of a far-off horizon.

Through what frame do you look at your Pacific? Do you look across the backyard of people who were thinking something else when they dumped their garbage down the cliff in their own backyard, spewed it over the miraculous rock gardens, tossed it into the surge of surf, where an old shoe now floats among the waving sea palms? I saw this once on a cove where an elite could put up their houses and fences and preëmpt the vantage points. If you were lucky yourself, if you got there first and could afford it, you actually own the frame and see to it that few intrude upon the solitude that was so hard to find. If you are less lucky, came later, and have to skimp, you may have no frame at all.

Whoever you are, the ocean wildness that confronts you in the few places a beach is open to you may be so new, so all-encompassing, so limitless that you haven't thought about its rarity or its jeopardy. In your once-in-a-year seaside weekend the beach-fire embers can easily be left, the beer enjoyed fully and the cans tossed, the bottles caromed off the sea-worn stone, the razor edges left to last almost forever underfoot. The wild bird is a moving target to be shot at (try to explain to your child why the gull that soared so gracefully in the sea wind now lies dead in the surf—because some kid didn't think about what his .22 was doing). It doesn't seem to matter. Here is freedom, space, the wild world you can still move in, not so crowded you need permission to run or throw or shoot. You do what you wouldn't do had you thought about the speed with which man is diminishing wildness, no matter what his income bracket.

It doesn't take much conjecturing to understand the resenting of people by one group and of fences by another. Perhaps we can avoid a stalemate by looking into what England has learned. There, in favorite places, the British could establish national parks of a special kind, to serve people and to respect a place, made available by people who happened to own it, who happened to love it and the things that belong in it, the tough and the fragile. They let you in if you will share their emotional attachment for it, if you will contribute toward what it takes to keep the place intact, if you will close the gate behind you when you enter to enjoy and when you leave to remember.

We could use this approach. We are fast running out of the great expanses of original wilderness that can be preserved by government. We still have many places privately owned, protected by sensitive people now —but soon to be broken up as their own lives break or end. These are places we love, or that our children may come to love if we leave them the chance; and they are places we are not finding it possible to buy or to vote protection for.

We can still try to purchase preservation. Meanwhile, or instead, we can borrow from the British. They borrowed the national park concept from us. We can now learn from them. Nathaniel Owings is one man who has already learned and who has added refinements the British may borrow back and refine further. His chief allies were Fred Farr, a member of the California Senate; Tom Hudson, a Monterey County Supervisor; and Nicholas Roosevelt, who lives high up on Partington Ridge and is genetically a conservationist. Assuming that there was bound to be development now that the Coast road had been built and improved, they wondered if that development might strive to augment the natural beauty of the coast, not clobber it.

What are the priorities? For the highway traveler as well as the resident, the seascape comes first; it must be kept uncluttered, or the clutter removed soon. The sense of openness, the wild sweep of ridges from the Santa Lucias to the sea, is almost equally important. These things come first because they affect so many people—those who drive by and who can only pause, not linger.

But on this, one of the most remarkable coasts of all, there must also be something lasting for those who would linger. Astride the highway is wilderness that should be kept intact. It belongs to everyone who drives the highway whether or not he owns it, whether he climbs to run its ridges or descends to walk its beaches. It is wild and he knows it is *his*, as all wildness is everyone's—something everyone can delight in, knowing that there are still good places where man has the sense to leave things alone, letting the forces that created them keep on creating.

How, then, to let man's works lie lightly on the land, in pools of development, not in an all-pervading drizzle. How to avoid the usual slash and spill, with a slab to mark the spot where beauty died? Can architecture respect the slope that is there? Can the ever-changing chaparral itself be spared and not supplanted with a scooped-out terrace begreened in clichés. Can one part of a house be high and another low because that's the way the land lies? Can houses be clustered, mindful of man's built-in need for at least some congregating, leaving broad spaces open to fulfill still another need? And can the seascape be kept clear?

Imaginative architecture and landscaping can help; so can zoning; so can the separation of development rights and scenic easements from the ownership of the surface itself; so can sensible innovation in taxation, with the public giving an advantage to the owner who gives the public an advantage. Later there may need to be some further governmental ownership of places that get the greatest public impact—even as the British are now finding it necessary to do. There can be established by law a body representative of various kinds of landowners, private and public, cognizant of the integrity of the whole stretch of coast and its back country and empowered to act in its behalf.

A beter course may appear, but here is something to aim at, and Nathaniel Owings has supplied the creative force and dynamic effort it took to make a start. He and his associates sought out the best man might do with an environment he wants to live in as well as preserve. Private owners might yet join forces with the Forest Service, which manages the wilderness and recreational lands in the area, with the Defense Department and its inland reservation and coastal installations, with the State and its parks, and with the Division of Highway, challenged here to move people but not mountains. Pico Blanco might still remain as uniquely beautiful as it was to Jeffers and not be reduced by the removal of its common limestone. A dramatic system of coastal ridges could be encompassed in a Ventana Wilderness established under the provisions of the new Wilderness Act.

The choice is still open. The Big Sur Coast can be the place where, from here on out, man asks not what he can do to hurt the earth, but what to do so as not to hurt it but to achieve restraint instead, leaving marks that are faint, or that aren't there at all.

## Introduction to *This Is the American Earth*

MAN'S MARKS ARE STILL FEW here, but they are being made faster and faster. The cabin hewed with patient care has mellowed and the road to it has not burgeoned beyond the two tracks that led there when it was new. The stream has claimed the bridge that once crossed it; twenty-year-old pines grow on one of the approaches and beavers have built and used

*Reprinted from* THIS IS THE AMERICAN EARTH *with permission of the Sierra Club.*

and abandoned a lodge on the other. The power line is hardly more permanent than the rail fence that fell and now moulders in the meadow. The highway is so far away that the drone of cars can hardly be heard above the stream music. Silence closes in soon after the sightseeing planes pass by the front of the great range.

But each year these silences are briefer. The throng that comes grows larger, needs more, and forest and meadow make way to accommodate them. Wider highways speed people through faster and crowd out the places where the cow has dropped her calf for all the generations since the ice retreated, and where the trumpeter swan could inform her cygnets of those few things the evolutionary force had not already told them. Here where the blue vault arches over the wildest and least limited open space and beauty, even here man's numbers are taming and limiting with greater and greater speed, heedless of the little losses which add up to deprivation.

Again and again the challenge to explore has been met, handled, and relished by one generation—and precluded to any other. Although Thomas Jefferson argued that no one generation has a right to encroach upon another generation's freedom, the future's right to know the freedom of wilderness is going fast. And it need not go at all. A tragic loss could be prevented if only there could be broader understanding of this: that the resources of the earth do not exist just to be spent for the comfort, pleasure, or convenience of the generation or two who first learn how to spend them; that some of the resources exist for saving, and what diminishes them diminishes all mankind; that one of these is wilderness, wherein the flow of life, in its myriad forms, has gone on since the beginning of life, essentially uninterrupted by man and his technology; that this, wilderness, is worth saving for what it can mean to itself as part of the conservation ethic; that the saving is imperative to civilization and all mankind, whether or not all men yet know it.

Ansel Adams probably knew this in his marrow when he first began to capture the image of wilderness with his camera. Wilderness, let's say, responded unstintingly to this understanding; if a cloud were needed for a given composition, or a highlight or a lowlight, wilderness would provide it, in exactly the right place, to reveal not only breadth and width, but depth and feel too. The symbiosis went uninterrupted for some twenty-five years and led to this book's conception. The book was assisted when the National Park Service expressed a wish that something functional be done with the little building the Sierra Club had in Yosemite Valley as a memorial to Joseph LeConte, a pioneer conservationist. Ansel Adams suggested an exhibit of photographs and text that would combine to explain what national parks were really all about.

# FURTHER READING

Edward Abbey  *Desert Solitaire* (New York: McGraw Hill Book Co., 1968).

Mary Austin  *The Land of Little Rain* (Garden City, N.Y.: Doubleday and Co., 1961).

J. Frank Dobie
*The Voice of the Coyote* (Boston: Little, Brown and Co., 1949).
*The Longhorns* (Boston: Little, Brown and Co., 1941).
*The Mustangs* (Boston: Little, Brown and Co., 1952).

Colin Fletcher  *The Man Who Walked Through Time* (New York: Alfred A. Knopf, Inc., 1968).

Joseph Wood Krutch
*The Desert Year* (New York: The Viking Press, 1952).
*The Voice of the Desert* (New York: William Sloane Associates, 1955).
*Grand Canyon* (New York: William Sloane Associates, 1958).

George Laycock  *America's Endangered Wildlife* (New York: W. W. Norton and Co., Inc., 1969).

Robert M. McClung  *Lost Wild America* (New York: William Morrow and Company, 1969).

Robert Murphy  *Wild Sanctuaries* (New York: E. P. Dutton and Co., 1968).

John Muir
*The Mountains of California* (Garden City, N.Y., Doubleday and Co., 1961).
*The Yosemite* (Garden City, N.Y.: Doubleday and Co., 1962).

Adolph Murie  *A Naturalist in Alaska* (Garden City, N.Y.: Doubleday and Co., 1963).

Roderick Nash  *Wilderness and the American Mind* (New Haven: Yale University Press, 1967).

Roger Tory Peterson and James Fisher  *Wild America* (Boston: Houghton Mifflin Co., 1955).

Terry and Renny Russell  *On the Loose* (San Francisco: Sierra Club, 1967).

William Schwartz  *Voices for the Wilderness* (New York: Ballantine Books, 1969).

Paul Shepard  *Man in the Landscape* (New York: Alfred A. Knopf., 1967).

Paul Shepard and Daniel McKinley   *The Subversive Science: Essays Toward an Ecology of Man* (Boston: Houghton Mifflin Co., 1969).

Wallace Stegner   *The Sound of Mountain Water* (Garden City, N.Y.: Doubleday & Co., 1969).

Ann and Myron Sutton   *The American West: A Natural History* (New York: Random House, Inc., 1970).

Edwin Way Teale
*Journey Into Summer* (New York: Dodd, Mead and Co., 1960).
*Autumn Across America* (New York: Dodd, Mead and Co., 1956).
*Wandering Through Winter* (New York: Dodd, Mead and Co., 1965).

The Sierra Club publishes some of the finest nature books available in its Exhibit Format Series. Two of the best of these are *Navajo Wildlands* and *Baja California*. The same books are available in paperback in the Sierra Club-Ballantine Books.

# SEVEN

# The Adventure Narrative

JEFFERSON'S LETTER TO LEWIS shows his imaginative grasp of the significance of the great transcontinental expedition and a realistic awareness
of the hazards he is asking Lewis to face. Lewis' letter to Clark and Clark's
acceptance show that they share Jefferson's commitment.

Jedediah Smith has been called "intelligent, mule-tough, religiously inclined;" his letter to Clark recounts one of his many stirring adventures.
Almost all writers of fiction about the mountain man since Ruxton published his vivid accounts of life in the West have drawn deeply on his
portrayal of the moutain man's personality and language. Ruxton and
Garrard have written some of the most lively and interesting accounts of
mid-nineteenth-century adventure in the West.

The old folk song, *Across the Wide Missouri*, captures the spirit of the
compelling urge for adventure in the West.

> Oh, Shennydore, I long to hear you.
> Away, you rolling river!
> Oh, Shennydore, I can't get near you.
> Away, away, I'm bound away
> Across the wide Missouri.
>
> 'Tis seven long years since first I seed 'ee.
> Away, you rolling river!
> 'Tis seven long years since first I seed 'ee.
> Away, away, I'm bound away
> Across the wide Missouri.
>
> Oh, Shennydore, I love your daughter.
> Away, you rolling river!
> I'll take her across the yellow water.
> Away, away, I'm bound away
> Across the wide Missouri.

# MERIWETHER LEWIS
# THOMAS JEFFERSON
# WILLIAM CLARK

## *Plans for the Great Adventure*

### *Lewis to Clark*

**D**EAR CLARK,                                   Washington, June 19th 1803

Herewith inclosed you will receive the papers belonging to your brother Genl. Clark, which sometime since you requested me to procure and forward to you; pray excuse the delay which has taken place, it has really proceeded from causes which I could not control; Mr. Thompson Mason[1] the gentleman in whose possesion they were, is a member of the Virginia legislature, and was absent of course from his residence untill March, previous to his return I was compelled to leave this place on a matter of business, which has detained me in Lancaster & Philadelphia untill the day before yesterday and since my return haveing possessed myself of the papers I sieze the first moment to forward them to you: In this claim I wish you sucess most sincerely.

From the long and uninterupted friendship and confidence which has subsisted between us I feel no hesitation in making to you the following communication under the fulest impression that it will be held by you inviolably secret untill I see you, or you shall hear again from me.

During the last session of Congress a law was passed in conformity to a private message of the President of the United States, inti[t]led 'An Act making an appropriation for extending the external commerce of the United States." The object of this Act as understood by it's framers was to give the sanction of the government to exploreing the interior of the continent of North America, or that part of it bordering on the Missourie & Columbia Rivers. This enterprise has been confided to me by the President, and in consequence since the begining of March I have been engaged in making the necessary preparations for the tour, these arrangements

The following abbreviations are used in the text; ADS, autograph document, signed; ALS, autograph letter, signed; DLC, Library of Congress; MoSHi, Missouri Historical Society Library, St. Louis; RC, receiver's copy; SC, sender's copy; [ ], word supplied or corrected. Editorial comment italicized; [?], conjectural reading; < >, word or phrase deleted from manuscript, usually by sender; . . . . unrelated matter deleted by the editor (Donald Jackson).

[1] Stevens Thomson Mason (1760–1803), U.S. Senator from Virginia.

*From* LETTERS OF THE LEWIS AND CLARK EXPEDITION WITH RELATED
DOCUMENTS 1783–1854, *edited by Donald Jackson. Editor's title.
Reprinted with permission of the University of Illinois Press,
publisher. Letters were numbered by Mr. Jackson;
nos. 46, 47 and 74 are reprinted here.*

being now nearly completed, I shall set out for Pittsburgh (the intended point of embarcation) about the last of this month, and as soon after as from the state of the water you can reasonably expect me I shall be with you, say about the 10th of August. To aid me in this enterprise I have the most ample and hearty support that the government can give in every possible shape. I am armed with the authority of the Government of the U. States for my protection, so far as its authority or influence extends; in addition to which, the further aid has been given me of liberal pasports from the Ministers both of France and England: I am instructed to select from any corps in the army a number of noncommissioned officers and privates not exceeding 12, who may be disposed voluntarily to enter into this service; and am also authorized to engage any other men not soldiers that I may think usefull in promoting the objects or success of this expedition. I am likewise furnished with letters of credit, and authorized to draw on the government for any sum necessary for the comfort of myself or party. To all the persons engaged in this service I am authorized to offer the following rewards by way of inducement—1st the bounty (if not a soldier) but in both cases six months pay in advance; 2dly to discharge them from the service if they wish it, immediately on their return from the expedition giving them their arrears of pay clothing &c. & 3dly to secure to them a portion of land equal to that given by the United States to the officers and soldiers who served in the revolutionary army. This is a sho[r]t view of means with which I am intrusted to carry this plan of the Government into effect. I will now give you a short sketch of my plan of operation: I shall embark at Pittsburgh with a party of recruits eight or nine in number, intended only to manage the boat and are not calculated on as a permanent part of my detatcment; when descending the Ohio it shall be my duty by enquiry to find out and engage some good hunters, stout, healthy, unmarried men, accustomed to the woods, and capable of bearing bodily fatigue in a pretty considerable degree: should any young men answering this discription be found in your neighborhood I would thank you to give information of them on my arivall at the falls of the Ohio; and if possible learn the probability of their engaging in this service, this may be done perhaps by holding out the idea that the direction of this expedition is up the Mississippi to its source, and thence to the lake of the Woods, stating the probable period of absence at about 18 months; if they would engage themselves in a service of this discription there would be but little doubt that they would engage in the real design when it became necessary to make it known to them, which I should take care to do before I finally engaged them: The soldiers that will most probably answer this expedition best will be found in some of the companies stationed at Massac, Kaskaskias & Illinois: pardon this digression from the discription of my plan: it is to descend the Ohio in a keeled boat of about ten tons burthen, from Pittsburgh to it's mouth, thence up the Mississippi to the mouth of the Missourie, and up that river as far as it's navigation is practicable with a boat of this discription, there to prepare canoes of bark or raw-hides, and proceed to it's source, and if practicable pass over to the waters of the Columbia or Origan River and by descending it reach the Western Ocean; the mouth of this river lies about one hundred and forty miles South of Nootka-Sound, at which place there is a considerable European Tradeing establishment, and from which it will be easy to obtain a passage to the United States by way of the East-Indies in some of the trading vessels that visit Nootka Sound anually, provided it should be thought more expedient to do so, than to return by the rout I had pursued in my outward bound journey. The present season being already so far advanced, I do not calculate on geting further than two or three hundred miles up the Missourie before the commencement of the ensuing winter. At this point wherever it may be I shall make myself as comfortable as possible during the winter and resume my journey as early in the spring as the ice will permit: should nothing take place to defeat my progress altogether I feel confident that my passage to the Western Ocean can be effected by the end of the next Summer or the begining of Autumn. In order to subsist my party with some degree of comfort dureing the ensuing winter, I shall engage some French traders at Illinois to attend me to my wintering ground with a sufficient quantity of flour, pork, &c. to serve them plentifully during the winter, and thus be enabled to set out in the Spring with a healthy and vigorous party—so much for the great outlines of this scheem, permit me now to mention partially the objects which it has in view or those which it is desirable to effect through it's means, and then conclude this lengthy communication. You must know in the first place that very sanguine expectations are at this time formed by our Government that the whole of that immense country wartered by the Mississippi and it's tributary streams, Missourie inclusive, will be the property of the U. States in less than 12 Months from this date; but here let me again impress you with the necessity of keeping this matter a perfect secret—in such a state of things therefore as we have every reason to hope, you will readily concieve the importance to the U. States of an early friendly and intimate acquaintance with the tribes that inhabit that country, that they should be early impressed with a just idea of the rising importance of the U. States and of her friendly dispositions towards them, as also her desire to become usefull to them by furnishing them through her citizens with such articles by way of barter as may be desired by them or usefull to them—the other objects of this mission are scientific, and of course not less interresting to the U. States than to the world generally, such is the ascertaining by celestial observation the geography of the country through which I shall pass; the names of the nations who inhabit it, the extent and limitts of their several possessions, their relation with other tribes and nations; their languages, traditions, and monuments; their ordinary occupations in fishing, hunting, war, arts, and the implements for their food, clothing and domestic accomodation; the diseases prevalent among them and the remidies they use; the articles of commerce they may need, or furnish, and to what extent; the soil and face of the country; it's growth and vegetable productions, its animals; the miniral productions of every discription; and in short to collect the best possible information relative to whatever the country may afford as a tribute to general science.

My Instruments for celestial observation are an excellent set and my supply of Indian presents is sufficiently ample.

Thus my friend you have so far as leasure will at this time permit me to give it you, a summary view of the plan, the means and the objects of this expedition. If therefore there is anything under those circumstances, in this enterprise, which would induce you to participate with me in it's fatiegues, it's dangers and it's honors, believe me there is no man on earth with whom I should feel equal pleasure in sharing them as with yourself; I make this communication to you with the privity of the President, who expresses an anxious wish that you would consent to join me in this enterprise; he has authorized me to say that in the event of your accepting this proposition he will grant you a Captain's commission[2] which of course will intitle you to the pay and emoluments attached to that office and will equally with myself intitle you to such portion of land as was granted to officers of similar rank for their Revolutionary services; the commission with which he proposes to furnish you is not to be considered temporary but permanent if you wish it; your situation if joined with me in this mission will in all respects be precisely such as my own. Pray write to me on this subject as early as possible and direct to me at Pittsburgh. Should you feel disposed not to attatch yourself to this party in an official character, and at the same time feel a disposition to accompany me as a friend any part of the way up the Missouri I should be extremely happy in your company, and will furnish you with every aid for your return from any point you might wish it. With sincere and affectionate regard Your friend & Humble Sevt.

MERIWETHER LEWIS

ALS, RC, (MoSHi).

## *Jefferson's Instructions to Lewis*

[20 June 1803]

TO CAPTAIN MERIWETHER LEWIS ESQ. Capt. of the 1st regimt. of Infantry of the U.S. of A.

Your situation as Secretary of the President of the U.S. has made you acquainted with the objects of my confidential message of Jan. 18, 1803 to the legislature; you have seen the act they passed, which, tho' expressed

---

[2] Jefferson, of course, could only nominate officers for appointment; his selections had to be confirmed by the Senate. He routinely made these nominations on the recommendation of the Secretary of War. For a note on the red tape that thwarted Clark's appointment to a captaincy, see No. 110. For Clarke's own reaction voiced many years later, see No. 345, in which he answers an inquiry put to him in No. 342 by Nicholas Biddle.

in general terms, was meant to sanction those objects, and you are appointed to carry them into execution.

Instruments for ascertaining, by celestial observations, the geography of the country through which you will pass, have been already provided. Light articles for barter and presents among the Indians, arms for your attendants, say for from 10. to 12. men, boats, tents, & other travelling apparatus, with ammunition, medecine, surgical instruments and provisions you will have prepared with such aids as the Secretary at War can yield in his department; & from him also you will recieve authority to engage among our troops, by voluntary agreement, the number of attendants above mentioned, over whom you, as their commanding officer, are invested with all the powers the laws give in such a case.

As your movements while within the limits of the U.S. will be better directed by occasional communications, adapted to circumstances as they arise, they will not be noticed here. What follows will respect your proceedings after your departure from the United states.

Your mission has been communicated to the ministers here from France, Spain & Great Britain, and through them to their governments; & such assurances given them as to it's objects, as we trust will satisfy them. The country <*of Louisiana*> having been ceded by Spain to France, <*and possession by this time probably given,*> the passport you have from the minister of France, the representative of the present sovereign of the country, will be a protection with all it's subjects; & that from the minister of England will entitle you to the friendly aid of any traders of that allegiance with whom you may happen to meet.

The object of your mission is to explore the Missouri river, & such principal stream of it, as, by it's course and communication with the waters of the Pacific ocean, whether the Columbia, Oregan, Colorado or any other river[1] may offer the most direct & practicable water communication across this continent for the purposes of commerce.

Beginning at the mouth of the Missouri, you will take <*careful*> observations of latitude & longitude, at all remarkeable points on the river, & especially at the mouths of rivers, at rapids, at islands, & other places & objects distinguished by such natural marks & characters of a durable kind, as that they may with certainty be recognised hereafter. The courses of the river between these points of observation may be supplied by the compass the log-line & by time, corrected by the observations themselves. The variations of the compass too, in different places, should be noticed.

The interesting points of the portage between the heads of the Missouri, & of the water offering the best communication with the Pacific ocean, should also be fixed by observation, & the course of that water to the ocean, in the same manner as that of the Missouri.

Your observations are to be taken with great pains & accuracy, to be entered distinctly & intelligibly for others as well as yourself, to compre-

[1] The words "whether the Columbia, Oregan, Colorado or any other river" are omitted from the fair copy.

hend all the elements necessary, with the aid of the usual tables, to fix the latitude and longitude of the places at which they were taken, and are to be rendered to the war-office, for the purpose of having the calculations made concurrently by proper persons within the U.S. Several copies of these as well as of your other notes should be made at leisure times, & put into the care of the most trust-worthy of your attendants, to guard, by multiplying them, against the accidental losses to which they will be exposed. A further guard would be that one of these copies be on the paper of the birch, as less liable to injury from damp than common paper.[2]

The commerce which may be carried on with the people inhabiting the line you pursue, renders a knolledge of those people important. You will therefore endeavor to make yourself acquainted, as far as a diligent pursuit of your journey shall admit, with the names of the nations & their numbers;

the extent & limits of their possessions;

their relations with other tribes of nations;

their language, traditions, monuments;

their ordinary occupations in agriculture, fishing, hunting, war, arts, & the implements for these;

their food, clothing, & domestic accomodations;

the diseases prevalent among them, & the remedies they use;

moral & physical circumstances which distinguish them from the tribes we know;

peculiarities in their laws, customs & dispositions;

and articles of commerce they may need or furnish, & to what extent.

And, considering the interest which every nation has in extending & strengthening the authority of reason & justice among the people around them, it will be useful to acquire what knolledge you can of the state of morality, religion, & information among them; as it may better enable those who may endeavor to civilize & instruct them, to adapt their measures to the existing notions & practices of those on whom they are to operate.

Other objects worthy of notice will be

the soil & face of the country, it's growth & vegetable productions, especially those not of the U.S.

the animals of the country generally, & especially those not known in the U.S.

the remains or accounts of any which may be deemed rare or extinct;

the mineral productions of every kind; but more particularly metals, limestone, pit coal, & saltpetre; salines & mineral waters, noting the temperature of the last, & such circumstances as may indicate their character;

volcanic appearances;

climate, as characterised by the thermometer, by the proportion of

---

[2] The last sentence in this paragraph appears in smaller letters, as if added later. A fragment of the text exists in Clark's hand, slightly abridged, on a two-page manuscript in MoSHi, extending from the beginning of this paragraph to superscript numeral 2.

rainy, cloudy, & clear days, by lightning, hail, snow, ice, by the access & recess of frost, by the winds prevailing at different seasons, the dates at which particular plants put forth or lose their flower, or leaf, times of appearance of particular birds, reptiles or insects.

Altho' your route will be along the channel of the Missouri, yet you will endeavor to inform yourself, by enquiry, of the character & extent of the country watered by it's branches, & especially on it's Southern side. The North river or Rio Bravo which runs into the gulph of Mexico, and the North river, or Rio colorado which runs into the gulph of California, are understood to be the principal streams heading opposite to the waters of the Missouri, and running Southwardly. Whether the dividing grounds between the Missouri & them are mountains or flat lands, what are their distance from the Missouri, the character of the intermediate country, & the people inhabiting it, are worthy of particular enquiry. The Northern waters of the Missouri are less to be enquired after, because they have been ascertained to a considerable degree, & are still in a course of ascertainment by English traders, and travellers. But if you can learn any thing certain of the most Northern source of the Missisipi, & of it's position relatively to the lake of the woods, it will be interesting to us.

<*Two copies of your notes at least & as many more as leisure will admit, should be made & confided to the care of the most trusty individuals of your attendants.*> Some account too of the path of the Canadian traders from the Missisipi, at the mouth of the Ouisconsing to where it strikes the Missouri, & of the soil and rivers in it's course, is desireable.

In all your intercourse with the natives, treat them in the most friendly & conciliatory manner which their own conduct will admit; allay all jealousies as to the object of your journey, satisfy them of it's innocence, make them acquainted with the position, extent, character, peaceable & commercial dispositions of the U.S.[,] of our wish to be neighborly, friendly & useful to them, & of our dispositions to a commercial intercourse with them; confer with them on the points most convenient as mutual emporiums, and the articles of most desireable interchange for them & us.[3] If a few of their influential chiefs, within practicable distance, wish to visit us, arrange such a visit with them, and furnish them with authority to call on our officers, on their entering the U.S. to have them conveyed to this place at the public expence. If any of them should wish to have some of their young people brought up with us, & taught such arts as may be useful to them, we will receive, instruct & take care of them. Such a mission, whether of influential chiefs or of young people, would give some security to your own party.[4] Carry with you some matter of the kinepox; inform those of them with whom you may be, of it's efficacy as

[3] End of version in Clark's hand (MoSHi).

[4] This sentence is inserted in smaller letters, as if added later. Jefferson's reference to the security of the party may have given rise to the common belief that the group of Osages which left St. Louis for Washington in the spring of 1804 were "hostages" for the safety of the expedition. The sending back of Indian delegations was done for a much different reason, and even when there were reports that Lewis and Clark had been killed in the West, no one in Washington treated these delegations as hostages.

a preservative from the smallpox; & instruct & encourage them in the use
of it. This may be especially done wherever you winter.

As it is impossible for us to foresee in what manner you will be recieved
by those people, whether with hospitality or hostility, so is it impossible
to prescribe the exact degree of perseverance with which you are to pursue
your journey. We value too much the lives of citizens to offer them to
probable destruction. Your numbers will be sufficient to secure you against
the unauthorised opposition of individuals or of small parties: but if a
superior force, authorised, or not authorised, by a nation, should be arrayed against your further passage, and inflexibly determined to arrest it,
you must decline it's farther pursuit, and return. In the loss of yourselves,
we should lose also the information you will have acquired. By returning
safely with that, you may enable us to renew the essay with better calculated means. To your own discretion therefore must be left the degree
of danger you may risk, and the point at which you should decline, only
saying we wish you to err on the side of your safety, and to bring back
your party safe even if it be with less information.

As far up the Missouri as the white settlements extend, an intercourse
will probably be found to exist between them & the Spanish posts of
St. Louis opposite Cahokia, or Ste. Genevieve opposite Kaskaskia. From
still further up the river, the traders may furnish a conveyance for letters.
Beyond that, you may perhaps be able to engage Indians to bring letters
for the government to Cahokia or Kaskaskia, on promising that they shall
there recieve such special compensation as you shall have stipulated with
them. Avail yourself of these means to communicate to us, at seasonable
intervals, a copy of your journal, notes & observations, of every kind,
putting into cypher[5] whatever might do injury if betrayed.

Should you reach the Pacific ocean inform yourself of the circumstances
which may decide whether the furs of those parts may not be collected
as advantageously at the head of the Missouri (convenient as is supposed
to the waters of the Colorado & Oregan or Columbia) as at Nootka sound,
or any other point of that coast; and that trade be consequently conducted
through the Missouri & U.S. more beneficially than by the circumnaviga-
tion now practised.[6]

On your arrival on that coast endeavor to learn if there be any port
within your reach frequented by the sea-vessels of any nation, & to send
two of your trusty people back by sea, in such way as <*they shall judge*>
shall appear practicable, with a copy of your notes: and should you be of
opinion that the return of your party by the way they went will be eminently dangerous, then ship the whole, & return by sea, by the way either
of cape Horn, of the cape of good Hope, as you shall be able. As you will
be without money, clothes or provisions, you must endeavor to use the
credit of the U.S. to obtain them, for which purpose open letters of credit[7]

[5] No enciphered messages from Lewis have been found.

[6] This paragraph and the preceding one were written longitudinally in the right-hand
margin, as insertions.

[7] For the text of the letter of credit, see No. 67.

shall be furnished you, authorising you to draw upon the Executive of the U.S. or any of it's officers, in any part of the world, on which draughts can be disposed of, & to apply with our recommendations to the Consuls, agents, merchants, or citizens of any nation with which we have intercourse, assuring them, in our name, that any aids they may furnish you, shall be honorably repaid, and on demand. Our consuls Thomas Hewes at Batavia in Java, Wm. Buchanan in the Isles of France & Bourbon & John Elmslie at the Cape of good Hope will be able to supply your necessities by draughts on us.[8]

Should you find it safe to return by the way you go, after sending two of your party round by sea, or with your whole party, if no conveyance by sea can be found, do so; making such observations on your return, as may serve to supply, correct or confirm those made on your outward journey.

On re-entering the U.S. and reaching a place of safety, discharge any of your attendants who may desire & deserve it, procuring for them immediate paiment of all arrears of pay & cloathing which may have incurred since their departure, and assure them that they shall be recommended to the liberality of the legislature for the grant of a souldier's portion of land each, as proposed in my message to Congress: & repair yourself with your papers to the seat of government <*to which I have only to add my sincere prayer for your safe return*>.

To provide, on the accident of your death, against anarchy, dispersion, & the consequent danger to your party, and total failure of the enterprize, you are hereby authorised, by any instrument signed & written in your own hand, to name the person among them who shall succeed to the command on your decease, and by like instruments to change the nomination from time to time as further experience of the characters accompanying you shall point out superior fitness: and all the powers and authorities given to yourself are, in the event of your death, transferred to, & vested in the successor so named, with further power to him, and his successors in like manner to name each his successor, who, on the death of his predecessor, shall be invested with all the powers & authorities given to yourself.

Given under my hand at the city of Washington this 20th day of June 1803.

Th: J. Pr. U.S. of A.

ADS, SC (DLC). This is a draft which Jefferson later incorporated into the draft of his memoir on Lewis (No. 362), and which is now filed with that document in DLC. A letterpress impression of the fair copy, in Jefferson's hand, is also in DLC.

[8] Thomas Hewes, consul for the port of Batavia, was appointed 24 Nov. 1801; William Buchanan of Maryland, commercial agent for the Isles of France and Bourbon, was appointed 9 July 1801; John Elmslie, Jr., consul at the Cape of Good Hope, was appointed 21 Feb. 1799.

# Clark to Lewis

DEAR LEWIS                                              Clarksville July 18th 1803

I received by yesterdays Mail, your letter of the 19th ulto. The Contents of which I recived with much pleasure. The enterprise &c. is Such as I have long anticipated and am much pleased with—and as my situation in life will admit of my absence the length of time necessary to accomplish such an undertaking I will chearfully join you in an "official Charrector" as mentioned in your letter,[1] and partake of the dangers, difficulties, and fatigues, and I anticipate the honors & rewards of the result of such an enterprise, should we be successful in accomplishing it. This is an undertaking fraited with many difeculties, but My friend I do assure you that no man lives whith whome I would perfur to undertake Such a Trip &c. as your self,[2] and I shall arrange my matters as well as I can against your arrival here.

It may be necessary that you inform the President of my acceding to the proposals, so that I may be furnished with such Credentials as the nature of the Toure may require, which I suppose had best be forwarded to Louisville. The Objects of this Plan of Governments are Great and Worthey of that great Chaructor the Main Spring of its action. The Means with which we are furnished to carry it into effect, I think may be Sufficiently liberal. The plan of operation, as laid down by you (with a Small addition as to the outfit) I highly approve of.

I shall indeaver to engage (temporally) a fiew men, such as will best answer our purpose, holding out the Idea as stated in your letter—The subject of which has been mentioned in Louisville several weeks agoe.

Pray write to me by every post after recving this letter, I shall be exceedingly anxious to hear from you. With every sincerity & frendship Yr. Obt. Sevt.

WM. CLARK

Capt. Merriwether Lewis
at Washington City or on
his way to Pittsburgh.

Note this letter
forwarded to Pittsburgh.

ALS, RC (DLC). Addressed, "Captain Meriwether Lewis." Reply is No. 80. Clark's first draft is in MoSHi, with several false starts and minor changes in wording. Two such changes are noted below. The third page of the MoSHi version contains two drafts of Clark's letter of 24 July 1803 to Jefferson (No. 77).

[1] Here, instead of "as mentioned in your letter," Clark first wrote "on equal footing &c."

[2] In the first draft, Clark wrote here, "I reserve nothing from you that will add either to Yr. profit or satisfaction, and. . . ."

# JEDEDIAH STRONG SMITH

## Explorations in the Western Desert

LITTLE LAKE OF BEAR RIVER, July 17th 1827. Genl. Wm. Clark, Supt. of Indian Affairs

Sir, My situation in this country has enabled me to collect information respecting a section of the country which has hitherto been measurably veiled in obscurity to the citizens of the United States. I allude to the country S.W. of the *Great Salt Lake* west of the Rocky mountains.

I started about the 22d of August 1826, from the Great Salt Lake, with a party of fifteen men, for the purpose of exploring the country S.W. which was entirely unknown to me, and of which I could collect no satisfactory information from the Indians who inhabit this country on its N.E. borders.

My general course on leaving the Salt Lake was S.W. and W. Passing the Little Uta Lake and ascending Ashley's river, which empties into the Little Uta Lake. From this lake I found no more signs of buffalo; there are a few antelope and mountain sheep, and an abundance of *black tailed hares*. On Ashley's river, I found a nation of Indians who call themselves *Sampatch;* they were friendly disposed towards us. I passed over a range of mountains running S.E. and N.W. and struck a river running S.W. which I called *Adams River*, in compliment to our President. The water is of a muddy cast, and is a little brackish. The country is mountainous to East; towards the West there are sandy plains and detached rocky hills.

Passing down this river some distance, I fell in with a nation of Indians who call themselves *Pa-Ulches* (those Indians as well as those last mentioned, wear rabbit skin robes) who raise some little corn and pumpkins. The country is nearly destitute of game of any description, except a few hares. Here (about ten days march down it) the river turns to the South East. On the S.W. side of the river there is a *cave*, the entrance of which is about 10 or 15 feet high, and 5 or 6 feet in width; after descending about 15 feet, a room opens out from 25 to 30 in length and 15 to 20 feet in width; the roof, sides and floor are solid rock salt, a sample of which I send you, with some other articles which will be hereafter described. I here found a kind of plant of the prickly pear kind, which I called the cabbage pear, the largest of which grows about two feet and a half high and 1½ feet in diameter; upon examination I found it to be nearly of the substance of a turnip, altho' by no means palatable; its form was similar to that of an egg, being smaller at the ground and top than in the middle; it is covered with pricks similar to the prickly pear with which you are acquainted.

---

*Reprinted from* MISSOURI REPUBLICAN (*St. Louis, Mo.*),
*October 11, 1827.*

There are here also a number of shrubs and small trees with which I was not acquainted previous to my route there, and which I cannot at present describe satisfactorily, as it would take more space that I can here allot.

The *Pa Ulches* have a number of marble pipes, one of which I obtained and send you, altho it has been broken since I have had it in my possession; they told me there was a quantity of the same material in their country. I also obtained of them a knife of *flint*, which I send you, but it has likewise been broken by accident.

I followed Adams river two days further to where it empties into the Seedekeeden a South East course. I crossed the Seedskeeder, and went down it four days a south east course; I here found the country remarkably barren, rocky, and mountainous; there are a good many rapids in the river, but at this place a valley opens out about 5 to 15 miles in width, which on the river banks is timbered and fertile. I here found a nation of Indians who call themselves *Ammuchabas;* they cultivate the soil, and raise corn, beans, pumpkins, watermelons and muskmelons in abundance, and also a little wheat and cotton. I was now nearly destitute of horses, and had learned what it was to do without food; I therefore remained fifteen days and recruited my men, and I was enabled also to exchange my horses and purchase a few more of a few runaway Indians who stole some horses of the Spaniards. I here got information of the Spanish country (the Californias) and obtained two guides, recrossed the Seedskadeer, which I afterwards found emptied into the Gulf of California about 80 miles from this place by the name of Collarado; many render the river *Gild* from the East.

I travelled a west course fifteen days over a country of complete barrens, generally travelling from morning until night without water. I crossed a Salt plain about 20 miles long and 8 miles wide; on the surface was a crust of beautiful white salt, quite thin. Under this surface there is a layer of salt from a half to one and a half inches in depth; between this and the upper layer there is about four inches of yellowish sand.

On my arrival in the province of Upper California, I was looked upon with suspicion, and was compelled to appear in presence of the Governor of the Californias residing at San Diego, where, by the assistance of some American gentlemen (especially Capt. W. H. Cunningham of the ship Courier from Boston) I was enabled to obtain permission to return with my men the route I came, and purchased such supplies as I stood in want of. The Governor would not allow me to trade up the Sea coast towards Bodaga. I returned to my party and purchased such articles as were necessary, and went Eastward of the Spanish settlements on the route I had come in. I then steered my course N.W. keeping from 150 miles to 200 miles from the sea coast. A very high range of mountains lay on the East. After travelling three hundred miles in that direction through a country somewhat fertile, in which there was a great many Indians, mostly naked and destitute of arms, with the exception of a few Bows and Arrows and what is very singular amongst Indians, they cut their hair to the length of three inches; they proved to be friendly; their manner of living is on fish, roots, acorns and grass.

On my arrival at the river which I named the *Wim-mul-che* (named after a tribe of Indians which resides on it, of that name) I found a few beaver, and elk, deer, and antelope in abundance. I here made a small hunt, and attempted to take my party across the [mountain] which I before mentioned, and which I called *Mount Joseph,* to come on and join my partners at the Great Salt Lake. I found the snow so deep on Mount Joseph that I could not cross my horses, five of which starved to death; I was compelled therefore to return to the valley which I had left, and there, leaving my party, I started with two men, seven horses and two mules, which I loaded with hay for the horses and provisions for ourselves, and started on the 20th of May, and succeeded in crossing it in eight days, having lost only two horses and one mule. I found the snow on the top of this mountain from 4 to 8 feet deep, but it was so consolidated by the heat of the sun that my horses only sunk from half a foot to one foot deep.

After travelling twenty days from the east side of Mount Joseph, I struck the S.W. corner of the Great Salt Lake, travelling over a country completely barren and destitute of game. We frequently travelled without water sometimes for two days over sandy deserts, where there was no sign of vegetation and when we found water in some of the rocky hills, we most generally found some Indians who appeared the most miserable of the human race having nothing to subsist on (nor any clothing) except grass seed, grasshoppers, etc. When we arrived at the Salt Lake, we had but one horses and one mule remaining, which were so feeble and poor that they could scarce carry the little camp equipage which I had along; the balance of my horses I was compelled to eat as they gave out.

The company are now starting, and therefore must close my communication. Yours respectfully,

(signed) Jedediah S. Smith, of the firm of
Smith, Jackson and Sublette.

# GEORGE FREDERICK RUXTON

## From *Life in the Far West*

AWAY TO THE HEAD waters of the Platte, where several small streams run into the south fork of that river, and head in the broken ridges of the "Divide" which separates the valleys of the Platte and Arkansa, were

*Reprinted from* LIFE IN THE FAR WEST *by George Frederick Ruxton (William Blackwood and Sons, 1849).*

camped a band of trappers on a creek called Bijou. It was the month of October, when the early frosts of the coming winter had crisped and dyed with sober brown the leaves of the cherry and quaking ash belting the brooks; and the ridges and peaks of the Rocky Mountains were already covered with a glittering mantle of snow, sparkling in the still powerful rays of the autumn sun.

The camp had all the appearance of permanency; for not only did it comprise one or two unusually comfortable shanties, but the numerous stages on which huge stripes of buffalo meat were hanging in process of cure, showed that the party had settled themselves here in order to lay in a store of provisions, or, as it is termed in the language of the mountains, "to make meat." Round the camp fed twelve or fifteen mules and horses, their forelegs confined by hobbles of raw hide; and guarding these animals, two men paced backwards and forwards, driving in the stragglers, ascending ever and anon the bluffs which overhung the river, and leaning on their long rifles, whilst they swept with their eyes the surrounding prairie. Three or four fires burned in the encampment, at some of which Indian women carefully tended sundry steaming pots; whilst round one, which was in the centre of it, four or five stalwart hunters, clad in buckskin, sat cross-legged, pipe in mouth.

They were a trapping party from the north fork of Platte, on their way to wintering-ground in the more southern valley of the Arkansa; some, indeed, meditating a more extended trip, even to the distant settlements of New Mexico, the paradise of mountaineers. The elder of the company was a tall gaunt man, with a face browned by twenty years' exposure to the extreme climate of the mountains; his long black hair, as yet scarcely tinged with grey, hanging almost to his shoulders, but his cheeks and chin clean shaven, after the fashion of the mountain men. His dress was the usual hunting-frock of buckskin, with long fringes down the seams, with pantaloons simlarly ornamented, and moccasins of Indian make. Whilst his companions puffed their pipes in silence, he narrated a few of his former experiences of western life; and whilst the buffalo "hump-ribs" and "tender loin" are singing away in the pot, preparing for the hunters' supper, we will note down the yarn as it spins from his lips, giving it in the language spoken in the "far west:"—

" 'Twas about 'calf-time,' maybe a little later, and not a hundred year ago, by a long chalk, that the biggest kind of rendezvous was held 'to' Independence, a mighty handsome little location away up on old Missoura. A pretty smart lot of boys was camp'd thar, about a quarter from the town, and the way the whisky flowed that time was 'some' now, *I* can tell you. Thar was old Sam Owins—him as got 'rubbed out' by the Spaniards at Sacramenty, or Chihuahuy, this hos doesn't know which, but he 'went under'[1] any how. Well, Sam had his train along, ready to hitch up for the Mexican country—twenty thunderin big Pittsburg waggons—and the way *his* Santa Fé boys took in the liquor beat all—eh, Bill?"

[1] Died.

"*Well*, it did."

"Bill Bent—his boys camped the other side the trail, and they was all mountain men, wagh!—and Bill Williams, and Bill Tharpe (the Pawnees took his hair on Pawnee Fork last spring): three Bills, and them three's all 'gone under.' Surely Hatcher went out that time; and wasn't Bill Garey along, too? Didn't him and Chabonard sit in camp for twenty hours at a deck of Euker? Them was Bent's Indian traders up on Arkansa. Poor Bill Bent! them Spaniards made meat of him. He lost his topknot to Taos. A 'clever' man was Bill Bent as *I* ever know'd trade a robe or 'throw' a buffler in his tracks. Old St Vrain could knock the hind-sight off him though, when it came to shootin, and old silver heels spoke true, she did: 'plum-center' she was, eh?"

"*Well*, she wasn't nothing else."

"The Greasers payed for Bent's scalp, they tell me. Old St Vrain went out of Santa Fé with a company of mountain men, and the way they made 'em sing out, was 'slick as shootin'. He 'counted a coup,' did St Vrain. He throwed a Pueblo as had on poor Bent's shirt. I guess he tickled that niggur's hump-ribs. Fort William[2] aint the lodge it was, an' never will be agin, now he's gone under; but St Vrain's 'pretty much of a gentleman,' too; if he aint, I'll be dog-gone, eh, Bill?"

"He is *so-o*."

"Chavez had his waggons along. He was only a Spaniard any how, and some of his teamsters put a ball into him his next trip, and made a raise of *his* dollars, wagh! Uncle Sam hung 'em for it, I heard, but can't b'lieve it, nohow. If them Spaniards wasn't born for shootin', why was beaver made? You was with us that spree, Jemmy?"

"No *sirre-e;* I went out when Spiers lost his animals on Cimmaron; a hunderd and forty mules and oxen was froze that night, wagh!"

"Surely Black Harris was thar; and the darndest liar was Black Harris—for lies tumbled out of his mouth like boudins out of a buffler's stomach. . . ."

A prominent feature in the character of the hunters of the far west is their quick determination and resolve in cases of extreme difficulty and peril, and their fixedness of purpose, when any plan of operations has been laid requiring bold and instant action in carrying out. It is here that they so infinitely surpass the savage Indian, in bringing to a successful issue their numerous hostile expeditions against the natural foe of the white man in the wild and barbarous regions of the west. Ready to resolve as they are prompt to execute, and combining far greater dash and daring with equal subtlety and caution, they possess great advantage over the vacillating Indian, whose superstitious mind in a great degree paralyses the physical energy of his active body; and who, by waiting for propitious signs and seasons before he undertakes an enterprise, often loses the opportunity by which his white and more civilised enemy knows so well how to profit.

2 Better known as Bent's Indian Trading Fort on the Arkansas.

## III

[This chapter deals with La Bonte's first trip into the mountains. He left his home in Missouri and went first to St. Louis.]

. . . . To the wild and half-savage trapper, who may be said to exemplify the energy, enterprise, and hardihood characteristic of the American people, divested of all the false and vicious glare with which a high state of civilisation, too rapidly attained, has obscured their real and genuine character, in which the above traits are eminently prominent—to these men alone is due the empire of the West—destined in a few short years to become the most important of those confederate states composing the mighty union of North America.

Sprung, then, out of the wild and adventurous fur trade, St Louis, still the emporium of that species of commerce, preserves even now, [1848] in the character of its population, many of the marked peculiarities distinguishing its early founders, who were identified with the primitive Indian in hardihood and instinctive wisdom. Whilst the French portion of the population retain the thoughtless levity and frivolous disposition of their original source, the Americans of St. Louis, who may lay claim to be native, as it were, are as strongly distinguished for determination and energy of character as they are for physical strength and animal courage; and are remarkable at the same time, for a singular aptitude in carrying out commercial enterprises to successful terminations, apparently incompatible with the thirst of adventure and excitement which forms so prominent a feature in their character. In St Louis and with her merchants have originated many commercial enterprises of gigantic speculation, not confined to the immediate locality or to the distant Indian fur trade, but embracing all parts of the continent, and even a portion of the Old World. . . .

But perhaps the most singular of the casual population are the mountaineers, who, after several seasons spent in trapping, and with good store of dollars, arrive from the scene of their adventures, wild as savages, determined to enjoy themselves, for a time, in all the gaiety and dissipation of the western city. In one of the back streets of the town is a tavern well known as the "Rocky-Mountain House," and hither the trappers resort, drinking and fighting as long as their money lasts, which, as they are generous and lavish as Jack Tars, is for a few days only. Such scenes, both tragic and comic, as are enacted in the Rocky-Mountain House, are beyond the powers of pen to describe; and when a fandango is in progress, to which congregate the coquetish belles from "Vide Poche," as the French portion of the suburb is nicknamed,—the grotesque endeavours of the bear-like mountaineers to sport a figure on the light fantastic toe, and their insertions into the dance of the mystic jumps of Terpsichorean Indians when engaged in the "medicine" dances in honour of bear, of buffalo, or ravished scalp,—are such startling innovations on the choreographic art as would make the shade of Gallini quake and gibber in his pumps.

Passing the open doors and windows of the Mountain House, the stranger stops short as the sounds of violin and banjo twang upon his ears, accompanied by extraordinary noises—sounding unearthly to the green-horn listener, but recognised by the initiated as an Indian song roared out of the stentorian lungs of a mountaineer, who patting his stomach with open hands, to improve the necessary shake, choruses the well-known Indian chant:— . . . and polishes off the high notes with a whoop which makes the old wooden houses shake again, as it rattles and echoes down the street.

Here, over fiery "monaghahela," Jean Batiste, the sallow half-breed voyageur from the north—and who, deserting the service of the "North West" (the Hudson's Bay Company), has come down the Mississippi, from the "Falls," to try the sweets and liberty of "free" trapping—hobnobs with a stalwart leather-clad "boy," just returned from trapping on the waters of Grand River, on the western side the mountains, who interlards his mountain jargon with Spanish words picked up in Taos and California. . . .

La Bonté, on his arrival at St Louis, found himself one day in no less a place than this; and here he made acquaintance with an old trapper about to start for the mountains in a few days, to hunt on the head waters of Platte and Green River. With this man he resolved to start, and, having still some hundred dollars in cash, he immediately set about equipping himself for the expedition. To effect this, he first of all visited the gun-store of Hawken, whose rifles are renowned in the mountains, and exchanged his own piece, which was of very small bore, for a regular mountain rifle. This was of very heavy metal, carrying about thirty-two balls to the pound, stocked to the muzzle, and mounted with brass, its only ornament being a buffalo bull, looking exceedingly ferocious, which was not very artistically engraved upon the trap in the stock. Here, too, he laid in a few pounds of powder and lead, and all the necessaries for a long hunt.

His next visit was to a smith's store, which smith was black by trade and black by nature, for he was a nigger, and, moreover, celebrated as being the best maker of beaver-traps in St Louis, and of him he purchased six new traps, paying for the same twenty dollars—procuring, at the same time, an old trap-sack, made of stout buffalo skin, in which to carry them.

We next find La Bonté and his companion—one Luke, better known as Grey-Eye, one of his eyes having been "gouged" in a mountain fray—at Independence, a little town situated on the Missouri, several hundred miles above St Louis, and within a short distance of the Indian frontier.

Independence may be termed the "prairie port" of the western country. Here the caravans destined for Santa Fé, and the interior of Mexico, assemble to complete their necessary equipment. Mules and oxen are purchased, teamsters hired, and all stores and outfit laid in here for the long journey over the wide expanse of prairie ocean. Here, too, the Indian traders and the Rocky-Mountain trappers rendezvous, collecting in sufficient force to ensure their safe passage through the Indian country. At the seasons of departure and arrival of these bands, the little town presents a lively scene of bustle and confusion. The wild and dissipated mountaineers get rid of their last dollars in furious orgies, treating all comers to galore of drink, and pledging each other, in horns of potent whisky, to successful hunts and "heaps of beaver." When every cent has disappeared from their pouches, the free trapper often makes away with rifle, traps, and animals, to gratify his "dry" (for your mountaineer is never "thirsty"); and then, "hos and beaver" gone, is necessitated to hire himself to one of the leaders of big bands, and hypothecate his services for an equipment of traps and animals. Thus La Bonté picked up three excellent mules for a mere song, with their accompanying pack-saddles, *apishamores*,[3] and lariats, and the next day, with Luke, "put out" for Platte.

As they passed through the rendezvous, which was encamped on a little stream beyond the town, even our young Mississippian was struck with the novelty of the scene. Upwards of forty huge waggons, of Conostoga and Pittsburg build, and covered with snow-white tilts, were ranged in a semi-circle, or rather a horse-shoe form, on the flat open prairie, their long "tongues" (poles) pointing outwards; with the necessary harness for four pairs of mules, or eight yoke of oxen, lying on the ground beside them, spread in ready order for "hitching up." Round the waggons groups of teamsters, tall stalwart young Missourians, were engaged in busy preparation for the start, greasing the wheels, fitting or repairing harness, smoothing ox-bows, or overhauling their own moderate kits or "possibles." They were all dressed in the same fashion: a pair of "homespun" pantaloons, tucked into thick boots reaching nearly to the knee, and confined round the waist by a broad leathern belt, which supported a strong butcher-knife in a sheath. A coarse checked shirt was their only other covering, with a fur cap on the head.

Numerous camp-fires surrounded the waggons, and near them lounged wild-looking mountaineers, easily distinguished from the "greenhorn" teamsters by their dresses of buckskin, and their weather-beaten faces. Without an exception, these were under the influence of the rosy god; and one, who sat, the picture of misery, at a fire by himself—staring into the blaze with vacant countenance, his long matted hair hanging in unkempt masses over his face, begrimed with the dirt of a week, and pallid with the effects of ardent drink—was suffering from the usual consequences of having "kept it up" beyond the usual point, paying the penalty in a fit of "horrors"—as *delirium tremens* is most aptly termed by sailors and the unprofessional.

In another part, the merchants of the caravan and the Indian traders superintended the lading of the waggons, or mule packs. They were dressed in civilised attire, and some were even bedizened in St Louis or Eastern City dandyism, to the infinite disgust of the mountain men, who look upon a bourge-way (bourgeois) with most undisguised contempt,

---

[3] Saddle blankets made of buffalo calfskin.

despising the very simplest forms of civilisation. The picturesque appearance of the encampment was not a little heightened by the addition of several Indians from the neighbouring Shawnee settlement, who, mounted on their small active horses, on which they reclined, rather than sat, in negligent attitudes, quietly looked on at the novel scene, indifferent to the "chaff" in which the thoughtless teamsters indulged at their expense. Numbers of mules and horses were picketed at hand, whilst a large herd of noble oxen were being driven towards the camp—the wo-ha of the teamsters sounding far and near, as they collected the scattered beasts in order to yoke up.

As most of the mountain men were utterly unable to move from camp, Luke and La Bonté, with three or four of the most sober, started in company, intending to wait on "Blue," a stream which runs into the Caw or Kanzas River, until the "balance" of the band came up. Mounting their mules, and leading the loose animals, they struck at once into the park-like prairie, and were speedily out of sight of civilisation.

Camping the first night on "Black Jack," our mountaineers here cut each man a spare hickory wiping-stick for his rifle; and La Bonté, who was the only greenhorn of the party, witnessed a savage ebullition of rage on the part of one of his companions, exhibiting the perfect unrestraint which these men impose upon their passions, and the barbarous anger which the slightest opposition to their will excites. One of the trappers, on arriving at the camping-place, dismounted from his horse, and, after divesting it of the saddle, endeavoured to lead his mule by the rope up to the spot where he wished to deposit his pack. Mule-like, however, the more he pulled the more stubbornly she remained in her tracks, . . . After tugging ineffectually for several minutes, winding the rope round his body, and throwing himself suddenly forward with all his strength, the trapper actually foamed with passion; and although he might have subdued the animal at once by fastening the rope with a half-hitch round its nose, this, with an obstinacy equal to that of the mule itself, he refused to attempt, preferring to vanquish her by main strength. Failing so to do, the mountaineer, with a volley of blasphemous imprecations, suddenly seized his rifle, and levelling it at the mule's head, shot her dead.

Crossing Vermilion, the trappers arrived on the fifth day at "Blue," where they encamped in the broad timber belting the creek, and there awaited the arrival of the remainder of the party.

It was two days before they came up; but the following day they started for the mountains, fourteen in number, . . . In a few days, without any adventure, they struck the Platte River, . . .

. . . they now knew that they were in the country of meat; and a few miles farther, another band of stragglers [buffalo] presenting themselves, three of the hunters were in pursuit, La Bonté taking a mule to pack in the meat. He soon saw them crawling towards the band, and shortly two puffs of smoke, and the sharp cracks of their rifles, showed that they had got within shot; and when he rode up, two fine buffaloes were stretched upon the ground. Now, for the first time, he was initiated in the mysteries of "butchering." He watched the hunters as they turned the carcass on the belly, stretching out the legs to support it on each side. A transverse cut was then made at the nape of the neck, and, gathering the long hair of the boss in one hand, the skin was separated from the shoulder. It was then laid open from this point to the tail, along the spine, and then, freed from the sides and pulled down to the brisket, but still attached to it, was stretched upon the ground to receive the dissected portions. Then the shoulder was severed, the fleece removed from along the backbone, and the hump-ribs cut off with a tomahawk. All this was placed upon the skin; and after the "boudins" had been withdrawn from the stomach, and the tongue—a great dainty—taken from the head, the meat was packed upon the mule, and the whole party hurried to camp rejoicing.

There was merry-making in the camp that night, and the way they indulged their appetites—or, in their own language, "throw'd" the meat "cold"—would have made the heart of dyspeptic leap for joy or burst with envy. Far into the "still watches of the tranquil night" the fat-clad "depouille" saw its fleshy mass grow small by degrees and beautifully less, before the trenchant blades of the hungry mountaineers; appetising yards of well-browned "boudin" slipped glibly down their throats; rib after rib of tender hump was picked and flung to the wolves; and when human nature, with helpless gratitude, and confident that nothing of superexcellent comestibility remained, was lazily wiping the greasy knife that had done such good service,—a skilful hunter was seen to chuckle to himself as he raked the deep ashes of the fire, and drew therefrom a pair of tongues so admirably baked, so soft, so sweet, and of such exquisite flavour, that a veil is considerately drawn over the effects of their discussion produced in the mind of our greenhorn La Bonté, and the raptures they excited in the bosom of that, as yet, most ignorant mountaineer! . . .

. . . they proceeded quietly up the river, vast herds of buffaloes darkening the plains around them, affording them more than abundance of the choicest meat; but, to their credit be it spoken, no more was killed than was absolutely required,—unlike the cruel slaughter made by most of the white travellers across the plains, who wantonly destroy these noble animals, not even for the excitement of sport, but in cold-blooded and insane butchery. . . .

Wolves are so common on the plains and in the mountains, that the hunter never cares to throw away a charge of ammunition upon them, although the ravenous animals are a constant source of annoyance to him, creeping to the camp-fire at night, and gnawing his saddles and *apisha-mores*, eating the skin ropes which secure the horses and mules to their pickets, and even their very hobbles, and not unfrequently killing or entirely disabling the animals themselves.

Our party crossed the south fork [of Platte River] about ten miles from its juncture with the main stream, and then, passing the prairie, struck the north fork a day's travel from the other. . . .

If the reader casts his eye over any of the recent maps of the western country, which detail the features of the regions embracing the Rocky Mountains, and the vast prairies at their bases, he will not fail to observe that many of the creeks or smaller streams which feed the larger rivers,—as the Missouri, Platte, and Arkansa,—are called by familiar proper names, both English and French. These are invariably christened after some unfortunate trapper, killed there in Indian fight; or treacherously slaughtered by the lurking savages, while engaged in trapping beaver on the stream. Thus alone is the memory of these hardy men perpetuated, at least of those whose fate is ascertained: for many, in every season, never return from their hunting expeditions, but meet a sudden death from Indians, or a more lingering fate from accident or disease in some lonely gorge of the mountains, where no footfall save his own, or the heavy tread of grizzly bear, disturbs the unbroken silence of the awful solitude. Then, as many winters pass without some old familiar faces making their appearance at the merry rendezvous, their long protracted absence may perhaps elicit a remark, as to where such and such a mountain worthy can have betaken himself, to which the casual rejoinder of "Gone under, maybe," too often gives a short but certain answer.

In the forks of the northern branch of the Platte, formed by the junction of the Laramie, they found a big village of the Sioux encamped near the station of one of the fur companies. Here the party broke up; many, finding the alcohol of the traders an impediment to their further progress, remained some time in the vicinity, while La Bonté, Luke, and a trapper named Marcelline, started in a few days to the mountains, to trap on Sweet Water and Medicine Bow. They had leisure, however, to observe all the rascalities connected with the Indian trade, although at this season (August) hardly commenced. However, a band of Indians having come in with several packs of last year's robes, and being anxious to start speedily on their return, a trader from one of the forts had erected his lodge in the village.

Here he set to work immediately, to induce the Indians to trade. First, a chief appoints three "soldiers" to guard the trader's lodge from intrusion; and these sentries amongst the thieving fraternity can be invariably trusted. Then the Indians are invited to have a drink—a taste of the fire-water being given to all to incite them to trade. As the crowd presses upon the entrance to the lodge, and those in rear become impatient, some large-mouthed savage who has received a portion of the spirit, makes his way, with his mouth full of the liquor and cheeks distended, through the throng, and is instantly surrounded by his particular friends. Drawing the face of each, by turns, near his own, he squirts a small quantity into his open mouth, until the supply is exhausted, when he returns for more, and repeats the generous distribution.

When paying for the robes, the traders, in measuring out the liquor in a tin half-pint cup, thrust their thumbs or the four fingers of the hand into the measure, in order that it may contain the less, or not unfrequently fill the bottom with melted buffalo fat, with the same object. So greedy are the Indians, that they never discover the cheat, and, once under the influence of the liquor, cannot distinguish between the first cup of comparatively strong spirit, and the following ones diluted five hundred percent, and poisonously drugged to boot.

Scenes of drunkenness, riot, and bloodshed last until the trade is over. In the winter it occupies several weeks, during which period the Indians present the appearance, under the demoralising influence of the liquor, of demons rather than of men.

### IV

La Bonté and his companions proceeded up the river, the Black Hills on their left hand, from which several small creeks or feeders swell the waters of the North Fork. Along these they hunted unsuccessfully for beaver "sign," and it was evident the spring hunt had almost exterminated the animal in this vicinity. Following Deer Creek to the ridge of the Black Hills, they crossed the mountain on to the waters of the Medicine Bow, and here they discovered a few lodges, and La Bonté set his first trap. He and old Luke finding "cuttings" near the camp, followed the "sign" along the bank until the practised eye of the latter discovered a "slide," where the beaver had ascended the bank to chop the trunk of a cotton wood, and convey the bark to its lodge. Taking a trap from the "sack," the old hunter, after setting the trigger, placed it carefully under the water, where the "slide" entered the stream, securing the chain to the stem of a sapling on the bank; while a stick, also attached to the trap by a thong, floated down the stream, to mark the position of the trap, should the animal carry it away. A little farther on, and near another "run," three traps were set; and over these Luke placed a little stick, which he first dipped into a mysterious-looking phial containing his "medicine."

The next morning they visited the traps, and had the satisfaction of finding three fine beaver secured in the first three they visited, and the fourth, which had been carried away, they discovered by the float-stick, a little distance down the stream, with a large drowned beaver between its teeth.

The animals being carefully skinned, they returned to camp with the choicest portions of the meat, and the tails, on which they most luxuriously supped; and La Bonté was fain to confess that all his ideas of the superexcellence of buffalo were thrown in the shade by the delicious beaver tail, the rich meat of which he was compelled to allow was "great eating," unsurpassed by "tender loin" or "boudin" or other meat of whatever kind he had eaten of before.

Trapping with tolerable success in this vicinity, the hunters crossed over, as soon as the premonitory storms of approaching winter warned them to leave the mountains, to the waters of Green River, one of the affluents of the Colorado, intending to winter at a rendezvous to be held in "Brown's Hole"—an enclosed valley so called—which, abounding in game, and sheltered on every side by lofty mountains, is a favourite wintering-ground of the mountaineers. Here they found several trapping bands already arrived; and a trader from the Uintah country, prepared to ease them of their hardly-earned peltries.

Singly, and in bands numbering from two to ten, the trappers dropped into the rendezvous; some with many pack-loads of beaver, others with greater or less quantity, and more than one on foot, having lost his animals and peltry by Indian thieving. Here were soon congregated many mountaineers, whose names are famous in the history of the Far West. . . . Here, too, arrived the "Bourgeois" traders of the "North West"[4] Company, with their superior equipments, ready to meet their trappers, and purchase the beaver at an equitable value; and soon the trade opened, and the encampment assumed a busy appearance.

A curious assemblage did the rendezvous present, and representatives of many a land met there. A son of *La belle France* here lit his pipe from one proffered by a native of New Mexico. An Englishman and a Sandwich Islander cut a quid from the same plug of tobacco. A Swede and an "old Virginian" puffed together. A Shawanee blew a peaceful cloud with a scion of the "Six Nations." One from the Land of Cakes [*sic*]—a canny chief—sought to "get round" (in trade) a right "smart" Yankee, but couldn't "shine."

The beaver went briskly, six dollars being the price paid per lb. in goods —for money is seldom given in the mountain market, where "beaver" is cash, for which the articles supplied by the traders are bartered. In a very short time peltries of every description had changed hands, either by trade, or by gambling with cards and betting. With the mountain men bets decide every question that is raised, even the most trivial; and if the Editor of *Bell's Life* were to pay one of these rendezvous a winter visit, he would find the broad sheet of his paper hardly capacious enough to answer all the questions which would be referred to his decision.

Before the winter was over, La Bonté had lost all traces of civilised humanity, and might justly claim to be considered as "hard a case" as any of the mountaineers then present. . . . Right glad when spring appeared, he started from Brown's Hole, with four companions, to hunt the Uintah or Snake country, and the affluents of the larger streams which rise in that region and fall into the Gulf of California. . . .

The Indian women who follow the fortunes of the white hunters are remarkable for their affection and fidelity to their husbands, the which virtues, it must be remarked, are all on their own side; for, with very few exceptions, the mountaineers seldom scruple to abandon their Indian wives, whenever the fancy takes them to change their harems; and on such occasions the squaws, thus cast aside, wild with jealousy and despair, have been not infrequently known to take signal vengeance both on their faithless husbands and on the successful beauties who have supplanted them in their

[4] The Hudson's Bay Company is so called by the American trappers.

affections. There are some honourable exceptions, however, to such cruelty, and many of the mountaineers stick to their red-skinned wives for better or for worse, often suffering them to gain the upper hand in the domestic economy of the lodges, and being ruled by their better halves in all things pertaining to family affairs; and it may be remarked, that when once the lady dons the unmentionables, she becomes the veriest termagant that ever henpecked an unfortunate husband.

Your refined trappers, however, who, after many years of bachelor life, incline to take to themselves a better half, often undertake an expedition into the settlements of New Mexico, where not unfrequently they adopt a very "Young Lochinvar" system in procuring the required rib; and have been known to carry off, *vi et armis*, from the midst of a fandango in Fernandez, or El Rancho of Taos, some dark-skinned beauty—with or without her own consent is a matter of unconcern—and bear the ravished fair one across the mountains, where she soon becomes inured to the free and roving life fate has assigned her.

American women are valued at a low figure in the mountains. They are too fine and "fofarraw." Neither can they make moccasins, or dress skins; nor are they so schooled to perfect obedience to their lords and masters as to stand a "lodge-poleing," which the western lords of the creation not unfrequently deem it their bounden duty to inflict upon their squaws for some dereliction of domestic duty....

"Meat's meat," is a common saying in the mountains, and from the buffalo down to the rattlesnake, including every quadruped that runs, every fowl that flies, and every reptile that creeps, nothing comes amiss to the mountaineer. Throwing aside all the qualms and conscientious scruples of a fastidious stomach, it must be confessed that *dog-meat* takes a high rank in the wonderful variety of cuisine afforded to the gourmand and the gourmet by the prolific "mountains." Now, when the bill of fare offers such tempting viands as buffalo beef, venison, mountain mutton, turkey, grouse, wildfowl, hares, rabbits, beaver and their tails, &c. &c., the station assigned to "dog" as No. 2 in the list can be well appreciated—No. 1, in delicacy of flavour, richness of meat, and other good qualities, being the flesh of *panthers*, which surpass every other, and all put together.

"Painter meat can't 'shine' with this," says a hunter, to express the delicious flavour of an extraordinary cut of "tender loin," or delicate fleece.

La Bonté started with his squaw for the North Fork early in November, and arrived at the Laramie at the moment that the big village of the Sioux came up for their winter trade. Two other villages were encamped lower down the Platte, including the Brulés and the Yanka-taus, who were now on more friendly terms with the whites. The first band numbered several hundred lodges, and presented quite an imposing appearance, the village being laid out in parallel lines, the lodge of each chief being marked with his particular totem. The traders had a particular portion of the village allotted to them, and a line was marked out which was strictly kept by the soldiers appointed for the protection of the whites. As there were many rival traders, and numerous *coureurs des bois,* or peddling ones, the market promised to be brisk, the more so as a large quantity of ardent spirits was in their possession, which would be dealt with no unsparing hand to put down the opposition of so many competing traders.

In opening a trade a quantity of liquor is first given "on the prairie,"[5] as the Indians express it in words, or by signs in rubbing the palm of one hand quickly across the other, holding both flat. Having once tasted the pernicious liquid, there is no fear but they will quickly come to terms; and not unfrequently the spirit is drugged, to render the unfortunate Indians still more helpless. Sometimes, maddened and infuriated by drink, they commit the most horrid atrocities on each other, murdering and mutilating in a barbarous manner, and often attempting the lives of the traders themselves. On one occasion a band of Sioux, whilst under the influence of liquor, attacked and took possession of a trading fort of the American Fur Company, stripped it of every thing it contained and roasting the trader himself over his own fire.

The principle on which the nefarious trade is conducted is this, that the Indians, possessing a certain quantity of buffalo robes, have to be cheated out of them, and the sooner the better. Although it is explicitly prohibited by the laws of the United States to convey spirits across the Indian frontier, and its introduction amongst the Indian tribes subjects the offender to a heavy penalty; yet the infraction of this law is of daily occurrence perpetrated almost in the very presence of the government officers, who are stationed along the frontier for the purpose of enforcing the laws for the protection of the Indians.

The misery entailed upon these unhappy people by the illicit traffic must be seen to be fully appreciated. Before the effects of the poisonous "fire-water," they disappear from the earth like "snow before the sun." Although aware of the destruction it entails upon them, the poor wretches have not moral courage to shun the fatal allurement it holds out to them, of wild excitement and a temporary oblivion of their many sufferings and privations. With such palpable effects, it appears only likely that the illegal trade is connived at by those whose policy it has ever been, gradually but surely, to exterminate the Indians, and by any means to extinguish their title to the few lands they now own on the outskirts of civilisation. Certain it is that large quantities of liquor find their way annually into the Indian country, and as certain are the fatal results of the pernicious system, and that the American government takes no steps to prevent it. There are some tribes who have as yet withstood the great temptation, and have resolutely refused to permit liquor to be brought into their villages. The marked difference between the improved condition of these, and the moral and physical abasement of those which give way to the fatal passion for drinking, sufficiently proves the pernicious effects of the liquor trade....

---

[5] "On the prairie" is the Indian term for a free gift.

Horse-racing, gambling, and ball-play, served to pass away the time until the trade commenced, and many packs of dressed robes changed hands amongst themselves. When playing at the usual game of *"hand,"* the stakes, comprising all the vauables the players possess, are piled in two heaps close at hand, the winner at the conclusion of the game sweeping the goods towards him, and often returning a small portion "on the prairie," with which the loser may again commence operations with an-other player.

The game of "hand" is played by two persons. One, who commences, places a plum or cherry-stone in the hollow formed by joining the con-caved palms of the hands together, then shaking the stone for a few moments, the hands are suddenly separated, and the other player must guess which hand now contains the stone.

Large bets are often wagered on the result of this favourite game, which is also often played by the squaws, the men standing round encouraging them to bet, and laughing loudly at their grotesque excitement.

The village presented the usual scene of confusion as long as the trade lasted. Fighting, brawling, yelling, dancing, and all the concomitants of intoxication, continued to the last drop of the liquor-keg, when the re-action after such excitement was almost worse than the evil itself. During this time, all the work devolved upon the squaws, who, in tending the horses, and in packing wood and water from a long distance, had their time sufficiently occupied. As there was little or no grass in the vicinity, the animals were supported entirely on the bark of the cotton-wood; and to procure this, the women were daily engaged in felling huge trees, or climbing them fearlessly, chopping off the upper limbs—springing like squirrels from branch to branch, which, in their confined costume, ap-peared matter of considerable difficulty.

The most laughter-provoking scenes, however, were, when a number of squaws sallied out to the grove, with their long-nosed, wolfish-looking dogs harnessed to their *travées* or trabogans, on which loads of cotton-wood were piled. The dogs, knowing full well the duty required of them, refuse to approach the coaxing squaws, and, at the same time, are fearful of provoking their anger by running off. They, therefore, squat on their haunches, with tongues hanging out of their long mouths, the picture of indecision, removing a short distance as the irate squaw approaches. When once harnessed to the travée, however, which is simply a couple of lodge-poles lashed on either side of the dog, with a couple of crossbars near the ends to support the freight, they follow quietly enough, urged by bevies of children, who invariably accompany the women....

When the travées are laden, the squaws, bent double under loads suffi-cient to break a porter's back, and calling to the dogs, which are urged on by the buffalo-fed urchins in rear, lead the line of march. The curs, taking advantage of the helpless state of their mistresses, turn a deaf ear to their coaxings, lying down every few yards to rest, growling and fighting with each other, in which encounters every cur joins the *mêlée*, charging pell-mell into the yelping throng, upsetting the squalling children, and making confusion worse confounded. Then, armed with lodge-poles, the squaws, throwing down their loads, rush to the rescue, dealing stalwart blows on the pugnacious curs, and finally restoring something like order to the march.

"Tszoo-tszoo!" they cry, . . . and belabouring them without mercy, they start them into a gallop, which, once commenced, is generally continued till they reach their destination.

### TRAPPING COMPANIONS

From the point where we left him . . . we must jump with him over a space of nearly two years, during which time he had a most uninterrupted run of good luck; trapping with great success on the head streams of the Columbia and Yellow Stone—the most dangerous of trapping ground— and finding good market for his peltries at the "North-west" posts—beaver fetching as high a price as five and six dollars a "plew"—the "golden age" of trappers, now, alas, never to return, and existing only in the fond memory of the mountaineers. This glorious time, however, was too good to last. In mountain language, "such heap of fat meat was not going to 'shine' much longer."

La Bonté was at this time one of a band of eight trappers, whose hunting ground was about the head waters of the Yellow Stone, which we have before said is in the country of the Blackfeet. . . . the leader of the party was Bill Williams, that old "hard case" who had spent forty years and more in the mountains, until he had become as tough as the parflêche soles of his moccasins. . . .

Williams always rode ahead, his body bent over his saddle-horn, across which rested a long heavy rifle, his keen gray eyes peering from under the slouched brim of a flexible felt-hat, black and shining with grease. His buckskin hunting-shirt, bedaubed until it had the appearance of polished leather, hung in folds over his bony carcass; his nether extremities being clothed in pantaloons of the same material (with scattered fringes down the outside of the leg—which ornaments, however, had been pretty well thinned to supply "whangs" for mending moccasins or pack-saddles), which, shrunk with wet, clung tightly to his long, spare, sinewy legs. His feet were thrust into a pair of Mexican stirrups made of wood, and as big as coal-scuttles; and iron spurs of incredible proportions, with tinkling drops attached to the rowels, were fastened to his heel—a bead-worked strap, four inches broad, securing them over the instep. In the shoulder-belt which sustained his powder-horn and bullet-pouch, were fastened the various instruments essential to one pursuing his mode of life. An awl, with deer-horn handle, and the point defended by a case of cherry-wood carved by his own hand, hung at the back of the belt, side by side with a worm for cleaning the rifle; and under this was a squat and quaint-looking bullet-mould, the handles guarded by strips of buckskin to save his fingers from burning when running balls, having for its companion a little bottle made from the point of an antelope's horn, scraped transparent, which contained the "medicine" used in baiting the traps. The old coon's face was sharp and thin, a long nose and chin hob-nobbing each other; and his head was always bent forward giving him the appearance of being hump-backed. He *appeared* to look neither to the right nor left, but, in fact, his little twinkling eye was everywhere. . . .

VIII

Again we must take a jump with La Bonté over a space of several months; when we find him, in company of half a dozen trappers, amongst them his inseparable compañero Killbuck, camped on the Greenhorn creek, *en route* to the settlements of New Mexico. They have a few mules packed with beaver for the Taos market: but this expedition has been planned more for pleasure than profit—a journey to Taos valley being the only civilised relaxation coveted by the mountaineers. Not a few of the present band are bound thither with matrimonial intentions; the belles of Nuevo Mejico being to them the *ne plus ultra* of female perfection, uniting the most conspicuous personal charms (although coated with cosmetic *alegria*—an herb, with the juice of which women of Mexico hideously bedaub their faces), with all the hard-working industry of Indian squaws. The ladies, on their part, do not hesitate to leave the paternal abodes, and eternal tortilla-making, to share the perils and privations of the American mountaineers in the distant wilderness. Utterly despising their own countrymen, whom they are used to contrast with the dashing white hunters who swagger in all the pride of fringe and leather through their towns—they, as is but natural, gladly accept husbands from the latter class; preferring the stranger, who posessses the heart and strong right arm to defend them, to the miserable cowardly "pelados," who hold what little they have on sufferance of savage Indians, but one degree superior to themselves.

. . . . On the eleventh day from leaving the Huerfano, they struck the Taos valley settlement on Arroyo Hondo, and pushed on at once to the village of Fernandez—sometimes, but improperly, called Taos. As the dashing band clattered through the village, the dark eyes of the reboso-wrapped muchachas peered from the doors of the adobe houses, each mouth armed with cigarito, which was at intervals removed to allow utterance to the salutation to each hunter as he trotted past of *Adios Americanos*,—"Welcome to Fernandez!" and then they hurried off to prepare for the fandango, which invariably followed the advent of the mountaineers. The men, however, seemed scarcely so well pleased; but leaned against the walls, their serapes turned over the left shoulder, and concealing the lower part of the face, . . .

No sooner was it known that Los Americanos had arrived, than nearly all the householders of Fernandez presented themselves to offer the use of their "salas" for the fandango which invariably celebrated their arrival.

This was always a profitable event; for as the mountaineers were generally pretty well "flush" of cash when on their "spree," and as open-handed as an Indian could wish, the sale of whisky, with which they regaled all comers, produced a handsome return to the fortunate individual whose room was selected for the fandango. . . . [In the fandango,] at one end of a long room, are seated the musicians, their instruments being generally a species of guitar, called heaca, a *bandolin,* and an Indian drum, called *tombé*—one of each. Round the room groups of New Mexicans lounge, wrapped in the eternal serape, and smoking of course, scowling with jealous eyes at the more favoured mountaineers. These, divested of their hunting-coats of buckskins, appear in their bran-new shirts of gaudy calico, and close fitting buckskin pantaloons, with long fringes down the outside seam from the hip to the ancle; with moccasins, ornamented with bright beads and porcupine quills. Each, round his waist, wears his moun-tain-belt and scalp-knife, ominous of the company he is in, and some have pistols sticking in their belt.

The dances—save the mark!—are without form or figure, at least those in which the white hunters sport the "fantastic toe." Seizing his partner round the waist with the gripe of a grisly bear, each mountaineer whirls and twirls, jumps and stamps; introduces Indian steps used in the "scalp" or "buffalo" dances, whooping occasionally with unearthly cry, and then subsiding into the jerking step, raising each foot alternately from the ground, so much in vogue in Indian ballets. The Hunters have the floor all to themselves. The Mexicans have no chance in such physical force dancing; and if a dancing Peládo steps into the ring, a lead-like thump from a galloping mountaineer quickly sends him sprawling, with the considerate remark—"Quit, you darned Spaniard! you can't 'shine' in this crowd."

# LEWIS H. GARRARD

## From *Wah-To-Yah and the Taos Trail*

### THE START

HAVING MADE ALL necessary preparations, such as laying in a good store of caps, fine, glazed powder, etc.; and having seen the shot towers, French Town, public and private buildings; at the instance of Mr. St.

*Reprinted from* WAH-TO-YAH AND THE TAOS TRAIL, OR PRAIRIE TRAVEL AND SCALP DANCES, WITH A LOOK AT LOS RANCHEROS FROM MULEBACK AND THE ROCKY MOUNTAIN CAMPFIRE, *by* Lewis H. Garrard, H. W. Derby & Co., 1850.

Vrain, our worthy *chef du voyage,* I crammed my purchases, clothes, etc., in my trunk, put it in charge of the porter, and walked to the steamer Salude, bound for Kansas, on the Missouri River, with many kind wishes uttered in my behalf; and, after the third tolling of the bell, and in obedience to the signals of the pilot, we were stemming the uninviting, yellow Mississippi.

We had a pleasant trip to Kansas, but the turbid stream and mud bluff banks, destroy the pleasing effects generally attendant on northern rivers. Colonel Chick, the principal man at Kansas, treated me kindly during my stay, and with his clever sons, the horse ferry, skiffs, and duck shooting, afforded entertainment.

To my surprise, Mr. T. B. Drinker, formerly an editor of a paper in Cincinnati, advanced toward me, after looking at the name on my trunk, and introduced himself. We were together much of the time while waiting for Mr. St. Vrain and company to arrive from St. Louis, with whom we expected to traverse the prairies as far as Bent's Fort. . . .

On the first of September, Mr. St. Vrain's arrival infused some life into our proceedings, but nothing more worthy of note occurred, except riding and looking at horses, of which Drinker and I were in need; one of which, Frank De Lisle, "*le maitre de wagon*" sold me for fifty dollars, whom, from his fanciful color, brown and white spots, and white eyes, was designated, by the descriptive though not euphonious name of, "*Paint.*" He was a noted buffalo chaser, and I anticipated much excitement through his services.

In the afternoon, of the 12th of September, the train rolled out—the heavily laden, high before and behind, Pennsylvania wains careering from side to side in the ruts, the shouts of the drivers to the newly-yoked teams, and the *vaya, hu-a, caraho,* of Blas and his two fellow-Mexican herders, and the *caballada,*[1] imparted a freshness and added vigor to our movements; horsemen going to and fro for things forgotten and missing, Mr. St. Vrain and De Lisle, passing and re-passing from one end of the train to examine the strength and capabilities of the weaker wagons; and ourselves, with *new* companions, talking and chirruping to our horses, slowly bringing up the rear, gave an appearance of efficiency and progress. Amid the bustle the foremost teams and ourselves reached the "Delaware Spring" after dark, and the whips and shouts applied to the sluggish oxen, of the lagging teams, did not cease until far in the night. Our horses were turned out to graze, the blankets unstrapped from the saddles, and we laid down supperless.

As we are all collected, it would be well to state the size and intention of the company. It was commanded by St. Vrain, an old mountaineer of the firm of Bent, St. Vrain, & Co., Indian and Mexican traders. The firm is rich, and owner of several forts, of which Bent's, or Fort William, on the Arkansas river, is the principal. Mr. St. Vrain was a gentleman in the true sense of the term, his French descent imparting an exquisite, inde-

[1] Herd of horses and mules.

finable degree of politeness, and, combined with the frankness of an in-
genuous mountain man, made him an amiable fellow traveler. His kindness
and respect toward me, I shall always gratefully remember. Mr. Folger,
another of our company, was a gentleman, so wedded to a roving prairie
life, that he has accompanied Mr. St. Vrain, for several years, in pure love
of adventure. His mule, "David," was a comical, antiquated animal; the
study of the expression of his grizzled phiz, was truly laughable; and much
merriment was caused by the master's *sensible* and affectionate advice and
consolation to David.

Mr. Beauvais was a Frenchman, employed to trade with the Sioux
Indians; Frank De Lisle, a clever fellow, the wagon master, or director—
an officer of trust; Bransford was clerk to the company; and General Lee,
of St. Louis, Beaubien, of New Mexico, and Drinker and myself, of Cincinnati, constituted *our* mess. There were, besides, twenty-three teamsters,
and the same number of wagons; every man armed, equipped, and ready
(if forced upon us) for a fight with the "yellow skins." . . .

So soon as a faint streak of light appears in the east, the cry *"turn out,"*
is given by De Lisle; all rise, and, in half an hour, the oxen are yoked,
hitched, and started. For the purpose of bringing everything within a
small compass, the wagons are *coralled;* that is, arranged in the form of a
pen, when camp is made; and as no animals in that country are caught
without a lasso, they are much easier noosed if driven in the coral. There,
no dependence must be placed in any one but one's self; and the sooner
he rises, when the cry is given, the easier can he get his horse. . . .

We encamped on a slope, using "bois de vache" (dried buffalo excre-
ment), for want of better fuel. We, on horses, selected a camp before the
wagons came up; Mr. St. Vrain and I; Folger and Chadwick; and Drinker
and Bransford, each pair taking an *apishiamore* (saddle blanket), would
collect our blankets full of the fuel (for the "wood" lies in all directions),
bring up to the intended fire, and off again, until a pile several feet high
would be collected. It burns well and freely, catching the steel-sparks like
tinder; but, being light, is soon fanned into a hot coal, and turns immediately to ashes. Wind prevails to such an extent on the prairie that no ashes
are ever seen about a camp a day or two after the fire is made; nothing
but black spots on the ground mark the site. . . .

We never eat but twice a day, *very* often but once in twenty-four
hours, at which scarcity of food, of course, there was grumbling. Bransford, who disliked it very much, said, after having concealed his feelings
some length of time, "Darn this way of living, anyhow; a feller starves a
whole day like a mean 'coyote,' and when he *does* eat, he stuffs himself
like a snake that's swallowed a frog, and is no account for an hour after."
It was about the truth, for our ravenous appetites scarcely knew bounds.

More buffalo in sight the third day than heretofore—the plain literally

covered. We crossed "Big Cow Creek," but no cows were seen, and thinking best to secure meat, such as it was, while an opportunity presented,
our worthy leader approached a band of bulls and fired, bringing down
one. It is with difficulty that buffalo can be approached, it requiring a
skillful person who will not permit the keen-scented animal to get to his
leeward, or in sight; for they run when a person is in view as far as a
mile, and from the scent still further; so we waited, with suppressed
breathing, for the report of the rifle. There lay a fine, fat, young male—
ere long he was on his knees (for the hump prevents his being placed on
his back), and the hide off. The men ate the liver raw, with a slight dash
of *gall* by way of zest, which served *a la Indian*, was not very tempting
to cloyed appetites; but to hungry men, not at all squeamish, raw, warm
liver, with raw marrow, was quite palatable. Before the buffalo range was
half traversed, I liked the novel dish pretty well.

Returning to camp, the prairie was black with the herds; and, a good
chance presented itself, I struck spurs into *Paint,* directing him toward
fourteen or fifteen of the nearest, distant eight or nine hundred yards. We
(Paint and I) soon neared them, giving me a flying view of their unwieldy
proportions, and, when within fifteen feet of the nearest, I raised my rifle
half way to the face, and fired. Reloading, still in hot pursuit (tough work
to load on a full run), I followed, though without catching up. One feels
a delightfully wild sensation when in pursuit of a band of buffalo, on a
fleet horse, with a good rifle, and without a hat, the winds playing around
the flushed brow, when with hair streaming, the rider nears the frightened
herd, and, with a shout of exultation, discharges his rifle. I returned to
the party highly gratified with my first, though unsuccessful, chase; but
Mr. St. Vrain put a slight damper to my ardor, by simply remarking—

"The next time you 'run meat' don't let the horse go in a trot, and
yourself in a gallop" (I had, in my eagerness, leaned forward in the saddle,
and a stumble of the horse would have pitched me over his head); by
which well-timed and laconic advice, I afterward profited.

### THE VILLAGE

On the evening of the 8th of November, I started for the Indian village,
with John Smith. Yes! John Smith! the veritable John Smith! After leaving cities, towns, steam-boats, and the civilized world, and traversing the
almost boundless plains; here, at the base of the Rocky Mountains, among
buffalo, wild Indians, traders, and Spanish mules, have I found a John
Smith. And, probably, for fear the name might become extinct, he has
named his little half-breed boy, John, whom we called Jack, for brevity's
sake....

....Ours was a nice little camp. The sun, in setting, cast long shadows
through the trees on the gray grass so calm and solemn; the smoke curled
upward in a continuous blue line, losing itself high in the open space; and
the air was cool enough to be bracing, and to render the fire agreeable.

On an outspread robe, at one side of the fire, sat Jack and his mother; Smith sharing the seat with them; myself, cross-legged, looked around with silent satisfaction and admiration; and Piere, a short distance off, was gathering wood for the night.

The squaw lifted the coffeepot from the coals, and we unstrapped our tincups from the saddles; with dryed, pounded buffalo meat, and the *sine qua non* of the mountaineer—the pipe—we did well, talking and smoking until the fire grew dim, when we separated. Wrapping up in my blankets, and covering my nose from the frost, I watched the stars in the clear, blue vault above, and listened to the distant howl of the *coyote,* until I unconsciously fell asleep. . . .

At twelve o'clock the next day, we came to three Indian lodges, where we found William Bent's squaw and her mother, on their way to the Fort. We were invited to the back part of the lodge, where dried, pounded cherries, mixed with buffalo marrow, and a root, eaten raw, resembling, in taste and appearance, the *Jerusalem artichoke,* were set before us. Whiffing the long pipe, with the clever inmates, we remounted.

Toward evening, Smith pointed to some objects, inquiring of me what they were, but I could not guess aright. "That's the village," said he. Mountain men can distinguish objects, which to a novice in prairie ken, have no tangible form or size. By sundown we were at the lodges, whose conical shape and dusky yellow hue, looked oddly but welcome to our tired eyes and limbs.

It is Indian rule, that the first lodge a stranger enters, on visiting a village, is his home during his stay—whether invited or not, it is all the same—and, as we wished to be at the "Lean Chief's" we inquired for him. Without saying a word, or going in the lodge first, we unsaddled in front of it, putting our "possibles" in the back part, the most honored and pleasant place, for there is no passing by, or other annoyance.

The owner occupies the back of the lodge, which is given up for a guest; and the Lean Chief's squaw and daughters removed his robes, etc., to one side. The women and children crowded around us while unsaddling; the strange dress and appearance of the boys attracted my attention; which latter, from their infancy to the age of six and seven, go without a particle of clothing, *dans costume a l'Adam*—a string of beads around the neck. The girls are clothed from the earliest hour.

The white man is always welcome with the Cheyenne, as he generally has *mok-ta-bo mah-pe*—coffee. We went in the lodge; the grave-looking head, *Vip-po-nah,* or the Lean Chief, and his two solemn coadjutors, shook hands with us, with the salutation of, *Hook-ah-hay! num-whit!*—equivalent to *Welcome, how do you do;* and then they relapsed into silence. Water was handed us to drink, as they suppose a traveler must be thirsty after riding; then meat was set before us, as they think a tired man needs refreshment. When we had finished, the pipe was passed around, during which soothing pastime the news were asked.

There is much to admire in this praise-worthy forbearance; and, although the Indians are as curious as any people, yet, through their consideration, the cravings of hunger and thirst are first satisfied; then, under the communicative influence of the long pipe, the topics of the season are discussed.

A lodge, generally, is composed of seventeen or more slender poles of pine, three inches in diameter at the butts, finely tapering to the small ends, and eighteen to twenty-three or four feet in length. These poles are tied together a few inches from the small ends, with the butts resting on the ground, so that the frame resembles a cone, over which a covering of buffalo skin is neatly fitted, divested of hair and rendered pliant by means of the *dubber*—an adze-shaped piece of iron, fitted to an angular section of elk's horn—which chips off pieces of the hard skin, until it is reduced to the requisite thinness. Brains are then rubbed on it, making it still softer. The skins are then cut and sewed together with awl and sinew, so that they fit neatly the pole frame. By rolling up the lower edge of this covering, it makes a commodious, airy habitation in summer; and, by closing all the apertures, a warm shelter in winter. At the apex, an opening is left, through which the ends of the poles protrude, and by which the smoke finds its way out. The fire is built in the center; and, to prevent the smoke being driven back by the wind, there are two flaps or continuations of the upper skins, with poles attached on the outside. These flaps they shut, shift, or extend, as occasion requires. . . .

We sat in our places at the back part, and the Indians, according to rank, took seats to our left, on mother earth, or their own robes. To the right was our host; and, if a man entitled to notice by right of seniority or daring deeds of valor, entered, those inferior in honors gave place next the white man (us). Sometimes Indians of equal rank were in the lodge at the same time, and then a *sotto voce* dispute, as to the "upper seat," would be carried on with much gesticulatory motion. . . .

Early in the morning we sat round the fire, waiting for the host's meat to cook, to which we contributed the coffee—the most important and rare addition.

The Indians talked of moving to the "Big Timber," a few miles above, and soon the village was in commotion; the young men driving up their different bands of horses; the squaws catching them. Some took down the lodges, and tying the poles in two bundles, fastened them on either side of a mule or horse, like the shafts of a draw—the lower ends dragging the ground; and, behind the horse, a tray-shaped basket or hoop, latticed with hide-thongs, was tied on these poles, in which were put the children too young to ride alone, and other things not easily carried on a horse. Some of the mules were saddled, and on each side were slung square bags, of thick buffalo hide, divested of hair, in which stone hammers, dubbers, wooden bowls, horn spoons, etc., were thrown.

The skin, of which these convenient hampers are made, is called *par fleche*—a French term Anglicised, as are many other foreign words, in the mountains, by general usage. Its literal meaning is, "*arrow fender*," or "*warder*"; for, from it, the prairie Indians construct their almost impenetrable shields. Moccasin soles is the principal use, for which purpose it is admirably suited, it being pliant to the foot, while it serves as a protection from the cactus, growing so prolifically in this country. Without care, one in walking will stumble over these, and the long, slender thorns, penetrating with ease, cause an acute, stinging pain, worse even than nettles. Being without socks most of the time (and none to be had), often, while hunting, a hole would wear in the toe of my moccasin, and, unavoidably, the thorns would stick most painfully. My "big toe" looked like a lady's finger punctured in sewing.

The village was, ere long, in motion. Looking back, to the old site, we saw nothing but eighteen thin pillars of smoke, finding their way to the upper air, marking where had been the lodges; pieces of old, cast-off robes, and the usual *debris* of a deserted Indian camp; which, with a few snarling coyotes, and large gray wolves, were all the signs of life remaining of the noisy, bustling town.

We crossed a large bottom, where we had a fine opportunity of seeing the moving village to great advantage. First went four or five lodges; and, following after, our wagon, with fifteen or twenty Indians talking to *Po-ome*, or "signing" with me. Young men were scattered in every direction, galloping to and fro, chasing stray animals, or coursing over the prairie for amusement.

Each lodge had its own band of horses, which presented a strange appearance; eighteen or more bands close to each other, walking along but not mixing; each band following a favorite mare, or, perchance, a woebegone, scrawny mule, not worth the powder and ball to kill it. It is a strange and general fact, that *caballadas* are mostly led by a no-account mare or mule—the greatest devil in the drove. They follow their erratic leader everywhere, like sheep, whether jumping, running, or grazing.

The animals, with the lodge pole *travées*, jogged along, no care being taken of them, while the fat, little inmates laughed, or, with "wond'ring eyes," stared at us silently.

The young squaws take much more care of their dress and horse equipments; they dashed furiously past on wild steeds, astride of the high-pommeled saddles. A fancifully colored cover, worked with beads or porcupine quills, making a flashy, striking appearance, extended from wethers to rump of the horse, while the riders evinced an admirable daring, worthy of Amazons. Their dresses were made of buckskin, high at the neck, short sleeves, or rather none at all, fitting loosely, and reaching obliquely to the knee, giving a relieved, Diana look to the costume; the edges scalloped, worked with beads, and fringed. From the knee, downward, the limb was encased in tightly fitting leggin, terminating in a neat moccasin—both handsomely worked with beads. On the arms were bracelets of brass, which glittered and reflected in the radiant, morning sun, adding much to their attractions. In their pierced ears, shells from the Pacific shore, were pendant; and, to complete the picture of *savage* taste and profusion, their fine complexions were eclipsed by a coat of flaming vermillion.

Altogether it was a pleasing and desirable change, from the sight of the pinched waists and constrained motions of the women of the States, to see these daughters of the prairie dressed loosely—free to act, unconfined by the ligatures of fashion; but I do not wish to be understood that I prefer seeing our women dressed *a la Cheyenne*, as it is a costume forbidden by modesty; the ornaments gaudy and common, and altogether unfit for a civilised woman to wear; but here, where novelty constitutes the charm, 'twas indeed a relief to the eye.

Many of the largest dogs were packed with a small quantity of meat, or something not easily injured. They looked queerly, trotting industriously under their burdens; and, judging from a small stock of canine physiological information, not a little of the wolf was in their composition. These dogs are extremely muscular, and are compactly built.

We crossed the river on our way to the new camp; the alarm manifested by the *ki-kun*—the children—in the lodge-pole drays, as they dipped in the water, was amusing; the little fellows, holding their breaths, not daring to cry, looked imploringly at their inexorable mothers, and were encouraged by words of approbation from their stern fathers. Regaining the grassy bottom, we once more went in a fast walk.

The different colored horses, the young Indian beaux, the bold, bewildering belles, and the newness of the scene, was gratifying in the extreme, to my unaccustomed senses. After a ride of two hours, we stopped, and the chiefs, fastening their horses, collected in circles, to smoke the pipe and talk, letting their squaws unpack the animals, pitch the lodges, build fires, arrange the robes, and, when all was ready, these "lords of creation" dispersed to their several homes, to wait until their patient and enduring spouses prepared some food. I was provoked, nay, angry, to see the lazy, overgrown men, do nothing to help their wives; and, when the young women pulled off their bracelets and finery, to *chop wood*, the cup of my wrath was full to overflowing, and, in a fit of honest indignation, I pronounced them ungallant, and savage in the true sense of the word. A wife, here, is, indeed, a helpmate.

Once more ensconced in the back part of Vip-po-nah's lodge, we felt at home. A large wooden bowl of meat was set before us, to which with coffee, we did ample justice.

The horses belonging to an Indian community, are numerous; with us, there were nearly or quite two hundred, of different colors and sizes, scattered over the gentle hillsides, in picturesque groups.

### PECULIARITIES

The morning came, and we were somewhat occupied in trading, but robes were scarce, the buffalo hair not being in prime order.

We were invited to *Gray Eye's* lodge, to a feast, early in the day. Sitting down, after shaking hands, a wooden bowl of choice pieces of fat meat was set before us. We used our *own* knives and fingers. Gray Eyes has two wives, and twelve children, two of whom—fine looking boys of fifteen and thirteen summers, respectively—were in the lodge; their father's eye beamed on them fondly, when he spoke of their killing buffalo from horseback, with bow and arrow. . . .

It is Indian custom, that whatever is set before the guest, belongs to him; and, he is expected to take what he does not eat home with him; so we stuck our knives in some of Gray Eye's fat slices, when the pipe was finished.

Smith's son Jack took a crying fit one cold night, much to the annoyance of four or five chiefs, who had come to our lodge to talk and smoke. In vain did the mother shake and scold him with the severest Cheyenne words, until Smith, provoked beyond endurance, took the squalling youngster in hands; he "shu-ed," and shouted, and swore, but Jack had gone too far to be easily pacified. He then sent for a bucket of water from the river, and poured cupfull after cupfull, on Jack, who stamped, and screamed, and bit, in his puny rage. Notwithstanding the icy stream slowly descended until the bucket was emptied, another was sent for, and again and again the cup was replenished and emptied on the blubbering youth. At last, exhausted with exertion, and completely cooled down, he received the remaining water in silence, and with a few words of admonition, was delivered over to his mother, in whose arms he stifled his sobs, until his heart-breaking grief and cares were drowned in sleep. What a devilish mixture Indian and American blood is!

The Indians never chastise a boy, as they think his spirit would be broken, and *cowed* down, and, instead of a warrior, he would be a *squaw* —a harsh epithet, indicative of cowardice—and they resort to any method but infliction of blows, to subdue a refractory scion.

The visits of the Indians were divided between Mr. Bent's lodge, and our own; but we saw as many as we wished, for our coffee and sugar cost us a dollar a pound. To secure the good will and robes of the sensitive men, we had to offer our dear-bought Java at meal time—the period of the greatest congregation. Still, their company was acceptable, as their manners, conversation, and pipes, were agreeable.

So complete and comprehensive is their mode of communication by signs, that they can understand each other without a word being said, and with more facility than with the lips. . . .

I sat long—collecting and embodying the thoughts and actions of the past four months, summing up the whole, with a glance at my then present situation. My companions were rough men—used to the hardships of a mountaineer's life—whose manners are blunt, and whose speech is rude—men driven to the western wilds, with embittered feelings—with better natures shattered—with hopes blasted—to seek, in the dangers of the warpath, fierce excitement and banishment of care. The winter snow wreaths drift over them unheeded, and the nightwind, howling around their lonely camp, is heard with calm indifference. Yet these aliens from society, theses strangers to the refinements of civilized life, who will tear off a bloody scalp with even grim smiles of satisfaction, are fine fellows, full of fun, and often kind and obliging.

John Smith was a modified[2] specimen of this character. Ten years before, he left his employer, a tailor, and ran off from St. Louis, with a party of traders for the mountains; and so enamored was he with the desultory and exciting life, that he chose rather to sit cross-legged, smoking the long Indian pipe, than to cross his legs on his master's board. He first remained a winter with the Blackfeet; but, running too great a risk of "losing his hair" (scalp), at the hands of the impetuous, *coup*-anxious braves, he sojourned awhile with the more friendly Sioux; and, subsequently, wended his way, while pursuing the trail of a horse-stealing band of Arapahoes, to the headwaters of the Arkansas; and, in the quiet nooks and warm savannas of the Bayou Salade, took up his abode and a squaw, with the Cheyennes, with whom he has ever since remained. At times he lived as they did, with lodge, and horses, running buffalo, and depending on it, as did his new-found friends, entirely for subsistence; dressing robes for the trade; taking part in the council; looked up to as a chief, and exercising much authority. He became such an adept in the knowledge of the Cheyenne tongue, and such a favorite with the tribe, that his services as trader were now quite invaluable to his employers. Possessed of a retentive memory, he still spoke the dialects of the three nations just named; and, in addition, French like a native, Spanish very well, and his mother tongue. Though subject to privations of a severe nature, he thought it "better to reign in hell than serve in heaven" and nothing could persuade him to lead a different life.

The New Mexicans often came in small parties to his Indian village; their mules packed with dried pumpkin, corn, etc., to trade for robes and meat; and Smith, who knew his power, exacted tribute, which was always paid. One time, however, refusing, Smith harangued the village, and calling the young men together, they resolutely proceeded to the party of cowering Mexicans; and emptying every sack on the ground, called the women and children to help themselves, which summons was obeyed with alacrity. The poor *pelados* left for El valle de Taos, poorer, by far, than when they came: uttering thanks to Heaven for the retention of their scalps. This, and other aggravated cases, so intimidated the New Mexicans, and impressed them so deeply with a sense of Smith's supreme potency, that ever after, his permission to trade was humbly craved, by a special deputation of the parties, accompanied by peace offerings of corn, pumpkin, and *pinole....*

Smith was strange in some respects; his peculiar adaptation to surrounding circumstances, and perceptive faculties, enabled him to pick up a little knowledge of everything, and to show it off much to his own credit—an

---

[2] The meaning attached to *modified* is, that he is not one of the worst characters—rather peaceable than otherwise.

unaccountable composition of goodness and evil, cleverness and meanness, caution and recklessness! I used to look at him with astonishment, and wonder if he was not the devil incog. He and I often sang hymns, and a more sanctimonious, meek, at-peace-with-mankind look, could nowhere be found, than in his countenance; at other times, he *sacre-ed* in French, *cara-ho-ed* in Spanish-Mexican, interpolated with *thunder strike you* in Cheyenne, or, at others, he genuinely and emphatically damned in American.

The Cheyennes have quite a variety of dishes, some hard to stomach—others quite palatable. Among them, a favorite is of wild cherries, gathered in the mountains, in the summer, and pounded (stone and all) to a jelly, which, when dried, is put away for the winter, when the buffalo marrow is good—the time for a reunion of the small bands, to trade, feast, smoke, and deliberate. These cherries, incorporated by much manipulation, at the hands of the not particularly clean matrons, with marrow and pounded meat, and patted in balls, form a principal portion of the feasts.

A buffalo skin is quite thick, which, to make pliable, is stretched to its utmost, on the ground (the hair side down) as soon as it is brought in from the hunt, by means of wooden pegs. When it dries, the squaws take the adze-shaped instrument, fitted to the angle of an elk's horn, which has before been described, and, with repeated blows, chip off small shavings of the raw hide, until it is the requisite thinness. The shavings are carefully preserved, and, when a very nice feast is wished, these "chips" are put in a wooden bowl, and boiling water poured over them, which cooks and reduces the whole to a pulpy mass immediately. This dish tastes similar to boiled Irish potatoes—to which, with the addition of cherries, a fancy flavor is added.

The fungus growing on the sides of decaying logs is gathered by the squaws, and boiled with meat, for several hours; on tasting the poisonous stuff, as I previously supposed it to be, my thoughts instantaneously traveled to Galveston bay and its fine oysters. It was first rate, but the appetite soon cloys.

A root growing in the bottoms, is much eaten, raw or cooked, partaking both of the flavor of the potato and Jerusalem artichoke.

Before most of the lodges, are three sticks, about seven feet in length, and an inch in diameter, fastened at the top, and the lower ends brought out, so that it stands alone. On this is hung the shield, and a small square bag of "par flêche," containing pipes, with an accompanying pendant role of stems, carefully wrapped in blue or red cloth, and decorated with beads and porcupine quills. This collection is held in great veneration, for the pipe is their only religion. Through its agency, they invoke the Great Spirit; through it they render homage to the winds, to the earth, and to the sky.

It seems strange that these people remain the same untutored, blood-thirsty savages as ever; and so untameable are their natures, that contact

with missionaries and white men, make them only the greater demons—
to remain here, as wild, almost, as their favorite buffalo, with no settled
purpose; for no apparent good; with no cares but those of providing for
themselves and families in the savage way—their fine forms, their intelligent (in spite of their mental darkness) countenances, and noble eyes, used
for no intellectual purpose, or, in any way for the advancement of religion
or science. And, it appears that all christian efforts, with extremely few
exceptions, instead of humanizing, and rendering their homes peaceful,
and themselves industrious, are so much waste of valuable lives and time.

### THE FORT

William Bent, one evening, wished some one to go to the Fort. I proposed to oblige him; and in the morning, saddling Paint, I was off.…

The country in the Fort vicinity, assumed a bleak appearance; the short
grass scantily concealed the cold ground, and the white chalk bluffs, the
leafless trees, and the chill air made me feel lonely. The fort mud walls
were abominably cheerless. Near were some men digging a grave.

My own unenviable thoughts occupied me through the solitary day;
and, only when Paint was turned in the coral, behind the Fort, to chew
dry hay, and myself with numbed fingers, gradually thawing in the long,
low diningroom, drinking hot coffee, eating bread, buffler, and "State
doins," and listening to Charlotte, the glib-tongued, sable Fort cook, re-
tailing her stock of news and surmises, did I feel entirely free to throw off
care. Shortly following, did I sit by the bright woodfire, in the clerk's
office, in a *dolce far niente* state, puffing a Mexican shuck cigarrillo,
wondering whence originated the soothing luxury, until the combined
effects of dinner, tobacco, and great change from cold to warmth, threw
me in a doze, from which I awaked at dusk.

Mr. Holt, the storekeeper, and I, selected the goods and other articles—
the object of my mission—in time for supper.

Captain Enos, Assistant Quartermaster, and his clerk, Dyer, Doctor
Hempstead, Mr. Holt, the carpenter, blacksmith, and a few Fort and
Government employees, constituted the quantity and quality of the male
inmates. Rosalie, a half-breed French and Indian squaw (the wife of Ed.
the carpenter), and Charlotte, the culinary divinity, were, as a Missouri
teamster remarked, "the only female women here." They nightly were
led to the floor "to trip the light fantastic toe," swung rudely and gently
in the mazes of the contra dance—but such a medley of steps is seldom
seen out of the mountains—the halting, irregular march of the war dance;
the slipping gallopade, the boisterous pitching of the Missouri backwoodsman, and the more nice gyrations of the Frenchmen—for all, irrespective
of rank, age, and *color*, went pell-mell into the excitement, in a manner
that would have rendered a leveler of aristocracies and select companies
frantic with delight. It was a most complete democratic demonstration.
And then the airs assumed by the fair ones—more particularly Charlotte,
who took pattern from real life in the "States;" she acted her part to per-

fection. The grand center of attraction, the belle of the evening, she treated the suitors for the "pleasure of the next set," with becoming ease and suavity of manner. She knew her worth, and managed accordingly; and, when the favored gallant stood by her side, waiting for the rudely-scraped tune, from a screaking violin, satisfaction, joy, and triumph, over his rivals, were pictured on his radiant face.

Doctor Hempstead, however, did not join the festive throng; and, his well-stocked library afforded recreation and pastime during the dull intervals of the day.

In the following afternoon, Greenwood, Jean Batiste—a Canadian—and myself, left for the village, with a laden cart of goods. . . .

The village was in an uproar. The "opposition traders," a mile above, had conferred a present of liquor on several chiefs, who, in turn, disposed to their friends, and all were making "the night hideous," in honor of the "rosy god;" for they have songs adapted to their orgies, more noisy and fierce than which, none exist. No serious injury resulted from the revel. . . .

We began to trade briskly in robes—owing to the cold weather, plenty of buffalo, and liquor, which last seemed to open the Indians' hearts—causing us to drop the backgammon board often to serve the precise savages, who would look at and handle a blanket, or other commodity, an hour, before concluding a bargain. We would have to praise, and feel, and talk of the article in question, and seal the trade, by passing the long pipe, as a balm to their fastidious tastes. . . .

## THE DANCE

The Indian beaux are ridiculous personifications of vanity. With small looking-glasses, vermillion-streaked faces, and decorated robes, or blankets, they perambulate the village, with looks of supreme self complacency. I often laughed heartily at their unique costumes, and self-satisfied looks. One of the dandies painted my face in the most approved Cheyenne style, but, the squaws laughed so immoderately at the grotesque contrast of a white skin and red paint, I soon washed it off.

The trader is treated with much respect by the Indians, and is considered a chief—a great man. To retain this respect, he acts with as much dignity as the circumstances permit. Caring for none of the trader's assumed reservedness, I danced with the squaws, mixed in the gayeties, and, in every way, improved my time. It was more than probable, I never would wish to trade with them; and why deprive myself of amusement? The squaws were astonished to find a white person so careless of dignity, though they liked me the better for it. With emotions of pleasure, are recalled the happy hours passed with this nation—the bright faces of the girls—the pleasant, broad, good-humored countenance of the "Smiling Moon" (O-ne-o Missit's daughter), the dancing eye of "Morning Mist" (Vip-po-nah's daughter), and the low chuckle of the men, as they gained a triumph in the favorite game of "guess."

## EL RIO DE LAS ANIMAS

[Garrard is enroute to Nuevo Méjico, on the Santa Fe Trail]

The fellows were strung close along with their blankets and robes, for sleeping; our mules hobbled, jumped among the greasebushes, on the bluff above, for the sparse herbage, and by the expiring embers of the campfire sat Lajeunesse, without hat, which he never wore, or possessed, puffing the dear pipe thoughtfully. A queer genius was this same Lajeunesse. For years a voyageur, undergoing between the Platte and Arkansas even more than the usual hardships, he now was settled in the quiet vale of Taos, with a wife; but, like his brother Canadians, no better off in property than when a young man, he first came to the Far West.

True to the mountaineer's characteristic, he was kind-hearted; for, of seemingly unsociable dispositions, they are generous, even to a fault. The fewness of their numbers, seems to create an interchange of kindly feeling, and the more one learns the nature of the hardy frequenters of the Rocky Mountain hunting grounds, and beaver streams, the more will he be pleased. To judge by his frankness and reckless life, his sole aim appears to be freedom of person and speech in its fullest import. Considering his neighbor's "possibles" "on the prairie" with him—his own at their entire disposal; and, though coffee, sugar, tobacco, and other luxuries are high-priced, and often purchased with a whole *season's* trapping, the "black water" is offered with genuine free-heartedness, and the last plug of to-bacco subjected to the rapacious knife of the guest, as though it were plenty as the rocks around.

In consonance, with the divine provision, the mountaineer deems it not good that he should be alone, and, a visit to the Mexican settlements, or a trading tour to the Indian lodges, often results in his returning a quiet, contented Benedict, with, perhaps, the village belle, to grace his solitary campfire, to mend his moccasins, or, to spread the warm robes in the least smoky spot—the lonely pair as devoted in their love and as tranquil in their affection, in the midst of blood-thirsty enemies, howling wolves, and chilling snows, as in the saloons of a metropolis.

The easy manners of the harum-scarum reckless trappers in rendezvous, and the simple, unsuspecting hearts of these mountain nymphs, cause him to be ever jealous of the attentions bestowed on his wife; and, often serious difficulties arise, in the course of which, she receives a severe drubbing with the knot end of a lariat, or no very light lodgepoling, at the hands of her imperious sovereign. Sometimes, the affair ends in a more tragical way than a mere beating; not unfrequently, the gay gallant pays the penalty of interference with his life.

### THE FARM

This section of country I have often heard spoken of as uninteresting; but to me there were many attractions. Here, with mule and gun, and a few faithful friends, one experiences such a grand sensation of liberty and a total absence of fear; no one to say what he shall do; costumed as fancy, or comfort, dictates; his blanket his house, the prairie his home. Money he needs not, except to buy coffee, ammunition, and "Touse."[3] No conventional rules of society restrict him to any particular form of dress, manner, or speech—he can swear a blue streak, or pray; it is his own affair entirely. Here, too, one soon learns to say nothing, and do less, but for himself; and the greenhorn is often reminded, amid showers of maledictions, to confine his philanthropic deeds and conversations to his own dear self. I was quite amused by the kindly-intentioned remarks of an old mountaineer to me, shortly after my appearance in the country. "If you see a man's mule running off, don't stop it—let it go to the devil; it isn't yourn. If his possible sack falls off, don't tell him of it; he'll find it out. At camp, help cook—get wood an' water—make yourself active—get your pipe, an' smoke it—don't ask too many questions, an' you'll pass!"

[3] Probably short for "Taos Lightning"—a particularly virulent brand of liquor.

# FURTHER READING

Paul Russell Cutright   *Lewis and Clark: Pioneering Naturalists* (Urbana: University of Illinois Press, 1969).

Bernard DeVoto, ed.   *The Journals of Lewis and Clark* (Boston: Houghton Mifflin Co., 1953).

Josiah Gregg   *The Commerce of the Prairies* (Lincoln: University of Nebraska Press, 1967).

Noel M. Loomis   *Wells Fargo* (New York: Clarkson N. Potter, Inc., 1968).

Harold McCracken   *Roughnecks and Gentlemen* (Garden City, N.Y.: Doubleday and Co., 1968).

John G. Neihardt   *The River and I* (Lincoln: University of Nebraska Press, 1968).

Francis Parkman   *The Oregon Trail.* Edited by E. N. Fellskog. (Madison: University of Wisconsin Press, 1969).

John Wesley Powell   *The Exploration of the Colorado River and Its Canyons* (Flood & Vincent, 1895; New York: Dover Publications, Inc., 1961).

Joseph G. Rosa   *The Gunfighter: Man or Myth* (Norman: University of Oklahoma Press, 1969).

Marshall Sprague   *A Gallery of Dudes* (Boston: Little, Brown & Co., 1967).

Wallace Stegner   *Beyond the Hundredth Meridian* (Boston: Houghton Mifflin Co., 1954).

Karl E. Young   *Ordeal in Mexico: Tales of Danger and Hardship Collected from Mormon Colonists* (Salt Lake City: Deseret Book Company, 1968).


TWO ANTHOLOGIES THAT TREAT THE FRONTIER EXPERIENCE

C. Merton Babcock   *The American Frontier: A Social and Literary Record* (New York: Holt, Rinehart and Winston, Inc., 1965).

Philip Durham and Everett Jones   *The Frontier in American Literature* (New York: The Odyssey Press, 1969).

# EIGHT

## Myth and Legend

**N.** SCOTT MOMADAY is a Kiowa Indian who has written of the great Kiowa migration through the legends he has gleaned from his relatives and old-timers. He very effectively assimilates family traditions and his own reminiscences into the account. He has adapted much of the material in *The Way to Rainy Mountain* into his recent Pulitzer-Prize winning novel, *House Made of Dawn*.

*High Horse's Courting* is a humorous legend told to Neihardt by Black Elk, a Sioux Indian. *The Legend of the Pacing White Mustang* is a first-rate piece of western lore, and J. Frank Dobie is a master teller of western tales. His many books about the Southwest are masterpieces, and he was a legend himself long before his death in 1964. Larry McMurtry, also a Texan, has captured the myth of the cowboy as a kind of vanishing god on horseback as he observed the phenomenon in his own family.

# N. SCOTT MOMADAY

## From *The Way to Rainy Mountain*

THE JOURNEY BEGAN one day long ago on the edge of the northern Plains. It was carried on over a course of many generations and many hundreds of miles. In the end there were many things to remember, to dwell upon and talk about.

"You know, everything had to begin. . . ." For the Kiowas the beginning was a struggle for existence in the bleak northern mountains. It was there, they say, that they entered the world through a hollow log. The end, too, was a struggle, and it was lost. The young Plains culture of the Kiowas withered and died like grass that is burned in the prairie wind. There came a day like destiny; in every direction, as far as the eye could see, carrion lay out in the land. The buffalo was the animal representation of the sun, the essential and sacrificial victim of the Sun Dance. When the wild herds were destroyed, so too was the will of the Kiowa people; there was nothing to sustain them in spirit. But these are idle recollections, the mean and ordinary agonies of human history. The interim was a time of great adventure and nobility and fulfillment.

Tai-me came to the Kiowas in a vision born of suffering and despair. "Take me with you," Tai-me said, "and I will give you whatever you want." And it was so. The great adventure of the Kiowas was a going forth into the heart of the continent. They began a long migration from the headwaters of the Yellowstone River eastward to the Black Hills and south to the Wichita Mountains. Along the way they acquired horses, the religion of the Plains, a love and possession of the open land. Their nomadic soul was set free. In alliance with the Comanches they held dominion in the southern Plains for a hundred years. In the course of that long migration they had come of age as a people. They had conceived a good idea of themselves; they had dared to imagine and determine who they were.

In one sense, then, the way to Rainy Mountain is preeminently the history of an idea, man's idea of himself, and it has old and essential being in language. The verbal tradition by which it has been preserved has suffered a deterioration in time. What remains is fragmentary: mythology, legend, lore, and hearsay—and of course the idea itself, as crucial and complete as it ever was. That is the miracle.

The journey herein recalled continues to be made anew each time the miracle comes to mind, for that is peculiarly the right and responsibility of the imagination. It is a whole journey, intricate with motion and meaning; and it is made with the whole memory, that experience of the mind which is legendary as well as historical, personal as well as cultural. And the journey is an evocation of three things in particular: a landscape that is incomparable, a time that is gone forever, and the human spirit, which endures. The imaginative experience and the historical express equally the traditions of man's reality. Finally, then, the journey recalled is among other things the revelation of one way in which these traditions are conceived, developed, and interfused in the human mind. There are on the way to Rainy Mountain many landmarks, many journeys in the one. From the beginning the migration of the Kiowas was an expression of the human spirit, and that expression is most truly made in terms of wonder and delight: "There were many people, and oh, it was beautiful. That was the beginning of the Sun Dance. It was all for Tai-me, you know, and it was a long time ago."

## IV

They lived at first in the mountains. They did not yet know of Tai-me, but this is what they knew: There was a man and his wife. They had a beautiful child, a little girl whom they would not allow to go out of their sight. But one day a friend of the family came and asked if she might take the child outside to play. The mother guessed that would be all right, but she told the friend to leave the child in its cradle and to place the cradle in a tree. While the child was in the tree, a redbird came among the branches. It was not like any bird that you have seen; it was very beautiful, and it did not fly away. It kept still upon a limb, close to the child. After a while the child got out of its cradle and began to climb after the redbird. And at the same time the tree began to grow taller, and the child was borne up into the sky. She was then a woman, and she found herself in a strange place. Instead of a redbird, there was a young man standing before her. The man spoke to her and said: "I have been watching you for a long time, and I knew that I would find a way to bring you here. I have brought you here to be my wife." The woman looked all around; she saw that he was the only living man there. She saw that he was the sun.

*There the land itself ascends into the sky. These mountains lie at the top of the continent, and they cast a long rain shadow on the sea of grasses to the east. They arise out of the last North American wilderness, and they have wilderness names: Wasatch, Bitterroot, Bighorn, Wind River.*

*I have walked in a mountain meadow bright with Indian paintbrush, lupine, and wild buckwheat, and I have seen high in the branches of a lodgepole pine the male pine grosbeak, round and rose-colored, its dark, striped wings nearly invisible in the soft, mottled light. And the uppermost branches of the tree seemed very slowly to ride across the blue sky.*

## XIII

If an arrow is well made, it will have tooth marks upon it. That is how you know. The Kiowas made fine arrows and straightened them in their teeth. Then they drew them to the bow to see if they were straight. Once there was a man and his wife. They were alone at night in their tipi. By the light of the fire the man was making arrows. After a while he caught sight of something. There was a small opening in the tipi where two hides were sewn together. Someone was there on the outside, looking in. The man went on with his work, but he said to his wife: "Someone is standing outside. Do not be afraid. Let us talk easily, as of ordinary things." He took up an arrow and straightened it in his teeth; then, as it was right for him to do, he drew it to the bow and took aim, first in this direction and then in that. And all the while he was talking, as if to his wife. But this is how he spoke :"I know that you are there on the outside, for I can feel your eyes upon me. If you are a Kiowa, you will understand what I am saying, and you will speak your name." But there was no answer, and the man went on in the same way, pointing the arrow all around. At last his aim fell upon the place where his enemy stood, and he let go of the string. The arrow went straight to the enemy's heart.

*The old men were the best arrowmakers, for they could bring time and patience to their craft. The young men—the fighters and hunters— were willing to pay a high price for arrows that were well made.*

*When my father was a boy, an old man used to come to Mammedaty's house and pay his respects. He was a lean old man in braids and was impressive in his age and bearing. His name was Cheney, and he was an arrowmaker. Every morning, my father tells me, Cheney would paint his wrinkled face, go out, and pray aloud to the rising sun. In my mind I can see that man as if he were there now. I like to watch him as he makes his prayer. I know where he stands and where his voice goes on the rolling grasses and where the sun comes up on the land. There, at dawn, you can feel the silence. It is cold and clear and deep like water. It takes hold of you and will not let you go.*

## XIV

The Kiowa language is hard to understand, but, you know, the storm spirit understands it. This is how it was: Long ago the Kiowas decided to make a horse; they decided to make it out of clay, and so they began to shape the clay with their hands. Well, the horse began to be. But it was a terrible, terrible thing. It began to writhe, slowly at first, then faster and faster until there was a great commotion everywhere. The wind grew up and carried everything away; great trees were uprooted, and even the buffalo were thrown up into the sky. The Kiowas were afraid of that awful thing, and they went running about, talking to it. And at last it was calm. Even now, when they see the storm clouds gathering, the Kiowas know what it is: that a strange wild animal roams on the sky. It has the head of a horse and the tail of a great fish. Lightning comes from its mouth, and the tail, whipping and thrashing on the air, makes the high, hot wind of the tornado. But they speak to it, saying "Pass over me." They are not afraid of *Man-ka-ih*, for it understands their language.

## XVIII

You know, the Kiowas are a summer people. Once upon a time a group of young men sat down in a circle and spoke of mighty things. This is what they said: "When the fall of the year comes around, where does the summer go? Where does it live?" They decided to follow the sun southward to its home, and so they set out on horseback. They rode for days and weeks and months, farther to the south than any Kiowa had ever gone before, and they saw many strange and wonderful things. At last they came to the place where they saw the strangest thing of all. Night was coming on, and they were very tired of riding; they made camp in a great thicket. All but one of them went right to sleep. He was a good hunter, and he could see well in the moonlight. He caught sight of something: men were all about in the trees, moving silently from limb to limb. They darted across the face of the full moon, *and he saw that they were small and had tails!* He could not believe his eyes, but the next morning he told the others of what he had seen. They only laughed at him and told him not to eat such a large supper again. But later, as they were breaking camp, a certain feeling came over them all at once: they felt that they were being watched. And when they looked up, the small men with tails began to race about in the limbs overhead. That is when the Kiowas turned around and came away; they had had quite enough of that place. They had found the sun's home after all, they reasoned, and they were hungry for the good buffalo meat of their homeland.

*It is unnecessary to dilate on the revolution made in the life of the Indian by the possession of the horse. Without it he was a half-starved skulker in the timber, creeping up on foot toward the unwary deer or building a brush corral with infinite labor to surround a herd of antelope, and seldom venturing more than a few days' journey from home. With the horse he was transformed into the daring buffalo hunter, able to procure in a single day enough food to supply his family for a year, leaving him free then to sweep the plains with his war parties along a range of a thousand miles.—Mooney*

*Some of my earliest memories are of the summers on Rainy Mountain Creek, when we lived in the arbor, on the north side of my grandmother's house. From there you could see downhill to the pecan grove, the dense, dark growth along the water, and beyond, the long sweep of the earth itself, curving out on the sky. The arbor was open on all sides to the light and the air and the sounds of the land. You could see far and wide even at night, by the light of the moon; there was nothing to stand in your way. And when the season turned and it was necessary to move back into the house, there was a sense of confinement and depression for a time. Now and then in winter, when I passed by the arbor on my way to draw water at the well, I looked inside and thought of the summer. The hard dirt floor was dark red in color—the color of pipestone.*

## XX

Once there was a man who owned a fine hunting horse. It was black and fast and afraid of nothing. When it was turned upon an enemy it charged in a straight line and struck at full speed; the man need have no hand upon the rein. But, you know, that man knew fear. Once during a charge he turned that animal from its course. That was a bad thing. The hunting horse died of shame.

## XXII

Mammedaty was the grandson of Guipahgo, and he got on well most of the time. But, you know, one time he lost his temper. This is how it was: There were several horses in a pasture, and Mammedaty wanted to get them out. A fence ran all the way around and there was just one gate. There was a lot of ground inside. He could not get those horses out. One of them led the others; every time they were driven up to the gate, that one wheeled and ran as fast as it could to the other side. Well, that went on for a long time, and Mammedaty burned up. He ran to the house and got his bow and arrows. The horses were running in single file, and he shot at the one that was causing all that trouble. He missed, though, and the arrow went deep into the neck of the second horse.

*In the winter of 1852–53, a Pawnee boy who had been held as a captive among the Kiowas succeeded in running away. He took with him an especially fine hunting horse, known far and wide as Guadal-tseyu, "Little Red." That was the most important event of the winter. The loss of that horse was a hard thing to bear.*

*Years ago there was a box of bones in the barn, and I used to go there to look at them. Later someone stole them, I believe. They were the bones of a horse which Mammedaty called by the name "Little Red." It was a small bay, nothing much to look at, I have heard, but it was the fastest runner in that whole corner of the world. White men and Indians alike came from far and near to match their best animals against it, but it never lost a race. I have often thought about that red horse. There have been times when I thought I understood how it was that a man might be moved to preserve the bones of a horse—and another to steal them away.*

## XXIV

East of my grandmother's house, south of the pecan grove, there is buried a woman in a beautiful dress. Mammedaty used to know where she is buried, but now no one knows. If you stand on the front porch of the house and look eastward towards Carnegie, you know that the woman is buried somewhere within the range of your vision. But her grave is unmarked. She was buried in a cabinet, and she wore a beautiful dress. How beautiful it was! It was one of those fine buckskin dresses, and it was decorated with elk's teeth and beadwork. That dress is still there, under the ground.

*Aho's high moccasins are made of softest, cream-colored skins. On each instep there is a bright disc of beadwork—an eight-pointed star, red and pale blue on a white field—and there are bands of beadwork at the soles and ankles. The flaps of the leggings are wide and richly ornamented with blue and red and green and white and lavender beads.*

*East of my grandmother's house the sun rises out of the plain. Once in his life a man ought to concentrate his mind upon the remembered earth, I believe. He ought to give himself up to a particular landscape in his experience, to look at it from as many angles as he can, to wonder about it, to dwell upon it. He ought to imagine that he touches it with his hands at every season and listens to the sounds that are made upon it. He ought to imagine the creatures there and all the faintest motions of the wind. He ought to recollect the glare of noon and all the colors of the dawn and dusk.*

# JOHN G. NEIHARDT

## *High Horse's Courting*

YOU KNOW, in the old days, it was not so very easy to get a girl when you wanted to be married. Sometimes it was hard work for a young man and he had to stand a great deal. Say I am a young man and I have seen a young girl who looks so beautiful to me that I feel all sick when

I think about her. I can not just go and tell her about it and then get married if she is willing. I have to be a very sneaky fellow to talk to her at all, and after I have managed to talk to her, that is only the beginning.

Probably for a long time I have been feeling sick about a certain girl because I love her so much, but she will not even look at me, and her parents keep a good watch over her. But I keep feeling worse and worse all the time; so maybe I sneak up to her tepee in the dark and wait until she comes out. Maybe I just wait there all night and don't get any sleep at all and she does not come out. Then I feel sicker than ever about her.

Maybe I hide in the brush by a spring where she sometimes goes to get water, and when she comes by, if nobody is looking, then I jump out and hold her and just make her listen to me. If she likes me too, I can tell that from the way she acts, for she is very bashful and maybe will not say a word or even look at me the first time. So I let her go, and then maybe I sneak around until I can see her father alone, and I tell him how many horses I can give him for his beautiful girl, and by now I am feeling so sick that maybe I would give him all the horses in the world if I had them.

Well, this young man I am telling about was called High Horse, and there was a girl in the village who looked so beautiful to him that he was just sick all over from thinking about her so much and he was getting sicker all the time. The girl was very shy, and her parents thought a great deal of her because they were not young any more and this was the only child they had. So they watched her all day long, and they fixed it so that she would be safe at night too when they were asleep. They thought so much of her that they had made a rawhide bed for her to sleep in, and after they knew that High Horse was sneaking around after her, they took rawhide thongs and tied the girl in bed at night so that nobody could steal her when they were asleep, for they were not sure but that their girl might really want to be stolen.

Well, after High Horse and been sneaking around a good while and hiding and waiting for the girl and getting sicker all the time, he finally caught her alone and made her talk to him. Then he found out that she liked him maybe a little. Of course this did not make him feel well. It made him sicker than ever, but now he felt as brave as a bison bull, and so he went right to her father and said he loved the girl so much that he would give two good horses for her—one of them young and the other one not so very old.

But the old man just waved his hand, meaning for High Horse to go away and quit talking foolishness like that.

High Horse was feeling sicker than ever about it; but there was another young fellow who said he would loan High Horse two ponies and when he got some more horses, why, he could just give them back for the ones he had borrowed.

Then High Horse went back to the old man and said he would give four horses for the girl—two of them young and the other two not hardly old at all. But the old man just waved his hand and would not say anything.

So High Horse sneaked around until he could talk to the girl again, and he asked her to run away with him. He told her he thought he would just fall over and die if she did not. But she said she would not do that; she wanted to be bought like a fine woman. You see she thought a great deal of herself too.

That made High Horse feel so very sick that he could not eat a bite, and he went around with his head hanging down as though he might just fall down and die any time.

Red Deer was another young fellow, and he and High Horse were great comrades, always doing things together. Red Deer saw how High Horse was acting, and he said: "Cousin, what is the matter? Are you sick in the belly? You look as though you were going to die."

Then High Horse told Red Deer how it was, and said he thought he could not stay alive much longer if he could not marry the girl pretty quick.

Red Deer thought awhile about it, and then he said: "Cousin, I have a plan, and if you are man enough to do as I tell you, then everything will be all right. She will not run away with you; her old man will not take four horses; and four horses are all you can get. You must steal her and run away with her. Then afterwhile you can come back and the old man cannot do anything because she will be your woman. Probably she wants you to steal her anyway."

So they planned what High Horse had to do, and he said he loved the girl so much that he was man enough to do anything Red Deer or anybody else could think up.

So this is what they did.

That night late they sneaked up to the girl's tepee and waited until it sounded inside as though the old man and the old woman and the girl were sound asleep. Then High Horse crawled under the tepee with a knife. He had to cut the rawhide thongs first, and then Red Deer, who was pulling up the stakes around that side of the tepee, was going to help drag the girl outside and gag her. After that, High Horse could put her across his pony in front of him and hurry out of there and be happy all the rest of his life.

When High Horse had crawled inside, he felt so nervous that he could hear his heart drumming, and it seemed so loud he felt sure it would 'waken the old folks. But it did not, and afterwhile he began cutting the thongs. Every time he cut one it made a pop and nearly scared him to death. But he was getting along all right and all the thongs were cut down as far as the girl's thighs, when he became so nervous that his knife slipped and stuck the girl. She gave a big, loud yell. Then the old folks jumped up and yelled too. By this time High Horse was outside, and he and Red Deer were running away like antelope. The old man and some other people chased the young men but they got away in the dark and nobody knew who it was.

Well, if you ever wanted a beautiful girl you will know how sick High Horse was now. It was very bad the way he felt, and it looked as though he would starve even if he did not drop over dead sometime.

Red Deer kept thinking about this, and after a few days he went to High Horse and said: "Cousin, take courage! I have another plan, and I am sure, if you are man enough, we can steal her this time." And High Horse said: "I am man enough to do anything anybody can think up, if I can only get that girl."

So this is what they did.

They went away from the village alone, and Red Deer made High Horse strip naked. Then he painted High Horse solid white all over, and after that he painted black stripes all over the white and put black rings around High Horse's eyes. High Horse looked terrible. He looked so terrible that when Red Deer was through painting and took a good look at what he had done, he said it scared even him a little.

"Now," Red Deer said, "If you get caught again, everybody will be so scared they will think you are a bad spirit and will be afraid to chase you."

So when the night was getting old and everybody was sound asleep, they sneaked back to the girl's tepee. High Horse crawled in with his knife, as before, and Red Deer waited outside, ready to drag the girl out and gag her when High Horse had all the thongs cut.

High Horse crept up by the girl's bed and began cutting at the thongs. But he kept thinking, "If they see me they will shoot me because I look so terrible." The girl was restless and kept squirming around in bed, and when a thong was cut, it popped. So High Horse worked very slowly and carefully.

But he must have made some noise, for suddenly the old woman awoke and said to her old man: "Old Man, wake up! There is somebody in this tepee!" But the old man was sleepy and didn't want to be bothered. He said: "Of course there is somebody in this tepee. Go to sleep and don't bother me." Then he snored some more.

But High Horse was so scared by now that he lay very still and as flat to the ground as he could. Now, you see, he had not been sleeping very well for a long time because he was so sick about the girl. And while he was lying there waiting for the old woman to snore, he just forgot everything, even how beautiful the girl was. Red Deer who was lying outside ready to do his part, wondered and wondered what had happened in there, but he did not dare call out to High Horse.

Afterwhile the day began to break and Red Deer had to leave with the two ponies he had staked there for his comrade and girl, or somebody would see him.

So he left.

Now when it was getting light in the tepee, the girl awoke and the first thing she saw was a terrible animal, all white with black stripes on it, lying asleep beside her bed. So she screamed, and then the old woman screamed and the old man yelled. High Horse jumped up, scared almost to death, and he nearly knocked the tepee down getting out of there.

People were coming running from all over the village with guns and bows and axes, and everybody was yelling.

By now High Horse was running so fast that he hardly touched the ground at all, and he looked so terrible that the people fled from him and let him run. Some braves wanted to shoot at him, but the others said he might be some sacred being and it would bring bad trouble to kill him.

High Horse made for the river that was near, and in among the brush he found a hollow tree and dived into it. Afterwhile some braves came there and he could hear them saying that it was some bad spirit that had come out of the water and gone back in again.

That morning the people were ordered to break camp and move away from there. So they did, while High Horse was hiding in his hollow tree.

Now Red Deer had been watching all this from his own tepee and trying to look as though he were as much surprised and scared as all the others. So when the camp moved, he sneaked back to where he had seen his comrade disappear. When he was down there in the brush, he called, and High Horse answered, because he knew his friend's voice. They washed off the paint from High Horse and sat down on the river bank to talk about their troubles.

High Horse said he never would go back to the village as long as he lived and he did not care what happened to him now. He said he was going to go on the war-path all by himself. Red Deer said: "No, cousin, you are not going on the war-path alone, because I am going with you."

So Red Deer got everything ready, and at night they started out on the war-path all alone. After several days they came to a Crow camp just about sundown, and when it was dark they sneaked up to where the Crow horses were grazing, killed the horse guard, who was not thinking about enemies because he thought all the Lakotas were far away, and drove off about a hundred horses.

They got a big start because all the Crow Horses stampeded and it was probably morning before the Crow warriors could catch any horses to ride. Red Deer and High Horse fled with their herd three days and nights before they reached the village of their people. Then they drove the whole herd right into the village and up in front of the girl's tepee. The old man was there, and High Horse called out to him and asked if he thought maybe that would be enough horses for his girl. The old man did not wave him away that time. It was not the horses that he wanted. What he wanted was a son who was a real man and good for something.

So High Horse got his girl after all, and I think he deserved her.

# J. FRANK DOBIE

## The Legend of the Pacing White Mustang

EVERY SECTION OF THE mustang world had its notability—the subject of campfire talk and the object of chases. Supreme above all local superiors was the Pacing White Mustang. A superb stallion of one region in the beginning, he became the composite of all superb stallions of his color wherever wild horses ran. The loom of human imagination wove him into the symbol of all wild and beautiful and fleet horses. Riders everywhere over a continent of free grass came to know of him and many to dream of capturing him. His fame spread beyond the Atlantic. He passed from the mortality of the bounded and aging into the immortality of the legended.

It is now nearly thirty years since I took the trail of this ubiquitous stallion. Looking back, I am astounded at the sign he left and at my own trailing. The record is a kind of epic.[1]

The great horse went under varying names—the White Steed of the Prairies, the Pacing White Stallion, the White Mustang, the Ghost Horse of the Plains. His fire, grace, beauty, speed, endurance, and intelligence were exceeded only by his passion for liberty. He paced from the mesa of Mexico to the Badlands of the Dakotas and even beyond, from the Brazos bottoms of eastern Texas to parks in the Rocky Mountains.

### LITERARY PROLOGUE

The earliest account of the Supreme Mustang, so far as I have found, is in Washington Irving's *A Tour on the Prairies*. On October 21, 1832, somewhere west of the junction of the Cimarron with the Arkansas, he made this journal entry:

---

[1] In *Tales of the Mustang*, a book of 89 pages published in an edition of 300 copies by The Book Club of Texas, Dallas, 1936, I put all I knew at the time about the White Steed of the Prairies. Before that I had put parts of the tradition into several magazine articles: "Tales of the Mustang," *Country Gentleman*, October, 1926; "The Pacing White Mustang," *American Mercury*, December, 1927, "When the Mustangs Ranged the Plains," *New York Herald Tribune Magazine*, August 9, 1931. A chapter on "Mustangs," in my book *On the Open Range*, Dallas, 1931, contains the Little Gretchen story of the White Mustang. By 1940 I had accumulated other stories and facts, and under the title of "The Deathless Pacing White Stallion" I published these additions in *Mustangs and Cow Horses*, edited by J. Frank Dobie, Mody C. Boatright and Harry H. Ransom, Texas Folklore Society, Austin, 1940—a book that went out of print a year or so after it was issued. *Western Horseman*, March and April issues, 1949, published a retelling of the main episodes of the tradition. A contraction of this appeared in Zane Grey's *Western Magazine*, Vol. 5 (Dec., 1951), 103–113.

In the decade since 1940 I have accumulated only minor additions to the legend. Now, adding them, I have brought together all my findings.

"We had been disappointed this day in our hopes of meeting with buffalo, but the sight of the wild horse gave a turn to camp conversation for the evening. Several anecdotes were told of a famous grey horse which has ranged the prairies of this neighborhood for six or seven years, setting at naught every attempt of the hunters to capture him. They say he can pace . . . faster than the fleetest horse can run."

In 1841, nine years after Irving's tour, the Republic of Texas sent out what is known as the Santa Fe Expedition to annex New Mexico. It became lost in Texas territory and, when its members reached Santa Fe, they were prisoners on a walk to Mexico City. Among them was a New Orleans journalist named George W. Kendall. The most important result of the expedition was his journals, published first in the New Orleans *Picayune*, 1842, and then two years later in book form: *Narrative of the Texan Santa Fe Expedition.*

One evening after a drove of mustangs had galloped up near the Texan camp, stood with raised heads, wheeled and dashed off, Kendall heard "the older hunters tell of a large white horse often seen in the vicinity of the Cross Timbers and near Red River. . . . As the camp stories ran, he has never been known to gallop or trot, but paces faster than any other horse sent out after him can run; and so game and untiring is the White Steed of the Prairies, for he is well known to trappers and hunters by that name, that he has tired down no less than three race-nags, sent expressly to catch him, with a Mexican rider well trained to the business of catching wild horses. . . .

"Some of the hunters go so far as to say that the White Steed has been known to pace his mile in less than two minutes, and that he can keep up this pace until he has tired down everything in pursuit. Large sums have been offered for his capture, and the attempt has been frequently made. But he still roams his native prairies in freedom, always alone. One old hunter declared that he was too proud to be seen with other horses, being an animal far superior in form and action to any of his brothers. This I put down as a rank embellishment, although it is a fact that the more beautiful and highly formed mustangs are frequently seen alone."

Writers about a country, whether travelers or residents, usually note what their predecessors have noted. Kendall's *Narrative* was the most popular work pertaining to Texas published in the 19th century. For years after its appearance both fictionists and nonfictionists writing on the Southwest felt obliged to include the White Steed, sometimes alluding to him as "Kendall's." Even before Kendall's journal got into book form, Captain Marryat of *Mr. Midshipman Easy* fame plagiarized the story of the White Steed and clapped it into his rambling *Narrative of the Travels and Adventures of Monsieur Violet in California, Sonora and Texas.* Meantime J. Barber had been inspired to a ballad:[2]

> Fleet barb of the prairie, in vain they prepare
> For thy neck, arched in beauty, the treacherous snare;

[2] *The United States Magazine and Democratic Review*, New York, XII (1843), 367–368.

Thou wilt toss thy proud head, and with nostrils stretched wide,
Defy them again, as thou still hast defied.

Not the team of the Sun, as in fable portrayed,
Through the firmament rushing in glory arrayed,
Could match, in wild majesty, beauty and speed,
That tireless, magnificent, snowy-white steed.

Josiah Gregg had gone west over the Santa Fe Trail in 1831. He looked at life steadily and reported it faithfully. His *Commerce of the Prairies* appeared in 1844, the year Kendall's *Narrative* was published. He had heard, he wrote, "marvelous tales" of a "medium-sized mustang stallion of perfect symmetry, milk-white, save a pair of black ears, a natural pacer. The trapper celebrates him in the northern Rocky Mountains; the hunter on the Arkansas; while others have him pacing on the borders of Texas."

Among the "veracious memoranda" of François des Montaignes "taken during an expedition of exploration in the year 1845," the "celebrated snow-white pacer of the Canadian" has taken on the power of making himself "visible only to special and favorite individuals."[3]

With the appearance of *Moby Dick*, in 1851, the White Mustang entered with thundering hoofbeats into the ranges of true literature. In that great chapter on "The Whiteness of the Whale," wherein Herman Melville reviews the white objects of the earth, ranging from the snowy Andes to the sacred elephants of India, he reaches his climax in a panegyric on the White Stallion.

"Most famous," he exclaims, "in our Western annals and Indian traditions is that of the White Steed of the Prairies; a magnificent milk-white charger, large-eyed, small-headed, bluff-chested, and with the dignity of a thousand monarchs in his lofty, over-scorning carriage. He was the elected Xerxes of vast herds of wild horses, whose pastures in those days were only fenced by the Rocky Mountains and the Alleghenies. At their flaming head he westward trooped it like the chosen star which each evening leads on the hosts of light. The flashing cascade of his mane, the curving comet of his tail, invested him with housings more resplendent than gold- and silver-beaters could have furnished him. A most imperial and archangelical apparition of that unfallen, western world, which to the eyes of the old trappers and hunters revived the glories of . . . primeval times. . . . Whether marching amid his aides and marshals in the van of countless cohorts that endlessly streamed it over the plain, like an Ohio; or whether with his subjects browsing all around at the horizon, the White Steed gallopingly reviewed them with warm nostrils reddening through his cool milkiness; in whatever aspect he presented himself, always to the bravest Indians he was the object of trembling reverence and awe."

Melville had never seen mustangs or talked with mustangers; he had the transporting power of imagination. Mayne Reid, on the contrary, had

[3] "The Plains," by François des Montaignes, in *The Western Journal and Civilian*, St. Louis, X (1853), 443.

firsthand experience with the mustang world. He was an Irish Protestant twenty years old when he landed at New Orleans in 1838. He went out on the plains with traders, served as soldier of fortune with the American army in the Mexican War, and then, according to report, spent some time in southwestern Texas. Before he became an exceedingly popular inventor of adventure stories, he was well fortified with frontier traditions and with knowledge of native plant and animal life. In 1861, twenty-nine years after Washington Irving heard the first "anecdotes" of record concerning the Pacing Stallion, Reid published *The War Trail, or the Hunt of the Wild Horse.\** The scene is laid more or less along the Rio Grande, and the story of the book-long chase is told in the first person.

"I had heard of the White Steed of the Prairies," the narrator begins his description. "What hunter or trapper, trader or traveler, throughout all the wild borders of prairie-land has not? Many a romantic story of him had I listened to around the blazing campfire—many a tale of German-like *diablerie.* . . . That there existed a white stallion of great speed and splendid proportions—that there were twenty, perhaps a hundred such—among the countless herds of wild horses roaming over the great plains, I did not for a moment doubt. I myself had seen and chased more than one magnificent animal, but the one known as The White Steed of the Prairies had a peculiar marking that distinguished him from all the rest. His ears were black—only his ears, and these were the color of ebony. The rest of his body, mane and tail, were white as fresh-fallen snow."

In almost the last novel, *The Boy Hunters, or Adventures in Search of a White Buffalo,* that Captain Mayne Reid wrote, he was still chasing the White Steed of the Prairies. Only as samples of other iterations do I name *The Backwoodsman, or Life on the Indian Frontier* (1864), by Sir C. F. Lascelles Wraxall, Bart., in which the White Steed leaps a canyon forty feet wide; *The White Mustang* (1889) by Lieut. H. R. Jayne (Edward S. Ellis); *Wild Horses* (1924) by Henry Herbert Knibbs, wherein, "his mane like new-spun silk lifting in the breeze," the untamable stallion, gray now, still paces. The Zane Grey assembly line and pulp magazines have published stories on the horse without end.[4]

An exception to mere iteration is "The Pacing Mustang," by Ernest Thompson Seton in *Wild Animals I Have Known* (1898), which is beautiful and true to range men as well as horses. "The Ghost Horse," by Chief Buffalo Child Long Lance, in *Long Lance* (1928) is true also to mustangs and is in the best tradition of the Blackfoot Indians.

---

* "On this wonderful Sunday, I found the opening of a serial story called *The War Trail,* by Captain Mayne Reid. I did not know what a war-trail might be; I looked at the beginning: and then suddenly found that I was in a world of beauty and romance, a world that I understood from of old, where the landscape led on and on, and men rode with comrades seeking, and villainy tried to thwart, and savagery tried to scalp, but how could either triumph over comrades and beauty? I was in an extraordinary world that would be mine forever."—John Masefield, *So Long to Learn,* The Macmillan Company, New York, 1952, p. 40. Quoted by permission.

[4] I used to look for these stories but quit looking long ago. The last one I noted was "Beyond the Outposts," by Peter Henry Moreland, in *Western Story Magazine,* Feb. 14, 1925.

## FRONTIER TALES

Before the Mexican War brought so many listeners and lookers to Texas, the White Pacer had changed his range from the plains to regions far east and south. When, as descendants remember, J. L. Rountree[5] settled in Milam County on the Brazos River in 1839, the stallion and his band were ranging on adjacent prairies, never entering bottom woods. It was not long before Rountree joined with two other men to run him down. The horse's circuit was well known. The mustangers placed three relays of horses along it and added three packs of hounds. On the third day an expert Mexican roper on the fastest horse in the country was brought into the chase, but the White Stallion could not be made to break his pace. He simply tired down everything after him. The hunters set snares for him under trees where he was accustomed to stand in the shade in the heat of the day, but no device succeeded with the wary animal. He disappeared finally without anyone's knowing whether he had been killed, had died a natural death, or had left the country.

He had merely left the country. One of the veracious chroniclers with Taylor's army on the border was Captain W. S. Henry. In his *Campaign Sketches of the War with Mexico,* he recorded that in October, 1845, among numerous mustangs brought in to mount the troops at Corpus Christi, was one "reported to be the celebrated 'White Horse of the Prairies.' He was a fine flea-bitten gray, fourteen hands high, well proportioned, and built a good deal after the pattern of a Conestoga No. 2. His head and neck were really beautiful, perfect Arabian; beautiful ears, large nostrils, great breadth of forehead, and a throttle as large as any I have ever seen in a blooded nag. His white mane was two feet long. He looked about twenty-five years old. He had been driven into a pen with some hundred others and lassoed. Thus, by an artifice, was entrapped the monarch of the mustangs: no more will he lead the countless herds in their wild scampers of freedom; no more will be seen his noble form, with head up and eye dilated, standing on the prairie-knoll, snuffing danger in the breeze, and dashing off at lightning-speed when it becomes apparent."

Captain Henry no doubt saw a mighty fine stallion, but it was not *the* White Steed. A few years later, as a story of the brush country came down, the famous stallion led his mares into a mustang pen built at a lake, and a hidden mustanger shut the gate while they were drinking. Some ranch people said, however, that this horse was not a genuine mustang but a descendant of a white mare lost by Kentucky or Tennessee troops passing through the country on their way to join General Taylor's army.[6]

[5] Told me by L. S. Rountree, Austin, Texas, in 1929. This story was published in "The Deathless Pacing White Mustang," in *Mustangs and Cow Horses.*

[6] From "Mustangs and Mustanging in Southwest Texas," by G. C. Robinson, in *Mustangs and Cow Horses,* 11–12. Clabe Robinson had the best memory in Live Oak County, where I was reared. I encouraged him to write this article and sent it to the *Dallas Morning* News, which published it Sept. 9, 1928, paying him $25. He died in utter poverty a few years later.

Rumors often circulated in one part of the country that the famous horse had been captured in another part far away. One drifting story had it that during the California gold rush a gambler offered a thousand dollars for the horse and that some frontiersman crossing the plains saw him, captured him, and brought him to San Francisco, where the gambler rode him down the street every day and hitched him as an advertisement in front of his gambling house.

About the time Austin was established as the capital of the Republic of Texas, in the early '40's, John W. Young started ranching on Onion Creek ten miles or so to the southeast. He was a Kentuckian and raised horses. Not long after he settled, an extraordinary stallion appeared among the mustangs habitually watering on Onion Creek. His form was perfect; his alertness and vitality were superb. He was pure white. His tail brushed the short mesquite grass that carpeted the earth, and his tossing mane swept to his knees. His only gait out of a walk was a pace, and it was soon found that he never, no matter how hard pressed, broke that pace. His band of mares normally numbered from fifty to sixty.

He led them southward across the Blanco, the San Marcos and the Guadalupe. It was known that he even at times ranged down as far as the Nueces. He kept clear of the timbers, never crossed the Colorado to the east, and did not range into the rocky cedar hills to the west; he seemed to like the rich mesquite grass of rolling country edging the blacklands better than that on the blacklands themselves. Many men, alone or in parties, tried to capture him.

Because he usually moved southward when chased, it was generally supposed that he had come up from that direction. Some speculators held that he had been imported to Mexico from Spain or Arabia, had been brought up as far as the Texas border by one of the owners of the great horse ranches occupying that country, and then, after being established on this ranch, had quit it and the semi-domesticated horse stock to run with the mustangs.

No matter how hard or how far chased, he always in time came back to the waters of Onion Creek. The favorite point of view from which to see him was Pilot Knob, about four miles from McKinney Falls. Any mustanging party that proposed a chase generally sent a scout to Pilot Knob to locate their quarry. The White Stallion's color, his alert movements and the large size of his manada, all made him and the bunch he led conspicuous. If started, he would lead out pacing, the mares following at a dead run. In a mile's distance he would gain at least a hundred and fifty yards on anything behind him. Then he would stop and look back, keeping out of shooting, as well as roping, distance.

The Indians had spotted him and they gave him a few chases, but the most persistent chasers were from San Antonio. A certain doctor there who was a horse fancier heard of the White Stallion, saw him in action, and offered five hundred dollars for him "delivered in sound condition." Five hundred dollars in those days amounted to a small fortune.

A Spaniard named Santa Ana Cruz determined to win the prize. He had a ranch on Onion Creek, kept several vaqueros, and was engaged by neighboring ranchers to put the quietus on rustlers. One day his vaqueros ran the White Stallion seventy-five miles south, and when they got back home two days later, found him grazing with his mares on the accustomed range.

To win the five hundred dollars, Santa Ana Cruz picked twelve riders, furnished each of them with two horses, and disposed them in the direction that the White Stallion was expected to run. A scout on Pilot Knob saw the manada go in to water and signaled. Soon after the mustangs had drunk, the nearest of the twelve men began the chase. The White Pacer took out in the direction of San Antonio. That first day, however, he did not keep his direction, and before the morning of the second day he had circled back into his favorite range. On this second day he was crowded harder, his mares lagged more, and, leaving them behind, he crossed the Guadalupe. For three days and three nights under a full June moon the Santa Ana Cruz men ceaselessly pursued him.

By the end of the third day, every animal in his band had dropped away. He himself had not once lagged, had not once broken his rack, except to change from right to left and from left to right. Two men continued to trail him until he had crossed the Frio River, still pacing toward the Rio Grande. Then they quit.

He never returned to his old range. In time the Onion Creek country learned why.

South of the Nueces, the rolling land rises into rough hills cut by deep arroyos. About three miles from a waterhole in one of these dry arroyos was a Mexican ranch called Chaparro Prieto. The low rock house, with portholes against Indian attacks, and the adjacent corrals were located in a draw matted with mesquite grass. Nearby was a hand-dug well that supplied water for the ranch people and their saddle horses.

The arroyo waterhole was so boxed in by bluffs that only one trail led down to it, from the north. One hot afternoon a vaquero from the Chaparro Prieto saw a lone white horse approaching the waterhole at a slow pace. At the instant of observation he was hidden by chaparral and was considerably to one side of the trail the horse was traveling. The working of his ears and the lift of his muzzle indicated that he smelled water. He was gaunt and jaded, but still firm on his feet and alert. The wind was in the vaquero's favor. He slipped a hand over his mount's nostrils to prevent a possible whinny. As the horse passed, he recognized him from descriptions he had often heard as the Pacing White Stallion of the Mustangs.

Here was a chance to rope what so many riders had tried and failed to capture. The thirsty stallion would drink deep and come back up the bank loggy with water. After he had gone down the trail out of sight, the vaquero placed himself in position for a sure throw when the animal should emerge. He was riding a fresh pony.

Within a few minutes the long-sought-for lover of freedom emerged, his ears working, his body refreshed. He saw the man and made a dash so swift that he eluded the rope's throw. Quickly recoiling his reata for another cast, the vaquero spurred in pursuit. The Steed of the Prairies had come two hundred miles from his range on Onion Creek, besides pacing in great circles before he had finally headed straight for the Rio Grande. His marvelous endurance was at last wearing out; the water that had refreshed him now loaded him down.

The second loop thrown by the fast-running vaquero went over his head. But he did not run full speed on the rope and jerk himself down. His response showed that he had been roped before. He wheeled just as the rope tightened and with wide-open mouth rushed at his captor. He did not seem to see the horse ridden by the vaquero. He was after the man. He nearly seized him, but the agile cow pony had wheeled also. Fortunately for the vaquero's life, some scattered mesquite trees grew just ahead of him. He managed to get one of these mesquite trees between himself and the roped stallion. The mesquite served as a snubbing post for tying up the stallion. However worn by his long war of defense, he was, at close quarters, still magnificent.

The vaquero left in a long lope to get help. He returned with two other vaqueros. With three ropes checking the White Mustang's attempts to fight, they led and drove him to a grassy spot on the prairie near the ranch corrals. There they threw him, tied the ropes so that he could not choke himself to death, fixed a clog on one of his forefeet, and staked him. When night came, he was standing where they left him, not having taken a mouthful of grass. The next day they carried a sawed-off barrel, used as a trough, within the horse's reach and filled it with water. He did not notice it. For ten days and ten nights he remained there, grass all about him, water within reach of his muzzle, without taking one bite or one swallow. Then he lay down and died.

This story, in full detail, was told to me by John R. Morgan when he was past eighty-six years old. In 1868 he came from Kentucky to ride with his uncle John W. Young and learned the history of the wonderful horse from men who had chased him. To him it was a part of the Onion Creek land.[7]

In 1927 I got into correspondence with a frontiersman named Curly Hatcher then living at Myrtle Point, Oregon.[8] This is his story:

"While I was catching wild horses on the Kansas and Colorado line in 1868, I saw the famous mustang often. He never ranged with other mustangs but always alone. When I first saw him he was a beautiful gray with

[7] It must have been about 1939 when Mr. Morgan, then living in Wichita Falls, Texas, gave me the history. I published it in *Mustangs and Cow Horses*.

[8] I had seen a brief article by Curly Hatcher in *Frontier Times*, Bandera, Texas, May 27, 35. The present narrative is combined from that and a letter answering some of my inquiries.

long mane and tail, and many a time I ran him in an attempt to rope him. Always I rode the fastest horses I could get, but never one that could make this mustang break his pace. After I quit running him I heard of him drifting gradually south, through No Man's Land and New Mexico and then below the Staked Plains. He was known to many men of the frontier. In 1874 I laid eyes on him again.

"I was a Texas Ranger and while carrying dispatches came upon him about twenty miles east of Menard on the San Saba River. He was almost white now, but I recognized him immediately as the horse I had chased along the Kansas-Colorado line six years before. I took after him, but as usual got nothing but his dust. I had to go on and deliver the dispatches. The next day when I came back over the same trail I found him dead. Sign showed that a Mexican lion had jumped out of a live oak tree onto his back and bit him in the neck. The ground was torn up from a terrible struggle. I examined the beautiful horse closely but could find no brand or mark of any kind on him. I clipped his mane and tail and as soon as I got back to camp wove a small rope out of the hair. This I kept for years as a souvenir of the greatest mustang in the world. Some of the old boys yet living have no doubt seen the horse."

One of the "old boys" was Andy Mather, of Liberty Hill, Texas, long since dead. "Yes," he said to me, "I knew Curly Hatcher well and I know he was lying about finding the Pacing White Mustang dead in Menard County. In the early days I heard of that horse a thousand times but he was always on the plains and to the north."

Andy Mather was a hasty man. Another frontiersman, C. M. Grady, who rangered with Curly Hatcher corroborated him, in part at least. According to his testimony,[9] in 1875, he and some other men on a buffalo hunt sighted a band of wild horses near the Santa Anna Mountains, in Coleman County. "As we rode out towards them, the most beautiful stallion I had ever seen, iron-gray and a pacer, stepped into view. The race was on. The stallion took the lead, his long mane hanging on both sides of his neck. He skimmed through the air like a flying bird. We soon gave up the chase. . . .

"Months later we came upon his band again, and again he paced away, like a bird flying, like a spirit horse. After that, one day alone, I came upon him asleep at the edge of East Santa Anna Mountain. I drew rein and looked at him for several seconds. The thought came to me that as I could never hope to catch him I would just shoot him as he slept. I raised my gun to my shoulder, but could not find the power within me to shoot such a beautiful creature. We all wanted him. Two men, John and Will Hampton of Burnet County, quit our ranger company to try to catch him, but never succeeded. . . . All the settlers, Staffords, St. Clairs, Hardins, Livingstons and Robertsons, tried to catch the gray horse but in vain.

[9] "Fifty-eight Years in Texas," by C. M. Grady, in *Frontier Times,* Bandera, Texas, June 1934, 379 ff.

"The last I heard of him he had moved on west. His range lay west of Table Mountain, and he was seen there several years later by Curly Hatcher and others, who were still trying to catch him. He moved on into the Golden West and never more was seen on his old range."

Maybe Curly Hatcher just dreamed that the great steed had been killed by a panther. "He moved on into the Golden West." White Horse Plains in Colorado, south of Cheyenne, is named for him, they say. White Horse Plain, up the Assinboine from Winnipeg, was named for him too, they · say.[10]

In 1924 a veteran trail driver named J. H. Hill, then living in Long Beach, California, issued two meaty, paper-bound booklets entitled *The End of the Cattle Trail* and *The Passing of the Indian and the Buffalo* in which he said something about mustanging. I wrote to ask if he had ever come across the White Steed of the Prairies.

"I have heard many times," he replied, "of the Pacing White Mustang. When I heard of him first, in the seventies, I was a clabber-lipped cowboy. I was living in Bonham, Texas, just south of Red River. Various riders of the country kept bringing in word about a band of mustangs led by the Pacing Stallion. At that time he was ranging between Fort Sill and the Washita River, in the Indian Territory.

"Dick Bragg of Bonham kept race ponies that he would run against anything in Texas or the Territory for stakes as high as any man wanted to put up. In the fall of '79, after the round-ups were over, an extensive party organized to capture the stallion. With them they took the fastest of Dick Bragg's race stock as well as everything else in the country that could run. Dick Bragg himself was along, hoping to add the champion race horse of the world to his string. A number of reservation Indians were in on the hunt.

"The boys found their Mustang all right. They laid all kinds of traps for him and tried all kinds of dodges to run him down or hem him in. But when he was crowded he would break off from his manada, they said, and pace away like the wind. According to their report, he was not pure white but of a light cream color with snow-white mane and tail. The Indians believed him to be supernatural and called him the Ghost Horse of the Prairies or the Winged Steed. When running at a distance he showed nothing but a fast-flying snow-white mane and snow-white tail that looked like wings skimming the ground. The boys who got nearest to him said he had a piece of rawhide rope around his neck. They thought he had been snared at some watering and that the experience had helped to make him what he was—the most alert and the wildest as well as the fleetest animal in western America.

"Mustang hunters kept after him, and later I heard that he had changed

[10] Kupper, Winifred T., *Sheep and a Sheepman of the Southwest*, M.A. thesis, University of Texas, 1938, 209. Coues, Elliot, editor, *The Manuscript Journals of Alexander Henry and David Thompson*, New York, 1897, 288.

his range from the Washita to the South Canadian. Such a change showed wonderful cunning, for the ordinary mustang when chased would keep circling within certain limits until he was finally closed in. Some of the mustangers swore they would get the White Ghost of the Prairies even if they had to shoot him. Death from a rifle may have been his fate. I last heard of him in 1881."

The latest date I have is 1889. In that year, as a lost mine hunter with a "constructive memory" told me, down in the Sierra Madre, the White Steed was ranging out from Phoenix, Arizona. Some man in bonanza offered two thousand dollars for him alive and unharmed. When pursued, he always paced out into the desert wastes, where he could go without water for days. Finally a hunter creased him, haltered him, led him to a strong corral, and collected the reward. But no power could make the horse submit. He walked restlessly about the corral, gnawed on the logs, nickered occasionally to the far-beckoning mountains, and refused food or water until he died—the usual ten days after capture.

According to another story, P. T. Barnum offered a reward of five thousand dollars for the horse. This was at a time, as a frontiersman named George McNeill used to tell, when the Pacing White Stallion ranged along the Bosque River in central Texas—a region noted for good horses. About every three months fifty or sixty men would organize to win the reward. One day while George McNeill was running him, his horse fell in a badger hole, breaking McNeill's leg. With help from another rider he remounted and was angling towards the pacing stallion when he saw a man shoot to crease him—and break his neck.

In 1926 while I was attending a convention of cattlemen in Fort Worth —to write an article—I fell in with a former sheepherder from New Mexico named Sandy Morris. He had a guitar, about thirty cowboy songs in his memory, and sufficient powers of endurance to sing all day and nearly all night. He kept the lobby of the convention hotel musical as long as a single soul remained awake to listen. While he was resting between songs, we had considerable talk and later I received letters from him. This is one story he told me.

"Along about 1875, I was riding down a road in the Llano River country of Texas when I spied a newspaper on the ground half covered by sand. Of course I got down and picked it up. I paid no attention as to where it had been printed, but I can never forget the story it told of a snow-white mustang stallion.

"It seems that the stallion had been ranging in the vicinity of a frontier fort, when one day a soldier saw him against the corral fence. He went outside afoot to investigate. The stallion made a dash at him, caught him by the back of the neck and killed him. After that, cowboys joined the post cavalry in a hunt to take the stallion alive. Everybody knew him. They had got on to his way of running, and they placed men in relays every five miles over a distance of eighty miles. Well, the White Mustang struck the expected course all right—and he went through those eighty miles without breaking his pace, and not a man got close enough to swing his rope. Then some soldier shot him dead. Some of the men who knew his history had a superstitious turn of mind. They said he would show up on his old range the next day. Whether he did or not, I can't say."

This "superstitious turn of mind" belonged to the illimitable spaces of sky and grass, to the drifts of buffaloes, to the howls of the buffalo wolves and the star-tingling cries of the little coyotes that in the night intensified the silences, and to the glow of coals and the evanescence of grayish smoke where a few minuscular human beings camped. But not all mystery is superstition.

Along in the '50's, as the story goes,[11] a fiddling, yarning character called Kentuck reached Santa Fe and threw in with an Arkansas gambler under the name of Jake. They heard so much talk about the White Steed of the Prairies and Jake had such a run of good luck that he decided to take his partner and hunt down the horse. He bought pack mules, everything needed for a pack trip, and four New Mexican horses of speed and endurance.

"I don't know exactly whur to hunt," Jake said, "but we'll ride on the prairies till we find the hoss or till they are burned crisp by the fires of Jedgment Day." He had a kind of fever in his mind.

They rode east on the Santa Fe Trail, and then away north of the Arkansas plains; they criss-crossed the endless carpet of short buffalo grass back southward until they were on the Staked Plains of the Canadian. They shot buffaloes and lived on hump. They dodged Indians and met no white man. Wherever wild horse sign led, they followed. They saw many bands and many stallions without bands, with now and then a white or gray among them, but not the White Stallion.

Summer passed into fall and northers brought the fluting sandhill cranes. Kentuck, who had not from the start had any heart in this wild-goose chase, yearned for bed and bed-warmer in Santa Fe. The longer Jake hunted and the more mustangs he saw, the hotter he grew on the quest.

"Go back if you want," he said with a fixed hardness to his partner. "Go and rot. I hev sworn to git what I come to git. If I don't git him I'll keep on a-hunting till the Day of Jedgment."

The White Pacer and the Day of Judgment seemed linked in his mind, and nothing else in it came to the surface. As winter opened, he took it into his head that the White Stallion would appear pacing out of the southwest. Whether riding or camping, he seldom looked now in another direction.

One cold, misty day, visibility cut to only a few yards, their camp backed against a rise of ground to the north, near a lake, the men huddled and pottered about a feeble fire of wet buffalo chips. They existed only to ride on. About sunset the skies cleared. For an hour not a word had been said. Now, while Kentuck rustled for chips dry on the bottom side,

[11] The story, somewhat bastardized folklore, is from a collection entitled "Frontier Yarns," in *Putnam's Magazine*, New York, VIII (1856), 503–517.

Jake squatted in his serape, straining his eyes towards the southwest as if he expected to catch the movement of something no bigger than a curlew's head in the rim of grass blades. The glow of the sun had melted and a full moon was coming up in the clear sky when he yelled, "Yonder," and ran towards his staked horse.

"I supposed it was Indians and grabbed my rifle," Kentuck later told. "Then my eyes picked up the white horse. He stood there to the southwest, maybe a hundred yards off, head lifted, facing us, as motionless as a statue. In the white moonlight his proportions were all that the tales had given him. He did not move until Jake moved towards him. As I made for my horse, I saw that Jake was riding without saddle, though he had bridled his horse and held his reata. We kept our rawhide lariats well greased so that they would not get limp from water and stiffen when dry.

"The White Pacer paced east, against the moon, and against a breeze springing up. He seemed to glide rather than work his legs, he went so smoothly. He did not seem to be trying to get away, only to hold his distance. He moved like a white shadow, and the harder we rode, the more shadowy he looked."

After the run had winded his horse, Kentuck called out, "Jake, I don't like this. There's no sense to it. I'm remembering things we've both heard. Let's stop. We can't no more catch up with him than with our own shadows."

Jake had lost his hat. His long black hair was streaming back. His set features were those of a madman. He screamed out, "Stop if yer want. I've told yer I'm a-going to foller till the Day of Jedgment."

Not another word passed between the two. Kentuck did not stop. "Riding on and on out there in the middle of nowhere, not even a coyote breaking the silence, it didn't seem like this world," he said. Then he made out a long black line across the ground ahead. "It'll soon be settled now," he thought, "and we'll know whether the White Stallion can cross empty space like a ghost." Pulling back his horse, he yelled to Jake, "Watch out for the canyon—the bluff."

The word "Jedgment" came to his ears and he saw Jake using his coiled reata for a quirt. Then he disappeared over the bluff. Kentuck was watching him so intently that he did not see what became of the Pacing White Stallion.

Kentuck walked from his heaving horse to examine the canyon brink. He could hear nothing below. Downward in the moonlight he saw only jags of ground amid the stubby growth called *palo duro* (hard wood). He called, but there was no response. He hobbled his horse and about daylight found a buffalo trail leading down the turreted bluffs. Soon after sunup he came upon what was left of Jake and his horse, a full hundred feet below the jumping-off place. He did the best he could for a grave.

In Santa Fe his story was no novelty. Some who heard it had known more than one man to come back from far away with his partner's horses and an explanation.

The "superstitious turns" of the legend are mostly Indian. The Kiowas were sure that neither fire nor lead could injure the great White Horse. A prairie fire might burn to death the mares and colts under his domination, but he would emerge from it unsinged; a bullet might pass through his body but would not injure it. At a reunion of Texas Rangers on the San Saba River in 1929, a veteran named Fred B. Hambledon, then living in Denver, told me a good deal about what he had learned from Utes and Comanches while he lived among them. Individuals in both tribes, he said, had traditions of the Phantom White Stallion. He had heard Uncle Dick Wootton, the Mountain Man who made Raton Pass noted, tell about the Stallion's leaping an immense chasm; Uncle Dick inclined to believe with Indians that he was a ghost horse. Many years ago, E. E. Dale, Professor of Western History at the University of Oklahoma, asked an old Comanche named Julián how his tribesmen came to own so many white-spotted ponies. "They all came from the White Stallion of the Plains," the old Comanche answered.

However he might entice after him the paramours of other stallions, the White Mustang was not of a malevolent disposition. Only in the tale that Sandy Morris found in a newspaper half buried in the sand does he so appear, and in an exaggerated narrative called *Wild Jim, the Texas Cowboy and Saddle King* that a certain "Captain" W. J. French printed at Antioch, Illinois, in 1890. Herein the stallion appears as a man-killer. His captor, who went by the modest title of "Champion Wild Horse Breaker of Texas," "laid out on the prairie a whole year" following the White Stallion and and his drove of "a thousand or more" mares. Finally by an extraordinary ruse he captured the leader and then trained him to allow no other man to approach him and to fight any stranger "like a panther." He killed at least "half a dozen men," most of them horse thieves trying to cut his picket rope. But in the narratives of the soil the Pacing White Mustang is consistently generous and noble.

A half century back, Dr. J. O. Dyer of Galveston was pursuing an unsleeping passion for the lore of early days. Some of it he wrote down. Along in the '70s he heard the following story, which in his last years—and that was a long time ago, too—he transmitted to me. It was, according to Doctor Dyer, told by a woman who as a girl came with German colonists to settle Texas, about 1848.

They were moving up the Guadalupe River in wagons. Gretchen's family, at the end of the train, had a gentle old gray mare that followed their wagon without rope or halter, stopping every once in a while to grab a mouthful of particularly lush grass. She was stupid and lazy and her ears flopped, but she was faithful. She carried two big sacks of corn meal so arranged that they made a kind of platform.

The wagon was running over with such things as German settlers carried—beds and bedding, pots and pans, mugs and plates, a heavy chest of drawers, a sauerkraut keg, and a great many children. Gretchen, eight or nine years old, was the liveliest of these. One day she asked her father to let her ride the old gray mare. He could see no harm in this; in fact, her absence might lessen the constant hubbub. So he lifted Gretchen up on the platform of corn meal sacks and tied her there with a rope in such a way that she would be comfortable but could not fall off. The old mare hardly batted an eye, and with Gretchen on her back continued as usual to walk and pick grass along behind the wagon.

That afternoon at a gully the tire of a wagon wheel fell away from the felloes, shrunken by dry weather, and several spokes were broken. When the halt was made for repairs, Gretchen was asleep, firmly tied on her pillion of corn meal. She did not know when the old gray mare grazed out of sight down a draw. Her father was busy with the wheel; her mother, like the old woman who lived in a shoe, had so many children that she did not know what to do; and so neither of them noticed. It was only after the wagon was repaired and the other children were counted into it and the train started on, that little Gretchen was missed. Then the old gray mare could not be found. None of the German men, so new to the frontier, could follow her tracks in the maze of mustang tracks they now discovered. They struck camp to search. Night came and no little Gretchen; the next day came and passed and no little Gretchen. Then on the morning of the third day the old mare brought her in, and this is the explanation the little girl gave.

After dozing she knew not how long, she awoke with a start. The lazy old mare had come to life and was lumbering along in a gallop after a neighing, pacing white horse with cream-colored mane and tail. She tried to stop the old mare, but she had neither bridle nor halter. She tried to jump off, but she was tied on and the knots of the rope were beyond her reach.

After the old mare had trotted and galloped until nearly sundown, the white horse all the time pacing ahead "like a rocking chair," they came to a large bunch of mares. They came out full of curiosity to greet their new sister, and they were very cordial in their greeting.

The wild mares seemed not to notice little Gretchen at all. They were so cordial in their nosings of the old gray mare that soon their muzzles were touching the meal sacks. Probably the sacking was salty. Some of the meal had sifted through. The mares tasted it. No matter if it was the first taste of corn they had ever had, they liked it.

They began to nip at the meal sacks so eagerly that they nipped Gretchen's bare legs. She screetched. She expected to be chewed up right away, even if the mares meant no harm. But at her cry the Pacing White Stallion was with one bound beside her. He was as considerate as he was intelligent. He drove the wild mares off. Then he chewed in two the ropes that bound Gretchen. Next he took her gently by the collar of her dress, very much as a cat takes one of her kittens, and set her down upon the ground.

It was about dark now and the coyotes were beginning to howl. Little Gretchen howled too, but there was no danger. After a while she made a kind of nest in some tall fragrant grass near a Spanish oak and, having cried a while, fell asleep.

When she awoke, the sun was high and not a horse was in sight. She was hungry. She went down to a waterhole that she saw close by and drank water for breakfast. She had heard that a person lost away out in the wilds had better stay in one place until he "found himself" or until someone found him. She had no hope of finding herself; she wished her papa would come. She remained near the waterhole.

Noon came and still no horse or person appeared within sight. Gretchen was hungrier than ever. It was late spring, and she gathered some of the red agrito berries (called also wild currants) growing near, but the thorny leaves pricked her fingers so severely that she quit before she had eaten enough to satisfy her hunger. Evening fell and she was still alone. She gathered some sheep sorrel down in the bottom of the draw and drank more water. Darknes came, the stars came out, the coyotes set up their lonely howling. Little Gretchen lay down in her nest again and again cried herself to sleep.

When she awoke the next morning, there standing over her, sound asleep, ears flopped down and lower lip hanging shapeless like a bag of curd, was the old gray mare. Gretchen was as glad as the redbird singing over her head. She jumped up and ran to the mare and tried to get on her. But the old mare was too tall. Then Gretchen grasped her by the mane and tried to lead her to a log that lay near at hand. If she could get the old mare beside it, she could use it as a stepping block. But the stupid old mare would not budge. After vainly pulling, coaxing, and jumping about for a long time, Gretchen began to wail.

She was leaning against the shoulder of the old mare sobbing, when she heard swift hoofbeats, rhythmic and racking. She looked up and saw the beautiful White Steed. The sunshine was on his whiteness. He came arching his neck and pacing with all the fire of a mustang emperor, but there was something about him that prevented Gretchen from being in the least frightened. On the contrary, she stretched her arms towards him and gave a childish "oh" of welcome. He paced right up to where she stood, gently grasped the collar of her dress and the scruff of her neck in his teeth and lifted her upon the mare. Then he must have told the old gray mare to go home. At least she went—went with Gretchen but no corn meal.

Home was the camp by the gully where the wagon had broken down. Gretchen's parents were so happy at having her restored that they did not mind the loss of the meal. After she had told her adventures, she showed the nipped places on her legs.

In after years she told the story many, many times. If her children and grandchildren seemed doubtful of the facts, she would in a pet pull down her cotton stockings and show the small, faint scars on her legs where the wild mares had nipped her. Then the children would have to believe.

### 3 SPANISH PACERS AND WHITE COLOR

The Spaniards introduced a strain of natural pacers into the Americas. Describing the horses of Sonora as well-built, small-boned, comely, proud, swift and enduring, a historian who lived among these horses for eleven years in the mid 18th century classified them in ranchero style as *caballos de camino* (travelers) and *caballos de campo* (what later came to be called cow horses). The *caballos de camino*, he said, paced as fast as any other horse could gallop and some paced up with running horses. They were incapable of running or trotting. Their gait was so smooth that "the rider could hold a glass full of water in his hand without spilling a drop."[12]

The strain was better preserved in South than in North America. In 1888 the minister from the United States to Colombia wrote: "The native horses are rarely over fifteen hands high, and but few are of that height. They all pace from their birth."[13] Tracing directly back to colonial times, the *caballo nacional* of Peru still has a *paso* peculiar unto itself. Many of these small national horses are of a light color—gray, white, palomino, with black skins.[14] According to the best evidence, the Narragansett pacers of New England, famous long before the Revolutionary War and now vanished, were descended from a stallion imported from Spain.

Charles W. Webber, who is reputed to have been a Texas Ranger in the '40s and who was among the early writers on the Texas scene, admitted that he had never seen the White Steed of the Prairies, though he had "often heard" of him from mustang hunters. "All the white mustangs I have ever seen," he said, "were natural pacers."[15] How many white mustangs Webber had seen, nobody could swear. Most Spanish horses walked slow, trotted hard and galloped soft; some few had a running walk; fewer paced. Pacing horses have never been favored by ranch people; they are too apt to stumble.

A white mustang was never a rarity like a white buffalo. As late as 1882 a band of thirteen white mustangs ran between the Palo Duro Canyon and the Canadian River in the Texas Panhandle—so alert that nobody ever saw them standing.[16]

---

[12] Pfefferkorn, Ignaz, *Sonora: A Description of the Province* (published in Germany 1794–1795), translated and annotated by Theodore E. Treutlein, University of New Mexico Press, Albuquerque, 1949, 95–96.

[13] Maury, Dabney H., *Recollections of a Virginian*, New York, 1894, 268.

[14] "The Peruvian Horse," *The Western Horseman*, VI (Nov.–Dec., 1941), 5 ff.

[15] Webber, Charles W., *Wild Scenes and Wild Hunters*, Philadelphia, 1852, 470.

[16] L. Gough, Amarillo, Texas, in a letter dated Feb. 10, 1930, to Boone McClure, in Archives of the Panhandle-Plains Historical Society, Canyon, Texas. Orally, Judge L. Gough gave me the same fact.

Indians liked white-spotted horses, which blend leopard-like with the earth, but not white horses. They are too easy to see, especially at night. One of the favorite nighttime ruses of the Pawnees against their enemies was to picket a white horse a little out from camp and then wait in ambush for thieves, who could be relied upon to spot that horse first of all.[17] As soon as it was dark a party of Mountain Men in the vicinity of hostile Blackfeet covered a white horse with blankets.[18] One day in 1932 while I was driving from Austin to San Antonio, I picked up an oldish man carrying a pack on his back. He told me that his father had been a ranger with Captain L. H. McNelly. This noted captain, he said, would not allow a ranger to ride a white horse or a horse with a white face. White would make a target for Indians and bandits. The idea was common all during turbulent times on the frontiers.

Belief was widespread, furthermore, that white horses lack endurance. In many minds they were associated with weak-eyed albinos, though the prejudice did not extend to grays. It included, especially among range men outside of California, palominos. Captain John G. Bourke observed that in General Crook's campaign of 1876 against the Sioux, white horses ridden by a certain cavalry troop stood up better, contrary to superstition, than all others.[19]

Overwhelming all prejudice against the color, is the association of the white horse with power, pride, glory, with feared conquerors and adored deliverers. Vishnu of the Hindus skimmed the world on his white horse long before St. John the Divine saw the seals opened and beheld a crowned one going forth upon a white horse conquering and to conquer, beheld Death upon a pale horse, and then later beheld one called Faithful and True upon a white horse followed by the armies of Heaven, all on white horses. Joan of Arc rode a white horse. In the old Confederate rhyme, "Jeff Davis rode a white horse." On gray Traveler, Robert E. Lee epitomized a holy cause. Buffalo Bill, last in line of the traditional Men on Horseback, showed himself to the millions of America and Europe always upon a white horse. For thousands of years white has been the color of supremacy, of sublimity and of mystery, the color most stirring to imagination.

Only this color from among hues of infinite variety that clothed the wild horses could have been sublimated into the legend that in space and time transcends all other animal legends of the Western Hemisphere.

When Washington Irving first heard of the great White Mustang in 1832—though his color inclined to gray then—he had already tantalized wild-horse runners for "six or seven years," between the Arkansas and the Cimarron. From that time until 1889, when, according to story, he was

[17] David, Robert B., *Finn Burnett, Frontiersman*, Glendale, California, 1937, 76.
[18] Ferris, W. A., *Life in the Rocky Mountains*, Denver, Colorado, 1940, 331.
[19] Bourke, John G., *On the Border with Crook*, London, 1892, 379.

captured near Phoenix, Arizona, and stood in a pen for ten days without touching food or water, his ears pointed to the far mountains of freedom, neighing his death song, is a long time for any king to reign.

The tradition represents a lost culture, the culture of the Horse Age, before machinery outmoded it. It embodies the ideals of peoples who lived by the horse. It belongs now with the memories of Pegasus and Bucephalus.

# LARRY McMURTRY

## *Take My Saddle from the Wall: A Valediction*

*Stranger: "Mr. Goodnight, you have been a man of vision."*
*Charles Goodnight: "Yes, a hell of a vision."*—J. Frank Dobie, *Cow People*

*Oh, when I die take my saddle from the wall,*
*Put it on my pony, lead him from the stall,*
*Tie my bones to his back, turn our faces to the West,*
*And we'll ride the prairie that we love the best . . .*—*"Goodbye, Old Paint"*

For braiding i have no gift. During the time when I was nominally a cowboy I would sometimes try to braid a halter, a rope, or a bridle rein, usually with sad results. I could seldom make the strands I worked with lay easily or neatly together; and so it may be, I fear, with the braid of this book.

The reader who has attended thus far will have noticed a certain inconsistency in my treatment of Texas past and present—a contradiction of attractions, one might call it. I am critical of the past, yet apparently attracted to it; and though I am even more critical of the present I am also quite clearly attracted to *it*. Such contradictions are always a bit awkward to work with, but in this case there is even an added difficulty: the strands of subject which I have attempted to braid are not of equal width, and I have only managed to twist them into a very rough plait. That I have not been able to do a smoother job is probably due to the fact that I am a novelist, and thus quite unaccustomed to the strain of prolonged thought. My first concern has commonly been with textures, not structures; with motions, rather than methods. What in this book appear to be inconsistencies of attitude are the manifestations of my am-

---

*"Take My Saddle from the Wall: A Valediction" is from*
*Larry McMurtry's* in a narrow grave: essays on texas,
*published in 1968 by The Encino Press, Austin, Texas.*
*Reprinted by permission of the author and the publisher.*

bivalence in regard to Texas—and a very deep ambivalence it is, as deep as the bone. Such ambivalence is not helpful in a discursive book, but it can be the very blood of a novel.

I realize that in closing with the McMurtrys I may only succeed in twisting a final, awkward knot into this uneven braid, for they bespeak the region—indeed, are eloquent of it—and I am quite as often split in my feelings about them as I am in my feelings about Texas. They pertain, of course, both to the Old Texas and the New, but I choose them here particularly because of another pertinence. All of them gave such religious allegiance as they had to give to that god I mentioned in my introduction: the god whose principal myth was the myth of the Cowboy, the ground of whose divinity was the Range. They were many things, the McMurtrys, but to themselves they were cowboys first and last, and the rituals of that faith they strictly kept.

Now the god has departed, thousands of old cowboys in his train. Among them went most of the McMurtrys, and in a few more years the tail-end of the train will pass from sight. All of them lived to see the ideals of the faith degenerate, the rituals fall from use, the principal myth become corrupt. In my youth, when they were old men, I often heard them yearn aloud for the days when the rituals had all their power, when they themselves had enacted the pure, the original myth, and I know that they found it bitter to leave the land to which they were always faithful to the strange and godless heirs that they had bred. I write of them here not to pay them homage, for the kind of homage I could pay they would neither want nor understand; but as a gesture of recognition, a wave such as riders sometimes give one another as they start down opposite sides of a hill. The kind of recognition I would hope to achieve is a kind that kinsmen are so frequently only able to make in a time of parting.

I have never considered genealogy much of an aid to recognition, and thus have never pursued my lineage any distance at all. I remember my McMurtry grandparents only dimly, and in very slight detail, and only a few of the many stories I have heard about them strike me as generative. My grandfather, William Jefferson McMurtry, was the first man I ever saw who wore a mustache—a heavy grey one—and when I think of him I think of that mustache. He died when I was four and only three stories about him have stuck in my mind.

The first was that he was a drunkard in his middle age, and that my grandmother, burdened with many children and unburdened by any conveniences, had found his drunkenness tiresome and threatened to leave him if he didn't stop drinking. The threat was undoubtedly made in earnest, and he took it so immediately to heart that he stopped drinking then and there, with a jug half-full of whiskey hanging in the saddleroom of the barn. The jug of whiskey hung untouched for nineteen years, until the nail rusted out and it fell.

I remember, too, that it was said he could stand on the back porch of the ranch-house and give a dinner call that his boys could hear plainly in the lower field, two miles away. As a boy, riding across the lower field, I would sometimes look back at the speck of the ranch-house and imagine that I heard the old man's dinner call carrying across the flats.

My grandmother's name was Louisa Francis. By the time I was old enough to turn outward, she had turned inward and was deaf, chair-bound, and dying. She lived until I was nine, but I cannot recall that we ever communicated. She was a small woman, wizened by hardship, and I thought her very stern. One day when I was in my teens I went down the crude stone steps to the spring that had been for years the family's only source of water, and it occurred to me that carrying water up those steps year after year would make a lady stern. The children all spoke of William Jefferson as if they had liked him and got on with him well enough, but they spoke of Louisa Francis as one speaks of the Power. I have since thought that an element in her sternness might have been a grim, old-lady recognition that the ideal of the family was in the end a bitter joke; for she had struggled and kept one together, and now, after all, they had grown and gone and left her, and in that hard country what was there to do but rock to death?

William Jefferson, however, sustained himself well to the end, mostly I judge, on inquisitiveness. Since eleven of the twelve children were gone, my father bore the brunt of this inquisitiveness, and one can imagine that it became oppressive at times. When my father returned to the ranch late at night from a trip or a dance the old man would invariably hear his car cross the rattly cattleguard and would hasten out in the darkness to get the news, as it were. Generally the two would meet half-way between the barn and the backyard gate, William Jefferson fresh with queries and midnight speculations on the weather or this or that, my father—mindful that the morning chores were just over the hill—anxious to get to bed. By the time grandfather died the habit had grown so strong that three years passed before my father could walk at night from the barn to the back-yard gate without encountering the ghost of William Jefferson somewhere near the chickenhouse.

Pioneers didn't hasten to West Texas like they hastened to the southern and eastern parts of the state. At first glance, the region seemed neither safe nor desirable; indeed, it wasn't safe, and it took the developing cattle industry to render it desirable. My grandparents arrived in 1877 and prudently paused for ten years in Denton County, some sixty miles west of Dallas and not quite on the lip of the plains. The fearsome Comanche had been but recently subdued—in fact, it was still too early to tell whether they *were* subdued. The last battle of Adobe Walls was fought in the Panhandle in 1874, and Quanah Parker surrendered himself and his warriors in 1875. The very next year, sensing a power vacuum, Charles Goodnight drove his herds into the Palo Duro; Satanta, the last great war chief of the Kiowa killed himself in prison in 1878. Remnants of the two nations trickled into the reservation for the next few years; there were oc-

casional minor hostilities on the South Plains as late as 1879. The Northern Cheyenne broke out in 1878—who could be sure the Comanches
wouldn't follow their example? To those brought up on tales of Comanche
terror the psychological barrier did not immediately fall. The Comanche
never committed themselves readily to the reservation concept, and for a
time there remained the chance that one might awaken in the night in that
lonely country to find oneself and one's family being butchered by a few
pitiless, reactionary warriors bent on a minor hostility.

At any rate, in the eighties William Jefferson and Louisa Francis and
their first six children moved a hundred miles farther west, to Archer
County, where, for three dollars an acre, they purchased a half-section of
land. They settled near a good seeping spring, one of the favorite watering
places on a military road that then ran from Fort Belknap to Buffalo
Springs. The forts that the road connected soon fell from use, but cattle
drivers continued to use the trail and the spring for many years. The
young McMurtry boys had only to step out their door to see their hero
figures riding past.

Indeed, from the pictures I have seen of the original house, they could
have ignored the door altogether and squeezed through one of the walls.
Life in such a house, in such a country, must surely have presented for-
midable difficulties and the boys (there were eventually nine, as against
three girls) quite sensibly left home as soon as they had mastered their
directions.

The median age for leave-taking seems to have been seventeen, and
the fact that the surrounding country was rapidly filling up with farmers
merely served as an added incentive to departure. The cowboy and the
farmer are genuinely inimical types: they have seldom mixed easily. To
the McMurtrys, the plow and the cotton-patch symbolized not only tasks
they loathed but an orientation toward the earth and, by extension, a
quality of soul which most of them not-so-covertly despised. A "one-
gallus farmer" ranked very low in their esteem, and there were even
McMurtrys who would champion the company of Negroes and Mexicans
over the company of farmers—particularly if the farmers happened to be
German. The land just to the north of the McMurtry holdings was
settled by an industrious colony of German dairymen, and the Dutchmen
(as they were called) were thought to be a ridiculous and unsightly thorn
in the fair flesh of the range.

In later years two or three of the McMurtry brothers increased their
fortunes through farming, but this was a fact one seldom heard bruited
about. Indeed, I heard no discussion of the matter until fairly recently,
when one of the farms sold for an even million dollars, a figure capable
of removing the blight from almost any scutcheon.

The cowboy's contempt of the farmer was not unmixed with pity. The
farmer walked in the dust all his life, a hard and ignominious fate. Cowboys could perform terrible labors and endure bone-grinding hardships

and yet consider themselves the chosen of the earth; and the grace that redeemed it all in their own estimation was the fact that they had gone a-horseback. They were riders, first and last. I have known cowboys broken in body and twisted in spirit, bruised by debt, failure, loneliness, disease and most of the other afflictions of man, but I have seldom known one who did not consider himself phenomenally blessed to have been a cowboy, or one who could not cancel half the miseries of existence by dwelling on the horses he had ridden, the comrades he had ridden them with, and the manly times he had had. If the cowboy is a tragic figure, he is certainly one who will not accept the tragic view. Instead, he helps his delineators wring pathos out of tragedy by ameliorating his own loss into the heroic myth of the horseman.

To be a cowboy meant, first of all, to be a horseman. Mr. Dobie was quite right when he pointed out that the seat of the cowboy's manhood is the saddle. I imagine, too, that he understood the consequences of that fact for most cowboys and their women, but if so he was too kindly a man to spell out the consequences in his books. I would not wish to make the point crudely, but I do find it possible to doubt that I have ever known a cowboy who liked women as well as he liked horses, and I know that I have never known a cowboy who was as comfortable in the company of women as he was in the company of his fellow cowboys.

I pointed out in Chapter 4 that I did not believe this was the result of repressed homosexuality, but of a commitment to a heroic concept of life that simply takes little account of women. Certainly the myth of the cowboy is a very efficacious myth, one based first of all upon a deep response to nature. Riding out at sunup with a group of cowboys, I have often felt the power of that myth myself. The horses pick their way delicately through the dewy country, the brightness of sunrise has not yet fallen from the air, the sky is blue and all-covering, and the cowboys are full of jokes and morning ribaldries. It is a fine action, compelling in itself and suggestive beyond itself of other centuries and other horsemen who have ridden the earth.

Unfortunately, the social structure of which that action is a part began to collapse almost a hundred years ago, and the day of the cowboy is now well into its evening. Commitment to the myth today carries with it a terrible emotional price—very often the cowboy becomes a victim of his own ritual. His women, too, are victims, though for the most part acquiescent victims. They usually buy the myth of cowboying and the ideal of manhood it involves, even though both exclude them. A few even buy it to the point of attempting to assimilate the all-valuable masculine qualities to themselves, producing that awful phenomenon, the cowgirl.

If, as I suggested earlier, the cowboy is a tragic figure, one element of the tragedy is that he is committed to an orientation that includes but does not recognize the female, which produces, in day-to-day life, an extraordinary range of frustrations. Curiously, the form the cowboy's recognition does take is literary: he handles women through a romantic convention. The view is often proffered by worshippers of the cowboy that he is a realist of the first order, but that view is an extravagant and imperceptive fiction. Cowboys are romantics, extreme romantics, and ninety-nine out of a hundred of them are sentimental to the core. They are oriented toward the past and face the present only under duress, and then with extreme reluctance.

People who think cowboys are realists generally think so because the cowboy's speech is salty and apparently straight-forward, replete with the wisdom of natural men. What that generally means is that cowboy talk sounds shrewd and perceptive, and so it does. In fact, however, both the effect and the intention of much cowboy talk is literary: cowboys are aphorists. Whenever possible, they turn their observations into aphorisms. Some are brilliant aphorists, scarcely inferior to Wilde or La Rochefoucauld; one is proud to steal from them. I plucked a nice one several years ago, to wit: "A woman's love is like the morning dew: it's just as apt to fall on a horseturd as it is on a rose." In such a remark the phrasing is worth more than the perception, and I think the same might be said for the realism of most cowboys. It is a realism in tone only: its insights are either wildly romantic, mock-cynical, or solemnly sentimental. The average cowboy is an excellent judge of horseflesh, only a fair judge of men, and a terrible judge of women, particularly "good women." Teddy Blue stated it succinctly forty years ago:

> I'd been traveling and moving around all the time and I can't say I ever went out of my way to seek the company of respectable ladies. We (cowboys) didn't consider we were fit to associate with them on account of the company we kept. We didn't know how to talk to them anyhow. That was what I meant by saying that the cowpunchers was afraid of a decent woman. We were so damned scared that we'd do or say something wrong . . .[1]

That was written of the nineteenth century cowboy, but it would hold good for most of their descendants, right down to now. Most of them marry, and love their wives sincerely, but since their sociology idealizes women and their mythology excludes her the impasse which results is often little short of tragic. Now, as then, the cowboy escapes to the horse, the range, the work, and the company of comrades, most of whom are in the same unacknowledged fix.

Once more I might repeat what cannot be stressed too often: that the master symbol for handling the cowboy is the symbol of the horseman.[2] The gunman had his place in the mythology of the West, but the cowboy

---

[1] *We Pointed Them North*, p. 188.

[2] *Singing Cowboy*, ed. Margaret Larkin, Oak Publications, N.Y., 1963, p. 60. See in this regard the well-known song "My Love is a Rider," a song said to have been composed by Belle Starr: He made me some presents among them a ring. The return that I made him was a far better thing. 'Twas a young maiden's heart I would have you all know, He won it by riding his bucking bronco. Now listen young maidens where e're you reside, Don't list to the cowboy who swings the rawhide. He'll court you and pet you and leave you and go Up the trail in the spring on his bucking bronco.

did not realize himself with a gun. Neither did he realize himself with a penis, nor with a bankroll. Movies fault the myth when they dramatize gunfighting, rather than horsemanship, as the dominant skill. The cowboy realized himself on a horse, and a man might be broke, impotent, and a poor shot and still hold up his head if he could ride.

Holding up the head had its importance too, for with horsemanship went pride, and with that, stoicism. The cowboy, like Mithridates, survived by preparing for ill and not for good—after all, it sometimes only took a prairie-dog hole to bring a man down. Where emotion was concerned, the cowboy's ethic was Roman: emotion, but always emotion within measure. An uncle of mine put it as nicely as one could want. This one was no McMurtry, but an uncle-by-marriage named Jeff Dobbs. He had been a cowboy and a Texas Ranger, and when he had had enough of the great world he retired to the backwoods of Oklahoma to farm peanuts and meditate on the Gospels. He was a self-styled Primitive Baptist, which meant that he had a theology all his own, and he had honed his scriptural knife to a fine edge in some forty years of nightly arguments with his wife, my Aunt Minta. Neither of them ever yielded a point, and when my aunt was killed I don't think they even agreed on the book of Zechariah.

One morning not unlike any other, Aunt Minta went out in her car, was hit by a truck, and killed instantly. At this time I was in graduate school in Houston, doctoral longings in me, and I wrote Uncle Jeff to offer condolence. His reply is *echt*-cowboy:

> Will answer your welcome letter.
>
> Was glad to heare from you again, well it has rained a-plenty here the last week, the grass is good and everything is lovely . . .
>
> Would like for you to visit me, we could talk the things over that we are interested in. What does PhD stand for? to me its post-hole digger, guess that would be about what it would stand for with all the other old Texas cowpokes . . .
>
> I never could understand why a man wanted to spend all his life going to school, ide get to thinking about the Rancho Grandy, and get rambling on my mind, freedom to quote O. M. Roberts:
>
>> to what avail the plow or sail or land.
>> or life if freedom fail . . .
>
> going to school was always like being in jail to me, life is too short, sweet and uncertain to spend it in jail.
>
> Well, Larry, am still having trouble with my sore eye, have had it five months now, it looks like pinkeye to me, might have took it from the pink-eyed cow.
>
> Yes it was an awful tragidy to have Mint crushed in the smashup, my car was a total loss too.
>
> Things like that will just hoppen though. It is lonesome dreary out here in the backwoods by myself.

Don't ever join the army, if you do you will have to stay in for four years, that would be a long time to stay in the danged army, this conscription is not according to the constitution of the U.S. its involuntary servitude which is slavery . . .

Well I have just had a couple of Jehovah's witnesses visit me but I soon got them told, I think they are as crazy as a betsie bug and I don't like to be bothered with them, with this sore eye I am in a bad humour most of the time anyway, yours truly

Jeff Dobbs

I doubt that Seneca himself could have balanced the car and the wife that simply, and this about one week after she was gone.

But mention of horses and horsemanship brings me back to the McMurtrys, all of whom were devoted to the horse. Indeed, so complete was their devotion that some of them were scarcely competent to move except on horseback. They walk reluctantly and with difficulty, and clearly do not care to be dependent upon their own legs for locomotion. That a person might walk for pleasure is a notion so foreign to them that they can only acquaint it with lunacy or a bad upbringing.

Much as their walking leaves to be desired, it is infinitely to be preferred to their driving. A few of them developed a driver's psychology and a driver's skills, but most of them remained unrepentent horsemen to the end; and an unrepentent horseman at the wheel of a Cadillac is not the sort of person with whom one cares to share a road. That their names are not writ large in the annals of the Highway Patrol is only due to the fact that they lived amid the lightly-habited wastes of West Texas and were thus allowed a wider margin of error than most mortals get.

As horsemen their talents varied, but only one or two were without flair. When it came to riding broncs, Jim, the second eldest, was apparently supreme. If he ever saw a horse he was afraid of no one ever knew about it, and in early Archer County his only rival as a bronc-rider was a legendary cowpuncher named Nigger Bones Hook. If the latter's skills were as remarkable as his name he must indeed have been a rider to contend with, but there are those who considered Uncle Jim his equal. Unfortunately, Uncle Jim over-matched himself early in life and as a consequence was reduced to riding wheel chairs for some forty years. When he was fifteen, William Jefferson let him ride a strong, wild bronc that had been running loose for some years; Uncle Jim stayed on him, but he was not experienced enough to ride him safely and before the ride was over his head was popping uncontrollably. When the horse exhausted himself neither it nor Uncle Jim were able to bring their heads back to a normal position. William Jefferson took both hands and set his son's head straight, but Uncle Jim's neck was broken and he left the field that day with a pinched nerve which would eventually result in a crippling arthritis. Despite the kickback from that one early ride he went on to acquire a large ranch, a wife and family, a couple of banks and a commensurate fortune. The horse that crippled him never raised his head again and died within two days.

When Jim reached the Panhandle in 1900 he was far from done as a rider; indeed, his most celebrated feat was recorded shortly thereafter. He hired on with the ROs, a ranch owned by an extraordinary and very eccentric Englishman named Alfred Rowe, who was later to go down on the Titanic. Uncle Jim's wages were fifteen dollars a month. One day Rowe bought seventeen horses from the army, all incorrigibles that had been condemned as too wild to be ridden. Rowe offered Uncle Jim a dollar a head to ride them, and he rode them all that same afternoon, after which, convinced that he had made his fortune, he soon went into business for himself.

Roy McMurtry was apparently the only one of the nine boys to rival Jim's skill with a bucking horse, but few of the others were loath to try their hand (or their seat) with a bronc. It is quite clear that riding was the physical skill most crucially connected with the entrance into manhood. In the spring of 1910 Johnny McMurtry, then still in his teens, borrowed a horse and made his way to the Panhandle, looking for a job as a cowboy. He immediately found one with his brothers Charley and Jim, who were then partners in an operation which at times involved as many as 4,000 cattle. One would have thought that with that many cattle to hassle, a young and extraordinarily willing brother would have been an entirely welcome addition to the staff; but McMurtrys, like most cattlemen, take willingness for granted and judge solely on performance. On almost his first drive Johnny came near to achieving permanent disgrace through a lapse in horsemanship. Some eight hundred nervous yearlings were involved; the older brothers were in the process of calming them after several rather hectic stampedes, one of which had flattened a six wire fence. The cattle were almost quiet when the lapse occurred; the account I quote is from an unpublished memoir left me by Uncle Johnny:

> I rode up the bank of Sadler Creek on an old silly horse, he got to pitching and pitched under a cottonwood tree and dragged me off, then into the herd he went and stampeded them again, Jim didn't see it so thought the horse had pitched me off, he caught him and brought him back to me, he was as mad as a gray lobo wolf with hydrophobia, he told me that if I could't ride that horse I had better go back to Archer County and catch rabbits for a living, that was about the only horse I had that I could really ride pitching and I was proud of it and was down right insulted for Jim to think I couldn't ride him . . .

The distinction between being drug off and being pitched off might seem obscure to many, but not to a young man whose ego-needs were closely bound up with horsemanship.

At any rate, all the McMurtrys could ride well enough to get themselves out of Archer County at an early age. Invariably, the direction they rode was northwest, toward the open and still comparatively empty plains of the Panhandle. Specifically they rode to the town of Clarendon, near the Palo Duro canyon, a town which in those days serviced and supplied most of the great Panhandle ranches, among them the JAs and the ROs. For better or worse, Clarendon was their Paris. Charlie arrived in '96, Bob in '99, Jim in 1900, Ed in 1902, Roy in 1910, Lawrence, Grace and May at dates now unremembered, Jo and Jeff in 1916, and Margaret in 1919. Even the old folks went to Clarendon for a time (1919–1925), but doubtless found it impossible to live peacefully with so many of their children about, and soon retreated to the balmier latitudes of Archer County, my father with them.

That that bare and windy little town on the plains should have been so much to my family I find a bit sad, but not inexplicable. Youth is youth and a heyday a heyday, wherever one spends it, and it would appear that at the turn of the century Clarendon was to cowboys what Paris was soon to be for writers. It was the center of the action. If one merely wanted to cowboy, there were the great ranches; and if one was more ambitious the plains was the one place where land in quantity could still be had cheap.

In time the McMurtrys got—and no doubt earned—their share of that land. Most of them started as twenty dollar a month cowboys and quit when they were far enough ahead to buy some land of their own. Seven of the boys and two of the girls lived out their lives within a hundred miles of Clarendon, and in time the nine boys between them owned almost a hundred and fifty thousand acres of Texas land and grazed on it many many thousand head of cattle.

I do not intend here to attempt to describe the McMurtrys one by one. In truth, I didn't know them all that well, not as individuals, and individual character sketches would be neither very interesting nor very authoritative. Most of them were old men when I was very young, and I almost never saw them singly or for any length of time. When I saw them as a family, grouped with their wives and multitudinous progeny at the family reunions which were held more or less annually from the late forties until the middle sixties. Most of the reunions were held in Clarendon, or, to be more accurate, were held at the Clarendon Country Club, which fact alone is indicative enough of the direction the family had moved.

The Country Club sits some fifteen miles to the northwest of Clarendon, on a ridge not far from the Salt Fork of the Red. Fifteen miles is a short trot in that country and the wives of the local elite would think nothing of driving that far for some minor social function, though as I remember the clubhouse about the only social functions to which it could be adapted were dancing and drinking. Once long ago some cousins and I discovered a couple of rusty slot-machines in a broom closet, indicating that that porticular form of gambling had, in those regions at least, passed out of vogue. There was a swimming pool (the one essential of all country clubs), a grove of trees for shade, a windmill for water, and a pond, I suppose, for decor. Of the sights and sounds which one associates with big-city country clubs in Texas—the polished foliage, the liveried staff, the well-parked rows of Mercedes and Lincolns, the tinkle of ice and the ploop of badly-hit tennis balls—there was nothing.

Thus, when I saw the McMurtrys, I saw them on the ground that had always held them, the great ring of the plains, with the deep sky and the brown ridges and the restless grass being shaken by the wind as it passed on its long journey from the Rockies south. Teddy Blue mayhap and Old Man Goodnight surely had left their horsetracks on that ridge; there one might have witnessed the coming and going of the god. One by one the old men arrived, in heavy cars with predominantly heavy wives, followed now and then by cautious off-spring in Chevrolets. The day was given over to feasting and anecdotage, in almost equal division. The barbecuing was entrusted to a Negro and a County Agent and generally consisted of about a hundred chickens (for the women and youngsters) and a side of beef (for the men, who, being cattlemen, scorned all other meat if beef were available). Vegetables were irrelevant, but there was usually a washpot full of beans, and of course, twenty or thirty cakes brought by the twenty or thirty wives. Later, should the season be opportune, a pickup full of watermelons might arrive, easily sufficient to bloat such children as were not already bloated on soda pop. Gourmandry was encouraged, indeed, almost demanded, and I recall one occasion when the son of someone's hired hand put all the young McMurtrys to shame by consuming twenty-six Dr. Peppers in the course of a single day.

In the forenoon the family normally split itself into three groups, the division following the traditional dividing line of Western gatherings: men, women, and children, or each to his own kind. After lunch everyone was too stuffed to move and mingled freely if somewhat heavily. My hundred or so cousins and I found generally that we could do without one another with no ill effects, and in the afternoons I picked my way gingerly among the bulging uncles and aunts, eavesdropping on such conversations as interested me. With most of my uncles I had no rapport at all. To their practiced eye it must have been evident from the first that I was not going to turn out to be a cattleman. For one thing, I wasn't particularly mean, and in the West the mischief quotient is still a popular standard for measuring the appearance of approvable masculine qualities in a youngster. Any boy worth his salt was expected to be a nuisance, if not to the adults at least to the weaker members of his own age group. I was a weaker member myself; indeed, though I don't remember it, I believe at some early and very primitive reunion I was cast into a hog wallow or pelted with ordure or something; though the atrocity may be apocryphal it would not have been out of keeping with the spirit of such occasions. Mean kids meant strength in time of need, and how could the elders be sure that a bookish and suspiciously observant youngster like myself might not in time disgrace the line? I knew from an early age that

I could never meet their standard, and since in those days theirs was the only standard I knew existed I was the more defensive around them. Indeed, scared. One was mild and two were gentle: the rest, with one exception, were neither harder nor softer than saddle leather. The one exception, was, in my estimation, harder than your average saddle. Tolerance was a quality I think no McMurtry ever understood, much less appreciated, and though one or two of them came to understand mercy it was never the family's long suit.

Strength was quite obviously the family's long suit: strength of body, strength of will, and, over it all, strength of character. One of my difficulties with them was that their strength of character was totally and inflexibly committed to a system of values that I found not wholly admirable. The talk beneath the reunion tent was the talk of men whose wills had begun to resent their weakening bodies. They had all, like Hector, been tamers of horses once—adventure and physical hardship had been the very ground of their manhood. The talk was often of the hardships of their youth, hardships that time with its strange craft had turned into golden memories. As I listened and grew older I became, each year, more sharply aware of the irony of the setting: that those men, who in their youth had ridden these same plains and faced their winds and dangers, should in their age buy so puny a symbol as the Clarendon Country Club, the exultantly unbourgeois and undomestic ideal of the Cowboy expiring in the shade of that most bourgeois and most domestic institution. To give them credit, though, I doubt that any of them were happy about it.

Of all the hardship stories I heard, the one which remains most resonant in my mind is the story of the molasses barrel. It was, for all witnesses, a traumatic event. Late one fall, not long after the turn of the century, William Jefferson had gone to the small town of Archer City to purchase the winter's provisions. Archer City was eighteen miles from the ranch, a tedious trip by wagon. He returned late in the afternoon, and among the supplies he brought back was an eighty-pound barrel of good sorghum molasses, in those days the nearest thing to sugar that could be procured. Such sweetening as the family would have for the whole winter was in the barrel, and all gathered around to watch it being unloaded. Two of the boys rolled the barrel to the back of the wagon and two more reached to lift it down, but in the exchange of responsibilities someone failed to secure a hold and the barrel fell to the ground and burst. Eighty pounds of sweetness quivered, spread out, and began to seep unrecoverably into the earth. Grace, the oldest girl, unable to accept the loss, held her breath and made three desperate circles of the house before anyone could recover himself sufficiently to catch her and pound her on the back. Indeed, the story was usually told as a story on Grace, for most of them had suppressed the calamity so effectively that they could not remember how anyone else had responded. They could speak with less emotion of death and dismemberment than of that moment when they stood and watched the winter's sweetness soak into the chickenyard.[3]

Uncle Johnny, the seventh boy, was born in 1891. He was my favorite uncle and in many ways the family's darling, and I should like to write of him in some detail. Of them all, he fought the suburb most successfully, and hewed closest to the nineteenth century ideal of the cowboy. He was the last to be domesticated, if indeed he ever was domesticated, and at one point he almost abandoned the struggle to be a rancher in order to remain a free cowboy. Indeed, according to the memoir he left me, the desire to be a cowboy was his first conscious desire:

> Dad had built two log barns and we boys would climb on top of those barns and watch the herds go by, never since then have I wanted to be anything except a cowboy . . .

By the time he was twelve he could chop cotton well enough to consider himself financially independent, and after only a month or two of labor was able to buy a secondhand saddle. By that time he had completed such text-books as the little school-house on Idiot Ridge possessed, and he was not impeded by education until 1909, when Louisa Francis persuaded him to enroll in a business college in McKinney. The school was teeming with chiggers, but Uncle Johnny applied himself grimly and in only four months acquired a diploma stating that he was a Bachelor of Accounts. He was the only McMurtry to achieve such eminence, and was also, ironically, the only McMurtry ever to go formally broke.

As soon as his course was finished he had to begin to think about paying for it. He went home, borrowed a horse, and headed for the Panhandle, equipped with his original second-hand saddle and seven dollars in cash. He meant to hire on with the JAs, but stopped by first to visit Charley and Jim at their ranch on the Salt Fork of the Red. They were shrewd men and doubtless knew a good thing when they saw it riding up. They hired him immediately at twenty dollars a month and keep, which meant, apparently, that he was allowed to eat whatever small vermin he could catch. Not that Uncle Johnny cared: at this time his eagerness for the cowboy life was little short of mystical. He was willing to forego eating, if necessary, and fortunately had never much liked to sleep either. Fortunately, since to his brothers 3 A.M. was traditionally the end of the night.

He worked for Charley and Jim three years, much of that time in a

---

[3] It now appears that the uncle who first told me this sad story had added a few flowers of his own. What "really happened," it seems, is that the barrel of molasses had a wooden spigot, and was unloaded safely and laid across two supportbeams so that when the spigot was opened the molasses would drain into the molasses pitcher. Unfortunately, a sow came along one day, walked under the barrel, and rooted the spigot out. The molasses drained from the barrel and ran down a footpath all the way to the lots. The catastrophe was thus discovered and the children lined up beside the path to weep. As with many family stories, I think I prefer the fiction to the truth.

bachelor camp on the baldies, as the high plains were then called. His possessions consisted of a saddle, shirt, pants, and chaps, two quilts, a six-shooter, and a horse called Sugar-in-the-Gourd. In coolish weather his brothers generously provided him with a teepee, a small stove, and a bucket of sourdough. He spent his wages on cattle—there being nothing else in his vicinity to spend them on—and when his brothers phased him out in 1913 he had paid off the business college and was fifteen hundred dollars to the good.

The yen to work for a really big ranch was still strong in him, so he drifted southwest to the Matadors and hired on with them two days before the wagons pulled out for the spring roundup in 1913. The Matador, like the ROs, was English-owned; they then ran 50,000 head of cattle on slightly over a half-million acres of land. By August Uncle Johnny had helped in the rounding up and shipping of some 19,000 steers, and by early December had assisted in the branding of 11,000 calves.

From the minute he saw the Matador wagons he seemed to realize that he had found his blood's country, and he often said that if he could choose three years to live over they would be the years he had spent with the Matadors. Much of the memoir is devoted to those years, and to the men he worked with: Weary Willie Drace, his wagon-boss, Rang Thornton, Pelada Vivian, and the Pitchfork Kid, names which mean nothing now. In speaking of their departed comrades, men once renowned but soon to be forgotten, old cowboys invariably draw upon the same few images, all of them images taken from their work. Thus, here is Teddy Blue, speaking of the men who had gone with him in the seventies up the long trail to the Yellowstone:

> Only a few of us are left now, and they are scattered from Texas to Canada. The rest have left the wagon and gone ahead across the big divide, looking for a new range. I hope they find good water and plenty of grass. But wherever they are is where I want to go.[4]

And here, a generation later, is Uncle Johnny, speaking of his buddy the Pitchfork Kid:

> His equal will never be seen on earth again and if he is camping the wagon and catching beeves in the great perhaps and I am fortunate enough to get there I won't be foolish enough to try and run ahead of him and catch the beef, I know it can't be done . . .

By October of 1915 he had increased his savings to $2500 and he decided to take the leap from cowboying to ranching, clearly one of the harder decisions he ever made:

> I left the wagon at the Turtle Hole, I have never before or since hated to do anything as bad as I hated to leave that wagon and to this day when I go down through there I am filled with nostalgia, just looking at the old

[4] *We Pointed Them North*, p. 230.

red hill in Croton, the breaks on the Tongue River and the Roaring Springs, if I had known that leaving was going to be that hard I would have stayed and worn myself out right there . . .

Where he went was a ranch in the sandy country south of Muleshoe, near the New Mexico line, and he stayed there the rest of his life. He struggled for more than ten years to keep the first ranch he bought, lost it and went stone broke in 1930, struggled back, and died owning several thousand acres, several hundred cows, and a Cadillac.

I saw Uncle Johnny's ranch for the first time when I was in my early teens and went there for a reunion. Three times in all he managed to capture the reunion for Muleshoe, and for the children of the family those were high occasions, quite different in quality from anything Clarendon offered. To begin with, Uncle Johnny lived far out in the country—and such country. I thought the first time I saw it that only a man who considered himself forsaken of God would live in such country, and nothing I have found out since has caused me to alter that view. The more I saw of it the more I knew that he had been well-punished for casting over the Edenic simplicity of the Matador wagons.

Then too, the house in which he lived, or, at least, in which he might have lived, was a bit out of the ordinary. It was a towering three-story edifice, reminiscent of the house in *Giant*. Every grain of paint had long since been abraded away by the blowing sand. The house had been built by an extremely eccentric New York architect, who must also have considered himself forsaken of God. Indeed, in the long run he probably was, for solitude and his wife's chirpings eventually drove him mad and he came in one morning from chopping wood, called her into the basement, and killed her on the spot with the flat of his axe, or so legend had it. No one had ever bothered to remove the basement carpet, and the spot, or splotch, remained. Nothing could have had a more Dostoevskian impact on such simple Texas kids as we were than that large irregular stain on the basement rug. A good part of every Muleshoe reunion was given over to staring at it, while we mentally or in whispers tried to reconstruct the crime.

When we grew tired of staring at the spot we usually turned our attentions to the player piano. The architect had apparently been as nostalgic for Gotham as Uncle Johnny was for the Matador wagons, since the piano was equipped with duplicate rolls of "The Sidewalks of New York" and a number of other ditties that must have evoked really choking memories amid those wastes. There were also a few spiritual items such as "The Old Rugged Cross," meant, no doubt, for his wife's Bible group. Over the years Uncle Johnny had developed a keen distaste for the piano, or perhaps for the selection of rolls, and he was always dashing in and attempting to lock it, an endeavour in which he was somehow never successful.

He himself appeared not to care for the house, and slept in the little bunk-house. The only sign that he ever inhabited the big house was that the bed in the master bedroom had eleven quilts on it, compensation, no doubt, for having wintered on the baldies with one blanket, one soogan and a wagon sheet. He generally had in his employ a decrepit cook of sorts (male) and one or two desperately inept cowboys, usually Mexican. These slept in the bunk-house too, or did if they were allowed the leisure to sleep. All the McMurtrys were near-fanatic workers, but Uncle Johnny was by all accounts the most relentless in this regard. His brothers often said, with a certain admiration, that Johnny never had learned how much a horse or a human being could stand. Such humans as worked for him stood as much as he could stand, or else left; and he had to an extraordinary degree that kind of wiry endurance which is fairly common in the cow country. His health broke when he was thirty-three and he was partially crippled the rest of his life, but it hardly seemed to have slowed him down. He could not be kept in bed more than five hours a night, and even with one leg virtually useless sometimes branded as many as eight hundred cattle in one day; once, indeed, he vaccinated 730 off the end of a calf-draggers rope in one afternoon.

In the last ten years of his life he sustained an almost incredible sequence of injuries, one following on another so rapidly that he could scarcely get from one hospital to the next without something nearly fatal happening to him. His arthritis was complicated by the fact that his right leg had been broken numerous times. Horses were always falling with him and on him, or throwing him into trees, or kicking him across corrals. The McMurtrys seemed to consider that these minor injuries were no more than he deserved, for being too tight to buy good horses instead of young half-broken broncs. He appreciated good horses, of course, but when he had something to do would get on any horse that stood to hand. One leg was broken almost a dozen times in such manner and near the end he was so stiff that he had his cowboys wire him on his horses with baling wire, a lunatic thing to do considering the roughness of the country and the temperament of most of the horses he rode.

In the late fifties he got cancer of the throat and had his entire larynx removed. For a while he spoke with an electric voice-box, a device which rendered his dry, wry wit even dryer and wryer. He soon grew dissatisfied with that, however, and learned to speak with a esophigal voice; it left him clear but barely audible and greatly reduced his effectiveness as a raconteur. No sooner was he home from the hospital after his throat operation than he got out to shut a gate and let his own pickup run over him, crushing one hip and leg horribly. He managed to dig himself out and crawl back to his ranch, and was immediately flown back to the same hospital.

In time he recovered and went home to Muleshoe and got married, this in his sixty-fifth year. The day after his wedding, so I am told, he and Aunt Ida, his bride, spent some eleven hours horseback, sorting out a herd of cattle he had bought in Louisiana. Two years later, while on their way to Lubbock, a car ran into them on the highway and broke them both up like eggshells. Aunt Ida got a broken back and knee, Uncle Johnny two broken knees and a bad rebreakage of his crippled leg. In time they both recovered but Uncle Johnny was scarcely home before he allowed a whole feedhouse full of hundred-pound sacks of cattlefeed to fall on top of him, breaking his leg yet again.

In the days of the Muleshoe reunions, most of these disasters were still in the future and he was very much his vigorous self. He owned a Cadillac at this time, but did almost all of his driving in an army surplus jeep of ancient vintage, so ancient, in fact, that it lacked both roof and seats. The small matter of the seat Uncle Johnny took care of by turning a syrup-bucket upside down in the floor-boards and balancing a piece of two-by-four across it. This worked well enough for day-to-day driving, but once when he set out to haul a trailerful of pigs to Lubbock the arrangement proved imperfect. The pigs turned over the trailer, the wrench threw Uncle Johnny off the syrup bucket, and jeep, trailer, uncle and swine ended up in a heap in the bar-ditch. He was not much hurt in the accident but was very out of temper before he managed, afoot and with only one usable leg, to get the seven wild pigs rounded up again.

Few of the McMurtrys were devoid of temper and he was not one of those who lacked it, yet I think no child ever sensed his temper. Children found him extraordinarily winning, the perfect uncle and instant confidant. He brought a quality to uncleship that only certain childless men can bring—adult, and yet not domestic. I had always supposed him a truly gentle man and was very shocked, one night, to hear him say that the way to handle Mexicans was to kick loose a few of their ribs ever now and then. I had only to reflect on that awhile to realize that I had never known a cowboy who was also a truly gentle man. The cowboy's working life is spent in one sort of violent activity or other; an ability to absorb violence and hardship is part of the proving of any cowboy, and it is only to be expected that the violence will extend itself occasionally from animals to humans, and particularly to those humans that class would have one regard as animals.

One of the more dramatic manifestations of Uncle Johnny's temper occurred just prior to the last of the Muleshoe reunions. For nostalgia's sake he grazed a few animals of even greater vintage than his jeep, among them a large male elk and an aging buffalo bull. The two animals were never on very good terms, and indeed the old buffalo was regarded as a great nuisance by everyone attached to the ranch. A few days before the reunion someone, Uncle Johnny most likely, made the mistake of leaving the elk and the buffalo alone in the same pen for an hour. The two soon joined in battle, and the battle raged freely for quite some time, neither combatant able to gain a clear advantage. When Uncle Johnny happened on the scene, half of his corrals had been flattened and much of the rest knocked hopelessly awry. Enraged, he at once found in favor of the elk and shot the buffalo dead on the spot. An hour later, when he was some-what cooler, the Scotch took precedence over the Irish in him and he decided that it might be a novelty (as it would certainly be an economy) to barbecue the buffalo and serve him to the clan. He thus set free the fatted calf that had been meant for that fate and had the buffalo towed to the barbecue pit. It was barbecued, I believe, for forty-eight hours and on the day of the reunion its flesh proved precisely consistent with the McMurtry character: neither harder nor softer than saddle leather. How long one should have had to chew it to break down its resistance I did not find out.

There is yet one more story about Uncle Johnny, and it is the story which slides the panel, as Mr. Durrell might put it. We have seen him so far as the dashing young cowboy and the lovable family eccentric, and I should probably have always thought of him in those terms if the last story had not come to me. It came as I left for college and was offered as a safeguard and an admonition.

While still young, Uncle Johnny had the misfortune to catch what in those days was called a social disease. Where he got it one can easily imagine: some grim clapboard house on the plains, with the wind moan-ing, Model A's parked in the grassless yard, and the girls no prettier than Belle Starr. His condition became quite serious, and had my father not gone with him to a hospital and attended him during a prolonged critical period he might well have died.

Instead, he recovered, and in gratitude gave my father a present. Times were hard and Uncle Johnny poor but the present was a pair of spurs with my father's brand mounted on them in gold—extraordinary spurs for this plain country.

Since then, my father had worn no other spurs, and for a very long time Uncle Johnny took on himself the cloth of penance—the sort of penance appropriate to the faith he held. For all McMurtrys and perhaps all cowboys are essentially pantheists: to them the Almighty is the name of drought, the Good Lord the name of rain and grass. Nature is the only deity they really recognize and nature's order the only order they hold truly sacred.

The most mysterious and most respected part of nature's order was the good woman. Even the most innocent cowboy was scarcely good enough for a good woman, and the cowboy who was manifestly not innocent might never be good enough, however much he might crave one. Instead, he might choose just such a setting as Uncle Johnny chose: a country forsaken of God and women, the rough bunkhouse, the raw horses and the unused mansion, the sandstorms and the blue northers—accoutrements enough for any penance.

At sixty-five he married a woman he had known for a very long time. When he began to court her he discovered, to quote the memoir, that "she was a much better woman than I was entitled to." Even after they married it was some time before he considered himself quite worthy to occupy the same house with her. Perhaps when he did he let the penance go. Despite the series of injuries, his optimism grew, he bought new land, began to talk of a long-postponed world cruise, and wrote on the last page of his memoir:

> I have had my share of fun and am still having it, we have a lot of plans for the future and expect to carry them out . . .

Ruin had not taught him well at all. A short while after the feed fell on him he learned that he had cancer of the colon. From that time on he was in great pain. His will to live never weakened, indeed, seemed to increase, but this time the cancer was inexorable and he died within three years, his world cruise untaken.

In July of 1965, eight months before he died, Uncle Johnny attended his last reunion. It was held at the Clarendon Country Club, on a fine summer day, and as reunions went it was a quiet, sparsely attended affair. There was a light turnout of cousins and no more than a dozen or two small children scattered about. The food was catered this time, and just as well, too; the Homeric magnificence of some of the earlier feasts would have been largely wasted on the tired and dyspeptic McMurtrys who managed to drag themselves to the plains that day. Charlie and Jim were dead, several of the others were sick, and most of the survivors had long since ruined their digestions.

The talk was what the talk had always been, only the tones had more audible cracks and the rhythms were shorter. Once I saw Uncle Bob, who was just recovering from a broken hip, trying to talk to Uncle Johnny, who was still recovering from his final broken leg. It was a fine paradigm of the existential condition, for the two brothers were standing on a windy curve of the ridge, moving their mouths quite uselessly. Uncle Johnny had almost no voice and Uncle Bob even less hearing, and indeed, had they been able to communicate they would probably only have got in a fight and injured themselves further, for they were not always in accord and it was rumoured that only a few months earlier they had encountered one another on the streets of Amarillo and almost come to blows.

Uncle Johnny, all day, was in very great pain, and only the talk and the sight of the children seemed to lift him above it. Finally it was three o'clock and the white sun began to dip just slightly in its arch. It was time for he and Aunt Ida to start the two hundred mile drive back to Muleshoe. Uncle Johnny reached for his white Stetson and put it on and all of his brothers and sisters rose to help him down the gentle slope to the Cadillac. Most of the women were weeping, and in the confusion of the moment Aunt Ida had forgotten her purse and went back to the tables to get it, while Uncle Johnny, helped by the lame and attended by the halt, worked his way around the open door of the car and stood there a few minutes, kissing his sisters goodbye. Though he was seventy-five and dying there was yet something boyish about him as he stood taking leave of the family. He stood in the frame that had always contained him, the great circular frame of the plains, with the wind blowing the grey hair at his temples and the whole of the Llano Estacado at his back. When he smiled at the children who were near, the pain left his face for a second and he gave them the look that had always been his greatest appeal—the look of a man who saw life to the last as a youth sees it, and who sees in any youth all that he himself had been.

The family stood awkwardly around the car, looking now at Uncle Johnny, now at the shadow-flecked plains, and they were as close in that moment to a tragic recognition as they would ever be: for to them he had always been the darling, young Adonis, and most of them would never see him alive again. There were no words—they were not a wordy people. Aunt Ida returned with her purse and Uncle Johnny's last young grin blended with his grimace as he began the painful task of fitting himself into the car. In a few minutes the Cadillac had disappeared behind the first brown ridge, and the family was left with its silence and the failing day.

There, I think, this book should end: with that place and that group, witnesses both to the coming and going of the god. Though one could make many more observations about the place, about the people, about the myth, I would rather stop there, on the sort of silence where fiction starts. Texas soaks up commentary like the plains soak up a rain, but the images from which fiction draws its vibrancy are often very few and often silent, like those I have touched on in this chapter. The whiskey jug hanging in the barn for nineteen years; the children, rent with disappointment around the puddle of molasses; the whorehouse and the goldmounted spurs. And Uncle Jeff, alone in the back-woods with his bad eye and his memories of the Rancho Grandy; and Uncle Johnny, riding up the Canadian in 1911 on a horse called Sugar-in-the-Gourd, and, only four years later, riding away bereft from the Roaring Springs, the dream of innocence and fullness never to be redeemed.

Those images, as it happens, all come from Old Texas, but it would not be hard to find in today's experience, or tomorrow's, moments that are just as eloquent, just as suggestive of gallantry or strength or disappointment. Indeed, had I more taste for lawsuits I would list a few for balance. Texas is rich in unredeemed dreams, and now that the dust of its herds is settling the writers will be out on their pencils, looking for them in the suburbs and along the mythical Pecos. And except to paper riders, the Pecos is a lonely and a bitter stream.

I have that from men who rode it and who knew that country round— such as it was, such as it can never be again.

# CHARLES M. SKINNER

## *The Governor's Right Eye*

OLD GOVERNOR HERMENEGILDO SALVATIERRA, of Presidio, California, sported only one eye—the left—because the other had been shot out by an Indian arrow. With this sound one he was gazing into the fire, on a windy afternoon in the rainy season, when a chunky man in a sou'wester was ushered into his presence, and after announcing that he was no other than Captain Peleg Scudder, of the schooner General Court, from Salem, he was made welcome in a manner quite out of proportion in its warmth to the importance that such a disclosure would have for the every-day citizen.

He was hailed with wassail and even with wine. The joy of the commandant was so great that at the third bowl he sang a love ballad, in a voice somewhat cracked, and got on the table to teach the Yankee how to dance the cachuca. The law forbade any extended stay of Americans in Spanish waters, and the General Court took herself off that very night—for this, mind you, was in 1797, when the Spaniard ruled the farther coast.

Next day Salvatierra appeared before his astonished people with a right eye. The priests attached to the fort gave a special service of praise, and told the miracle to the red men of their neighborhood as an illustration of the effect of goodness, prayer, and faith. People came from far and near that they might go to church and see this marvel for themselves. But, alas, for the governor's repute for piety! It soon began to be whispered around that the new eye was an evil one; that it read the deepest thoughts of men with its inflexible, cold stare; that under its influence some of the fathers had been betrayed into confessing things that the commandant had never supposed a clergyman to be guilty of. The people feared that eye, and ascribed such rogueries to the old man as had been entirely foreign to his nature hitherto.

This common fear and suspicion reacted, inevitably, and Salvatierra began, unconsciously, to exhibit some of the traits that his subjects said he possessed. He changed slowly from the indulgent parent to the stern and exacting law-giver. He did not know, however, what the people had been saying about him, and never suspected that his eye was likely to get him into trouble.

It was a warm night and he had gone to bed with his windows open—windows that opened from his garden, and were level, at the bottom, with the floor. A shadowy form stole along the gravel path and entered one of these windows. It was that of a mission Indian. He had gathered from

*From* MYTHS AND LEGENDS OF OUR OWN LAND (*Philadelphia and London: J. B. Lippincott, 1896.*

the talk of the faithful that it would be a service to the deity as well as to men to destroy the power of that evil eye. He came beside the bed and looked attentively at the governor, sleeping there in the light of a candle. Then he howled with fright—howled so loudly that the old man sprang to his feet—for while the left eye had been fast asleep the evil one was broad awake and looking at him with a ghostly glare.

In another second the commandant was at the window whirling his trusty Toledo about his head, lopping ears and noses from the red renegades who had followed in the track of the first. In the scrimmage he received another jab in the right eye with a fist. When day dawned it was discovered, with joy, that the evil eye was darkened—and forever. The people trusted him once more. Finding that he was no longer an object of dread, his voice became kinder, his manner more gentle. A heavy and unusual rain, that had been falling, passed off that very day, so that the destruction from flood, which had been prophesied at the missions, was stayed, and the clergy sang "Te Deum" in the church. The old commandant never, to his dying day, had the heart to confess that the evil eye was only a glass one.

Hartley Burr Alexander *The World's Rim: Great Mysteries of the North American Indians* (Lincoln: University of Nebraska Press, 1953).

Natalie Curtis *The Indians' Book: Songs and Legends of the American Indians* (New York: Dover Publications, Inc., 1968).

J. Frank Dobie *Apache Gold and Yaqui Silver* (Boston: Little, Brown and Co., 1939).

Austin E. and Alta Fife *Saints of Sage and Saddle* (Bloomington: Indiana University Press, 1956).

Joe B. Frantz and Julian Earnest Choate, Jr. *The American Cowboy: The Myth and the Reality* (Norman: University of Oklahoma Press, 1955).

John Greenway *Folklore of the Great West* (Palo Alto: The American West Publishing Co., 1969).

Clyde Kluckholn *Navaho Witchcraft* (Cambridge: Harvard University Press, 1944).

Richard E. Lingenfelter and Richard A. Dwyer *Songs of the American West* (Berkeley: University of California Press, 1968).

John G. Neihardt *Black Elk Speaks: Being the Life Story of a Holy Man of the Oglala Sioux* (New York: William Morrow and Co., 1932).

E. D. Sayles *Fantasies of Gold* (Tucson: The University of Arizona Press, 1968).

Irwin Silber *Songs of the Great American West* (New York: The Macmillan Company, 1967).

N. Howard Thorp *Songs of the Cowboys.* Edited by Austin and Alta Fife (New York: Clarkston N. Potter, Inc., 1966).

Frank Waters
*Book of the Hopi* (New York: The Viking Press, 1963).
*Masked Gods* (Denver: Alan Swallow, 1950).
*Pumpkin Seed Point* (Chicago: The Swallow Press, Inc., 1969).

# NINE

## The Humorous Sketch

MARK TWAIN'S HOAX, *A Petrified Man,* was reprinted all over the world and was believed true by many people. Twain's deliberate incoherence at first prevents the casual reader from detecting the real point of the humor. J. Ross Browne wrote countless humorous sketches for *Harpers* about life in California, and as a compulsive traveller, about people and places around the world. Humorous sketches are even found in his government reports.

Ambrose Bierce wrote the most sardonic prose and verse to be found in American literature—Mencken is mild beside him. *The Humorist* is a good self-portrait, and *Fantastic Fables* show his social pessimism. One of his favorite targets was the "railrogues."

Bill Nye was a prolific, mildly ironic commentator on the human spectacle as he observed it in Laramie and the West. He enjoyed deflating the over-blown image of the cowboy in the very region where Wister was to make a hero of him. He used the pun with great skill and had an inspired facility in absurd word coinage.

Frederick Manfred's *Gitting Our Seed Back* is a peculiarly authentic piece of western humor.

# MARK TWAIN

## A Petrified Man

A PETRIFIED MAN was found some time ago in the mountains south of Gravelly Ford. Every limb and feature of the stony mummy was perfect, not even excepting the left leg, which has evidently been a wooden one during the lifetime of the owner—which lifetime, by the way, came to a close about a century ago, in the opinion of *savan* who has examined the defunct. The body was in a sitting posture and leaning against a huge mass of croppings; the attitude was pensive, the right thumb resting against the side of the nose; the left thumb partially supported the chin, the forefinger pressing the inner corner of the left eye and drawing it partly open; the right eye was closed, and the fingers of the right hand spread apart. This strange freak of nature created a profound sensation in the vicinity, and our informant states that, by request, Justice Sewell or Sowell of Humboldt City at once proceeded to the spot and held an inquest on the body. The verdict of the jury was that "deceased came to his death from protracted exposure," etc. The people of the neighborhood volunteered to bury the poor unfortunate, and were even anxious to do so; but it was discovered, when they attempted to remove him, that the water which had dripped upon him for ages from the crag above, had coursed down his back and deposited a limestone sediment under him which had glued him to the bed rock upon which he sat, as with a cement of adamant, and Judge S. refused to allow the charitable citizens to blast him from his position. The opinion expressed by his Honor that such a course would be little less than sacrilege, was eminently just and proper. Everybody goes to see the stone man, as many as 300 persons having visited the hardened creature during the past five or six weeks.

---

*Reprinted from San Francisco* DAILY EVENING BULLETIN, *October 15, 1862.*

# J. ROSS BROWNE

## From *The Great Port Townsend Controversy*

WHILE I HAD THE MISFORTUNE to be in public employ (for no disreputable act that I can now remember), it became my duty to inquire into conditions of the Indians on Puget's Sound. In the course of my tour I visited this unique city for the purpose of having a "wa-wa," with the Duke of York, chief of the Clallam tribe.

Some months after my visit to Port Townsend, in writing a report on the Indians of Puget's Sound, I took occasion to refer to the salient points of [an] interview with the Duke of York, and to make a few remarks touching the degraded conditions of himself and tribe, attributing it to the illegal practice on the part of the citizens of selling whiskey to the Indians. The report was printed by Order of Congress, though I was not aware of the fact till one day, sitting in my office in San Francisco, I received a copy of the "Olympia Democrat" (if I remember correctly), containing a series of grave charges against me, signed by the principal citizens of Port Townsend. I have lost the original documents, but shall endeavor to supply the deficiency as well as my memory serves. The letter was addressed to the "United States Special Agent," and was substantially as follows:

> "Sir,—The undersigned have read your official report relative to the Indians of Puget's Sound, and regret you have deemed it necessary to step so far aside from the line of your duty as to traduce our fair name and reputation as citizens of Port Townsend. You will pardon us for expressing the opinion that you might have spent your time with more credit to yourself and benefit to the goverment.
>
> "Sir, it may be that on the occasion of your visit here the Duke of York and his wives were drunk; but the undersigned are satisfied upon a personal examination, that neither Queen Victoria nor Jenny Lind suffered the loss of two front teeth as you state in your report; and they are not aware that Jenny Lind's eyes were ever blackened by the Duke of York.
>
> "The undersigned do not pretend to say that there is no whiskey sold in Port Townsend; but they do deny sir, that you ever saw any of them drunk, or that the citizens of Port Townsend, as a class, are at all intemperate.
>
> "We therefore enter our solemn protest against the unfounded charges made in your report, and respectfully recommend that in future you confine yourself to your official duties."

---

*Reprinted from* CRUSOE'S ISLAND *by J. Ross Browne, 1864.*

Here was a serious business.

Upon the whole, I felt that I was a little at fault, and had better apologize. There was no particular necessity for introducing Queen Victoria's front teeth and Jenny Lind's black eye to Congress.

I therefore prepared and published in the newspapers an Apology, which seemed to me ought to be satisfactory. The following is as close a copy of the original as I can now write out from memory:

San Francisco, Cal., April 1, 1858

"Gentlemen,—I have not the slightest recollection of having traduced 'your fair name and reputation' or made any reference to you whatever in my report. When I alluded to the 'beachcombers, rowdies, and other bad characters' in Port Townsend, I had no idea that respectable gentlemen like yourselves would take it as personal. You deny positively that either Queen Victoria or Jenny Lind had her front teeth knocked out by the Duke of York. Well, I take that back, for I certainly did not examine their mouths as closely as you seem to have done. But when you deny that Jenny Lind's eye was black, you do me a great injustice. I shall insist upon it to the latest hour of my existence that it was black—deeply, darkly, beautifully black, with a prismatic circle of pink, blue and yellow in the immediate vicinity. I cheerfully retract the teeth, but, gentlemen, I hold onto that eye as long as the flag of freedom waves over this glorious republic!

"While you do not pretend to say that there is no whiskey sold in Port Townsend, you do insist upon it that I never saw any of you drunk. Of course not, gentlemen. There are several of you that I do not recollect having ever seen, either drunk or sober. If I did see any of you under the influence of intoxicating spirits, the disguise was certainly effectual, for I am now entirely unable to say which of you it was. Besides I never said I saw any of you drunk. It requires a great deal of whiskey to intoxicate some people and I should be sorry to hazard a conjecture as to the gauge of any citizen of Port Townsend. I do not believe you habitually drink whiskey as a beverage—certainly not Port Townsend whiskey, for that would kill the strongest man that ever lived in less than six months, if he drank nothing else.

"That, 'it is not necessary for public officers to adhere strictly to the facts for their reports' is a melancholy truth. You have me there, gentlemen. Truth is very scarce in official documents. It is not expected by the public, and it would be utterly wasted upon Congress.

"The result of your inquiries on the subject of murder appears to be that only two murders were committed in Port Townsend during the past year, instead of six, as stated in my report. Well, gentlemen, I was not present, and did not participate in any of these alleged murders, and cheerfully admit that your sheriff, who gave me the information and whose name is appended to your letter, may not have counted them correctly. At all events, I take four of them back, and place them to the credit of Port Townsend for the ensuing year. Gentlemen, you need not take any further trouble about 'setting yourselves right before the world.' I trust you will admit that you are all right now, since I have duly made the amende honorable. I remain, etc."

Strange to say, so far from being satisfied with this apology, the citizens of Port Townsend were enraged to a degree bordering on insanity. For two years they did nothing else, in an official point of view, but write letters to the San Francisco papers denouncing the author of this Vile Kalumy, and assuring the public that his description of Port Townsend was wholly unworthy of credit; that Port Townsend was the neatest, cleanest, most orderly and most flourishing little town on the Pacific coast. By the time the Frazer River excitement broke out, the people of California were well acquainted, through the newspapers, with at least one town on Puget's Sound. Thousands who had no particular business there went to take a look at this wonderful town, which had given rise to so much controversy. The citizens were soon forced to build a fine hotel. Others thought it would soon be the great center of commerce for all shipping that would be drawn thither by the mineral wealth of Frazer River and bought city lots on speculation. Traders came there and set up stores; new saloons were built; customers crowded in from all parts; in short, it became a gay and dashing sort of place, and very soon had quite the appearance of a city.

During the following year I made bold to pay my old friends a visit. A delegation of the Common Council met me at the wharf. A most complimentary address was read to me by the mayor of the city, in which it was fully and frankly acknowledged that I was the means of building up the fortunes of Port Townsend. These gratifying public demonstrations over, we adjourned to the nearest saloon, and buried the hatchet forever in an ocean of the best Port Townsend whiskey. It is due to the citizens to say that not one of them went beyond reasonable bounds on this joyous occasion, by which I do not mean to intimate that they were accustomed to the beverage referred to. At all events I think it has been clearly demonstrated by these authentic documents that "whiskey built a great city."


# AMBROSE BIERCE

## *The Humorist*


"What is that, mother?"
                    "The humorist, child.
His hands are black, but his heart is mild."
"May I touch him, mother?"

---

*Selections by Ambrose Bierce reprinted from* THE COLLECTED
WORKS OF AMBROSE BIERCE, *Neale Publishing Co., 1909 and 1912.*

" 'Twere needlessly done:
He is slightly touched already, my son."
"O, why does he wear such a ghastly grin?"
" 'Tis the outward sign of a joke within."
"Will he crack it, mother?"
                              "Not so, my saint;
" 'Tis meant for the *Saturday Livercomplaint*."
"Does he suffer, mother?"
                              "God help him, yes!—
A thousand fifty kinds of distress."
"What makes him sweat so?"
                              "The demons that lurk
In fear of having to go to work."
"Why doesn't he end, then, his life with a rope?"
"Abolition of Hell has deprived him of hope."


## The Genesis of Embarrassment


When Adam first saw Eve he said:
"O lovely creature, share my bed."
Before consenting, she her gaze
Fixed on the greensward to appraise,
As well as vision could avouch,
The value of the proffered couch.
And seeing that the grass was green
And soft and scrupulously clean;
Observing that the flow'rs were rare
Varieties, and some were fair,
The posts of precious woods, and each
Bore luscious fruit in easy reach
And all things suited well her worth,
She raised her angel eyes from earth
To his, and blushing to confess,
Murmured: "I love you, Adam—yes."
Since then her daughters, it is said,
Look always down when asked to wed.

## Treasury and Arms

A Public Treasury, feeling Two Arms lifting out its contents, exclaimed:

"Mr. Shareman, I move for a division."

"You seem to know something about parliamentary forms of speech," said the Two Arms.

"Yes," replied the Public Treasury, "I am familiar with the hauls of legislation."

# BILL NYE

## The Lop-Eared Lovers of Little Laramie

### A Tale of Love and Parental Cussedness

#### CHAPTER I

THE SCENE OPENS with a landscape. In the foreground stands a house; but there are no honeysuckles or Johnny-jump-ups clambering over the door; there are no Columbines or bitter-sweets, or bachelor-buttons, clinging lovingly to the eaves, and filling the air with fragrance. The reason for this is, that it is too early in the spring for Columbines and Johnny-jump-ups, at the time when our story opens, and they wouldn't grow in that locality without irrigation, anyway. That is the reason that these little adjuncts do not appear in the landscape.

But the scene is nevertheless worthy of a painter. The house, especially, ought to be painted, and a light coat of the same article on the front gate would improve its appearance materially. In the door of the cottage stands a damsel, whose natural loveliness is enhanced 30 or 40 percent, by a large oroide chain which encircles her swan-like throat; and, as she shades her eyes with her alabaster hand, the gleam of a gutta percha ring on her front finger tells the casual observer that *she is engaged.*

While she is shading her eyes from the blinding glare of the orb of day, the aforesaid orb of day keeps right on setting, according to advertisement, and at last disappears behind the snowy range, lighting up, as it does so, the fleecy clouds and turning them into gold, figuratively speaking, making the picture one of surpassing loveliness. But what does she care for a $13.00 sunset, or the low, sad wail of the sage-hen far up the canon, as it calls for its mate? What does she care for the purple landscape and

*From* BILL NYE AND BOOMERANG.

the mournful sigh of the new milch cow which is borne to her over the green divide? She doesn't care a cent.

## CHAPTER II

It is now the proper time to bring in the solitary horseman. He is seen riding a mouse-colored bronco on a smooth canter, and, from his uneasiness in the saddle, it is evident that he has been riding a long time, and that it doesn't agree with him. He has been attending the spring meeting of the Rocky Mountain Roundup.

He takes a benevolent chew of tobacco, looks at his cylinder-escapement watch, and plunges his huge Mexican spurs into the panting sides of his bronco steed. The ambitious steed rears forward and starts away into the gathering gloom at the rate of twenty-one miles in twenty-one days, while a bitter oath escapes from the clenched teeth and foam-flecked lips of the pigeon-toed rider.

But stay! Let us catch a rapid outline of the solitary horseman, for he is the affianced lover and soft-eyed gazelle of Luella Frowzletop, the queen of the Skimmilk Ranche. He is evidently a man of say twenty summers, with a sinister expression to the large, ambitious, imported Italian mouth. A broad-brimmed white hat with a scarlet flannel band protects his Gothic features from the burning sun, and a pale-brown ducking suit envelopes his lithe form. A horsehair lariat hangs at his saddle bow, and the faint suspicion of a downy mustache on his chiselled upper lip is just beginning to ooze out into the air, as if ashamed of itself. It is one of those sickly mustaches, a kind of cross between blonde and brindle, which mean well enough, but never amount to anything. His eyes are fierce and restless, with short, expressive, white eyelashes, and his nose is short but wide out, gradually melting away into his bronzed and stalwart cheeks, like a dish of ice-cream before a Sabbath school picnic.

Such is the rough sketch of Pigeon-toed Pete, the swain who had stolen away the heart of Luella Frowzletop, the queen of Skimmilk Ranche. He isn't handsome, but he is very good, and he loves the fair Luella with a great deal of diligence, although her parents are averse to the match, for we might as well inform the sagacious and handsome reader that her parents are Presbyterians, whereas the hero of this blood-curdling tale is a hard-shell Baptist. Thus are two hearts doomed to love in vain.

## CHAPTER III

During all this time that we have been going on with the preceding chapter, Luella has been standing in the door looking away to the eastward, a soiled gingham apron thrown over her head, and a dreamy, far-away look in her mournful sorrel eyes. Suddenly there breaks on her finely moulded and flexible ear the sound of a horse's hoof.

"Aha!" she murmurs. "Hist! it is him. Blast his picture! Why didn't he have some style about him, and get here on time?" And she impatiently mashes a huge mosquito that is fastened on her swarthy arm.

Any one could see, as she stood there, that she was mad. She didn't really have any cause for it, but she was an only child, and accustomed to being petted and humored, and lying in bed till half past ten. This had made her high spirited, and she occasionally turned loose with the first thing that came to hand.

"You're a fine haired snoozer from Bitter Creek; ain't ye?" said the pale flower of Skimmilk Ranche, as the solitary horseman alighted from his panting steed, and threw his arms about her with great *sang froid*.

"In what respect?" said Pigeon-toed Pete, as he held her from him, and looked lovingly down into her deep, sorrel eyes.

"O fairest of thy sect," he continued, as he took out his quid of tobacco, preparatory to planting a long, wide, passionate kiss on her burning cheek, "you wot not what you fain would say. The way was long, my ambling steed has a ringbone on the off leg, and thou chidest me, thy erring swain, without a cause." He knew that she would pitch into him, so he had this little impromptu speech all committed to memory.

She pillowed her sunny head on his panting breast for an hour or so, and shed eleven or eight happy tears.

"O, lode star of my existence, and soother of my every sorrow," said he, with charming *naïveté*, "wilt thou fly with me to-night to some adjacent justice of the peace, and be my skipful gazelle, my little *ne plus ultra*, my own *magnum bonum* and *multum in parvo*, so to speak? Leave your Presbyterian parents to run the ranche, and fly with me. You shall never want for anything. You shall never put your dimpled hands in dishwater, or wring out your own clothes. I will get you a new rosewood washing machine, and when your slightest look indicates that you want forty or fifty dollars for pin money, I will make out a check for that amount."

He had just finished his little harangue, whatever that is, and was putting in a few choice gestures, when the old man came around from behind the rain-water barrel with a shot-gun, and told the ardent admirer of Luella that he had better not linger to any great extent, and as he said it in his quiet but firm way, at the same time fondling the lock on his shot-gun, the lover lingered not, but hied him away to his neighing steed, and lightly springing into the saddle, was soon lost to the sight. We will leave him on the road for a short time.

*       *       *       *       *

## CHAPTER IV

We will now suppose a period of three years to have passed. Luella had been sent to visit her friends in southern Iowa, partly to assuage her grief, and partly to save expenses, for she was a hearty eater. Here she met a young man named Rufus G. Hopper, who fell in love with her, about the first hard work he did, and when, metaphorically speaking, he laid his 40-acre homestead, with its wealth of grasshopper eggs, at her feet, she capitulated, and became his'n, and he became her'n.

Thus these two erstwhile lovers of the long ago had become separated, and the fair Queen of the Skimmilk Ranche had taken a change of venue with her affections. Still all seemed to be well to the casual observer, although at times her eyes had that far-away look of those who are crossed in love, or whose livers are out of order. Was it the fleeing vision of the absent lover, or had she eaten something that didn't agree with her?

Ah! who shall say that at times there did not flash across her mind the fact that she had sacrificed herself on the altar of Mammon, and given her rich love in exchange for forty acres of Government land? But the time drew nigh for the celebration of the nuptials, and still no tidings of the absent lover. Nearer and nearer came the 4th of July, the day set apart for the wedding, and still in the dark mysterious bosom of the unknown, lurked the absent swain.

*     *     *     *     *

These stars indicate the number of days which we must now suppose to have passed, and the glad day of the Nation's rejoicing is at hand. The loud mouthed cannon proclaims, for the one hundredth time, that in the little Revolutionary scrimmage of 1776, our forefathers got away with the persimmons. Flags wave, bands play, and crackers explode, and scare the teams from the country. Fair rustic maids are seen on every hand with their good clothes on, and farmers' sons walk up and down the street, asking the price of watermelons and soda water. Bye and bye the band comes down street playing "Old Zip Coon," with variations. The procession begins to form and point toward the grand stand, where the Declaration of Independence will be read to the admiring audience, and lemonade retailed at five cents a glass.

But who are the couple who sit on the front seat near the speaker's stand, listening with rapt attention to the new and blood-curdling romance, entitled the "Declaration of Independence?" It is Luella and her new husband. The casual observer can discover that, by the way he smokes a cheap cigar in her face, and allows the fragrant smoke from the five cent Havana to drift into her sorrel eyes. All at once the band strikes up the operatic strain of "Captain Jinks," and as the sad melody dies away in the distance, a young man steps proudly forth, at the conclusion of the president's introductory speech, and in a low, musical voice, begins to set forth the wrongs visited on the Pilgrim Fathers, and to dish up the bones of G. Washington and T. Jefferson, in various styles.

What is it about the classic mouth, with its charming *naïveté* and the amber tinge lurking about its roguish outlines, which awakes the old thrill in Luella's heart, and causes the vital current to recede from its accustomed channels, and leave her face like marble, save where here and there a large freckle stands out in bold relief? It is the mouth of Pigeon-toed Pete. Those same Gothic features stand out before her, and she knows him in a moment. It is true he had colored his mustache, and he wore a stand-up collar; but it was the same form, the same low, musical, squeaky voice, and the same large, intellectual ears, which she remembered so well.

It appeared that he had been to the Gunnison country, and having manifested considerable originality and genius as a bull whacker, had secured steady employment and large wages, being a man with a ready command of choice and elegant profanity, and an irresistable way of appealing to the wants of a sluggish animal. Taking his spare change, he had invested it in hand made sour mash corn juice, which he retailed at from 25 to 50 cents a glass. Rain water being plenty, the margin was large, and his profits highly satisfactory. In this way he had managed to get together some cash, and was at once looked upon as a leading capitalist, and a man on whom rested the future prosperity of the country. He wore moss-agate sleeve buttons, and carried a stem-winding watch. He looked indeed like a thing of life, and as he closed with some stirring quotation from Martin F. Tupper amid the crash of applause, and the band struck up the oratorio of "Whoop 'em up 'Liza Jane," the audience dispersed to witness a game of base-ball. Luella took her husband's arm, climbed into the lumber wagon, and rode home, with a great grief in her heart. Had she deferred her wedding for only a few short hours, the course of her whole life would have been entirely changed, and, instead of plodding her weary way through the long, tedious years as Mrs. Hopper, making rag-carpets during winter, and smashing the voracious potato bug during the summer, she might have been interested in a carbonate Bonanza, worn checked stockings, and low-necked shoes.

There are two large, limpid tears standing in her sorrel eyes, as the curtain falls on this story, and her lips move involuntarily as she murmurs that little couplet from Milton:

> "I feel kind of sad and bilious, because
> My heart keeps sighing, 'It couldn't was.' "

## One Kind of Fool

A YOUNG MAN, with a plated watch-chain that would do to tie up a sacred elephant, came into Denver the other day from the East, on the Julesberg Short line, and told the hotel clerk that he had just returned from Europe, and was on his way across the continent with the intention of publishing a book of international information. He handed an oilcloth grip across the counter, registered in a bold, bad way and with a flourish that scattered the ink all over the clerk's white shirt front.

*From* REMARKS BY BILL NYE.

He was assigned to a quiet room on the fifth floor, that had been damaged by water a few weeks before by the fire department. After an hour or two spent in riding up and down the elevator and ringing for things that didn't cost anything, he oiled his hair and strolled into the diningroom with a severe air and sat down opposite a big cattle man, who never oiled his hair or stuck his nose into other people's business.

The European traveler entered into conversation with the cattle man. He told him all about Paris and the continent, meanwhile polishing his hands on the tablecloth and eating everything within reach. While he ate another man's desert, he chatted on gaily about Cologne and pitied the cattle man who had to stay out on the bleak plains and watch the cows, while others paddled around Venice and acquired information in a foreign land.

At first the cattle man showed some interest in Europe, but after a while he grew quiet and didn't seem to enjoy it. Later on the European tourist, with soiled cuffs and auburn mane, ordered the waiters around in a majestic way to impress people with his greatness, tipped over the vinegar cruet into the salt and ate a slice of boiled egg out of another man's salad.

Casually a tall Kansas man strolled in and asked the European tourist what he was doing in Denver. The cattle man, who by the way, has been abroad five or six times and is as much at home in Paris as he is in Omaha, investigated the matter, and learned that the fresh French tourist had been herding hens on a chicken ranch in Kansas for six years, and had never seen blue water. He then took a few personal friends to the dining room door, and they watched the alleged traveler. He had just taken a long, refreshing drink from the finger bowl of his neighbor on the left and was at the moment trying to scoop up a lump of sugar with the wrong end of the tongs.

There are a good many fools who drift around through the world and dodge the authorities, but the most disastrous ass that I know is the man who goes west with two dollars and forty cents in his pocket, without brains enough to soil the most delicate cambric handkerchief, and tries to play himself for a savant with so much knowledge that he has to shed information all the time to keep his abnormal knowledge from hurting him.

# The Cow-Boy

So MUCH AMUSING TALK is being made recently anent the blood-be-draggled cow-boy of the wild West, that I rise as one man to say a few things, not in a dictatorial style, but regarding this so-called or so esteemed

---

*From* REMARKS BY BILL NYE.

dry land pirate who, mounted on a little cow-pony and under the black flag, sails out across the green surge of the plains to scatter the rocky shores of Time with the bones of his fellow-man.

A great many people wonder where the cow-boy, with his abnormal thirst for blood, originated. Where did this young Jesse James, with his gory record and his dauntless eye, come from? Was he born in a buffalo wallow at the foot of some rock-ribbed mountain, or did he first breathe the thin air along the brink of an alkali pond, where the horned toad and the centipede sang him to sleep, and the tarantula tickled him under the chin with its hairy legs?

Careful research and cold, hard statistics show that the cow-boy, as a general thing, was born in an unostentious manner on the farm. I hate to sit down on a beautiful romance and squash the breath out of a romantic dream; but the cow-boy who gets too much moist damnation in his system, and rides on a gallop up and down Main street shooting out the lights of the beautiful billiard palaces, would be just as unhappy if a mouse ran up his pantaloon-leg as you would, gentle reader. He is generally a youth who thinks he will not earn his twenty-five dollars per month if he does not yell, and whoop, and shoot, and scare little girls into St. Vitus's dance. I've known more cowboys to injure themselves with their own revolvers than to injure anyone else. This is evidently because they are more familiar with the hoe than they are with the Smith & Wesson.

One night, while I had rooms in the business part of a Territorial city in the Rocky Mountain cattle country, I was awakened at about one o'clock A.M. by the most blood-curdling cry of "Murder" I ever heard. It was murder with a big "M." Across the street, in the bright light of a restaurant, a dozen cow-boys with broad sombreros and flashing silver braid, huge leather chaperajas, Mexican spurs and orange silk neckties, and with flashing revolvers, were standing. It seemed that a big, red-faced Captain Kidd of the band, with his skin full of valley tan, had marched into an ice-cream resort with a self-cocker in his hand, and ordered the vanilla coolness for the gang. There being a dozen young folks at the place, mostly male and female, from a neighboring hop, indulging in cream, the proprietor, a meek Norwegian with thin white hair, deemed it rude and outre to do so. He said something to that effect whereat the other eleven men of alcoholic courage let off a yell that froze the cream into a solid glacier, and shook two kerosene lamps out of their sockets in the chandeliers.

Thereupon the little Y.M.C.A. Norwegian said:

"Gentlemans, I kain't neffer like dot squealinks and dot kaind of a tings, and you fellers mit dot ledder pantses on and dot funny glose and such a tings like dot, better keep kained of quiet, or I shall call up the policemen mit my delephone."

Then they laughed at him, and cried yet again with a loud voice.

This annoyed the ice-cream agriculturist, and he took the old axe-handle that he used to jam the ice down around the freezer with, and peeled a large area of scalp off the leader's dome of thought, and it hung down over his eyes, so that he could not see to shoot with any degree of accuracy.

After he had yelled "Murder!" three or four times, he fell under an ice-cream table, and the mild-eyed Scandinavian broke a silver-plated castor over the organ of self-esteem, and poured red pepper, and salt, and vinegar, and Halford sauce and other relishes, on the place where the scalp was loose.

This revived the brave but murderous cow-gentleman, and he begged that he might be allowed to go away.

The gentle Y.M.C.A. superintendent of the ten-stamp ice-cream freezers then took the revolvers away from the bold buccaneer, and kicked him out through a show-case, and saluted him with a bouquet of July oysters that suffered severely from malaria.

All cow-boys are not sanguinary; but out of twenty you will generally find one who is brave when he has his revolvers with him; but when he forgot and left his shooters at home on the piano, the most tropical violet-eyed dude can climb him with the butt-end of a sunflower, and beat his brains out and spatter them all over that school district.

In the wild, unfettered West, beware of the man who never carries arms, never gets drunk and always minds his own business. He don't go around shooting out the gas, or intimidating a kindergarten school; but when a brave frontiersman, with a revolver in each boot and a bowie down the back of his neck, insults a modest young lady, and needs to be thrown through a plate-glass window and then walked over by the populace, call on the silent man who dares to wear a clean shirt and human clothes.

## Early Day Justice

THOSE WERE TROUBLESOME times, indeed. All wool justice in the courts was impossible. The vigilance committee, or Salvation Army as it called itself, didn't make much fuss about it, but we all knew that the best citizens belonged to it and were in good standing.

It was in those days when young Stewart was short-handed for a sheep-herder and had to take up with a sullen, hairy vagrant, called by the other boys "Esau." Esau hadn't been on the ranch a week before he made trouble with the proprietor and got the red-hot blessing from Stewart he deserved.

Then Esau got madder and sulked away down the valley among the little sage brush hummocks and white alkali waste land to nurse his wrath. When Stewart drove into the corral at night, from town, Esau raised up

---

*From* REMARKS BY BILL NYE.

from behind an old sheep dip tank, and without a word except what may have growled around in his black heart, he raised a leveled Spencer and shot his young employer dead.

That was the tragedy of the week only. Others had occurred before and others would probably occur again. It was getting too prevalent for comfort. So, as soon as a quick cayuse and a boy could get down into town, the news spread and the authorities began in the routine manner to set the old legal mill to running. Someone had to go down to The Tivoli and find the prosecuting attorney, then a messenger had to go to The Alhambra for the justice of the peace. The prosecuting attorney was "full" and the judge had just drawn one card to complete a straight flush, and had succeeded.

In the meantime the Salvation Army was fully half way to Clugston's ranch. They had started out, as they had said, "to see that Esau didn't get away." They were going out there to see that Esau was brought into town. What happened after they got there I only know from hearsay, for I was not a member of the Salvation Army at that time. But I got it from one of those present, that they found Esau down in the sage brush down on the bottoms that lie between the abrupt corner of Sheep Mountain and the Little Laramie River. They captured him, but he died soon after, as it was told to me, from the effects of opium taken with suicidal intent. I remember seeing Esau the next morning and I thought there were signs of ropium, as there was a purple streak around the neck of the deceased, together with other external phenomena not peculiar to opium.

But the great difficulty with the Salvation Army was that it didn't want to bring Esau into town. A long, cold night ride with a person in Esau's condition was disagreeable. Twenty miles of lonely road with a deceased murderer in the bottom of the wagon is depressing. Those of my readers who have tried it will agree with me that it is not calculated to promote hilarity. So the Salvation Army stopped at Whatley's ranch to get warm, hoping that someone would steal the remains and elope with them. They stayed some time and managed to "give away" the fact that there was a reward of $5,000 out for Esau, dead or alive. The Salvation Army even went so far as to betray a great deal of hilarity over the easy way it had nailed the reward, or would as soon as said remains were delivered up and identified.

Mr. Whatley thought that the Salvation Army was having a kind of walkaway, so he slipped out at the back door of the ranch, put Esau into his wagon and drove away to town. Remember, this is the way it was told to me. Mr. Whatley hadn't gone more than half a mile when he heard the wild and disappointed yells of the Salvation Army. He put the buckskin on the backs of his horses without mercy, driven on by the enraged shouts and yells of his infuriated pursuers. He reached town about midnight, and his pursuers disappeared. But what was he to do with Esau?

He drove around all over town, trying to find the official who sighed for the deceased. Mr. Whatley went from house to house like a vegetable man, seeking sadly for the party who would give him a $5,000 check for Esau. Nothing could be more depressing than to wake up one man after another out of a sound sleep and invite him to come out to the buggy and identify the remains. One man went out and looked at him. He said he didn't know how others felt about it, but he allowed that anybody who would pay $5,000 for such a remains as Esau's could not have very good taste.

Gradually it crept through Mr. Whatley's wool that the Salvation Army had been working him, so he left Esau at the engine house and went home. On his ranch he nailed up a large board on which had been painted in antique characters with a paddle and tar the following stanzas: Vigilance Committees, Salvation Armies, Morgues, or young physicians who may have deceased people on their hands, are requested to refrain from conferring them on to the undersigned. People who contemplate shuffling off their own or other people's mortal coils, will please not do so on these grounds. The Salvation Army of the Rocky Mts is especially warned to keep off the grass!
James Whatley.

# FREDERICK MANFRED

## Gitting Our Seed Back

PA THOR LAUGHED and slapped his leg. He rolled in his chair. His pipe almost fell from his mouth. "That's a good one! A good one!" he roared. Then he narrowed his eyes. "I can just see him standing there, I kin. Just see him." He laughed again. "God, I did ask fer rain, but, Christ, this is ridiculous!" He slapped and rubbed his leg.

The womenfolk looked down, vainly trying to restrain their smiles.

"Reminds me," ruminated Pa Thor aloud, as if he hadn't noticed either Ma Thor or Kirsten. "Reminds me. Neighbor Grayson down the road a piece, had a wife ready to give with child. He was worried about her, worried more than most farmers are. Because, you see, she was awful small. So he took her to Sioux Falls. That's where all them rich an' high monkey-monks live. An' while he was waitin' fer the kid to come, another feller came out, an' sat down to wait too. He was a fat rich feller, had all the sugar in the coffee he wanted. An' they set there waitin'. Pretty soon

*Reprinted from* THE GOLDEN BOWL *by Frederick Manfred, Dakota Press, 1969, by permission of the author and publisher.*
*Editor's title*

a nurse came out. 'Mr. Jones?' That was the rich feller, an' he sings out, 'Here. Yes?' 'Mr. Jones, you're the father of a nice, fat, eight-pound baby boy.' 'Great guns!' he roars. 'That's wonderful!' He jumps up and down, an' kisses the nurse and offers my neighbor a cigar. 'Here. Take two. Celebrate with me. It's wonderful, having babies! You're waiting too, I suppose?' My neighbor nods a little, nervous, you know. The rich feller says, 'Say, just to show you what kind of a good sport I am I'll wait an' keep you company till you hear from your wife.' So they set there, an' pretty soon the nurse comes out, an' she says, 'Mr. Grayson?' 'Yes.' The nurse was a little nervous an' she acted kinda funny, an' then she said, 'Well, you had a boy.' 'Oh,' he said. 'Oh. An' how much did it weigh?' The nurse wasn't gonna answer him at first, but finally she said, 'Well, it was about a pound.' Grayson thanked her an' started to go out. 'Great guns!' yells the rich feller, 'only a pound? That's tough luck, feller. Tough!' 'Hell no,' says Grayson. 'That's not tough. Livin' out where I do, in the dust bowl, why hell! we're lucky to git our seed back.'"

Ramon F. Adams  *The Cowboy and His Humor* (Austin: University of Texas Press, 1968).

Philip H. Ault  *The Home Book of Western Humor* (New York: Dodd, Mead and Co., 1967).

Ambrose Bierce
*The Devil's Dictionary* (1911) (New York: Dover Publications, Inc., 1970).
*The Sardonic Humor of Ambrose Bierce*. Edited by George Barkin. (New York: Dover Publications, Inc., 1970).

Walter Blair  *Native American Humor* (New York: American Book Company, 1937).

B. A. Botkin  *A Treasury of American Humor* (New York: Crown Publishers, 1944).

Wells Drury  *An Editor on the Comstock Lode* (Palo Alto: Pacific Books, 1948).

Ben K. Green
*Wild Cow Tales* (New York: Alfred A. Knopf, Inc., 1969).
*Horse Tradin'* (New York: Alfred A. Knopf, Inc., 1967).

Stan Hoig  *The Humor of the American Cowboy* (Lincoln: University of Nebraska Press, 1970).

T. A. Larson, ed.  *Bill Nye's Western Humor* (Lincoln: University of Nebraska Press, 1968).

Mark Twain
*Autobiography*. Edited by Charles Neider. (New York: Harper & Bros., 1961).
*Letters From Earth*. Edited by Bernard DeVoto. (Greenwich, Conn: Fawcett Publications, Inc., 1963).
*Roughing It* (Hartford, Conn.: The American Publishing Company, 1871).

# Index